FDR

AND THE
Jews

RICHARD BREITMAN

ALLAN J. LICHTMAN

FDR
Jews
AND THE

THE BELKNAP PRESS of
HARVARD UNIVERSITY PRESS
Cambridge, Massachusetts
London, England
2013

Library of Congress Cataloging-in-Publication Data

Breitman, Richard, 1947–
　　FDR and the Jews / Richard Breitman and Allan J. Lichtman.
　　　　pages　cm
　　Includes bibliographical references and index.
　　ISBN 978-0-674-05026-6 (alkaline paper)
　　　1. Roosevelt, Franklin D. (Franklin Delano), 1882–1945—Relations with Jews.
　2. Roosevelt, Franklin D. (Franklin Delano), 1882–1945—Political and social views.
　3. Jews—Government policy—United States—History—20th century.　4. Jews, European—Government policy—United States—History—20th century.
　5. Holocaust, Jewish (1939–1945)　6. Jews—Persecutions—Europe—History—20th century.　7. United States—Foreign relations—Germany.　8. Germany—Foreign relations—United States.　9. United States—Foreign relations—1933–1945.
　I. Lichtman, Allan J.　II. Title.　III. Title: F.D.R. and the Jews.
　E807.B745　2013
　973.917092—dc23　　　　2012038166

Contents

FDR
AND THE
Jews

Introduction

Four Roosevelts

DURING WORLD WAR II, the Nazis and their collaborators shot, gassed, starved, and worked to death some six million Jewish men, women, and children in order to destroy the biological substance of the Jews. They perpetrated what remains to date the only systematic effort by a modern state to exterminate an entire people across all national frontiers.

Upon gaining power in 1933, Adolf Hitler and other leading Nazis targeted for persecution alleged blood enemies of the German race. Yet before the war Nazi oppression of German Jews followed a jagged trajectory. Some Nazi activists physically assaulted Jews in the early exuberant days of Hitler's semilegal revolution. Once secure in their authority, Nazi officials curbed personal violence, but enacted a series of discriminatory laws and decrees, what contemporary observers called Hitler's "cold pogrom" against Jews. Only in late 1938 did central authorities instigate the violence known as *Kristallnacht*—the Night of Broken Glass—wiping out synagogues across the country in a matter of days. For the first time, the Gestapo imprisoned tens of thousands of German Jews in concentration camps that also held other alleged enemies of Hitler's new Reich.

Some scholars have condemned Franklin Delano Roosevelt, the president of the United States from 1933 to 1945, for callously standing by while Hitler persecuted German Jewry and then exterminated nearly two-thirds of Europe's Jews. Playwrights, filmmakers, and political figures have replayed this story of ironic betrayal by a famously humane president whom Jews of his time revered. Others claim that Roosevelt did everything feasible to rescue European Jews and saved millions of potential victims by orchestrating the defeat of Nazi Germany in World War II. The titles alone of prominent works illustrate the two extremes that have dominated debates about FDR and the Jews. Critics wrote *The Abandonment of the Jews* and *The Jews Were Expendable.* Defenders countered with *The Myth of Rescue* and *Saving the Jews.*

This ongoing quarrel is unforgiving, passionate, and politically charged. Conservative backers of modern-day Israel hold FDR out as an exemplar of indifference to Jewish peril and the horror of genocide. The survival of Israel, they claim, depends upon avoiding his errors. Liberals, in turn, defend their iconic president from what they see as unfounded smears. Our work challenges both extremes in this dispute. We seek to capture the contemporary reality of FDR and other leaders, whose decisions were constrained by the past and projected into what the poet Longfellow called "the shadowy future."[1]

For most of his presidency Roosevelt did little to aid the imperiled Jews of Germany and Europe. He put other policy priorities well ahead of saving Jews and deferred to fears of an anti-Semitic backlash at home. He worried that measures to assist European Jews might endanger his political coalition at home and then a wartime alliance abroad. FDR usually avoided singling out the Jews in public. When he engaged Jewish issues, he maneuvered, often behind the scenes. When he hesitated, other American officials with far less sympathy for Jews set or carried out policies.

Still, at times Roosevelt acted decisively to rescue Jews, often withstanding contrary pressures from the American public, Congress, and his own State Department. Oddly enough, he did more for the Jews than any other world figure, even if his efforts seem deficient in retrospect. He was a far better president for Jews than any of his political adversaries would have been. Roosevelt defied most Republican opponents and some isolationist Democrats to lead political and military opposition to Nazi Germany's plans for expansion and world domination.

As biographer Kenneth Davis has noted, Roosevelt could "turn empathy on or off at will, as if it were water in a faucet." FDR believed that he must act "like a physician who must daily operate in life-and-death situations" and "simply could not afford to let himself feel too acutely the pain of those who suffered; doing so would impair his professional performance." Like a triage physician, FDR gave urgent attention to some priorities at times in his presidency, while putting others aside.[2]

The most dramatic accusations against FDR, his unwillingness to admit to American soil the Jewish refugees aboard the SS *St. Louis* in 1939 and to order the bombing of gas chambers and crematoria at Auschwitz, do not withstand close scrutiny. His critics have given them emblematic moral weight. We have restored their actual historical significance.

Roosevelt went through four different phases on Jewish issues as the conditions of his presidency radically changed. Only during his first term was he a bystander to Nazi persecution. FDR refused to jeopardize his political future or his large agenda in domestic and foreign policy by rubbing raw the wounds of ethnic antagonism in the United States at a time of massive economic suffering. Much like Lincoln facing the political need to hold the Union together while wrestling with the humanitarian imperative to abolish slavery, a first-term president put political realism above criticism of Nazi Germany and efforts to admit persecuted Jews into the United States. He declined to meet with Jewish leaders until shortly before the 1936 election.

After his reelection had released some political pressure and Hitler grew bolder in his cruelty, a second Roosevelt shifted course and ministered to Jewish concerns. This now-activist Roosevelt used his executive powers to loosen immigration restrictions and to promote his own ambitious plans to resettle the Jews of Europe in other lands. He publicly backed a Jewish homeland in Palestine and pressured the British to keep Palestine open to Jewish immigrants.

FDR's activism diminished during 1939, especially after Hitler provoked the European war by invading Poland in September. A third Roosevelt put internal security, foreign policy, and military concerns well above Jewish issues. FDR sought to insulate the homeland from foreign spies and saboteurs and overcome domestic resistance to revising America's restrictive Neutrality Acts and aiding nations resisting Hitler's aggression by all means short of war. He feared that undue attention to the "Jewish Question" would benefit his isolationist adversaries and stymie his foreign policies. America's entrance into the war created intense pressures for a swift and decisive victory. It generated new fears about enemy subversion within the United States, and once more diverted attention from Nazi atrocities against Jews. Diplomatic and military officials worried about appearing to fight a war for the Jews and insisted that America could save the Jews only by defeating Hitler's armies.

In late 1943, a fourth Roosevelt changed direction again and addressed Jewish issues with revived interest. He established a War Refugee Board to help rescue the surviving Jews of Europe and pursued plans for the postwar resettlement of refugees. Shortly before his death, a gravely ill president met personally with the influential king of Saudi Arabia in an effort to secure a Jewish homeland in Palestine. Roosevelt also denounced organized anti-Semitism as an integral part of Hitler's brutal attempt to rule Europe and the Western world. Any American who condoned or participated in anti-Semitism was "playing Hitler's game," he said in February 1944. "There is no place in the lives or thoughts of true Americans for anti-Semitism." FDR's record on Jewish issues would look better to the twenty-first century if he had spoken out this forthrightly years earlier and acted decisively on the consequences of his words.[3]

Still, Roosevelt's initiatives to aid imperiled Jews after his first reelection and in the late stages of the war were not empty gestures. Even his failed proposal in 1938 for removing Jews en masse from Europe was a bold and visionary idea that he had formulated himself. Although Roosevelt's proposal won little support across the Western world, his continued push for Jewish resettlement in Latin America facilitated the immigration of some 40,000 Jews there. Other measures such as the easing of immigration restrictions in the mid to late 1930s and the formation of the War Refugee Board likely helped to save the lives of many more Jews.

The "Jewish Question" that Roosevelt confronted had in milder forms haunted Western civilization for centuries. Throughout the history of the West, diverse peoples had persecuted ethnic and religious minorities. Still, as nationalism intensified in the late nineteenth century, majority peoples perceived Jews as a unique and troublesome presence. Jews of the Diaspora, who lived in many lands, were the ultimate wanderers, allegedly more loyal to each other than to their adopted states. Many Christians feared that Jews were plotting to take over the Christian world by fomenting revolution and controlling international finance. Anti-Semitism became widespread in Germany well before Hitler's rise to power, and took its most oppressive form in Eastern Europe. Despotic regimes there severely limited political, social, and economic opportunities for Jews, including their places of residence. Mobs in these lands, often encouraged by officials of the state, took Jewish lives and destroyed Jewish homes, synagogues, and businesses. Leaders in democracies like the United States and Great Britain lacked the will or the political and military strength to hold these regimes accountable for anti-Semitic oppression.[4]

Between 1880 and 1920, maltreatment of Jews contributed to an influx of some two million mostly Southern and Eastern European Jews to the United States. Several hundred thousand more Jews fled to other Western Hemisphere nations, Western Europe, and Palestine. The new arrivals in the United States, like other strangers, faced suspicion and discrimination in jobs, housing, and education. Even at its worst, however, American anti-Semitism fell far short of the more virulent versions in Europe.

Given his years of experience in the politics of New York State, home to nearly half of American Jews, and his European travels, Roosevelt grasped the significance of the "Jewish Question." As governor of New York, he denounced discrimination against Jews in 1930 and backed Palestine as a Jewish homeland. In 1932, he became the first presidential candidate in history to criticize anti-Semitism. Yet, FDR knew that many Americans held prejudicial views of Jews and that during times of economic depression and world war, Congress and the public would resist making sacrifices for oppressed people in foreign lands.

The urgency of the "Jewish Question" in the early twentieth century prompted Jews to found new advocacy groups in the United States. Most Jewish leaders of this time remained active in the Nazi era, including such luminaries as Louis D. Brandeis and Stephen S. Wise. Established Jewish advocates have received much criticism, and little defense, for their allegedly timid response to the perils of European Jews. Although focused on FDR, we also seek to reconsider Jewish leadership in a balanced way.

FDR was a public man, reveling in campaign oratory, sparkling conversation, and the company of adoring women. Yet, for all the familiarity of his public profile, FDR was one of the most private leaders in American history. He wrote no memoirs and left precious few revealing letters, notes, or memos. He frequently gathered information from informal emissaries and contacts, relied on verbal communications, and sent sensitive messages through private back channels. He often used banter and bonhomie to avoid scrutiny, perfecting the talent of telling people what they wanted to hear and then following his own inclinations. No contemporary, including Eleanor Roosevelt, knew whether FDR had a hidden center to his personality or only shifting peripheries.

Unlike the five presidents who followed him, from Harry Truman to Richard Nixon, FDR did not regularly tape conversations in the Oval Office. The Secret Service installed a taping system there in mid-1940, but recordings cover only four months of press conferences and some accidental snippets of conversation. Roosevelt also banned any official transcript of cabinet sessions or note-taking during other presidential meetings, so that participants could speak freely, assured that their remarks would not appear in the newspapers. Much of what is written about FDR's thinking on controversial matters comes from other people's letters and papers, which often include reconstructions of meetings with the president or recollections of conversations over a drink as he poured his favorite martini at the cocktail hour.

Our research took us to numerous manuscript collections in libraries and archives across the country. We have drawn on more primary sources than any previous study about Roosevelt's responses to Jewish issues before and during the Holocaust. Unlike other authors, we examine FDR's decision-making as president from the perspective of his life experiences and full political career.

Roosevelt's handling of the crisis of European Jewry may offer the best opportunity to understand the political dynamics of American responses to persecution and genocide in foreign lands. FDR was a man of faith. He recognized both moral issues across the globe and the practical concerns of governing a great nation. He served in office more than four years longer than any other president and was the only leader to confront both an economic depression and a major war on his watch. Not just Americans, but suffering peoples across the world looked to FDR for inspiration and relief from their hardships. How he responded, and why, reveal much about the strengths and limitations of the American presidency.

The story of FDR and the Jews is ultimately a tragic one that transcends the achievements and failures of any one leader. Even if FDR had been more willing to override domestic opposition and twist arms abroad, he could not have stopped the Nazis' mass murder of some six million Jews. For Hitler and his followers, the annihilation of Jews was not a diversion from the war effort, but integral to its purpose. For America and Britain, the rescue of Jews, even if practical, was ultimately subordinate to the overriding priorities of total war and unconditional surrender of the enemy. "Action expresses priorities," Mahatma Gandhi said while engaged in a freedom struggle of his own.

CHAPTER ONE

The Rise and Fall of FDR

AT THE AGE of eighty-six, four months before her death, Mrs. Roosevelt traveled to Toronto, Canada, to address a Jewish women's group. Three years earlier, the Jewish Forum had awarded her the Einstein Medal for lifetime humanitarian service to the Jewish people. This Mrs. Roosevelt was not Franklin's wife Eleanor, who became renowned for her human rights advocacy. Rather, it was Franklin's mother, the Grand Dame Sara Delano Roosevelt, who died in 1941, just four years before her son.

In the warm and nurturing home of Sara and his father James Sr., at Hyde Park, ninety miles north of New York City, young Franklin seemed to have gained the self-assurance and wise counsel needed to escape the anti-Semitism that was so common among upper-class Protestants. Like his parents, Franklin took pride in his Protestant heritage, and would later proclaim his membership in the "Aryan races." Yet, this pride did not translate into disdain for Jews. James Sr., who was fifty-three years old at the time of Franklin's birth in 1882, had business dealings with Jews. He counseled his son about the immorality of anti-Semitism and his contempt for it. Sara was a proper patrician woman with an acute sense of class, who made friends with Jews and engaged in charitable work for Jewish causes. Throughout his adult life, FDR would be open to Jewish contacts and concerns.[1]

As an only child, Franklin's life revolved around gaining the attention and admiration of adults, especially his parents. James and Sara cultivated in their son the qualities of self-confidence and compassion for the less fortunate. From his formative years through struggles with paralysis in early middle age, Roosevelt loved to be the center of attention and believed that he was destined to perform great deeds in the service of humanity. He developed stoical traits of character that stressed discipline, responsibility, and trust in his own judgment. He learned how to set firm priorities, to give others no more than what he considered their due, to keep his inner thoughts private, and to deflect external pressure with winning charm and subtle persuasion so as not to be swayed from his course. Jewish leaders, like other supplicants, would find the future president Roosevelt equally sympathetic and elusive.[2]

Young Franklin learned well from private tutors and worked hard to meet or exceed expectations. Sara and James introduced him to sports and sailing, shooting, family history, foreign languages, culture, and travel. He developed lifelong interests in stamp collecting, geography, and history, which later provided him an independent vision of the world. Franklin's parents told him stories about his Dutch and Belgian Huguenot (Protestant) and early American ancestors. For this family, the Protestants were the heroes of Enlightenment Europe who challenged the reactionary Catholic Church and oppressive monarchs. Already, FDR had a sense of the "rights" and "wrongs" of history.[3]

In 1896, the fourteen-year-old Franklin entered the small Groton boarding school in Massachusetts. Like English public schools, Groton sought to train a privileged white Protestant class of boys to be disciplined and tough enough for God's work as leaders of the nation. After years of his family's adoration, Franklin had to face merciless adolescent peers, some of whom called him the "feather duster" (after his initials F. D.) because they found him shallow and conceited. Groton's headmaster, the Reverend Endicott Peabody, put athletic competition above academics as the best preparation for leadership. Although Franklin did not excel at sports, the resourceful young man earned a team letter as equipment manager for the baseball team.[4]

Like all but two of his Groton classmates, FDR went on to college at Harvard. There he might have encountered Jews in the student body, but not on the faculty. Although Jewish students comprised 6 percent of Harvard's enrollment in 1906, two years after FDR's graduation, FDR's social life revolved exclusively around Protestant, high-society clubs. His prolific extracurricular agenda showed diverse interests, a strong work ethic, and a humanitarian conscience. He helped found the Political Club, which promoted interest in politics and good government, and served as an officer of Harvard's Social Service Committee, the Harvard Union. He demonstrated compassion for persecuted peoples by signing on to the Boer Relief Fund, formed by students to "assist in relieving the distress of the Boer women and children confined in British concentration camps in South Africa." FDR was one of three students to whom contributors could send donations.[5]

Roosevelt participated in Christian religious and charitable activities through the Christian Association and the Episcopalian St. Paul's Society. FDR's Hyde Park family had attended the local Episcopalian Church. Roosevelt's mentor, Reverend Peabody, was an Episcopal priest, and young Roosevelt identified as an Episcopalian throughout his life. For FDR, religion was a matter of private faith and public service in the Peabody tradition. He did not proclaim his beliefs to the world, seek to convert others, or regularly attend church. He held a flexible view of Christianity, attuned to its ethical teaching, and adapted to the findings of modern science and enlightened social thought. FDR despised doctrinal disputes and, for his time, held a tolerant view of other faiths.[6]

Although Roosevelt earned mediocre grades, he studied with such noted history and government professors as Edward Channing, A. Lawrence Lowell, William Z. Ripley, Silas Marcus MacVane, Roger Bigelow Merriman, and visiting professor Frederick Jackson Turner. Roosevelt enrolled in several courses with Professor MacVane on constitutional government, English and European history, and studied English and German history with Professor Merriman. These big thinkers reinforced FDR's vision of history as Protestantism and liberty versus Catholicism and despotism. Merriman and FDR became friends and correspondents. "Your ancient teachings," FDR wrote in November 1933, "have stood your old pupil in good stead in the development of more modern history."[7]

FDR's work as editor in chief of the *Crimson* late in his Harvard career reflected his service ethic and a disdain for supercilious wealth and privilege. His editorial admonishing students who failed to join the Harvard Union, blamed not "men really unable to afford" the dues, but "those who fail to do so solely from laziness, meanness, or lack of interest in the University." Another editorial defended academics: "Of late years, however, the prominence of the unacademic side of university life has, perhaps, been unduly emphasized . . . the purely scholarly side has not been given enough importance." Still, FDR never pursued scholarship. His twenty-fifth Harvard Reunion statement in 1929 said that he planned to "defer serious writing until after the Class of 1904 had had its 50th Reunion." Yet, Roosevelt genuinely respected scholarly achievement and ultimately relied more on close academic advisers than any prior president.[8]

In 1938, during dinner-party conversation, FDR confided to Courtney Letts de Espil, the American-born wife of the Argentine ambassador, private thoughts about his high school and college years. Both he and Sumner Welles, his undersecretary of state, Roosevelt said, "were disliked heartily now by most of those with whom we went to school [Groton] or to Harvard." He added, "I don't believe they liked either of us very much at the time. . . . They disliked anyone who even took the trouble to read a daily newspaper and wonder what was going on in the world—and to inquire how the other half lived." This attitude within Harvard's elite may explain why FDR never received an invitation to join Porcellian, the university's most exclusive club, which included his father and Theodore Roosevelt as members. This snub rankled FDR for years and may well have fueled his political ambitions.[9]

FDR did not subscribe to a strict meritocracy. He later confided to his Hyde Park neighbor (and secretary of the treasury) Henry Morgenthau Jr. that in the 1920s he had supported efforts to reduce the number of Jews at Harvard because each group should have its share of places and no group should gain undue representation.[10]

In 1900, during Franklin's first year at Harvard, his father died. The following year, cousin Theodore became the Republican vice president of the United States and then, after anarchist Leon Czolgosz assassinated President William McKinley, assumed the presidency. President Theodore Roosevelt brought a progressive domestic program to his Republican Party. TR's ideas and personality impressed young Franklin, who prompted some derision at Harvard by mimicking TR's mannerisms. But he remained loyal to his father's Democratic Party.

After Harvard, FDR entered Columbia Law School. Although he performed poorly in classes, he passed the bar exam during his third year, dropped out, and began to practice law. Yet the impatient and politically ambitious young man lacked interest in the practice or theory of the law. His thought tended to the factual and the anecdotal rather than the conceptual or analytic. Franklin's self-confidence, composure, and interest in public life kept him from probing deeply into philosophical or religious matters.

While at Columbia, in 1905, Franklin married his twenty-year-old distant cousin Eleanor Roosevelt, TR's niece. Despite her adoration of Franklin, Eleanor fretted over his neglect of home life and the meddling in her husband's life of her domineering mother-in-law Sara, who never remarried and still doted on her son. Eleanor, who viewed herself as painfully tall, awkward, and plain, worried about holding the romantic attention of the strikingly handsome Franklin. He stood about six feet, one inch tall with a lean, athletic build. He had blue eyes, dark wavy hair, a strong jaw, and a jaunty manner. As a young man, he also had a disconcerting habit of throwing back his head and looking down his nose at others through his eyeglasses. Yet for Franklin his marriage to Eleanor was a step up. She was the niece of the president of the United States, whereas he came from the obscure side of the Roosevelt clan. The press gushed about President Roosevelt giving away the bride, but fairly ignored the groom.[11]

FDR suspended his unhappy law practice in 1910 and entered politics. He confounded the conventional wisdom by winning a State Senate election as a Democrat in his Republican-leaning rural district. FDR had barely located his seat in the back benches of the Senate chamber when he led an insurgent crusade against the Democratic machine, taking a big risk with potentially big rewards. In 1911, two years before the Seventeenth Amendment required the direct election of U.S. senators, the New York State Legislature was poised to select as senator the former lieutenant governor, William F. Sheehan, an Irish Catholic and the handpicked candidate of New York City's corrupt Democratic machine, Tammany Hall. Some twenty bolting Democrats, led by the twenty-eight-year-old first-term senator FDR, blocked Sheehan's selection. Like Democratic governor Woodrow Wilson of New Jersey, who fought the U.S. Senate appointment of party boss James Smith Jr., young FDR framed the battle against Sheehan as a lofty progressive crusade to give ordinary Americans a say in their government.

Tammany leaders insinuated that anti-Catholic bigotry drove Roosevelt to oppose Sheehan's appointment. The bishop of Syracuse, Patrick Ludden, seconded the charges. FDR responded by urging his opponents "not to let race or religion enter into this fight." He briefly backed the candidacy of another Catholic, John D. Kernan, a former state railroad commissioner, to prove his point. The still callow Roosevelt was learning how to play religious politics with the masters of the game.[12]

As an alternative to Sheehan, Roosevelt vetoed Samuel Untermyer, a Jewish civic leader and lawyer. The combative Untermyer, a self-made millionaire, attributed Roosevelt's opposition not to prejudice against Jews, but to the subterranean influence of J. P. Morgan and Company and other magnates. Roosevelt's insurgents were not selfless reformers, he charged, but venal politicians like the Tammany Democrats. FDR predictably denied that "the influence of any special interest affected in any way the choice of a United States Senator."[13]

Ultimately, in late March 1912, the bosses ditched Sheehan, but induced the bolters to support another Irish Catholic, State Judge James A. O'Gorman, who also had close ties to Tammany Hall. FDR, who was learning how to spin events, hailed O'Gorman's selection as a victory over the machine. The *New York Times* lauded Roosevelt as one of a handful of young Americans "unknown four years ago who have jumped into fame and become factors in national affairs."[14]

Young senator Roosevelt articulated his first progressive philosophy in a March 3, 1912, speech at Troy, New York. He grounded civilized progress in the "Aryan races," which had for "the past thousand years . . . been struggling to obtain individual freedom." With this battle won, he said, new times required a "struggle for the liberty of the community rather than liberty of the individual," with progressive government advancing reforms for the common good. Most American Jews would have scoffed at Roosevelt's equation of Aryan races with civilized progress. Still, FDR had a commonplace white Anglo-Saxon Protestant racial vision for his times.[15]

FDR might have faded from history at the age of 30 if not for the assistance of an indispensable new aide, the brilliant, acerbic, chain-smoking, and chronically disheveled journalist Louis McHenry Howe. When Roosevelt fell ill with typhoid fever, Howe so skillfully ran his absentee campaign for state senator that FDR won reelection despite recycled Republican rumors about his anti-Catholic bigotry. It was another lesson in FDR's education about the toxic mixing of politics and religion. Yet the religiously charged words he chose after the election showed that his education remained incomplete. "Any candidate who brings any question of religion into politics," he wrote, "acts in a manner wholly un-American and un-Christian, and is not fitted to be the holder of any office."[16]

The amateur yachtsman was learning to navigate the religious politics of New York State. Catholics and Jews accounted for about a quarter of the voters in the state and a much larger percentage of Democrats. Two of the brightest young stars within the Democratic Party of 1912 were Catholics and Tammany Hall regulars: Robert F. Wagner, president pro tem of the State Senate, and Al Smith, Democratic leader of the State Assembly. These men represented a new generation of machine-bred politicians who favored policies to increase the efficiency of government, curb the abuses of business, and improve the conditions of labor. Several Jews also represented New York City in the state legislature. FDR joined with Jewish assemblyman Mark Goldberg of New York City to cosponsor the Roosevelt-Goldberg Bill on civil service reform.[17]

The Democratic Party relied considerably on Jewish money. In 1912, nine Jewish donors from New York State donated some $85,000 to the National Democratic Campaign Fund. Bernard Baruch, Abram Elkus, Hy Goldman, Charles Guggenheim, Henry Morgenthau Sr., Jacob Schiff, James Speyer, Nathan Straus Sr., and Untermyer contributed 24 percent of Democratic funds collected from New York State and 7.5 percent of funds raised nationwide. Morgenthau served as finance chair of the Democratic Party in 1912 and 1916. Jewish money for Democratic coffers would continue to matter significantly during FDR's years in national politics.[18]

In 1912, FDR backed the winning presidential campaign of fellow progressive Democrat Woodrow Wilson. On March 11, 1913, the new president nominated Roosevelt as assistant secretary of the navy. Naval officers wondered whether FDR would imitate his cousin TR, who as assistant secretary in the late 1890s, became "the most insubordinate subordinate ever known in the [navy] department." However, the strong and restraining hand of FDR's boss, Secretary of the Navy Josephus Daniels, a progressive newspaper editor and publisher from North Carolina, kept him in check.[19]

Roosevelt stretched too far the following year when he agreed to seek the party's nomination for U.S. senator on an anti-Tammany slate. FDR badly lost the primary, but learned to balance reform politics with practical calculation. In New York State, this meant deference to the powerful Tammany machine. Still, his political independence and reform credentials impressed progressive Jewish leaders in New York City, including Rabbi Stephen S. Wise, who wrote that the "Hennessey-Roosevelt people . . . represent all that is best in the make-up of the Democratic Party in the state." This exchange began a lasting, if occasionally stormy relationship between the politician and the rabbi.[20]

Born in Budapest in 1874, Wise immigrated to the United States with his family as an infant. He was ordained as a rabbi and also earned a PhD from Columbia University. He rose to leadership positions in several Zionist organizations that sought a Jewish homeland in Palestine. Wise was a cofounder of the National Association for the Advancement of Colored People in 1909 and the American Civil Liberties Union in 1920. In 1907, he founded the Free Synagogue in New York City, which he dedicated to the idea of the "free pulpit," where the spiritual leader preaches "the truth as he sees it." Unlike Orthodox Jews who insisted on adherence to time-tested religious laws and doctrine, Wise followed the Reform movement, which upheld freedom of conscience in belief and practice. Wise's piercing stare, his shiny upswept black hair, his limitless energy, his passion, and his inspirational oratory made him a natural leader. Wise would become the most important advocate for Jewish causes during FDR's four terms in the White House.[21]

After the outbreak of World War I in the summer of 1914, Roosevelt worked on upgrading the navy for an anticipated conflict with Germany. He lauded President Wilson's goal of spreading America's socially and morally responsible system of democratic capitalism across the world. He also backed the American occupations of the Philippines and Panama as humanitarian ventures and supported the invasion and occupation of Haiti in 1915 and Santo Domingo in 1916 as rescue missions

In 1916, President Wilson nominated Louis D. Brandeis to the U.S. Supreme Court. The first Jew to secure a place on the court, Brandeis was a leader of the Zionist movement, an outspoken progressive, and a close confidant of the president. His controversial nomination predictably stirred conservative opposition with undertones of anti-Semitism. It also divided Jewish leaders, with some objecting to having a Zionist and a progressive—a radical in their eyes—becoming the nation's first Jewish justice. The *New York Times*—owned by assimilated Reform Jew Adolph S. Ochs—blasted the nomination, saying, "Brandeis was essentially a contender, a striver after changes and reforms that under our system of government can be properly achieved only through legislation, not through the judgment of courts."

The Senate brushed aside this opposition and confirmed Brandeis 47 to 22. Roosevelt knew and admired Brandeis; they had served together as officers of the New York chapter of the progressive American Association for Labor Legislation. However, FDR took no part in the struggle over Brandeis's confirmation or other Jewish affairs at this time.[22]

Secretary of the Navy Daniels forged relationships with Jewish leaders and bolstered their relief efforts in Palestine. In early 1915, to prevent famine and epidemics within Jewish settlements in Palestine, Daniels dispatched the U.S. Navy supply ship *Vulcan* with some 900 tons of foodstuffs and medicine. Daniels arranged for the *Vulcan* to carry traditional Passover foods such as matzoh and potatoes and ordered the captain to "race across the ocean" and dock in the Holy Land by the Jewish holiday. This was the first time that the U.S. government had officially provided aid to Jews in Palestine. Daniels also worked with Jewish organizations to offer regular religious services for Jews in the military. Although FDR was aware of such initiatives, Jewish-related issues were not a priority for the ambitious assistant secretary.[23]

FDR avoided state politics in 1916 and campaigned for Wilson's reelection. Two days after the election, Wilson carried the Electoral College when he won California by less than 4,000 votes. "The Republican Party has proved to its own satisfaction I hope that the American people cannot always be bought. I hope to God I don't grow reactionary with advancing years," FDR wrote. Age would not diminish either Roosevelt's conviction that business controlled the Republican Party or his commitment to progressive policies.[24]

In April 1917, provoked by Germany's unrestricted submarine warfare in the Atlantic, the United States declared war on Germany. FDR reveled in his new status as an administrator of the American war effort, although he unsuccessfully sought a military commission. As with Abraham Lincoln in the Civil War and Wilson in World War I, Roosevelt would lead the nation through World War II without having had any combat experience himself. World War I, though, stoked his political ambition as he watched President Wilson exercise executive power to shape the great events of the times.

During the war years, FDR became acquainted with a brilliant Jewish lawyer of about his own age. Felix Frankfurter, a Harvard law professor, took a leave of absence to serve as assistant to the secretary of war and chair of the War Labor Policies Board, on which Roosevelt served. He was a nonobservant Jew who married the daughter of a Protestant minister. Supreme Court justice Brandeis would convert him to the Zionist cause. Frankfurter was a small, energetic man with spectacles and the owlish appearance of a reclusive professor. He was both a brilliant scholar and a tireless and colorful public advocate for progressive causes. In the 1920s, Frankfurter would earn fame by rallying public opinion behind Nicola Sacco and Bartolomeo Vanzetti, two radicals controversially charged with murder in conjunction with a payroll robbery. Frankfurter shared FDR's intense ambition, but sought achievement through the law, education, and influence with America's political leaders. He had little use for criticism and could be ruthless and cutting to legal or political adversaries.[25]

Franklin's wife Eleanor was less accepting of Frankfurter and other Jews. She had acquired harsh and commonplace stereotypes of Jews as pushy, social inferiors, much like Edith Wharton's iconic Simon Rosedale, who connives and buys his way into high society. She described Frankfurter as "an interesting little man but very Jew." After reluctantly attending a party for Jewish financier Bernard Baruch, head of the War Industries Board, she complained, "The Jew party was appalling. I never wish to hear money, jewels, and sables mentioned again." Such attitudes were rife among FDR's family and friends.[26]

In mid-1918, FDR toured the European war zone and gained his first encounter with warfare, which he would draw upon during his presidency. Once safely home, Roosevelt insisted that only a strong peacetime military and universal military training would deter future wars.[27]

About this time, FDR's personal life unraveled. Eleanor discovered that he was having an affair with Lucy Mercer, her part-time social secretary. Franklin was deeply in love and might have given up his marriage and his career for Lucy. Sara Roosevelt and Louis Howe successfully intervened to avoid scandal and to hold the marriage to Eleanor together. In 1920, Lucy married an older, wealthy widower, Winthrop Rutherfurd, who died in 1944. Although FDR promised Eleanor that he would not see Lucy again, the two resumed a personal relationship—concealed from Eleanor—certainly in the 1940s and likely much earlier. After the affair, FDR's marriage would never be the same, and his relationship with Eleanor became a professional one. FDR would continue to enjoy the company of other attractive and adoring women such as his personal secretary Marguerite "Missy" LeHand and his cousin Margaret "Daisy" Suckley, but Lucy remained his true love.[28]

FDR's affinity for women mattered politically. More than most men of his generation, he worked comfortably with intelligent, talented, and professional women. He later told Frances Perkins, his secretary of labor and the first woman cabinet member in U.S. history, "I am willing to take more chances. I've got more nerve about women and their status in the world." FDR also had more nerve than most American leaders about working with Jews and moving them into government.[29]

At the war's end, President Wilson hoped to implement his plans for shaping a postwar international order based on self-determination, free trade, and collective security as alternatives to "atavistic imperialism and revolutionary socialism." Instead, the modern American conservative movement surged forth in response to the national crisis that followed a brutal war and a failed peace. The war unleashed a wave of nativism at home that brought on the government's repression of dissent and spread civil and racial strife across the nation. Wilson's Democratic coalition cracked in 1918 when an increasingly conservative Republican Party recaptured the U.S. House and Senate a week before Armistice Day.

Then Wilson's peace plans collapsed amid the diplomatic crosscurrents of a devastated Europe. The president managed to include his proposal for a League of Nations as a peace-keeping organization in the Versailles Treaty with Germany. But Wilson refused to consider compromising with Republican opponents on a treaty that would specify that the U.S. could not intervene in foreign domestic disputes or commit troops abroad without the approval of Congress. The Senate then rejected the treaty, thereby blocking American participation in the League, perhaps presenting Roosevelt with another lesson in the contest between principle and pragmatism as well as sending a warning about the strength of noninterventionist sentiment in the United States. Amid these struggles, Wilson suffered a debilitating stroke, which dashed his hopes for another presidential run. Failure abroad, social unrest and fears of radical subversion at home, and a postwar recession made 1920 a bad year for any Democratic candidate.

Before his postwar decline, Wilson had privately endorsed Britain's "Balfour Declaration." British foreign secretary Lord Arthur Balfour had said that Britain would "view with favour the establishment in Palestine of a national home for the Jewish people." His 1917 declaration pledged Britain's "best endeavours" to establish this national home, although not explicitly a Jewish state. It also said, "nothing shall be done which may prejudice the civil and religious rights of existing non-Jewish communities in Palestine" or "the rights and political status enjoyed by Jews in any other country." After Balfour publicly announced his declaration, Secretary of State Robert Lansing proposed to Wilson several reasons for rejecting this promise to the Jews. He said the United States was not at war with Turkey and should not be complicit in taking Turkish territory (Palestine had been part of the Ottoman Empire). He argued that American Jews did not uniformly support Zionist aspirations "to reestablish their race as an independent people." He claimed that "many Christian sects and individuals would undoubtedly resent turning the Holy Land over to the absolute control of the race credited with the death of Christ." Lansing's arguments, however, failed to change the president's mind about the Balfour Declaration.[30]

In 1922, the League of Nations formally authorized the British Mandate or trusteeship over Palestine to implement the Balfour Declaration. Independently, in 1922, the U.S. Congress passed and President Warren Harding signed a resolution backing the Balfour Declaration. In 1919, American Jewish leader Julian W. Mack prophetically wrote, "The powers of the world cannot create a Jewish Homeland; the powers of the world can give the Jews of the world the opportunity to create a Jewish Homeland, but only the Jewish people can make Palestine a real Jewish Homeland." Even before the league formalized the mandate, Arabs rioted against Jewish settlers in 1920 and 1921. Jews, not for the last time, decried the anemic British response.[31]

Assistant Secretary Roosevelt remained offstage as Wilson stumbled in Paris and failed in Washington. His payoff came quickly. In July 1920, the Democratic National Convention chose FDR, a noted progressive with a magic name, as the vice presidential candidate on the ticket headed by Ohio Governor James Cox. At age thirty-eight, Franklin was three years younger than Teddy Roosevelt when he ran for vice president in 1900.[32]

Conservative senator Warren Harding of Ohio won the Republican nomination against a crowded field that included long-shot candidate Herbert Hoover, who had impressed Jewish leaders with his work as director of food relief for postwar Europe, which encompassed Eastern European lands with large populations of Jews. Hoover's backers included Frankfurter. "I am for Hoover first and last and will do anything to help," Frankfurter wrote to Hoover's Jewish aide on food relief Lewis L. Strauss. Harding represented the conservative consensus of the 1920s that locked together support for private enterprise and white Protestant cultural values. He promised a "return to normalcy" for Americans tired of liberal reform, war, and waves of Catholic and Jewish immigrants. He pledged to end "ineffective meddling" by government in business affairs and to govern as an "America First" president, who, mindful of "racial differences" among people, would open the nation's golden door to "only the immigrant who can be assimilated and thoroughly imbued with the American spirit."[33]

To show well in an apparently losing campaign, FDR had only to perform creditably, not a Herculean task when paired with the lackluster Cox. Roosevelt campaigned energetically and effectively. He improved his speaking skills and mastery of national issues. The man who juggled at least two women and balanced reform leadership and deference to Tammany Hall had no trouble advocating preparedness, patriotic "Americanism," and U.S. participation in the League of Nations. On Election Day, conservative Republicans strengthened their hold on Congress, and Harding won 60 percent of the popular vote to just 34 percent for Cox.

The vice presidential contest rewarded Roosevelt with national campaign experience, invaluable contacts, and the gratitude of party leaders. After the election, he worried only that the Harding administration would become "so tremendously reactionary as to fan the flames of Radicalism." Meanwhile, he could await an inevitable turning of the political tide. "Thank the Lord we are both comparatively youthful!" FDR wrote to campaign advance man Stephen T. Early, later his White House press secretary.[34]

Congress and the Harding administration acted quickly to restrict European immigration to the United States, with Jews a target. Some two million Jewish immigrants who had arrived since the 1880s from places such as Russia, Poland, and Lithuania faced hostility from Protestants and Catholics who harbored negative stereotypes of Jews and doubted their loyalty to the United States. These "new" Jewish immigrants were divided by places of origin in the Old World, communities of settlement in America, religious beliefs and affiliations, and political ideology. Unlike their more established brethren, most recent arrivals from Southern and Eastern Europe struggled economically in adjusting to their adopted nation. Many, if not a majority, turned to socialism as a means for uplifting the working class. Still, outsiders easily missed this diversity and viewed Jewish newcomers as a unified group inclined to support radical politics and resist assimilation. The new arrivals quickly learned not to rely on the goodwill of most Christians.

The Bolshevik Revolution of October 1917 in Russia and America's Red Scare of 1919–1920 led many Americans to associate Jewish socialism with communism abroad and subversion at home. In 1919, U.S. Senate hearings on radical propaganda focused on alleged Jewish agitators. Reverend G. A. Simons, the former head of the Methodist Episcopal Church in Russia, told receptive senators that Jews had perpetrated the Bolshevik Revolution, with many "having come over from the lower East Side of New York." These revolutionaries were now returning to finish the job of revolution in the United States.

Simons pointed to a book recently published in the United States, *The Protocols of the Elders of Zion,* which told of a "secret Jewish society" that used the Bolsheviks "to make a conquest of the world." Although a crude forgery, *Protocols* reinforced the fear that rootless Jews, loyal only to one another, were plotting to raise up their race from outcasts to the masters of the world. Henry Ford, America's leading brand-name producer, prolifically marketed conspiracy theories and menacing stereotypes of Jews. In a four-volume set of books, collectively titled *The International Jew: The World's Foremost Problem,* Ford drew upon the fabricated *Protocols* to warn of a Jewish conspiracy already advanced in America through alleged Jewish control over industry and finance, and most insidiously the news media and the movies.[35]

Reports of the U.S. State Department and the army's military intelligence unit also charged that Jews fostered revolution. A whispering campaign in 1919 accused Justice Brandeis of leading a Jewish plot that pushed the Wilson administration to the far left. Jewish leader Cyrus Adler said that his sources in the press noted the "strong belief that Brandeis was a powerful influence in the administration and that he stood for extremely radical opinions; that he went outside his business as a member of the Court; and had a circle of radicals around him," among them Frankfurter. Similar anti-Semitic innuendos would reemerge during the Roosevelt administration, with Frankfurter perceived as spinning the conspiratorial web.[36]

Contemporary science lent credence to anti-Semitic stereotypes. Leading academic, research, and professional associations within the United States propagated the notion that inherited traits determined the capacities of races. Magazines, including *Scientific American,* which FDR began subscribing to at Groton, newspapers, and best-selling books gave racial theory popular reach. Most racial theories branded Jews as a distinct race. Although scientists subjected no other religious group to racial classification, they claimed to discern the genetic traits of Jews through their long noses, oily skin, and distinctive crania, and common personality types. Others claimed they could recognize Jews through their distinctive "non-white" appearance. Both racial science and ingrained customs sustained negative and contradictory stereotypes about Jews in the popular media. Jews were both able competitors to America's Christian civilization and a source of racial pollution through inferior genes.[37]

When the House Committee on Immigration considered restrictive legislation after the 1920 elections, a report by Wilbur J. Carr, director of the State Department's Consular Service, singled out Eastern European Jews as "filthy un-American and often dangerous in their habits," "economically undesirable," "socially undesirable," "abnormally twisted," and prone to become "political and labor agitators." Only the two Jewish Democrats on the fourteen-person committee signed a minority report that objected to these aspersions. "There is nothing in the entire [Carr] report which suggests careful or impartial study," wrote immigration authority Max J. Kohler. "There are many judgments of a most superficial character, all of them expressing prejudice rather than knowledge. The spirit of anti-Semitism is marked throughout, and represents a very ugly turn in the treatment of public questions." The Emergency Immigration Act, which raced through Congress in 1921, temporarily restricted European immigration to 3 percent of each nationality in the U.S. under the census of 1910, with a total annual quota of 357,000. The Act sharply limited the immigration of Jews who resided primarily in Eastern European nations with meager quotas.[38]

Three months after Congress restricted immigration, on August 10, 1921, following several days of draining activity, FDR crawled into bed at his retreat on Campobello Island with no inkling that he would never walk without assistance again. The local family physician, E. H. Bennett, first diagnosed a cold. After Roosevelt's paralysis grew worse, he brought in a consultant, William W. Keen, the nation's first brain surgeon, who had participated in a secret operation to remove a cancerous tumor from President Grover Cleveland's jaw. Vacationing nearby, Keen examined Roosevelt and diagnosed a blood clot on the lower spinal cord, urging massage of the leg muscles, the painfully wrong remedy for FDR's real illness that a specialist, Robert Lovett, diagnosed on August 25. Dr. Lovett confirmed that Franklin Roosevelt at age thirty-nine had contracted polio, colloquially known as infantile paralysis. Five years earlier, with his thoughts on his children, FDR had written to warn Eleanor, "The infantile paralysis in N.Y. and vicinity is appalling."[39]

After the family received the diagnosis of polio, Louis Howe stepped in to help Eleanor cope with FDR's business and political affairs, while the two of them kept FDR's illness hidden for several weeks. As he struggled with his affliction, the jaunty, youthful-looking FDR of 1920 soon disappeared. His face took on a new gravity and maturity with thinner hair and the lines of middle age. FDR read more widely, especially in American history. He developed greater patience and determination than before and came to put the challenges of politics into broader context and perspective.

FDR's illness also changed the life of Eleanor Roosevelt. She challenged the authority of her domineering mother-in-law and in doing so gained confidence and self-assurance in her marriage and her professional life. Eleanor became a leader of progressive women's groups. Like other reform-minded, upper-class, white Protestant women of her generation, she embraced a liberal maternalism that would apply principles of the household economy to improving the health, welfare, and living conditions of modern society. She was becoming an exemplar of the new female social and political engagement with the world outside the home.[40]

Roosevelt rejected his doctors' opinion that he would never regain the use of his legs. He intended to overcome paralysis and return to politics through persistence, faith, and determination. Despite the conventional wisdom of his time that would exclude a disabled man from electoral politics, Roosevelt battled for physical mobility not merely to live comfortably, but to make his mark on history. He discovered the heated waters at Warm Springs, Georgia, and he found them to be restorative. In 1926, he purchased the Warm Springs resort and, with the assistance of his friend and confidant Basil O'Connor, established the Georgia Warm Springs Foundation as a nonprofit center for polio research and rehabilitation. Immersion in the waters at Warm Springs did not cure the paralysis that afflicted both of FDR's legs. But it contributed to his recovery of sufficient health and vigor to run for high office again in 1928.[41]

After contracting polio, FDR was better suited than before to assume the role of a successful national leader. The continuities in FDR's political career are too compelling to suggest that a new man emerged from the crucible of his illness. Before, he had been a progressive, a reformer who challenged entrenched power, a vigorous and innovative campaigner, and a celebrated wartime administrator of a large, complex, and important department of government. Roosevelt's ordeal strengthened qualities already present within him, while smoothing out rough spots in his character. His lonely battle against paralysis both enriched his inner life and stiffened his resolve to insulate private struggles from public view. His illness taught him how to respond to unexpected twists of fate. It reinforced his inclination to keep aspects of his life in separate compartments and to set and keep firm priorities. As a leveler of class and privilege, polio enlivened Roosevelt's sense of noblesse oblige with empathy for the destitute, exploited, and oppressed. His early botched treatment by the eminent Dr. Keen honed his distrust of conventional experts and his faith in his personal judgment. It prompted him to seek advice and assistance from private sources and persons outside the conventional mainstream. In time, FDR's circle would come to include many Jews.

CHAPTER TWO

FDR Returns

A PARTLY PARALYZED FDR eased back into New York politics by endorsing Al Smith for governor in 1922. Smith had lost his governorship in the Republican landslide of 1920 and faced stiff Democratic opposition from publisher William Randolph Hearst. In a nifty maneuver, FDR also backed for senator Dr. Royal S. Copeland, the author of a medical column for the Hearst newspaper syndicate. Both Smith and Copeland won the Democratic nomination and the general election. Still, Hearst never quite forgave Roosevelt for backing Smith.

In the midterm elections of 1922, the Democratic Party gained an extraordinary seventy-four House seats and six Senate seats, coming close to recapturing control of Congress. Then in 1923, the "Teapot Dome" scandal exposed high officials in the Harding administration as profiting from the illegal sale or use of government property, including federal oil reserves at Elk Hill, California, and Teapot Dome, Wyoming. After Harding's death in August 1923, the untainted vice president Calvin Coolidge stepped in as a surprisingly popular president at a time of peace and prosperity. Republican confidence rose and Democratic prospects for 1924 plummeted.[1]

As the capstone of his abbreviated term, Coolidge and the Republican Congress culminated efforts to restrict immigration. In 1924, Congress limited permanently European immigration to nationality quotas of 2 percent, based on the census of 1890. Jewish leaders protested discrimination against U.S. citizens who had arrived since 1890, but they also endorsed restrictions based on mental and physical fitness, moral character, and political ideology. "My associates and I are very vigorously opposed to unrestricted immigration," prominent social worker and fundraiser Jacob Billikopf testified before the U.S. House of Representatives. "We are opposed to the type of immigrant whose physique and mentality are impaired; to the immigrant with criminalistic tendencies; to any man or woman who comes with ideas and ideals which are not in harmony with the ideals governing our own country." In their testimony, Jewish leaders avoided identifying Jews as a distinct race. Jews, they said, belonged to the "white race," unlike unassimilable nonwhite Asiastics, who were not eligible for naturalized American citizenship.[2]

The new legislation slashed the 1921 quotas for Europe and heavily favored Western and Northern Europe at the expense of Southern and Eastern Europe. Taken together, the quotas for nations in the heart of Eastern Europe—Russia, Poland, Romania, Lithuania, Latvia, and Yugoslavia—totaled only about 10,000. The law required entry visas, backed by supporting documents such as birth certificates, police records, and bank reports. It excluded Japanese and other Asians, but exempted most of the Western Hemisphere from restrictions so that Mexico could continue supplying western farmers with cheap labor.[3]

A House-Senate conference committee revised the law by creating a cabinet-level commission to set new, permanent quotas based on the "national origins" of the American population. Secretary of Commerce Herbert Hoover objected that the government lacked reliable data to fix national origins quotas "accurately and without hardship." Congress nonetheless maintained this new provision that increased quotas for Great Britain and Northern Ireland and reduced them for other Northern and Western European countries. The new system had by far the greatest impact on Germany, which saw its quota sliced in half, from 51,227 to 25,957. It maintained the meager quotas for Southern and Eastern Europe. By excluding blacks, Asians, Latinos, and American Indians from calculations of America's national origins, American immigration policy enshrined whites as a privileged category, legally and culturally. Jewish leader and prominent attorney Louis Marshall said that national origin quotas established "a difference between black and white" and then subdivided whites "on the theory that in the one case the cradle was rocked in Nordic territory and in the other in non-Nordic territory and that one group represents all that is noble in mankind and the other all that is ignoble."[4]

For restrictionists, the quota system insulated America from the effects of foreign persecution that had sent waves of Jewish immigrants fleeing to the United States. For long-suffering Jews in Eastern Europe, it meant finding places of refuge elsewhere in the New World.

In 1927, Peruvian and Paraguayan consuls in the U.S., encouraged by first-term Senator Copeland of New York, a critic of immigration quotas, officially welcomed projects to resettle Jews in their sparsely populated lands. Two years later, a non-Jewish syndicate obtained a land grant of 2.5 million acres in Peru, which it offered to Jewish organizations for settlement by Eastern European Jews. Surveyors pronounced the land fit for settlement, and the Peruvian government pledged subsidies and tax breaks to foster the economic development promised by an influx of Jewish labor. Ironically, Jewish leaders in Germany took the lead on implementing this plan to rescue their brethren in the lands of pogroms to the south and east. They had no inkling at this time that German Jews might soon need to find refuge abroad. Their proposal ambitiously envisioned the emigration of some 250,000 Eastern European Jews per year to Peru. However, political unrest in Peru and the economic hardships of the Great Depression that began in 1929 killed the plan.[5]

FDR took no part in debates over immigration restriction. Rather, he returned to public prominence only later in the year by nominating New York governor Al Smith as a presidential candidate at the National Democratic Convention in New York City. FDR mastered a text largely written by Smith's Jewish speechwriter, Judge Joseph M. Proskauer, which dubbed Smith the "Happy Warrior" of American politics. It was his first national appearance since being struck by polio, and he painfully made his way to the rostrum on crutches. With his hands gripping the podium, he stood for forty-five minutes, ending his speech to a thunderous ovation that lasted for more than an hour. Some may have been applauding for Smith, potentially the party's first Catholic presidential candidate. Surely others cheered for the raw courage and brilliance of FDR's performance.

FDR's party divided along regional and cultural lines in the convention; eastern delegates backed Smith and southern and western delegates favored California senator William Gibbs McAdoo. Smith and his allies failed by a single vote to pass a resolution that denounced the racist Ku Klux Klan. After McAdoo and Smith deadlocked for a record 103 ballots, the delegates compromised on corporate lawyer John W. Davis. FDR was one of very few Democrats to emerge from the convention with his standing enhanced nationwide. Rabbi Stephen S. Wise, who attended the convention as a New York delegate, wrote, "A few more Franklyn [sic] Roosevelts and a few less of other kinds of people might have turned the scale" for Smith.[6]

Smith stayed in the political arena and won reelection as governor, but Coolidge prevailed in a presidential contest that also included Senator Robert F. La Follette of Wisconsin, the nominee of a new Progressive Party sponsored by labor and farm groups. The Democratic share of the vote sank to an historic low of 29 percent, with La Follette winning 17 percent. "The problem with the Democrats was that they were neither radical enough for the radicals nor conservative enough for the conservatives," said Thomas W. Hardwick, former Democratic senator from Georgia.[7]

FDR preferred a liberal direction for the party. Five years earlier, he had anticipated modern political alignments and terminology by branding Republicans as America's "conservative" party and Democrats the "liberal" party. By 1924, Roosevelt and his adviser Louis McHenry Howe were developing a critique of Republican policies similar to later assaults on "trickle-down" economics. "Prosperity from the Republican standpoint," Howe wrote to FDR, "means the prosperity of a few great corporations and such crumbs of prosperity as drop from their table for the benefit of the country at large."[8]

After Coolidge surprisingly declined to run for president in 1928, leadership smoothly passed to Hoover, secretary of commerce since 1921. Hoover had gained the admiration of Jewish leaders for his postwar relief work. Yet he believed in preserving the white "Nordic" basis of American society through immigration restriction. In 1923 he said, "Social considerations involved in the immigration problem far outweigh any economic considerations or arguments that might be made for allowing unchecked immigration." Hoover's belief in social harmony left no room for attacking the structural discrimination that religious and racial minorities faced in education, jobs, housing, and social life. Throughout his years at Commerce, and during his campaign for president in 1928, he made no condemnation of anti-Semitism.

At the 1928 Democratic Convention in Houston, Roosevelt showed his growing mastery of ethnic politics when he arranged for a rabbi to deliver the convocation on the day he again nominated Smith for president. Henry Morgenthau Jr. profusely thanked FDR, saying, "I believe our party would have been criticized, and justifiably so, if they had every religion represented expect [sic] the Jewish." FDR responded with the quip, "'Yes, we have no rabbi today!'" He explained that "four policemen and several firemen" had scoured Houston in vain for a rabbi to open the convention. "Apparently, the rabbies [sic] in Houston, like the Catholic priests were backward about coming forward," FDR wrote. "The other sky pilots [Protestants] were so anxious to pray for our souls (or rather to make political speeches to us) that the authorities had to draw lots!" Just before Roosevelt introduced "a willing baptist to meet the emergency . . . your good rabbi was led in handcuffed, delivered over to me and the day was saved."[9]

The convention nominated Smith for president, making him the first Catholic on a major party ticket in the United States. Later, the New York State Democratic Convention met in October 1928 with the preferred candidate for governor absent—Roosevelt, who had fled to his retreat in Warm Springs. He had disappeared because he wanted to avoid running for governor in what he viewed as another grim year for Democrats, given peace, prosperity, and Republican control over national government. By avoiding electoral politics in 1928, FDR expected to lead his party after the election and choose his time to run for high office. Howe suspected that Roosevelt's zest for the political game might make him reconsider. He cabled his boss, "If they are looking for goat why don't Wagner [U.S. senator Robert F.] sacrifice himself." He advised, "a definite final and irrevocable statement that your health will not permit you to run."[10]

Smith wanted Roosevelt's help to carry their state. He ultimately appealed successfully to FDR "on a personal basis," while assuring him a strong lieutenant governor nominee in Jewish banker Herbert H. Lehman. Smith believed that if the polio-stricken FDR won the election, Lehman would assume most executive duties, leaving Smith in effective control of the state. Smith even doubted whether FDR would live through a term as governor.

Like Republican Party bosses who hoped to put the troublesome Theodore Roosevelt in a useless office by nominating him for vice president in

1900, Smith's miscalculations about another Roosevelt changed the course
of history. Smith lost the presidency, but FDR won the governor's mansion.
He then vaulted ahead of Smith as a contender for the presidency, after political fortunes had brightened for Democrats in 1932.

Antipluralist white Protestants bitterly opposed the election of a Catholic president in 1928. Although Hoover personally avoided anti-Catholic
appeals, other Republicans and southern Democrats opposed to Smith's
election did not. American Jews recognized bigotry and backed Smith in
response. Jewish financier Bernard Baruch wrote to Winston Churchill of
his surprise that "intolerance in the Land of the Brave and the Free would
hold such sway." Billikopf said that "the great, if not the greatest issue in
American life is the one which concerns itself with the problem or problems
of race and religious prejudice." Thus, "the vote for Smith . . . is a blow at
Prejudice." Jewish leader Cyrus Adler told Roosevelt, "it was about time that
the American people should show that they are willing to put their professions of religious liberty in practice." Republican Roger W. Straus, the son
of pioneering Jewish cabinet member Oscar Straus, warned Hoover of the
many desertions by Jews who felt compelled "to vote for religious freedom."
The Yiddish-language Jewish press uniformly deplored religious bigotry,
although most newspapers declined to choose between two appealing candidates. Three Yiddish papers endorsed Smith and two endorsed Hoover.[11]

FDR believed that Smith had made an uphill battle steeper by campaigning on his opposition to Prohibition. He told Daniels, "I am more and
more disgusted and bored with the thought that in this great nation, the
principle issue we may be drawn into is what we do or do not put into our
stomachs." On fundamentals, FDR worried that Smith moved too far to
the right in appeasing big business. Smith's appointment of Jewish General
Motors magnate John Jacob Raskob as campaign manager, Roosevelt
wrote, was "a bold stroke to try to end the 99% of business (big and little)
preference for the Republican Party." FDR said he told Smith "to make it
clear that . . . Raskob would be merely a business manager and have nothing to say about issues. But Smith would not agree to this." In July, Raskob
wrote to conservative industrialist Irénée Du Pont that Smith agreed with
them on the goal of "protecting big business."[12]

Despite FDR's misgivings about the fate of Democrats in 1928, he ran
for governor with gusto. FDR confided to Senator Wagner his preference
for executive leadership. "It seems to me that for you and me things have

worked out very well," he wrote. "I know that you would rather be Senator than Governor and if I had to be either I would rather be Governor than Senator."[13]

Lehman readily accepted his role as FDR's running mate. Earlier, some Jewish leaders had promoted Lehman as a candidate for governor, especially after the Republicans seemed poised to nominate Jewish attorney general Albert Ottinger. Responses to what Billikopf called "behind the stage" maneuvers to nominate Lehman, illustrate how fears about anti-Semitism could paralyze Jewish leaders. Billikopf said that Roosevelt, who was "protestant and prominent," could "have the nomination," but would decline "because of his health." Although Lehman hoped to run against Ottinger and keep Jewish voters in line for the Democrats, Jewish leaders who calibrated political decisions to mollify anti-Semites opposed his nomination. Federal judge and Jewish leader Julian W. Mack wrote that prominent Jewish columnist Walter Lippmann "is absolutely clear that it would be a most terrible mistake to nominate any Jew for Governor this year. He feels strongly that it would intensify Protestant religious bigotry . . . and arouse or intensify latent anti-Semitism." *New York Times* publisher Adolph Ochs said, "It would be unwise to have a Catholic and Jew on the same ticket, believe it would be a political mistake, and a liability to Smith throughout the country."[14]

After FDR's nomination, Felix Frankfurter expressed relief about avoiding "a rivalry between two Jews for the Jewish votes. There are people who are playing with fire in this country, and it is a source of great relief and satisfaction that a candidate so superbly fit, wholly on the merits, as Franklin Roosevelt was available." Billikopf said, "Although I should love to have seen Herbert Lehman nominated for the governorship . . . the choice of Franklin Roosevelt was highly desirable."[15]

Roosevelt's campaign against Attorney General Ottinger posed both political jeopardy and opportunity. FDR knew that his opponent might attract normally Democratic Jewish voters in New York City, but might also lose anti-Semitic Republican votes upstate. The balance between Jewish solidarity and Christian anti-Semitism, which neither candidate could readily control, might decide the election.

During a brief five-week campaign, in which FDR dashed across the state to dispel doubts about his health, he first denounced anti-Catholic bigotry and urged the election of Smith. Soon he and Smith both realized that he had to cater to state concerns if he hoped to beat Ottinger and help the national ticket. For the first time, Roosevelt recruited Jewish talent, enlisting former state assemblyman Samuel I. Rosenman as a speechwriter and authority on state issues. Rosenman would remain an influential adviser for the remainder of FDR's life.

In New York, open agitation of the religious issue came not from anti-Semites, but from contentious Jews. The day after FDR's nomination, Robert Daru, a Jewish assistant attorney general in New York City, warned him that Jewish Republicans, led by Marshall, were playing a game of double deception to help Ottinger: denying the existence of a Jewish bloc vote while making "the indirect appeal for the Jews to vote for Ottinger." Daru said, "Mr. Marshall knows that any attempt to obtain Jewish support for the Republican gubernatorial candidate because of his religious faith cannot be done openly. . . . But there is an indirect way in which Jews can be improperly influenced to vote for a Jew, and Mr. Marshall knows how. Tell them they are being oppressed,—discriminated in certain ways—even if they are not."[16] Marshall was, in fact, secretly coordinating the release of such material with the Republican Party, although he complained, "apparently the Republican organization has no idea as how to distribute its news matter."[17]

FDR wrote back to Daru, saying, "I sincerely hope that one religious issue at a time will be all that we will be burdened with in this campaign." Consistent with his view of Jewish identity, Roosevelt added, "in this particular case the issue is not so much religious as racial, which is, if anything 'worse.'" Religion publicly surfaced in the campaign about two weeks later when Benjamin E. Greenspan, former assistant corporation counsel for New York City, warned in a published letter to FDR about an effort led by bigots to help Roosevelt by prompting anti-Semites to vote against Ottinger. He added that "another class of bigots is attempting to induce the Jewish people to vote for the Republican nominee for Governor as well as the Democratic candidate for Lieutenant Governor."[18]

A week later, Democrat Samuel Untermyer, FDR's former critic, publicly claimed that Ottinger "was nominated solely because he is a Jew and a foil or cover to the campaign of bigotry that the Republican Party is waging throughout the nation. He is a Jew only as a stalking horse to attract the Jewish votes that would otherwise go to the Democratic national and state tickets." Untermyer insisted that Lehman was a "better" Jew than Ottinger and more deserving of Jewish votes. Reverend Edward L. Hunt, a Hoover supporter, responded that the GOP had nominated the attorney general because of his qualifications, not his religion. He implored Hoover loyalists not to abandon Ottinger. Hearst then charged that Roosevelt had deliberately used Untermyer "to drag a religious issue into politics." Roosevelt, he said, had encouraged Jews to assail Ottinger because he lacked qualifications for governor, other than his last name.[19]

FDR carefully walked the line between retaining Jewish support and exploiting upstate anti-Semitism. He knew that his progressive views appealed to New York's heavily left-wing Jewish voters and said only that the state's "Jewish citizens" would vote according to "the fitness of the candidates and the great issues involved." Roosevelt declined comment about prospects for a "silent" anti-Semitic vote against Ottinger, but the practical politician also indirectly encouraged such support in an interview with the press on October 21. "There are a great many Republicans," he said, "openly coming out and supporting the Democratic ticket, or coming around privately and saying 'I can't announce this publicly, but don't worry about where I am going on election day.'" A reporter asked, "Like that man at church this morning?" FDR answered, "Yes—'We can't say that out loud.'"[20]

Late in the campaign, Rabbi Wise delivered an important pro-Roosevelt speech at Madison Square Garden. Wise agreed with Frankfurter's suggestion to expose "the irrelevant appeal widely and quietly made in behalf of Ottinger as a Jew" and persuade "Jews to show their patriotism as well as their discernment" by voting for FDR. Wise told the Garden crowd that he would vote for "men of all faiths," the Catholic Smith, the Protestant Roosevelt, and the Jewish Lehman, "not as a Jew . . . but as an American choosing the best candidates." For the remainder of his long career in the public eye, Wise would balance carefully his special pleading for Jewish causes with a devotion to common American ideals.[21]

Sectarian politics played out predictably in the gubernatorial vote, but with less effect than religiously charged rhetoric would suggest. Smith narrowly lost New York State and overwhelmingly lost the national popular and Electoral College vote. Although religion did not decide the outcome, Smith benefited from a pro-Catholic vote and Hoover from an anti-Catholic Protestant vote. About 75 percent of white Protestants outside the South voted for Hoover and an equal percentage of northern Catholics for Smith. A majority of Jews nationwide also supported the Democratic ticket.

Although Smith sufficiently mollified business to gain near parity in fund-raising, affluent voters still favored Hoover. As Roosevelt had anticipated, class voting reflected the role of Republicans as the guardians of pro-business policies during the 1920s.[22]

In New York, Roosevelt beat Ottinger by a thin statewide plurality of some 25,000 votes. Three of the other five Democrats running statewide also prevailed, including Lehman, who proved that a Jewish candidate could win high office in New York. Statistical analysis of election returns by county shows that FDR, the three other winning Democrats, and Smith easily carried the Jewish and Catholic vote, with FDR slightly behind the other candidates. Roosevelt won more upstate white Protestant voters than any other Democrat did. Thus, Ottinger's religion seems to have slightly diminished FDR's Jewish vote and more substantially expanded his white Protestant vote.[23]

The elusive Roosevelt did not record his reflections on his 1928 victory over a Jewish opponent. Still, as a shrewd politician, he likely drew lessons from this religiously sensitive campaign. First, non-Jewish politicians should avoid entanglement in conflicts among Jewish leaders. Second, Jews respond to nonreligious issues and do not necessarily vote en masse for Jewish candidates or Jewish causes. Third, no Jewish leader or group can turn on or off a Jewish bloc, although some may threaten to do so. To serve their interests, Jewish leaders may also deny the existence of a Jewish vote. Fourth, anti-Semitism can be present even when hidden from view, as evidenced by the so-called "silent" Republican vote. Fifth, non-Jewish leaders could lean on Jewish talent like Rosenman.

The elections of 1928 likely reinforced FDR's aversion to religious-based politics. In an unpublished statement, FDR recognized "an absolute separation of temporal authority from spiritual authority," which "applies as a fundamental doctrine of America to Protestant, Catholic, Jew, and the followers of all other religions and sects." Consistent with his Christian social service at Harvard, he adhered not to an inward-looking religion, but to the Social Gospel ideal of religion in the service of humanity. He said, "While I am unalterably in favor of keeping the Church and the State separate, I am just as much in favor of putting some religious ideals into our political life."[24]

After his election, the pragmatic governor-elect continued to draw on the skills and expertise of Jewish professionals. Roosevelt cared only that these aides and advisers had the experience, brains, and liberal values to help him navigate the treacherous waters of New York politics and guide state policy. Rosenman remained as speechwriter and policy consultant. Henry Morgenthau Jr. provided guidance on farm issues; Proskauer, Smith's former campaign chair, advised on criminal justice matters, as did Anna Rosenberg on labor issues. The election of 1928 also revived Roosevelt's dormant relationship with Frankfurter, who had become the Harvard Law School's only Jewish tenured faculty member. Frankfurter began corresponding with Roosevelt after his nomination for governor; a friendship and working partnership between the two men thrived thereafter.

Although Roosevelt retained most appointees from Smith's tenure, he rejected the exiting governor's plea that he should employ Belle Moskowitz, Smith's chief strategist, as his personal secretary, and retain the brilliant but prickly Robert Moses as secretary of state. Eleanor Roosevelt, who had a closer relationship to Smith than Franklin did, warned her husband that Smith planned to keep control of state government through these two Jewish appointees. Her advice reflected lingering stereotypes of assertive Jews. "You will wake up and find R. M. Secretary of State and B. M. running Democratic Publicity at her old stand unless you take a firm stand," she told her husband. "Gosh, the race has nerves of iron and tentacles of steel."[25]

Soon after his inauguration as president, Hoover faced a test internationally when Arab riots in the summer of 1929 killed more than 130 Jewish settlers in Palestine, including some Americans. Leaders of American Jewry demanded that the United States should honor its commitment to the Balfour Declaration by protesting Great Britain's inadequate security for Jews, sending a warship to Palestine in support of Jewish settlers, and insisting that an American serve on the British commission charged with investigating the riots. The Hoover administration rejected all three requests. For the president and his foreign policy advisers, the costs of antagonizing Arabs and other Muslims by intervening in Palestine outweighed the benefits. Walter Knabenshue, America's counsel general in Jerusalem, explained that "It would appear to be inadvisable for the United States to make official representations in this matter to the British Government, for such action would undoubtedly create resentment against us here and in other Moslem countries." Hoover acceded to such advice.[26]

In October 1929, the American stock market crashed, beginning the worldwide Great Depression. In response, President Hoover sought to preserve American jobs for Americans. After the president discussed immigration with his cabinet, he directed the State Department to issue new instructions to American consuls abroad. Without seeking new legislation, the president slashed immigration to the United States in September 1930 by having the State Department tighten the existing provision of law that banned entry visas to foreigners likely to become a public charge.[27]

Previously, U.S. officials considered aliens who lacked the physical or mental capacity for employment as likely to become public charges. Now, the State Department applied this label to the vast majority of visa applicants who lacked the substantial means needed to support themselves in Depression-ridden America. Aliens could not compensate for inadequate funds by arranging for work in the United States; immigration law also barred "contract labor." The new restrictions cut immigration from European countries on average to about 10 percent of quota levels, reducing the already limited opportunities for Jews to seek refuge in the United States. In 1931, for the first time in the country's history, the outflow of residents leaving for other lands exceeded the inflow of immigrants.[28]

Neither the reduction of immigration nor other Hoover remedies improved an ailing economy. The Great Depression shattered the Republican Party's image as the reliable guardian of prosperity and created an opening for their long-suffering Democratic rivals. Nationally, FDR's Democrats notched big victories in the 1930 U.S. Senate and House elections. In New York, Roosevelt easily won reelection as governor, with a nearly 60 percent majority. Statistical analysis shows that FDR again swept the Catholic and Jewish votes. This time he also won the white Protestant vote. Only highly affluent voters and traditionally Republican Negroes backed his Republican opponent Charles Tuttle. Two days after the election, voters from Warm Springs, Georgia, formed the nation's first Roosevelt for President Club.[29]

The Great Depression devastated New York State's Jewish community, which was still adjusting to life in the United States and burdened with discrimination in jobs and education. In late June 1930, Governor Roosevelt denounced both these forms of intolerance in an interview with the Jewish Telegraphic Agency. FDR was in Sarasota Springs at the time, addressing the convention of the Independent Order of B'rith Abraham. Roosevelt called for "continuous education work" to combat discrimination against Jews, but declined to support legislation that would make it a misdemeanor for an employer to discriminate against a job applicant on account of race, creed, or color. "Such a law," he said, "would be just as difficult to enforce as the Volstead Act," which prohibited the manufacture and sale of alcoholic beverages.[30]

Hundreds of thousands of Jews in New York City lost their savings when the Jewish-owned and recklessly mismanaged Bank of United States collapsed in late 1930. This was the biggest bank failure to date in American history. Desperate Jews pleaded with Roosevelt for help. The governor expressed his sympathy for the depositors but failed to deliver a vigorous investigation of wrongdoing at the bank. He could not restore vanished deposits after Jewish bankers Felix Warburg and Lehman (FDR's lieutenant governor) failed in behind-the-scenes efforts to merge the troubled bank with stronger institutions. The non-Jewish commercial banking community showed little interest in rescuing a bank run by Jews primarily for immigrant Jewish workers and small merchants. The Republican legislature rejected the governor's belated and modest proposals for banking reform, enabling FDR to shift blame to his opposition. Disgruntled depositors mounted a few demonstrations and protests but lacked political clout. Both Republican hostility to Jewish concerns and FDR's sympathy without sufficient follow-up would foreshadow episodes of his presidency.[31]

In Germany, the worldwide depression benefited Adolf Hitler and his Nazi Party. In 1923, Hitler had led a failed coup against the German Republic, but received a light sentence for treason from anti-Republican judges. Hitler disclosed his obsessive hatred for Jews in his memoir and political tract, *Mein Kampf,* which he wrote in prison. Hitler emerged from prison as a political force in Germany during the late 1920s. He skillfully exploited resentment over the draconian peace treaty that the Allies had imposed on Germany after World War I and promoted a toxic mix of German expansionism and virulent anti-Semitism. For Hitler and his Nazi followers, the Jews were a deadly international menace that threatened the German race. In the September 1930 elections, the Nazis stunned the world by winning the second-largest number of seats in the Reichstag, the lower house of the German legislature.

The American press extensively covered the Nazi gains as a threat to democracy and Jewish rights in Germany. Yet the mainstream media and even the left-wing Yiddish press doubted that the Nazis had staying power in Germany. The day after the 1930 Reichstag election, the *Yiddish Forward,* edited by the respected Abraham Cahan, dismissed Hitler as "no more than a windbag, stupid, filled with *chutzpah,* yet not one to be worried about." Politically active Jews shared some of this disdain for Hitler, but heard troubling news from private sources that the Nazis could come to rule Germany, persecute Jews, and threaten world peace.[32]

In October 1930, when the recommendations of a British White Paper—a statement of government policy—threatened to curtail Jewish immigration to Palestine, the Hoover administration stayed aloof. It ignored demands from some 40,000–50,000 protestors in New York City and many thousands more in cities across America. Governor Roosevelt sent a message to the New York rally that affirmed a "moral obligation" to establish a Jewish national home in Palestine. Eventually, for reasons of his own, British prime minister Ramsay MacDonald decided to preserve Jewish access to Palestine, although he did not formally rescind the White Paper. Meanwhile, Jewish lawyer Benjamin Ammerman, a Republican candidate for Congress in New York, asked the president to protect the "property, liberty and lives of those of the Jewish faith" in Germany. Secretary of State Henry L. Stimson replied negatively for the president, saying, "This Government is not in a position to intercede on behalf of persons other than American citizens." Jewish leaders asked the president to participate in meetings on the welfare of European Jewry, to protect Jewish students studying at the University of Vienna, including some Americans, from assaults by hostile German students, and to use his influence to stop the persecution of Jews in Poland. Hoover did not respond positively to any of these petitions.[33]

Many leaders of American Jewry still admired Hoover for his relief work after World War I and for his nomination of Jewish New York State Judge Benjamin Cardozo for the U.S. Supreme Court in January 1932. Hoover defied advisers who had warned against selecting a second Jewish justice. The president knew that unlike Justice Brandeis, Cardozo was neither controversial nor active politically. A unanimous Senate confirmed his nomination by voice vote.[34]

As the Depression deepened after the 1930 elections, FDR emerged as the clear frontrunner for the Democratic presidential nomination in 1932. Roosevelt defended liberal policies, but also avoided a confrontation with Tammany Hall by ignoring the pleas of reformers to force from office the machine-backed, corrupt mayor of New York City, Jimmy Walker. FDR's one-time admirer Rabbi Wise sharply criticized the governor's irresolute approach to reforming state politics. Still, conservative Democrats opposed his nomination. They hoped instead to deadlock the convention on the model of 1924, and broker the choice of a nonthreatening conservative. The opposition failed to settle on an appealing candidate and FDR won a fourth-ballot victory after offering the vice presidential nomination to favorite son John Nance Garner of Texas. Smith and his allies reluctantly backed the heavily favored Democratic ticket.[35]

Shortly after his nomination, FDR selected Henry Morgenthau Sr. as vice chairman of his Executive Finance Committee. Six other New York Jews also served on the committee: Bernard Baruch, Herbert Bayard Swope, Jessie I. Straus, Sidney Weinberg, Walter Weinstein, and Laurence A. Steinhardt. Although Republicans collected a larger share of business dollars during FDR's presidential campaigns, Jewish businessmen primarily supported Democrats.[36]

Only with the presidential nomination in hand did FDR finally pressure the corrupt mayor Walker to resign from office. Such maneuvering prompted Wise to complain to Frankfurter that the governor is "utterly untrustworthy" regarding any "decision or action which may adversely affect his own political fortunes." Even if FDR were "surrounded by the right men," Wise wondered if he would "heed their counsel" or just "bind them to his magisterial will once he becomes president?" Ironically, critics would later charge that Wise had fallen victim to FDR's "magisterial will." Frankfurter responded, by saying that despite some "limitations and inadequacies" FDR would take America in "the right [liberal] direction." All leaders, he said, defer at times to expediency, "not excluding Woodrow Wilson." Circumstances would test FDR's moral backbone many times during his presidential years.[37]

Roosevelt was one of the most cosmopolitan presidential candidates in the history of the Republic. He had traveled frequently to Europe and could read both German and French. FDR had visited Germany many times in his youth. When he and Eleanor later honeymooned there in 1905, his letters home warned of German militarism, which he believed had outweighed the liberal side of German culture and society. When war erupted in Europe in 1914, Assistant Secretary of the Navy Roosevelt wrote of his disappointment that the German Kaiser "has left the U.S.

out—he has declared war against everybody else. . . . Everybody here feels that this country as a whole sympathizes with the allies against Germany." His anti-German orientation, his detestation of religiously based politics, and his reliance on Jewish advisers all suggested that FDR would strongly respond to the rise of Hitler and the Nazis to power in Germany. However, the Great Depression and the dire threat it posed to American prosperity and social stability overrode other considerations.[38]

CHAPTER THREE

The Democrat
and the Dictator

AFTER FDR'S NOMINATION for president in 1932, some Democratic politicians, like Louis Howe in 1928, advised him to use his disability as cover for avoiding a political challenge. Convinced that Roosevelt could lose to Herbert Hoover only with a colossal blunder on the stump or a physical collapse, they argued that his health justified conducting an old-style "front-porch" campaign in Hyde Park. Roosevelt firmly rejected such advice. "I have suggested to Governor Roosevelt the dangers attending around the country public speaking," wrote Democratic senator Key Pittman of Nevada. But "he does not feel the dangers."[1]

Not for the first or the last time, Roosevelt was right and his cautious advisers were wrong. FDR delivered more than 100 speeches during the campaign and seemed to enjoy every one of them. The campaign invigorated him, honed his rhetorical skills, and built momentum for the reform program—the New Deal—that he began during his first hundred days in office. With more than a fifth of the workforce unemployed, farms and businesses bleeding red ink, and the financial system collapsing, FDR focused on domestic issues during the campaign.

James G. McDonald, the head of the American Foreign Policy Association, who considered himself an "unqualified pessimist" about the state of world affairs, secured a rare private interview with candidate Roosevelt on October 16. McDonald recorded his impression "that he [FDR], having made up his mind it would be inadvisable to speak about foreign affairs in the campaign, was paying little attention to them." McDonald was "disappointed not to get any assurance from him as to any particular line of policy" and regarded FDR "as being almost 100 percent political minded." Roosevelt would continue this wary approach to world affairs and immigration during his first term as president.[2]

With vast unemployment at home, no candidate would dare to challenge America's immigration quotas. Still, in a remarkable interview with Joseph Brainin, editor of an English-Yiddish news service, FDR called for "humanizing" the immigration regulations. Although FDR generally backed immigration restrictions at a time of economic hardship, he challenged Hoover's policies, saying, "The spirit of the regulations must be carried out with tact, discretion, and human understanding." FDR opposed plans circulating in Washington and state capitals for the registration of aliens. He became the first major party presidential candidate to condemn prejudice against Jews. "It is foolish to call the Jews a materialistic race," FDR said. "The Jews are idealists primarily. The trouble is that people are slow to perceive realities and prefer to cling to old—even if untrue—proverbs." He added, "I come to the conclusion that racial and religious prejudice hasn't a chance in the world to survive. . . . The more contact the non-Jew gains with the Jew, the quicker the old prejudices, based on ignorance, will vanish." These comments, together with FDR's liberal policies and record in New York politics, earned him the admiration of most Jewish voters.[3]

Hoover countered by distributing lists of Jewish appointees, issuing endorsements from prominent Jews, and publishing campaign material in Yiddish and Hebrew. Jewish Republican banker, philanthropist, and civic leader Felix Warburg endorsed Hoover, whom he praised for appointing Benjamin Cardozo to the Supreme Court and leading "the nation successfully through the most severe and prolonged depression in our history. . . . The next years are too important and the conditions too dangerous to take a chance on educating a new president." It was too little, too late for a president who had failed to meet Jewish requests, condemn anti-Semitism, or advocate the liberal policies favored by most Jewish voters. During the campaign, Hoover had boasted of his "rigid restriction of immigration to protect American jobs for Americans."[4]

On Election Day, Roosevelt won 57 percent of the popular vote and all but six states. With working majorities in Congress, Democrats gained unified control of national government for the first time since 1918. In New York, FDR's former lieutenant governor, Herbert Lehman, succeeded him as the state's first Jewish governor. Northern white Protestants, African Americans, and affluent voters comprised the diminished Republican base. Democrats were already putting together strands of what became America's politically dominant "Roosevelt Coalition." FDR won the votes of white southerners, Catholics, Jews, and union members. Within two years, African Americans would also abandon their traditional loyalty to the party of Lincoln and begin voting for Roosevelt's Democrats. In 1932, some 70 to 80 percent of Jewish voters backed FDR, topping all other religious or ethnic groups. Rabbi Stephen S. Wise, who had quarreled with Roosevelt over reforming New York politics and opposed his nomination and election, quickly wrote a conciliatory letter to the president-elect.[5]

Adolf Hitler became chancellor of Germany on January 30, 1933, during the interregnum between the Hoover and Roosevelt administrations. In the July 1932 parliamentary elections, the Nazi Party had become the largest party in Germany's Reichstag. Lacking a majority, Hitler needed a backroom deal and German president Paul von Hindenburg's approval to form a minority coalition government. After an arsonist burned down the Reichstag in late February 1933, Hitler assumed broad emergency powers. By this time, some Jews had shed their illusions about Hitler. New York City rabbi Jacob Katz denounced Hitler's ascendancy as an affront to civilization. American Jews, he said, could only "pray that our co-religionists in Germany will not be harmed."[6]

Hoover's former aide Lewis Strauss tried to broker a deal for Hoover and Roosevelt to issue a joint statement protesting Hitler's treatment of Jews. Strauss's initiative failed, in part because FDR sought a fresh start for his presidency and declined to cooperate on any policy matters with the lame duck Hoover.[7]

On March 3, the last day of the Hoover administration, Secretary of State Henry Stimson wrote to the American ambassador in Berlin Frederic M. Sackett of a newspaper report about an impending pogrom in Germany. He said, "This government is disinclined to lend credence to this report."

But Stimson did give Sackett discretion to inform the German government privately of American "apprehension and distress." Given the concern of Americans over the survival of their democracy during the Great Depression, it is not startling that the nation's leaders stayed publicly silent about the misdeeds of a foreign dictator whose tenure remained uncertain.[8]

The day after FDR took the oath of office as president, Nazis won a plurality of nearly 44 percent in the German parliamentary elections. Other parties quickly lost power as Hitler tightened his grip on Germany. In the midst of a worldwide depression and at the very beginning of FDR's New Deal, a twelve-year-long nightmare for European Jews had begun.

The last thing Roosevelt needed was a foreign policy crisis. Eager to stanch the bleeding of a run on the banks, FDR reassured Americans in his inaugural address that "the only thing we have to fear is fear itself—nameless, unreasoning, unjustified terror which paralyzes needed efforts to convert retreat into advance." Roosevelt wanted to focus on fighting the Depression, reforming the economy, and making Democrats the nation's majority party.

In Germany, gangs of Nazi thugs targeted Jews with random acts of violence. Hitler did not disavow this savagery, but turned their street tactics into official policy, beginning his "cold pogrom" that slowly froze Jews out of German economic, political, and cultural life. To contemporary observers abroad, it seemed remarkable that the government of a supposedly modern and enlightened nation would direct such wrath against peaceful, loyal, and useful citizens.

Nazi ideology challenged the liberal faith in free will, tolerance, and equality. In the New Reich, biology was destiny. For Nazis, Jews were a distinct race, with criminality, greed, radicalism, mental instability, and loathsome diseases genetically programmed into their blood. Regardless of any surface appearance as law-abiding German citizens, Jews were the eternal enemy of the Aryan race, dedicated to its ultimate destruction.

Hitler and other leading Nazis may have had no predetermined plan to slaughter German Jews, but their animus was apparent, even from the outside. As early as 1933, a few observers raised the grim prospect that the Nazis would eventually turn from discrimination to mass murder. McDonald told confidants that Hitler had boasted to him in a private April interview, "I will do the thing that the rest of the world would like to do. It doesn't know how to get rid of the Jews. I will show them." Hamilton Fish Armstrong, another American who edited *Foreign Affairs,* also visited Germany to survey the Nazi revolution. In a June 1933 radio broadcast, he quoted Hitler as saying that if he expelled Jews from Germany, his nation's economic troubles would be over. Armstrong's original draft said "killed or expelled." Perhaps he later decided not to risk charges of exaggeration or feared raising undue alarm. After attending the annual Nazi Party rally in Nuremberg during early September 1933, *New York Times* correspondent Frederick T. Birchall reported, "Aryanism is now the keystone of Nazi policy" and "the most popular of Nazi principles. . . . Its corollary is persecution even to extermination—the word is the Nazis' own—of the non-Aryans, if that can be accomplished without too much world disturbance." Most observers of the early Nazi regime did not foresee such a catastrophe, but still recognized the precarious situation of German Jews.[9]

Nazi plans for a racial community required expanded living space that Germany could achieve only through war and conquest. Hitler's central ideas revolved around race and space. Nazi leaders sought to eliminate restrictions of the Treaty of Versailles and build a powerful military to conquer foreign lands. Hitler's ultimate goals, spelled out loosely in his well-known work *Mein Kampf* and more specifically in an unpublished second book, were to dominate Europe and acquire a vast empire in the East, at the expense of both Poland and the Soviet Union. German expansion would bring millions of additional Jews under Nazi control and Hitler would likely abandon all restraint on their oppression.[10]

Although few paid sufficient attention to Hitler's writings and speeches, the Nazis worried American Jewish leaders. Long-standing divisions within the American Jewish elite thwarted a unified response. In the words of an old Jewish proverb, "Where there are two Jews, there are three opinions." These diverse opinions, even during times of peril to Jews, had their own prior history in the United States.

In 1903, during Theodore Roosevelt's first term, a murderous pogrom in the Russian city of Kishinev had shocked and outraged the world. "Rivers of Jewish blood ran in Kishinev streets," the *Atlanta Constitution* reported. The *Los Angeles Times* told of "little girls raped, eyes cut out and nails driven into the brains of victims." TR met with Jewish leaders and condemned pogroms, but not the Russian government. He instructed his secretary of state to request that the tsar receive a petition of protest drafted by B'nai B'rith, the largest Jewish fraternal organization. After the tsar refused to receive the petition, the secretary buried it in a State Department vault. Secretary of War William Howard Taft also spoke informally to Nicholas II on a visit, but the last emperor of Russia was unmoved. Later, perhaps with this example in mind, TR concluded that the United States "is too apt to indulge in representations on behalf of weak peoples which do them no good and irritate the strong and tyrannical peoples to whom the protest is made."[11]

In late 1905, Russian Jews suffered from another outbreak of yet more violent and deadly pogroms, with casualties in the thousands. Both Jews and sympathetic Christians again demanded action from TR. "These frightful holocausts have appalled the world," said the *Washington Post,* using words later reserved for Hitler's extermination of Jews. "President Roosevelt is the logical intervener in this unspeakable pandemonium." Simon Wolf, former president of B'nai B'rith, wrote to TR. "The man that sidetracked precedent by ending the coal strike, that conjured peace between Russia and Japan, that in a hundred ways showed marvelous versatility and courage," Wolf asked, "can he not take the initiative and bring about concert of action to stem the cruelties in Russia?" The White House noted the principle of respecting foreign sovereignty and observed that the situation for Jews in Russia was hopeless, given the disarray of the tsarist government.[12]

With America dithering in the face of Russia's pogroms, Jewish leader and scholar Cyrus Adler wrote prophetically about the limitation of humanitarian appeals to presidents:

> What I deprecate is the futile appeal at such a time as this to Kings and Presidents. Every refusal of such interference works harm and not good and if you knew, as no doubt you did know, or if Lord Rothschild knew, as he undoubtedly did know, that the President and King Edward would undoubtedly find themselves unable to interfere, what under heaven could come of these requests. Would not their effect rather be ill giving, as it would, an assurance of international immunity to the people who have engaged themselves in this hellish work?[13]

Given the dismal record of world leaders, some Jews in the United States concluded that only Jewish self-defense could counter anti-Semitic violence abroad. In November 1905, Jews in New York City, many of them newcomers from Eastern Europe, formed the Jewish Defense Association, which drew

6,000 persons to a rally supporting American intervention in Russia and the purchase of arms for persecuted Jews there.

This program of self-defense alarmed established Jews from Central Europe who had already achieved prosperity and even renown in their chosen American homeland. Worried that impoverished new immigrants, with their foreign folkways, strange language, and radical politics, would spur an anti-Semitic backlash in the United States and cast doubt on the good citizenship of all Jews, they rejected armed self-defense for Jews. Instead, they sought to expand Jewish influence in the backrooms of American power and to preempt leadership from the Eastern European Jews. In 1906, these elite Jews founded the American Jewish Committee. Although the Jewish Defense Association faded quickly, the committee emerged as America's leading advocacy group for Jewish interests worldwide.[14]

Pennsylvania state judge Mayer Sulzberger served as the committee's first president. Lawyer Louis Marshall succeeded him in 1912. Other founders included Adler; Oscar S. Straus, whom TR made the first Jewish cabinet member as secretary of commerce and labor; Sears, Roebuck CEO Julius Rosenwald; Illinois and later federal appeals court judge Julian W. Mack; businessman Cyrus L. Sulzberger; and financiers Jacob Schiff and Felix Warburg. These prominent assimilated Jews considered the masses of new Jewish immigrants from Eastern European lands in need of mature wisdom and responsible stewardship, not democratic representation.[15]

The bespectacled, short, and slightly portly Marshall became the preeminent leader of American Jewry. A tireless advocate, eloquent speaker, and master negotiator, Marshall knew how to get coverage in the press and access to decision-makers. Like other committee leaders, Marshall believed that all Jews should blend invisibly into American life as another religious denomination. Marshall also worshipped "the Republican Party almost as much as he does his religion," his son-in-law Jacob Billikopf said.[16]

The American Jewish Committee lobbied with some success against restrictive immigration laws. Most notably, it used publicity and political pressure to move the American government, between 1908 and 1912, into abrogating an 1832 commercial treaty with Russia. Led by Marshall, the committee charged that Russia had violated the treaty by refusing to honor the passports of Russian-born, naturalized American Jews. Marshall had to overcome opposition from both Theodore Roosevelt and his Republican successor President William Howard Taft, both of whom told Jewish leaders that continued agitation against the treaty would inflame anti-Semitism in the United States. Marshall rejected this argument saying, "We can point to no triumph as a result of a policy of silence." He sought to make Russia's treaty violation "not a Jewish but an American question" of equal treatment for its citizens.[17]

Unable to move President Taft with publicity alone, the committee warned him that he could lose hundreds of thousands of Jewish votes when running for reelection in 1912. It also worked for a congressional resolution on abrogation that Taft would dare not ignore. The committee rained letters and petitions on Congress, worked with sympathetic members, and threatened opponents with agitation in their districts. In mid-December, after the U.S. House overwhelmingly endorsed abrogation, a chastened President Taft terminated the 1832 treaty by executive action. The treaty abrogation did not technically interfere in the affairs of foreign powers, because it involved U.S. citizens and a bilateral treaty.[18]

This victory was anything but robust, failing to ameliorate Russian hostility to Jews or turn American diplomacy in a more humanitarian direction. In a new crisis for imperiled Jews in Romania shortly afterward, the American Jewish Committee could not persuade new Democratic president Woodrow Wilson to offer help. The committee also failed to persuade either Wilson or his successor Warren Harding to aid Polish Jews suffering from official discrimination and mob violence in the early 1920s. Still, for the first time in history, the American government had shifted its foreign policy in response to Jewish demands.[19]

This Jewish campaign demonstrated the power of strategic planning, public relations, and political pressure. Rather than follow this precedent, the American Jewish Committee reverted to backroom diplomacy and self-censorship to avoid antagonizing anti-Semites. They failed to grasp that an open struggle for Jewish rights could expand support for their cause and that they could play Democrats off against Republicans and Congress against the president. This retreat would profoundly influence the American Jewish response to Hitler's oppression of the Jews.[20]

A more combative alternative to the American Jewish Committee arose out of the American Zionist movement, which represented primarily newcomers from Eastern Europe. World War I transformed Zionism. For Zionists, Palestine was the historic home of the Jews, the land that the Bible promised to the Jewish people. Secular Zionists looked to Palestine as a haven for persecuted Jews and an opportunity to establish a model state. Religious Zionists, including a small Orthodox group called the Mizrachi, hoped to create a Jewish commonwealth based on biblical law and tradition. The rise of American Zionism and the continued immigration of working-class Jews from Eastern Europe unleashed a democratic spirit among Jews and recast Jewish advocacy politics in the United States. During World War I, Zionists leaders pushed for the formation of a democratically elected American Jewish Congress.

War and economic privation disrupted the Zionist movement on the continent in 1914. By default, American Zionism gained new prominence, especially after renowned lawyer Louis D. Brandeis agreed to coordinate Zionist affairs from an unscathed America. Brandeis, a progressive icon and presidential adviser, helped make the intellectual and religious Wilson a player in the Zionist cause. Reorganizing the feeble Federation of American Zionists, which depended on support from unreliable affiliated groups, Brandeis formed a unified Zionist Organization of America. Based on individual membership, this organization quickly attracted Jews from Eastern Europe who saw in its platform a haven for their brethren left behind in Russia and Poland. Brandeis served as honorary president and Judge Julian W. Mack as president.[21]

For Brandeis, Zionism flowed logically from the progressive politics of the Wilson era. In Palestine, Zionists could build afresh an exemplary state—a beacon for the world—upon the best Jewish and American traditions. Brandeis insisted that Zionism did not promote dual loyalty, but strengthened Jewish devotion to America's ideals of democracy and social justice. American Jews who had already adopted one homeland and did not want to choose another could comfortably embrace his Zionism. Still, for American Zionists, loyalty to Jewry meant loyalty to a people, not just identification with a religious denomination.[22]

Leaders of the American Jewish Committee and of Reform Judaism, despite some notable exceptions such as Rabbi Wise, rejected a racial or national conception of Jewish identity. "Zionism sets the Jews apart as a national group," said prominent Reform Rabbi and committee member David Philipson of Cincinnati. "We American Jews, who, in contradistinction to the Zionists, teach and believe that the Jews constitute a religious community and not a nation, are Americans in nationality and Jews in religion."[23]

An ethnic or racial conception of Jewish identity edged close to the beliefs of anti-Semites who would fence Jews out of the white mainstream. It resonated with the views of most white Protestant patricians, including the young Franklin and Eleanor Roosevelt, who distinguished Jews from so-called "Aryans." Jewish sociologist Stephen G. Rich compared the idea of a "Jewish race" with " 'Nordic' propaganda." During the 1924 hearings on immigration restriction, Jewish advocates had publicly avoided identifying Jews as a race or people and instead had insisted that Jews belonged to the "white race." Yet according to historian Eric L. Goldstein, the notion that Jews shared a racial identity had an emotional appeal that tugged against the benefits of joining America's privileged white majority.[24]

Leaders of the American Jewish Committee united with Zionists to support the Balfour Declaration of November 1917, in which Britain pledged a "national homeland" for Jews in Palestine, but not explicitly a Jewish state (which committee leaders mostly opposed). They also agreed on proposals to establish a "bill of rights" for Jews living in newly created European states at the end of the war. Postwar treaties incorporated both the Balfour Declaration and on-paper protection for Jewish minorities, although not the full safeguards of a Jewish bill of rights.

In December 1918, shortly after the Armistice ending the war, an American Jewish Congress met at last in Philadelphia, with major factions of American Jewry participating. In June 1917, some 335,000 Jewish women and men, living in more than eighty cities and belonging to more than thirty Jewish organizations, had voted to choose representatives to the congress. Its mission was to form a Jewish delegation to the Paris Peace Conference. Among 400 delegates, lawyers, businessmen, and financiers from the American Jewish Committee shared space with socialists, labor leaders, and rabbis. In the election for congress president, an American-born federal judge, the aforementioned Mack, defeated a Lithuanian-born Yiddish-language poet, Solomon Bloomgarten, known by his pen name Yehoash. Nathan Straus, co-owner of Macy's and Abraham & Straus department stores, who would give most of his fortune to Zionist causes, served as honorary president. Marshall headed the Jewish delegation to the great power deliberations in Paris. At the insistence of the American Jewish Committee, though, the congress convened as a temporary body that adjourned in 1920.

Jewish unity shattered after American delegates returned home from Paris. Despite the leadership of American Jewish Committee members such as Marshall, Mack, and Straus at the American Jewish Congress's inaugural 1918 meeting, the committee shunned the congress when it reconvened as a permanent body in 1922. Leaders of the committee also denounced proposals to expand "Jewish democracy" into a World Jewish Congress, which they said would inflame anti-Semitism in the United States and Europe. No longer could the American Jewish Congress claim success for its goal "to unify American Jewry."[25]

The American Zionist movement also splintered under stress. Chaim Weizmann, president of the World Zionist Organization, quarreled with Brandeis over fundraising and control of the movement. He charged that Brandeis led a secular, soulless movement that aimed at economically developing Palestine but lacked a distinctively Jewish component. Some Zionists also objected to Brandeis as the puppet master who pulled the strings of the movement without taking personal responsibility. Jewish activists futilely implored Brandeis to leave the bench and lead American Jewry.[26]

When Brandeis and his allies lost control of the Zionist Organization of America during the 1920s, membership and fundraising plummeted. Into the vacuum came Hadassah, the Women's Zionist Organization of America. Henrietta Szold founded the group in 1912, both to aid Jewish settlers of Palestine and to carve out a place for women within the Zionist movement. By 1927, Hadassah had 34,466 reported members, compared to just 21,806 for the once-dominant main Zionist group.[27]

Jewish factions in the United States briefly unified again in 1929. After protracted negotiations, the Zionist Organization of America endorsed a proposal to add non-Zionists, represented primarily by the American Jewish Committee, to the international Jewish Agency. Under Chaim Weizmann's leadership, the Jewish Agency represented Jewish interests in Palestine. Under the authority of the League of Nations mandate, it worked to establish a Jewish homeland in Palestine and to administer the outside aid that sustained its Jewish population. Rabbi Wise had objected that Zionists had betrayed their ideals for non-Zionist money and seemed "content to be a tolerated auxiliary and beneficiary of the philanthropic process in American Jewish life." Although most Zionists endorsed cooperation with prosperous, well-connected Jews, Jewish unity quickly collapsed after Marshall's death in September 1929 and the Arab riots that summer in Palestine. In the wake of the riots, the Brandeis group led by Wise and Bernard Deutsch regained control of the Zionist Organization of America.[28]

Even a common enemy like Hitler failed to unify leaders of American Jewry. Few understudies came of age in the 1930s to challenge the old guard of Felix Frankfurter, Brandeis, Samuel Untermyer, Wise, Adler, Deutsch, Joseph Proskauer, Mack, Warburg, and Lehman and his influential brother, Judge Irving Lehman. All these men—women had barely cracked the inner circle of Jewish political leadership—were more than fifty years old in 1933 and set in their ways. Adler, Marshall's successor as president of the American Jewish Committee, lacked renown among both Jews and Christians. Primarily a scholar and administrator, Adler could not match Marshall's polemical skill and did not easily tolerate those with whom he disagreed. Nazi persecution only inflamed the long-smoldering power struggle between his group and the American Jewish Congress. "This particular American Jewish Congress is an organization which was created for the purpose of disunion," Adler wrote. "It was created with the intention of destroying the American Jewish Committee. . . . It never drew an honest breath and to me it has been almost a matter of besmirching myself even to have to sit down with these gentlemen."[29]

After the Nazis came to power, the American Jewish Committee and B'nai B'rith preferred quiet diplomacy with the Roosevelt administration; aid to German Jews through the American Jewish Joint Distribution Committee (founded in 1914 to raise and distribute funds for aiding suffering Jews in the European "war zones"); and a broad alliance with non-Jews in a campaign against Nazi oppression. They feared that identifiable Jewish-sponsored rallies, demonstrations, and boycotts would lack credibility, intensify anti-Semitism, and provoke reprisals against Germany's Jews.

Nazi persecution of Jews trapped Jewish advocates within a painful double bind. For Nazi leaders, foreign demonstrations against Germany's anti-Semitic policies confirmed the power of a worldwide Jewish conspiracy and justified the repression of German Jews. Yet silence abroad signified tacit approval of those same oppressive policies. "Silence is acquiescence," Rabbi Wise warned. "Agitation serves only to furnish the persecutors with a pretext to justify the wrongs they perpetuate," the American Jewish Committee countered.[30]

In a joint statement released on March 20, 1933, the American Jewish Committee and B'nai B'rith expressed "horror at the anti-Jewish action in Germany" and called for the "American Government to make proper representations to the government of Germany." However, they condemned "boycotts, parades, mass meetings and other similar demonstrations." Adler telegraphed Jewish organizations on March 22 to discourage participation in rallies or demonstrations. The committee said that its Jewish contacts in Germany had "unanimously" advised that Jewish mass meetings and other public displays did more harm than good.[31]

On March 26, Secretary of State Cordell Hull reported progress for Jews in Germany. He was "hopeful" that Germany "will soon revert to normal." President Roosevelt advised Attorney General Homer S. Cummings to decline an invitation to attend a protest in his home state of Connecticut.[32]

By telephone, Rabbi Wise futilely sought to persuade New York governor Herbert Lehman, a member of the American Jewish Committee's Executive Board, to speak at his planned rally in New York City's Madison Square Garden. Lehman said, "I am working in many directions on this thing and I hope helpfully. I think it would be a mistake for me to go to that meeting." Wise warned that his rally offered the only alternative to unruly protests by radical, left-wing Jews. He said, "If we do not have this meeting there will be Socialist Jewish meetings, Communist Jewish demonstrations, instead of that we are to have an orderly, dignified representative dominantly Christian protest meeting under our auspices." Lehman responded, "I believe it should be a dominantly Christian protest meeting." He nonetheless declined to attend the rally or to specify what he was doing on behalf of persecuted Jews. Their telephone conversation shows the distance between these two men.[33]

Wise and his allies insisted that the United States, with the world's largest population of Jews, and its riches and power, lead the fight against the Nazi pestilence. Wise said, "What is happening in Germany today may happen tomorrow in any other land on earth unless it is challenged and rebuked." Wise's group planned a flagship rally at Madison Square Garden for late March, with kindred demonstrations in other cities. The protestors sought to proclaim their moral outrage, weaken the Nazi regime, and move President Roosevelt to take on the cause of Germany Jewry. They realized only their first goal.[34]

On March 27, more than 20,000 persons packed the Garden, while 35,000 rallied outside and at nearby Columbus Circle; 10,000 more protestors marched in Brooklyn. As Wise had promised, the rally featured Christian speakers such as Al Smith, Senator Robert F. Wagner, Episcopalian bishop William T. Manning, Methodist bishop Francis J. McConnell, and New York mayor John P. O'Brien. President William Green of the American Federation of Labor, and Charles H. Tuttle, FDR's gubernatorial opponent in 1930, also spoke.[35]

Smith recalled the prejudice he had encountered as a Catholic candidate for president. He said, "the only thing to do" with bigotry "is to drag it out into the open sunlight and give it the same treatment that we gave the Ku Klux Klan." Bishop Manning said, "none of us who call ourselves Americans have the right to be indifferent to such acts" of "religious persecution." Bishop McConnell warned unless Americans protest "the anti-Semitic movement . . . we will come to a place after awhile when the situation becomes intolerable, and then we resort to force." Green opposed interference in the "political affairs" of another "great nation," but said that "when any nation violates the laws of humanity . . . the voice of the American Federation of Labor will be heard in solemn protest." Rabbi Wise exempted the German people from blame for Hitler's tyranny. He called for "justice and even magnanimity from [Germany's] erstwhile foes" of World War I, but also warned that "Germany cannot hope to secure justice through injustice to its Jewish people." Telegrams of support for the rally poured in from U.S. House Speaker Henry T. Rainey, Senate majority leader Joseph T. Robinson, three other senators, and eight governors; all but one were Democrats.[36]

Elsewhere, residents of Chicago jammed the Auditorium Theatre while thousands more spilled into the streets. Protesters packed the Philharmonic Auditorium in Los Angeles, while 10,000 clamored outside for admission; 6,000 filled the Lyric Theater in Baltimore; 3,000 gathered in Newark; 3,000 in Washington, D.C.; and 2,500 in Atlantic City. On March 27 alone, the United Press estimated that some 1,000,000 persons participated in hundreds of protests nationwide, one of the largest political demonstrations to date in American history. As in New York, organizers recruited Christian speakers: U.S. senators, governors, and mayors, the editor of the *Christian Century,* and the dean of the University of Chicago Divinity School.

Still, opposition from cautious Jewish groups and the State Department took a toll on the protests. Smith said he chose to speak at Madison Square Garden despite many "pussyfooting" telegrams and cables "telling me there wasn't any reason for a meeting." Missing persons at the Garden included not only Governor Lehman (he spoke to a small group in Albany), but also his brother Irving, Warburg, and other members of New York's fabled Jewish families. John J. Dunn, the auxiliary Roman Catholic bishop of New York, informed Rabbi Wise through an intermediary that he had withdrawn from the program after receiving "private advice" from the State Department "that the reports have been grossly exaggerated and the action to be condemned has ceased." His retreat left the rally bereft of Church officials in a city of more than 2 million Catholics.[37]

Also absent from the platform at Madison Square Garden was any African American speaker. African Americans had a mixed response to Hitler's persecution of Jews. The National Association for the Advancement of Colored People (NAACP) denounced his anti-Semitic policies and urged America to boycott the 1936 Summer Olympics in Berlin, but did not join with other non-Jewish groups in sponsoring anti-Nazi demonstrations. Commentary in the black press condemned the Nazis, but also suggested that Americans should fight to end racial discrimination at home before tackling oppression abroad. "We'd Like a Break Too, Mr. Alfred E. Smith," read the headline for the *Chicago Defender*'s commentary on the March rally.[38]

Jews gained more support for the campaign against Hitler from liberal white Protestants more like FDR than leaders of the Catholic Church or the African American community. Members of the Catholic hierarchy did not assail Hitler until he appeared to be threatening Church interests. Black leaders remained largely outside the anti-Nazi movement. Jews had long supported the crusade against racial discrimination; Wise had helped found the NAACP and Marshall had argued two cases for the organization before the U.S. Supreme Court. Yet Jewish groups in the 1930s engaged in little outreach to African Americans. Friction between blacks and Jewish landlords and merchants in their communities also soured relations between the groups.[39]

News about Nazi persecution of political enemies and Jews traveled quickly, prolifically, and mostly accurately across the Atlantic. During FDR's first hundred days in office, the *New York Times,* the *Chicago Tribune,* the *Los Angeles Times,* the *Atlanta Constitution,* and the *Washington Post* published some 485 articles and editorials on Hitler and the Jews (more than half in the *New York Times*). Nearly a third of the news stories appeared on the front page. Even the *Chicago Tribune,* tightly controlled by its anti-Semitic, conservative, and anticommunist owner Colonel Robert R. McCormick, published seventeen front-page stories on Hitler's oppression of Jews during this period. The two major national newsweeklies, *Time* and

Newsweek, published twenty-one stories on Hitler and the Jews, and some 200 local newspapers across America published more than 2,600 articles on this topic during FDR's first hundred days. Editorial opinion in the national and local press was almost uniformly negative.[40]

Rival Jewish leaders Adler and Wise, who rarely agreed on anything, lauded the mainstream press. Adler wrote to British Jewish leader Neville Laski that American press coverage of events in Germany was "very full and very fair." Wise told publisher Adolph S. Ochs, "how profoundly we, of the American Jewish Congress, appreciate the editorial utterances of the New York Times. . . . The Times has rendered a great service to the cause of human justice and human freedom."[41]

The Nazi regime sought to turn the American protests to its advantage. On the day of the New York rally, the Nazi Party announced a boycott of Jewish businesses, supposedly to answer "this Jewish international hymn of hate against Germany." According to Jay Pierrepont Moffat, chief of the State Department's Western European Division, Secretary Hull had to calm down a tense situation inflamed by extremists on both sides. The State Department informed German foreign minister Konstantin von Neurath that if Germany canceled the boycott, Hull would issue a conciliatory statement (drafted by Moffat). The draft read, "I have reason to believe that many of the accounts of acts of terror and atrocities and terror which have reached this country have been exaggerated, and I fear that the continued dissemination of exaggerated reports may prejudice the friendly feelings between the peoples of the two countries." Protests in the United States "would adversely affect our economic relations with Germany." This concession, the foreign minister responded, came too late to cancel the boycott, but the Nazis would limit it to a single day. Hull's abject statement stayed buried in the files.[42]

Judge Proskauer, an increasingly important committee leader with some influence in Democratic circles, warned that Jewish agitation would "cause a repercussion on the Jews of America for interfering in these larger concerns" to control arms and improve the world economy. Like committee leaders during World War I, he said, "We are Americans first and must be loyal above all else, to America."[43]

The most militant early response to the Nazis came from the small but vocal Jewish War Veterans. In March 1933, the group initiated a movement to boycott German goods. The Veterans insisted that Jews must unite in self-defense regardless of others. The boycott "is the moral substitute for war," the only reality that Hitler understood, they said. The aging but still influential lawyer Untermyer led the boycott as head of a new American League for the Defense of Jewish Rights. It was quickly renamed "Non-Sectarian Anti-Nazi League to Uphold Human Rights" to mask its Jewish leadership. The league recruited another star in Rabbi Abba Hillel Silver, a prominent Zionist and, at age forty, one of the younger leaders of the American Jewish Congress. Silver said that Nazi politics "must be attacked with political weapons and the strongest political weapon, when all others fail is the boycott." He feared that if Hitler crushed the Jews of Germany, other tyrants would follow his lead.[44]

For tactical reasons, the American Jewish Congress initially opposed the economic boycott. Rabbi Wise sought to be both outsider and insider. He hoped to put mass pressure on the White House but also to exert inside influence. Wise looked to FDR for salvation in early 1933 and did not want to appear as if he led a band of "unmanageable radicals." He also distrusted any movement not controlled by his congress.[45]

The American Jewish Committee vehemently opposed the boycott on principle and pressured Untermyer to abandon the effort. Untermyer responded that "your Committee offers no hope for relief. . . . The Hitler Party is bent on the extermination of the Jews in Germany, or upon driving them out of the country." Neither "reason, justice nor humanity makes the slightest appeal . . . nothing but the fear of consequences will affect them." Untermyer insisted that only militant resistance gave Jews any hope to gain non-Jewish support. The boycott, he said, "is not a fight of Jews, but of humanity."[46]

In the summer of 1933, the American Jewish Congress endorsed the boycott. Jews needed a "measure of self-defense" against German authorities who "have neither ears for pleas nor minds for persuasion," the congress said. Shortly thereafter, Hadassah, which had grown to 40,000 members, endorsed the boycott. So did the American Federation of Labor, although it kept its activities separate from Jewish groups. The boycott took hold among some major Jewish merchants, in both the United States and Europe. It did not gain support from non-Jewish enterprises and had slight prospect of significantly harming a German economy that exported little to the United States.[47]

To Wise's dismay, the World Zionist Organization subverted the anti-Nazi boycott through the Haavara (transfer) agreement that arranged for

Jews to pay for German exports to Palestine as a means for promoting immigration there. The Haavara agreement, which eventually helped perhaps 20,000 German Jews find refuge with some capital in Palestine, presented Jewish leaders with a painful dilemma. Many European Zionists saw Palestine as the only safe refuge for Jews. They put a higher priority on expanding Jewish immigration to Palestine and on strengthening the Jewish community there than on protecting Jewish rights in any Diaspora nation, including Germany. Wise denounced the Haavara agreement as "a filthy inexcusable breaking of the Jewish front against Germany."[48]

Hitler and his inner circle knew little about the United States, but detested any foreign criticism, which they usually blamed on Jewish machinations. Regardless, the Nazis forged ahead with their ideological revolution recorded by McDonald, who traveled to Berlin during Hitler's first months in power. McDonald thought that American newspapers were, if anything, underestimating the potential for Nazi violence against Jews. He gave FDR a firsthand account of the dangers inherent in Hitler's regime.[49]

Frankfurter, who spent the weekend of April 7 at the White House, and Supreme Court justice Brandeis, who met with FDR the following Tuesday, both believed that Roosevelt "was alert to the meaning of events in Germany especially in relation to the peace of the world." At the right moment, Frankfurter told Wise by telephone that weekend, the president would morally condemn Germany and help Jews to escape the Nazi regime. McDonald gained a different impression after his overnight stay at the White House on May 1. He inferred correctly that, despite Roosevelt's concern, the administration would not publicly reprimand Germany and jeopardize international economic negotiations and disarmament efforts. As compared to the persecution of Jews, he said, FDR had "larger fish to fry in Germany."[50]

In an ironic twist of history, FDR relied on three Jews—Herbert Feis, James P. Warburg, and Bernard Baruch—to plan for the London Economic Conference, scheduled for the summer of 1933. The president also hoped to avert war, which many feared was imminent, by keeping Hitler engaged in the ongoing Geneva Disarmament Conference. Even if disarmament efforts failed, FDR believed that it was important for domestic and world opinion to sustain negotiations. He feared that a breakdown of talks might lead to war. On April 24, after meeting with the president, Secretary of State Hull wrote to Norman Davis, the American representative at

Geneva, that public opinion would regard adjournment of the conference as equivalent to a breakdown.[51]

Like his predecessors, Hull firmly backed the principle of nonintervention in foreign domestic matters. A lean and dignified six-footer, sixty-one years old at the time of his appointment, his snow-white hair thinning, Hull was married to a woman from a Jewish family. The former Tennessee senator had presidential ambitions, and he did not wish to highlight any Jewish connections. He was a cautious, middle-of-the-road Democrat with limited foreign policy experience and a penchant for avoiding controversy and would remain so throughout the crisis in Europe. His abiding passion was the promotion of free trade agreements, which made him wary of human rights issues that antagonized powerful senators. Hull said shortly after his appointment, "I am of the opinion that outside intercession has rarely produced the results desired and has frequently aggravated the situation." Hull and Vice President John Nance Garner were the only powerful southern Democrats in the upper administration, and FDR did not lightly challenge his leadership. "Cordell Hull is the only member of the Cabinet who brings me any political strength that I don't have in my own right," FDR said.[52]

Feis, a holdover from the Hoover administration, was the only appointed Jewish official in the Department of State. He had earned a PhD from Harvard University, where his informal mentors included Frankfurter and Brandeis, whose daughter he courted for a time. Later, Feis chaired the Economics Department at the University of Cincinnati. He was a nonpracticing Jew who had married the granddaughter of President James A. Garfield. Still, he remained acutely aware of his singular position as the only Jew of any influence at State and never felt fully integrated into the Christian, patrician, and quietly anti-Semitic world of American diplomacy. Like other well-placed Jews in the administration or FDR's circle of advisers, he sought to avoid the appearance of pushing Jewish concerns, even though he believed that Hull put too low a priority on the humanitarian crisis of German Jewry.[53]

Feis's superior at State, Undersecretary William Phillips, posed a more immediate barrier to aiding Jews than the distant and indifferent Hull. The suave, sophisticated, and impeccably tailored Phillips traced his American ancestry to the era of Governor John Winthrop and the Massachusetts Bay Colony. Like many other high officials at State, he was a restrictionist who opposed any initiative on behalf of imperiled Jews abroad. Phillips had considerable influence through his mastery of bureaucratic politics, his many years of diplomatic experience, and his direct pipeline to President Roosevelt. The two men had overlapped at Harvard and socialized together during the Wilson administration, when FDR served as assistant secretary of the navy and Phillips served as assistant secretary of state. Phillips met more frequently with FDR during the president's first term than Secretary Hull or any other diplomatic official.[54]

Under the influence of their own cultural bigotry and their commitment to nonintervention in the internal politics of foreign powers, the high officials in Roosevelt's State Department discouraged all protests, demonstrations, and boycotts against Hitler's persecution of Jews. They resisted any presidential or diplomatic rebuke of the Nazi regime.

Instead, FDR met privately with Hjalmar Schacht, Hitler's economic adviser, who was visiting the United States in May 1933. Roosevelt sought to lobby against German rearmament and to send a message to Berlin that Nazi persecution of Jews endangered German-American relations. Shortly after these meetings, Roosevelt said in a letter to Judge Lehman that "At last the German Government now knows how I feel about things. . . . It is probably better to do it this way rather than to send formal notes of protest, because, frankly, I fear that the latter might result in reprisals in Germany." FDR's informal conversations with Schacht typified his inclination to convey his views to foreign leaders through backdoor channels. He would continue such private diplomacy throughout his presidential years.[55]

FDR likely believed that his discreet scolding of Schacht would help German Jews. In turn, Schacht, who was anti-Semitic, opportunistic, and devoted to Hitler, could deflect protest against Germany by serving as a sounding board for critics. Justice Brandeis saw through Schacht's deceptions and told Rabbi Wise, "I hope none of our people will talk privately with Schacht. If he is to hear what we think it should be said publicly; and under no circumstances should we dine with him anywhere. . . . Schacht is evidently trying to reach privately influential Jews." Wise could not resist attending a private dinner for Schacht, hosted by David Sarnoff, the Jewish founder of the National Broadcasting Corporation (NBC). Proskauer, Irving Lehman, and Bernard Baruch also attended, but Frankfurter and Felix Warburg declined invitations.[56]

FDR's personal diplomacy with Schacht followed the cautious, behind-the-scenes strategy of the American Jewish Committee. Judge Lehman, a

leader of the committee, responded to news of the Roosevelt-Schacht meetings with enthusiasm, writing to FDR that he had "brought a ray of hope
into a very dark situation." He noted that at the Sarnoff dinner Schacht had
said, "'I was deeply impressed by the President. Such charm; such tact; such
courage; such sincerity!—He reminded me in every way of Hitler.' You can
imagine that it was somewhat difficult for me to restrain myself."[57]

Wise, who had urged American intercession on behalf of Armenians
during World War I, hoped that Roosevelt would publicly condemn Nazi
outrages. He feared that without forceful action by the president, events in
Germany "may be the beginning of a worldwide movement against us, a
worldwide conflagration, a worldwide undertaking against the Jews." Based
on his sources in Berlin, Frankfurter agreed "that what we hear from and
about Germany is really under-statement rather than exaggeration." Wise
whipped up another round of protests, scheduled for May 10, 1933, the day
that Nazi activists burned "objectionable" books. He disregarded a personal
plea from Adler "to abandon this parade on May 10 because the situation is
so tense that the present German government may use any pretext for reprisals." Warnings against demonstrations coming from German Jews, Wise
said, were "not worth reading" because "a pistol is held at their heads" and
they "are made desperate by their fears."[58]

On schedule, some 100,000 protestors marched in New York City led by
the Catholic World War I hero General John F. O'Ryan. More than 50,000
marched in Chicago, 20,000 in Philadelphia, and 10,000 in Cleveland. In
Ohio, both Republican senator Simeon D. Fess and his Democratic colleague Robert J. Bulkley backed the protest. Many thousands of letters and
telegrams demanding succor for persecuted Jews poured into White House
and congressional offices.[59]

This second round of anti-Nazi demonstrations did not stiffen White
House policy toward the Nazis. Instead, FDR chose to conciliate Germany.
In a major foreign policy address on May 16, 1933, he offered Germany the
prospect of parity with other powers by reducing military strength to a
common level. He proposed that nations sign a nonaggression pact and indicated that the United States would not stand in the way of international
enforcement. The next day Hitler made a conciliatory speech of his own.
After the two speeches, Roosevelt boasted to Henry Morgenthau Jr., "I
think I have averted a war . . . I think that sending that message to Hitler
had a good effect." Rabbi Wise agreed that FDR "has saved Germany from

France. He has saved the world from war. In heaven's name, why can't he be moved to save the Jews of Germany?" However, Roosevelt's adviser Samuel Rosenman told the American Jewish Committee that if the economic and disarmament conferences "fail, the result for the world at large and for the Jews in particular would be extremely unfavorable."[60]

From his experience in New York politics, Roosevelt understood well the rivalries among Jewish groups. On May 19, he met with Democratic representative Henry Ellenbogen of Pennsylvania, a naturalized citizen from Vienna who wanted the administration to act more aggressively on Germany. FDR allegedly told him, "There are two kinds of Jews—those who want me to spread-eagle [the Nazis] and those who want me to be silent." After speaking with Ellenbogen, Wise noted ruefully that his kind of Jews had no access to FDR and remarked, "So now we have it from the lips of the President that there are those want him to be silent!"[61]

According to an August 2, 1933, article in the *New Republic* magazine, Felix Warburg led those who wished the president to "remain silent." The editors wrote, "We are reliably informed that President Roosevelt was dissuaded from intervening in Berlin against Jewish persecution by Mr. Felix Warburg, who warned him that such a step on the part of the American government would harm rather than help the German Jews." Frankfurter also believed that Roosevelt was ready to make a public statement condemning Nazi persecution, but one or more members of the American Jewish Committee, perhaps Warburg, had dissuaded him. The evidence is inconclusive. Regardless, the president would not likely have listened to a lifelong Republican who backed Hoover in 1932, unless, of course, Warburg told him what he wanted to hear.[62]

FDR had no lack of wary counsel from Jews within his circle of advisers. After Governor Lehman and Judge Rosenman dined and stayed over at the White House on May 25, Rosenman passed the word to Jewish leaders, "You should not ask the President to make any declaration now or any public act." After hearing this warning, Wise believed that an opportunity had been irretrievably lost: "Had we acted publicly six weeks ago in demanding action by the President we might have had it. Now it is almost certain that it is too late." Like Frankfurter, Wise would not blame the president for inaction. He faulted the timid Jews of the American Jewish Committee and B'nai B'rith.[63]

The president was willing to let Congress condemn the persecution of Jews in Germany, although he would not back a formal resolution. Getting

Congress to act was not an easy alternative. Many members of Congress shared State Department concerns about the Jewish immigration agenda, and some were outright anti-Semites. Republican representative Louis Mc-Fadden of Pennsylvania gave one speech essentially endorsing the notion of a worldwide Jewish conspiracy contained in the spurious *Protocols of the Elders of Zion*. Even Wise hoped to avoid an uncontrollable debate on the floor of the House. Roosevelt likely encouraged a Senate statement. He invited Senate majority leader Joseph Robinson to a working Potomac River cruise on June 4. Six days later, on the floor of the Senate, Robinson decried Germany's "cruelty and inhumanity" to the Jews, but also opposed American intervention in German domestic affairs. Colleagues from both parties seconded his remarks. Journalists wrote that Robinson had responded to a nudge from FDR, a belief that Proskauer and Adler shared.[64]

Even a unified Jewish leadership would not likely have compelled the president to shift course. From working in New York politics and running against Jewish opponent Albert Ottinger in 1928, FDR knew that Jewish organizations were paper tigers politically. The elitist American Jewish Committee, which had some 350 members in the early 1930s, lacked a grassroots constituency. The supposedly mass-based American Jewish Congress was not a true membership organization, but a loose federation of primarily Eastern European fraternal and Zionist groups. These affiliates contributed little besides their names to the congress, which raised a pitiful $98,000 in 1933. Like other ethnic and religious organizations of this era, Jewish groups had not yet built strong political infrastructures. The American Jewish Congress could sponsor protest rallies and parades, but lacked the funding, field staff, organizing skill, and community infrastructure to sustain a mass-based political campaign. Neither the congress nor the committee had formal lobbying or legislative branches, an office in the nation's capital, or political committees that endorsed or contributed to candidates. No leader had the power to sway Jewish voters, who comprised only a few percent of the electorate. FDR expected continued support from liberal Jewish voters and donors, regardless of his response to demands from organized Jewry.[65]

The conservative and isolationist Republican Party, which worried more about communism than Nazism, offered no alternative for most Jews. The GOP was a predominantly white Protestant party, which appealed to traditional "Americanism" and backed rigid restrictions on immigration. Few

Jews had voted Republican in national elections since 1928, and among thirteen Jews serving as a governor or congressional representative in 1933, only two were Republicans.

The day after Robinson's speech, FDR's first hundred days in office ended without a strong American response to Hitler's persecution of the Jews, despite widespread public outrage in the United States. Even some Republicans, including the staunchly conservative senator Fess, past chairman of the Republican National Committee, had backed Wise's protests. Five weeks later, after continued White House silence, McDonald wrote to Eleanor Roosevelt, asking "whether the time has come when, in harmony with many precedents in American history, the American government should take the initiative in protesting against the prevailing violations of elementary civil and religious rights in Germany. Such a protest would, I anticipate, evoke enthusiastic and grateful response from millions of Americans." He received no response to this plea.[66]

In part, the precedent for nonintervention and opposition from his State Department explain FDR's quiescence, as did a conservative opposition that alienated Jewish voters or donors. FDR had long recognized dangerous tendencies in Germany, and he no doubt detested Hitler, Nazi ideology, and the persecution of German Jews. In his first term, FDR struggled to find responses to Nazi policies and actions without thwarting higher priorities at home and abroad, expending precious political capital, or aggravating religious issues. He found no adequate answers to this dilemma. The precedent followed by Theodore Roosevelt and other presidents of nonintervention in the internal affairs of foreign powers served FDR's need to focus on programs for domestic economic recovery and reform. He knew that without progress in fighting the Depression he could become, like Hoover, a failed one-term president.

Roosevelt's New Deal was the most ambitious reform program in American history. In part, Roosevelt overrode business opposition, enacted his program, and won reelection by respecting the social conservatism of his time. The New Deal reforms that transformed the nation on so many different levels were, in fact, a function of the political support of millions of northern industrial workers and southern working-class whites who had their own attachments to social conservatism and suspicions about Jews, foreigners, and racial minorities. New Deal programs helped redefine the standing of many Americans once perceived as outsiders and set the stage for later civil rights initiatives. Yet the president refused to put his economic reforms at risk by stirring up racial and religious animosities. He was determined not to lose political support by letting his New Deal programs appear to become minority programs.

FDR's liberal policies may have been incremental and designed to rescue the capitalist economy. Nonetheless, his New Deal was a transforming moment in American life. It challenged old structures of power, threw up new ones, and created new social roles and opportunities for millions of Americans who worked for government, labored in offices and factories, or farmed for a living. It advanced American pluralism by offering jobs and power to Catholics and Jews and a few African Americans without disrupting local traditions. The New Deal reversed prior insular and protective international economic policies. It challenged old dogmas about upholding the gold standard, balancing the federal budget, and keeping government small and unobtrusive. The New Deal shifted the center of American politics by taking on responsibility for steering the economy, promoting social welfare, regulating labor relations, and curbing the abuses of business. It expanded federal spending and the deficit, although not as much as some critics on his left would have preferred.

The economic effects of FDR's new policies were swift and significant. Within the first six months of his term, investment, industrial production, and stock prices dramatically increased. For liberal American Jews, the New Deal was a program worth fighting for even if it meant deferring concerns about the fate of German Jews.[67]

Roosevelt followed the precedent of his gubernatorial years in drawing upon Jews of ability. Some 15 percent of his appointees were Jews, far exceeding the Jewish percentage of the population, and his informal group of outside advisers included several Jews. Most officials held middle-level positions in the economic agencies and departments of government. Henry Morgenthau Jr. was part of FDR's economic team from the beginning, and became secretary of the treasury in early 1934, serving as the only Jewish cabinet member during FDR's four terms. Other Jews in the administration included legislative craftsman Benjamin V. Cohen, Charles E. Wyzanski Jr., solicitor general in the Labor Department, Mordecai Ezekiel, economic adviser to the secretary of agriculture, and the aforementioned Feis, an economic adviser in the State Department. All would eventually play some role in shaping the administration's response to the plight of German Jews.

The Jews who figured prominently in FDR's inner circle of informal advisers included the speechwriter Rosenman, Frankfurter, and banker James P. Warburg, an authority on international economics. Frankfurter turned down an offer to become solicitor general, the government's primary legal advocate. From his post at the Harvard Law School, he preferred to continue as a consultant on economic and legal matters and chief New Deal talent scout. Rosenman usually followed the lead of the cautious American Jewish Committee; although highly deferential to FDR, Frankfurter took a bolder approach.

For all their rising influence in American politics, Jews did not change Roosevelt's political calculus. Supreme Court justice Brandeis, the most prestigious of American Jews, whom Roosevelt respectfully called Isaiah, had influence with the president despite his position in the judiciary. Leadership from Brandeis, Rabbi Wise said, "would be not a battle won but half the war." But Brandeis, understanding the limits of FDR's options, again rejected the idea, more plausible in 1933 than in earlier years, of resigning from the bench to become the new Moses, the savior of his people. Brandeis, like other Jews in FDR's circle, put a higher priority on participating in what Secretary of the Interior Harold Ickes called Roosevelt's "bloodless revolution" in national policy and politics than on what the justice called "our, in a sense lesser problem" of endangered German Jews.[68]

FDR's tepid response to the Nazi persecution of Jews in 1933 did not deter the German press from denouncing him as an anti-German friend of the Jews. Reflecting the views of high Nazi officials, the Berlin newspaper *Deutsche Nachrichten* declared in July 1933 that no one, not even the president of the United States, could induce Germany to alter its policies toward the Jews. Despite his back-channel expressions of displeasure to Nazi officials, Roosevelt did not seriously test this proposition early in his first term.[69]

CHAPTER FOUR

Immigration Wars

ON APRIL 7, 1933, the Nazi government enacted a measure that allowed it to remove Jews and political opponents from civil service jobs. The usually cautious Cyrus Adler, dean of American Jewish leaders, wrote, "The best thing that can happen for the Jews of Germany if at all possible would be to take every last one of them out. . . . The situation in Germany is indescribably bad." A month later, after visiting Germany and learning of sporadic violence against Jews, prominent Jewish fundraiser Rabbi Jonah B. Wise (no relation to Rabbi Stephen S. Wise) called the long-term situation of German Jews hopeless. Some American Jewish activists hoped that the United States could admit many who wished to leave, but America was coping with its own crisis. Sober people pondered whether American democracy could survive the severe social and economic strains of the Great Depression.[1]

Nonetheless, several Jewish insiders tried to clear the way for Jewish immigration. Presidential adviser Felix Frankfurter thought that he had "set the train in motion" for easing visa requirements when meeting with the president on the morning of April 7. Judge Irving Lehman had met with Roosevelt three weeks earlier. He urged FDR to modify President Hoover's interpretation of the clause in immigration law prohibiting admission of those likely to become a public charge, the main obstacle to filling the German quota. On the afternoon of his meeting with Frankfurter, FDR suggested to his cabinet that the administration might facilitate the entry of some carefully chosen German refugees, not all of them Jewish. However, he did not issue follow-up instructions. As president, the former naval administrator ran a loose ship. He controlled grand strategy but allowed subordinates flexibility on details, often without indicating his preferences.[2]

Frankfurter first drafted executive orders that gave FDR the option to reverse with the stroke of a pen Hoover's strict interpretation of the public charge clause. On April 16, Frankfurter sent to the president a wire from Rabbi Stephen S. Wise (that Frankfurter may have written in Wise's name) which warned that pressure for action was increasing and may "seriously embarrass White House."[3]

At the next cabinet meeting Secretary of Labor Frances Perkins reintroduced Frankfurter's ideas on visa reform. Secretary of State Cordell Hull expressed mild opposition, and Roosevelt, suffering from a cold, did not make his own view clear. On April 19, presidential press secretary Steven Early called the State Department asking why it had not sent over a draft of the necessary executive order. Undersecretary of State William Phillips went to the White House to explain State's position. The anti-Semitic Phillips may simply have pointed to the unfilled quota as evidence that there was no need for a new policy. Roosevelt apparently agreed with him: whether he believed it or simply deferred to State Department opponents is unclear. He did ask Phillips to talk to Perkins.[4]

Moved by abuses against Jews and the Nazis' political opponents, the knowledgeable Perkins also understood that the public charge clause, not the quota limit, blocked Jewish immigration from Germany. America had traditionally admitted persecuted refugees, she told Phillips, and her department, not State, would gauge the impact of immigration on economic conditions and the labor market. If the administration failed to act soon, formidable Jewish pressure would be unleashed on it. State Department official Jay Pierrepont Moffat wrote, "In fact she quite blew our poor Under Secretary off his end of the telephone."[5]

Officials at State quickly found an old veto statement, one in which President Woodrow Wilson had objected to American consuls determining whether a foreign country was engaging in persecution; this kind of judgment would interfere with American foreign policy. Assistant Secretary of State Wilbur J. Carr, the State Department's immigration expert and the author of the derogatory 1920 report on Eastern European Jews, skillfully used Wilson's argument at the next cabinet meeting.[6]

These April 1933 exchanges began a long battle between two departments, having opposite views of the world, over arcane points of immigration laws and regulations. Perkins, deeply religious, idealistic, and liberal, had forged relationships with immigrants and FDR during her years as a pro-labor activist and official in New York. Phillips, Carr, and Moffat were all restrictionists and held anti-Semitic beliefs in a department rife with such sentiments.

When President Hoover had toughened the interpretation of the public charge clause, the justification was the Depression—an economic emergency. Many State Department officials favored the reduction of immigration below levels allowed by the quota system regardless of economic conditions. They were so committed to keeping aliens out of the United States that they discounted real Jewish concerns about Nazi Germany. Moffat reflected a consensus among these officials when he wrote in his diary, "Many of the Jewish leaders here are less actuated by what is happening in Germany than by using it as an excuse to lower the bars on our immigration restriction policy in favor of refugees."[7]

Secretary Hull could have shifted State Department policy. However, Hull, who worked best behind the scenes, dreaded controversy. He wanted German cooperation at the World Economic Conference, and he shied away from anything that might seem critical of the new Nazi government. The former senator from Tennessee knew well that Southern Democrats and many Republicans in the Senate adversely viewed immigration, especially Jewish immigration. He deferred to his subordinates, except in early September, when Hull asked Moffat to draft a statement approving the settling of (German) Jews *outside* the United States. Moffat responded that any encouragement of Jewish resettlement anywhere would implicitly "reverse the policy [of restrictive immigration] for which we have fought for twelve years." Always sensitive to criticism, Hull backed off.[8]

Roosevelt could not alienate either Perkins or Hull and Phillips. This meant a balancing of views, although State weighed more heavily on the scales. Perkins told Frankfurter that State would instruct consuls confidentially to be more liberal in determining whether political and religious refugees would become public charges. Frankfurter saw that his proposal on refugees had died in the bureaucracy. He told Perkins, "It grieves me beyond words that the humane and wise forthrightness of Franklin Roosevelt should be impeded." He added, "For once in my life I wish that, for a brief period, I were not a Jew. Then I would not have even the appearance of being sectarian. . . . What is happening in Germany is essentially no more the concern of Jews than it is of Gentiles. The interests that are at stake are not narrower than those of 'civilization.'" Roosevelt had let the State Department win by default the first engagement in the war over immigration. The combatants would battle again later in 1933.[9]

The new American ambassador to Germany, William E. Dodd, formerly history professor at the University of Chicago, did not help German Jews emigrate to the United States. A prominent liberal Democrat, Dodd had received his doctorate from the University of Leipzig. He had no expertise on Germany in recent years—he was an historian of the American South. In early July, before he sailed to Europe, Dodd told a Jewish delegation that FDR had a keen interest in the situation of German Jews. According to Dodd, the president had refrained from openly criticizing Germany in order not to make life worse for Jews, and he was expecting Dodd to report firsthand about how America could unofficially moderate Germany's persecution of Jews. By late August, Dodd inaccurately claimed that the German quota was full, so Jews could not qualify for visas. (He was probably misinformed.) Dodd was an inexperienced diplomat most often at odds with his colleagues at State, who lacked respect for him and paid him little heed.[10]

In the summer of 1933, the State Department loosened visa restrictions for foreigners with American relatives able and willing to provide financial support. Then, in September, it suggested special consideration for visa applicants who lacked access to immigration documents such as passports, police records, marriage certificates, and financial statements. However, it did not issue regulations on document requirements until early 1934, and American consuls usually continued to demand full documentation. The new instructions on financial support applied only to the few aliens with immediate family in the United States. FDR told Governor Herbert Lehman that he backed this limited initiative.[11]

Organized labor, a far more important Democratic constituency than American Jewry, stood resolutely against any loosening of immigration restrictions. On September 10, FDR met with William Green, president of the American Federation of Labor, the nation's leading labor organization. Green then wrote to Roosevelt, urging him to keep immigration tightly restricted "in the name of the 11,000,000 now unemployed." Commissioner of Immigration and Naturalization Daniel MacCormack said that the American Federation of Labor had protested against any relaxation of immigration laws and regulations. Perkins told Green that Labor and State had not yet decided how to handle cases of political and religious refugees "so numerically small as to be unimportant."[12]

In early September, Judge Julian W. Mack reported to Governor Lehman that during a trip to Germany he learned that Jews who had "for generations thought of themselves as Germans" no longer "had any illusions as to the future" and were ready to leave the country even with meager possessions. Their longing, he said, was to be " 'allowed into your great country.' " When Mack noted "the difficulties connected with our immigration laws" and the "large number of unemployed," they responded, " 'but our children would never become a burden on public charities." They pointed out that even tiny Holland had taken in some 3,000–4,000 Jewish refugees.[13]

In mid-September, Jewish insiders renewed their campaign on behalf of Jewish refugees. On September 12, Henry Morgenthau Jr. brought Judge Irving Lehman for tea at the White House with FDR. Lehman again requested a public statement by the president condemning Nazi persecution, but Roosevelt had no intention of breaking precedent. He would not interfere in the domestic affairs of foreign powers. The president agreed, however, to bring together quickly Jewish leaders and officials at State and Labor while letting Mack serve as a liaison between them. According to a later report by author Marvin Lowenthal, "Judge Lehman had gotten a promise from F.D. that about ten thousand [German Jewish refugees] would be allowed to enter if adequate bond were given so they would not become public charges." He noted that "the details are still to be worked out by Philips [sic] and the State Department."[14]

Hull, Phillips, and A. Dana Hodgdon (chief of the Visa Division) from State; Perkins and MacCormack from Labor; and Judge Joseph Proskauer,

Irving Lehman, and Max Kohler, an immigration authority for the American Jewish Committee, met on September 20. FDR decided not to participate; he apparently hoped to avoid choosing sides openly or getting embroiled in a fight over details. Proskauer asked the State Department group to "take the curse off" Hoover's interpretation of the public charge clause that sharply cut immigration. He urged the administration to recognize officially "the existence of tragic conditions in Germany." The group discussed the option, mentioned in the Immigration Act of 1917, of having someone put up money (a bond) in advance as a guarantee that an immigrant would not go on welfare. Once someone posted a bond, a consul would have no financial reason to deny a visa application. To make matters worse, from the State Department's perspective, the Labor Department had jurisdiction over the bond.[15]

For the next month, the various parties fought over the bonding proposal and other details. Labor and State wrote formal legal opinions defending their positions for and against the bonding procedure respectively, and then took the dispute to Attorney General Homer Cummings. Labor's solicitor, twenty-seven-year-old Charles E. Wyzanski Jr., believed that the president had suggested this solution. Wyzanski hoped a favorable decision would allow for the admission of 25,000 German refugees, Jews and non-Jews. Cummings turned the task of writing a decision over to Assistant Attorney General Alexander Holtzhoff, who, praising the excellent opinion written by Wyzanski, decided in favor of Labor.[16]

During his five years as attorney general, the loyal Cummings gave Roosevelt whatever he wanted. He would not have ruled against FDR's preference. However, the president had no visible role in the outcome. He would not risk antagonizing his State Department and organized labor. He did not want to provoke Congress into enacting new restrictive laws or let critics charge him with giving away American jobs to foreigners.

Restrictionist and, in some cases, anti-Semitic State Department officials predictably opposed the bonding procedure. One consular official said that the Americans "look to us to protect their rights, and if ships begin to arrive in New York City laden with Jewish immigrants, the predominant Gentile population of the country will claim they have been betrayed through a 'sleeping' State Department." Another official argued, "Jews are persistent in their endeavors to obtain immigration visas" and "allege that they are the subjects of either religious or political persecution. . . . Unrestrained acceptance of bonds of Jewish aliens would soon develop the common understanding that for some reason the immigration laws of the United States operated to admit nothing but Jews."[17]

In early January 1934, Wyzanski had fearful second thoughts about lowering immigration barriers. Secretary of Labor Perkins "was most anxious to act at once to entertain applications from anyone to the full limit of the German quota," he wrote to his parents. Wyzanski then described his discomfort as a Jew urging his non-Jewish boss to desist from helping Jews escape Hitler. At the risk of being "charged at least by Jews with having betrayed my co-religionists," he warned of "the effect of the admissions upon Jews already here and upon the increasing wave of anti-Semitism." He also opposed any public statement by the president on Jewish refugees, saying that it would encourage "opposition from the Congress, KKK elements, AF of L and other restrictionists." FDR, he said, "has been more than generous to the Jews," despite the political risks involved. "Unless the gain is very clear I should not advocate having him champion their cause again."[18]

MacCormack, the commissioner of immigration, also feared that widespread use of the bonds would provoke a public backlash against Jews and the Labor Department. After left-wing Australian immigrant Harry Bridges organized a dockworker's strike on the West Coast that led to violent clashes between strikers and police, MacCormack worried about "a wave of hysterical hate" against immigrants. He seemed willing to accept legislation reducing quotas to 40 percent of existing levels. He also told James G. McDonald that although Labor had accepted in principle the idea of public charge bonds, it had not yet implemented the proposal. If the administration was to issue bonds, he said, they should be sharply limited in number—in effect creating a "labor bond" quota within the broader immigration quota. The Labor Department also kept confidential, for fear of a negative public response, negotiations for the admission of 250 refugee children from Germany.[19]

By March 1934, MacCormack had decided that any use of the bonding procedure would incite Congress to cut immigration quotas drastically. Restrictionist pressure in Congress came not just from Republicans, but from Democrats such as Representative Martin Dies of Texas, who sponsored legislation to slash all immigration quotas by 60 percent. Under pressure from the administration, the House Immigration Committee killed the Dies bill. Still, Congress remained a treacherous place for any consideration of immigration policy.[20]

Quota immigration from Germany rose slightly from 1,919 in the fiscal year ending June 30, 1933, to 4,392 (most of it Jewish), in the year ending June 30, 1934, about 17 percent of the quota limit. An increased demand for visas, not slightly liberalized policies, accounted for most of this uptick. Even the usually pro-immigrant Conference on Immigration Policy concluded that continuation of the Hoover's restrictive policy on granting immigration visas remained advisable. It proposed only small changes in procedure to aid relatives of U.S. citizens and resident aliens.[21]

One small but significant private effort worked around the quota. In April 1933, Alvin Johnson, founder of the liberal New School for Social Research in New York City, launched an initiative for refugee scholars and professionals. Johnson founded the University in Exile for primarily Jewish scholars threatened by Nazi persecution. Scholars and members of the clergy could enter the United States outside of quota limits. Johnson told Frankfurter that despite worries about anti-Semitism, he believed that the advisory committee for his enterprise should contain at least some Jews. The university recruited fourteen scholars in 1933 and ultimately 180 by 1945. These refugee academics helped keep alive the tradition of German scholarship and made notable contributions to American intellectual and political life. Economist Gerhard Colm, political scientist Arnold Brecht, and sociologist Hans Speier served as policy advisers to the Roosevelt administration during World War II. Max Wertheimer was a founder of Gestalt psychology, and political philosopher Leo Strauss became an inspiration for the American conservative movement.[22]

MacCormack remained steadfast in his fears of an anti-Semitic upsurge in the United States. In June 1934, Mack told Jewish leaders of a conversation with MacCormack. Mack found MacCormack preoccupied with "the tremendous growth of anti-Semitism in this country . . . and also the lack of sympathy with any liberalizing tendencies in immigration laws and regulations, even on the part of non-Jewish liberals." MacCormack told Mack that American Jews had to choose between protecting 4.5 million Jews in the United States or aiding many fewer German Jews.[23]

Mack's report dismayed Judge Irving Lehman who, like Frankfurter, worried that misconceptions about anti-Semitism justified inertia on refugees. Lehman said that conservatives raised the specter of Jewish control "to insist that the Administration is un-American . . . that its inspiration comes from those who have not inherited American traditions." Lehman was "disturbed, not by the supposed danger, but by the fact that Colonel MacCormack believes it exists and the reasons he has given for his belief." As befitted a member of the American Jewish Committee, Lehman still urged caution. He favored only the admission of "five or even ten thousand German Jews a year," about 20 to 40 percent of the German quota. He warned against "other matters advocated by groups of Jews," likely referring to public protests and official denunciations of Nazi persecution. Later in the year, McDonald noted that during a private discussion about refugees, MacCormack "reverted to the theme which I was to hear so often during my stay at home—the increase in anti-Semitism and the danger of its accentuation."[24]

Conservative activist John B. Trevor and eugenicist Harry H. Laughlin, who had teamed up in support of the 1924 quota bill, reunited to oppose any concessions for admitting Jewish refugees. Trevor chaired the Committee on Immigration and Alien Insane of the New York State Chamber of Commerce, which called for denying admission to all aliens lacking "a definite country to which they could be deported"—in effect excluding all refugees. The committee distributed a report on immigration prepared by Laughlin, which called for excluding all "low-grade Jews" and asserted that "with modern dumping of inadequates . . . the United States if it continues to be the world's asylum and poorhouse, would soon wreck its present economic life and its future [biological] inheritance." Laughlin called it inconceivable to relax the Hoover administration's standard of who was likely to become a public charge.[25]

Thus by mid-1934, the option to admit larger numbers of Jews into the United States through public charge bonds or other new policies seemed to have died within the Roosevelt administration. In fiscal 1935, when tens of thousands of German Jews clamored to enter the United States, immigration from Germany only ticked up slightly to 5,201 persons, just 20 percent of quota levels.

Nonetheless, by 1934 America's own "Jewish Question" became more openly political and public, with anti-Semites targeting the Roosevelt administration for its alleged subservience to Jews. Never before in U.S. history had such a small fragment of the population (about 4 percent) stirred such political strife. Some Jewish leaders hoped to protect the president and his liberal agenda from a political opposition that they saw as isolationist, reactionary, and hostile to Jewish concerns.

Fascist movements that rose up during the Depression made the most anti-Semitic noise. William Dudley Pelley, a gifted self-promoter, headed the Silver Shirts. Its "one issue" crusade for "the forcible removal of the Jew from power" may have recruited as many as 25,000 members nationwide. Gerald Winrod of Kansas, "the Jayhawk Nazi," pledged to battle the "hidden hand" of the Jewish conspiracy that worked to "overthrow, the religious, moral, and governmental systems of the world." His newspaper, the *Defender,* had a circulation of some 100,000. Remnants of the Klan mutated into virulent anti-Jewish groups, and more than a hundred other small anti-Semitic groups formed in the 1930s. The larger tides of politics washed aside such extremist groups, but they still gained headlines that added to an impression of growing anti-Semitism in America.[26]

Friends of New Germany, the puppet of an American branch of the German Nazi Party, packed 20,000 Nazis and sympathizers into Madison Square Garden on May 17 to extoll Hitler's contributions to civilization. When speakers denounced boycott leader Samuel Untermyer, the crowd shouted, "Hang him! Hang him!" That same day, the Special Committee on Un-American Activities Authorized to Investigate Nazi Propaganda and Certain Other Propaganda began its hearings. Although Congress had formed the committee at the request of Jewish Democratic representative Samuel Dickstein of New York, Dickstein did not believe that a Jew should lead investigations of Nazis and deferred to Democrat John McCormack of Massachusetts as chairman. The committee probed overtly pro-Nazi groups, but otherwise paid little heed to anti-Semitism in the United States. Labor solicitor Wyzanski presciently warned the American Jewish Committee, "The investigation is going to be diverted to a general assault upon Communism . . . instead of an inquiry into Nazi propaganda." Opposing a Labor Department investigation of the race or religion of those deported as subversives, Wyzanski said that if the result was a very small number of Jews among deportees, the critics would simply explain away the result— the solicitor of the department (Wyzanski) was after all a Jew.[27]

Less extreme or vocal forms of anti-Semitism were more important and widespread in the 1930s. Some business leaders charged that Jews controlled the New Deal. Robert Ruliph Morgan "Ruly" Carpenter, a family member and director of the DuPont Corporation, suggested that the family finance a new organization to bring down the New Deal, which "Frank-furter and his thirty-eight hot dogs—a gang of fanatical and communistic Jew professors" directed. Frank W. Buxton, editor of the *Boston Herald,* wrote privately about "Substantial men who sympathized with anti-Semitism. . . . I was amazed at the intensity with which highly intelligent men argued that the Jews were controlling the President."[28]

The Republican Party rallied its white Protestant base through appeals to traditional Americanism, which raised warning flags for Jews. In its 1934 meeting, the Republican National Committee ratified a "Statement of Principles" that avoided analysis of policy for a morally charged, nation-alist critique of the New Deal. "We must not see destroyed in four years a civilization which has been centuries in building," the party manifesto said. It invoked the word "American" three times in half a sentence, advocating "American democracy, working along American lines, in accordance with the spirit of American institutions." In a radio address broadcast from the meeting, Republican chairman Henry P. Fletcher urged listeners to reject FDR's "inexperienced theorists who have lost their American faith." It was a baby step from the committee's deliberations to a one-line platform that a local activist proposed: "ONE GOD, ONE COUNTRY, ONE RELIGION, ONE LAW, ONE FINANCE, ONE PUBLIC SCHOOL, ONE LANGUAGE, ONE VOTE, ONE TICKET."[29]

Some Republican leaders openly warned of Jewish radical influence on the Roosevelt administration. New York Republican representative Hamil-ton Fish Jr., who represented FDR's home district, named six Jews on his list of sixteen alleged pro-communists in the Roosevelt administration. He denounced "young radicals, so-called economic experts and lawyers, of Fe-lix Frankfurter's school of thought, most of whom are disciples of Karl Marx." Republican representative Frederick Britten of Illinois charged that Reds planned their mischief at a "little red house down in Georgetown where are held the meetings that promote the communistic legislation . . . every night of the week from ten to eighteen young men of communistic minds meet. . . . They call them Frankfurter's hot dogs."[30]

Frankfurter responded to this raising of the "Jewish Question" in Amer-ica with a warning to his former Harvard protégé and White House insider Thomas "Tommy the Cork" Corcoran, an Irish Catholic who lived in the little red house with FDR's Jewish adviser Benjamin V. Cohen. Frankfurter told him that the fear of anti-Semitism was more insidious than its real-ity. Opponents of the New Deal he warned, would "spread rumors about

Jewish influence" in the hope of weakening liberal resolve for both domestic reform and Jewish causes. He insisted that concern about an anti-Semitic backlash should not deter the administration from advancing the New Deal or aiding imperiled Jews. Other advisers and officials, including some Jews, disagreed.[31]

The *American Hebrew* newspaper rebutted charges of a "Jew Deal" with statistics showing that "the much discussed Jewish influence on the national administration is more myth than fact." Henry Morgenthau Jr. was the only Jewish cabinet member, and no Jews headed any of the twenty-five independent offices of government or the twenty emergency relief administrations. No Jews held high positions in the departments of justice, war, the navy, and commerce, and few Jews represented America abroad.[32]

Jewish organizations tried to counteract suspicion of Jewish causes by presenting a uniting American front against Nazi evil. On March 10, the American Jewish Congress and the American Federation of Labor presented "The Case of Civilization against Hitlerism," before 20,000 "jurors" at Madison Square Garden. They put on trial Hitler's dictatorship as an affront to all civilized peoples, not just Jews. Christians headlined the event. President Wilson's former secretary of state Bainbridge Colby presided, and Judge Samuel Seabury of New York summed up the case against Hitler. Twenty "witnesses" testified against the Nazis. Al Smith and New York mayor Fiorello H. LaGuardia testified for the American public. Few Americans knew that this famous Italian American had a Jewish mother. Author Miriam Beard, daughter of the well-known progressive historians Charles and Mary Beard, testified for women; American Legion official Edward J. Neary for war veterans; *Commonweal* editor Michael Williams for Catholics; and Reverend Arthur Brown for Protestants. Once again missing was any Catholic Church official or a witness for African Americans. Reverend John Haynes Holmes, Rabbi Stephen S. Wise's ally in New York reform politics, announced the inevitable guilty verdict.[33]

Simultaneously, B'nai B'rith, following the precedent of its petition to Nicholas II in 1903, sent a petition to FDR with 250,000 signatures protesting Germany's treatment of Jews. The organization asked the president to forward the petition to Hitler, along with a diplomatic note backing the protest. Undersecretary of State Phillips wrote in his diary that the petition "is, of course a movement by American Jews, but the signature [*sic*] are not confined by any means to Jewish names." The petition and other pleas went unanswered. A despairing Rabbi Wise wrote in May to Jacob Bil-likopf, "One goes on working here and it is all so difficult. In the end I sup-pose the counsel of cowardice and silence that prevailed in Germany will prevail here."[34]

The American labor movement, which provided indispensable voters, volunteers, and contributions for Democrats, lacked a consistent response to Hitler's oppression of the Jews. The American Federation of Labor de-nounced Hitler's anti-Semitic policies and backed the anti-Nazi boycott, but opposed the easing of immigration restrictions. Baruch C. Vladeck, a socialist and editor of the *Jewish Daily Forward*, recruited Jewish leaders of unions and independent left-wing groups for a new Jewish Labor Commit-tee in February 1934. The committee claimed to represent the interests of half a million Jewish workers, but its leaders rarely consulted the ordinary laborer. It viewed Hitler's anti-Semitic policies as part of a broad anti-labor campaign by fascists in Europe and reactionaries in America.[35]

The Jewish Labor Committee endorsed the anti-Nazi boycott and finan-cially aided left-wing democratic leaders in Europe. "The Jewish question must be solved in the countries where the Jews live," Vladeck said. The committee supported President Roosevelt as a bulwark against the Ameri-can right wing. It drew its strength primarily from the clothing trades unions in New York City, especially the International Ladies Garment Workers Union. David Dubinsky, the union's influential Jewish president, served as secretary of the committee. Although the Amalgamated Clothing Workers of America also affiliated with the committee, its Jewish president, Sidney Hillman, FDR's closest ally in the labor movement, stayed aloof from committee affairs.[36] Vladeck shunned affiliation with established Jew-ish groups, which he said failed to represent the Jewish working class and put exclusively Jewish concerns above the larger battle against fascism. In December 1934, Vladeck rejected an invitation by the American Jewish Congress to participate in elections for congress members. The congress, he said, "stressed the fight against Hitlerism as a purely Jewish issue" rather than "only one angle of Fascism." In an article in the *Jewish Daily Forward* Vladeck called the election a political move motivated not by a "desire to serve the Jewish community but by a desire to clinch leadership in Jewish life."[37]

Bernard Deutsch responded in kind. He said that his congress had broadly defended human rights as evidenced by the mock trial of Hitlerism. "But on whom else but Jews does the duty to defend Jews fall first?" he asked. He assailed the "groups of influential Jews" who had "objected to public action, to public protest, and to public demonstration." Rabbi Wise backed Deutsch and disparaged critics of his congress as "self crowned 'grand dukes' who . . . believe only in dictatorship, in their own dictatorship." In an article in the Yiddish newspaper the *Day,* he condemned that "hush-hush policy which these noble gentlemen follow always." He said that the Jews in Germany followed this same policy. They naively believed if they "devoted themselves to assimilation" and "denied their Jewishness . . . they would escape persecution."[38]

To some observers, it appeared that Jewish leaders hated each other almost as much as they hated Hitler. Reverend Holmes wrote that "the long controversy between the American Jewish Congress and the American Jewish Committee" was "a tragedy only second to that of the German tragedy, although a long way removed." This friend and political ally of Wise, found "Wise and his associates wholly right in their protest, denunciation, agitation, boycott organization, etc., and by the same token Dr. Adler and his group wholly wrong as it seems to me that they have come perilously near to taking the Nazi horror lying down."[39]

Despite Frankfurter's warning, fears of growing anti-Semitism reached into the White House. In a letter to Wise on May 13, Walter White, secretary of the National Association for the Advancement of Colored People, said that during a discussion of anti-lynching legislation, the president brought up anti-Semitism. FDR, White wrote, "is quite apprehensive of the growing anti-Semitic and Nazi sentiment in the United States. . . . This sentiment, especially in its manifestations of the strong tendency to find a scapegoat for the ills and suffering of the depression, may result in very serious clashes, the President seems to fear."[40]

Rising isolationism in the United States also deterred the administration from criticizing Germany. Not only conservatives, but some liberal Democrats such as Senator Burton K. Wheeler of Montana and Representative Maury Maverick of Texas, and progressive Republicans such as Senators Hiram Johnson of California and Gerald Nye of North Dakota demanded that America avoid entanglement in foreign political and military affairs. FDR needed their support for his domestic reforms. In his January 4, 1934, message to Congress, FDR had declared, "I have made it clear that the United States cannot take part in political arrangements in Europe."

International cooperation might have advanced the resettlement of German Jews. In October 1933, the Geneva-based League of Nations had created a new refugee office, the High Commission on Refugees (Jewish and Other) Coming from Germany. Its history foreshadowed twelve years of the Western world's frustration and failure in responding to Nazi persecutions of Jews. Germany began by winning a major concession, when the league agreed that the high commissioner would report only to a governing board of representatives from interested nations, which included the nonmember United States, not the league itself. Thus, the League of Nations opted out of officially managing the problem of Jewish refugees. It diminished the power and prestige of the office in other ways, too. At the insistence of the British, it omitted Palestine from the high commissioner's sphere of activity. The commissioner could deal only with exiles who had left Germany—as of late 1933 about 60,000 primarily Jewish persons—and could not interfere with German domestic matters. He had to raise his own funds, absent financial support from the league.[41]

The British had a prestigious candidate for high commissioner in Lord Robert Cecil, a renowned architect of the league who would win the Nobel Peace Prize in 1937. However, as Felix Warburg explained in a telegraph to Otto Schiff in London, "appointment should go to American because large amounts to be raised here and such party should by nationality be independent of pressure government which has mandate of Palestine." The league secretary general appointed McDonald after prominent Americans such as Smith and Hoover declined interest. The Rockefeller family vetoed another American candidate, Raymond Fosdick, president of the Rockefeller Foundation. John D. Rockefeller III even tried to dissuade McDonald from taking the job. "He evidently was impressed by the invitation, but being instinctively rather anti-Semitic, he had difficulty in realizing that the job to be done was one of potentially large scope," McDonald said.[42]

McDonald's job presented formidable challenges. Many world leaders in public and private life knew and respected the new commissioner. He was a man of high moral conscience and vast energy who believed that Hitler's persecution of Jews affronted all civilized peoples. Jewish refugees could not have found a more stalwart advocate. Yet, like later heads of organizations dealing with resettling and rescuing Jews, McDonald lacked the influence and prestige of more prominent figures considered for the position.

"A great figure like Lord Robert Cecil," Adler wrote, "might be able to accomplish even more."[43]

The first meeting of McDonald's governing board on December 8 anticipated events to come. The French representative said that France had too many refugees and New World nations had too few. Britain's Lord Cecil, who became chairman of the board, said that Europe generally was swamped with refugees and that hope for the future rested on settlement overseas. The views of FDR's representative, Columbia law professor Joseph P. Chamberlain, reflected the political and economic situation in the United States. Although typically an advocate for Jewish refugees, he said that the United States would tightly restrict immigration as long as economic hard times continued. The representative for Uruguay said that his country was too small to absorb refugees and that Brazil and Argentina offered brighter prospects. Yet neither nation, although invited to do so, had sent representatives to the board. With understated passive voice, the *New York Times* reported, "A general impression of disappointment with the session was given, although no discouragement was voiced."[44]

Three weeks later, McDonald told Jewish leaders in London that he despaired of solving the refugee problem as long as nations saw new arrivals as burdens and Christians viewed the plight of refugees as a Jewish problem— the latest version of the West's "Jewish Question." Advocates for refugees must awaken "non-Jews as to a sense of their responsibility," he said, and must somehow "turn the refugees into assets for the various countries to which they might be expected to go." McDonald fretted about the dim prospects for raising large sums of money. Already he began considering settlement possibilities in far-flung parts of the world, another sign of the major powers' obstinacy on refugee issues.[45]

State Department officials regarded McDonald and the League High Commission as irritants who would flood the United States with Jewish refugees. In his summary of a conversation with Chamberlain, Assistant Secretary Carr wrote, "He thinks there will be a great drive for placing over 200,000 Jews who are probably to be driven out of Germany. . . . Europe thinks they should, many of them, come here. . . . I fear a general onslaught on our restrictive immigration laws. So there seems to be trouble ahead." When McDonald spoke to Moffat, chief of the department's Western European Division, about American cooperation in resettling refugees, Moffat consulted Assistant Secretary R. Walton Moore, a former Virginia representative who was a friend and political ally of Secretary of State Hull. Moore warned against the United States signing on to any international agreement on refugees. Among other problems, he said, to do so would limit America's sovereign powers on the admission or expulsion of aliens. The humanitarian challenge posed by refugees, he said, was already "handsomely served by our laws which do not discriminate against refugees, or stateless persons as such."[46]

During FDR's first two years in office, any decisive response to Jewish concerns seemed to risk negative repercussions for foreign policy, economic reform, social comity, and domestic politics. Not surprisingly, Roosevelt preferred to handle any adjustment of immigration policy behind closed doors, not in public: open debate would only unite his enemies and divide his supporters. When back-room negotiations left the State Department with control over immigration, the president did not intervene to fulfill promises he had made to Jewish advocates.

FDR had likely envisioned a compromise between State and Labor that would modestly admit more German Jews to the United States. When MacCormack backed away from the use of public charge bonds, Perkins found herself isolated within the administration, and Labor lost its leverage. Only the president's forceful intervention might have shifted the balance in favor of expanded immigration. Sensitive to supposedly rising anti-Semitism and worried about collateral political damage, Roosevelt remained in the background. He missed an opportunity to ease visa restrictions imposed by a former president whose policies FDR had otherwise repudiated.

CHAPTER FIVE

Transitions

THE YEAR 1934 began auspiciously for FDR with a sparkling fifty-second birthday celebration in January. Some 5,000 guests joined him on his birthday at New York City's posh Waldorf-Astoria hotel. Fifty-two young women clad in white satin carried candles and formed themselves into the shape of a giant birthday cake to sing "Happy Birthday, Mr. President." More than 300,000 birthday greetings poured into the White House, while Americans of every class, race, religion, and political affiliation attended some 6,000 parties across the land. The celebrations raised more than $1 million, not for FDR's Democratic Party, but for his Warm Springs Foundation that aided victims of crippling disease.[1]

Roosevelt would have much to celebrate in the second year of his presidency. He could claim credit for the economy's continuing recovery from the Great Depression. He would extend his New Deal program of domestic reform, and his Democrats would become the first party since the Civil War to gain U.S. House and Senate seats in a midterm election. In foreign policy, however, Congress moved to limit his discretion, particularly in Europe, where German power increasingly threatened the peace.

Having long dispensed with any domestic political opposition, Adolf Hitler had no internal restraints. He launched vicious new measures against perceived enemies at home and embarked on risky foreign policy ventures. Hitler's successes and Germany's growing aggressiveness only highlighted Roosevelt's foreign policy constraints and added to his problems. For the time being, the president could only signal his convictions that some combination of nations had to rein Germany in.

In the midterm elections that fall, Democrats campaigned successfully for continued economic progress and against Wall Street and the Hoovervilles of Republican times. Their victories swelled Democratic majorities to beyond 70 percent in both chambers of Congress. In a little-noted election in Missouri, New Deal critic Senator Roscoe Patterson lost to an obscure Democrat, Harry S. Truman.[2]

The 1934 elections continued a realignment of party loyalties. Many Americans who had voted against Hoover in 1932 voted for Democrats in 1934 and converted to the New Deal party. First-time and newly eligible voters likewise flocked to the Democrats. The Democratic percentage of the two-party registration rose in five representative states from 41 percent in 1932 to 48 percent in 1934. In nine major cities, the Democratic percentage soared from 48 percent to 58 percent. The midterm elections also began the conversion of African American voters from staunch Republicans to loyal Democrats. For the first time in history, Democrats captured a majority of the African American vote. Jews still remained the most loyal supporters of FDR and his party. Roosevelt's failure to act publicly against Nazi persecution of German Jews did not diminish Jewish loyalty to his party. Jews supported the New Deal and regarded Republican alternatives as unpalatable or worse. Not a single Jewish Republican remained as governor or member of Congress after the election.[3]

After the successful midterms, FDR pursued three major related goals: winning reelection in 1936, extending the New Deal, and battling isolationists in Congress. He anticipated a difficult election campaign in 1936, with Senator Huey Long of Louisiana leading a third-party campaign, backed perhaps by the "radio priest," Father Charles Coughlin of Royal Oak, Michigan. Both Long and Coughlin, despite their authoritarian bent, looked to outflank FDR from the left on economic policy. Coughlin advocated government control over the financial system. In 1935, he began citing Jewish bankers as prime villains who controlled the world economy, which led Jewish leaders to complain of his anti-Semitism. Long claimed some five million members for his "Share Our Wealth" clubs, based on taxing the rich and giving to the poor. Coughlin gained a weekly radio audience of some twenty million listeners and said that six million had joined his National Union of Social Justice. Emil Hurja, FDR's pollster, reported that Long could lure some 10 percent of voters away from the president, enough to turn several key states from Democratic to doubtful.[4]

Despite the recovery, unemployment remained stubbornly high. In April 1935, the president signed legislation roughly based on his employment program in New York that established a Works Progress Administration (WPA) for unemployed workers. Harry Hopkins, who had directed the New York operation, also ran the WPA. A month later, the Supreme Court stunned the president by unanimously striking down the National Industrial Recovery Act, which authorized the executive to negotiate binding industry-wide economic codes. The court found that the law illegally regulated commerce within states and delegated to the president law-making authority reserved for Congress. In a second case, the court ruled that the Frazier-Lemke Act, which limited the repossession of farms, unconstitutionally deprived creditors of property rights. Finally, on that "Black Monday," the court also decided that FDR could not fire without cause a member of the Federal Trade Commission.

The three rulings appeared to crimp future social and economic legislation and curtail presidential power. Although Louis D. Brandeis wrote the Frazier-Lemke opinion, some critics saw it as a blow against Jewish elements linked to the White House—the comeuppance of Felix Frankfurter's too-clever Jewish conspirators. *Atlanta Constitution* columnist Arthur Sears Henning said, "The happy hot dogs . . . were commissioned to get around the constitution." Their master was Frankfurter, "the most influential single individual in the United States," who is frequently "coming and going through the backdoor" of the White House. Still, "the Supreme Court justices were not taken in" and "the cunning of the Frankfurter lawyers proved a boomerang."[5]

Brandeis had backed all three decisions as needed restraints on government-sponsored monopolies and bureaucratic intrusions on the states and private business. Shortly after the court released its opinions, Brandeis summoned Benjamin V. Cohen into his office. "The Justice was visibly excited and deeply agitated," Cohen said in handwritten notes on the meeting. The decisions "change everything," Brandeis told Cohen. "The president has been living in a fool's paradise. . . . I would not be surprised if everything would have to be redrafted." He insisted that Cohen "make sure that Felix [Frankfurter] is here in the morning to advise the president. Everything that you [the administration] has been doing must be changed."[6]

The president and his advisers abandoned the industrial planning of the National Recovery Administration but moved ahead with liberal programs that bumped the edges of constitutional restraints. In July, the president signed the National Labor Relations or Wagner Act, named after FDR's friend and prime mover of the bill, Senator Robert F. Wagner of New York. The act created a National Labor Relations Board that prohibited various unfair labor practices and protected workers' right to collectively bargain with employers. It led to the formation of the Congress of Industrial Organizations, which recruited millions of industrial workers without regard to craft affiliations and strengthened the ranks of the Democratic Party. Both Sidney Hillman and David Dubinsky were major organizers of the congress, which William Dudley Pelley of the Silver Shirts derided as "a synagogue." In August 1935, the president put in place the third major pillar of what some historians called the "Second New Deal," when he signed the Social Security Act. The act created the modern federal welfare program of old-age pensions, unemployment compensation, financial assistance for the disabled, and aid for mothers with dependent children. It established the principle that Americans had certain entitlements from government in addition to rights as individuals. Jewish leaders hailed the new welfare system, which Jewish social service activists had helped to put in place. Economist Abraham Epstein headed the American Association for Old Age Security, which had been calling for old-age pensions since the late 1920s. Physician I. M. Rubinow, the secretary of B'nai B'rith and a long-standing advocate of social security, served as a consultant to the President's Committee on Social Security.[7]

In foreign policy, FDR clashed with a heavily Democratic but isolationist Congress. The Senate rejected his recommendation that the United States join the World Court in January 1935. Later, prompted by the Senate hearings on how munitions makers had influenced American entry into World War I and reports that Italy was about to invade Ethiopia, isolationists in Congress passed a temporary six-month Neutrality Act. The act embargoed the shipment of war materiel to belligerent nations and gave the president no leeway to punish only the aggressor. FDR bent to prevailing winds and his dependence on progressive isolationists and signed the restrictive bill in August 1935. He issued an ambiguous statement that appeased isolationists, but called for a more flexible approach to foreign crises. FDR applied the act to both belligerents when Italy invaded Ethiopia in October. Despite the president's call for a "moral embargo," of Italy, American business continued to supply the Italians with vital oil supplies, which the act did not cover. Then Congress passed the Neutrality Act of 1936, which FDR signed on March 1. The act imposed mandatory embargoes on the export of war materiel to belligerents and banned the granting of American loans and credits, with no presidential discretion to punish aggressor states.

The rejection of U.S. participation in the World Court and the passage of the Neutrality Acts of 1935 and 1936 signaled a retreat from American involvement in world affairs and a repudiation of the leadership role for the nation that Roosevelt had proposed in a 1928 article in *Foreign Affairs.* Congressional and public support for stringent neutrality legislation warned FDR that he could pay a heavy price for any entanglement in the politics of foreign nations. In Germany, the semiofficial government newspaper, the *Diplomatische Korrespondenz,* hailed America's approach to neutrality as a model for the world.[8]

Some observers had anticipated that Hitler's consolidation of power and an improving German economy would moderate Nazi extremism. Events proved otherwise. On June 30, 1934, selected squads of Heinrich Himmler's SS murdered more than eighty officers of the rival SA force, as well as other political enemies of Hitler. The Nazi-controlled press justified these summary executions by charging that the SA was planning a coup, and that its leader, Ernst Röhm, was a notorious homosexual. The following month leaders of the Nazi movement in Austria, working with at least one Nazi diplomat in the German legation in Vienna, murdered Austrian chancellor Engelbert Dollfuss and launched a failed coup. Hitler then dissociated himself from the conspirators and deferred his hope of seizing his Austrian homeland. In March 1935, Germany reinstituted the military draft, violating a provision of the Treaty of Versailles. A year later, Hitler overrode the fears of his military leadership and sent German troops into the Rhineland, a demilitarized area of Germany according to another provision of the peace settlements. The reoccupation of the Rhineland eliminated France's buffer zone in case of war. The move capped Germany's transformation into the dominant diplomatic and military power on the continent. Germany could now pressure smaller European countries to bend to its wishes.

Escalating Nazi persecution of German Jews paralleled Germany's growing strength and influence. At the annual Nazi Party rally held in Nuremberg during September 1935, Hitler issued new anti-Semitic decrees. To uphold Germany's racial purity, the Nuremberg Laws banned marriage or sexual intercourse between Jews and persons of "German or kindred blood" and prohibited Jews from employing German women under the age of forty-five as domestic workers. In effect, Jews also lost the rights of citizenship under the new decrees. Authorities within the United States continued to debate whether the Nazi "radicals" or "moderates" controlled events in Germany. Yet the only difference between them, the American Jewish Committee noted, was whether to "crush the Jews by so-called 'legal means' alone" or by more violent measures.[9]

On immigration, the American Jewish Committee and its allies continued their backdoor diplomacy. In November 1935, New York governor Herbert Lehman wrote confidentially to FDR requesting the admission of a few thousand more Jewish refugees from Germany, which would clearly redeeem the president's pledge from 1933. He sent to the president a letter from James G. McDonald to Felix Warburg, which said "it is the President alone who can get the thing done" on easing visa restrictions and "he only if he is prepared to take personal responsibility to see that it is done." FDR shunted the matter off to the State Department, which prepared a noncommittal response for him. The president added that the State Department had already instructed consuls to provide visa applicants "most generous and favorable treatment" and in some cases to waive document requirements.[10]

Jewish author Harold Fields reported at the end of October 1935 that the American public still opposed easing immigration restrictions even for refugees; any change in policy had to be a quiet one. The idea of admitting refugees through public charge bonds continued to languish. Daniel W. MacCormack, commissioner of immigration and naturalization, placed blame everywhere but on his own agency and department. In a meeting with Jewish leaders on November 6, 1935, he warned that any "liberalization of the present procedure" for visas would antagonize restrictionists in Congress, who opposed any "liberalization of immigration which would favorably affect Jews in particular." He said that State had undermined the

Labor Department by throwing upon it all responsibility for any easing of visa restrictions. Southern congressmen and patriotic organizations would block any initiative on public charge bonds and in the process strengthen the existing prejudice against the Labor Department. A week later, in a letter to Governor Lehman, according to a summary by a sympathetic Cyrus Adler, FDR said "that the bars on the immigration of German Jews to America had been greatly relaxed." The president may have been misinformed or perhaps he was seeking to deflect Jewish pressure on the administration. In fiscal 1936, some 6,346 Germans (mostly Jewish) immigrated to America, well short of FDR's purportedly promised 10,000 per year and less than a quarter of quota limits.[11]

By the end of fiscal year 1936, 97,352 Germans, according to State Department data, intended to immigrate. In the three fiscal years 1934–1936, some 60,000 potential German immigrants, most of them Jewish, may have failed to find refuge in the United States because the Roosevelt administration continued policies that denied them visas despite available quota slots.[12]

The assassination of Huey Long in September 1935 dashed prospects for a significant third-party campaign in the 1936 presidential election. Pollster Hurja reported that no other third-party candidate would win more than 2 percent of the popular vote. Still, FDR faced concerted opposition from most business groups and conservative organizations. With Jewish immigration at very modest levels, it was not a sensitive issue during the 1936 elections.[13]

In part, American Jews admired Roosevelt for the enemies he made, especially after new revelations of anti-Semitism within the conservative opposition. A Senate investigation of lobbying activities by liberal Democratic senator Hugo Black of Alabama uncovered anti-Semitic correspondence from Alexander Lincoln, president of the influential conservative group, Sentinels of the Republic. In response to a letter about the "Jewish brigade that Roosevelt took to Washington," Lincoln responded, "I am doing what I can as an officer of the Sentinels. I think, as you say, that the Jewish threat is a real one." Lincoln pleaded not guilty to anti-Semitism, but undercut his cause by saying that he was referring only to "those of Jewish origin active in the communistic movement." Lincoln's allies on the right inflamed the scandal. Sentinel official Thomas Cadwalader denied "that the Jews as a race or religion were trying to pull down civilization," but added that "many conspicuous Jews in the world are engaged in that effort." Outspoken conservative Henry Joy, president of Packard Motors, joined the debate, denouncing Jewish influence in government "by presidential appointment and approval." The controversy forced Lincoln out of the Sentinels and tainted the broader conservative movement.[14]

Other conservative groups, if not overtly anti-Semitic, defended America's Christian civilization from the "un-American" New Deal. Major corporate heads, led by E. F. Hutton, the chairman of General Foods, converted the Crusaders, originally an anti-Prohibition group, into an important conservative lobby group. The Crusaders called for a Christian spiritual revival in America and pledged "to fight vigorously any attempts to have the majority of Americans ruled by organized minorities seeking special advantages." Pierre du Pont, a founder of the American Liberty League, the most richly funded and prominent conservative organization of the 1930s, corresponded with Hiram Evans, the grand wizard of the Ku Klux Klan about joining forces to fight America's "Red menace."[15]

Early in the election year of 1936, Rabbi Stephen S. Wise breached what he called "General Headquarters" and finally met with President Roosevelt. According to some sources, the failing health and waning influence of Roosevelt's trusted aide Louis Howe opened the way for the meeting. Howe apparently had never forgiven Wise for opposing FDR's presidential ambitions in 1932. Wise told Reverend John Haynes Holmes that he had hoped to get FDR to "see the light and the right about the Nazi situation" and surmount the caution of his "timorous Jews." Wise found that Roosevelt had a prepared excuse for inaction. In typical fashion, FDR turned to a private source, saying, " 'But Max Warburg [a German-Jewish businessman and brother of Felix Warburg] wrote to me that the situation in Germany is so hopeless that nothing can be done!" Wise said, "I confess I have been cussing Max Warburg's head off." Given that Max was Felix's brother, Wise was likely also cursing his nemesis, the American Jewish Committee. Some critics would later charge that Wise fell under the influence of FDR's "magnetic personality." However, as Wise later explained in a letter to Holmes, even before the meeting "I was giving my full moral support to the Administration despite its obvious shortcomings and multitudinous defects." In March 1936, Wise confided to Frankfurter, "There are only two things I am thinking of at present—Hitlerism that must go and FDR who must stay." A month later, he told Frankfurter, "There seems to be a much better and warmer feeling for FDR, that the danger of his being defeated has been virtually reduced to zero. But no mistakes must be made least of all in relation to those racial antagonisms."[16]

In October, FDR again deflected Wise from a serious discussion of German Jewry. "He said this disturbing thing," Wise recalled after meeting with the president. "'I have just seen two people who have toured through Germany. They tell us that they saw that the Synagogues were crowded and apparently there is nothing very wrong in the situation at present.'" FDR ignored what he had told Wise earlier about the hopeless situation for Jews in Germany. This time it was Wise who "then explained to him how grave conditions were. . . . He listened carefully; but I could see that the tourists (whoever they were, the Lord bless them not) had made an impression on him."[17]

In Palestine, a new Arab revolt led to small-scale civil war. When the British considered curtailing Jewish immigration, President Roosevelt responded. In late July 1936, he instructed Secretary of State Cordell Hull to send a back-channel signal to Britain via Robert W. Bingham, American ambassador in London, that the United States opposed the suspension of Jewish immigration to Palestine. On August 5, FDR publicly declared that "men and women of Jewish faith have a right to resettle the land where their faith was born and from which much of modern civilization has emanated." Partly in response to American pressure, Britain did not impose new formal restrictions on Jewish immigration to Palestine, but in practice impeded the entry of Jews. At his second meeting with FDR in October 1936, Rabbi Wise expressed his appreciation for "the matter of intervention in Palestine. . . . I told him that my joy was shared by Justice Brandeis, Felix [Frankfurter], and Judge Mack." Jewish immigration to Palestine, of course, posed far less political jeopardy for FDR than Jewish immigration to the United States. Still, FDR had done more than other world leaders to keep Palestine open to Jewish immigrants.[18]

FDR knew that liberal Jewish leaders and voters would not abandon his campaign. For Jewish leaders, with the exception of a few lifelong Republicans like Felix Warburg, support for the conservative and isolationist Republican Party, backed by anti-Semitic groups, was unthinkable. He also knew that his isolationist opposition would press charges of undue Jewish influence on the administration, rather than upbraid his failure to challenge the Nazis.

In seeking a candidate to face the president, Republicans chose the little-known Alf Landon of Kansas, the lone Republican governor who won reelection in 1934. Landon had roots in the GOP's progressive past, but the party's mainstream conservatives found him sufficiently pliable for their purposes. With the exception of brewers and distillers and Jewish and southern businessmen, most business dollars flowed to the GOP in 1936. Father Coughlin and Dr. Francis Townsend, the champion of generous old-age pensions, organized a third-party movement that melded liberal economics with Coughlin's increasingly authoritarian and anti-Semitic appeals. Gerald L. K. Smith, an anti-Semitic former minister, joined their campaign. Without Long to head their ticket, the allies chose an obscure progressive Republican representative, William "Liberty Bell" Lemke of North Dakota, a champion of debt relief for farmers.[19]

From the camps of both major parties in 1936 came charges and countercharges about anti-Semitism and Jewish plots. According to press reports, both Democrats and Republicans encouraged whispering campaigns of the kind that plagued Al Smith in 1928. Democrats whispered that Landon was at worst anti-Semitic and at best tolerant of right-wing anti-Semitic groups, like the Sentinels and the Crusaders. The German American Bund also endorsed Landon to counter President "Rosenfield's" Jewish New Deal.[20]

Landon had a history of opposing anti-Semitism. He repudiated all groups associated with "racial prejudices and religious bigotry." He said, "I think the Democratic Party is not above trying to misrepresent my attitude on this matter." Rabbi Wise told FDR in October "of the pressure that was being brought to bear upon me to give Landon a clean bill of health on the matter of his alleged anti-Jewish feeling." Wise did not give in. He said, "Whether Landon was or was not racially prejudiced back of him stood Pugh and many of the Sentinels of America and the Liberty Leaguers who were anti-Jewish and he was getting the benefit of their support and I saw no reason to exonerate him." Zionist activist Samuel Rosensohn told Frankfurter that Republican Jews who try "to tell us that the Democrats are injecting the Jewish question into the campaign" are placing "the blame for the evil upon the persons who pointed out its existence." On October 8, a less partisan figure than Wise, Sigmund Livingston, chairman of the Anti-Defamation League of B'nai B'rith, finally gave Landon his Jewish clearance.[21]

Republicans in turn recycled stories about Jewish control over the New Deal and whispered that Jewish leaders had regimented their followers to vote en masse for President Roosevelt. Given this controversy, Wise told

FDR at their October meeting that he would keep quiet about the president's "supremely important service to us" on Palestine. Public revelations, Wise said, "might be used against you at this time by the other Party." Wise also helped FDR by denying charges of a Jewish bloc vote. In a reprise of his 1928 address that endorsed FDR for governor, Wise told a crowd at Carnegie Hall that there is no such thing as a "Jewish vote." He said that while speaking for FDR in twenty-five cities, he had never "made any allusion to the Jews. I addressed my hearers not as a rabbi or as a Jew, but as an American citizen."[22]

Roosevelt swept 60 percent of the popular vote to only 37 percent for Landon. Lemke limped in with 2.5 percent. As Roosevelt's campaign chair Jim Farley had famously predicted, FDR won every state except Maine and Vermont. Postelection polls showed that a majority of African Americans backed Roosevelt in 1936, ratifying their turn to the Democrats in 1934. The GOP still polled better among women than men, but for the first time since suffrage, a majority of women voted Democratic. The American electorate sharply divided along religious lines. More than three-quarters of Jews and Catholics voted for FDR; white northern Protestants split their votes between Roosevelt and Landon.[23]

In 1936, Democrats won overwhelming control of Congress and achieved their goal of becoming America's majority party. Since 1928, the party had gained some 175 U.S. House seats, forty Senate seats, and nineteen governors' mansions. The GOP retained a meager eighty-nine House members and sixteen senators. After losing New Jersey in 1937, the party held seven governorships with a combined population of less than New York State. From 1928 to 1936, the Democrats' share of the two-party registration soared from 31 percent to 55 percent in five representative northern states and from 36 percent to 65 percent in nine major cities.[24]

With his election triumph behind him and the economy continuing to improve, FDR finally broke the bureaucratic logjam on Jewish refugees. In late 1936, Foreign Service Inspector Jerome Klahr Huddle toured American consulates in Germany. He reported to Washington that many potential immigrants came from better-class families, and even their distant relatives in the United States sought to aid them in escaping persecution. In January 1937, the Department of State issued new regulations for granting immigrant visas. The revised instructions told consuls to reject only applicants who were probable public charges, not just possible public charges. In addition, consuls could accept affidavits of support from distant relatives as well as close relatives. John Wiley, the consul general in Antwerp, Belgium, wrote to his counterpart Homer Brett in Rotterdam about the import of these new instructions. Brett replied that, "I understand it as a radical change in policy and I am sending an enthusiastic acknowledgement. . . . I personally think that a strained definition of the LPC clause has been enforced ever since September 1930, and that this instruction signifies that 'likely' is to mean what is meant when the law was written."[25]

FDR left no presidential fingerprints on the new regulations, which the State Department quietly implemented. The press did not report any change in policy, and the increase in German immigration, although significant, was not large enough to provoke a public outcry or raise the ire of Congress. In fiscal 1937, German immigration to the United States increased to 10,895, still well below 50 percent of quota limits, but finally reaching FDR's purported target of 10,000 admissions. For the first time, the Roosevelt administration had done something decisive to help persecuted Jews escape from Germany.

FDR's successes at home still did not carry over into foreign policy. In March 1937, the president privately discussed with Canadian prime minister Mackenzie King a plan to excise the causes of war through an international New Deal. World leaders, though, had no interest in such joint ventures. British chancellor of the exchequer Neville Chamberlain, a Conservative Party leader who soon became prime minister, wrote to Secretary of the Treasury Henry Morgenthau Jr. that the United States could best contribute to world peace by amending its neutrality legislation, which "constitutes an indirect but potent encouragement to aggression." However, FDR could not stop Congress from handcuffing him again with the "permanent" Neutrality Act of 1937. On May 1, FDR reluctantly signed the third unwanted Neutrality Act since 1935. The United States seemed both unwilling and unable to counter potential German expansion through cooperation with other nations.[26]

FDR pondered the conundrum of how to prevent another world war with isolationists cuffing his wrists at home. He confronted his critics directly in a speech on October 5, 1937, which drew on metaphors from epidemiology to warn "The epidemic of world lawlessness is spreading" and required a "quarantine" that would isolate aggressors from peace-loving nations of the world. At the next cabinet meeting, Roosevelt explained his thinking, but offered no specific proposals. Afterwards, Attorney General Homer Cummings, a close political ally of FDR, recorded in his diary the president's comments, likely mixed with his own thoughts: "It is also idle to assume that, by following such an ultra-isolationist policy, we are thereby avoiding trouble. If the pirate nations of the world are able to get the jump on the Democratic Governments of the world—the latter always being slow to act—the consequences are too far reaching and too terrifying to be ignored." The president believed that "great and far-reaching events hang on a hair trigger" and that "the friends of the Neutrality Act and those who regard that act as insane are seeking the same purpose. The problem is not whether we shall keep out of war but how shall we keep out of war."[27]

Isolationist opinion—undaunted by the president's quarantine speech— and the weakness of America's peacetime military deterred the president from punishing "pirate nations" or taking a more active role in the world. Gallup Polls conducted during 1937 showed that 70 percent of respondents thought that it was a mistake for America to enter World War I. In addition, 73 percent agreed that Congress should hold a referendum of the American people before declaring war and 71 percent agreed that if one foreign nation attacked another, the United States should not "join with other nations to compel it to stop." In a survey of America's "most vital issue," respondents ranked neutrality second only to unemployment."[28]

Still, the emerging second-term Roosevelt endorsed Jewish settlement in Palestine and worked behind the scenes to keep the British from restricting Jewish immigration. With the pressures of reelection behind him, FDR had finally delivered on his promise from 1933 of loosening visa restrictions and admitting at least 10,000 German immigrants to the United States. Unlike other timid heads of state and most leaders of the U.S. Congress, FDR in his "quarantine" speech also challenged aggressor nations. Yet international aggression and religious persecution were spiraling out of control. World leaders and lawmakers in the United States lacked the will and the means to deter Germany from massively rearming and threatening neighbor states, or to stop Japan from waging a war of conquest in China. The Arab revolt and uncertain British policy threatened Jewish settlement in Palestine. Jews continued to suffer under Hitler's cold pogrom and anti-Semitic persecutions had spread to Eastern Europe.

Rabbi Wise proposed in November 1937 that prominent Jews should meet with Jewish members of Congress "to tell them the whole story of what is happening in Germany, Austria, Hungary, and above all, Poland and Rumania." The legislators would go "to the President, putting the Jewish question before him and asking him whether something cannot be done to bring to European lands a sense of American horror." Realistically, Wise recognized that Gentile America had grown weary of his cause. "Alas, it must be added parenthetically that there is not too much of such American horror."[29]

CHAPTER SIX

Moving Millions?

FDR'S NEW DEAL programs softened the rough edges of capitalism, a historic achievement that nearly all American Jewish leaders applauded. Still, despite a 60 percent mandate in the 1936 election and expansive Democratic majorities in the U.S. House and Senate, FDR could not necessarily bend Congress to his will. In 1937, Roosevelt sought to protect his New Deal reforms from the Supreme Court with a plan to appoint additional justices, but the Senate decisively rejected his "court-packing" proposal. This battle divided the Democratic majority, reopened criticism of his alleged dictatorial ambitions, and breathed life into a moribund Republican opposition at a time when a nasty recession called the economic recovery into question. With equal stubbornness, Congress also resisted a loosening of America's rigid neutrality laws or an expansion of immigration to the United States.

Although FDR lost his campaign to expand the size of the Supreme Court, it nonetheless upheld the Wagner Act and the Social Security Act, leveling constitutional barriers to federal welfare and regulatory laws. By 1938, FDR had secured his legacy at home. In contrast, his achievements in foreign policy were meager at a time of growing world crisis. With a weak military and a diplomatic role limited by Congress, he had little chance of halting the collapse of order in Europe and Asia. In the remainder of what he must have thought was his last term he still might intervene to assist Jews in Europe threatened by rising persecution in Germany and other countries. Soon, however, FDR learned that his willingness to seek solutions for imperiled Jews left him isolated internationally and domestically. Other world leaders, such as Britain's Neville Chamberlain, preferred to ignore the plight of Jews or even blame the victims of Nazi persecution. In the United States, Congress and the public opposed expanded immigration or involvement in Old World quarrels. Roosevelt tempered his aims and avoided anything that required congressional approval, but he kept pushing.

If timing and circumstances partly explain Roosevelt's new activism on the Jewish crisis in Europe, he also benefited from replacing William Phillips as undersecretary of state with Sumner Welles. FDR could rely on Welles, unlike Phillips, to supervise initiatives on Jewish refugees and square them with the broad goals of American foreign policy.

From a well-off family, Welles, like FDR, attended Groton and Harvard. The Welles and Roosevelt families were friendly, and Welles had been a page at the wedding of Franklin and Eleanor as a twelve-year-old. FDR sponsored Welles's entry into the Foreign Service, where he advanced up the ranks as a specialist in Latin America. Unlike most Foreign Service personnel, Welles opposed the deployment of military force to support American business interests. In 1933, FDR appointed Welles assistant secretary of state for Latin America, and then undersecretary, State's number-two position, in 1937. Welles was politically liberal, knew the bureaucratic machinery at State, and got along well with the president, despite a personality that many others found formal to the point of being cold. Welles's frequent contact with, and loyalty to, FDR antagonized Secretary of State Cordell Hull and others in the department. Welles would work with a president who effectively wanted to be his own secretary of state.[1]

Welles had limited qualifications for managing Jewish issues. During his youth, he had little contact with Jews. In his Maryland home his best Jewish contact was Rabbi Morris Lazaron of Baltimore, a non-Zionist aligned with the far-right faction of internal Jewish politics. Welles epitomized the wealthy, mannered WASP. Still, other than the economic specialist Herbert

Feis, who was Jewish, Welles was the best man Roosevelt could find at State to handle Jewish initiatives.[2]

The president also needed an ally among American Jewish leaders. On January 22, 1938, in a meeting with Rabbi Stephen S. Wise, head of the American Jewish Congress, FDR signaled his intention to seek new areas of settlement for European Jews: "Don't you think the time has come for your people, in the light of these difficulties, to think about this:—If we can stave off war for another two years or three at most, we will have a world Conference on re-allocation of territories, especially unoccupied territories, and re-apportionment of raw materials. In that case we might find some large areas as a second choice [after Palestine] for the Jews." Wise parried by asking whether FDR would be willing to swap his Hyde Park estate for the huge King Ranch in Texas. Palestine, he said, was the Jewish homeland. FDR responded, "I am not offering a substitute for Palestine, but Palestine possibilities are going to be exhausted." As the president put it, "You ought to have another card up your sleeve." Wise had earlier told a correspondent that once Britain gave Jews in Palestine enough land, it might be possible to ask for additional territory in Kenya or Uganda. Wise reaffirmed this view in May 1938, adding, however, that he did not trust Britain.[3]

FDR's comments about Palestine thrust him into the midst of bottomless disputes within the American Jewish community. Zionists, some favoring Britain's 1937 plan for partition, some opposed to it, all gave Palestine priority as a haven for Europe's Jews and the destination for charitable funds. Non-Zionists generally sought more direct aid for Jews in Europe. Many of them opposed partition of Palestine as an unwise move toward a Jewish state. Roosevelt believed the pressing need for emigration meant keeping open a range of options whatever the political balance among Jews, especially after Adolf Hitler expanded his domain in early 1938.

On February 12, 1938, in a meeting at his private headquarters at Berchtesgaden, Hitler browbeat Austrian chancellor Kurt von Schuschnigg with insults, threats, and demands. The overwhelmed Austrian leader agreed to concessions that enabled Germany to annex his country. Then in early March, Schuschnigg fought back, announcing a plebiscite on maintaining an independent Austria. Hitler would not risk the outcome of a popular vote. After he demanded postponement of the vote and Schuschnigg's resignation, German troops marched unmolested into Austria on March 12.

The next day Hitler announced the *Anschluss:* his Austrian homeland, with more than 200,000 Jewish residents, was now part of Germany.[4]

Nazi authorities and police in Austria quickly arrested thousands of alleged dissidents. Press across the world covered the spectacle of mobs beating and robbing Jews and forcing them to kneel and try to scrub the streets free of pavement slogans favoring the ousted regime. A *New York Times* story on March 16 quoted a "Berlin Nazi" who "expressed some astonishment at the speed with which anti-Semitism was being introduced here." A few days later Nazi authorities showed their contempt for world opinion by raiding the home of Vienna's most renowned citizen, the eighty-one-year-old Jewish founder of modern psychoanalysis Sigmund Freud. Many Austrian Jews saw no alternative to survival other than emigration. High-level negotiations enabled Freud and his immediate family to gain refuge in England. No such smooth path opened for other Austrian Jews, however, including Freud's four sisters, who remained trapped in Vienna. In the first few days after the *Anschluss* 1,500 to 3,500 Austrians, mostly Jews, applied for immigration visas to the United States.[5]

In taking this first step toward realizing his dream of a vast German empire, an elated Hitler encountered only token resistance from democratic nations. The British government decided not to contest the takeover of Austria, and France followed suit. With an army smaller than that of Belgium, and an isolationist Congress and public, the United States remained unprepared to intervene in European affairs.

In a March 17 speech before the National Press Club, Secretary of State Hull steered a middle course between "policing the world," and withdrawing into an isolationist shell. Hull urged rapid American rearmament to protect the nation, drastic revision of the Neutrality Acts, and ad hoc cooperation with other nations on matters of mutual interest. "Isolation is not means to security," he said, 'it is a fruitful source of insecurity." Without naming aggressors, he warned of the danger that "international anarchy based on brute force will inundate the world and ultimately sweep away the very bases of civilization and progress." Assistant Secretary of State George Messersmith wrote privately that the president endorsed this line of policy: "there will be no swerving from it in any detail."[6]

At the cabinet meeting on March 18, less than a week after the *Anschluss,* Roosevelt asked what the United States could do for Austria's political refugees. The Nazis persecuted political opponents in Austria, but they directed most of their hatred against Austrian Jews. Yet Roosevelt preferred the term "political." Secretary of the Interior Harold Ickes, a staunch anti-Nazi, thought that FDR wanted to make it as easy as possible for refugees to enter the country, while postponing decisions on whether they could stay under the quota law. Henry Morgenthau Jr. recorded the president as saying, "After all, America had been a place of refuge for so many fine Germans in the period of 1848 and why couldn't we offer them again a place of refuge at this time." Roosevelt proposed two immigration initiatives: combining the quotas of Germany and Austria, and introducing a bill to increase the quotas. When the president asked the cabinet whether Congress would vote to increase the German quota, Vice President Garner said that if Congress could vote in secret, it would halt all immigration. No one challenged this assessment.[7]

FDR apparently concluded that he should bypass Congress. Despite some cabinet reservations, the president combined the small immigration quota for Austria with the much larger German quota for a single annual quota of 27,370. Since America had not come close to filling the German quota, the combined quota would give Austrian applicants a much better chance of getting visas. Roosevelt could say that the laws remained unchanged, but Jewish immigration from the new Greater Germany would increase if American consuls cooperated. In fiscal 1939, the United States filled this combined quota, substantially increasing Jewish immigration. Still, there was an eleven-year waiting list for American visas: by then, some 300,000 Germans and Austrians sought entry to the United States.[8]

In line with what he told Rabbi Wise in January, the president also advanced an ambitious proposal to ease the plight of refugees internationally: the United States would become one of a number of havens. On March 22, after discussion with Morgenthau and Welles, FDR launched the idea of a new international committee to facilitate and finance emigration of "political refugees" from Germany and Austria. Hull presented this idea publicly on March 24, when he invited twenty nations from Latin America and nine from Europe, including Italy but not Germany or the Soviet Union, to an international conference on admitting German and Austrian refugees to nations that would accept them, presumably the invited Latin American states. He also invited Canada, Australia, and New Zealand. A day later, at an outdoor press conference from behind the wheel of his open car at Warm Springs, Georgia, a freelancing president expanded the scope of the proposal to include oppressed peoples in lands other than Austria and Germany. It signaled both his hopes for a large and broad effort and for avoiding the label "Jewish refugees." When a reporter asked FDR whether the main purpose of his proposal was to benefit Jews in Germany and Austria, he said yes, but that a large number of Christians would also benefit. For the first time, the president had publicly put his imprimatur on a major effort to save Jews from Nazi persecution.[9]

The *New York Times* reported on March 26 that "indications increased that the suggestion [for an international conference] originated with President Roosevelt." Wise heard the same thing from White House adviser Benjamin V. Cohen. Wise also said that before Hull's announcement the president had telephoned Irwin Steingut, the Jewish Democratic minority leader in the New York State Assembly, saying, "keep your shirt on. We are going to do something big." Welles indicated that he wrote and redrafted the memo on refugees specifically to "meet the President's wishes as expressed to us [Welles and Morgenthau]."[10]

Feis, an economic adviser and the only Jew in the State Department's upper levels, said, "I have been worn down not so much by exertion as by a sense of futility. The last week or ten days I have been doing my best to awaken my colleagues to the plight particularly of the Jews in Austria." He added, however, that "something may happen" because "the president seems definitely interested and the Secretary quite acquiescent."[11]

FDR authorized Ickes to deliver an address on the CBS radio network blasting countries persecuting Jews. Ickes scheduled the speech for April 3, the fiftieth anniversary of the Chicago-based *Daily Jewish Courier.* Hull wanted him to delete some specific references to fascism and current dictators, and Ickes complied. Even then, Hull was unhappy, but suspected that "the president wanted members close to the Administration to refer critically to fascism." Ickes went directly to FDR, who said criticizing fascism was fine. He made a few minor changes, and Welles asked for a few more, but they did not defuse Ickes's bombast.[12]

On April 4, in a private meeting with his old friend Arthur Sweetser, the senior American in the League of Nations at Geneva, FDR claimed personal ownership of the proposed international effort at resettling refugees. Sweetser still hoped he could persuade the president to engage the United States with the League of Nations.[13]

The president began the conversation by unexpectedly asking Sweetser how he liked "my refugee proposal. . . . That was *my* proposal." FDR then quickly interjected, tapping his chest with obvious pleasure. "I worked that out myself." He continued:

> We had the matter up at the Cabinet to see if we could not do something for these unfortunate people [the Jews]. But some of them [the cabinet members], particularly Ickes, objected on account of the immigration laws, said it couldn't be done. Then suddenly it struck me: why not get all the democracies to share the burden? After all, they own most of the free land of the world, and there are only . . . what would you say, fourteen, sixteen million Jews in the whole world, of whom about half are already in the United States. If we could divide up the remainder in groups of 8 or 10, there wouldn't be any Jewish problem in three or four generations.[14]

Roosevelt apparently wanted at least eight to ten places of Jewish settlement outside Europe.

What Sweetser sought was greater U.S. involvement with the League of Nations, but the president did not want the League of Nations High Commission for Refugees to handle his new initiative. He wanted a new organization, given the failures of the league during the past five years. Sweetser had not expected to talk about Jews in Europe, and he was not pleased at the direction in which FDR led the conversation. The two men ended up agreeing that war in Europe was not likely for at least another year, but that eventually Germany would collide with either the Soviets or the British and French. FDR concluded with an account he had heard of Hitler's February 12 tirade to Schuschnigg: Hitler had compared himself to Julius Caesar and Jesus Christ.

The Roosevelt administration tried to make its initiative attractive for foreign leaders. It asked for no financial commitments from any government for refugees; rather, private organizations would support the effort. Moreover, "no country would be expected to receive more immigrants than were permitted under existing laws." At the insistence of the British, the administration also kept Palestine off the agenda of the refugee conference.

FDR had sent a strong message of disapproval to Germany without breaching diplomatic relations or openly denouncing Hitler's regime. The press generally hailed the initiative, and it also united usually feuding Jewish groups. Rabbi Wise wrote to Felix Frankfurter, "You will, I am sure, be glad learn to learn that the American Jewish Committee, the B'nai B'rith, the Zionist Organization and we of the Congress are meeting together in the hope of evoking nation-wide support for the Skipper's [FDR's] proposal to which he is abundantly entitled." The Federal Council of Churches backed the conference proposal, as did the National Association for the Advancement of Colored People, the National Catholic Welfare Conference, and the American Federation of Labor, with the proviso that it did not breach the quota limits on immigration. In response to a letter of congratulations from Governor Herbert Lehman in New York, FDR said, "I only wish we could do more."[15]

In part, opposition from an isolationist, restrictionist Republican Party and a minority faction of like-minded Democrats kept FDR from doing more. Conservative Democratic representative Martin Dies of Texas denounced FDR's plans for an international conference and increasing immigration from Germany and Austria. He said, "our first duty is to our own people" and that immigrants either "will take jobs that Americans are now holding or taxpayers of America will be compelled to support them." Two months later, Dies became chair of the House Committee on Un-American Activities and shifted its primary focus from investigating fascists to communists, including alleged Reds in the Roosevelt administration. Republican representative Thomas A. Jenkins of Ohio said the president has gone "on a visionary excursion into the warm fields of altruism," and using FDR's own words, that he has forgotten "the 'one-third' of our people who are ill-clothed, ill-fed and ill-housed." The prestigious Republican senator William E. Borah of Idaho, an authority on foreign affairs and the dean of the Senate, discounted the political significance of Hitler's seizure of Austria and called those who stressed Austria's plight actors.[16]

On April 13, 1938, FDR brought ten interfaith leaders to the White House to discuss refugee matters. Sweetser's friend James G. McDonald and Columbia Professor Joseph P. Chamberlain were the most knowledgeable of the non-Jews. Wise, Henry Morgenthau Sr., and financier Bernard Baruch represented the Jewish community. Christian representatives included Samuel McCrea Cavert, secretary of the Federal Council of Churches, and Reverend Michael J. Ready, secretary of the National Catholic Welfare Conference. Secretary of State Cordell Hull, Welles, Messersmith, and Secretary of Labor Frances Perkins also attended. The president called Hitler "a maniac with a mission."[17]

Chamberlain suggested that the United States and other governments would have to fund any large-scale refugee resettlement. Virtually everyone else dissented, because public funding meant going to a hostile Congress. Someone asked FDR whether "political refugees" was really the right term. FDR answered that they were actual or potential refugees because of political conditions in their country. Those present understood that he wished to avoid using the term *Jewish* refugees.[18]

In an off-the-record session, Welles told the American Society of Newspaper Editors that immigration to the United States would not exceed quota limits, and private organizations, not the government, would fund resettlement. Welles added that the United States seeks "to make it possible for these populations in certain central European countries to find a refuge to which they can go and I am not at all sure that if this proves successful in the future one of the causes for European war in the future will be, if not completely avoided, can be greatly alleviated." He reached out to both isolationists and liberal internationalists by lauding the initiative as a means for avoiding war.[19]

Only Italy declined an invitation to participate in the conference, which cooperating nations set for July 6–14, 1938, at the Hôtel Royal in Évian on the French side of Lake Geneva. Roosevelt reached outside the administration for a representative to the international conference with bipartisan appeal. Welles tried to talk former secretary of state Henry Stimson, a Republican, into heading the American delegation.

Crusty at age 71, Stimson was still practicing law in New York. He was a prominent statesman whom FDR respected; in 1940, the president would tap him to become secretary of war. This time Stimson declined in very diplomatic language. In a conversation with *Foreign Affairs* editor Hamilton Fish Armstrong and in his own diary, Stimson said that the United States had not done the "proper preparation" to make such a conference productive. Germany probably would not cooperate, most likely dooming the effort to failure. What most bothered Stimson was that the German/Austrian refugee problem was a Jewish problem, which made it politically perilous. He feared that the conference would validate anti-Semitism rather than help Jews. Stimson said he regretted having to decline a presidential request for the first time in his career.[20]

FDR then turned to Myron C. Taylor, a Republican moderate like Stimson, though less renowned and experienced in government. Taylor had just retired from his position as president of U.S. Steel. He had earned recognition as a competent administrator and an authority on industrial efficiency. He was a philanthropist and a Quaker.

Taylor worked with the April 13 White House group of interfaith representatives and advisers. With some new members, this group became the President's Advisory Committee on Political Refugees, chaired by McDonald. Drawing upon his experiences as League of Nations High Commissioner for Refugees, McDonald discounted the chances of getting the German government to cooperate with arrangements for orderly emigration.[21]

Frankfurter was willing to propose means for advancing FDR's initiatives on refugees, and perhaps had some inkling of what FDR thought was feasible or how far he could press. On July 1, Frankfurter wrote McDonald about the need for a lasting international refugee agency that would supervise refugees from departure through resettlement. Frankfurter thought that the task had become too large for private philanthropy: "The problem may not unfairly be likened to our own unemployment problem. Government, both federal and local, had to step in to deal with the relief problem when it assumed dimensions that it did in 1933. It exceeded the capacities of a private effort." Having talked with the president, Frankfurter apparently thought that the government might assist refugees despite congressional opposition.[22]

Numbers and geography would affect decisions about resources and means. State Department officials had originally opposed expanding the mandate of the conference beyond German and Austrian refugees. Count Jerzy Potocki, Polish ambassador to the United States, implied to Assistant Secretary Messersmith that the upcoming Évian Conference should help Poland deal with *its* Jewish problem. Messersmith said that Poland could send a representative to the conference, but otherwise gave Potocki no encouragement. Then at a June 4 meeting State Department official Robert Pell said, "after further consideration in Washington," the international refugee conference should be free to consider "the problems of refugees from all countries." From the beginning, the president had favored a European-wide approach.[23]

Feis, who despaired for the future of Jews in Austria, Romania, and Poland, endorsed this broad approach to refugees. He did not believe that a new international organization, useful as it might be, would be able to "meet the situation of the massed millions. Neither will Palestine even though the doors are kept somewhat open." He asked William C. Bullitt, American ambassador to France, to suggest to the French government that it should open its African colony of Madagascar to settlement by European Jews.[24]

Welles thought Germany's hard-pressed political refugees should come first, but "the work of the Committee, in his [FDR's] belief, should continue for several years to facilitate the emigration of surplus populations from Central Europe to other parts of the world." Welles reiterated that FDR's initiative complemented efforts to maintain world peace: "If it can be undertaken, the successful carrying out of such a program would do a great deal to make for European appeasement and peace in the generations to come."[25]

"Appeasement" was a common term in British diplomatic parlance during the 1920s—long before the Nazis came to power. As the rectification of imbalances and perceived treaty injustices, appeasement might bring lasting European stability. The opposite of appeasement was rigid defense of the status quo, which could lead to war with Germany. By including the resettlement of Jews in "appeasement," Welles suggested an additional construction. If Germany really wanted to expel Jews and force them to emigrate, the West could help satisfy this demand on an issue of great passion for Hitler and perhaps avoid war.[26]

The Évian Conference was an extraordinary undertaking for a president facing a nasty recession, ongoing struggles with Congress over recovery measures, internal battles against conservatives in his party, and a difficult midterm election. No hidden political motive underlay Roosevelt's humanitarian initiative. To the contrary, with the Jewish vote secure for his party, he had little to gain and much to lose politically from potentially antagonizing anti-Semites and restrictionists.

In late June 1938, on the eve of Évian, pollster George Gallup reported that the president's popularity had fallen to 54 percent, down from 63 percent in October 1937. Meanwhile, the American Jewish Committee commissioned two private polls (taken by the Gallup organization) of about 3,000 people each during the spring of 1938. About 45 percent of the samples felt that Jews had too much power in the United States. Some 25 percent said there was likely to be a campaign against the Jews. About 26 percent thought Germany would be better off if it drove the Jews out, which nearly doubled the percentage from a *Fortune* poll in late 1936. The Gallup pollsters concluded that anti-Semitism had risen during 1938. Nazi propaganda attributing the world's problems to Jews resonated among some circles in the United States, and the economic recession led others to look for scapegoats. Such attitudes made it doubly difficult for Roosevelt to confront Nazi Germany and to muster support for aiding German or European Jews.[27]

In early July, some 200 delegates, diplomatic observers, journalists, and representatives of Jewish and other organizations from various countries, including Germany, gathered in Évian, creating a circus atmosphere for public speeches directed to home consumption. Quarrels among the many Jewish representatives from different groups, each seeking a visible role and with little agreement on priorities, led to disillusionment. A confidential memo for the American Jewish Committee noted the failure of Jewish leaders to present a united front. The author said that, "the difficulty in getting to any sort of agreement and the insistence on points of disagreement rather than points of accord must have proved a spectacle far from edifying to the non-sectarian organizations also present. I think it was at this point in the conference that somebody discovered that Evian written backwards becomes 'naïve.' "[28]

The fundamental problem at Évian was not Jewish dissension, but the resistance of world leaders to assuming responsibility for resettling refugees, most of them Jewish. Nicaragua, Costa Rica, Honduras, and Panama stated that they wanted no traders or intellectuals, code words for Jews. Argentina said it had already accommodated enough immigrants from Central Europe. Canada cited its unemployment problem. Australia said that it had no "racial problems" and did not want to create any by bringing in Jewish refugees. Imperial countries such as Britain, France, and the Netherlands said that their tropical territories offered only limited prospects for European refugees. League of Nations High Commissioner Sir Neill Malcolm was openly hostile to the idea of a new refugee organization. The high point of the conference was perhaps the offer by the representative of the Dominican Republic to take in 100,000 refugees. The *Washington Post* headlined one story on the conference, " 'Yes, But—'." It noted, "it has been a disappointment, if not altogether a surprise . . . that delegates take the floor to say, 'We feel sorry for the refugees and potential refugees but—.' " Benito Mussolini's press spokesman, Virginio Gayda, said that FDR had called the conference only because he was of Jewish origin: its only message was "nobody wants the Jews."[29]

The Évian Conference produced some concrete results. The delegates decided to consider Jews still in Germany, not just those who had already fled, as potential refugees and of proper concern. They agreed to establish a new international organization, the Intergovernmental Committee on Refugees, rather than rely on the ineffectual League of Nations High Commission. On both points, the liberal American view prevailed over British opposition. The British representatives preferred not to infringe on German sovereignty, and the government may well have worried about too many refugees fleeing to Palestine.

Still, there was enough progress to keep hope alive for imperiled Jews. After the conference, the State Department authorized Taylor to announce that the United States would likely continue to accept 27,370 Germans and Austrians per year, so that, over a five-year period, nearly 140,000 could enter the United States under the German quota—a substantial commitment.[30]

Washington lawyer George Rublee, director of the new Intergovernmental Committee on Refugees, assumed the unenviable task of negotiating with the Nazis for the emigration of German Jews. In London, prominent German-Jewish banker Max Warburg, who long had ties with Hjalmar Schacht, former economics minister and still head of the *Reichsbank*, told Rublee that Nazi Germany would allow Jews to emigrate with resources only if the world community offered Germany an opportunity to expand exports, presumably to the United States. In effect, the Nazis offered to ransom Jews in return for aiding Germany's economy and its war-making capacity. Most American Jewish organizations and the American officials resisted making this deal. In a letter to Justice Brandeis, Rabbi Wise reflected, "You are right about not advantaging Hitler through giving up of boycott or its equivalent. But what of the tens of thousands who will never escape, unless Hitler gets some trade advantage?"[31]

The United States and other democracies also worried that concessions for the resettlement of German Jews would encourage regimes in Eastern Europe to oppress their "surplus" Jews in the hope of dumping them elsewhere. Hull deprecated FDR's earlier promise of a broad approach to resettling persecuted peoples. He said that the United States had convened the Évian Conference primarily "to meet the particular acute situation created by the *Anschluss*. . . . The reception which has so far met our efforts to meet the problem in Germany and the limited opportunities for settlement . . . do not give any hope whatever that a 'global' solution of the problem might be possible." American diplomats abroad had sent the secretary reports detailing the anti-Semitic policies of governments in Eastern European lands. Hull also told Taylor and Rublee that negotiations with Germany must not "break up this [free trade] policy or create additional spheres of bilateral trade influence through the medium of specially constructed currency or credit arrangements." At their London meeting, Rublee told Warburg that the State Department firmly opposed any linkage between the treatment of German Jews and American trade policies.[32]

During a trip to Europe in September, Benjamin V. Cohen investigated the Jewish crisis for American Jewish organizations, following the suggestion of Justice Brandeis. Cohen went through the files of the Intergovernmental Committee on Refugees with "a fine tooth comb." Although seemingly satisfied, Cohen hinted to State Department official Pell that Frankfurter had planned the Évian Conference and the Intergovernmental Committee on Refugees as a way to unite the democracies against Germany, but that "Fascists in the State Department" and Taylor had muddied the waters. Cohen said that he personally favored negotiations with Germany, but was not optimistic about their chances of success. Unsuccessful negotiations over German Jews would at least demonstrate Germany's bad faith. Cohen could not sort out a way to mobilize opposition to Nazi Germany and simultaneously facilitate Jewish emigration on a large scale.[33]

Hitler's demands on behalf of ethnic Germans in the Czechoslovakian border region known as the Sudetenland raised the threat of imminent war. Hitler actually sought to gut Czechoslovakia's border defenses and open it for conquest. France had a treaty obligation to protect Czechoslovakia, but the French preferred not to honor it without British backing. British prime minister Chamberlain and French premier Édouard Daladier urged Mussolini to suggest that Chamberlain and Daladier join Hitler and Mussolini in Munich for a last-minute summit conference in late September. Roosevelt joined the British-French appeal.

At Munich, the British and French leaders gave in to Hitler's demands for immediate annexation of the Sudetenland as the price of maintaining the peace. Germany and the European democracies imposed the Munich Agreement upon Czechoslovakia, which found itself deserted by its allies. Crucial Czech border fortifications and industry fell into German hands.

Leading American Jews deplored this settlement. Their outrage over appeasement limited their willingness to deal with Nazi Germany on Jewish refugees. Zionists worried that British appeasement would extend to Palestine and result in the closing down of Jewish immigration. New York Rabbi William F. Rosenblum, among other Zionists, appealed to the American public by warning that British appeasement in Palestine would "so encourage the forces of dictatorship and fascism" that they would extend their methods of divide and conquer "to this continent and this country."[34]

Important backing for the British policy of appeasement of Germany came from financier Joseph P. Kennedy, whom FDR had appointed American ambassador to Great Britain, allegedly to get him out of Washington. Arriving in London earlier in 1938, Kennedy had flamboyantly ingratiated himself with the circle around Lady Astor popularly known as the "Cliveden Set," a pro-appeasement aristocratic crowd that FDR detested. Kennedy built a close personal relationship with Chamberlain and tried repeatedly to persuade the president to support Chamberlain in accommodating Germany. The two men disagreed politically. In private, Kennedy spoke critically about FDR's New Deal and expressed some sympathy for fascism. He even told the German ambassador to Britain that the problem with Nazi Germany was less its goal of getting rid of Jews and more the loud "clamor" of the process. FDR confided to Ickes he did not think Kennedy would last as ambassador. Still, Kennedy was in an important position to undercut FDR's refugee initiative.[35]

FDR came to regret his brief support for the Munich negotiations. Speaking to the cabinet in mid-October, the president first attributed British and French weakness to an airplane gap—Germany was far out-producing both of them combined. "With England and France it was, therefore, a question of peace at any price." Attorney General Homer Cummings wrote in his diary that the president had "entered into quite a dissertation" about foreign policy. FDR forecast German domination of Europe as far as the Black Sea and into the Middle East. If Turkey and the Arabs came into their orbit, England would have difficulty in retaining control over Egypt. German domination of Europe would strangle the British Empire. The next day the president told Cummings that the United States had to be militarily prepared for whatever came: "He said he did not propose, if he could help it, to leave the office of President, and leave his country, as totally unequal to dealing with an international bully as England and France were in these last few weeks." The United States would no longer countenance any effort to accommodate the appeasement of Germany.[36]

Shortly after the cabinet session, FDR bypassed Kennedy and sent a secret message to Chamberlain through Scottish liberal Arthur Murray, one of the president's World War I friends. FDR gave Chamberlain and Britain another option besides the continued appeasement of Germany. His message: If Chamberlain confronted Germany and it led to war, Britain could count on the entire economic might of the United States. Roosevelt believed that the Nazis threatened the survival of freedom everywhere in the West. Aiding the world's remaining democracies was now his primary foreign policy goal, but he still had to persuade Congress to release him from the shackles of America's Neutrality Acts.[37]

Appeasement might have one benefit: perhaps Chamberlain would have some influence with Hitler. Roosevelt sent a note to Chamberlain via Kennedy, asking Chamberlain to use his newfound relationship with Hitler on behalf of refugees. The Nazi government needed to show some flexibility and allow emigrants to retain sufficient resources to begin life in a new land. Time was of the essence, and Hitler should allow the Intergovernmental Committee on Refugees to negotiate with German officials. Kennedy chose not to deliver the president's message personally, but sent it in writing to the prime minister. *The Nation* reported that Kennedy had told Rublee he was willing to give the committee moral support, but not to the point of endangering other causes. Chamberlain gave a polite reply for the record, saying he would consult the British ambassador in Berlin, but would leave the matter to formal diplomatic channels. Rublee notified Hull and Welles that the president's message had no impact on Chamberlain.[38]

Rublee termed the refugee problem "insoluble" and vented his frustration in a letter to his friend Dean Acheson. "Nor do I know whether the [American] Government will give me the effective support which I need," Rublee wrote. "[Ambassador] Kennedy tells me that the British will do nothing unless the American Government will contribute something positive, and they have contributed nothing but words. In what manner am I going to come out of this adventure?" Acheson had clashed with FDR in 1933 and left the Treasury Department, but was repairing his relationships within the administration by 1938. Perhaps he sent the letter to Justice Brandeis, for whom he had clerked—Brandeis met often with FDR. In any case, it reached the president, who wanted to discuss the situation with Welles and Hull.[39]

A new crisis on the evening of November 9, 1938, complicated plans to negotiate with Germany. In reaction to the assassination of a German diplomat

in Paris by a distraught young Jew seeking to draw attention to Nazi persecution, the Nazi regime authorized the violent punishment of Jews in
Greater Germany. Stormtroopers and their imitators destroyed more than a
thousand synagogues as well as Jewish businesses across the country. Approximately 100 German Jews were killed, and 30,000 Jewish men were arrested and sent to concentration camps. Although the violence continued for
several days, it was termed *Kristallnacht,* the Night of Broken Glass. This officially sponsored pogrom ended all hopes that the Nuremberg Laws marked
the high point of persecution, and it foreshadowed wartime tragedies.[40]

Kristallnacht shocked the Western world. For three successive days, the
New York Times covered the violence in Germany on its front page; one
article compared it to the Thirty Years' War of the seventeenth century and
the Bolshevik Revolution of 1917. The *Times* even ran an article encapsulat-
ing coverage in other American papers. The *Washington Post* used the anal-
ogy of the Catholic slaughter of thousands of French Huguenots—the St.
Bartholomew's Day Massacre of 1572. Nothing in recent Western European history seemed appropriate.[41]

If the events in Germany dramatized the need for a strong American
response, the November congressional elections, just before *Kristallnacht,*
impeded it. On Election Day, without abandoning isolationist ideas, the
GOP nearly doubled its contingent in the House, picking up eighty-one
seats along with eight Senate seats and eleven governorships. Democrats retained 60 percent of House and 70 percent of Senate seats, but the large contingent of southern Democrats would not support liberalized immigration.

On Saturday, November 13, Armstrong called Assistant Secretary Messersmith to recommend against officially protesting the Nazi brutality or
breaking diplomatic relations. Instead, Armstrong suggested calling Ambassador Hugh R. Wilson home for "report and consultation" and adopting
at least some modest initiatives to help refugees. Messersmith asked whether
the major newspapers would cover Wilson's departure as an important political statement. Armstrong's soundings indicated yes. Finally, he called
Frankfurter, who had been lobbying FDR to denounce Nazi Germany.
Armstrong said that practical action would be more effective.[42]

In response to *Kristallnacht,* FDR summoned home his ambassador to
Germany, becoming the only world leader to do so. At his Tuesday press
conference, the president said that the news from Germany was scarcely

believable in a twentieth-century civilization. Although he did not use the word Jews, no one could have missed what he meant. FDR did not mention any new ideas for resettling refugees. In deference to public opinion and congressional sentiment, he endorsed the quota limit.[43]

In a meeting with Secretary of Labor Perkins on November 17, FDR agreed to do something practical for German Jews in the United States, even though he could not persuade Congress to raise the already filled German quota. Perkins wanted the president to extend indefinitely the temporary visitors' visas of thousands of German Jews. In an angry memorandum, Messersmith called this plan illegal, saying that it would sabotage the immigration laws and antagonize the public and Congress. Roosevelt adopted it anyway and said at a November 18 press conference, "it would be a cruel and inhuman thing to compel them [those on visitors' visas] to leave. . . . There being no adequate law on the subject, we shall simply present the facts to the Congress. If the Congress takes no action, these unfortunate people will be allowed to stay in this country. . . . I cannot, in any decent humanity, throw them out." Again, the president overrode State Department views.[44]

FDR told a group visiting the White House that he could not enlarge the immigration quota, but he could use his presidential powers to allow German Jews with visitors' visas to make new homes in America. This "Machiavellian" maneuver impressed one of his guests, Canadian prime minister Mackenzie King. Roosevelt then suggested settling German exiles in former German colonies, now under the mandate of other European countries. He also spoke of relocating Jews in South America and other underpopulated areas. FDR said that the United States must prepare to defend itself against Germany and Japan, and must produce enough airplanes to help the British and the French.[45]

King wrote that the president went into much more detail about refugees (detail he did not record), but that "I said nothing one way or the other. Just listened. I felt more than ever that we, in Canada, cannot afford to close our doors to those who are being persecuted in other parts of the world while great countries like Britain and the United States, on whose cooperation our existence depends, are doing what they are, and have more crowded areas." The next day he reflected that only powerful personal Jewish influence surrounding FDR could explain the president's commitment to aiding refugees. Other world leaders found it difficult to comprehend that humanitarian impulse, not political pressure, might have motivated Roosevelt to adopt the cause of persecuted peoples abroad.[46]

Yet there is no other sound explanation. FDR had acted on his own inclinations with little support from his foreign policy team and with political calculation cutting in the opposite direction. On November 16, after the president had broached with him resettlement prospects for refugees, Henry Morgenthau Jr. recorded in his diary that, "The point is the President has this. Nobody is helping him. I am going at least to do the spade work. The thing to do is have it ready before Congress comes."[47]

American outrage against Germany did not translate into support for increased immigration. A week after *Kristallnacht* Armstrong told a correspondent who wanted to try to expand the German quota, "I haven't met anyone yet connected with the refugee work, or any representative of a Jewish organization, who isn't definitely and entirely opposed to discussing the quota in Congress for fear that a discussion would result in lowering the quota rather than raising it. Even if it were raised, the antagonism aroused would, these people fear, tremendously aggravate anti-Semitic feeling in this country." After FDR's November 18 press conference, Senator Borah quickly objected to any increase of immigration quotas and questioned whether the president could legally extend visitors' visas. According to a Roper/Fortune poll in January 1939, two months after *Kristallnacht*, 83 percent of respondents opposed "a bill to open the doors of the U.S. to a larger number of European refugees than now admitted under our immigration quotas." Only 9 percent supported such a bill, with the remainder undecided. A May 1938 Roper/Fortune survey had found only 5 percent support for raising U.S. quotas to admit more political refugees. The president had reason to worry about Congress and public opinion.[48]

A renewed effort to persuade other countries to admit Jews had to consider the costs of transportation, housing, and subsistence aid. On Wednesday, November 16, McDonald, his assistant George Warren, Armstrong, and Taylor met with the president and Welles. The refugee delegation noted that FDR's Évian venture had bogged down: the German government would not even let Rublee come to Berlin. In effect, the Nazis were confiscating most of what Jewish property remained in Germany. German Jews would never be able to emigrate with enough resources to surmount economic barriers to entry in other countries. The delegation wanted the United

States to appropriate public funds for the resettlement of Jews, a most unlikely prospect in the isolationist Congress.

Even after *Kristallnacht*, FDR backed negotiations for the emigration of German Jews, but balked at unilateral American funding. He told a delegation of refugee advocates on November 16 that he might get funds from Congress once practical plans had emerged, with others participating. FDR sketched out the possibility of governments supplying $400 million for refugee settlement, $150 million of which might come from the United States over a four-year period. The president and Welles did not share this unlikely request for a large and controversial congressional appropriation with other State Department officials.[49]

The subject of Palestine arose at the informal international meeting on November 17. British ambassador Sir Ronald Lindsay cunningly suggested to Welles that Britain would allow the United States to take in more German Jews by waiving most of its unfilled immigration quota to the United States (about 65,000). Lindsay may have sought to deflect American pressure on the British to admit more Jews to Palestine. Only Congress could approve an exchange of quotas and FDR had just publicly reaffirmed the quota limit for Germany. Welles said that many American Jews opposed a risky attempt to change the German quota.[50]

Earlier—just before *Kristallnacht*—Britain had repudiated its 1937 endorsement of partition. In yet another postponement of a final decision, Britain announced that it would sponsor a round-table conference between Jews and Arabs in London in 1939. If they failed to reach agreement, Britain would unilaterally decide Palestine's future.

In response, FDR told Lindsay that the British should instead tell some of the Arab leaders from Palestine and some adjoining countries that

Palestine and Transjordan constituted only a small portion, probably not over 5% of their territories. Some Jews were in Palestine and others were clamoring to go there. Their coming to Palestine and Transjordan would not hinder the Arabs as there was plenty of land for all. Some of the Arabs on poor land in Palestine could be given much better land in adjoining Arab countries. The struggle between the Jews and the Arabs in Palestine was self-defeating for both Arabs and Jews. Lindsay spoke of the opposition of the Arab world and the Moslem world, and the Chief [FDR] belittled this opposition and thought it due largely to British indecision and conflicting policy.

FDR suggested that Britain could designate all former German colonies for Jewish settlement. If the Germans really wanted to resettle the Jews, they could not object to this solution.[51]

The British embassy in Washington prepared an informal response to FDR regarding Palestine, but delayed it for a month. The British denied that there was vacant arable land in other Arab territories and rejected any forcible transfer of Arabs from Palestine on political and moral grounds "in order to make room for immigrants of a race which has, in great part, not lived in Palestine for many centuries."[52]

During his press conference on November 18, the president plugged the efforts of the Intergovernmental Committee on Refugees and put pressure on Berlin to receive Rublee. That afternoon the cabinet discussed refugee issues, but the only detail Attorney General Cummings recorded in his diary was FDR's swipe at Ambassador Kennedy. Press reports indicated that Kennedy had his own refugee plan. The president said sarcastically that Kennedy had not taken him into his confidence.[53]

In a meeting with Justice Brandeis, FDR continued to show enthusiasm for Jewish settlements outside Palestine. The president envisioned settlement(s) elsewhere of 100,000 families costing $3,000 per family. The total cost ($300 million) could be shared equally by the U.S. government, the British and French governments, and private subscribers—largely Jewish.[54]

Morgenthau's subordinates called upon Mordecai Ezekiel, economic adviser in the Agriculture Department, to formulate an ambitious plan to resettle refugees. This Jewish economist had worked with Morgenthau on New Deal agricultural policy. Ezekiel sought to rescue up to half a million people from Greater Germany quickly by having leading countries, including the United States, commit themselves to using five years of immigration quotas immediately (mortgaging future quotas). They would also admit other refugees temporarily, pending settlement elsewhere. He thought Latin American countries would cooperate in absorbing refugees if they received loans for industrialization, which would help wean them from dependence on "certain European countries." Even more optimistically, Ezekiel proposed that Congress establish a government-sponsored corporation to carry out the plan. He estimated the overall cost at more than half a billion dollars, financed through government, private sources, and a long-term interest-bearing loan floated to the public. The sketch showed the scope of efforts needed to deal with a growing refugee problem, but Ezekiel's plan had no chance of winning congressional approval, especially after the 1938 elections. The cost estimate must have tempered Morgenthau's enthusiasm.[55]

Roosevelt pursued lesser measures. From Warm Springs FDR approved a long memo to Taylor, which said that the resettlement of Jews with at least some capital would both respond to a humanitarian crisis and benefit sparsely settled lands. FDR and Welles looked for multiple outlets across the world. FDR authorized Taylor to state publicly that the United States had a sizeable immigration quota from Germany and that, beyond the quota, it could take in a certain number of clergy and members of learned professions under existing laws. FDR did not think it "desirable or practical" to recommend any specific change in U.S. immigration quotas.[56]

In mid-October, FDR responded to a private inquiry from Herbert Lehman on British threats to Jewish immigration to Palestine, saying, "We have left no stone unturned—and will leave no stone unturned—to persuade the British government to adopt a liberal policy with regard to the refugees." Then, the night before Thanksgiving, Roosevelt issued an unexpected announcement from his cottage at Warm Springs. He said he was gratified to read reports, whose accuracy he could not confirm, that Britain would increase the number of Jews allowed to enter Palestine. Just the previous day, he had told reporters that he never commented on unconfirmed newspaper reports; his November 23 late-night announcement was even more surprising in that context. This was another attempt to force Britain's hand. Frankfurter deciphered this move very quickly, writing FDR: "Let me break in on your holiday just long enough to thank you on the courageous resourcefulness with which you are making the Chamberlain Government do its duty in utilizing Palestine as the obvious first line of relief for the victims of the latest and largest Nazi barbarities."[57]

After Thanksgiving, the president asked Welles to send to Warm Springs all available information about conceivable places for Jewish colonization in any part of the world. Messersmith, Phillips, now the ambassador to Italy, and Wilson joined FDR in Georgia to discuss resettlement in Africa. The president wanted Phillips to explore with Mussolini the possibility of settling Jews in Ethiopia. In his diary, Secretary Ickes recorded what FDR related at a cabinet meeting afterwards. The president had a twofold purpose in instructing Phillips to confer with Mussolini—to try to drive a wedge between him and Hitler, and to have Mussolini lobby Hitler to let Jews take property with them to other lands.[58]

At the end of November, Perkins floated publicly the kind of vast resettlement scheme that Roosevelt had earlier discussed with Morgenthau, McDonald, and Brandeis. Her initiative likely had FDR's tacit approval; he preferred to have subordinates test out controversial ideas before he endorsed them in public. Obviously, it was better politically for Perkins, rather than Morgenthau, the only Jew in FDR's cabinet, to suggest an ambitious plan for moving Jews from Europe to havens elsewhere. Perkins discussed a plan for a giant international relief corporation to train the younger Jews in Central and Eastern Europe and remove them to available lands where they could pursue farming. Britain, the United States, and individuals of all races and creeds would have to combine their efforts to supply the funding. Critics feared that such a program would play into Hitler's hands and only encourage other countries to imitate the Nazis. Zionist leaders also looked askance on large Jewish settlements other than in Palestine.[59]

Roosevelt tinkered. Over lunch, he asked Morgenthau how many Jews needed prompt rescue from perilous circumstances in Europe. It was an extraordinary question put not to the secretary of state, but to the highest-ranking Jew in government. Morgenthau estimated 500,000 from Greater Germany and 250,000 from Romania and Poland. Roosevelt sketched out a cost of $1,000 per person and asked Morgenthau whether a goal of resettling 100,000 per year for five years would be sufficient? Morgenthau responded that it was better than what anyone else had proposed. Roosevelt again suggested apportioning the costs into a U.S. contribution ($100 million over five years), funds from other countries, private contributions, and proceeds from the sale of bonds. He was prepared to recommend the annual admission of 20,000 Jews into the United States within the quota, which could not be reserved for only Jews; he would push for at least 15,000 a year for Palestine, and another 65,000 a year elsewhere.[60]

By this time, American consul general Raymond Geist, the most knowledgeable American diplomat in Berlin, had sent a bleak forecast to Messersmith, writing, "The Germans are in a mood of triumph and victory over their success in Czechoslovakia; and they consider that their course forward is positively irresistible." He stressed that, "They have embarked on a program of annihilation of the Jews and we shall be allowed to save the remnants if we choose; but I am afraid that the chances of getting any cooperation from the persons who are now firmly in power are slight indeed." Geist speculated that it might be necessary to sacrifice half a million people

[German Jews] to uphold justice and the principles of human dignity—this meant giving up on saving German Jews in order to confront Nazi Germany, but then the United States should be preparing to "attack the oppressor and bring about his destruction." Failing that, the government ought to try to come to some kind of "working arrangement with the German authorities regarding the evacuation of the victims on a scale sufficiently great to make the Nazis think that by some show of moderation they can accelerate the exodus."[61]

Equally dire forecasts came from Rublee, who wrote Acheson that "There are two factions in Germany. One headed by Goering, the Minister of Economics [Goering actually held a powerful position that overlapped with the Ministry of Economics] and Schacht, want to arrive at a settlement of the Jewish question and want to talk with me to see if a settlement is possible. The other composed of Himmler, Goebbels, and Ribbentrop want[s] to exterminate the Jews and to make no concession to foreign countries." Like Geist, Rublee took this information seriously; there is no sign that he discounted it as Nazi hyperbole.[62]

Although stymied in his effort to reach Berlin, Rublee still clung to the dim hope of negotiating successfully with the German government. After a meeting with Rublee in London on December 14, Schacht suggested that Germany might allow many Jews to emigrate in return for expanded purchases of German goods through funds raised by "international Jewry." As Jewish advocates had feared, Schacht had once again proposed to ransom Jews in exchange for bolstering the German economy. Without an increase in German exports, German Jews would lack the funds they needed to settle elsewhere.[63]

Messersmith decried this cynical deal as unacceptable, even as a basis for further negotiation. However, Ambassador Kennedy favored making substantial concessions to Germany. In a remarkable conversation with British Jewish activist Neville Laski in early December 1938, Kennedy defended his support for appeasing Hitler and expanding economic relations with his regime. By increasing trade with Germany, Britain and the United States would enmesh the Nazi government in a mutually profitable relationship that would moderate its behavior in the future, he claimed. Secretary of State Hull disagreed, but Kennedy promised to work on Hull when he returned to Washington soon. Kennedy believed that if trade barriers remained and bad will prevailed, war would follow.[64]

The ambassador also said that anti-Semitism was rising in Britain and America partly because of a perception that "the Jews" wanted Germany punished by force of arms. Citing his many intimate conversations with the prime minister, Kennedy claimed that Chamberlain held the Jews responsible for the "serious setback and possible destruction" of his policy of appeasement. As a result, the prime minister had little sympathy for Jewish concerns, Kennedy noted. Chamberlain believed that if the United States did not increase its immigration quota or provide territory for Jewish settlement, it had no right to ask Britain to do so.

Kennedy declared that Congress would block any appropriation request from FDR; even to ask for public funding would be a serious mistake. Anti-Semites would exploit any such effort to undermine the position of Jews in America, which he thought "very delicate." He cited FDR as having said that if foreign nations dragged the United States into a war with Germany, there might even be a pogrom in America. Kennedy said (probably correctly) that the president preferred as little publicity as possible about the level of immigration to the United States. Still, Kennedy and other anti-Semites had their own reasons for extracting Jews from Germany and Eastern Europe. The ambassador thought the Jews in Germany were "a festering sore leading to international complications straight along the path of war. . . . the world's most difficult and dangerous problem." If there was war, Kennedy forecast, "the fate of millions of Jews in Central Europe was not worth much, if anything."[65]

After meeting with FDR in mid-December, Kennedy wrote that "FDR dreams of moving Jews not only out of Germany but out of all Central and Eastern Europe. This would mean a new homeland. Palestine wouldn't hold them all, so FDR thinks of Angola, which Portuguese offered for Jewish settlement in 1912." These comments are consistent with what FDR had said to Rabbi Wise in January, to Sweetser in April, and to Morgenthau in November.[66]

In the six months from the Évian Conference until the end of the year, members of the Roosevelt administration from the president to the most experienced American diplomat in Berlin put serious time and energy into the long-shot effort of removing hundreds of thousands of Jews in an orderly fashion from Germany and Austria. At first, they hoped for some cooperation from Nazi leaders who wanted to rid themselves of Jews. In a reversal of the Shylock myth, even "moderates" like Schacht wanted their pound of flesh in return for releasing Jews; higher Nazi officials, even more anti-Semitic, refused to let Jews take any property with them even if that meant keeping them in Germany. So American strategy shifted to raising outside money to sustain Jewish immigrants in new lands and assuming that the Nazi would confiscate German-Jewish property. Roosevelt largely worked in isolation with little aid or encouragement from any other leader of conse-quence across the Western world.

In 1938, FDR foresaw a looming humanitarian disaster: Welles had said that FDR considered the situation of Jews in Germany an emergency. He had seen and heard enough about Hitler over the years to expect the worst. The Nazis hated Jews and believed in an international Jewish conspiracy against Germany, and they saw Jewry as a hostile element across the conti-nent. FDR had heard all this from McDonald. Removing Jews from Europe might not slake Hitler's thirst for land and blood, but FDR, Morgenthau, Welles, and Perkins thought the effort was worthy for its own sake.[67]

After Munich and *Kristallnacht,* the president used refugee issues to ex-pose the horrors of a regime determined to punish and persecute Jews, rather than let them emigrate. Appeasement of such a regime would never work. In late October, FDR declared, "There can be no peace if national policy adopts as a deliberate instrument the dispersion all over the world of millions of helpless and persecuted wanderers with no place to lay their heads." After Munich and *Kristallnacht,* FDR refused to endorse any con-cessions that would help Germany prepare for war and divide the potential democratic opposition.[68]

Welles had argued that extracting Jews from Germany might help to prevent war. In April, he had encouraged newspaper editors to spread this notion. There is no clear evidence about how seriously FDR took this rather different form of appeasement; given his view of Hitler, he most likely ex-pected to delay war, rather than to prevent it. Still, in attempting to recruit Stimson, appointing Taylor, and in declining to break openly with Ken-nedy on refugee issues, he hoped to mobilize support for his international refugee effort among at least some Republicans and proponents of a negoti-ated settlement with Germany.

By late 1938, the United States had filled the immigration quota for Germany, which represented considerable progress for the advocates of ref-ugees. FDR's reluctance to try to go much beyond the immigration quota limits reflected reasonable political judgment and concerns about domestic anti-Semitism. Moreover, looking back in 1946, Morgenthau detected a major shift in FDR's electoral ambitions during 1938. In early 1938, he said, FDR had no intention of running for president again. By the end of the year, Morgenthau thought, Roosevelt expected a war and believed he would have to run again to save the country. No contemporary (and no historian) knew exactly when Roosevelt decided to seek an unprecedented third term. Still, the evidence indicates that war drove his decision, and by late 1938, he expected war. If Morgenthau was right, Roosevelt's rekindled concern about his political standing added to the reasons for not pushing Congress hard on Jewish refugees after *Kristallnacht.*[69]

Contemporaries thought FDR had done a great deal for persecuted Jews. In December 1938, a panel of distinguished Jews and Christians awarded him the American Hebrew Medal, noting, "he took the initiative at every crisis in Jewish affairs" and "was responsible for the Évian Conference and for aiding refugees of Central Europe." They would not have given such an award to the first-term Roosevelt, but by December 1938, the award seemed fitting.[70]

In retrospect, one may ask why FDR did not do more to accomplish his vision of moving millions of Jews out of Europe. There was a real political tension between stiffening opposition to Nazi Germany and promoting Jewish emigration—heightened by Nazi Germany's determination to strip Jews of their property. The more Roosevelt risked on initiatives for Jews, the less he thought he could carry Congress and the public with him on broad issues of foreign policy. Instead of acting boldly, in the absence of domestic or international support he cautiously threaded his way through competing priorities.

CHAPTER SEVEN

Resettlement in Latin America?

IN SEEKING DESTINATIONS for Jewish refugees, FDR had reason to look southward. Most Latin American countries had expanses of undeveloped land, and shortages of both investment capital and skilled professionals. Many thousands of Jews from Eastern Europe had migrated to Argentina and Brazil during the 1920s, after the United States had imposed its immigration quotas. Just before the Great Depression, Peru had offered land for the settlement of hundreds of thousands of Jews.

On immigration issues, Latin America posed both promise and contradictions. Latin countries shared in the Western world's nativist and anti-Semitic currents of the times, and the Great Depression hardened opposition to Jewish immigration. Many Latin Americans believed that their cities were already overcrowded and unhealthy. In the 1930s, most Latin American countries discouraged or prohibited the immigration of middle-class Jews hoping to live and work in towns and cities. In early 1935, Argentinean and Brazilian officials rebuffed the efforts of League of Nations High Commissioner on Refugees James G. McDonald to secure the admission of even small numbers of Jewish refugees to their lands. Jews, they told him, were politically radical and useless for agricultural labor. Roosevelt was aware of McDonald's efforts and the dismal results.[1]

Still, FDR had a romantic attachment to farming, and agricultural settlement represented the path of least resistance for Jewish immigration to Latin America. Johns Hopkins geographer and sporadic presidential adviser Isaiah Bowman threw his influence behind agriculture. In October 1938, Roosevelt read Bowman's book *Limits of Land Settlement* with great interest; he asked Bowman to assess prospects for refugee settlements in the plateau region north and south of the Orinoco River in Venezuela.[2]

As an adviser on resettlement issues Bowman had impeccable academic credentials tempered by practical experience in Latin America. Born in Canada, Bowman grew up in rural Michigan, never losing his attachment to the land. He became an American citizen at age twenty-one and, aspiring to become a geographer, attended Harvard a year behind Roosevelt. He then taught geography at Yale and later earned his doctorate. Fashioning himself as a geographical explorer, he undertook three major and arduous expeditions to uncharted areas of the Andes Mountains in South America. He left Yale to become director of the American Geographical Society, a position that one biographer described as his ticket to the "higher ranks of the professional classes and simultaneously his entrée into New York's ruling class." A champion of detailed maps, he became an important adviser to Woodrow Wilson in the last stages of World War I and at the Paris Peace Conference. Although he was more conservative than Wilson, the two men shared a belief in a new world order of free nations and free trade, sustained by the economic power of the United States.[3]

During the interwar period, Bowman ambitiously leapfrogged from position to position in organizations that overlapped scholarship and policy-making—president of the Association of American Geographers, chairman of the National Research Council, and founding member of the Council on Foreign Relations. In 1935, he became president of Johns Hopkins University, where he hoped to build a geography department. In 1936, he appeared on the cover of *Time*. Roosevelt had an avid interest in geography. Bowman was the most prominent geographer in the country, and he believed in using science to serve humanity. He was a natural resource for FDR—another former Wilsonian committed to economic progress and American ideals.[4]

Bowman's racist views biased his analysis of resettlement prospects for Jews in Latin America and elsewhere. He believed in encouraging modern pioneers to settle on vacant or underused land. This romantic vision of a recreated America worldwide came more from his own roots—a kind of agrarian idealism—than from any practical knowledge or experience with economic development. Despite the evidence of Jews working on kibbutzes in Palestine and European Zionist groups training to become farmers, Bowman believed that Jews lacked the skills and fortitude required of pioneers. A lifelong eugenicist, Bowman regarded perceived racial and genetic differences as established scientific facts. He shared the negative stereotype of the urban Jew. The Protestant work ethic had a racial component, he thought, and neither Jews nor blacks had the capacity to overcome the hardships of developing untamed land in hostile climes.[5]

Once Bowman established his supremacy on the Baltimore campus, he instituted a formal Jewish quota at Hopkins in 1942. Jewish students, he explained, came there only to make money or to marry non-Jews. He refused to reappoint the talented young Jewish historian Eric Goldman despite unanimous backing from the History Department, the intervention of noted historian Charles Beard, and a university-wide protest campaign. Bowman told the History Department that there were already too many Jews on the faculty at Hopkins.[6]

In October 1938, Bowman gave FDR a discouraging response about opportunities for Jewish emigration to Venezuela. Although he had in his writings championed pioneer belts of territory around the globe, he thought "The strongest bar to settlement from the outside is the combination of extreme environmental conditions and the unfamiliar character of the life. . . . Decidedly the llanos [plains] are not adapted to large-scale immigration." FDR persisted, asking again about sparsely settled agricultural land for Jewish colonies—suitable for 50,000–100,000 people. Whether or not FDR recognized Bowman's opposition to measures benefiting Jewish refugees, he did not want the geographer to make public any presidential interest in such matters. FDR said that he had no specific plans—he just wanted to be prepared. Bowman ruled out entire regions of South America based on the allegedly unsuitable climate for Europeans or the undue cost of development. He mentioned a couple of small possibilities in South America, and clearly endorsed only Costa Rica as a plausible haven for numerous refugees. As a prospect, he said, it had no rival in Latin America.[7]

Roosevelt pressed ahead anyway. As always, he sought multiple sources of advice and information. Roosevelt and Sumner Welles urged McDonald,

George Warren, and Hamilton Fish Armstrong of the President's Advisory Committee on Political Refugees to speed up their consideration of possibilities, particularly in Latin America, for Jewish immigration. Far closer to the president than Bowman, Welles believed that large numbers of Jews had to leave Europe. The undersecretary gave the president reassurance that he was not alone on this issue.[8]

The men of the President's Advisory Committee on Political Refugees turned to Bowman, who hired other authorities on Central America. They focused on prospects for agricultural workers, with other kinds of immigrants following over time. These analysts agreed that Costa Rica offered the best short-term prospects, because of its available land and sympathetic politics. Henry Morgenthau Jr. alerted the president that Costa Rica had large debts and needed $5 million to avoid default.[9]

Within days, however, Bowman began dismantling prospects for a Costa Rican project. A large foreign immigrant group would create political turmoil in a small Central American country, and Latin American leaders might well blame the United State for importing European problems into American affairs, he argued. No supporter of Nazism, Bowman hardly empathized with its victims.[10]

Bowman relished the opportunities for himself and Johns Hopkins that came from access to the White House and refugee organizations. On November 16, Morgenthau told him that FDR had approved his hiring of Karl Pelzer as a researcher, with Treasury to pay his monthly salary. A recent University of California, Los Angeles PhD in geography, Pelzer was himself a refugee from Germany who steered resettlement hopes toward Africa. Bowman noticed Welles's interest in Portugese Angola and proposed it as a second Jewish homeland if Portugal cooperated.[11]

Meanwhile, after the Rockefeller Foundation declined funding, Bowman obtained a grant from the Refugee Economic Corporation for the scientific study of settlement carried out by a team within the Walter Hines Page School of International Affairs at Johns Hopkins. Bowman met in New York with members of the President's Advisory Committee on Political Refugees, discussing possible Jewish agricultural settlements in Brazil and Bolivia. When Welles heard that the Brazilian government would accept no more than 3,000 refugees for a tract in northeastern Brazil larger than the size of Texas, he pushed for a larger number. Bowman conceded that communities of refugees "could be made self-sustaining if sites were chosen by experts in water engineering and citrus-fruit husbandry."[12]

Pelzer soon issued a discouraging assessment of Africa. He concluded that the continent could absorb about half a million settlers (excluding South Africa and Ethiopia), but at a minimum price of $5,000 per family. In addition, governments would need to fund railway construction, so the total cost would be prohibitively large. In his comments to FDR, Bowman denigrated plans for large-scale settlement of Jewish refugees in Africa or anywhere else. His alternative vision of small settlements at numerous places across the globe looked fine on paper, but represented a dead end for refugees, given the difficulty of managing all its moving parts. Bowman made the scale of settlement dependent upon political factors: "the absorption must be on such a limited scale in any one area that the people already established in the area will welcome the new settlers."[13]

Bowman's firm opposition might have blocked any hope for major Jewish settlements outside Europe, except for the fact that grand projects appealed to Roosevelt's imagination. Sometime after *Kristallnacht,* Samuel Rosenman, a close and influential presidential adviser, sketched out ambitious ideas, possibly for a speech by Roosevelt or his adviser Harry Hopkins. The Jewish problem was a worldwide problem in ethics, Rosenman wrote. Policy-makers needed to translate the good wishes of the Évian Conference into action, providing a homeland or a protectorate for refugees—not a Jewish state, but a refuge run by "a non-racial committee, the country offering the land to have the preponderant voice." In contrast to Bowman's plan for scattered, small settlements, Rosenman envisioned a new Jewish refuge large enough for five million people.[14]

Secretary Morgenthau sought to turn Rosenman's thinking into action. He suggested to FDR that the United States would cancel the World War I debts of Britain, France, and the Netherlands in return for their ceding the British, French, and Dutch Guianas to the United States as havens for refugees. Roosevelt responded that a hostile environment and perilous diseases made the Guianas unsuitable for Jewish settlement—a remark that may have come straight from Bowman. Welles opposed American sovereignty over the Guianas, but he thought it worth studying whether hemispheric governments could establish a joint protectorate there until incoming refugees set up their own government.[15]

Probably to deflect American pressure for the use of other British colonies for refugees, in early 1939 Britain offered British Guiana. Technicians dispatched to the territory by the President's Advisory Committee on Political Refugees proposed a pilot settlement of some 3,000–5,000 refugees at a cost of about $3 million. British-Jewish backers, however, balked at putting money into Guiana; they wanted government financing from Britian or the United States. In June 1939, a high official in the Department of Agriculture suggested that Secretary Henry Wallace bring the subject of refugee settlement in all the Guianas to a cabinet discussion, given FDR's interest in the matter. However, the outbreak of war a few months later ended any chance of government funding, and construction in British Guiana ceased.[16]

Still, the idea lived on. In the spring of 1940, a New Yorker wrote Eleanor Roosevelt to suggest joint development of the Guianas for refugees. She passed the idea on to the president, who still thought the climate along the coast and lowlands vile—"so vile that it would cost huge sums to make life there inhabitable for white people." Still, as options faded, FDR noted that with careful planning the Guianas might sustain an influx of several million immigrants over a number of years. His view was more flexible than Bowman's, but what would the British, French, and Dutch charge the buyer, and who could take control? Roosevelt ruled out direct American possession for political/foreign policy reasons, and Welles agreed. FDR continued to contemplate some form of Pan American trusteeship, especially if the war in Europe forced the Western Hemisphere nations to take responsibility for European possessions there. FDR's unstated supposition was that Germany might well conquer the imperial nations of Netherlands, France, and even Britain.[17]

Even after the war began, settlement prospects remained alive in the Dominican Republic. At the Évian Conference, the spokesman for this small Caribbean country had announced that it would admit up to 100,000 refugees. The American chargé d'affaires in Santo Domingo thought dictator Rafael Trujillo wanted some white settlers, outside financing for development projects, and likely other concessions from the United States. Given the lack of options for refugees, Welles swallowed his distaste for the brutal Trujillo regime and encouraged American attorney Albert Houston to explore possibilities for colonization. Welles authorized Houston to tell Dominican officials that the United States viewed Dominican resettlement efforts with great sympathy, but he could not promise any concessions on trade negotiations with the United States.[18]

A team of four experts explored lands, half of which Trujillo owned, that Dominican officials offered for settlement. The American analysts found some of the property suitable for settlement of more than 28,000 families. Because of the difficulties of starting new settlements and uncertainties about which crops settlers would produce, they recommended starting with a modest pilot project.[19]

James N. Rosenberg, a key member of the American Jewish Committee, and Dr. Joseph Rosen, who had years of experience with Jewish colonization in the Soviet Union, took the lead in forming the Dominican Republic Settlement Association. The American Jewish Joint Distribution Committee (the foremost Jewish relief organization), and the President's Advisory Committee on Political Refugees backed their efforts. Without support from the Roosevelt administration, the venture could not have overcome even the initial obstacles. After receiving a discouraging report from the chargé d'affaires in Santo Domingo, the head of the Foreign Service told him, "you may or may not realize how deeply this Government is committed to finding a solution of the problem of German refugees and how strong an interest in it the President and Mr. Welles have."[20]

Both Roosevelt and Welles were willing to pay a price for establishing a successful farming enterprise in the Dominican Republic. They overlooked Trujillo's 1937 mass murder of some 17,000 Haitian residents of the Dominican Republic. Ferdinand Mayer, the U.S. minister in Santo Domingo, reported that Trujillo's dictatorship was "of the same ruthless character as that in Germany, Italy, and Russia." Trujillo hoped that his offer to welcome Jews on his land would help repair his damaged image, while FDR hoped it would establish a precedent for Jewish resettlement in Latin America. In a July 1939 visit to Washington, Trujillo discussed Dominican debts with FDR and Hull, and was feted as a celebrity by members of Congress, the military, and the State Department. Later, Dominican and American officials spoke about Export-Import Bank loans, improved trade with the United States, and cooperation against potential German aggression. In January 1941, FDR met with Rosenberg in the White House before he left for the Dominican Republic to sign a settlement contract.[21]

Virtually everything that could have gone wrong with the Dominican project did. American diplomats in the Dominican Republic were hostile to the project or skeptical of Trujillo's sincerity in fulfilling his grandiose promises. Most potential Jewish immigrants had no interest in working on less than fertile land and preferred to use Trujillo's domain as a way station for entry into the United States. American Jewish organizations battled one another over supporting this project at the expense of other pressing demands. As the war progressed and American officials increasingly feared that Nazis would infiltrate German agents into Latin America, they withdrew support for resettling refugees in the Dominican Republic or elsewhere in the hemisphere. Ultimately, only 757 refugees made it to the Jewish settlement called Sosúa.[22]

The difficulties at Sosúa highlighted the obvious limitations of agricultural settlement plans. Some younger Jews had trained or retrained themselves to become farmers in Palestine or elsewhere—partly a break with the notion of assimilation in Europe, partly a conscious strategy for maximizing the chance of receiving visas to somewhere. In the eighteen months before war began in Europe, desperation spread from most German Jews to Austrian Jews and then to Czech Jews, many of whom lacked the skills, inclination, or physical capacity for farm work. Most refugees could not transform themselves into plausible farmers.[23]

One vision for refugee-farmers evolved into an effective rescue program. Mauricio (Moritz) Hochschild, a native German Jew who became wealthy through his mining interests in several South American countries, had sought to resettle Jews from Germany since he and McDonald had discussed these possibilities in 1935. Bolivian citizen Hochschild benefited from American efforts at the Évian Conference and the accelerated effort to find new homes for Jews after *Kristallnacht*.[24]

Despite the indifference of American diplomats in Bolivia, Hochschild used sympathetic officials in Washington for leverage; he conferred with Herbert Feis in the State Department and met with members of the President's Advisory Committee on Political Refugees. On December 10, 1938, in response to an American inquiry, the Bolivian government declared that it would freely admit all farmers, businessmen with at least $5,000 in assets, family members of refugees already in the country, plus fifty technicians and fifty professionals. Bolivian consuls rarely vetoed potential immigrants for a lack of farming skills, so many German Jews qualified and obtained visas.[25]

It was a good start. Hochschild impressed the Refugee Economic Corporation and the President's Advisory Committee on Political Refugees. In January 1939, Hochschild founded an organization to provide temporary assistance, loans, and employment assistance to refugees in Bolivia. The Joint Distribution Committee and the Refugee Economic Corporation backed this effort, which ultimately aided a large majority of refugees who came to Bolivia. Even Bowman ultimately endorsed Hochschild's proposed agricultural settlement, known as *Nueva Terra*.[26]

As 9,000–10,000 refugees clustered in La Paz, Hochschild and his Bolivian allies hit a wall of political opposition, resulting from rising anti-Semitism, corruption in the sale of visas, and domestic political upheaval. Still, at least 20,000 European Jews reached Bolivia between 1938 and 1941. Some remained there; others slipped across loose borders to Brazil, Paraguay, Argentina, Chile, or Peru. Prompted by Hochschild, Bolivia became, per capita, the largest rescuer of Jews in the Western Hemisphere.[27]

Hochschild's influence reached across Bolivian borders. He recruited the Joint Distribution Committee to support the activities of the Argentinean Association for German-Jewish Aid. When Chile suspended Jewish immigration in 1939, Hochschild said that he hoped for a chance to persuade Chilean officials to lift the ban. An official of his firm dispensed relief to Jewish refugees in Peru.[28]

Peru illustrated the diminishing prospects for Jewish immigration to Latin America. In 1929, the Peruvian government had agreed in principle to subsidize the settlement of at least 250,000 Polish Jews on undeveloped land. By the late 1930s, economic distress and fears of radicals had chilled the climate for immigrants. In a spring 1938 communiqué Peruvian officials said its cooperation "is naturally conditioned upon the legal prescriptions in force in this country with respect to immigration, as well as upon the measures which hereafter may be adopted in the national interest." American ambassador Laurence Steinhardt, the only sitting Jewish American ambassador, told Washington that Peru feared that a flood of Jewish refugees might bring radical ideas with them.[29]

Peruvian officials reacted decisively when the local press published a September 1938 dispatch about a ship with 250 Jewish refugees seeking to land on the west coast of South America. The Ministry of Foreign Affairs issued a confidential instruction to Peruvian diplomats to deny visas to all Jews. The government set the bar for entry so high that a British pharmaceutical company could not get a visa for an employee whom it planned to deploy in Peru, because the Peruvian consul thought he was Jewish. The man was actually Welsh.[30]

The Peruvian minister of foreign affairs told Ambassador Steinhardt that Peru had actually given 176 visas to Jews over a four-month period, but they had all settled in Lima, which was not desirable. He declared that Peru was willing to admit farmers, certain specialists, and industrialists possessing capital. Steinhardt optimistically suggested that Peru would more than proportionately issue visas in these categories.[31]

In Chile, newly elected pro-U.S. president Manuel Prado y Ugarteche tried to facilitate the immigration of Jewish refugees in late 1938 and early 1939. His conservative opponents accused Chilean officials of selling visas to Jews. By July 1939, an estimated 7,000–8,000 Jewish refugees had entered the country, prompting so many complaints that the Chilean minister of foreign affairs submitted his resignation. Although the president persuaded the foreign minister to stay on, he announced new measures to prevent Jews from becoming street peddlers or taking other disreputable jobs. Another decree banned all new immigrants except for close relatives of legal residents. In December 1940, after the SS *Augustus* landed in Chile with 870 Jewish refugees, the Chilean government closed its ports to Jewish refugees and tried to keep those admitted from migrating to the cities.[32]

For a time Cuba served as a promising destination for Jewish refugees. On November 11, 1938, Cuban strongman Colonel Fulgencio Batista talked for a half-hour with President Roosevelt in the White House. Although generally seeking to improve Cuba's image in the United States, Batista also had the specific agenda of persuading FDR to reduce the tariff on Cuban sugar. As a result, he sought to make a good impression in Washington. Roosevelt or someone close to him seems to have expressed the hope that Cuba would be able to accommodate additional Jewish refugees. During a speech in New York a week later, Batista announced that he was "deeply moved by the sad plight of the political refugees" and that "Cuban officials would heartily cooperate with President Roosevelt in his plan to relieve the terrible situation abroad." He called upon other Central and South American countries to join with Cuba to facilitate the entry of German political refugees. In a column in the *Washington Post* Leonard Lyons revealed that Batista had delayed his return to Cuba because "he and Roosevelt are working upon a plan for Cuba to receive some German refugees."[33]

The president did not personally formulate any Cuban plan. If any American did, it was Lawrence Berenson, president of the Cuban Chamber of Commerce in the United States. Berenson was a friend of Batista who later helped the dictator find a place of exile after Fidel Castro's revolutionaries toppled his regime in 1959.

Independent evidence corroborates Roosevelt's personal interest. During FDR's Thanksgiving vacation at his retreat in Warm Springs, Georgia, Welles sent a confidential and urgent message to all American ambassadors to the Latin American republics, asking them to meet personally with the foreign minister of their host countries to stress American interest in refugees. He told American diplomats that the United States hoped that each American republic would make a "specific and generous statement which all of our peoples must feel for the tragic situation of their fellow men and women."[34]

Several hundred thousand German Jews, who feared that their situation in Germany could only deteriorate, clustered on a ten-year waiting list for American immigration visas. If they escaped Germany, wherever they went, they remained eligible for a spot to enter the United States under the substantial German quota. They simply had to wait their turn. If it became harder for other Jews in Germany to pay for transportation across the Atlantic or otherwise qualify for visas, that would only produce more quota slots for refugees already outside the country.

Cuban officials had their own selfish reasons for admitting Jewish refugees temporarily. The government charged heavy fees for visas or tourist landing permits. Whether as a quid pro quo or not, Batista gained agreement from the Roosevelt administration to reduce the tariff on Cuban sugar and to back a program of economic, technical, and military assistance to Cuba. A steady stream of ships with Jewish passengers began to leave German ports for Havana.[35]

By the summer of 1939, estimates of the total number of German-Jewish refugees in Cuba ranged from 5,000 to 6,000 in a country with a population of about 4.5 million. The Joint Distribution Committee guaranteed that Jewish "tourists" who stayed on would not become public charges in Cuba. Nonetheless, Cuban anti-Semites, some of them inflamed by pro-Nazi elements, objected to the influx of Jews. Tensions rose among Batista, the corrupt Cuban director of immigration, and President Federico Laredo Brú, who sought to crack down on the immigration traffic. The Cuban Jewish Committee's relief organization had foreseen the danger of a backlash, and asked their American counterparts for assistance.[36]

This backlash emerged in May 1939 when Cuban authorities denied admission to Jews aboard the SS *St. Louis*. Through the popular Hollywood movie *The Voyage of the Damned,* the plight of 937 German Jewish passengers on the *St. Louis* entered American popular culture. In the process, the *St. Louis* and its passengers acquired mythical traits and shed important real ones. The *St. Louis* passengers also failed to gain entry into the United States, which, for some, symbolizes U.S. government indifference to the fate of persecuted Jews during the Holocaust. However, the voyage of the *St. Louis* preceded the Holocaust, and it was an exception, not the rule.

Most of the passengers on the *St. Louis,* which sailed from Hamburg on May 13, had what they thought were valid Cuban tourist landing permits, purchased from the German shipping line Hapag: twenty-two had Cuban immigration visas, and 734 were on the waiting list for American visas. While the ship was en route, the Cuban government, in response to pressures from Cuban anti-Semites, invalidated these tourist documents, which were not technically valid for long-term stay. When the ship arrived on May 26 in Havana, harbor authorities allowed only twenty-eight passengers to come ashore. Two additional ships with smaller numbers of refugees who had similar documents and problems arrived within days. They departed without leaving passengers in Havana, but the *St. Louis* remained.

If forced back to Germany, the *St. Louis* passengers faced the grim fate of imprisonment in concentration camps—extermination camps would not exist for another two-and-a-half years. One veteran of Buchenwald slit his wrists and plunged into the harbor. The international press picked up a political story with spectacular human interest. Berenson and Cecilia Razovsky of the National Coordinating Committee rushed to Havana to try to resolve the impasse. They bypassed the Cuban Jewish Committee and tried to deal directly with the Cuban government, some of whose officials reacted with hostility to Razovsky, either because of her manner or her gender.[37]

Berenson fared no better. His relationship with Batista did not help: the colonel chose not to intervene, and Berenson alienated President Laredo Brú. Meanwhile, Berenson ignored other offers, including one from the Dominican Republic, to admit the passengers. Dominican officials asked for irrevocable fees of $500 per passenger, little different than Cuba. Berenson and Razovsky rejected this extortion. They also ignored a possibly less onerous overture from Honduras. Even after Cuban authorities forced the ship to leave Havana on June 2, Berenson believed he could negotiate a face-saving compromise that settled the passengers temporarily somewhere in Cuba. He preferred to deal with the Cubans he knew rather than unfamiliar officials elsewhere.[38]

As the German captain marked time by sailing along the Florida coast, telegrams from friends and relatives of passengers bombarded the White House and the State Department. Some wanted the United States to pressure Cuba; others wanted the United States to admit the passengers at least temporarily. Roosevelt was in Hyde Park when the deadlock in Havana Harbor occurred. After he returned to Washington on May 31, illness confined him to his room for several days. The State Department handled most of the *St Louis* affair. Undersecretary Welles, a veteran of dealing with difficult and corrupt Cuban regimes, knew that an official American attempt to force Cuban acceptance of the *St. Louis* passengers would have ruined FDR's Good Neighbor Policy and undermined America's standing in Latin America generally at a time when war seemed near.[39]

Once the ship began to meander toward Miami, Secretary Morgenthau intervened. Worried friends in New York had called him, he told Hull in a phone conversation on June 5. Hull said he had just talked to the Cuban ambassador and Roosevelt about the *St. Louis*. The State Department rejected as illegal a proposal for using the Virgin Islands as a holding area: the Virgin Islands could not take in tourists who lacked a permanent home to which they could return. A disappointed Morgenthau asked Hull if he could keep calling to monitor the situation. After the Joint Distribution Committee lost contact with the ship, Morgenthau asked the coast guard to locate and track it without any publicity. Phone calls between Morgenthau and Hull and Morgenthau and the coast guard commander—the transcripts survive—made it plain that the point of this tracking was to keep alive the chance to find a solution.[40]

There is no truth to the notion, found in some literature, that American officials ordered the coast guard to prevent any passengers from reaching American shores. Still, they could not legally enter the United States without jumping ahead of other Jews on the waiting list. They could not enter as visitors without a place of return. The administration's political calculus was almost as clear as the legal situation. If the president tried to evade immigration laws, his opponents in Congress would exploit his vulnerability to reduce chances of revising the Neutrality Acts.[41]

On June 7, after Laredo Brú had escalated Cuban financial demands and set a final deadline, negotiations in Havana neared the point of collapse.

The Joint Distribution Committee in New York seemed willing to meet the Cuban demands of nearly half a million dollars beyond sums already pledged, but Berenson was not. Visa Division Chief Avra Warren told American embassy officials in Havana that the secretary of state and the White House had ruled out intervention if the Cuban president gave a final no, which he did that evening.[42]

As the *St. Louis* and two smaller refugee ships steamed back across the Atlantic, the Joint Distribution Committee and the Intergovernmental Committee on Refugees persuaded Belgium to agree to take in the passengers as a special case. Britain, France, and the Netherlands followed; each took a share. Through Robert Pell, its representative with the Intergovernmental Committee on Refugees, the State Department facilitated the European solution, which satisfied Jewish leaders and sympathetic officials in the Roosevelt administration.[43]

Leaders of the Joint Distribution Committee told Morgenthau that their intervention on behalf of the *St. Louis* passengers was exceptional and not a precedent. Their committee had expended extraordinary sums of money on resettling these refugees. Without sharply curtailing its aid to suffering Jews in Europe, it could not bear the future burdens of chaotic, forced and disorganized emigration. The committee would continue to warn Jews against any "attempt to gain admission to Cuba or to any other country" without documents "fully acceptable to the receiving countries."[44]

Many of these homeless Jews found refuge in Western Europe preferable to Latin American alternatives to Cuba. As the *St. Louis* steamed back across the Atlantic, the passengers cabled Morris C. Troper, European head of the Joint Distribution Committee, saying, "Our gratitude is as immense as the ocean on which we are now floating." After the settlement Berenson wrote, "I am weary and tired, but am coming to rapidly. Thank God those sad refugees have landed in safe places." In the prewar summer of 1939, they were safe, and those passengers with American quota numbers could still wait for their turn for entry into the United States.[45]

A final footnote in Hollywood's version of the story says that more than 600 of the 937 passengers eventually perished in concentration camps. A recent careful investigation showed that 254 eventually died, most of them at the extermination camps of Auschwitz or Sobibor, the rest in internment camps or in attempting to evade the Nazis. Other versions overlook basic facts. In a recent play by Janet Langhart Cohen, *Emmett and Anne,* Emmett

Till, the now famous African American teenager tortured and murdered in 1955 for talking to a white woman in Mississippi, and Anne Frank have a conversation in heaven. Anne recounts the *St. Louis* story, in which the passengers return to Germany and the Nazis send them to the death camps. Yet none actually returned to Germany, and in June 1939, the Holocaust had not yet begun. The *St. Louis* passengers themselves, Jewish aid workers, and American officials all believed that the refugees had escaped Nazi persecution.[46]

Relatives or friends of those *St. Louis* passengers who landed on the continent and later fell victim to the Holocaust had a right to feel betrayed. The Cuban government and Berenson bear much of the responsibility. Roosevelt, politically pragmatic, decided not to risk political jeopardy through an uncertain battle with Congress over the fate of the *St. Louis*—which could have cost him capital with Congress in his battle to revise the Neutrality Acts. It was a debatable judgment, but cannot be interpreted as indifference to Jewish refugees. If not for his intervention, 5,000–6,000 other Jews would not have found refuge in Cuba.

The expulsion of the *St. Louis* passengers did not end Jewish immigration to Cuba. As many as 2,000 Jews entered the island in the subsequent two and a half years primarily by paying exorbitant fees and bribing Cuban officials. Many of the new arrivals were Polish diamond workers stranded in Belgium who would found the diamond industry in Cuba.[47]

Mexico, Brazil, and Argentina, the most populous nations in Latin America, might have seemed more logical destinations than Cuba, but they raised political obstacles to the admission of Jewish refugees. In 1938, Mexican president Lázaro Cárdenas imposed a quota of 5,000 German immigrants, with preference to Catholic Germans and members of some Protestant groups. Fewer than a thousand German Jews entered Mexico during the next three years.[48]

The Brazilian government had issued a secret circular in 1937 that essentially barred the admission of virtually all Jews. The number of Jews legally admitted to Brazil in 1938 fell to 500, despite expressions of sympathy by the Brazilian delegate to the Évian Conference. Under pressure from the United States, Brazil modified this policy in September 1938 to admit select Jews with substantial capital or valuable skills. At first, Welles called for a number larger than the total of 3,000 offered by Brazilian officials, only to learn that Brazilian representatives in Washington had made the outrageous claim that 200,000 European Jews had entered illegally between 1934 and 1937. American diplomats, consulting privately with Brazilian experts, came up with revised figures of nearly 12,000 legal immigrants and perhaps 2,000 illegal entrants.[49]

The appointment of Oswaldo Aranha, former Brazilian ambassador to the United States, as foreign minister of Brazil improved the prospects for Jewish immigration. In March 1939, Aranha attended a dinner given by the Council of Foreign Relations in New York, where one of the guests asked him whether Brazil would accept Jews who could assimilate and had financial resources. Although no one succeeded in working out a plan tying an increased number of visas for Jews to a reduction of Brazilian debts, the new foreign minister apparently decided to purchase American goodwill. Meanwhile, American diplomats in Brazil disingenuously exaggerated the political, economic, and media influence of American Jews in order to create a political rationale for a more generous policy. Despite inconsistent policies and decisions, Brazil gave visas to about 10,000 Jewish refugees between 1939 and 1942.[50]

Argentina, which had the largest Jewish population in Latin America, moved in the other direction. In 1938, Argentina adopted new immigration policies that restricted the admission of Jews. In August 1939, Argentinean cabinet ministers explained to the Chamber of Deputies that they saw a major distinction between immigrants and refugees: refugees had undesirable qualities and came unwillingly to their shores. The Ministries of Agriculture, Foreign Affairs, and Interior collaborated to apply temporary measures to block those who might not be able to adapt to Argentinean conditions. The number of Jews directly entering Argentina declined to 1,873 from 4,919 in 1938 (some Jews also reached Argentina from other Latin American countries), and dropped again the following year.[51]

Although Roosevelt operated mostly through others, he told Morgenthau that he intervened directly in one Latin American case. On April 30, 1939, General José Félix Estigarribia, the Paraguayan minister to the United States, was elected president of Paraguay. Before he left the United States, he sought to meet FDR in order to straighten out difficulties that had arisen over a proposed loan from the Export-Import Bank to Paraguay. Roosevelt agreed to host a lunch for the general. Although there is no direct record of their conversation, Roosevelt later said that he had asked the president-elect to take in refugees, and Estigarribia agreed to admit 5,000.[52]

From 1938 to 1941, at least 40,000 Jews from all nations emigrated to Latin America—about half of them to Bolivia—although many would eventually seek permanent refuge elsewhere. It was far from a token number, although it was not nearly enough to make much of a dent in the burgeoning refugee crisis of the era. The many barriers to the increased admission of Jews to nations south of the border included anti-Semitism, nationalism, resistance to immigrants competing for jobs, the lack of local Jewish leadership comparable to Hochschild in Bolivia, and in some cases pro-fascist sentiment. Latin American consuls in Europe issued visas in spite of these obstacles—usually with the approval of their governments.[53]

American-sponsored resettlement or migration efforts in Latin America were poorly conceived and badly managed. Some diplomats and State Department officials simply refused to consider resettlement of refugees as consistent with the interests of the United States. To be sure, some refugees found safety through their own desperate efforts or through purchasing visas from corrupt officials acting against the wishes of their governments. Still, Bolivia, Cuba, and Brazil are clear cases where governments temporarily admitted Jewish refugees in the hope of earning goodwill with the United States. Despite Bowman's sabotage and Trujillo's corruption, in the face of anti-Semitism in Latin America and Roosevelt's fascination with farming, during the 1930s more German Jews may have reached Latin American countries than Palestine. Even limited resettlement in Latin America would not have taken place if the Roosevelt administration had looked on with indifference to the plight of Jews trapped in Hitler's Europe as war approached.[54]

CHAPTER EIGHT

Toward War

ON MARCH 15, 1939, Germany occupied Bohemia and Moravia, encouraging Slovak politicians to secede and set up a Nazi satellite state. Adolf Hitler had wiped out the once formidable nation of Czechoslovakia. Angry about unopposed Nazi aggression, FDR warned fellow Democrat Tom Connally, a member of the Senate Foreign Relations Committee, that invoking the Neutrality Act in case of another German invasion would turn America into Hitler's tacit ally. On March 17, the United States condemned the destruction of Czechoslovakia and reimposed import duties on subsidized German goods. On March 20, Democratic senator Key Pittman, chair of the Senate Foreign Relations Committee, proposed a revision of the Neutrality Act that dropped the mandatory arms embargo and made all trade cash-and-carry.[1]

The German takeover of Czech lands made many Czech Jews desperate to escape their homeland. A Czech Jewish textile manufacturer soon came to the United States with his wife and two children on six-month visitors' visas. As their remaining time in the United States dwindled, the mother despaired for the future of her family. She and her children leaped to their deaths from the thirteenth floor of a Chicago hotel. Representative Adolph Sabath of Chicago discussed this August 1939 tragedy with the president, who condemned the Nazi persecution that led to such desperation and promised as he had before to extend visitors' visas of refugees in the United States until they had found permanent residence somewhere.[2]

During 1939, FDR rested on what he had already done in loosening immigration restrictions to the United States, rather than risk fanning congressional opposition to his increasingly anti-Nazi foreign policy. He relied more and more on hopes and efforts to move German Jews to other countries. With few governments willing to participate so far in resettlement, Roosevelt and his envoys cast a broad net, looking at a range of unlikely possibilities to find new homes for the persecuted.

On January 4, 1939, Ambassador William Phillips personally delivered to Italian dictator Benito Mussolini a letter from President Roosevelt asking the *Duce* to persuade Hitler that Jews should retain some assets when emigrating abroad. FDR told Phillips also to raise the possibility of settling Jews on a large plateau region that included part of Ethiopia, Kenya, and adjoining territory. Mussolini had recently returned from a skiing vacation. Either to show his vitality or his contempt for the subject of the meeting, he remained dressed in his ski clothes. His son-in-law, Foreign Minister Galeazzo Ciano, was present but stood mute throughout the discussion. Mussolini responded that Jews had rejected his offer of another area in Ethiopia. He said that rather than dispersing small numbers of Jews across the world, the Jewish people should be given a homeland of their own, although not in a large or important area. Then those Jews who continued to live elsewhere would be treated formally like the foreigners they were.

Phillips limited himself to presenting American criticism of Nazi Germany's methods of dealing with its Jews. However, Mussolini would have none of this.

> The Duce interrupted me [Phillips] by recounting the iniquities of the German Jews and of Jews in general, their lack of loyalty to the country of their residence, their intrigues, and the fact that they never could assimilate with any other race. . . . He told me of the financial frauds which were being practiced by the Jews and showed me a little book in German containing photographs of counterfeit bills for huge amounts of German marks. I was impressed by his apparently genuine antagonism to the Jews. He went on to

say that, in his opinion, there would not be one Jew left in Germany, and that other European countries—and he mentioned in particular Rumania and Hungary—were confronted with the same problem and were finding it necessary to rid themselves of their Jewish elements. There was no room for the Jews in Europe, and eventually, he thought, they would all have to go.[3]

Clearly, Hitler had convinced Mussolini that Jewish behavior merited banishment.

Hitler also played upon suspicions in the West that the Jews and Jewish sympathizers were leading the world toward war. On January 30, 1939, during a long address to the Reichstag, he declared that Germany did not hate England, America, or France. "Jewish and non-Jewish agitators" had stirred up anti-German passions in the West. Despite Jewish manipulation, he said, Western nations refused to take in these "splendid people." Hitler claimed that Europe would achieve peace and stability only if it resolved the "Jewish Question." He ominously forecast: "If the international Jewish financiers in and outside Europe should succeed in plunging the nations once more into a world war, then the result will not be the bolshevization of the earth, and thus the victory of Jewry, but the annihilation of the Jewish race in Europe!"[4]

Hitler's strategy of raising the "Jewish Question" in order to cast suspicions on Jews across the world achieved some success in the United States. In heated foreign policy debates, many conservatives harped on the alleged link between Jews and communism, and on Jewish influence in the Roosevelt administration and in the American media. Republican William R. Castle Jr., former undersecretary of state, complained in his diary of "Jewish control everywhere. Where the Jews do not actually own the newspapers or the radio stations, they could nonetheless dominate policy because they do own the establishments that do the advertising, and any paper understands that if it publishes something that the Jews do not like, the result will be no more Jewish advertising. The same thing is true of radio stations." Castle's diary indicates that these views were commonplace within his wide circle of friends and acquaintances in politics, business, and finance—mostly Republicans, but with a sprinkling of Democrats.[5]

A New York advertising executive who claimed to support the New Deal wrote the White House that many of his colleagues opposed Roosevelt's foreign policies, and none of them understood why the president seemed preoccupied with attacking the Germans. Roosevelt responded that they should visualize businessmen in Germany and Italy, who breathed and slept only with government permission. If the United States did not assist other democracies in resisting German and Italian plans for expansion, America might find itself hemmed in by authoritarian regimes.[6]

Courtney Letts de Espil, the American-born wife of the Argentine ambassador, wrote in her diary that her close friend Frances Hull, wife of the secretary of state, must have hated an article revealing that she had "sprung from an old Jewish family who are now Episcopalian." She added, "In these days of Jew baiting in Europe it makes even a half-Jew feel more than ordinarily self-conscious about his race—when among gentiles. Particularly in public life. The Germans use Morgenthau and his friendship with F.D.R. as insidious propaganda against the U.S., its president and its form of gov't." She believed that politics had become so poisoned in America that if Hull were to be nominated for president in 1940, the Republicans would target him for pro-Jewish bias.[7]

Nazi propaganda disseminated by American right-wing extremists gave the impression that Jews led and inspired all anti-Nazi sentiment in the United States. Someone sent Secretary of the Interior Harold Ickes a copy of a broadside headlined "Onward Christian Soldiers—to Your Death," claiming that the American people had no quarrel with Germany and Japan, or vice versa. The only people who wanted war, according to "The American Eagles," were the Jews. "The Baruch-Frankfurter-Rosenman-Morgenthau-B'nai-B'rith administration of this Christian Republic," the ad claimed, insulted Germany for acting against the Jews and Japan for defending itself against communism.[8]

Roosevelt tested this climate when he appointed his friend Felix Frankfurter to the Supreme Court. Although Justice Benjamin Cardozo—one of two Jews on the Court—had died in July 1938, FDR seemed to be waiting for the other Jewish justice, eighty-two-year-old Louis D. Brandeis, to resign before he nominated Frankfurter. Attorney General Homer Cummings told the president that the Senate might reject Frankfurter, and Cummings feared the nomination would lend credibility to charges that Roosevelt had "Red" sympathies. In a replay of the Brandeis nomination, a number of prominent Jews, including Arthur Hays Sulzberger of the *New York Times,* organized what Benjamin V. Cohen called the "Jewish protest against Felix's appointment." They urged the president not to encourage anti-Semitism by putting another Jew on the Court. The clamor was sufficiently loud that FDR asked Sumner Welles to draft a letter in the president's name to Julian W. Mack. It said, "Whatever the fears of some timid persons may be . . . citizens of the United States are elected or appointed to positions of responsibility solely because of their qualifications, experience, and character, and without regard to their religious faith." Frankfurter privately expressed his concern about "the number of prominent Jews who are unwittingly embracing Hitlerism. . . . Their suggestion that Jews should not be called to public life because they are Jews is for me completely undistinguishable from Nazism." After *Kristallnacht,* the controversy in Jewish circles died down. On January 5, 1939, FDR announced Frankfurter's nomination, even though Brandeis remained on the Court.[9]

As if to justify fears of a backlash, Democratic senator Pat McCarran of Nevada, a fervent anticommunist and opponent of New Deal programs, attempted to snarl confirmation. He charged that Frankfurter, born in Vienna, was not technically an American citizen, though he arrived at the age of eight and became naturalized five years later, along with his parents. Henry Morgenthau Jr. and Samuel Rosenman located the ship records giving Frankfurter's age, in effect, validating his naturalization. That calmed the storm over Frankfurter, whom the Senate confirmed on a voice vote.[10]

Some 1939 polls show fairly widespread anti-Semitism, with nearly half of Americans agreeing that Jews had too much influence in their country. Yet its most virulent form was limited to fewer than 20 percent of Americans. According to a May 1939 Gallup Poll, just 29 percent of respondents thought there was likely to be "a widespread campaign against Jews" in the United States. Twelve percent admitted they would support such a campaign, with another 8 percent in sympathy.[11]

Both the president and Jewish advocates feared the contagious effect of anti-Semitism on controversial foreign policy issues. As a result, the president avoided new initiatives for refugees. Even proponents of Jewish immigration to the United States sought to adjust the quotas, not fundamentally challenge them. In a late February 1939 speech before the American Committee for the Protection of the Foreign-Born, New York congressman Emanuel Celler praised the Roosevelt administration for admitting 20,000 refugees above the German quota. (This figure apparently lumped together the extension of visitors' visas and the admission of professionals and members of the clergy not subject to the quota limit.) He claimed another 5,000 had entered illegally, and he was working to help some of them stay in the country. Celler and other Jewish members of Congress sought to pool unused immigration quotas from countries other than Germany to admit refugees. He said that some southern and western congressmen had warned him that, in response, they would press to stop all immigration or cut the quotas by half. He urged the delegates to try to change public opinion and build support for refugee bills.[12]

What might appeal to people's consciences, refugee advocates calculated, were the child victims of Nazi Germany. Since 1934, an organization known as German Jewish Children's Aid had helped hundreds of distressed children resettle in the United States. Until mid-1938, the United States could fit some children within the German quota. In 1939, adults and families filled the quota, effectively shutting out unaccompanied children.[13]

Britain had already set a precedent for a special children's measure by admitting 10,000 German-Jewish children in the aftermath of *Kristallnacht*. The first of them arrived in Britain in early December 1938. New York social worker Marion Kenworthy and Francis Pickett of the humanitarian American Friends Service Committee led the campaign for a similar initiative in America, hoping that the children's plight would stir public sympathy. Kenworthy's circle of friends included political and philanthropic figures in New York and Washington, among them Eleanor Roosevelt, whose advice and backing she sought. At a meeting of the President's Advisory Committee on Political Refugees James G. McDonald suggested that by supporting a children's bill in Congress, the administration would stave off more contentious proposals to expand the quotas, which would backfire, he implied.[14]

Secretary of Labor Frances Perkins seems to have taken the lead within the administration to push for an American bill to admit Jewish children outside the quota. In early December 1938, Labor Department official Isador Lubin told Lessing Rosenwald, son of the founder of Sears, that Perkins would back a children's bill in the next Congress. Her intentions alarmed Assistant Secretary of State George Messersmith, still smarting from having lost the last battle with her. They also prompted Undersecretary Welles to write "nothing could be less advisable" than more steps by Labor to expand the quota. Welles pledged to convey his views to the president.[15]

Eleanor Roosevelt talked to her husband and reported that it would be best to "get two people of opposite parties in the House and in the Senate and have them jointly get agreement on the legislation. . . . The State

Department is only afraid of what Congress will say to them. . . . He [FDR] advises that you choose your people rather carefully and if possible get all the Catholic support you can." History and political calculation guided the focus on Catholics. Most Catholics and Jews had chosen different sides during the Spanish Civil War, and American Catholics were not nearly as anti-Nazi as American Jews. Father Charles Coughlin had a large following for his frequently anti-Semitic, anti-Roosevelt broadcasts. The presence of Catholic support thus would help neutralize Catholic fears or resentments about a partisan Jewish cause.[16]

Kenworthy followed FDR's advice. On January 9, fifty religious leaders delivered a petition to the White House and released it to the press. George Cardinal Mundelein of Chicago then became cochairman of what soon became the Non-Sectarian Committee for German Refugee Children. New York senator Robert F. Wagner, the consummate New Deal liberal and a Catholic, sponsored the bill in the Senate.[17]

In late January, Messersmith learned that Wagner's proposed bill would allow anywhere from 10,000 to 30,000 children into the country. Messersmith complained that the draft proposal was too broad and administratively infeasible. An anti-immigration group, Messersmith wrote, was lobbying senators and trying to collect information about the percentage of Jews among current immigrants: "It is quite obvious that under the surface a good deal is brewing which can have very undesirable effects." The assistant secretary believed that "thoughtful and informed Jews" almost unanimously supported his view that such a bill would lead to denunciations of Jews in Congress and in the press. Most ominously, Messersmith implied that support for a children's bill would stymie the administration's foreign policy agenda in Congress.[18]

After apparently concluding that he could not stifle a children's bill, Messersmith advised FDR to let Congress, not the administration, take the initiative. When Jewish comedian Eddie Cantor asked the president to endorse the idea of a children's bill, Messersmith prepared a discouraging response, which presidential secretary Marvin McIntyre sent to Cantor. Michigan Democrat John D. Dingell (father of the contemporary Michigan congressman), who had met with FDR a few days before Wagner did, introduced the first version of the children's bill in the House. Dingell lacked the right political profile for a bipartisan effort. Edith Nourse Rogers, a Massachusetts liberal Republican, then became Wagner's cosponsor of a bill they introduced in both houses on February 9 to allow 10,000 children into the country outside the quota for each of the next two years.[19]

Eleanor Roosevelt endorsed the bill on February 13, the first time she had openly backed any measure on behalf of persecuted Jews. She then asked the president if she could tell Welles that they both supported the children's bill. FDR, who was away on a cruise, said that he would review his options when he returned. On March 6, back in Washington, he received the American Hebrew Medal award, acknowledging it with a letter praising the Constitution for upholding religious freedom and calling for Christians and those who follow the "ancient teachings of Israel" to find unity in the heritage of the Old Testament. He cautiously remained silent about the children's bill.[20]

On March 21, Senator Wagner visited the White House. There is no record of his talk with the president, but after Republican gains in the 1938 midterm elections, FDR preferred to bypass rather than challenge congressional restrictionists directly. The president had not yet won a battle with Congress to revise the Neutrality Acts. He did not relish alienating swing votes over the sensitive issue of immigration quotas. If the two men spoke about the Wagner-Rogers effort, they might have discussed ways to dissuade Americans from thinking that it benefited only Jews.

On March 31, Kenworthy announced that the Quakers would select the 20,000 children—Protestant, Catholic, and Jewish—to be admitted over two years. In truth, many of the non-Jewish candidates were of Jewish descent and considered Jews by the Nazis. An impressive group of intellectuals, churchmen, and labor leaders testified for the bill in hearings before a special joint congressional committee. Former president Herbert Hoover and Republican Senator Arthur Capper of Nebraska endorsed the bill. Roosevelt's 1936 opponent Alf Landon hedged: he supported the idea, but wanted to lower the age limit to children below fourteen and warned of potential future abuse. In addition to Cardinal Mundelein, Catholic support came from Bishop James Edward Freeman of Washington, D.C., and Archbishop John J. Cantwell of Los Angeles.[21]

Critics of the bill charged that any breach of the quota, including an exception for children, was a step on the path to unrestricted immigration. Most Americans apparently agreed. Two-thirds of respondents to a Gallup Poll in March 1939 opposed letting in additional refugee children. Representatives of the American Coalition of Patriotic Societies, the American

Legion, and the Daughters of the American Revolution denounced the Wagner-Rogers bill. Opponents barraged members of Congress and the administration with letters and telegrams of protest. Jacob Billikopf said that although Representative Rogers introduced the bill, she was getting "cold feet" because of protests in her district. At a dinner party, Castle spoke with Rogers about what he called her "miserable bill." Unmoved by the plight of Jewish children, he told Rogers, "I should prefer to let in 20,000 old Jews who would not multiply." Efforts to expand Jewish immigration, he said, "had created a terrible anti-Semitic sentiment throughout the country which might break out in riots if her bill went through." Texas Democratic representative Martin Dies declared that Americans should "stay on our shores and mind our own business." Democratic senator Robert Reynolds of North Carolina claimed that refugees were "systematically building a Jewish empire in this country." He founded a new organization dedicated to shutting out all immigrants. Democratic Congressman Martin Sweeney of Ohio was a strong supporter of Father Coughlin. They represented the outer edge of vocal congressional opposition from FDR's own party that reflected public sentiment.[22]

Retired General George Van Horn Moseley, once a contender for army chief of staff, was among those spreading scare stories about Jews. He declared that one Sears Roebuck store had discharged 200 employees and replaced them with German-Jewish refugees. Others claimed that the Chicago Sears had done the same with 500 employees. A check revealed that there were three German Jewish refugees on the payroll of Sears in Chicago, and all had been additions, not replacements. The Anti-Defamation League found similar rumors about Sears in the South, the Northwest, and the Midwest. Other rumormongers victimized Macy's, Abraham and Straus, and Bloomingdale's.[23]

Expected allies of the Wagner-Rogers bill retreated. Myron C. Taylor declined a request by the wife of retired Supreme Court justice Brandeis to testify before Congress in favor of the bill. Taylor said that advocacy would interfere with his efforts to raise money for resettling Jews abroad. Monsignor Michael Ready, general secretary of the National Catholic Welfare Conference and a member of the President's Advisory Committee on Political Refugees, doubted that conditions in Germany justified bringing German children to the United States. Pickett could not convince him otherwise.[24]

A special House-Senate joint committee reported the bill favorably, but then it followed a tortuous route through the immigration committees of both houses. A late March private poll of senators revealed substantial opposition to the Wagner-Rogers bill, both in the full Senate and in the Senate Immigration Committee. The influential conservative Robert A. Taft, a Republican senator from Ohio, professed sympathy for German refugees and children, but refused to encourage additional immigration. The United States, he claimed, was already doing more than its share. With Wagner rejecting compromise proposals, the American Legion (at least according to Pickett) swayed the House Immigration Committee, dominated by restrictionists, against the bill. Only four of nineteen members there clearly favored it, and eleven seemed firmly opposed.[25]

When Representative Caroline O'Day of New York wrote the president to ask his view in early June, all chance for passage had vanished. He wrote, "File, No Action." During June, the Senate Immigration Committee gutted the bill, giving the children preference but counting them under the quota. The committee also favorably reported bills to halt all immigration for five years and to fingerprint all aliens currently in the United States. Wagner disowned the mutilated version of his bill. It only shuffled refugees within the existing quota, putting children ahead of adults and families at the top of the waiting list. Neither of the other two anti-alien committee bills came up for a final vote in 1939.[26]

Early and forceful support from the president might possibly have salvaged the children's bill before the opposition mobilized effectively, but there would have been a price to pay on foreign policy initiatives. Roosevelt dodged the the moral issue of saving children, perhaps with the rationalization that it benefited only limited numbers. It would not be the only such case. FDR avoided positions that might put at risk his broader goals of mobilizing anti-Nazi opposition and gaining freedom to act in foreign affairs.

The administration still hoped to revive stalled efforts at negotiating with Germany to release and resettle Jews outside the United States. Intergovernmental Committee director George Rublee traveled to Berlin on January 10 and opened a dialogue with German officials. On January 20, Hjalmar Schacht informed Rublee that Hitler had dismissed him as head of the Reichsbank: Schacht indicated that Nazi leaders would thwart any reasonable effort to negotiate the orderly emigration of Jews.[27]

American consul general Raymond Geist arranged for Rublee and his two assistants to meet with Hermann Göring and his financial adviser Helmut Wohlthat. Both men apparently backed further negotiations in spite of opposition from the German Foreign Office and the SS. In the final stage of negotiations Rublee wrote Dean Acheson, "I am amused that I am to receive Brandeis' instructions. What power does he think I have to give effect to them?"[28]

German negotiators pledged to allow 150,000 Jewish emigrants to use a portion of their assets, put into a Nazi-controlled trust, to make some purchases of German-made supplies or equipment, as had been done earlier in the 1933 German agreement with the Jewish Agency for Palestine. However, a large loan from foreign Jewish sources had to cover all costs of resettlement (such as purchases and development of land): the German-Jewish property in trust could only serve as collateral. There was no assurance that the Nazis would allow any Jewish assets to leave Germany.

Nazi intransigence was not the only barrier to freedom for German Jews. Even if negotiations succeeded in authorizing the release of many German Jews, the question remained: Where could they go? The world community had not committed itself to places for resettlement. As a result, the Intergovernmental Committee did not specify the numbers of Jews it could resettle, but only agreed to work on finding havens for them. It was soon to turn over fundraising responsibilities to a new organization (named the Coordinating Foundation). The Intergovernmental Committee and Germany avoided any mutually binding commitments: each side agreed to act independently.[29]

Upon returning to the United States, Rublee told the President's Advisory Committee on Political Refugees that Germany would deny departing Jews access to any foreign exchange. He could hope for a better deal only under the remote scenario that the international climate brightened, outside attacks against Germany died down, the anti-Nazi boycott diminished and German exports improved, and new havens for Jews opened up. Rabbi Stephen S. Wise thought that the Nazis had fooled and trapped Rublee, but Messersmith was relieved that Rublee had not acceded to Germany's demands and offered commercial concessions. Having had enough of an impossible job, Rublee also announced that he planned to resign, with Sir Herbert Emerson of Great Britain replacing him.[30]

Nazi Germany seemed determined to confiscate all Jewish assets, and never made clear how many Jews it would allow to emigrate. If the Intergovernmental Committee found havens for substantial numbers of Jews, Geist, the most knowledgeable American official in Berlin, thought that

Nazi officials would go along. He believed that Göring and Hitler favored the idea of getting rid of Jews soon: Heinrich Himmler, Julius Streicher, and Joseph Goebbels would not venture to oppose them. The Nazis would strip departing Jews of their assets, but they would get out. If American Jews rejected these arrangements and refused to raise money for the proposed new foundation, Geist foresaw chaos. The Gestapo was applying such pressure on German Jews to emigrate that orderly emigration could become impossible. That meant forcing Jews across borders at night, putting Jews without visas on ships nominally sailing to Trinidad or Shanghai, and throwing the burdens of arranging entry and support to others, such as the Joint Distribution Committee.[31]

Rublee believed that even a lopsided agreement was better than a collapse of negotiations. After meeting with Welles and FDR at the White House, Rublee optimistically told reporters that he hoped that orderly emigration would likely replace the current chaotic conditions. He surmised that countries such as Australia, the Dominican Republic, South American nations, and the Philippine Islands, among other places, might shelter emigrating German Jews, although he lacked guarantees from a single prospective refuge. "I was very glad that what I was able to tell him [FDR] was of an encouraging nature," Rublee said, both putting a bright public face on a grim situation and hoping to keep alive flickering prospects for meaningful negotiations with Germany.[32]

If international efforts failed to find places of refuge for Jews, Geist wrote that the Nazis would scuttle negotiations and handle the "Jewish Question" "entirely in their own way." He said, "It will, of course, consist in placing all the able-bodied Jews in work camps, confiscating the wealth of the entire Jewish population, isolating them, and putting additional pressure on the whole community, and getting rid of as many as they can by force." Drawing upon confidential sources within the SS, he had described in rough outline the strategy the SS would pursue during the war and the Holocaust.[33]

Geist was not alone in forecasting catastrophe for German Jewry. On February 22, Lord Anthony de Rothschild, a founder and leader of the Central British Fund for German Jewry, attended the meeting of the President's Advisory Committee on Political Refugees. Rothschild had recently conferred with a number of Jews whom the Nazis had imprisoned in Buchenwald after *Kristallnacht* and who had gone to Britain after their release.

He told the committee that he thought all Jews in Germany would be dead within two years. Refugee advocate Solomon Adler-Rudel, who had fled Germany for Britain, also warned that plans for large-scale immigration were moving so slowly that by the time delegates submitted reports, "the last Jew will have been buried in Germany."[34]

At the request of Wise and Paul Baerwald, both of them members of the President's Advisory Committee, James N. Rosenberg hosted an April 15 meeting of about seventy prominent American Jews to discuss the so-called Rublee plan. A split within the American Jewish Committee blurred the usual divisions between Jewish groups. The conservative advertising magnate Albert D. Lasker was the strongest critic. He charged that the Nazi proposals compelled Western Jews to finance the enslavement of their brethren forced to remain in Germany. Acceptance of massive Nazi confiscation of Jewish assets would also encourage other governments to plunder their Jews. Only governments, not private philanthropists, could finance costly resettlement proposals. Although agreeing with much of Lasker's analysis, Governor Herbert Lehman opposed rejecting outright the initiative of FDR, Taylor, and Rublee. Wise spoke strongly in favor of moving forward: at worst, the Rublee plan was a variant of the Haavara agreement. The group compromised: if Taylor favored the Rublee plan, the Jewish leaders would help to establish a private foundation that would finance resettlement efforts under general, but not purely Jewish, auspices. Taylor quickly agreed to this stipulation.[35]

On April 29, Welles briefed FDR about the divisions among American Jewish leaders. The American Jewish elite did not want to reinforce or sustain the Nazi contention that Jewry was organized internationally; they feared that the Rublee plan condoned Nazi confiscation of Jewish property; and they worried that it might strengthen Nazi Germany. Welles explained that the proposed foundation would have an international and interdenominational board to finance and execute settlement projects. He then hoped to find the still-elusive havens for refugees.[36]

Roosevelt called a White House meeting on May 4 with Taylor, McDonald, McDonald's deputy George Warren, Welles, Jay Pierrepont Moffat, head of the Division of European Affairs in the State Department, and some prominent American Jews. Taylor pointed out that "Goering had as much as said that he had been given six months to come to an understanding with outside Jewry, and that if nothing happened by the end of that time the authorities would chart another [more dire] course." Welles had also earlier read the latest telegram from Geist, which warned that unless places of settlement were opened up very shortly, "the radicals would again gain control in Germany and try to solve the Jewish problem in their own way."[37]

Rosenman recounted the difficulties encountered "in reaching a meeting of minds" regarding a foundation. He wanted an interdenominational body, with the Jews probably in a minority. Taylor said that the Nazis posed the greatest danger to Jews, implying that the refugee crisis represented another manifestation of Europe's enduring "Jewish Question." Moffat wrote in his diary that the president urgently sought the most immediate and practical means for rescuing Jews:

> The President then pointed out that the conversation had convinced him of one essential fact,—namely, that haste was essential. Perhaps some existing organization could be used which would obviate the long delays necessary to setting up a new body. As this was a new idea to most of those present, there was considerable emotion and all the disadvantages were brought out towards using a foreign organization, or a relief organization, or an organization with existing commitments. The President, however, stuck to his point, and said that in his opinion we should tell the Germans in a fortnight,—not one day longer,—that an organization was in existence which could deal with the German Trust. It was not so much a question of the money as it was of actual lives, and the President was convinced that the warnings given by our Embassy in Berlin were sound and not exaggerated.

The group ended up assuring FDR that they would take action within that time.[38]

By May 20, Taylor had a list of ten Jewish and non-Jewish nominees for a board of directors of a private refugee foundation. He offered to go back to London to link this new organization with the Intergovernmental Committee on Refugees. However, the founders failed to raise the start-up capital, and illness delayed Taylor's departure until the end of June. On June 22, Welles summed up FDR's views for the convalescing Taylor. The launching of a new foundation would defuse Germany's charge that its Western critics had obstructed the resettlement of Jews. Even the placement of some funds in bank accounts represented a step forward. Finally, FDR criticized the growing defeatist attitude among leaders of free nations on the challenges posed by refugees. He said that the settlement of refugees—Christian and

Jewish—in new homes throughout the world "would be a tremendous factor in bringing about peaceful conditions in the world during the years to come." This was Roosevelt looking for ways to sell his program to opponents of confrontation with Germany—and looking past the immediate threat of war. In late July, Welles told other State Department officials that the Intergovernmental Committee on Refugees had to consider all refugees present or future, not limited to Germany: "this had always been the President's idea and . . . it was a constructive idea,—more prevention than cure."[39]

Jewish officials and their non-Jewish allies took more than two months to establish the Coordinating Foundation, and it did not choose its director, former Belgian prime minister Paul van Zeeland, until August, just before the outbreak of war in Europe. Private initiative had proven no substitute for concerted action by governments, but world leaders had declined to act collectively or to put resources into resettlement proposals.[40]

FDR's political strategy failed to adapt to the approach of war. He believed that Americans would back rescue efforts only if persuaded that a solution of the "Jewish Question" in Germany would help keep the peace and aid persecuted Christians as well. The president and refugee advocates failed to generate much interest outside Jewish circles in resettlement plans. Moreover, the larger the scope of FDR's vision, the more difficult it became to muster support or to implement a limited program to rescue German Jews before the advent of war. FDR wanted to have it both ways: a long-range solution to an overcrowded, boiling Europe and a short-range rescue plan for German Jewry in advance of war. He achieved neither objective in 1939.

As signs of impending war swept across Europe during the summer of 1939, Roosevelt indicated that he still expected the Intergovernmental Committee on Refugees to convene as planned in Washington during October. On August 23, McDonald met with Welles about the president's agenda. Germany and the Soviet Union announced a nonaggression treaty—the Hitler-Stalin Pact—on that day, and Poland now seemed doomed. Though preoccupied with the general crisis, Welles recited now familiar goals: dramatizing the needs of refugees; finding places of settlement; gaining international cooperation; and possibly securing government financing. McDonald complained that if the United States refused "to throw something into the pot," it should cancel the international meeting. He reminded Welles that in November FDR had spoken of possibly requesting substantial funds from Congress. Welles noted the administration's dearth of victories on the Hill lately: FDR would not ask for an appropriation without at least an even chance of success. McDonald noticed Welles's general pessimism, concluding that if war broke out, all intergovernmental activity for refugees would cease.[41]

On September 1, Germany invaded Poland and the British and French declared war on Germany two days later. As Poland under Nazi rule descended into darkness and Italy and Eastern European countries persecuted Jews in their midst, many Jewish organizations expanded relief efforts where feasible. Other Jewish leaders believed that only a Jewish-controlled Palestine could finally resolve Europe's urgent and recurring "Jewish Question." The executive secretary of the non-Zionist American Jewish Committee explained,

> There is less ground today for opposition to the "Jewish National Home" development and even to political Zionism than there was before Hitler's accession to power, because in spite of the many mistakes made by the Zionists in the past, it is widely recognized that had there been no Zionist movement, Palestine today would still largely be a desert, with as little opportunity for the settlement of Jews as British Guiana or Madagascar.[42]

Despite the war, both the president and members of his Political Advisory Committee on Political Refugees hoped to continue the Intergovernmental Committee on Refugees and the Coordinating Foundation. Even with diminished capacity, these organizations could assist roughly 200,000 refugees who had already fled Germany but lacked permanent homes, becoming the modern world's wandering Jews. Their ranks would likely swell as more refugees clamored to flee war-torn Europe. Still, advocates for refugees faced opposition at home and abroad from those who opposed what they saw as special treatment for Jews amid the ravages of war.[43]

Leading members of the President's Advisory Committee on Political Refugees urged the White House to cancel the October meeting of the Intergovernmental Committee on Refugees. They warned that a public meeting between the president and Lord Winterton, a member of both the committee and the British government, would undercut FDR's claim that America intended to remain neutral in the war. Beyond that, the war seemed to guarantee that neither the British nor the American government would appropriate funds for refugees. Finally, Jewish leaders feared a public backlash if policy-makers seemed preoccupied with helping the Jews.[44]

The British sought to kill international rescue efforts outright. Two weeks before the war, Lewis L. Strauss, Hoover's former aide and confidant, traveled to London. He related to Hoover that both British cabinet members and "prominently placed private citizens" shared widespread skepticism about any "larger project" for resettling refugees. They thought Germany would permit Jews to leave during the war only to relieve an economic burden in Germany or to send them abroad as German agents. Consequently, the British balked at encouraging further Jewish emigration from Germany. For financial and political reasons, Britain ruled out any settlement of refugees in any British possession during the war, including in British Guiana. A few days later, Kennedy reported a British compromise offer: neutral countries might carry on the remigration efforts of the Intergovernmental Committee on Refugees, but countries at war with Germany should not.[45]

FDR could easily have abandoned contentious refugee issues without paying a political price. Instead, the Roosevelt administration held the Intergovernmental Committee on Refugees meeting at the White House on October 17. Neither the British nor the French sent formal government representatives. Roosevelt told the group that refugee initiatives had been going well, if slowly, until war broke out. He put a bright face on a tortuous process that had not yielded significant results.

Roosevelt said he wanted to help immediately displaced persons in countries of temporary refuge who needed permanent homes—perhaps 200,000–300,000 people. A more daunting task awaited the end of the war—the resettlement of perhaps ten or twenty million displaced persons. The president hoped to populate sparsely settled areas of the world, and said that ambitious economic and engineering studies must begin during the war. After van Zeeland later proposed to raise with government guarantees loans of $20 million for resettlement immediately and $80 million later for long-term projects, Roosevelt responded to Welles,

> Mr. van Zeeland's plan is on the whole good but I think misses the *psychology* which is necessary to success. . . . The outline does not stimulate my imagination or that of the average individual in the civilized world to picture the huge rounded out project which could affect many millions of our fellow beings. . . . Somebody has to breathe heart and ideals on a large scale into this whole subject if it is to be put into effect on a world-wide basis.

Again, Roosevelt overlooked the immediate problems for a long-term program—in effect, giving up on emergency rescue.[46]

Hope for one daring American settlement proposal lingered into the early months of the war. Secretary of Labor Perkins had supported moving Jewish refugees into vacant Alaskan lands by instituting a separate Alaskan quota, and Lubin, commissioner of the Bureau of Labor Statistics, hosted a strategy meeting in early 1939 for interested Jewish immigration advocates. Interior Department official Felix Cohen presented a report indicating that industrious immigrants would boost the Alaskan economy and an expanded population would bolster the national defense.[47]

Michael Chabon's creative 2007 novel *The Yiddish Policemen's Union,* about an imaginary Alaska peopled by millions of Jews descended from resettled refugees, has brought renewed attention to this 1939–1940 Alaskan territory scheme. The novelist represented the darkest fears of a State Department legal adviser at the time: "these refugees would, nearly all of them, belong to a particular race. If they should remain in the territory they would sooner or later obtain control thereof, . . . and this would raise various problems."[48]

The plan did not get far. Despite his own Jewish roots, Ernest Gruening, an official in the Interior Department and then the appointed governor of the Alaskan territory, rejected the scheme. Undersecretary of the Interior Henry Slattery became its official sponsor, rather than Nathan Margold or Cohen, its senior proponents in Interior: for domestic consumption, the "Slattery plan" sounded better politically than the "Cohen plan." Secretary of the Interior Ickes strongly backed the plan. For the State Department, no matter what the name, it was another end-run around immigration restrictions. Even Welles advised FDR that implementation would require new laws limiting immigration from Alaska into the forty-eight states. Roosevelt clearly liked the idea of developing sparsely settled lands, mixing Jews with others, and using private funds. FDR surprised Ickes by the amount of thought he had put into "a minor matter."[49]

In typical fashion, Roosevelt did not back either Interior or State decisively. To reduce his political jeopardy, he suggested limiting Jewish refugees in Alaska to 10 percent of the incoming population. That restriction deprived the Slattery plan of much of its "rescue value." Jewish leaders did not unanimously favor the plan. Billikopf wrote to Maurice Hexter that Albert Einstein was enthusiastic about possibilities in Alaska, but that his own attitude was "distinctively negative." He said that he had forwarded "a copy of a super-confidential report which my brother-in-law Bob Marshall, and two associates had prepared for Secretary Wallace—a report about Alaska and which pointed out the insuperable difficulties involved in set-tling refugees." An official of the Emergency Committee for Zionist Affairs reported Brandeis's view that Alaska might boomerang as the Wagner-Rogers bill had done: "It will be understood that admitting refugees to Alaska means admitting them to the United States."[50]

In February 1940, Senator William H. King of Utah and Representative Frank Havenner of California, both Democrats, introduced a bill for Alas-kan settlement that the Interior Department had helped to draft. As with the Wagner-Rogers bill of 1939, the White House neither endorsed nor op-posed the legislation. Many Alaskans vocally opposed an influx of Jews, and Gruening lobbied effectively against the bill, which remained stalled indefinitely in committees of both the House and the Senate.[51]

During 1939, FDR knew that his political opponents would thwart any proposal to appropriate large sums for the resettlement of Jewish refugees in other lands or expand American quotas. Any attempt to breach the quota system would both give nativists and anti-Semites ammunition and em-power the isolationist bloc in Congress that bitterly opposed loosening the Neutrality Acts. Whether or not he was fully correct in these judgments, he was not far off, as demonstrated by the failure of Congress to pass the Wagner-Rogers bill, a measure with bipartisan sponsorship and humanitar-ian appeal.

Despite sympathy for the cause of Jewish refugees, during 1939 Roose-velt avoided any public moral stands that would endanger his standing with Congress and his capacity to conduct an increasingly anti-Nazi foreign policy. The outbreak of war made all practical resettlement efforts far more difficult. The war also transformed FDR from a sponsor of humanitarian action into a hard-fisted guardian of national security and opponent of Nazi and fascist aggression—the third Roosevelt.

CHAPTER NINE

Tightened Security

DURING WARS, AMERICANS often feared subversion by aliens. Even before the United States formally entered World War I, President Woodrow Wilson had decried those immigrants who allegedly "have poured the poison of disloyalty into the very arteries of our national life. . . . They are not many but they are infinitely malignant, and the hand of our power should close over them at once." FDR had personally experienced this fear of an alien threat while serving in 1917 as assistant secretary of the navy. Informed of a possible German plot against him, the thirty-five-year-old Roosevelt began to carry a revolver. His concerns two decades later about a German "Trojan Horse" in the United States grew out of his World War I experiences.[1]

In 1938, the Federal Bureau of Investigation (FBI) reminded FDR of the dangers of German espionage when it uncovered a Nazi spy ring in New York City. The operation included German military intelligence agents, one codenamed "Sex"; German American volunteers, including a femme fatale; and a German American veteran of the U.S. Army who hoped to steal Army mobilization plans for the East Coast. The FBI's tracking of the network and the arrest and trial of four of the hapless spies triggered one of the biggest news stories of 1938. On October 8 that year, after a meeting with New York district attorney Lamar Hardy, FDR told the press that government needed better coordination and increased funds to deal with rising foreign espionage.[2]

The *Washington Post* observed that in free and open America "spies can operate with more impunity than in any other large nation." It said that international espionage had reached unprecedented peacetime levels and that in the event of war, "control of the espionage business is certain to become a major problem for the American government far surpassing in gravity the racketeering and kidnapping challenges to the Federal Bureau of Investigation." The German spy case inspired the Warner Brothers film *Confessions of a Nazi Spy,* released in April 1939. Jack and Harry Warner both supported FDR politically, and Hollywood insiders dubbed Warner Bros. the "Roosevelt studio." Their movie, the first direct critique of Nazi Germany to hit American screens, also exposed Hitler's mania for global conquest. It prompted protests and threats of retaliation from the German government even before its release in theaters.[3]

After the outbreak of war in Europe, the president put the FBI, which he bolstered with 150 new agents, in charge of all investigations of espionage, sabotage, subversion, and violations of Neutrality Acts. He told the press that he was guarding against a repeat of the subversive activity that had plagued the nation before America's entry into World War I. Attorney General Frank Murphy promised that the FBI would chase enemy agents from their "happy hunting ground." The *New York Times* warned that the nation was in the grip of a potentially dangerous "spy mania" that could threaten "people's rights and privileges."[4]

In early January 1940, Commissioner of Immigration James Houghteling reported to Roosevelt that the House had passed a bill to fingerprint immigrants six months earlier, but other controversial clauses stymied it in the Senate. Houghteling mentioned that his boss, Secretary of Labor Frances Perkins, opposed the fingerprinting of aliens. He also noted that Congress seemed inclined to cut immigration quotas, a goal that he apparently shared.[5]

Perkins, the administration's most forthright champion of refugees, made a good target for Roosevelt's opponents, some of whom falsely claimed that she was Jewish. In late January, FDR overrode Perkins and asked her in consultation with the attorney general and secretary of state to issue an executive order for the fingerprinting of immigrants, some of whom might be criminals, spies, or saboteurs. Some political refugees might also become targets for assassination by agents of their home countries, Roosevelt argued. Ready identification would protect the country and keep refugees safe, he told Perkins. FDR diminished Perkins's control over refugees and other immigration issues when he transferred Immigration and Naturalization from the Labor Department to Justice in June.[6]

Robert Jackson, whom FDR had appointed attorney general earlier that year, declared that the transfer would achieve "a more strict control of the privilege of entering this country." He pledged that no alien "shall be admitted unless it affirmatively appears to be for the American interest." Like FDR's previous attorney generals, Homer S. Cummings and Frank Murphy, Jackson was a Roosevelt loyalist. He had taken a lead role in advocating on behalf of FDR's ill-fated Supreme Court packing plan. It is unlikely that Jackson would have made such statements without at least the president's tacit approval.[7]

By then, the war had taken an ominous turn that took the world by surprise. After Germany conquered Poland and Germany and the Soviet Union partitioned it between them, the fighting virtually ceased on the continent. FDR had told his British friend Arthur Murray that the French and British must have used the delay to prepare for German attacks. However, in the spring of 1940, Germany launched lightning attacks—the *Blitzkrieg*—across much of Western Europe. On April 9, Germany invaded neutral Denmark by land, sea, and air, and German troops landed in Norway, another neutral nation. On May 10, Germany attacked the Low Countries (the Netherlands, Belgium, and Luxembourg) and France. By invading France through neutral Belgium, the Nazi armies outflanked France's supposedly impregnable Maginot Line of defense. Within days, German forces penetrated deeply into France, and by late May had trapped 340,000 British and French troops at Dunkirk. Only a near miraculous evacuation by sea across the English Channel saved most from slaughter or capture and left Britain with an army to continue the war. On June 14, triumphant German troops entered Paris. A new authoritarian French government quickly replaced the collapsed Third Republic and set up headquarters in the resort town of Vichy. In barely more than a month, one of the world's great democratic powers had become a hapless partitioned state. An armistice with Germany splintered France it into a northern and western coastal zone that Germany occupied, a southern zone controlled by the new Vichy regime, and a small slice of southeastern France occupied by the Italians.[8]

Some observers believed that subversion led to the defeat of the Nazis' targets. American reporters attributed Hitler's rapid conquest of Norway not to German military prowess, but to a "Fifth Column" of German spies and sympathizers betraying Norway from within; they warned that the same thing could happen in the United States. Overlooking the French military mistakes, Ambassador to France William Bullitt largely blamed a Nazi and communist Fifth Column for the fall of France. Returning to the United States in the summer of 1940, Bullitt pressed this message upon America's highest government officials. He specifically claimed that many Nazi agents had entered France as Jewish refugees.[9]

British intelligence officials, operating in the United States under the organization called British Security Coordination, spread fears about the dubious loyalties of refugees. Britain itself interned enemy aliens, including German Jews, en masse, screening them carefully. British Security Coordination head William Stephenson developed a close relationship with the FBI, which harbored its own suspicions of aliens. For J. Edgar Hoover, fears of an internal enemy also justified a major expansion of the FBI, and he fought against military intelligence officials to preserve the FBI's jurisdiction over internal security. Sherman Miles, head of American military intelligence, also believed that internal subversion had weakened France and could similarly afflict the United States.[10]

FDR's World War I crony Breckinridge Long, brought into the State Department recently as assistant secretary of state for special war problems, noted that Sumner Welles, at FDR's request, led a discussion of how to shield the United States from German and Soviet agents. Long claimed that German agents on temporary visas had infiltrated America, and that most Labor Department officials refused to cooperate in weeding them out. He saw Visa Division chief Avra Warren and Hoover as allies in his crusade against alien spies and agents.[11]

Long was a Princeton graduate and a scion of the renowned Breckinridge family that claimed six members of the U.S. House of Representatives, two U.S. senators, and a vice president of the United States. He had served in the State Department during World War I where he met and became friends with FDR. Like Roosevelt, Long ran as a Democrat for high office in 1920, losing a bid to become U.S. senator from Missouri. He contributed generously to Roosevelt's 1932 campaign and served as his floor manager at the Democratic Convention that year. The president rewarded him with an appointment as ambassador to Italy. Long had ties to members of Congress in both parties, particularly among isolationists. He was ambitious, anti-immigrant, and underhanded.

Long memorialized his xenophobia and his prejudices in his diary. In retrospect, his influence just before and during the Holocaust was so damaging to humanitarian efforts and so visible to posterity that some have personified him as *the* villain responsible for an immoral American policy. Others have cast Long as symbolic of the retrograde State Department, although he was not a career State Department official.

In late 1938, White House adviser Benjamin V. Cohen had written a savage critique of some key Foreign Service personnel and State Department officials. Cohen claimed that Ambassador to Germany Hugh Wilson and other officials in the embassy in Berlin had become unwitting tools of the Nazis. The wife of State Department Adviser on Political Relations James Dunn openly expressed pro-Nazi views, and Dunn was not much better. Cohen editorialized:

> If we are going to fight this Nazi disease, which is spreading quickly through their mad ambition, we must fight it with all the means we have. It is not only a question of spending billions for defense that is important, but it is just as important to fight them with right ideas[.] [W]e must have men in our State Department who represent our ideas. . . . Can't something be done to clean out just a few State Department men or must this go on? I don't see why the President permits it.

By mid-1940, the climate in the State Department was, if anything, more hostile than before to Jewish immigrants, because the country moved to the right.[12]

Still, the State Department included some outliers. FDR's confidant, the politically liberal Welles, shared his concern for the plight of refugees. Through meetings with the president and connections with other policymakers, Herbert Feis had backed FDR's refugee initiatives. Assistant Secretary of State Adolf A. Berle was more conservative and less anti-Nazi than Welles, but occasionally sympathetic to Jewish concerns. In February 1940, he had suggested an official American protest "based on straight humanity" after Germany had deported virtually the entire Jewish population of the city of Stettin to the Lublin region in eastern Poland. Arguing that any public expression would open the United States to charges of interfering with German sovereignty, Long blocked Berle's initiative. Months later, Justice Department solicitor general Francis Biddle sought Berle's assistance in enabling three psychoanalyst professors to obtain visas as professionals outside the quota. They had not worked recently, and a strict interpretation of immigration law called for them to show continuous employment. Berle recognized that by stripping Jews of jobs, Nazi persecution made such regulations unworkable; he intervened to try to remove the obstacle.[13]

Pervasive fears of threats to American security in the spring and summer of 1940 resembled the climate of opinion in the United States after the terrorist acts against the World Trade Center on September 11, 2001. Within popular culture, newsreels, radio broadcasts, documentaries, and popular books echoed dire warnings about a Nazi Fifth Column operating within the United States. In validation, a Roper Poll in June 1940 found that only 2.7 percent of the public thought the government was doing enough about the Fifth Column threat. New watchdog groups arranged antifascist rallies and publicity campaigns. Such emotions stiffened resistance to immigration in the Roosevelt administration and among the political elite.[14]

In late April, Berle wrote that he had become increasingly wary of subversive refugees. These fears heightened after Berle became the State Department's coordinator of intelligence. In this capacity, he dealt with leaders of the FBI, military intelligence, and naval intelligence, all of whom fretted about German and communist espionage abetted by Jewish refugees.[15]

In May, Welles, who also believed that Fifth Column subversion contributed to Norway's conquest, asked Long to help tighten the scrutiny of immigrants. Long claimed, probably correctly, that this shift in policy had FDR's support. George Messersmith, now ambassador to Cuba, found that many Germans and Italians who had left their countries because of persecution spoke positively about their native governments. In some cases, Messersmith claimed, government officials had coerced their cooperation by threatening relatives at home. He suggested that Washington should examine every visa case "with a fine toothcomb" even after consular approval. Even Secretary of the Interior Harold Ickes, who thought some "superpatriots" were going crazy, favored the careful scrutiny of aliens.[16]

Hoover sent almost daily reports to the president on Nazi and communist subversion. Some of them were farfetched, but FDR could not ignore their cumulative weight. On May 21, in a confidential memo he personally drafted for Attorney General Jackson, FDR asserted that the defense of the nation justified wiretapping without court order against persons suspected of "subversive activities against the Government of the United States, including suspected spies. You are requested . . . to limit these investigations . . . to a minimum and to limit them in so far as possible to aliens."[17]

Roosevelt believed Republcians would exploit politically any lapses in guarding the nation. GOP strategists expected that the 1940 elections would extend their gains from 1938 and perhaps even create an opportunity to recapture the presidency. FDR would let different agencies and individuals dispute the trade-off between protecting the nation and rescuing refugees, while adjudicating where necessary. Still, the general wartime direction was clear: a security-conscious administration would curtail the admission of immigrants and visitors to the United States. In theory, Roosevelt remained committed to resettlement efforts abroad. In practice, his government could not credibly press other Western Hemisphere countries to take in Jewish refugees while reducing its own admissions.

At a June 5 press conference, in response to a question about refugees, FDR said that, as in other countries, American authorities had uncovered some cases of refugees serving involuntarily as spies, because the Nazis threatened their relatives: "It has been spying under compulsion, and it is an amazing story that we have rather fully. Of course, it applies to a very, very small percentage of refugees coming out of Germany, but it does apply, and therefore, it is something that we have to watch. Isn't it rather a horrible thing?"[18]

Some of Roosevelt's Republican opponents saw Jewish spying as the natural result of Jewish greed. After hearing that many Jews staying at the Warwick Hotel in Philadelphia had German maids, William R. Castle wrote in his diary, "I have always said that if you want to find the German Fifth Column in the United States look among the Jews because that is where you would least expect to find them. . . . You talk about a great deal of the loyalty of Jews to other Jews but I think that is bunk, at least when it comes to balancing the loyalties with the lure of money"—presumably payoffs from Hitler's government.[19]

In early June, the State Department tightened visa controls. Applicants now had to show a legitimate purpose for entering the United States, not just good reasons for leaving Europe. American consuls in Europe had to determine that applicants were not likely to engage in radical activities that might endanger public safety. In order to "safeguard the best interests of the United States" consuls must withhold visas unless they had "no doubt whatsoever concerning the alien."[20]

Later that month, Long and Warren devised additional means for delaying and preventing both the permanent and temporary entry of Europeans into the United States. The State Department had spent years asserting and defending the discretion of the individual consul to grant or withhold visas according to the merits of each case. But now, Long wrote, consuls could issue nonimmigrant visas only if they had prior authorization from Washington. Private instructions could exclude specific nationalities. With regard to immigration visas, State could advise "consuls to put every obstacle in the way and to require additional evidence and to resort to various administrative advices which would postpone and postpone and postpone. . . ." Long wrote triumphantly in his diary, "The cables practically stopping immigration went!"[21]

Despite Long's declaration of victory, Solicitor General Biddle suggested using a small part of a relief appropriation to bring children victimized by war to the United States. Biddle wanted to send an American ship to Bordeaux, France, to pick up displaced children, who, unlike adults, posed no threat to U.S. security. At the same time, German bombing of British cities created a groundswell of American support for evacuating British children to the United States. Eleanor Roosevelt supported both ventures. The president asked her to delay any action until the State Department could formulate a clear policy on children in danger. On June 20, refugee advocates conferred in New York and established the United States Committee for the Care of European Children, which chose Eleanor as honorary president and department store magnate Marshall Field as president. This committee and other groups sought to arrange sponsors in the United States and to push for visas for children, an initiative that Long predictably opposed, but Justice officials supported. Although it was often difficult to get Vichy France or Nazi Germany to grant exit permits, some organizations occasionally succeeded. As late as April 1941, German Jewish Children's Aid secured visas for a small number of German-Jewish children.[22]

James G. McDonald and the President's Advisory Committee on Political Refugees offered to screen applicants for visitors' visas and to present affidavits of financial support and vouchers of good character from American sponsors of adult refugees. In effect, they backed an emergency program to issue visitors' visas to those who faced death after the German conquest of France. The emergency visitors' visas might have helped bring Jews and others imperiled by the Nazis to the United States. On June 19, McDonald and two other members of the committee met with Eleanor Roosevelt in New York; she later conferred with the president, who suggested that the members meet with Welles and Biddle. If these two failed to satisfy the committee, FDR said the committee could report to him. Hamilton Fish Armstrong, editor of *Foreign Affairs,* wrote to FDR's secretary Edwin "Pa" Watson: "I am sure that the President is anxious for our laws to be interpreted liberally in this crisis. . . . Certainly Secretary Hull and Under-Secretary Welles are in entire sympathy with the President. . . . I am not sure that the same is true of all the subordinate officials, in the Department or abroad." This struggle for influence and for visas played out over many months. A few sponsors of visas got their candidates through; most did not.[23]

In August 1940, Rabbi Max Nussbaum and his wife arrived in the United States from Berlin, showing that it was still possible for some German Jews to escape Nazi Germany and relocate. Nussbaum spoke about the dangers for Jews within Nazi reach at a luncheon for authorities on foreign policy at the *New York Times.* He said that the Nazis were considering a plan to ship four million Jews to the island of Madagascar—if France agreed to cede it to the Germans. This contingency plan represented one means for satisfying Nazi hopes of cleansing Europe of Jews. A year later, the Nazis would turn to more efficient and horrific methods. Then Arthur Sulzberger arranged for Nussbaum to brief Treasury Secretary Henry Morgenthau Jr., who asked Nussbaum whether he knew any Jews who worked for the Gestapo. Nussbaum conceded that in Paris the Gestapo did put pressure on Jews who had relatives remaining in Germany—mostly to carry out small tasks, such as reporting on conversations of emigrants in cafés. In Germany, the Gestapo targeted Polish Jews who needed official permission to stay. Nussbaum said that the Gestapo had better ways of sending spies abroad, such as giving Gestapo agents the names of Jews who had died in concentration camps and equipping them with false passports stamped with the "J" required for Jews. His answers probably did not reassure Morgenthau about safely admitting refugees to America.[24]

On the day Morgenthau received Nussbaum, the Portuguese steamship SS *Quanza* docked unexpectedly in Norfolk, Virginia. The eighty-six passengers, all German Jews, had Mexican transit visas, and some had permanent visas for Venezuela. In an eerie replay of the *St. Louis* affair, Mexican authorities had refused them permission to land. This time, however, Hitler had already overrun much of Europe, and American quotas were largely unfilled. The *Quanza* passengers also numbered less than 10 percent of those aboard the *St. Louis.* According to an account by Rabbi Stephen S. Wise at the time, the president offered American asylum for the *Quanza* refugees in response to an appeal from Field and Eleanor Roosevelt. Still, the passengers had to overcome bureaucratic obstacles. The President's Advisory Committee on Political Refugees won approval for its allies in the Justice Department to admit the passengers to the United States. Long then reluctantly gave his approval to accept some of the refugees temporarily. He tried too late to rescind this authorization after learning that Justice officials had cleared all the passengers for admission.[25]

If Long lost the *Quanza* battle, he quietly won the war on refugees. On July 15, Visa Division chief Warren arrived in Lisbon and, according to American minister Herbert Pell, "explained in detail the policy which had been adopted by the Department to meet the situation caused by the turn of military events in France. . . . Visas should be granted only when there was no doubt whatsoever concerning the alien." Warren went on to the American consulates in Switzerland, Germany, Sweden, and perhaps elsewhere, where he apparently affirmed the same tough interpretation of previous State Department instructions and telegrams. This squeeze from Washington made visas very scarce even for those few whom the President's Advisory Committee on Political Refugees had preapproved.[26]

Margaret Jones, representative of the American Friends Service Committee in Vienna, wrote to friends: "I had a conference with Warren when he was in Vienna a few weeks ago—there is absolutely no chance for *anyone,* except in most unusual cases. FDR doesn't want any more aliens from Europe—refugees have been implicated in espionage—and so forth. All part of the spy hysteria. (What kind of a USA am I coming back to??? I am almost afraid to face it.)" She returned to a country not only fearful of aliens, but also rife with ethnic and religious tensions.[27]

In the late 1930s, Father Charles Coughlin had stirred up considerable Catholic anti-Semitism when he founded a right-wing, paramilitary group known as the Christian Front, which urged patriots to "act, buy and vote Christian." Coughlin's sermons and magazine, *Social Justice,* became overtly pro-Nazi. Although Coughlin's radio audience shriveled, his still sizable following included Irish, Italian, and Polish Catholics anxious to prove their Americanism by enlisting in an anticommunist campaign laced with attacks on Jews. The Catholic Church's top media star, Bishop Fulton J. Sheen of *The Catholic Hour* on NBC, backed the Christian Front. So did the Church's most outspoken editor, Father Patrick Scanlon of the widely circulated *Brooklyn Tablet.* Like Coughlin, Scanlon thought Jews had gained "influence, affluence, and power—and so often use it against Christians." The nation's leading prelate, Cardinal Francis J. Spellman of New York, ignored pleas to denounce the Christian Front. Father James Gillis, another "radio priest" who also edited *The Catholic World,* wrote a syndicated column, and contributed to *The Catholic Hour,* joined Coughlin in opposing Roosevelt's foreign and domestic policies. In 1940, the FBI arrested seventeen Christian Front thugs for sedition. However, Coughlin's standing with anticommunist churchmen insulated him from official reprisals. Both Congress and the FBI declined to investigate Coughlin's involvement in the Christian Front.[28]

Roosevelt sought to dampen anti-Jewish sentiment and strengthen his standing among Catholics. He wrote to Myron C. Taylor, now his envoy to the Vatican, that "there is a great deal of anti-Jewish feeling in the dioceses of Brooklyn, Baltimore, and Detroit and this feeling is said to be encouraged by the church." Probably influenced by his experience in the state and national campaign of 1928, he asked Taylor to spread the word that "if anti-Jewish feeling is stirred up, it automatically stirs up anti-Catholic feeling and that makes a general mess." He also summoned home Ambassador Joseph Kennedy from Britain to assure Catholic voters of his peaceful intent.[29]

In late 1939, a nationwide Gallup Poll had found that respondents preferred Roosevelt to any challenger, although most said that they would have backed a Republican candidate in the absence of war abroad. Secretary of State Cordell Hull hoped to replace FDR as the Democratic nominee in 1940, and Texas conservatives promoted Vice President John Nance Garner as their choice for president. None of his Democratic challengers matched Roosevelt's anti-Nazi record.

After Roosevelt decided to run for an unprecedented third term, he dropped Garner from his ticket in favor of liberal visionary Henry A. Wallace, his secretary of agriculture. When the Republican Convention convened on June 24, just after Nazi troops marched into Paris, delegates hoped for salvation from George Washington's two-term tradition. The retired but still astute National Committee member Charles Hilles wrote, "The campaign will boil down to two issues, the international and the third term. But for the third term it would be difficult to beat Roosevelt. But for the world crisis Roosevelt would fade from the scene."[30]

Among GOP contenders, Senator Robert A. Taft of Ohio had become FDR's most incisive critic, but Taft lacked popular appeal and lagged in the polls. Thomas Dewey, the district attorney in New York City, had a certain romantic allure and swept the party primaries. However, the thirty-eight-year-old New York crime-fighter had never held public office above county prosecutor and was a risky candidate in perilous times. With no candidate breaking clear of the pack, dark horse Wendell Willkie outraced the field. Although a utility executive, Willkie was an internationalist, a civil libertarian, and a Democrat until 1939. Yet Willkie earned conservative stripes as a warrior for private enterprise. He benefited from a skillful publicity campaign guided by industrialists, bankers, and publishers who opposed the New Deal but favored preparedness and aid to Britain. "The election of Willkie will result in no diminution of assistance to the British," Columbia University alumnus George A. Ellis assured his alma mater's president, Nicholas Murray Butler, during the campaign. "Roosevelt's reelection will almost certainly precipitate this country into a war for which it is in no way prepared, and the result of which may be disastrous rather than beneficial to the British."[31]

Right-wing anti-Semites such as Gerald L. K. Smith, Father Coughlin and anticommunist author Elizabeth Dilling closed ranks behind Willkie, although he repudiated such support. Dilling declared it "a Christian's duty" to ignore the moderate Republican's me-too campaign and "protest at the polls against New Deal dictatorship, Red treason and war, by voting for Willkie." Two thousand delegates to the World Christian Fundamentals Association, founded by anti-Semitic minister William Bell Riley, denounced the president for pushing "to involve us in the European war for the express purpose of perpetuating their unconstitutional regime." The real "fifth column," the association claimed, consisted of "third termites who seek to sacrifice youth on a foreign battlefield in order to advance their greed for political power."[32]

Roosevelt believed that some of his isolationist opponents, notably national hero Charles Lindbergh, had turned disloyal to democracy. He wrote to the Republican Henry Stimson (whom he appointed as his new secretary of war), "Lindbergh has completely abandoned his belief in our form of government and has accepted Nazi methods for America because apparently they are efficient." With his friend Morgenthau, FDR was even blunter: he was "absolutely convinced that Lindbergh was a Nazi." Although unfair to Lindbergh, the president was not completely off-target about all isolationists. Months earlier, Castle had written, "When democracy degenerates into socialism a form of dictatorship of the right is better for the nation."[33]

Inside battles over refugees erupted during the campaign. In late September, Long bypassed his adversary, Solicitor General Biddle, and convinced Attorney General Jackson that there should be meticulous supervision of immigration, that visa requirements were inadequate, and that Justice should defer to State on visa questions. On October 2, Ambassador to the Soviet Union Laurence Steinhardt, the only American ambassador who was Jewish, gave Long invaluable support. In a long cable, Steinhardt opposed loosening visa regulations for anyone and rebuked the President's Advisory Committee on Political Refugees for undermining America's security. He also accused unnamed (Jewish) organizations of using subterfuge to bring in persons of dubious citizenship potential. Steinhardt argued that so many Jews and others in Soviet territory had friends or relatives in the United States that any liberal program would overwhelm the capacities of his embassy. He hoped for a firmer State Department stance against the visa-sponsoring organizations after the elections.[34]

In Rabbi Wise's diametrically opposite view, the State Department made many promises, but delivered little or nothing for refugees. He correctly feared that State had privately instructed the consuls to withhold visas. Wise thought State Department officials were trying to protect FDR before the elections by keeping out any conceivably disruptive radicals. Wise put the reelection of Roosevelt above the admission of a small number of refugees. Earlier, he had written Cohen that the country needed FDR: "no one else can serve the country today, and after 1941, as he can." Wise wanted to do battle over refugee policy only after the election.[35]

McDonald continued to press the administration on refugee issues. Through Eleanor Roosevelt, he arranged a meeting with FDR to question Long's visa maneuvers. However, Long had the president read Steinhardt's telegram beforehand. FDR told Long he approved policies to exclude any suspicious aliens, no matter how prestigious their sponsors. When McDonald and his executive secretary George Warren joined Biddle and Henry Hart from Justice at the White House on October 9, Roosevelt read aloud from Steinhardt's telegram. It appears that the president cut off McDonald's attempt to criticize Long. Yet FDR also expressed concern about the visa delays that the committee reported. He asked Justice and State to reduce the delays in clearing carefully screened immigrants. The president took the time for this hearing less than a month before Election Day.[36]

Long seemed to get the better of the clash and recorded his satisfaction in his diary, but the president left the Justice Department as a minimal check on the State Department. On October 18, Welles, Long, Biddle, and Hart agreed that the President's Advisory Committee on Political Refugees should retain semiofficial status and could continue to back the admission of intellectual and political refugees and persons in imminent physical danger. The October discussions skirted the basic issue of whether Jews in conquered territories or within Nazi reach were imperiled simply because they were Jews—and therefore eligible for visitors' visas. Long soon managed to implement a narrow interpretation of political refugees as prominent figures whose achievements or activities had antagonized the Nazis. FDR had originally used the term "political refugees" to avoid talking about Jewish refugees. Now Long seemed on the point of limiting both the absolute number of those classified as political refugees and the percentage of Jews among them.[37]

In November, FDR garnered some 55 percent of the popular vote, and his Democrats retained 69 percent of the U.S. Senate and 61 percent of House. With war neutralizing opposition to a third term, voters lacked incentives for rejecting the party in power. Postelection polling showed that like Alf Landon in 1936, Willkie did best in small towns and farm communities, among women, professionals and upper-income earners, and white Protestants outside the South. FDR and his party overwhelmingly carried the Jewish vote and retained a majority of African Americans. As compared to 1936, most defections came from German and Irish Americans unhappy with the president's pro-British policies.

After the November elections, Justice Department officials proposed using the Virgin Islands as a way station for refugees, granting visitors' visas
to the islands for wait-listed, would-be immigrants to the United States.
Long feared that easy entry into the American possession would bypass the
strict scrutiny of applicants by consuls and enable German spies to pene-
trate America's defenses. After Secretary of the Interior Ickes backed the
plan, Long appealed to the president. FDR supported Long, although
nominally on jurisdictional grounds. Roosevelt told Ickes that the president
and the State Department had the final say over any matter that involved
foreign policy: "The Virgin Islands . . . present to this Government a very
serious social and economic problem not yet solved. If the Interior Department could find some unoccupied place not now a social and economic
problem where we could set up a refugee camp . . . , that would be treated
with sympathy by the State Department and by me."[38]

Four years earlier, after winning reelection, Roosevelt had loosened visa
regulations to the United States. Two years earlier, after unsuccessful midterm elections, Roosevelt had approved politically riskier proposals for extending visitors' visas. Now, after winning an unprecedented third term, he
professed more concern for American citizens in the Virgin Islands than for
desperate European refugees.

Clearly, the war and security fears had shifted both his priorities and the
views of most presidential advisers and officials. In Berle's words, "There is
considerable question as to whether we want a large contingent of German-
Jewish refugees in the Caribbean just now, since we know automatically
that a certain percentage of them will go sour." Ickes believed that the president might support policies to help refugees find jobs in the Virgin Islands,
but legal snags and State Department opposition stymied progress. The
governor of the Virgin Islands, Lawrence William Cramer, who had supported the scheme publicly, resigned his post.[39]

On February 27, 1941, the American consul in Basel, Switzerland, reported that German officials in Switzerland and likely elsewhere were bribing potential Jewish immigrants to the United States into working secretly
for Germany. This dubious cable gave Long and other restrictionists in the
State Department new evidence for their alarmist claims and worried even
Assistant Secretary of State Berle, who had just criticized the Visa Division.
The State Department decided to concentrate visa approvals in Washington, where diligent intelligence officials could weed out potential spies and

subversives. Officials soon began screening about 100 applicants a day, under all quotas, rejecting more than 40 percent of the applications that made it to their desks.[40]

With his increased power, Long shut down the State Department office that dealt with the Intergovernmental Committee on Refugees and the President's Advisory Committee on Political Refugees. Robert Pell, the most senior official in this bureau, wrote that for months, Long had "indulged in an unrelenting attack on the work and the officers who had the misfortune, not of their own choice, to be connected with it. There is just no use going on. . . . I am sorry that all of our good work of the past three years has ended this way, but there it is."[41]

Long's early 1941 diary gives the impression that Nazi Germany flooded the United States with tens of thousands of Jewish refugees, with a legion of spies lurking among them. (Long sloppily exaggerated the size of the German quota by some 10,000.) According to Visa Division records, in the period from July 1, 1940 to March 31, 1941, American consulates in Germany issued only 2,126 immigration visas. American consulates in other countries (e.g., Great Britain, Cuba) free of German influence, issued about 10,000 visas to refugees who fell under the German quota. In fiscal 1941, the previously filled immigration quota for Germany (27,370 for the fiscal year) was less than half subscribed, even as hundreds of thousands of Jews desperately sought exit from Europe.[42]

Long pushed ahead with more ways to keep America free of foreign intruders. He proposed to bar persons on visitors' visas or diplomatic visas from engaging in political activity or fundraising for political causes. Hull typically dodged controversy and referred Long to Welles. Foreign influence and foreign quarrels could only disturb Americans. Welles approved orders for central visa control, but rejected the ban on political activity. On March 19, FDR had told Welles that he favored allowing nationals of the occupied countries to take a constructive interest in their political reconstruction. A month later, FDR approved the basic plan for central visa control, but trimmed the size of the proposed expansion of the Visa Division's personnel budget.[43]

A disheartened McDonald asked Eleanor Roosevelt whether the President's Advisory Committee on Political Refugees should disband voluntarily. She spoke to her husband, who denied that the State Department wanted to terminate the committee or its work: he still wanted to admit the proper refugees to the United States, and he needed the committee for future contingencies. Eleanor said, "He [FDR] feels that if a few of the people are turned down you should not become discouraged, because sometimes things are discovered in an investigation which make it necessary to refuse, and these investigations have to be made." She did not personally dissent from her husband's position.[44]

In late May, Eleanor asked Welles whether the State Department could help rescue Jewish children from Vichy France. Welles telegraphed Ambassador William D. Leahy to ask if Vichy France would grant them exit visas. Leahy replied that even making the request might backfire, resulting in further restrictions against Jews. In the portion of France not occupied by Germany, only native Frenchmen, not refugees, were eligible for American visas, according to instructions that the State Department issued in June.[45]

On June 20, FDR signed bill S. 913, which had raced through both houses of Congress in a month. It directed consuls to refuse a visa "whenever any American diplomatic or consular officers knows or has reason to believe that any aliens seeks to enter the United States for the purpose of engaging in activities which will endanger the public safety." This legislation virtually equated political activity with subversion. "The measure is considered broad enough," a *New York Times* report said, "to give the president power to suspend all immigration quotas, if he desires." Still, it did not focus only on Jews trying to escape Europe.[46]

Confident that Congress would not interfere, Long had already used executive powers to crack down against visas applications from Jews in Greater Germany and Soviet territories. On May 2, State Department legal adviser Richard W. Flournoy had approved a proposed telegram instructing consuls abroad to deny visas to applicants who had close relatives living in totalitarian countries, subsequently listed as Germany, Italy, and the Soviet Union. In effect, the instruction barred from entry Jews in greatest peril from despotic rulers. State dispatched that admonition to consuls on June 6. On June 17, a second instruction required officials in Washington to pre-approve visas for anyone in Germany or German-controlled territories.[47]

The State Department hardly kept these measures secret. The new chief of the Visa Division, Julian Harrington, announced publicly that the close relatives rule was essential because pressure on their relatives in Germany had compelled some refugees to spy for the Nazis. He cited an alleged case in Havana, where a German-Jewish refugee was reporting daily to the German embassy: "it was understood that Nazi authorities were bringing pressure upon him to act for them despite his race." The *New York Times* carried this sensational story on the front page the next day. A day later, the *Washington Post,* noting that consuls could exempt meritorious persons who were not dangerous, termed it another move to combat the Fifth Column. A *Post* editorial commended the State Department for thwarting the machinations of the Gestapo.[48]

Reports of new State Department restrictions on visas surprised Biddle, who had become acting attorney general when FDR appointed Jackson to the Supreme Court. Biddle angrily noted that American law did not justify the practice of denying visas to all those with close relatives in certain countries. The State Department had failed to consult Justice in advance, as the two departments had previously agreed. He claimed that in any legal dispute, the attorney general's view must prevail.[49]

Long warned Welles against Justice officials "whose liberal attitude discounts the 'risk' involved in admitting refugees not clearly proven to be Nazi, Italian, or Communist agents." The State Department had to retain control of policy, not surrender it to Justice. On July 18, Biddle again challenged the legality of new procedures for visa control. However, Hull spoke to the president, who reaffirmed that State should keep control over visas.[50]

Critics of the close relatives rule made enough noise to worry the ever-cautious Secretary Hull. Long wrote a long memo to FDR recounting his version of the measure's history. Both sides convened at the White House on September 4. Most of the members of the President's Advisory Committee on Political Refugees attended, along with State and Justice officials. Rabbi Wise and Archbishop Joseph Rummel of New Orleans, himself a German immigrant to the United States, presented a united Jewish-Catholic front against the close relatives rule. Long defended himself badly, falsely claiming that immigration quotas were full (those for Germany and Poland were nowhere near full), and that the close relatives rule had not significantly reduced the number of visitors' visas. The committee effectively made the point that consuls had delayed issuing even those visas approved in Washington. McDonald wrote afterwards to Eleanor Roosevelt that, though the president did not commit himself definitively, he believed that FDR would approve most of the committee's recommendations. The Visa Division did streamline its procedures to avoid delays, and it agreed that the mere presence of close relatives in German territory was not enough by itself to disqualify an applicant as a threat to security. A furious Long dismissed all the criticism as part of a personal vendetta against him. He labeled his opponents "sanctimonious hypocrites."[51]

In practice, the State Department had already cut off most visas to Jews seeking them. The compromises in Washington made only a marginal difference. Among those ensnared by the centralization of visa control in Washington and the close relatives instruction was the family of Anne Frank, still living openly in Amsterdam. Anne's father Otto had futilely asked his teenage friend Nathan Straus Jr., now head of the Federal Housing Authority, to get American visas for himself and his family. Under the new restrictions, even such a high official could not deliver them to the Franks.[52]

Long and some others like him in the State Department edged the limits of respectable anti-Semitism. About a quarter of Americans polled in 1940 had judged Jews to be more radical than other Americans. About a third of Americans in 1941 thought Jews were trying to force the United States into the war. The American public shared negative stereotypes of Jews and feared for national security. Alien Jews suffered on both counts.[53]

Despite his security fears and concerns about domestic anti-Semitism, FDR liked to have subordinates who disagreed with each other, leaving him to adjudicate where necessary. In late August 1941, he appointed Long's adversary Biddle as attorney general. The president chose him, Jackson's own preference, after a delay of several months, even though he worried that the solicitor general might be too "soft."[54]

Very close to the start of the Holocaust, in an August 1941 speech in Brazil, Nahum Goldmann, president of the World Jewish Congress, declared that most of European Jewry was beyond help. Why had this happened?, Goldmann asked. In 1933, German Jews had failed to recognize Nazi designs for extermination: they thought only of protecting themselves. "Our friend" Roosevelt was prepared to withdraw the American ambassador and to break relations with Germany unless Hitler withdrew his decrees against the Jews.

> Roosevelt visualized that this fight to wipe out the Jews would spread into a war against Europe and the whole world, because of Hitler's mania of world domination. Do you know why this ultimatum [Roosevelt's to Hitler] was not delivered? Because of those Jews. They did not know that there existed a world-wide Jewish problem. They said that Roosevelt would only worsen the

situation by his intervention. Thus, since Roosevelt "could not be more papal than the pope," it was impossible for him, despite his sincere friendly feelings for the Jews, to carry through this action, and that thanks to those Jews who did not know how to protect the interests of the Jewish people.

Goldmann said he expected the death of some three million Jews in the war, although he did not blame Roosevelt for this tragedy.[55]

In order to strike a blow at his non-Zionist competitors, primarily the American Jewish Committee, Goldmann focused on the "good Roosevelt" of 1937–1939, giving him a decisiveness and commitment he did not possess in 1933 and which he no longer had in 1941. The leaders of the American Jewish Congress and the World Jewish Congress had invested in a pro-Roosevelt political strategy, but not so heavily that they would simply falsify reality. They backed FDR, in gratitude for his prewar initiatives and his anti-Nazi policies.

Beginning in the second half of 1940, FDR launched a series of daring foreign policy ventures. While campaigning for president, he narrowly pushed the first peacetime draft through Congress, through the teeth of Republican opposition. On his own initiative, he sent fifty aging American destroyers to Britain in exchange for bases in British possessions in the Western Hemisphere. Still, when Willkie accused the president of plotting America's entry into the war, FDR responded by pledging to the "mothers and fathers" of America that "your boys are not going to be sent into any foreign wars."[56]

After winning an unprecedented third term, the president, in a letter to Judge Samuel Rosenman, called the 1940 elections "a narrow escape—not for personalities [including himself], but for ideals." FDR worried that his Republican opponents would not stoutly defend Western civilization from a growing Nazi threat: "I have learned a number of things which make me shudder—because there were altogether too many people in high places in the Republican campaign who thought in terms of appeasement of Hitler— honest views of most of them, and views based on the materialism in which they view not only themselves but their country." The day after the election Secretary of the Interior Ickes, very likely attuned to FDR's views, urged Rabbi Wise to forgo a mass protest against Vichy's anti-Semitic laws. Instead, Ickes suggested a mournful commemoration of the death of the French Republic. Ickes thought protestors should connect anti-Semitism with all forms of repression, brutality, and injustice: "What we are striving for is a world where everybody—Jews and non-Jews, white and colored, men of all nationalities and creeds—will have a chance to live in safety and with dignity." Nonetheless, Wise went ahead with his protest meeting at Carnegie Hall a week later. The rally featured a message from French resistance leader General Charles de Gaulle, forwarded in code from London, which promised that Vichy's anti-Jewish laws "would have no validity in Free France."[57]

FDR then proposed that America should become "the great arsenal of democracy" by lending or leasing weapons and supplies to nations resisting Nazi and fascist aggression. Critics denounced the administration's March 1941 Lend-Lease Bill as "a war dictatorship bill" that would prolong the fighting in Europe, strip bare our homeland defense, and eventually drag America into war. "It is clear as sunlight that he [FDR] is getting us into war," said Republican representative Dewey Short of Missouri. "War is worse than a German victory," Senator Taft said. Still, most Americans viewed aiding the British as a preferable alterative to joining in the war. Lend-Lease cruised through Congress, backed by 99 percent of House Democrats but only 15 percent of Republicans. In the Senate, 69 percent of Democrats voted yes, compared to 37 percent of Republicans.[58]

America opened its arsenal of democracy to one totalitarian country in order to check the Axis powers. On June 22, 1941, Germany and its allies poured about 3.5 million men into what Hitler called Operation Barbarossa, a crusade to destroy the Soviet Union and conquer its European domain. Joseph Stalin had trusted in the Nazi-Soviet Pact and the benefits to Germany of economic and political cooperation with the Soviets. He had dismissed numerous intelligence warnings of an impending German attack, and he chose to believe Hitler's word of honor that he had not deployed German forces in Poland to attack the Soviet Union. As a result, Hitler took the Soviet forces by surprise. Massive German spearheads in the north, center, and south struck quickly and deeply into Soviet territory, while the Soviet armies suffered huge casualties. Western analysts stopped calculating whether the Soviet Union could survive, and began estimating the weeks before its inevitable collapse.[59]

Before Germany launched its attack, Winston Churchill and Roosevelt had exchanged messages about a coordinated response. Unlike Stalin, they each trusted their intelligence reports about an impending German attack.

Reversing decades of anticommunist views and rhetoric, Churchill encouraged the Soviets and gave what little aid Britain could spare. With his private secretary, Churchill was more vivid: "If Hitler invaded Hell he [Churchill] would at least make a favorable reference to the Devil [in the House of Commons]." Through the new American ambassador, New Hampshire Republican John G. Winant, no anti-Semite or freelancer like Kennedy, Roosevelt responded that he personally would support any Churchill announcement of "welcoming Russia as an ally."[60]

Given American anticommunism, Roosevelt stayed low-key in public, though he announced that Hitler's forces posed the gravest danger to the Americas. He unfroze Soviet funds in the United States—frozen since the Soviet attack on Finland—and sent his closest adviser Harry Hopkins to meet with Stalin and assess whether the United States should extend Lend-Lease aid to the Soviets. After a series of unusually open meetings with Stalin, Hopkins decided that the Soviets would ultimately prevail and that the United States should supply all necessary aid. On July 29, Churchill told the House of Commons that the Americans were giving Britain aid on a gigantic scale and was advancing "in rising wrath and conviction to the very verge of war." When reporters questioned the president about this impolitic statement, FDR feigned ignorance and then joked that he could not hear follow-up questions.[61]

Britain's accidental alliance with Stalin and America's deepening involvement in the war enraged Roosevelt's isolationist opponents. Ever since passage of Lend-Lease, isolationists, led by conservative women's groups and a new America First Committee, had intensified their campaign against the president. Antiwar elements viewed communism, not fascism, as America's real enemy and worried about pro-war Jews and radicals. The extension of Lend-Lease aid to the Soviet Union magnified these sentiments.

Contemporary Jewish leaders such as Goldmann and Wise judged Roosevelt by different standards than some observers use today. Given his firm and politically risky anti-Nazi policies, they gave him the benefit of the doubt on other issues. They regarded FDR as a bulwark against further German expansion and against anti-Semitism in the United States. On every matter of concern to Jews FDR eclipsed his Republican and conservative Democratic rivals.

Jewish leaders failed to recognize that Roosevelt's ongoing campaign against Nazi Germany led him to avoid appearing pro-Jewish. That image would only impede his task of mobilizing the country. An emphasis on Jewish concerns might also jeopardize his political fortunes, which he equated with the effort to save civilization, given the strength of his isolationist opposition. Thus he did not react publicly as the Nazis transformed the persecution of Jews into mass murder.

Roosevelt believed that national security and public opinion required that his administration must seriously scrutinize all potential newcomers to the United States; he used Long as his tool to achieve that goal. Ultimately, he accepted a sharp reduction in visas and kept Long in place, despite his biases and flaws. Long's commitment to reducing the influx of purportedly dangerous foreigners effectively undermined FDR's professed commitment to the cause of Jewish and non-Jewish refugees.

CHAPTER TEN

Wartime America

IN EARLY 1941, Theodore N. Kaufman, the Jewish proprietor of a small advertising firm in Newark, New Jersey, self-published a short book that called for sterilizing all German men and dividing up Germany among neighboring states. An alert corps of Nazi propagandists saw in Kaufman and his book the perfect foil for their myth-making. They transformed this obscure self-publisher into the president of a bogus "American Peace Federation," a leader of "international Jewry," and a "close associate" of Judge Samuel Rosenman, FDR's speechwriter and confidant. On July 24, 1941, the headline of a front-page story in the central Nazi Party newspaper, the *Völkischer Beobachter,* blared: "A Monstrous Jewish Extermination Plan: Roosevelt's Guidelines." The story claimed that President Roosevelt had inspired Kaufman's *Germany Must Perish,* and personally dictated key sections. Two months later, the Nazi propaganda ministry published a pamphlet that cited Kaufman's book as proof of an international Jewish conspiracy to exterminate the German people, abetted by Roosevelt and Winston Churchill. It said that Germany faced a stark choice with an obvious answer: "Who should die, the Germans or the Jews?"[1]

Throughout the summer and fall of 1941 Nazi propagandists charged that FDR's subservience to Jews supposedly explained his thirst for a "Jewish war" against Germany. In October, German newspapers claimed that FDR was himself a Jew. Nazi officials sincerely believed that Jews dominated the Roosevelt administration, but they also saw that this anti-Semitic propaganda resonated in Eastern Europe and the Middle East.[2]

Actually, it was Adolf Hitler who welcomed war with America, but not immediately. Germany boasted growing U-boat squadrons, but lacked a powerful surface fleet. Hitler planned for a war in alliance with Japan, whose formidable navy could bog the United States down in a draining two-front war. He pledged that Germany would support the Japanese in a conflict with the Americans. Unless Japan attacked the United States, Hitler believed that American entrance in the war would only help Britain and the Soviet Union stave off German domination of Europe.[3]

Psychologists might label Nazi charges about a Jewish "extermination policy" projection or more mundanely camouflage for Germany's own policies. Heinrich Himmler's SS and police had closely followed German troops invading the Soviet Union. Their mission was to murder Jews and other designated enemies. By early August, they were shooting all Jews—men, women, and children—in some parts of conquered Soviet territory.[4]

On September 28, Ukrainian auxiliary police posted notices ordering all Jews in Kiev to appear at 8:00 a.m. the next day at a central city location. More than 30,000 Jews complied. German police and Ukrainian auxiliaries led them toward a ravine in the northwest part of the city. As they walked, the Jewish men, women, and children chanted religious songs, seeking comfort in their faith. The commander of a mobile killing unit known as Sonderkommando 4a watched from the top of the ravine as armed policemen forced the first group of Jews, now stripped to their underwear, to lie face down at the base of the ravine. His men tried to shoot each victim, aiming for the back of the head, per instructions. Then the executioners repeated the process, piling new batches of victims on top of the first. The commander frequently exhorted his men to speed up their work; they were not killing the Jews quickly enough. The policemen, supplied with ammunition and rum, worked in shifts. They reported killing 33,771 Jews in the course of two days at the now infamous ravine called Babi Yar—the largest Nazi mass murder of the first phase of the Holocaust.[5]

Nazi officials offered some public clues about their murderous violence against Jews in the East. In his radio broadcast of November 16, Propaganda Minister Joseph Goebbels declared the Jews guilty for bringing about war and responsible for Germany's self-defense: "Now it [world Jewry] is suffering a gradual process of extermination that it had intended for us. . . . It is now perishing as a result of its own law: An eye for an eye, a tooth for a tooth." Still, the covert construction of extermination camps, just underway, remained among the Nazi regime's greatest secrets. For high Nazi officials, Germany's war of extermination complemented its war of conquest. Their singular purpose was to kill every Jew within their reach because they believed that the Jewish people did not deserve to survive on this earth.[6]

Preoccupied with aiding the Allies and preparing for a possible American entry into the war, Roosevelt sought to avoid giving any speck of credibility to the charge that Jews dictated his pro-Allied policies. He knew that America was not yet ready, politically or militarily, to fight Germany, Japan, and Italy. These three dictatorships had been formally allied since the Tripartite Pact of September 27, 1940, forming a united front against the threat of American intervention in the war. FDR wanted time to rearm and to mobilize public support for increased aid to Britain and the Soviet Union.[7]

Nearly a year before Pearl Harbor, British and American officials began coordinating plans for defeating the Axis powers. American military authorities concluded that victory over Germany required an invasion of Europe, which in turn demanded American participation and a vast increase in American military forces. Joint British-American military staff conversations led to agreement that the Allies must first defeat Germany, their most dangerous foe. Officials also agreed to defend the Western Hemisphere and British Commonwealth nations. This consensus on strategy in a lengthy conflict did not commit the United States to enter the war immediately or at any specific time in the future. Though he approved of what the military called the "ABC agreement," Roosevelt stayed aloof, largely to avoid the political complications of what FDR's speechwriter Robert Sherwood later called a "common-law alliance with the British." Facing three hostile powers and the possibility of war in either the Atlantic or the Pacific, the commander in chief simply planned for a war instigated by the Axis.[8]

Occasional naval incidents pushed America to the edge of a shooting war and fed the propaganda war with Germany. On October 16, 1941, German submarines threatened a convoy of merchant ships and their Canadian escorts about 350 miles south of Iceland. When the destroyer USS *Kearney* came to their rescue the following day, German *U-568* torpedoed it, killing eleven sailors and crippling the ship. Hours later, the U.S. House of Representatives approved a revision of the Neutrality Act to allow the arming of American merchant ships crossing the Atlantic. The idea of peace with "the Nazi Neanderthals" had become a delusion, declared Wendell Willkie, now a staunch interventionist. In a national radio broadcast on October 27, Navy Day, Roosevelt declared, "The shooting has started. And history has recorded who fired the first shot." Unlike the first shot fired on Union forces at Fort Sumter in 1861, the torpedo launched by *U-568* did not start a war. The canny president believed that only graver provocation would enable him to lead a unified nation in battle against enemies abroad.[9]

The president warned Americans, however, that Hitler's blueprint for world conquest extended to the Americas. He claimed to possess secret Nazi documents showing plans to subjugate Central and South America as vassal states and to replace all traditional religions with a Nazi church that worshipped Hitler as God and revered *Mein Kampf* as its bible. He named the many religions that Hitler sought to abolish—Protestant, Catholic, Mohammedan, Hindu, Buddhist, and Jewish. These charges contained some kernels of truth. Nazi objectives stretched into the Western Hemisphere, and Hitler and the Nazi elite despised traditional religion and sought blind German faith in Hitler and Nazi ideology.[10]

Nazi shortwave radio responded to Roosevelt's charges with more venom than ever. A veteran Nazi broadcaster who had once taught at New York's Hunter College called FDR's statements about Nazi plans to abolish religion "silly nonsense." There was only one explanation, he claimed: FDR had a screw loose.[11]

The most prominent American isolationist, whom FDR hated, had by then undercut his own cause. In a speech delivered in the American heartland at Des Moines, Iowa, on September 11, 1941, Charles Lindbergh explicitly charged Jews with pushing America into war. Speaking on behalf of the America First Committee, Lindbergh said, "Leaders of both the British and Jewish races . . . for reasons which are not American, wish to involve us in the war." He claimed that America's tolerance of Jews could not survive the tensions of war, and that Jews endangered America through "their large ownership in our motion pictures, our press, our radio, and our government." By crossing the line between private mutterings and public prejudice,

Lindbergh unwittingly discredited both the anti-interventionist movement and claims that Jews led the push for war. However, the *Christian Century* noted the irony that, "One hundred clubs and hotel foyers rang with denouncement of Lindbergh on the morning after his Des Moines speech—clubs and hotels barring their doors to Jews."[12]

Criticism of Lindbergh and America First filled the media. Interventionists seized on the speech as proof that the antiwar movement mimicked Nazi propaganda. Although leaders of America First rallied behind Lindbergh, such prominent Republicans as Willkie and Thomas Dewey criticized his comments, as did some figures in the antiwar movement. FDR's critic Herbert Hoover lamented, "Lindbergh has put us all in difficulty. I cannot bear to criticize him, although it would be better for me if I did so." A Gallup Poll showed that public approval of Lindbergh's ideas on U.S. foreign policy had plunged to a low of 15 percent.[13]

In Phillip Roth's counterfactual historical novel *The Plot against America,* Lindbergh defeats FDR in the presidential election of 1940. He then signs a treaty of friendship with Germany and persecutes Jews at home. When Hitler invades the Soviet Union in the novel, the fictional President Lindbergh declared, "Adolf Hitler has established himself as the world's greatest safeguard against the spread of Communism and its evils." The historical Lindbergh had, in fact, said at the time of the German invasion, "I would a hundred times rather see my country ally herself with England, or even with Germany, with all her faults, than the cruelty, the godlessness, and the barbarism that exists in Soviet Russia."[14]

Critical reaction to Lindbergh may have deflated a Senate investigation of alleged pro-war propaganda in Hollywood movies initiated by isolationist senators. Unlike Lindbergh, senators avoided overt expressions of anti-Semitism. Still, their clear subtext was to investigate whether Jews were using their influence in Hollywood to push the United States into war. The hearings generated more negative than positive press and much ridicule. When investigators called actor Charlie Chaplin, who was not Jewish, to testify about his part in the *The Great Dictator,* a widely circulated cartoon showed Chaplin with a subpoena in his hand saying, "Now what I could possibly tell these past-masters about comedy?" The hearing ended inconclusively without any bombshell revelations.[15]

FDR joined with those mocking the Senate investigation of Hollywood. He read an apocryphal telegram from an unidentified senator about a subversive book: "Written entirely by foreign born, mostly Jews. First part full of war-mongering propaganda. Second part condemns isolationism. That fake story about Samaritan dangerous. Should be added to your list and suppressed." The book was the Bible.[16]

New polling data showed that the American people rejected the notion that Jews were pushing the nation into war. A Gallup survey released on October 24 found that only one in sixteen respondents mentioned Jews among the groups striving to get America into the war. Jews finished fifth among the most frequently mentioned pro-war groups, behind the Roosevelt administration and the Democratic Party, big business, British organization and agents, and American pro-British groups.[17]

The president did not heed this latest twist in the polls. He continued to believe he could unite America for the inevitable war with Germany only by branding the Nazis as a threat to all of humanity. Talking publicly about Nazi killings of Jews would only supply ammunition to both Nazi propagandists and isolationists. The Nazis wanted to harp constantly on the Jewish threat; Roosevelt wanted to make Nazism itself the issue in ways that hundreds of millions of people at home and abroad could grasp. FDR believed that it made no political sense to single Jews out as special victims of Nazi terror.

On October 24, a reporter asked FDR about the failed Nazi bombing of ships in the Red Sea. The president responded that he had heard only that Hitler was trying to get "one of the few prominent Jews left in Germany" to explain how Moses parted the Red Sea. The reporters at the press conference laughed heartily, but the joke soured with those who knew that the Nazis had begun deporting German Jews to the East, as the American embassy in Berlin had already reported.[18]

Isolationist efforts to paint Roosevelt as a warmonger culminated several days before Pearl Harbor. As evidence of Roosevelt's intent to wage war against the Axis, Robert McCormick's *Chicago Tribune* published the military's response to Roosevelt's top-secret order to estimate the level of American manpower and production needed for victory in a global war. An army officer had given the order and estimates to Senator Burton Wheeler, who leaked it to a *Tribune* reporter. Under the banner page one headline, "FDR's War Plans!," the story claimed that the president was planning to mobilize "10 million armed men" and devote the American economy to wartime production. FDR was still discussing the political repercussions of this embarrassing story with his advisers on the evening of December 6, when aides rushed him a decoded version of a portion of the latest Japanese cable to the Japanese ambassador in Washington: Tokyo thought further negotiations pointless and was sending a long statement that would break relations with the United States. Recognizing that war was inevitable, the president rejected Harry Hopkins's plaintive suggestion that the United States should strike first. The president still lacked any information about where or when Japan would attack.[19]

Despite his shock at finding the U.S. military unprepared for the Japanese attack on December 7, Pearl Harbor united Americans behind Roosevelt's leadership. The public overwhelmingly backed his now famous day-after speech, which declared December 7 "a date which will live in infamy." The Senate unanimously approved a declaration of war against Japan, which only one House member opposed: Jeannette Rankin of Montana, who had also voted against declaring war on Germany in 1917. Although Congress would have granted any presidential request, FDR did not ask for an immediate declaration of war against Germany. In his fireside chat on December 9, FDR explained that the Axis powers relied on each other's triumphs and that the United States had to fight a global conflict, but he still waited for Germany to move first.[20]

Although Hitler quickly ordered U-boat commanders to sink American ships, he did not declare war against the United States until a December 11 speech to the Reichstag. Hitler admitted that 160,000 Germans had already died in the campaign against the Soviet Union, but he still boasted of German triumphs in the war. The führer then blasted Roosevelt, claiming that his failures to revive the American economy, combined with prodding by American Jews, led him to seek war as a solution to his domestic problems. Benito Mussolini followed Hitler in declaring war on the United States. Roosevelt quickly sent a written message to Congress asking it to recognize the state of war with Germany and Italy. Again, Congress's decision was nearly unanimous.[21]

Pearl Harbor elicited little remorse from isolationist leaders, some of whom still had hoped the United States would fight only Japan and avoid war with Germany. "Our principles were right," said former general Robert E. Wood, the head of America First Committee. "Had they been followed, war could have been avoided." According to Lindbergh, "The final judgment of our policies must be left to the future and to more objective time; but in this final judgment, I have complete confidence." Hoover wrote, "I have not approved the policies towards Japan and have felt that this constant sticking of pins in rattlesnakes would produce just such a result. . . . If this had not been done, Japan, from her own internal exhaustion, would have totally collapsed without the loss of a single American life."[22]

The Japanese attack, along with the German and Italian declarations of war, hardened American attitudes toward alleged enemies at home. On December 8, even before Germany declared war against the United States, Federal Bureau of Investigation (FBI) Director J. Edgar Hoover ordered the Immigration and Naturalization Service to detain more than 4,000 German and Italian aliens and American citizens sympathetic to Germany, previously identified as potential security threats, as soon as the United States declared war on Germany. FDR authorized the arrest of enemy aliens and the confiscation of their property even before a declaration of war. Allowed to operate without warrants, Hoover's men arrested more than a thousand Germans and Italians within a few days. The Justice Department detained for questioning about 60,000 aliens, most of them Germans. Journalist John Franklin Carter, FDR's semiofficial intelligence analyst, predicted an Axis sabotage campaign in the United States by the spring of 1942, abetted by a wealthy and well-entrenched fifth column. Carter thought that some German agents had already become American citizens. Influential columnists such as Walter Winchell and Walter Lippmann criticized the administration for being too soft on internal enemies. One high Justice Department official thought the army was planting such notions in the minds of journalists; he worried that Justice was losing the battle for the president's favor.[23]

By mid-1942, the Justice Department had apprehended some 8,000 enemy aliens, more than half of them Japanese. Although federal authorities interned few German-Jewish refugees, they remained on the list of enemy aliens subject to restrictions. Among them was the fourteen-year-old (future historian) Gerhard L. Weinberg, who had to register and obtain permission to compete on his Albany, New York, high school debate team.[24]

FDR also asked J. Edgar Hoover to shut down several publications he thought seditious: notably, William Dudley Pelley's new magazine, *The Galilean*. The Justice Department began to use grand juries to move against "seditious newspapers," including Father Coughlin's *Social Justice*. Attorney General Francis Biddle discussed these cases personally with FDR, who wanted to prosecute Coughlin himself. After the Church hierarchy forbade

Coughlin to engage in politics or continue his radio broadcasts, Biddle advised the president against proceedings. Administration insiders Leo Crowley, Jimmy Byrnes, and Tommy Corcoran—all Catholics—thought an indictment "would merely stir up the old anti-Semitic, anti-Administration fight between the Catholics and the Jews." Roosevelt, who still worried about the leanings of Catholic voters, agreed to leave a silenced Coughlin alone.[25]

In July 1942, about six weeks after federal agents rounded up eight German saboteurs landed by Nazi submarines on the East Coast, the Justice Department indicted for sedition twenty-eight German agents, Bund members, and anti-Semitic right-wing activists, including Pelley, Gerald Winrod, and Elizabeth Dilling. The sweeping indictment named the America First Committee and several of the isolationist mothers' groups, but did not include any left-wing opponents of the war. Trial did not begin until 1944 after rewritten indictments dropped the antiwar organizations, but added new individual defendants. Prosecutors charged these Americans with violating the Smith Act by conspiring with Nazi agents to overthrow the government of the United States. The government intended to employ new social science techniques of content analysis to show that the Nazis and the defendants used parallel language. The trial dragged on inconclusively for eight months. The presiding judge died. In 1946, a new judge dismissed all charges, ruling that continuation would be a "travesty on justice."[26]

Ironically, both anti-Semites and Jewish visa applicants became victims of fifth column fears. Breckinridge Long and his subordinates in the State Department reached a nominal compromise with the President's Advisory Committee on Political Refugees regarding refugees with close relatives remaining in German territories. The State Department and the interdepartmental visa screening committees would not reject such applicants automatically—only if there was additional evidence against them. Still, the committee complained that the practice of rejecting all such applicants persisted. An interagency board that included representatives of the FBI, the Military Intelligence Division, and the Office of Naval Intelligence reviewed all visa applications. The FBI and the intelligence agencies, which cared only about keeping out possibly dangerous aliens, had veto power—anything derogatory in their files about sponsors or potential immigrants meant rejection. Highly dubious charges were common, including complaints and suspicions about mainstream Jewish organizations that aided immigrants. Roosevelt established an appeals board with two presidential appointees, but that new level of review only led to more administrative squabbles with few positive results for aliens seeking visas.[27]

The President's Advisory Committee on Political Refugees rejected the charge that fifth columnists came into the country under the guise of Jewish refugees. The committee claimed in vain that federal authorities had documented only a single isolated example of a German refugee of Jewish origin serving as a German agent. Cases of espionage in France, it said, had little bearing on the American experience since American Jewish immigration organizations carefully screened the refugees they sponsored for admission and assistance.[28]

One case of a refugee-spy was indeed exceptional. Paul T. Borchardt was a Catholic (since 1908) of Jewish descent and an authority on the Arab world who spied for Germany during World War I. The Nazis expelled him as a non-Aryan and briefly imprisoned him in Dachau in 1938. He traveled to Britain in 1939 as a refugee and offered his services to British intelligence, claiming to be anti-Nazi, although he apparently remained loyal to his fatherland. British authorities neither accepted his offer nor deported him from their country. In 1940, he came to the United States and joined a small spy ring of German agents and German American Nazis. U.S. Attorney Matthew Correa in New York, who prosecuted Borchardt and others for espionage, declared, "I can think of nothing more despicable than to capitalize on the misery of thousands of others who really are refugees." A jury convicted Borchardt, and the judge sentenced him to twenty years in prison. The publicity from such a case, including front-page coverage in the *New York Times,* loomed larger than the loyalty of many tens of thousands of anti-German Jewish refugees.[29]

To glean intelligence, William J. Donovan, director of a special government unit blandly titled the Office of the Coordinator of Information, hired scholars and even some émigrés from Germany to debrief recent immigrants from Europe. As a result, at least some U.S. intelligence officials had a ground-level picture of intensifying Nazi persecution of Jews in Germany.[30]

Donovan, a multidecorated World War I veteran, was becoming an increasingly important figure in FDR's circle of advisers and informants. He had seen war conditions firsthand, and he knew how to tell a tale. Before becoming America's "coordinator of information" in June 1941, the Irish-Catholic Republican Donovan had gone to Britain in mid-1940 to confer with British intelligence and to study Nazi fifth column methods. In late

1940, under British sponsorship, he toured the Mediterranean theaters, the Balkans, and the Middle East. Upon his return, he met with FDR in March 1941 and urged the president to send war materiel directly to the Middle East to enable the British to hold Egypt.[31]

Later, Donovan wrote about that visit to the White House, "You will remember that the day I returned home from the Middle East, I said this to you [FDR]: 'Unless what I say is understood, the fight of the small nations of this world will not be understood. While these small nations look upon Churchill as the great defender, they look upon you as the great liberator.'" Donovan did not want America to fight a war in defense of the British Empire. As in World War I, the United States had to support freedom and self-determination for peoples abroad, which meant political independence for territories and colonies held by the British. This commitment dovetailed with FDR's own vision of decolonization after the war.[32]

The U.S. media reported most prominently on dramatic battles of the war. Yet mainstream American newspapers, which FDR closely followed, covered the escalating Nazi atrocities against Jews in the fall of 1941. Headlines included: "Death Rate Soars in Polish Ghettoes" (*New York Times,* September 14); "New Anti-Jewish Drive Seen" (*New York Times,* October 5); "200 Jews Kill Selves Over Nazi Order to Wear a Star" (*Chicago Tribune,* October 13); "Berlin Is Swept by New Wave of Anti-Semitism" (*Chicago Tribune,* October 16); "Nazis Will Move Jews to Poland" (*Washington Post,* October 19); "German Atrocities" (*Washington Post,* October 24); and "Nazis Seek to Rid Europe of All Jews" (*New York Times,* October 28). Whatever the press failed to report or highlight later, it captured part of the first phase of what soon became a continent-wide Nazi campaign for exterminating Jews.

Beyond press reports, there is little to indicate precisely what the president knew about the Nazis' early mass killings of Jews and when he knew it. Before the war, Roosevelt had warned repeatedly that war would place Jews in Germany and Eastern Europe in great peril, and he had read *Mein Kampf.* Reports that the Nazis were shooting Soviet Jews in large numbers or that Jews were dying in ghettos in Poland in 1941, if they reached him, could hardly have surprised him. He thought Hitler capable of unspeakable evil, and he knew that the Nazis persecuted and murdered civilians in occupied nations. But Roosevelt lacked the kind of near-perfect real-time intelligence that Churchill received for a time—decodes of intercepted German police radio messages, in which SS and police authorities proudly announced to their superiors the shootings of tens of thousands of Jews in the Soviet Union. At this time, the British government did not share these most sensitive sources with their American counterparts out of fear that leaks might prompt Germany to change its coding system.[33]

Still, some of FDR's confidants had detailed knowledge of Nazi atrocities. In early November 1941, William D. Hohenthal, the American military attaché in Berlin, conveyed to Hopkins an informant's report that SS units had segregated Jews and then shot them in many cities, towns, and villages in occupied Soviet territory. We can only guess whether Hopkins had privately discussed this report with Roosevelt, and if so, how the president reacted to news of what historians now call the first phase of the Holocaust.[34]

On October 25, 1941, the White House denounced in scathing terms German executions of innocent hostages in France. Rosenman had arrived at the White House that morning, and he likely helped to prepare this statement, which warned that Nazi frightfulness would one day bring "fearful retribution." The British government received little advance notice of this sudden awakening of American outrage. Churchill scrambled to issue a companion statement declaring that retribution for Nazi crimes must become a major goal of the war. France was on the minds of the American political elite, in part because the *New York Times* had run a number of articles about French resistance to the German occupation and Nazi reprisal killings. The *Times'* fascination with reprisals against French resistance fighters stood in marked contrast to its neglect of stories about Jews targeted by these same Nazi and Vichy authorities.[35]

At the end of October, *Congress Weekly,* an organ of the American Jewish Congress, described with horror: "From Kovno in the North to Odessa in the South, a wave of outright slaughter, mass deportations and incarceration of Jews in concentration camps." *Congress Weekly* noted that the general British and American press as well as Jewish newspapers had reported, among other killings, the deportation of 15,000 Hungarian and Galician Jews from Hungary, now Germany's ally, to Ukraine, where they were murdered in cold blood. The unnamed author wondered how President Roosevelt and Prime Minister Churchill could condemn reprisal killings of a hundred hostages in Nantes and Bordeaux and remain silent about these much larger crimes. The author then supplied his own answer, even if he rejected its validity: "Condemnation of Nazi atrocities in France are a weapon against isolationism . . . [but] condemnation of the atrocities against Jews would add fuel to the isolationist propaganda that the war against Hitler is a 'Jewish war.'" The general secretary of the Jewish National Workers' Alliance sent a copy of this editorial to presidential press secretary Stephen T. Early, calling for FDR to speak out on behalf of millions of suffering Jews.[36]

Some knowledgeable American Jews, however, believed that the Nazis were baiting a trap for Americans. Richard C. Rothschild, head of the American Jewish Committee's Survey Committee on Anti-Semitism, explained that "the Nazis are just as desirous of having the Jews defended as they are of having them attacked, since both defense and attack fuel the flames of the controversy. . . . In line with this strategy, the Nazis promote all sorts of misconceptions."[37]

By mid-1942, the mainstream press in Britain and America had begun to publish stories about massive Nazi killings of Jews. On June 16, the *New York Times* reported that Nazis had murdered 60,000 Jews in Vilna, Lithuania, although the story noted that accounts of the massacre from an eyewitness refugee could not be confirmed. Sources associated with the Polish-Jewish Bund, an ally of the Jewish Labor Committee in the United States, estimated Nazi murder and brutality had claimed the lives of 700,000 Polish Jews by the spring of 1942. The sources said that the Nazis had deployed mobile gas chambers in Poland to exterminate Jews systematically. Bund leaders called for reprisals against Germans living in allied countries as the only way to save "millions of Jews from certain destruction." The British Broadcasting Corporation carried these reports, as did the *New York Times,* first in a brief notice on June 27 and then in a full-page story (on page 6) on July 2. The mainstream press also widely covered a World Jewish Congress estimate in late June 1942 that the Nazis had killed more than a million Jews since 1939. Still, the sources cited in these stories lacked the kind of detached standing or visible evidence needed to dispel the doubts of the dubious.[38]

Reliable information obtained by American intelligence sources that could have confirmed Nazi atrocities remained buried within the bureaucracy. Donovan's organizations, the Coordinator of Information and then, in mid-1942, the larger Office of Strategic Services, gathered military, political, and economic information about Nazi Germany from a wide array of informants and other sources. In the process, they uncovered reports about specific incidents of Nazi killings of Jews and about Nazi gassing of disabled patients deemed genetically defective.[39]

Donovan also sent experienced reporters to parts of the world lacking regular correspondents. Their stories could guide opinions in the right direction—either through shortwave radio broadcasts to overseas audiences or through domestic use. Allen Dulles, who many years later became the longest-serving director of the Central Intelligence Agency, seems to have coordinated the operation initially until Donovan reassigned him to Switzerland in the fall of 1942.[40]

The government hired former NBC correspondent Gerald M. Mayer, once based in Berlin, among others. In April 1942, Mayer received a cover appointment as special assistant to the American minister to Switzerland. He was the most likely author of a series of three largely accurate and dramatic would-be articles in the summer and fall of 1942 regarding Nazi extermination of Jews. The first one began:

> Germany no longer persecutes the Jews. It is systematically exterminating them. The new racist policy, which in cold calculated cruelty surpasses the horrors of Magdeburg [destroyed during the Thirty Years War in the seventeenth century] or Carthage, was revealed to me by a British officer who escaped the hell of the Himmler ghetto in Warsaw. For several months now, the Third Reich has been brutally destroying the Jewish population by two effective means: starvation and mass execution.[41]

To the best of our knowledge, this piece and its two follow-up stories never emerged from the bureaucracy. Perhaps the reports became lost when the government transferred information policy to the Office of War Information (OWI); perhaps they simply contradicted the dominant line in the American propaganda war.

Donovan and officials in the State Department engaged in psychological warfare hoped to break the will of the enemy by driving wedges between the Nazi regime and the German public. In late April 1942, Roosevelt told Assistant Secretary of State Adolf A. Berle that such a strategy could work against Germany. Many officials in the Coordinator of Information also thought that democracies could counter the manipulative propaganda of dictatorial regimes only with similar material of their own. In their view, this meant avoiding the "Jewish Question."[42]

An interagency committee advising the OWI concluded in early September 1942 that "atrocity material relating to atrocities perpetrated upon citizens of other countries may produce in the minds of our people morbid results rather than desirable results. . . . Barbarous actions and cruelties not serving directly to illuminate the nature of the enemy, but merely to excite horror and hatred . . . would not be released." This committee did not recommend an outright ban on exploiting information about Nazi killings of Jews, but it cautioned against the public use of such intelligence.[43]

Jewish organizations engaged in lonely and frustrating efforts to expose Nazi crimes against Jews. On July 21, 1942, the American Jewish Congress, B'nai B'rith, and the Jewish Labor Committee drew 20,000 people to a rally in Madison Square Garden to protest Nazi atrocities. Roosevelt and Churchill both sent statements for the organizers to read at the rally. Roosevelt hailed the determination of the Jewish people to make every sacrifice for an Allied victory. Americans of all religions, he said, shared in the sorrow of Jewish fellow citizens over the savagery of the Nazis against helpless victims. He also forecast that the Nazis would not succeed in "exterminating their victims any more than they will succeed in enslaving mankind." In a typical Rooseveltian compromise, this wording melded Nazi policies toward Jews with the Nazi threat to humanity. Nonetheless, it appears to have represented the president's first public mention of Jews as Nazi victims.[44]

Churchill noted (not quite accurately) that the Jews were Hitler's first victims and had joined the vanguard of resistance to Nazi aggression. He pointed to the service of 10,000 Palestinian Jews in the British military, and another 20,000 carrying out police duties in Palestine. Both Roosevelt and Churchill pledged that the Allies would punish the perpetrators of crimes in the peace settlement. Neither leader offered any plans for thwarting the killing of Jews or other victims of Nazi terror; they had no military means for interfering with German forces.[45]

Roosevelt used the term "extermination"—but not necessarily because he had a full appreciation of Nazi policies against Jews. Rabbi Stephen S. Wise had suggested this statement, and Roosevelt, according to Wise, accepted it almost word for word. Actually, Roosevelt's advisers toned Wise's draft down, but still adopted most of his language. Wise rejoiced that FDR had finally spoken out on Jewish problems, even though no action had accompanied his words.[46]

On August 21, Roosevelt had issued a broad statement condemning barbaric crimes of the invaders in Europe and Asia. He warned the criminals that the United States and the "United Nations"—the term Roosevelt had coined to describe all countries opposing the Axis—would win the war and force them to answer for their acts in court. A. Leon Kubowitzki, an official of the World Jewish Congress, complained that this statement would not help "us; there is not a word about the Jews, nor a word about the deportations."[47]

Kubowitzki correctly concluded that the Nazis were cleansing Western Europe of Jews through mass deportations to the East, rather than conspicuously executing Jews in places like France or the Netherlands. He recommended trying to get the State Department, the American Red Cross, the pope, and neutral governments to press the French not to allow deportations of French Jews to the East. At home, he sought the advice and counsel of prominent non-Jews. He also hoped to lobby sympathetic congressmen, and to hold a press conference for weekly and monthly periodicals to break through what he called the conspiracy of silence in the major newspapers. "Our people in Europe are being exterminated in cold blood," Kubowitzki said. "We must take chances."[48]

A week later Wise received a now-famous cable from Gerhart M. Riegner, representative of the World Jewish Congress in Switzerland, via Member of Parliament Sidney Silverman in London. From an unimpeachable unidentified source within Germany—now known to be German industrialist Eduard Schulte—Riegner had received word that the Nazis were considering a plan to exterminate 3.5–4 million Jews with the use of prussic acid to resolve definitively the "Jewish Question" in Europe.[49]

For Wise, this telegram addressed two burning questions. First, was Hitler indeed engaged in the systematic murder of all Jews in all areas of Nazi control or influence? Second, if so, could such crimes be established authoritatively? Positive answers led naturally to a third query: Could the United States and its allies stop the carnage?

On September 2, Wise rushed to Washington and laid his cable before Undersecretary of State Sumner Welles. At the time, neither man knew of the irony created by Wise's approach. Nearly a month earlier Riegner had asked American diplomats in Switzerland to send his cable directly to Wise through diplomatic channels. They complied, despite their skepticism about the accuracy of Riegner's spectacular charges. But State Department officials in Washington, dubious about such an outlandish claim, convinced that they had no means for stopping the Nazis from killing Jews, and worried that Wise might create damaging publicity, declined to send him the cable. They sat on the information for three weeks.[50]

Welles consulted the State Department's authorities on European matters, who emphatically doubted the report of a Nazi plan for mass murder. They believed that the Nazis were putting Jews deported to the East to work, as they had done with Russian prisoners of war. Welles accepted this seemingly plausible opinion: Why should they waste valuable labor? He called Wise to question the information in Riegner's cable. Wise asked, "May we feel reassured?" Welles responded cautiously, "Who can tell, seeing that you are dealing with that madman [Hitler]?" He asked Wise not to publicize Riegner's cable until the State Department thoroughly investigated the evidence of Nazi atrocities.[51]

If his conversations with the undersecretary at all calmed Wise a new cable from Agudath Israel sources in Bern on September 4 revived his horror: in recent days 100,000 Warsaw Jews had been killed, with their corpses used to make soap—that part of the story turned out to be inaccurate. Wise spread the news of both cables to his friends and allies, meeting with the President's Advisory Committee on Political Refugees and with Jewish organizations. He hoped that someone would tell Roosevelt, even if the president would be unable to do much: "Roosevelt cannot intervene, because Hitler will rightfully do nothing for him. Hitler would have won the war if it had not been for our President and America."[52]

The Union of Orthodox Rabbis in the United States called an urgent meeting of American Jewish organizations to devise a strategy for responding to reports detailing the systematic mass murder of Jews. This first meeting was inconclusive, and the American Jewish Congress arranged a second meeting on September 6. Wise told the representatives about his meeting with Welles and his request to avoid publicity until the State Department completed its investigation. Participants considered three ideas: (1) Roosevelt should appeal directly to the German government to stop the killing; (2) neutral governments should be asked to intervene on behalf of Jews in Poland; and (3) the U.S. government should threaten to take reprisals against German aliens in the United States unless the massacres ceased. The Jewish organizations agreed only that Wise should set up a committee to study the matter. Another meeting on September 9 added several ideas, such as placing the evidence of mass murder before Democratic senators Robert F. Wagner and Tom Connally, getting other members of Congress in both houses to denounce Nazi crimes against Jews, and marshaling important church and lay opinion to influence a broad public audience. These lobbying efforts in the United States had no prospect of changing Nazi policies.[53]

Wise described these weeks as the unhappiest days of his life. He had difficulty sleeping. He struggled to explain "the uniquely tragic fate," "the extermination of the whole Jewish population of Europe" to Reverend John Haynes Holmes. He returned to Washington for more meetings with State Department officials. They said again that the Nazis were most likely deporting Jews from the Warsaw Ghetto for slave laborers. Nevertheless, James G. McDonald backed up Wise's sources: "much evidence here deportation means extermination." He also warned that Switzerland might close its border to Jews fleeing France unless the United States began admitting more refugees.[54]

Roosevelt must have learned of Riegner's horrific information and of the State Department's investigation, perhaps in conversations with Felix Frankfurter or Henry Morgenthau Jr. FDR often met with Rosenman, but the record does not establish whether Rosenman received the grim news in September. Roosevelt also met with Welles once in early September. FDR tended to believe the worst about Hitler and Nazi Germany, but explosive information about the murder of millions of Jews required careful handling.

On a late September mission to the Vatican, Myron C. Taylor suggested that the pope should speak out publicly against German treatment of refugees and hostages—especially Jews. Cardinal Maglione, the pope's secretary of state, said that the pope had repeatedly called for humane treatment, using what he thought was clear, if general language: "the blessing or the malediction of Almighty God would descend upon rulers according to the manner in which they treat the peoples under their rule." He insisted that without documentary proof, the pope could not and should not descend to particulars.[55]

On October 7, in a formal presidential statement, FDR declared that the Allies would punish war criminals when hostilities ceased. The United States, Britain, and other Allied countries would convene a war crimes commission to gather the needed evidence. The president also indicated that Nazi crimes were ongoing. Some of the governments in exile of countries conquered by the Nazis had wanted the Allies to condemn Germany's criminal occupation policies. An Allied statement might help to deter future crimes, they hoped. Roosevelt avoided threats to the German people as a whole and disavowed "mass reprisals" against them. "The number of persons eventually found guilty," he said, "will undoubtedly be small, compared to the total enemy populations."[56]

The United States had no military presence on the European continent and no weapons to deploy against Germany, its conquered territories, or its allies. The administration never seriously considered the idea of reprisals against German aliens in the United States. It had no diplomatic leverage with the enemy either, although it maintained diplomatic relations with Vichy France, a government collaborating with Germany, but not formally allied with it. France offered at least a slim chance for saving some Jews. In response to an August 27 letter from the American Jewish Committee, the American Jewish Congress, B'nai B'rith, and the Jewish Labor Committee protesting deportations of Jews from France, Welles wrote that the State Department had made the most vigorous representations possible through the American embassy at Vichy.[57]

Bolstered by information and support from private American organizations operating in France, the American chargé d'affaires at Vichy, S. Pinkney Tuck, had already condemned the deportations in a meeting with Premier Pierre Laval. Tuck also appealed for the lives of 4,000 Jewish children separated from their deported parents; Laval showed no interest in this plea. Tuck then told Washington that Americans could save the children only by admitting them to the United States. Laval might accept such a proposal to lessen widespread criticism of the deportations of adults; otherwise, the children would perish. The State Department authorized the American Jewish Committee to publicize Welles's letter to increase the pressure on the French.[58]

Long called these Jewish children derelicts, and thought the precedent of bringing them to the United States dangerous. Nevertheless, after he returned from a cross-country trip, FDR personally approved the granting of visas to 5,000 children, not the 1,000 State had originally contemplated. It was only a gesture, but it likely reflected some awareness of Nazi policy. Welles told McDonald that there would be and should be no public statement about this decision.[59]

At an October 15 press conference, a journalist asked Welles whether Vichy had accepted an American offer to take in 5,000 Jewish refugee children. Welles equivocated, saying they were not of a particular race or nationality. Private organizations were bringing these destitute children to the United States under the terms of existing immigration laws. He declined to confirm the number. Even so, his statements enraged Laval, who threw up roadblocks to the children's rescue. After some delay, Vichy authorities decided to authorize exit visas only for bona fide orphans, not including the children of parents the Nazis had deported to Eastern Europe. These officials falsely implied that their parents remained alive.[60]

Prospects for the orderly rescue of Jewish children ended when German troops entered unoccupied France after the Allies invaded North Africa in November 1942. Vichy France no longer had full control of its Jews. Relief workers smuggled an estimated 500 Jewish orphans from France into Spain and Portugal. Some of them, along with other refugee children in North Africa, eventually received visas and came to the United States, but it was a far cry from 5,000. The Vichy government blamed the West more than Germany for infringing on French sovereignty, and it severed relations with the United States. In a November 20 speech, Pierre Laval said that he hoped for a German victory in the war to forestall control of France by communists and Jews, who would extinguish French civilization.[61]

While in Rome, Taylor had received additional evidence from Switzerland of Nazi mass murder. Two refugees from Poland reported from asylum in Switzerland that the Nazis had sent Jews from the Warsaw ghetto to special death camps, one of which they identified as Belzec. Jews deported from other countries to the East were also earmarked for death, not slave labor. Taylor then traveled to London, where the British section of the World Jewish Congress provided him with corroborating information. After he reached Washington, he and Welles received a follow-up response from the Vatican to his inquiries: unconfirmed reports of "severe measures against non-Aryans" had reached the Holy See, but it was not possible to verify them. Taylor's assistant Harold Tittmann said the Vatican had no practical suggestions, believing that only military force, not moral suasion, could check Nazi barbarism.[62]

Based on what Taylor later said to Wise and others, Taylor gave the president the documentary evidence he had gathered abroad and affirmed the accuracy of reports about Nazi atrocities in France, Poland, and Yugo-slavia. Only a change in the "war situation in Europe might affect the Nazi plan of extermination of many and the removal of others from given terri-tories," Taylor said. Nonetheless, Taylor favored additional condemnation of Nazi inhumanity by the president, the secretary of state, the cardinal secretary of state, and the pope. If FDR was willing to do this, Taylor could get Tittmann to try again with the pope.[63]

If the pope first issued a statement denouncing Nazi killings of Jews, Roosevelt could follow him without fear of adding to Catholic voter defec-tions. FDR and his Democrats were facing a difficult midterm election, scheduled for November 3, 1942. A clearly worded papal statement might have had many benefits abroad, for example, helping to convince French officials in North Africa that they should aid, not hinder, an Allied inva-sion. We have no direct evidence about how Roosevelt analyzed this situa-tion, but with the pope remaining silent, he waited discreetly until after the November elections and the Allied invasion of North Africa while State Department amassed evidence about Nazi killings.

The midterm elections stung the Democrats and the president. Roose-velt's bitter foe, Congressman Hamilton Fish, won his own home congres-sional district in Dutchess County in spite of Willkie's repudiation of him. Republican Thomas Dewey won the governorship of New York. A Repub-lican isolationist candidate in Illinois won a U.S. Senate seat by about 200,000 votes. The Democrats barely held control of the House, losing forty-seven seats. In the Senate, they lost nine seats. FDR had very limited control over the new Congress, in which a conservative coalition of Repub-licans and right-wing Democrats held the balance of power.

After the election, Congress rejected FDR's request for including in the Third War Powers Act a provision authorizing the president to suspend laws or regulations hampering "the free movement of persons, property and in-formation into and out of the United States." Such presidential authority would have spared the wrangling over how to manage the admission of 5,000 Jewish children from France. There, time saved would have meant lives saved. In the House Ways and Means Committee's hearings on the Third War Powers bill members worried that FDR would use this provision "to open the doors to indiscriminate immigration." After a subcommittee stripped out the clause on immigration, Attorney General Biddle accepted the change and reported his decision to FDR at the November 20 cabinet meeting. A few days later Roosevelt met with Vice President Henry Wallace, House Speaker Sam Rayburn, Majority Leader John McCormack, and Senate Majority Leader Alben Barkley. FDR tried to persuade them of the need to loosen restrictions on immigration and imports. Rayburn said that Congress would not support any such initiative. Roosevelt then retreated; Congress would have to decide the matter on its own. Afterwards, he attended a religious service held in the East Room of the White House and broadcast nationally.[64]

By then, additional reports about the mass extermination of Jews had reached the West. The American Legation in Switzerland had probed Riegner's sources and added evidence from independent sources. On November 13, Welles asked Wise to visit him in order to discuss the information received from Switzerland. When he returned from a trip to Mexico, Wise arranged an appointment for November 24.[65]

Also in November, Polish underground courier Jan Karski arrived in London and reported to government officials what he had seen and heard in the Warsaw Ghetto and at a site near the Belzec extermination camp. His testimony was also conveyed to the British section of the World Jewish Congress. Karski delivered his information just after the Polish government-in-exile in London released a report about a Heinrich Himmler–run program to kill Polish Jews at Belzec, and two other such camps, Sobibor, and Treblinka: the Nazis spared only able-bodied Jews suitable for slave labor.[66]

On November 24, Welles told Wise that the evidence arriving from Switzerland and elsewhere confirmed his deepest fears. Welles, acting on his own, said that Wise could release the information to the press as long as he omitted all names in the documents from Switzerland: "For reasons that you will understand, I cannot give these [facts] to the press, but there is no reason you should not. It might even help if you did." This authorization did not bind the State Department to vouching for the reliability of reports on the Nazi slaughter of Jews, but it gave Wise leeway to act.[67]

In late October, officials of the World Jewish Congress had decided to seek a meeting with the president and the secretary of state to discuss Nazi barbarities. Afterwards, they planned to hold a press conference with the goal of reaching a broad audience and dispelling public doubts about the Nazis' mass murder of Jews. However, Roosevelt shunned any such meeting.

To avoid putting himself in the difficult position of having to respond either positively or negatively to Jewish pleas, he let Welles serve as his emissary to Jewish leaders.[68]

Welles was isolated within his own Department. European specialists in the State Department had flatly rejected Riegner's original cable; it would take much more evidence than Welles had gathered to pry open their closed minds. Welles's always precarious relationship with his nominal boss, Secretary of State Hull, had also deteriorated. He could expect no backing from Hull in an internal conflict with other officials. Assistant Secretary Berle, a possible ally, was preoccupied with political problems related to the Allied invasion of North Africa. William Bullitt, a Hull ally who despised Welles, was plotting to use evidence of Welles's homosexual behavior to oust him from government. Finally, the wartime Roosevelt had shied away from taking risks on Jewish issues, except for small steps taken behind the scenes. On Jewish issues in the public eye, Welles had no allies. An unofficial report by Rabbi Wise represented his only recourse for releasing information on the precarious survival of European Jewry.[69]

At a press conference that Wise quickly arranged for two days before Thanksgiving, he announced that the Nazis had killed about two million Jews as part of a campaign to exterminate every Jew still alive in Europe. The *New York Herald Tribune* ran a front-page story on Wise's report, which mentioned the State Department's confirmation of the evidence. (State Department experts soon distanced themselves from Welles on this point.) The Associated Press also circulated a major story, but most of the reporters present attributed the information to Wise.[70]

Critics later singled out the *New York Times,* America's de facto newspaper of record, for carrying this story on page 10, tucked in behind related stories. Yet other major American newspapers also failed to highlight the story. The *Washington Post* placed it on page 6, the *Los Angeles Times* on page 2, and the *Atlanta Constitution* on page 4. Few publishers wanted to take the risk of splashing on their front pages spectacular claims that the Nazis were systematically slaughtering millions of European Jews, especially when a private citizen, not officials of the United States government, had presented the pertinent evidence.

After Wise's revelations, various Jewish organizations prepared to hold a day of mourning for the Jews killed by the Nazis, which they set for December 2. Meanwhile, Wise awaited a call from the White House. On November

30, Welles had told him that FDR would wish to see him and a few other Jewish officials—not more than four. However, when Edwin "Pa" Watson checked with the president the next day, FDR declined to hold the meeting.[71]

Typically, Roosevelt did not put on record his reasons for avoiding this meeting, but circumstances suggest his motives. For two years, he had limited his direct exposure to Jewish issues. With America in the war, he continued to rally public support through powerful but unifying, non-Jewish, themes such as Nazi slavery versus American freedom. Now Wise wanted him to discuss something catastrophic *and* sensational with a Jewish delegation. When Morgenthau asked Roosevelt privately about two or three million Jews trapped in the heart of Europe, FDR summarized some recent conversations with Isaiah Bowman and the president of Colombia for the resettlement of large numbers of European peoples. Again, he wanted Jews to be only a small fraction of the total refugee population. The ever-loyal Morgenthau was too deferential to the president to say bluntly that, under the circumstances, this kind of speculation about postwar plans for resettling members of diverse ethnic groups was no longer enough.[72]

FDR feared that his involvement in publicity about what we call the Holocaust would divide the American people and add to the widespread perceptions at home and abroad that Jews manipulated his policies. The U.S. government's most ambitious propaganda initiative, the documentary series *Why We Fight*, directed by Frank Capra, illustrates this caution. The seven-part documentary released between 1942 and 1945 barely touches upon the Nazis' persecution or slaughter of Jews.[73]

In addition, Roosevelt had no remedies for Nazi mass killings beyond the ultimate threat of retribution. The United States had no leverage with the Nazi regime at all and no military capacity to do more than it was already doing to win the war. It was far easier for the Nazis to kill than for any outside power to intervene against them.

Most importantly, FDR believed that the fortunes of war had shifted in favor of the Allies. Their successful invasion in Northwest Africa meant that the Allies could think about moving on to Europe. Although the outcome in the East remained uncertain, Germany's increasingly dire difficulties at Stalingrad looked promising for the Soviets. Roosevelt hoped that this combination of defeats would break the morale of the German people. On December 5, he told visiting Canadian prime minister Mackenzie King that he thought the German situation resembled that of 1917–1918: Germany "might crumple up at any moment."[74]

FDR had misread the lessons of World War I, which Germany lost on the battlefields, not at home. His private view of a collapsing Germany was wildly optimistic at the end of 1942. He could not express this view, but he wanted to avoid pushing all Germans to fight to the finish. Any emphasis on Nazi atrocities against Jews would not go over well in Germany and in German-dominated Europe, first, because it seemed to support Nazi propaganda about the Roosevelt administration, and second, because of anti-Semitism among Germans and others.

On December 2, Wise wrote both to FDR and to Jewish White House adviser David Niles, saying, in effect, that FDR had to receive a small Jewish group and to speak out: "it would be gravely misunderstood if, despite your overwhelming preoccupation, you did not . . . receive our delegation . . . [or] utter what I am sure will be your heartening and consoling reply." Wise begged Niles to help to avert a moral defeat for Jewish leaders. Niles relayed the message; FDR relented, and reluctantly agreed to a meeting.[75]

On December 8, the first anniversary of FDR's speech about Pearl Harbor, four American Jewish representatives entered the Oval Office at noon. The president sat behind his cluttered desk, smoking a cigarette. He greeted Wise—the only one whom he knew personally, and Wise introduced the others: Adolph Held of the Jewish Labor Committee, Rabbi Israel Rosenberg of Agudath Israel, and Henry Monsky, representing B'nai B'rith. A representative of the American Jewish Committee, Maurice Wertheim, was scheduled, but could not make it in time.[76]

Rabbi Wise said: "Mr. President, we have an orthodox Rabbi in our midst. It is customary for an orthodox rabbi to deliver a benediction upon the head of his country, when he comes in his presence. Will you, therefore, permit Rabbi Rosenberg to say the prayer of benediction?"

"Certainly," the President answered.

Rabbi Rosenberg rose and put on his scull-cap. We all rose. The President remained seated, and, as Rabbi Rosenberg commenced to recite the prayer in Hebrew, the President bowed his head.

"O, God Lord of Kings, blessed be Thy name that Thou bestowest a share of Thy glory upon the son of men."

"Thank you very much"—the President said.

The President seemed to be moved, and so were we all.

Wise read a portion of a memorandum about the Nazi policy of exterminating Jews. He appealed to FDR to bring this to the world's attention and
"to make an effort to stop it." Roosevelt responded:

> The government of the United States is very well acquainted with most of
> the facts you are now bringing to our attention. Unfortunately we have re-
> ceived confirmation from many sources. Representatives of the United
> States government in Switzerland and other neutral countries have given up
> proof that confirm[s] the horrors discussed by you. We cannot treat these
> matters in normal ways. We are dealing with an insane man—Hitler, and
> the group that surrounds him represent an example of a national psycho-
> pathic case. We cannot act toward them by normal means. That is why the
> problem is very difficult. At the same time it is not in the best interest of the
> Allied cause to make it appear that the entire German people are murderers
> or are in agreement with what Hitler is doing. There must be in Germany
> elements, now thoroughly subdued, but who at the proper time will, I am
> sure, rise, and protest against the atrocities, against the whole Hitler system.
> It is too early to make pronouncements such as President Wilson made, may
> they even be very useful. As to your proposal, I shall certainly be glad to is-
> sue another statement, such as you request.

When Roosevelt asked the delegation for other suggestions, Held suggested
asking neutral countries to intercede with Germany on behalf of Jews.
There were few others.

FDR then shifted the discussion to North Africa, which was foremost
on his mind. He mentioned that he had given orders to free Jews from concentration camps there and to abolish Vichy's special laws against Jews. He
then balanced this statement with another complaining that Moslems had
also suffered discrimination by the French—they had had fewer rights than
Frenchmen and Jews, and there were seventeen million Moslems. The
United States would fight for equal rights for all—it would not elevate
one group over another. Indirectly, FDR had signaled to the assembled
leaders that the concerns of Jews would not override those of other peoples.
At the close of the twenty-nine-minute meeting, as the group stood up,
FDR said that they could issue a statement about the meeting, drawing
on what he had told Wise in July—if they quoted him exactly. He added,
"We shall do all in our power to be of service to your people in this tragic
moment."

This was the first and last meeting FDR held with a delegation of Jews outside of his inner circle to discuss what we call the Holocaust. Wise, who had a stake in the meeting's success, was outwardly pleased afterwards. In a thank you note to Niles, who had brought about the meeting, Wise praised FDR, who, he said, could not have been more friendly or helpful: "The word he gave us will carry through the country and perhaps serve in some degree as warning to the beasts. . . . Thank God for Roosevelt. We ought to distribute cards throughout the country bearing just four letters, TGFR, and as the Psalmist would have said, thank Him every day and every hour."[77] Wise had demonstrated to other Jewish leaders his access to the president, and Roosevelt had seemed to understand their concerns. He did not mention FDR's comments on balancing the rights of Moslems and Jews in North Africa. (We treat that subject further in Chapter 12.)

FDR's sympathetic but essentially noncommittal response to Rabbi Wise and his delegation typified the wartime president's approach to Jewish issues. Either Roosevelt did not see the plight of European Jews as one that compelled decisive presidential engagement, or he continued to worry that whatever he might do or say would backfire, impairing the war effort. During FDR's first term the struggle to rebuild a shattered economy had kept him from risking political capital on Jewish priorities. In 1942, the urgency of world war had the same deterrent effect. This cautious wartime Roosevelt was politically and emotionally stingy when it came to the plight of Jews— even given that he had no easy remedies for a specific Jewish tragedy in Europe. He hoped that the sudden collapse of Germany and the end of the war would resolve all ancillary issues, but Germany did not crumble under pressure and FDR would not live to see the war to its conclusion.

Franklin Roosevelt with father James and mother Sara. Franklin's parents instilled in him religious tolerance and an ambition to make his mark on the world. In 1941, at the age of eighty-six, Sara traveled to Toronto, Canada, to address a Hadassah meeting. *Franklin Roosevelt Library, 4796170 and 47967178.*

Franklin and Eleanor Roosevelt. Their marriage became a working relationship after Eleanor discovered her husband's affair with Lucy Mercer in 1918. More idealistic and less political than Franklin, Eleanor had to pick her battles and spoke out more boldly on domestic civil rights than on the plight of European Jews. *Library of Congress, Prints and Photographs Division, LC-USZ62-111583.*

Louis Dembritz Brandeis, the first Jewish justice of the U.S. Supreme Court. An ardent Zionist, he refrained from openly advocating for Jewish causes until he retired from the court in 1939. *Library of Congress, Prints and Photographs Division, LC-DIG-ppmsca-06024.*

Samuel Rosenman is sworn in as a New York State judge. Rosenman was an important adviser to FDR from 1928 until the latter's death in 1945 and he edited the public papers of FDR's presidency. He frequently urged caution on Jewish issues. *Library of Congress, Prints and Photographs Division, NYWTS-BIOG-ROSENMAN.*

Felix Frankfurter and his wife. Frankfurter was a key adviser to FDR and a talent scout for the administration until his appointment to the Supreme Court in 1939. Some critics falsely charged that he manipulated the administration on behalf of left-wing and Jewish interests. *Library of Congress, Prints and Photographs Division, LC-USZ62-109697.*

Frances Perkins, secretary of labor throughout FDR's presidential years and the first woman cabinet member in American history. She staunchly advocated for the admission of additional Jewish refugees to the United States. *Library of Congress, Prints and Photographs Division, LC-DIG-hec-21834.*

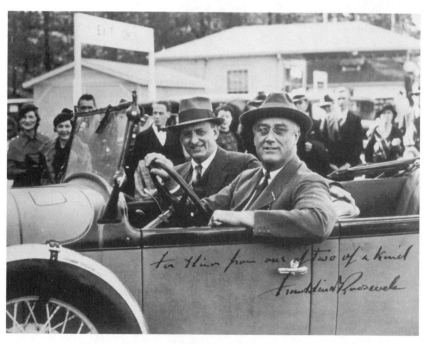

FDR and Henry Morgenthau Jr., influential presidential confidant and secretary of the treasury for most of FDR's time in office. The only Jewish cabinet officer, Morgenthau persuaded the president to form the War Refugee Board in early 1944. *Franklin Roosevelt Library, 8176.*

Chicago protest against Nazi book-burning and the oppression of Jews, 1933. Similar mass protests across the nation in 1933 and later years did not alter American policy or influence the Nazis' persecution of Jews. *United States Holocaust Memorial Museum, 76508.*

Three leaders of the U.S. State Department: from left to right, Secretary of State Cordell Hull, Undersecretary Sumner Welles, and Assistant Secretary Adolf A. Berle. While Hull distanced himself from Jewish causes, Welles promoted FDR's agenda at State, including some initiatives to aid the Jews of Europe. *United States Holocaust Memorial Museum, 04638.*

From left to right, Senator Robert F. Wagner (D-NY), actress Helen Hayes, and Representative Edith Nourse Rogers (R-MA). The Senate's most outspoken advocate for Jewish concerns, Wagner teamed with Rogers to sponsor unsuccessfully a 1939 bill to admit additional refugee children to the United States outside of quota limits. *Library of Congress, Prints and Photographs Division, LC-H22-D-6377.*

This cartoon shows Nazi leader Hermann Göring holding up Jews for money. Nazi efforts to strip Jews of their resources were a major impediment for Jews seeking to emigrate from Germany in the 1930s. *Simplified Finance"—A 1938 Herblock Cartoon,* © *The Herb Block Foundation, courtesy Library of Congress, Prints and Photographs Division, LC-DIG-hlb-00156.*

This cartoon illustrates the unwillingness of world leaders to admit Jewish refugees to their shores. *"Still No Solution"—A 1939 Herblock Cartoon,* © *The Herb Block Foundation, courtesy Library of Congress, Prints and Photographs Division, LC-DIG-hlb-01250.*

Isaiah Bowman, a prominent geographer and adviser to FDR on potential havens for imperiled Jews. He discounted the capacity of foreign lands to accommodate Jewish refugees. *Library of Congress, Prints and Photographs Division, NYWTS-BIOG-BOWMAN.*

Passengers aboard the SS *St. Louis.* The 937 Jewish refugees on this ship were turned away from Cuba in 1939 and failed to gain emergency admission to the United States. They were resettled in what seemed to be safe havens in Western Europe, although later Nazi conquests resulted in the deaths of some 254 of the original passengers. *United States Holocaust Memorial Museum, 38577, courtesy Fred Buff.*

America First Rally, featuring Charles Lindbergh (center). In a September 1941 speech, Lindbergh accused Jews of pushing America into war. *Library of Congress, Prints and Photographs Division, LC-USZ62-111262.*

Breckinridge Long, assistant secretary of state during much of World War II. He played an instrumental role in limiting Jewish immigration to the United States. *Library of Congress, Prints and Photographs Division, LC-USZ62-127905.*

General William Donovan, head of the Office of Strategic Services, the predecessor to the Central Intelligence Agency. An important presidential adviser during the war, Donovan sought to avoid inflaming Arab opinion in the Middle East and North Africa. *Library of Congress, Prints and Photographs Division, NYWTS-BIOG-DONOVAN.*

THE COMPANY WILL APPRECIATE SUGGESTIONS FROM ITS PATRONS CONCERNING ITS SERVICE   1280

WESTERN UNION
CABLEGRAM (27)

CLASS OF SERVICE	SYMBOLS	
This is a full-rate Cablegram unless its deferred character is indicated by a suitable symbol preceding the address.	LC	Deferred Cablegram
	NLT	Cable Night Letter
		Ship Radiogram

R. B. WHITE PRESIDENT   NEWCOMB CARLTON CHAIRMAN OF THE BOARD   J. C. WILLEVER FIRST VICE-PRESIDENT

1942 AUG 29

NV15 CABLE=LIVERPOOL 122 1/63 NFD   8/29/42

NLT STEPHEN WIS (CARE MRS SCHNEEBERGER
250 WEST 94 ST) WORLD JEWISH CONGRESS NYK
(330 WEST 42 ST SEE SPL INSTNS ON FILE (RELAY VIA SI)=

HAVE RECEIVED THROUGH FOREIGN OFFICE FOLLOWING MESSAGE FROM
RIEGNER GENEVA STOP (RECEIVED ALARMING REPORT THAT IN FUHRERS
HEADQUARTERS PLAN DISCUSSED AND UNDER CONSIDERATION ALL JEWS
IN COUNTRIES OCCUPIED OR CONTROLLED GERMANY NUMBER 3-1/2 TO
4 MILLION SHOULD AFTER DEPORTATION AND CONCENTRATION IN EAST
AT ONE BLOW EXTERMINATED TO RESOLVE ONCE FOR ALL JEWISH
QUESTION IN EUROPE=

CFM 3-1/2 4.   QUICKEST, SUREST AND SAFEST WAY TO SEND MONEY IS BY TELEGRAPH OR CABLE

Critical Holocaust information sent by Gerhart M. Riegner to Jewish leader Rabbi Stephen S. Wise in August 1942, through American diplomatic channels. Although State declined to release the information to Wise, he received the telegram weeks later from sources in London. *The Jacob Rader Marcus Center of the American Jewish Archives, Cincinnati, Ohio, americanjewisharchives.org.*

Joseph Kennedy and his son Ted, later U.S. senator from Massachusetts. As American ambassador to Britain in the late 1930s, Kennedy favored a policy of appeasing the Nazis. *Library of Congress, Prints and Photographs Division, LC-USZ62-112082.*

GHETTO

ARTHUR SZYK
N.Y. '43.

WHO TOLD YOU I AM NOT VICTORIOUS ANY MORE?!.....

This cartoon illustrates Adolf Hitler's war on the Jews. For Hitler and his collaborators, the destruction of the biological substance of the Jewish people was a key aim of the war, not a diversion from military operations. The Nazis were more dedicated to killing Jews than the Allies were to saving Jews. *Reproduced with the cooperation of The Arthur Szyk Society, www.szyk.org, courtesy Library of Congress, Prints and Photographs Division, LC-USZ62-133552.*

Peter Bergson, a transplanted Palestinian who lobbied for American assistance to oppressed Jews in Europe. Although denounced as a divisive figure by mainstream American Jewish leaders, he pioneered dramatic public relations methods and influenced some members of Congress and other celebrities. *Library of Congress, Prints and Photographs Division, NYWTS-BIOG-BERGSON.*

Jewish leaders who met with FDR in December 1942. At the center is Rabbi Stephen S. Wise, a strong FDR partisan and the leading American Jewish spokesman of the times. FDR gave the delegates permission to quote him on the plight of the Jews. It was the first and last meeting that FDR held about the Holocaust with a delegation of Jews outside his inner circle. *United States Holocaust Memorial Museum, 03912.*

A protest march by Orthodox rabbis in Washington, D.C., on October 6, 1943. The group failed in its efforts to gain a meeting with President Roosevelt. FDR did reaffirm at the time his support for additional Jewish immigration to Palestine, up to the limit of the territory to absorb refugees. *United States Holocaust Memorial Museum, 49332.*

John Pehle, the first director of the War Refugee Board, which likely helped rescue up to 200,000 Jews. Created late in the war the board lacked significant resources and leverage within government. *Library of Congress, Prints and Photographs Division, NYWTS-BIOG-PEHLE.*

SCHUTZ-PASS

Nr. 28/69.

Name: **Lili Katz**
Név:

Wohnort: **Budapest**
Lakás:

Geburtsdatum: **13. Sept. 1913.**
Születési ideje:

Geburtsort: **Budapest**
Születési helye:

Körperlänge: **164 cm.**
Magasság:

Haarfarbe: **blond** Augenfarbe: **grau**
Hajszín: Szemszín:

Unterschrift:
Aláírás:

SCHWEDEN   SVÉDORSZÁG

Die Kgl. Schwedische Gesandtschaft in Budapest bestätigt, dass der Obengenannte im Rahmen der — von dem Kgl. Schwedischen Aussenministerium autorisierten — Repatriierung nach Schweden reisen wird. Der Betreffende ist auch in einen Kollektivpass eingetragen.

Bis Abreise steht der Obengenannte und seine Wohnung unter dem Schutz der Kgl. Schwedischen Gesandtschaft in Budapest.

Gültigkeit: erlischt 14 Tage nach Einreise nach Schweden.

A budapesti Svéd Kir. Követség igazolja, hogy fentnevezett — a Svéd Kir. Külügyminisztérium által jóváhagyott — repatriálás keretében Svédországba utazik.

Nevezett a kollektiv útlevélben is szerepel.

Elutazásáig fentnevezett és lakása a budapesti Svéd Kir. Követség oltalma alatt áll.

Érvényét veszti a Svédországba való megérkezéstől számított tizennegyedik napon.

Reiseberechtigung nur gemeinsam mit dem Kollektivpass. Einreisewisum wird nur in dem Kollektivpass eingetragen.

Budapest, den **25. August** 1944

KÖNIGLICH SCHWEDISCHE GESANDTSCHAFT
SVÉD KIRÁLYI KÖVETSÉG

Kgl. Schwedischer Gesandte

Antiqua Nyomdai és Irodalmi Rt. Budapest

Protective document for a Hungarian Jew issued by Swedish diplomat Raoul Wallenberg, who cooperated with American authorities to rescue thousands of Jews in Budapest. Wallenberg died under mysterious circumstances in a Russian prison after the war. *United States Holocaust Memorial Museum, 71944, courtesy of Lena Kurtz Deutsch.*

Prime Minister Winston Churchill, President Franklin Roosevelt, and Premier Joseph Stalin at Yalta in February 1945, the last wartime conference that FDR attended. After Yalta, a seriously ill Roosevelt traveled to Egypt and met with King Ibn Saud of Saudi Arabia in a futile effort to reconcile the Arab leader to Jewish settlement in Palestine. Roosevelt died less than two months later on April 12, 1945. *Franklin Roosevelt Library, 48223659(69).*

CHAPTER ELEVEN

Debating Remedies

AFTER REVEALING NAZI plans to exterminate the Jews of Europe, Rabbi Stephen S. Wise told the press that FDR had offered American and Allied assistance to these imperiled people. He quoted FDR as saying that the United Nations were prepared to take every step "which will end these serious crimes against the Jews and against all other civilian populations of the Hitler-ruled countries and to save those who may yet be saved." Roosevelt had made no such statement at his meeting with Jewish representatives, according to surviving notes, but the president had given Jewish leaders latitude to speak for him. Wise made the most of that opportunity. Still, the question remained: What could or would the Allies do?[1]

In Britain, public pressure and lobbying by the Polish government-in-exile moved the normally unsympathetic foreign secretary Anthony Eden to endorse an Allied declaration against Nazi killings of Jews. Roosevelt undoubtedly preferred a joint statement, which the Nazis could not so easily ascribe to his alleged pro-Jewish bias. London drafted a statement for the three big powers; eight other governments of the United Nations quickly cosigned. On December 17, 1942, following a prepared script, Member of Parliament Sidney Silverman rose in the House of Commons to ask the British government what it knew of the Nazi policy regarding Jews. Eden then read the joint declaration that German authorities were carrying out Adolf Hitler's oft-repeated threat to exterminate the Jewish people.[2]

Political leaders, not officials in the Foreign Office and the State Department, initiated this first Allied declaration on crimes specifically against Jews. The press gave it much more prominent coverage than Wise's press conferences, including a page 1 article in the *New York Times*. The Allies now recognized and condemned Nazi policy, and they threatened to punish war criminals, but publicity alone could save few Jewish lives. They offered no hint of a rescue strategy.[3]

Americans had once before used publicity and pressure from a distance against fanatics intent on genocide. In mid-1915, Turkish nationalists within the Ottoman government had begun the first systematic effort in modern history to annihilate a minority people in their realm—the Armenians. Organized killing squads, filled with thugs deliberately released from prison, murdered Armenians and deported them to desert wastelands where many died of disease, famine, and exposure. The death toll quickly surpassed the carnage of the Russian pogroms during Theodore Roosevelt's years in the White House.[4]

On April 27, 1915, America's Jewish ambassador to the Ottoman empire, Henry Morgenthau Sr., informed his superiors in Washington of Turkish persecution of Armenians, and received instructions to "urge Turkish government to protect both Armenians and Zionists." On June 18, Morgenthau reported that his informal efforts had failed. The Turkish head of state, he said, had expressed his "resentment at attempted interference by foreign government with the sovereign rights of the Turkish government over their Armenian subjects" that they justified on grounds of military necessity. On July 16, 1915, Morgenthau wrote, "It appears that a campaign of race extermination is in progress under a pretext of reprisal against rebellion." American consuls in the Ottoman empire, Morgenthau, and his successor as ambassador, Abram I. Elkus, kept the Wilson administration informed about the fate of Armenians.[5]

America's mainstream press published hundreds of articles on the plight of the Armenians. Newspapers closely tracked the body count of Armenians, reporting in late October 1915 that the Turks had already slaughtered nearly one million civilian victims. Also in October, many thousands rallied at New York City's Century Theatre to protest this mass murder. Speakers included representatives of Protestant missionaries in Turkey, Catholic luminaries, and Rabbi Wise, who decried "inhumanity whether committed by Germans against Belgians, by Russians against Jews, or by Turks against Armenians." Participants called upon all officials with "influence in the Turkish Empire to put an end to these wrongs."[6]

Former president Theodore Roosevelt, in full rhetorical bluster, demanded a decisive American response "to this crowning iniquity of the wholesale slaughter of the Armenians." He thought mass meetings amounted to nothing more than a safe emotional outlet; only sentiment followed by action was honorable. President Wilson followed not the politically motivated words of the out-of-power Roosevelt, but his example during his presidency—he had not risked other priorities to aid the oppressed Jews of Russia. The Wilson administration did not break relations with the Ottoman empire, denounce Turkish atrocities, or threaten economic sanctions or military intervention. Wilson and his advisers sought to maintain strict neutrality so that Wilson could attempt to broker a peace agreement among belligerents. They hoped to sustain good relations with Turkey, avoid reprisals against U.S. missionaries there, and preserve long-standing American commercial interests in the region. The president also would not pay the price of dispatching the very limited numbers of American troops to a far-off nation with which the United States had no direct quarrel.[7]

In February 1916, the State Department finally publicly protested against the oppression of Armenians in the Ottoman empire. A *Los Angeles Times* correspondent noted ruefully, "Although approximately 1,000,000 Armenians have already been massacred or starved to death by the Turks, the United States government dispatched today its first actual protest against the continuation of such atrocities." The statement expressed the State Department's "confidence that the authors of such atrocities will be punished" and warned that if crimes against the Armenians continued, "the American government will be compelled to take action of a more drastic character." This vague warning had no impact in Turkey, especially when three weeks later the State Department publicly repeated assurances from the Ottoman government that deportations had ceased and the situation of Armenians had visibly improved. In fact, atrocities against the Armenians continued through the end of the war and beyond, with no vehement American response.[8]

Despite bold wartime declarations by Allied powers, those who ordered or carried out vast crimes largely escaped punishment, except for a few revenge killings of high-level perpetrators by Armenian vigilantes. The world responded so feebly to the Armenian genocide that many authorities give credence to a disputed Hitler statement shortly before World War II began: "After all, who remembers today the extermination of the Armenians?"[9]

Franklin Roosevelt, a leader of the Harvard Committee for Boer Relief, continued to demonstrate a concern for persecuted minorities abroad when in 1921 he began a ten-year stint as a trustee of Near East Relief. This organization aided Armenian and other suffering people in the region. One Near East Relief official who toured the disputed Caucasus territory in the summer of 1921 wrote FDR that he had stood beside "heaps of human bones and half-decomposed [Armenian] bodies representing the remains of 500 women and children killed in one spot" that year. This report, however, arrived just after Roosevelt came down with polio, and he likely paid it little if any attention.[10]

Henry Morgenthau Jr. certainly remembered the human catastrophe in the Ottoman empire. At age twenty-three he had visited his father, the ambassador, in Constantinople, as Ottoman persecution of Armenians and threats to Jews in Palestine mounted. Ottoman authorities reportedly considered sending Jews to concentration camps, and they enacted a law stipulating the death penalty for any Jew owning Zionist stamps. The young Morgenthau had returned home, missing the worst phase of killing and deportation of Armenians in 1915. His father summoned him back late that year to help the embassy deal with desperate situations in the Ottoman empire. The scale of the Armenian tragedy could not have escaped the young would-be public servant.[11]

We lack any records of Roosevelt and the two Morgenthaus discussing the Turkish genocide or what it meant for European Jews. When in 1918 the former ambassador published his diary of his service in Constantinople, the matter could easily have come up in social gatherings of the two families, who were neighbors in Hyde Park. Roosevelt used to call Morgenthau Sr. "Uncle Henry." The senior Morgenthau's experiences in the Ottoman empire turned him into an ardent opponent of Zionism. He believed that the push for a Jewish state in Palestine would inflame the hatred of Jews that already existed across the world. Morgenthau Jr. did not share his father's anti-Zionist passion, but at least until 1940 he was a non-Zionist who avoided taking positions on Jewish aspirations in Palestine.[12]

When the treasury secretary learned about the Nazi Final Solution, it was the second such cataclysm Morgenthau Jr. had experienced. He must have felt deeply about what the Nazis were doing to members of his own faith. Yet his position in the cabinet at first made him leery of advancing Jewish concerns. He served at Roosevelt's pleasure, and he represented all Americans, not European Jews. Treasury officially had little involvement in responding to foreign crises. Only after seeing compelling evidence of how the State Department obstructed efforts to aid and rescue Jews did Morgenthau turn to his friend in the White House.

Important officials in the State Department and in the British Foreign Office initially opposed any public statement on Nazi crimes against Jews. Some continued to doubt whether the Nazis truly intended to exterminate every Jew within their reach. Elbridge Durbrow of the European Division agreed that Nazis cruelly mistreated the Jews, but he insisted that the State Department had received no information from official sources about mass murder and therefore could not confirm such crimes. Perhaps he expected Hitler to send the State Department a memo.[13]

To avoid further pressure to aid Jews, the State Department sought to cut off the source of information about Nazi extermination. State Department bureaucrats who knew that Wise and others had received reports from Switzerland sent through the diplomatic pouch closed down this channel. Durbrow drafted a telegram prohibiting the American Legation at Bern from sending private messages through official channels, with the pretext that they might offend the Swiss. Undersecretary of State Sumner Welles tried to strike a balance between State Department views and Gerhart M. Riegner's need to send highly confidential information from Switzerland through protected routes. Contradictory telegrams left Riegner without clear guidance on what information he could dispatch to the United States.[14]

Foreign Office parliamentary undersecretary Richard Law told an American diplomat in London that the British government could not simply ignore persistent public demands to aid Jews threatened by the Nazi policy of annihilation. Britain wanted to confer confidentially with the United States and then approach other Allied governments about limited measures on behalf of refugees. The British government suggested that both nations might issue some special visas for refugees and guarantee that neutral countries could eventually release wartime refugees. When pressed, Law said he only meant to guarantee refugees repatriation to their countries of origin, not admission to Britain or the United States.[15]

The British were talking big, but doing little. State Department officials noted publicly how much the United States had already done and claimed the initiative for holding a joint conference. After some squabbling, the two countries agreed to send delegations to Bermuda in mid-April 1943 for a confidential gathering that might usefully consider ideas for aiding Jews and deflect political pressures for unilateral action.[16]

American Jewish organizations mobilized to formulate plans for rescuing Jews. At a meeting that Wise arranged in mid-February, Jewish leaders proposed that the Allies guarantee financial support for all refugees who escaped to Turkey, Sweden, Switzerland, Spain, and Portugal. Britain could admit any who reached the British Isles. The United States could house refugees in some place such as the Virgin Islands for the duration of the war.[17]

A rally in Madison Square Garden on March 1, organized by the American Jewish Congress in cooperation with non-Jewish organizations, attracted an overflow crowd. Ten thousand people stood outside the packed Garden and listened through amplifiers as Rabbi Wise, Chaim Weizmann, Mayor Fiorello LaGuardia, Senator Robert F. Wagner, and other speakers pleaded for support to "stop Hitler now." The meeting ratified an eleven-point resolution addressed to President Roosevelt and Allied leaders. They wanted the Allies to guarantee financial aid and postwar repatriation to neutral countries taking in refugees. They called upon America to ease the admission of refugees to the United States within the quota system and the British to open wider the gates of Palestine. They also urged the United Nations "to establish an appropriate inter-governmental agency to which authority and power shall be given to implement the program of rescue outlined here."[18]

Shortly afterwards, most of the Jewish organizations agreed to form a Joint Emergency Committee on European Jewish Affairs. One subcommittee focused on arranging mass demonstrations outside New York; another on influencing the media. The committee also prepared a list of demands, similar to those of the March 1 rally, to present to Welles, and through him, to FDR.[19]

Welles declared that President Roosevelt and the American government had shown deep interest in the fate of European Jews and that the United States would do everything possible to "prevent further persecution of the oppressed race." The State Department would promptly consider the resolution backed by the March 1 meeting, and Britain and the United States would convene a bilateral conference on refugee problems.[20]

Another Jewish-led emergency committee spoke independently, with a louder public voice. It had an unusual pedigree. Linked to the right-wing, anti-British Irgun in Palestine, Palestinian Hillel Kook, who took the name Peter Bergson in the United States, had earlier launched the nonsectarian Committee for a Jewish Army, recruiting support from several senators. Bergson was a gifted fundraiser and publicist. His innovations included dramatic newspaper ads written by playwright Ben Hecht calling for a Jewish army of 200,000: "The Jews of Palestine and the stateless Jews of the world do not only want to pray: THEY WANT TO FIGHT!!!!"[21]

After reading about Wise's press conference of November 24, 1942, Bergson changed his focus from raising a Jewish army to rescuing Jews still alive in Europe. His new Emergency Committee to Save the Jewish People of Europe planned its own meeting at Madison Square Garden for March 9, an event cast as a memorial service or pageant called "We Will Never Die." With his knack for securing celebrity assistance, Bergson persuaded Hecht to write the script for his pageant, composer Kurt Weill to arrange the score, and producer Billy Rose to seek White House support. Rose asked FDR in a February letter for a two-paragraph statement to be read as part of the pageant—in effect, a pledge that a "David of Democracy" was riding to the rescue of millions of Jews still under the executioner's blade in Nazi-dominated Europe. Henry F. Pringle of the Office of War Information advised the White House that such a message would "raise a political question." Wallace Murray, the Near East specialist in the State Department, now adviser on political relations, more pointedly asked Secretary of State Cordell Hull, Welles, and Assistant Secretary of State Adolf A. Berle to block the pageant, which he claimed the Axis propaganda machine would exploit. The White House simply declined to send a message, saying the president did not issue statements for pageants and presentations. "We Will Never Die" filled Madison Square Garden twice in a single day.[22]

Hecht's pageant played again on April 12 in Washington, D.C.'s Constitution Hall, where the audience included Eleanor Roosevelt, six members of the U.S. Supreme Court, more than 200 members of Congress, and many foreign diplomats. Despite opposition from established Jewish groups, large audiences attended performances of "We Will Never Die" in Philadelphia, Boston, Chicago, and ultimately in the Hollywood Bowl, where Governor Earl Warren joined many Hollywood figures in the audience. Bergson charged that Rabbi Wise had resented the appearance of a rival group and obstructed the performance of his pageant in other cities. Relations between the two Jewish emergency committees, already strained by tactical disputes and competition for contributions, outside support, and media attention, further deteriorated. Still, the Bergson group sustained a vigorous lobbying and advertising campaign for rescue measures.[23]

In interviews decades after the war, Bergson criticized American Jewish leaders no less than the government. The only Americans who feared the impression of a Jewish war, he charged, were timid Jewish leaders, obsessed with defending their organizational turf and with the danger of anti-Semitism in the United States. Had these leaders militantly lobbied for rescue measures, they might have compelled a positive response from the Roosevelt administration. However, Bergson, a recent arrival in the United States, had little understanding of American political culture. Roosevelt did not easily succumb to outside pressure. He would have shunned any actions that gave the impression that the United States was fighting a Jewish war regardless of views expressed by Jewish advocates either within or outside his circle of advisers.

Ironically, the split between Bergson and mainstream Jewish leaders like Rabbi Wise may have inadvertently helped their cause. Each side could present rescue measures and organize its own events, which attracted somewhat different followers. Bergson could operate as an outside agitator and publicist, while Wise could work both from within and outside the Roosevelt administration. It was Wise who had publicly released credible reports of the Nazis' mass murder of Jews, alerting Bergson among others to the horrors of the Holocaust. Wise could also present Jewish concerns and proposals directly to Welles and occasionally FDR himself.[24]

Jewish leaders competed for the backing of Eleanor Roosevelt with mixed success. Eleanor had worked primarily behind the scenes to assist in efforts to rescue Jewish children and individual refugees who sought her intervention. She had supported the decision to take in the passengers from the SS Quanza, advocated the admission of a small number of German

Jewish scholars and intellectuals, and had become honorary president of the private U.S. Committee for the Care of European Children and a Hadassah group that promoted the immigration of Jewish youth to Palestine. She had not publicly denounced the Nazis oppression of Jews, endorsed a Jewish homeland in Palestine, or pressed openly for any specific rescue measures. Wise failed to persuade Eleanor to back his March 1 rally, although she lauded Hecht's pageant "We Will Never Die" in her regular "My Day" column after attending its Washington performance. She also sent an encouraging message to Bergson's Emergency Committee to Save the Jewish People of Europe, but declined a request to back the organization.[25]

Eleanor followed the line that the Allies could best save Jews by winning the war as rapidly as possible. In August 1943, she specifically addressed the oppression of Jews—which she called a "race issue"—for the first time in her "My Day" column, which she had been writing nearly without interruption since late 1935. She noted that, Jews "have suffered in Europe as has no other group" and "called upon the world as a whole to protest in its own interest against wholesale persecution." However, she added, "I do not know what we can do to save the Jews in Europe and to find them homes." In contrast to her bold public advocacy on domestic civil rights, Eleanor was not an innovator on solutions for Hitler's Jewish victims. It is possible, although not plausible given her public silence, that Eleanor pressured Franklin privately on rescue measures for Jews. There is no reliable evidence on this matter, only much later second- and third-hand reconstructions by interested parties.[26]

In mid-March 1943, the President's Advisory Committee on Political Refugees presented proposals that paralleled those of Jewish organizations. The committee suggested moving refugees out of Spain, so that the Spanish government might accept new arrivals from France. It recommended that the Allies should persuade Turkey to admit refugees from the Balkans temporarily. They should also guarantee to all neutral countries that accepted refugees the costs of maintenance and postwar repatriation, and resume admission of refugees to sites in Western Hemisphere countries and territories. Separately, James G. McDonald, chairman of the committee, wrote that for most Jews remaining in Europe, Palestine offered the only alternative to death. He believed that Palestine, no longer threatened by Erwin Rommel's army, could absorb more Jews, and that the British White Paper was not immutable.[27]

Talk of Palestine as an essential destination for Jews only stiffened British resistance to rescue measures. In March 1943, British foreign secretary Eden traveled to Washington for talks on managing the alliance with the Soviet Union and planning the postwar peace settlements. On March 27, Wise and Joseph Proskauer asked Eden to join with the Allies in calling upon Hitler to release all Jews in Europe. Eden called this "fantastically impossible." He also deprecated virtually every other specific suggestion, such as using Turkey as a haven for Bulgarian Jews and shipping food to starving Jews in Europe, which he deemed a violation of the Allied economic blockade of Axis territory.[28]

At a meeting later that day Hull urged Britain to help rescue about 60,000–70,000 Bulgarian Jews threatened with extermination. Eden then warned that if the Allies assumed responsibility for Bulgarian Jews, Hitler might then offer to release Jews from Poland and Germany, and "there are not enough ships and means of transportation in the world to handle them." In reality, Hitler was hardly going to authorize the release of large Jewish populations under direct German control, but the Bulgarian government was less rigid, especially in 1943. Still, Eden probably feared that masses of Bulgarian Jews might crash the British gates of Palestine.[29]

Welles hoped to keep Bulgarian Jews on the Bermuda Conference agenda. He told Jewish leaders that he would consider the event successful if it rescued 50,000 people. He even endorsed "dignified" mass meetings sponsored by Jews. Welles said that only Roosevelt had a chance of overriding the current negative Allied view of an appeal to the Nazis to release Jews. By contrast, Breckinridge Long wrote in his diary that Jewish agitation lent color to Hitler's charges that the Allies fought the war on behalf of the Jews, a distortion that gained believers in Turkey, Palestine, and North Africa.[30]

Public protests, combined with continued appalling reports about Nazi killings and deportations, moved Alben Barkley, the Senate majority leader, to sponsor a resolution expressing America's indignation about Nazi-inflicted atrocities upon the civilian populations in occupied countries. The resolution cited "especially the mass murder of Jewish men, women, and children" and declared that those guilty should be punished commensurately for their crimes. The measure passed both houses easily, but given a lack of remedies beyond postwar trials of the perpetrators, Congress had merely ratified the statement issued months earlier by the United Nations. In March and April, seven state legislatures passed resolutions of support for the plight of Jews, calling in some cases for the opening of Palestine to Jewish refugees.[31]

On March 30, Senator Barkley gave the keynote speech at a packed conference of the Joint Emergency Committee on European Jewish Affairs. He called upon the U.S. government to demand that Nazi Germany cease its practice of exterminating Jews: "never before has the world known or witnessed such sheer brutality, such beastly barbarism, such cruel inhumanity." If the Nazis continued, the United States should urge neutral countries to ask Germany to release all Jews from its territories. He said that the United States should arrange sanctuaries for them in America, Palestine, and neutral countries.[32]

Roosevelt happened to meet with leaders of Congress the next morning and might have spoken to Barkley about his speech, which the press covered widely. At lunch with Supreme Court Justice Owen Roberts later that day, the president likely asked Roberts to chair the American delegation to the Bermuda Conference. Roberts, a Republican whom Hoover had appointed to the bench, fit the bipartisan mold of Henry Stimson and Myron C. Taylor as the kind of representative Roosevelt preferred for a politically sensitive mission. Roberts declined after he learned that this meeting would overlap with the Supreme Court session. Taylor had earlier turned down an offer to chair the delegation. He foresaw that the conference would likely fail because neither side was willing to admit refugees, pay for transportation, or guarantee resettlement from neutral countries that temporarily sheltered Jews.[33]

Harold Dodds, president of Princeton University, finally agreed to chair the delegation. Long did not select Barkley as the Senate's representative, choosing instead Scott Lucas, a first-term Democrat from Illinois. Lucas was an up-and-coming supporter of the New Deal, but in 1943 he was known more for listening than for taking initiatives. From the House, Long chose Representative Sol Bloom, chairman of the House Foreign Affairs Committee, who had regularly deferred to and defended the State Department.[34]

On April 1, the president received seven Jewish members of Congress. They requested simplified procedures for immigration and the appointment of Jewish authorities on refugees to the American delegation to Bermuda—or the admission of a separate Jewish delegation. Roosevelt arranged a meeting for the representatives with Long to consider revising the immigration process. The president also said it might be possible to issue visitors' visas again. Representative Emanuel Celler tried to warn FDR that the Bermuda Conference would probably not achieve any breakthroughs for imperiled Jews. According to information passed to Weizmann and Moshe Shertok (later Sharett) of the Jewish Agency for Palestine (who were visiting the United States), Roosevelt promised the congressman that he would push for the rescue of Jewish children. He also said he would support sending food into Europe through the blockade. The Joint Emergency Committee on European Jewish Affairs tried to get a follow-up appointment with FDR, but apparently failed.[35]

Like Celler, mainstream Jewish leaders held out little hope for a successful conference: the scope of Bermuda was too narrow, and neither Senator Lucas nor Representative Bloom would likely challenge State Department views. They met privately with Bloom to goad him into action. The committee also sought a Jewish delegation to the conference; they secured only the last-minute addition to the American delegation of two outside technical advisers with useful knowledge, but no political influence.[36]

On April 14, just five days before the Bermuda Conference, Wise and his allies organized another mass protest in Chicago. Wise delivered the keynote address to a capacity crowd of more than 20,000 in the Chicago Stadium. He demanded concrete action, not just study and exploration, at the upcoming conference. Missouri senator Harry S. Truman passionately told the crowd, "the people of that ancient race, the Jews, are being herded like animals into the Ghettoes, the concentration camps, and the wastelands of Europe. The men, women, and the children of this honored people are being . . . actually murdered by the fiendish Huns and Fascists." He added that "today—not tomorrow, we must do all that is humanly possible to provide a haven and a place of safety for all of those who can be grasped from the Nazi butchers." Like Barkley, who would become Truman's second-term vice president in 1949, Truman could use strong language in a way FDR felt he could not. The rally adopted a twelve-point program similar to that of the March 1 gathering in New York. It included pressure on German satellite states, the setting aside of refugee havens in neutral countries, the opening up of Palestine to Jewish immigrants, and the establishment of an international agency to implement rescue measures.[37]

Shortly before the Bermuda Conference opened, Sweden offered to try to persuade Germany to release Jews without ransom payments. The Swedish cabinet approved a proposal to take in 20,000 Jewish children if the Allies paid to maintain them and guaranteed their removal at war's end. Some Jews had already escaped Denmark and arrived in Sweden, which allowed them to stay there. The Swedish cabinet thought this ambitious proposal would impress officials in London and Washington, but neither government offered the required guarantees.[38]

Another possible opportunity for rescue or relief lay in Romania. The Romanian government had deported and killed Jews side by side with Nazi forces in 1941. Then, prompted by Allied warnings, it began to hesitate and quarrel in September 1942 about future policies toward Romanian Jews. In July 1942, Roosevelt and Winston Churchill had released stern statements for Rabbi Wise to read to the mass meeting in Madison Square Garden, and on August 21, 1942, Roosevelt had denounced barbaric crimes in Europe and Asia and threatened punishment of war criminals in court after the war. In October 1942, Marshal Ion Antonescu, Romania's anti-Semitic dictator, postponed plans to deport about 300,000 Jews to the Belzec death camp and by November his government was internally debating plans for allowing some Romanian Jews to emigrate. The Russian decimation of Romanian troops fighting with the Germans at Stalingrad and the massive German disaster there in January only strengthened Romanian reservations about handing Jews over to Germany.[39]

In early 1943, Bergson's Emergency Committee to Save the Jewish People of Europe had suggested that the Romanian government would release Jews in return for a payment of $50 per person. Zionist leaders denounced as misleading and unethical Hecht's ad about Jews in Romania, which appealed for donations to pay ransom for the release of 70,000 Jews deported to Romanian-occupied Transnistria. In fact, Romanian intermediaries wanted more money ($350 per person), the Romanian government did not guarantee release of the Jews, and Germany firmly opposed Romanian plans to allow some Jewish emigration. The scheme required the Allies to repudiate their economic restrictions against financial transactions with an enemy nation, and to overcome their resistance to paying ransom. Wise thought that perhaps the Bergson group had fallen for a hoax. It seems, however, that it took the most optimistic interpretation of a middleman's ability to work with Romanian officials.[40]

Any plan to secure the emigration of Romanian Jews had to run a gauntlet of political, diplomatic, and practical obstacles. Nazi officials sought to block any Jewish emigration to Palestine, and the British resisted taking in adults there. In the absence of Allied pressure, Turkey was reluctant to admit more Jews, even temporarily. The British adamantly opposed efforts to rescue Romanian Jews. The Foreign Office called the Romanian offer "a piece of blackmail, which if successful, would open up an endless process on the part of Germany and her satellites in southeastern Europe of unloading, at a given price, all their unwanted nationals on overseas countries." No practical Allied plan emerged for the rescue of Romanian Jews.[41]

Through a cruel twist of fate, the opening of the Anglo-American conference at Bermuda coincided with Passover and with an uprising of thousands of Jews in the Warsaw ghetto. Nazi authorities had already deported most ghetto inhabitants to the gas chambers at Treblinka.

At Bermuda, Law, the most senior British official present, pointed out the folly of offering to assume responsibility for any sizable portion of twenty to thirty million "useless" people who were a liability to Hitler. Protected by an enduring commitment to confidentiality, the American and British delegations agreed to respect each other's sensitive areas—the tight immigration policy of the United States and British opposition to negotiating with Germany or sending aid into Europe through the blockade. Both sides hoped to avoid inflaming Arab opinion on Palestine, the British even more so than the Americans. One of the very few publicized decisions to emerge from the conference was Britain's reaffirmation of the White Paper of 1939, which meant only 29,000 more Jews could enter Palestine, the remainder from the five-year quota of 75,000. For security reasons, however, British representatives refused to admit any Jewish adults into Palestine from the Balkans; they spoke only of accepting 4,000 children, accompanied by 500 adult escorts, and wanted the Americans to share the costs of transporting them. Leaders of the Jewish Agency for Palestine feared that Britain did not intend to fulfill even this limited commitment. In their view, British policy would in practice end Jewish immigration to Palestine.[42]

Among U.S. delegates, Senator Lucas was particularly forthright in rejecting any diversion from the war effort: "I am thinking about the millions of boys in this country who are fighting on every front in this war. I am thinking of the mothers. . . . Every day you postpone bringing this war to a conclusion you just take upon your hands the blood of American boys." Refugee specialist Robert Borden Reams added that if one Nazi spy or saboteur entered the country, Congress would bar the door to all future refugees.

With such adverse views, the Bermuda Conference produced minimal results, missing opportunities for at least attempting to rescue Jews in German satellite states like Bulgaria and Romania.[43]

In a May 4 speech in Boston, Assistant Secretary of State Berle reiterated the canonical Allied view that only "the invasion of Europe, the defeat of German arms, and the breaking of German power" could help stop the mass murder of civilians. A refugee specialist in the British Foreign Office commented approvingly that at least American officials now appreciated the British perspective on German atrocities. Nearly six months after the Allied declaration of December 17, both the State Department—apart from Welles and Herbert Feis—and the Foreign Office still folded the "Jewish Question" into the broader imperative of smashing the Axis war machine.[44]

By then, the Allies had realized that Germany would not soon collapse militarily or psychologically. They abandoned any hope of invading France during the summer of 1943. Instead, the Allies planned an easier invasion of Sicily and then, if successful, Italy. FDR later told his aide William Hassett that decisive action in Europe would come in September 1943, after Anglo-American forces consolidated their gains in North Africa. That meant another year or more of delay in military operations that might disrupt the killing of Jews.[45]

The idea of sending relief to suffering civilians in Europe had divided Britain and the United States for years. In January 1943, President Roosevelt had appointed former New York governor Herbert Lehman as director of European relief. "The appointment of a Jew to an office which is going to play a decisive role in the reconstruction of Europe is a fact of the most far-reaching significance," wrote Maurice Perlzweig, political director of the World Jewish Congress. It showed that "more than any statesman living he [FDR] appreciates the full moral horror of anti-Semitism and is determined to make no sort of compromise with it." Lehman favored relief to mitigate suffering, save lives, and earn goodwill. However, he also found that he lacked both independent resources and the authority to compel cooperation from reluctant wartime officials. On August 30, 1943, he detailed these frustrations in a ten-page letter to FDR. Lehman would later gain greater resources and authority as head of a joint United Nations Relief and Rehabilitation Administration, but most of its work would take place after the war's end.[46]

Lehman also failed to overcome Churchill's commitment to maintaining an economic blockade as a tactic for weakening Germany and shortening the war. Beyond relief shipments to Greece that Britain had already approved, the cabinet would not authorize or even study relief programs. These British policies reduced the likelihood of aiding or rescuing Jews.[47]

During his meetings with FDR in May 1943, Churchill wrote triumphantly to Eden, "In fact I can safely say that there is no chance of [the] President taking any strong line against our [blockade] policy and views." Yet Roosevelt remained skeptical of British policy; State Department official Francis Sayre said afterward that the president tried to persuade Churchill to relent on shipments of food through the blockade. Churchill would not relent, and the president conceded that Britain should have the final word on maintaining the blockade. To mask the military rationale for their blockade, the Allies publicly blamed Germany for not cooperating with the Allies on relief shipments.[48]

Mainstream Jewish organizations in the United States, which still hoped to work with the administration on rescue initiatives, had some internal allies. Oscar Cox, general counsel of the Foreign Economic Administration, proposed that the administration establish a new American rescue organization with the authority of government behind it—acting alongside the State Department. On June 18, Cox and his staff circulated within the bureaucracy a revised draft plan for an independent U.S. board, headed by prominent officials, to deal with "all aspects of the war refugee problem which are not the direct responsibility of the State Department."[49]

Wise wrote FDR on behalf of a coalition of organizations to express their disappointment with the "inexplicable absence of active measures to save those Jews who can still be saved—without, of course, in the slightest degree impairing our war effort." He asked for an early appointment to present practical proposals for rescuing Jews. Hearing that the next step might be a meeting of the Intergovernmental Committee on Refugees, Celler called for American delegates unlike the "Charlie McCarthys [dummies] who represented us at Bermuda." He also tried to revive the notion of holding a meeting of receptive senators and representatives; only extreme pressure on the authorities, he believed, could yield results.[50]

In a late July meeting, Wise urged Roosevelt to warn Nazi satellites such as Hungary and Romania, which had most of the surviving European Jews, against further cooperation with Germany. FDR avoided a firm commitment, but Wise left hopeful that the president and Churchill would issue a joint statement aimed at satellite states. Roosevelt responded weeks later with a letter to Wise reaffirming past commitment to punishing those who perpetrated atrocities, and noting, "I intend again, on suitable occasions, to revert publicly to this subject, as I am sure the heads of the other United Nations Governments will also do."[51]

On July 28, Polish ambassador Jan Ciechanowski and Jan Karski, a lieutenant in the Polish underground, met with Roosevelt in his study. Earlier in London, Karski had already informed the Polish government-in-exile, the Allied governments, and Polish Jewish leaders about the continuing Nazi slaughter of Jews. After Cox had met Karski, he told Harry Hopkins about him, which smoothed the way for Karski to visit the White House.[52]

Karski said later that Roosevelt expressed interest in the Polish underground, the Jewish underground, and many other subjects. Eventually, Karski steered the conversation around to concentration camps and to Nazi treatment of the Jews. He said that despite the brutality of Nazi occupation policies in general, they treated the Jews differently—they intended to destroy their biological substance. Without Allied intervention, Polish Jewry would cease to exist. Roosevelt thanked Karski and commented on the importance of his story. In one of Karski's recollections, the president's final words were a noncommittal, "Tell your people we shall win the war."[53]

Something more came out of Wise's and Karski's meetings with Roosevelt. Wise had told FDR about a World Jewish Congress proposal to supply money indirectly for relief and rescue of Jews in Romania and France. Wealthy Jews in both countries would lend money for these purposes, and Jewish organizations abroad would reimburse them through deposits in American or Swiss banks, with the accounts blocked until the end of the war. Thus, no outside funds would reach enemy nations to help them carry on the war, but Jewish sources could make money available for emigration or relief. Wise doubted that the Treasury would approve this plan, but Roosevelt personally intervened. He phoned Morgenthau to advocate it and sent over the written request as well.[54]

On August 5, Morgenthau asked Hull to join with him in approving the World Jewish Congress proposal for facilitating the possible evacuation of up to 70,000 Jews from Romania at a cost of about $170,000 deposited to blocked accounts. American officials did not intend to dedicate this modest sum for paying ransom, but only for covering the costs of emigration if that proved possible. Even so, lower-level State Department officials had challenged Treasury about the principles and the process involved.[55]

Welles might have been able to steer such a controversial policy through State's obstacle course, but he was on his way out of government—the victim of Hull's long-smoldering resentment at the president's reliance on him. William Bullitt, himself out of favor with FDR, had determined to turn Welles's homosexual episodes into a security threat. When FDR refused to fire Welles, Bullitt teamed up with Hull and began to talk indiscreetly about Welles's escapades. Berle later called Welles's forced resignation a tragedy of Greek proportions.[56]

With Welles gone, imperiled Jews no longer had a powerful ally within a generally hostile agency. Hull let the World Jewish Congress proposal sit, and then his subordinates told Treasury that State refused to comment on the scheme. It first appeared that Treasury could proceed unilaterally by getting American diplomats in Switzerland to issue a license for the transaction. Then Morgenthau learned from Lehman that State had not sent the authorization to Bern and later that American diplomats in Switzerland insisted on consulting the British, who were predictably opposed. These tactics postponed this potentially life-saving initiative for several months.[57]

Berle dissented from the majority view in his department. He justified a license for the Joint Distribution Committee to supply relief to impoverished Jews in a Shanghai ghetto because "the blockade has now reached a point at which it probably hurts our friends almost as much as it hurts our enemies." He believed that the Allies could aid suffering people without collaterally benefiting Germany and Japan.[58]

In September, following a Bergson group conference on rescue measures, Pierre van Paassen addressed a long letter to the president. He urged FDR to focus on the situation of Jews in the Balkans and to warn Nazi satellites against cooperating with Germany. Van Paassen also called for formation of a new Anglo-American agency to carry out rescue efforts. In mid-September, Bergson sent Cox a blueprint for action passed by an emergency conference a couple of months earlier: its proposal for an American rescue agency differed from recommendations by mainstream Jewish organizations for an international agency, but paralleled an initiative that Cox had already put forward on his own. Bergson then recruited a number of senators and representatives to back Senator Guy Gillette, Democrat of Iowa, and Representative Will Rogers Jr., Democrat of California, cosponsors of the Gillette-Rogers resolution that urged the president to establish a commission to formulate plans for saving Jewish survivors from extinction at Nazi hands. It drew support also from some unlikely quarters, such as the Hearst newspaper chain.[59]

The Gillette-Rogers resolution exposed another point of dispute between the Bergson group and mainstream American Zionists. Bergson and his allies believed that Jewish leaders should put aside the controversial issue of Palestine in order to unite Jews and Christians behind urgent rescue plans. Mainstream Zionists deemed it necessary for practical rescue measures and the future well-being of Jews to sustain pressure on the public and the government for opening Palestine to Jewish refugees and ultimately establishing a Jewish state there. Thus, Rabbi Wise testified before the House Committee on Foreign Affairs that while he favored the Gillette-Rogers resolution, he also wanted to include a section on keeping Palestine open to Jewish immigration. The plans adopted at the Wise-sponsored mass rallies of March 1 and April 14, Wise's July meeting with FDR in July, and his gaining of presidential approval for the initiative on rescuing Romanian Jews demonstrate that mainstream Zionists combined advocacy of rescue measures and Jewish rights in Palestine.[60]

As the Gillette-Rogers resolution gained support, Cox warned Welles's replacement, Undersecretary of State Edward R. Stettinius Jr., that Congress might seize the initiative and do what the administration should do and "should have done a long time ago." In early October, however, Long's subordinate Reams reinforced Stettinius's caution on Jewish concerns by telling him that most critics of the State Department inside and outside Congress were ill-informed or irresponsible.[61]

Some of the external critics showed up on the streets of Washington. In concert with the Orthodox rescue group Vaad ha-Hatzala, the Bergson group organized a protest march by a delegation of rabbis who would seek to meet the president. The two groups agreed on the urgent need for rescue measures that could be achieved only by challenging the Roosevelt administration. These similarities overcame past differences—Bergson's advocacy for a Jewish army in Palestine and the non-Zionist views of the Vaad ha-Hatzala. Bergson sponsored the rabbis' march to rally support for the Gillette-Rogers resolution, which faced uncertain prospects in Congress, given the lack of administration support. He also pushed for the resolution on rescue through the tactic he had pioneered of placing large dramatic ads in major newspapers.[62]

Rabbi Wise and other Bergson opponents discouraged the march planned for October 6. According to Hassett's firsthand account, on that morning,

Judge Samuel Rosenman told the president that "he had tried—admittedly without success—to keep the horde from storming Washington." Rosenman said the group behind this petition did not represent "the most thoughtful elements in Jewry" and that "the leading Jews of his acquaintance opposed this march on the Capitol." Although the group had tried for weeks to arrange a meeting with FDR, he decided, apparently that morning, not to receive representatives of the rabbis. Instead, Roosevelt talked about letting more Jews into Palestine to the limit of its capacity to absorb them—if necessary, with a barbed-wire fence to keep Jews in and Arabs out.[63]

Most Jewish members of Congress also opposed the march. When Representative Bloom told one of the rabbis that a march of such un-American-looking people in Washington was undignified, his comment backfired. About 400 Orthodox rabbis from New York, Philadelphia, and Baltimore showed up, joined by close to fifty from elsewhere. The mostly bearded rabbis dressed solemnly in black recited psalms as they marched to the Capitol. Vice President Henry Wallace and Jewish representatives in the House received seven rabbis, who presented a petition to the president demanding immediate action to rescue European Jews, creation of a special agency for this purpose, and the opening of Palestine to Jewish immigration. Wallace and House Speaker Sam Rayburn also participated in a ceremony on the steps of the Capitol in which Rabbi Eliezer Silver of Cincinnati read the petition in Hebrew and Rabbi Aaron David Burack of Brooklyn read an English translation. Wallace noted the timing of the event—three days before Yom Kippur—and said he was moved. Nevertheless, he also stated that only an Allied military victory would solve the larger Nazi problem, of which the Jewish tragedy was a part. Bergson and four leading rabbis saw presidential secretary Marvin McIntyre, while Roosevelt went off to Bolling Field, where he dedicated four Liberator bombers for a Yugoslavian combat unit serving with American forces. The press generally followed the president.[64]

An indirect source claims that Roosevelt subsequently asked World Jewish Congress executive Nahum Goldmann whether anything could be done to "liquidate" the notorious Bergson. According to White House logs, FDR did not meet with Goldmann in the fall or winter of 1943. Still, FDR undoubtedly disliked Bergson's methods and strategy, which the trusted Rosenman and mainstream Jewish advocates condemned, and which challenged his own cautious approach to Jewish issues. From the president's perspective, Bergson and his allies gave Jewish issues undue publicity and detached Jewish concerns from broader Allied priorities and principles.[65]

On November 5, Roosevelt met privately with left-wing columnist Samuel Grafton, associate editor of the *New York Post,* who had some ties to Bergson. Although there is no record of their conversation, three months earlier Grafton had written a scathing critique of contradictions in the Allied response to the slaughter of Jews. When the Nazis gassed Jews in the "execution caravans" located in Poland, the world considered them a special problem, and Allied warnings to the Nazis against the use of poison gas did not apply. When the Allies considered rescue, they perceived Jews as part of a general problem, for which the only real solution was military victory. But Hitler would not let the Jews wait, Grafton argued. The first step was to put an independent agency in charge of rescue.[66]

A few days after meeting with Grafton, Roosevelt considered the prospect of a sudden German military collapse, which would impose on occupying armies the burden of providing relief to millions of displaced persons. In a November 10 memo to Secretary of War Stimson he asked the army to ship and distribute relief supplies to liberated areas, even in the midst of active military operations. He referred Stimson to the State Department and the Treasury for assistance.[67]

On November 11, Stettinius told State Department officials that FDR believed America should do more to help the Jews. Perhaps Grafton had changed his thinking or perhaps it was Cox, who had been trying for some time to do so. Perhaps he was responding to pressure from Congress as well. FDR mentioned opening offices in Algiers, Naples, Portugal, Madrid, and Ankara; creating an additional refugee camp such as that in North Africa; and appropriating some funds for these purposes. State Department official Ray Atherton objected and Stettinius temporized by asking Long to discuss details with Hull.[68]

Days later, Roosevelt began a long trip to Cairo, before proceeding to Tehran for the first summit conference with Joseph Stalin. He was out of the country for about a month. During that time, Congress and the Treasury Department challenged the State Department's mismanagement of refugee issues.

Bloom asked Long to testify before the House Foreign Affairs Committee to rebut the critics of the State Department's refugee policies. Long insisted on a closed session, allegedly to avoid giving the Nazis inside information they could use to block rescue efforts. On November 26, he energetically defended all policies of the State Department since 1933 and of the Intergovernmental Committee on Refugees since its inception in 1938. If Congress passed the Gillette-Rogers resolution, he said, it would repudiate all this fine work, but Long refused to put his opposition on the record.[69]

Letting the Gillette-Rogers resolution die in committee would turn the wrath of the resolution's supporters upon committee members. Therefore, on December 10, the House Foreign Affairs Committee released Long's testimony. This tactic backfired. To fit his preconceptions, Long had misrepresented the facts on the admission of refugees to the United States. He confused the number of visas issued with the number of people admitted: many visas expired because of delays. Long also assumed that every visa that any consul had issued anywhere in Europe was for "refugees." Long claimed that the United States had admitted 580,000 refugees since 1933—an exaggeration by at least 250 percent. Representative Celler circulated Long's report and data, which immigration experts shredded during the latter half of December. Celler called for Long's resignation.[70]

Shortly before Thanksgiving, Morgenthau, Treasury's general counsel Randolph Paul, Foreign Funds Control chief John Pehle, Assistant General Counsel Josiah DuBois Jr., and two other Treasury officials—Ansel Luxford, and Harry Dexter White—met to plan strategy for a decisive battle with the State Department and the British over efforts to save Jews. Morgenthau warned his subordinates, none of them Jewish, that they confronted a generation of patricians in the State Department "who don't like to do this kind of thing. . . . But don't think you are going to be able to nail anybody in the State Department . . . to the cross." Luxford responded, "I am not so sure. . . . They will go too far."[71]

The weight of Morgenthau's cabinet responsibilities made him more cautious than his Treasury team. In a December 6 meeting, Pehle said, "I feel especially sore at all these Jewish episodes in the State Department and I'm convinced that it's just a gang in there that are blocking everything." Morgenthau responded, "Well, I, of all people appreciate the sympathetic interest of you boys; on the other hand, I've got to be a balance wheel." On December 17, he explained that as secretary of the treasury, he had to represent all Americans: "But if Mr. [Representive] Hamilton Fish was to go after me, he goes after me because I am a Jew. Let's use plain, simple language.

He doesn't go after me because I am Secretary; he goes after me because he thinks that I have done something for the Jews because I am a Jew."[72]

On December 9, former State Department official Bernard Meltzer recounted to DuBois the State Department's delaying tactics that stalled the World Jewish Congress's proposals for rescuing Jews in the Balkans and France. Hull had signaled that the State Department did not stand behind the cables it sent out for Treasury on providing funds for the rescue of Jews. This equivocation at the top helped to explain why subordinate American diplomats withheld their cooperation. Only Meltzer and Feis had backed relief and rescue proposals; everyone else at State had opposed them. Meltzer said that he could not prove that anti-Semitism accounted for the Foreign Service crowd's position, but their opposition, allegedly on grounds of economic warfare, which was his responsibility, was "striking."[73]

Treasury officials tried to get a sympathetic ambassador, John G. Winant, in London to clear away British obstruction of the World Jewish Congress proposals. They learned, however, that "The [British] Foreign Office are concerned with the difficulties of disposing of any considerable number of Jews should they be rescued from enemy-occupied territory. . . . For this reason they are reluctant to agree to any approval being expressed even of the preliminary financial arrangements." In effect, the Foreign Office preferred to let Jews die in place, rather than try to find havens for them elsewhere.[74]

Morgenthau and Paul asked for a showdown appointment with Hull and Long. By then, Stettinius had met with both men (December 17) and had called for approving licenses for relief and rescue programs and setting up asylums for refugees. The Treasury group put Hull in the uncomfortable position of siding with the British or the Treasury.[75]

On December 18, Hull sent out a telegram to London, saying that Winant's previous cable about the British Foreign Office's standpoint was read "with astonishment." After five months of delay, Long suddenly approved a license for the World Jewish Congress to set up its blocked account in Switzerland; in Treasury's view, "they saw the record being built up against them." Cox told the Treasury group that widespread criticism from inside and outside the administration had made the State Department "very very sensitive."[76]

Cox said that the president favored the idea of a new organization, which Cox had championed since June, to handle refugee matters, but that the

State Department had opposed this plan. Luxford summarized, "Oscar has a whale of a good plan, but he has to have an excuse to get it to the President. We have a beautiful issue here to take it to the President and say, 'We want a solution to it. The British have taken a dogmatic attitude. . . .' There is where you marry them [the two conceptions]." This marriage brought the War Refugee Board into existence.[77]

On Monday morning, December 20, Hull and Long thought "the decks were clear" when Morgenthau and Paul walked in for a meeting. Explaining what actions they had just taken, the two State Department officials blamed a cast of others—the Nazis, the Latin American countries, the British—for thwarting previous American initiatives for refugees. Hull even claimed he was trying to get the British to revise their White Paper policy on Palestine. When Long took Morgenthau aside and criticized Treasury's informant Meltzer, who was Jewish, for delaying the World Jewish Congress proposal, Morgenthau shot back, "Well, Breck, as long as you raise the question, we might be a little frank. The impression is . . . that you, particularly, are anti-Semitic." Morgenthau "took his gloves off." He termed State Department attitudes identical with those expressed in the cable of the British Foreign Office. Citing the American tradition of sheltering the persecuted, Morgenthau said he was acting as secretary of the treasury, not as a Jew. He knew too much to accept Long and Hull's self-serving fiction. He knew that Roosevelt had approved of the World Jewish Congress plan, and the State Department had done nothing but stall it.[78]

DuBois spent much of Christmas Day drafting a report for Morgenthau, entitling it "Report to the Secretary on the Acquiescence of this Government in the Murder of the Jews." He charged Long with creating the bottleneck in granting visas and reiterated how State had obstructed the presidentially approved rescue plan. He related how the State Department deliberately suppressed information from Switzerland on the Nazi killings of Jews and then sought to cover up this treachery. He warned that without drastic changes in America's approach to Nazi atrocities, the United States would have to share historic responsibility for this extermination of an entire people. Privately, DuBois later told Morgenthau that if the president did nothing, DuBois would resign and take his story to the press.[79]

For a time, Morgenthau deliberated over how best to proceed. He dropped DuBois's inflammatory title, substituting "Personal Report to the President." However, he retained comments about the widespread perception that some State Department officials were anti-Semitic and that publicity about their obstructionist policies might spark a nasty political scandal. With the assistance of Benjamin V, Cohen, Cox meanwhile sent Morgenthau and later Rosenman a copy of a proposed executive order and accompanying press release setting up a new refugee board supervised by Leo Crowley, head of the Foreign Economic Administration, Morgenthau, and Hull. While not strictly necessary, Cox wrote, an executive order might forestall criticism from the administration's opponents on the Hill.[80]

At another Treasury meeting, White summarized the politics of refugee policy. In the past, the United States had allowed Britain to dominate Allied decisions on the "Jewish Question" in Europe. Only Roosevelt could change that tacit policy and only Morgenthau could persuade the president to do so. If the president felt keenly enough, he could overcome British resistance and other obstacles to helping Europe's surviving Jews. Morgenthau's staff reasoned that if they went to Hull and requested his cooperation, he might well misinform the president. Morgenthau should get to FDR first.[81]

At 12:40 p.m. on January 16, 1944, Morgenthau, Pehle, and Paul brought their report to the White House, which Roosevelt asked them to summarize orally. He did not believe that Long had intentionally tried to prevent rescue measures, but admitted that the assistant secretary had "soured" on refugees as security risks. Morgenthau reminded the president that Attorney General Francis Biddle had reported to the cabinet that only three Jews admitted to the United States during the war had presented any security issues. He warned that Congress might act if the president did not. In any case, FDR quickly approved the concept of a War Refugee Board: it did not take much persuasion. Since only the army had the capacity to distribute relief or supply immediate care for refugees in liberated areas, he wanted Secretary of War Stimson, rather than Crowley, to serve on the board. He also urged Morgenthau to consult with Undersecretary of State Stettinius, perhaps because he was better organized and more sympathetic to Jewish concerns than Hull. The implication was that Stettinius, rather than Hull, might represent, in practice, the State Department on the new War Refugee Board. Roosevelt also wanted Judge Rosenman informed. He and Morgenthau then discussed the possibilities of getting Jews into Turkey, Spain, and Switzerland.[82]

Despite the change in the composition of the board—Stimson was no liberal—the meeting proceeded more smoothly than Morgenthau expected.

The task of persuading FDR may have been easier than Morgenthau believed. An increasingly isolated Roosevelt had come to rely heavily on his Treasury Secretary as a confidant.

Hull was a weak and distant secretary of state. Critics had forced Welles out of government. The Republican Stimson was a powerful figure, but lacked a close personal relationship with the president. Once the most consequential of vice presidents, Wallace had lost responsibility and favor after feuding with more conservative members of the administration. FDR could no longer depend on his previously robust support team in the White House. Louis McHenry Howe, his aide for a quarter century had died in 1936. Thomas "Tommy the Cork" Corcoran, FDR's chief political operative, feuded with the president and entered private law practice in 1940. Marguerite "Missy" LeHand, his indispensable personal secretary and companion who lived in the White House, suffered a major stroke in 1941. Adviser Hopkins remained important, but ended his more than three-year residence at the White House in late 1943. He never regained his earlier intimacy with the president. FDR had minimal support or trusted advice during the last year and a half of his life and presidency.[83]

The Treasury's efforts over a period of six months, combined with key assistance and advice from the unheralded Cox and Cohen, produced a small new organization dedicated to saving Jews and other civilian lives during the remainder of the war. The Bergson group had helped to shape opinions in Congress, but congressional critics of the State Department lacked sufficient leverage to shift policies on their own.[84]

Stettinius then reorganized the State Department, stripping Long of most of his functions. Ironically, in view of his misbegotten testimony on the Gillette-Rogers resolution (which sponsors withdrew after the establishment of the War Refugee Board), Long was left with congressional relations—he still had many friends in Congress. The Visa Division went to Assistant Secretary of State Berle, who was strict on security issues, but also a frequent critic of past visa practices. Berle thought State must "work itself into the clear" on rescue and relief proposals and get something done quickly.[85]

Roosevelt had always disliked the State Department, and he liked it even less with Welles gone. FDR's strengths were in politics, leadership, oratory, and policy-making, not administration. When those in charge of an agency botched a problem, he tended to add people or organizations to the task: he was not very good at subtracting. Roosevelt's approval of plans for a War

Refugee Board did not necessarily mean that he would compel cooperation from his wartime bureaucracy.

From December 1942 until January 1944 Roosevelt very gradually shifted away from the position that only a military victory could save the victims of Nazi terror. His hopes for a quick end of the war dashed, FDR began to listen to friends and critics who wanted him, in effect, to break with Britain on Jewish issues. He came to realize that at least some Jews could be rescued during the war. It took him too long, but he did learn from the clash of views among agencies and subordinates. Morgenthau and his subordinates, as well as the unheralded Cox, did the president and the Jews of Europe a great service, in the process converting the third Roosevelt into the fourth. Morgenthau moved into the vacancy created by Welles's ouster: he would handle most Jewish issues and, if necessary, take them to FDR. Whether the fourth Roosevelt would subtract enough from State and the War Department to rescue as many Jews as possible remained an open question.

CHAPTER TWELVE

Zionism and the Arab World

IN LATE NOVEMBER 1943, en route to a conference of Allied leaders in Tehran, Iran, FDR flew in an army transport plane over parts of Palestine. The president recorded his impressions in a rare personal diary that he kept during the trip: "On Saturday we passed over Bethlehem and Jerusalem & the Dead Sea—everything very bare looking—& I *don't want* Palestine as my homeland." FDR understood that many Jews looked upon this barren desert as the promised land of their people, and, potentially, the only place where Jews could control their destiny and welcome their own without restriction. However, Britain, not America, held stewardship over Palestine under the Mandate of the League of Nations. FDR's State Department also put access to Middle East oil and good relations with the vast Moslem world well above advancing Jewish settlement in Palestine.[1]

During the Nazi era, when access to Palestine became urgent for Jews, Britain tightened restrictions on Jewish immigration and stifled expectations for a Jewish state. Before the war, British policies in the Middle East aimed at securing access to Arab oil and maintaining the integrity of the British empire, which included well more than half the Moslems of the world.

During the war German military conquests in North Africa and German propaganda threatened Britain's hold—and the lives of Jews in Palestine, Egypt, and North Africa. Britain sought to dampen Arab unrest that could hamper military operations and require a diversion of troops for pacification. In the presidential election year of 1944, policies on the future of Palestine also became a point of competition between Democrats and Republicans in the United States. Despite his sympathy for Jewish aspirations in the Holy Land, FDR had to tread carefully on Palestine, weighing political priorities and competing interests such as military strategy during the war and good relations with Britain and oil-rich Arab states.

Violence in Palestine preceded the war in Europe. In 1936, Arabs began a multi-year revolt against British rule and Jewish settlements there. In turn, members of a breakaway underground splinter group of the Revisionist Zionist movement known as the Irgun launched violent reprisals. This turmoil, which claimed hundreds of Jewish and British lives, and thousands of Arab lives, weakened Britain's already tenuous commitment to continued Jewish immigration.

In late 1938, Roosevelt used his friend and cousin Arthur Murray to convey his private views to Prime Minister Neville Chamberlain and Colonial Secretary Malcolm MacDonald. FDR suggested to Murray that "the old firm hand of British policy [in the Middle East] is gone," with the result that the Arabs had lost respect for the British. He was not willing to risk a breach in relations with Britain over policy toward Palestine, but he believed Britain should admit Jewish refugees there.[2]

In January 1939, Benjamin V. Cohen told the president that the British War Office, which sought to achieve friendly relations with the Arabs, was pressuring the British cabinet to shut down Jewish immigration to Palestine, but the British also knew they would need American aid in the event of war. Roosevelt, he implied, might have some leverage on British policy. The need for cooperation between the world's most important democracies flowed in both directions across the Atlantic.[3]

Two weeks after resigning from the Supreme Court, Louis D. Brandeis began lobbying on Palestine. He reproached Chamberlain about rumors that the forthcoming British White Paper would repudiate the Balfour Declaration, writing, "I cannot believe that your Government has fully considered how gravely shattered would be the faith of the people of this troubled world . . . if Great Britain so drastically departed from her declared policy."

Ambassador Joseph P. Kennedy reported that the British indeed intended to reject the Balfour Declaration, not just by halting immigration, but by sponsoring a future Palestinian state with Jews as a minority: "He [Foreign Secretary Lord Halifax] just wanted to give me [Kennedy] a bare outline. . . . They are still talking it over [but] . . . giving the Arabs the better of it." Brandeis told FDR that the forthcoming White Paper on Palestine would call for making the territory independent within ten years; limiting Jewish immigration to 10,000 a year for five years, with any further immigration dependent upon Arab consent; and sharply restricting land purchases by Jews. Roosevelt said he had managed to postpone any announcement of a new British policy, but that the British hoped to use the White Paper to blunt German and Italian influence in the Moslem world. In contrast to his earlier reticence on Nazi persecution of Jews in Germany, Brandeis lobbied FDR on Palestine at least four times in the months before the White Paper appeared.[4]

According to an Arab source who participated in an Arab-British-Jewish conference in London in early 1939, Britain was at first generous to his people, but then tilted back toward the Jews in the midst of negotiations with the Arabs. Chamberlain told the Arab delegation in London that the United States had asked Britain to not unduly favor the Arabs: "they were further told that while as yet America was not an ally, still the world was on the verge of another World War, and England could not therefore neglect the wishes of her friends." When Ambassador Kennedy denied exerting any such influence, the Arabs learned that the pressure on behalf of Jews seeking refuge in Palestine had come directly from Washington through the British ambassador there. A British official said unofficially that Roosevelt was responding to Jewish influence, perhaps because he was hoping for a third term in office.[5]

On May 10, 1939, FDR wrote to Secretary of State Cordell Hull and Assistant Secretary of State Sumner Welles that any new British announcement on Palestine was a mistake. FDR already knew the contents of the White Paper; the British had sent advance notice to the State Department. Two days later, Ambassador Kennedy again tried to win a British delay—or Welles asked him to—without success.[6]

The White Paper did indeed limit Jewish immigration to 10,000 per year for five years, adding another 25,000 refugees admissible over the five years, with special consideration given to refugee children and their dependents. Restrictions on Jewish purchases of land and the immigration cutoff remained: after five years, Jewish immigration would effectively end because the British would require Arab consent.[7]

In an unusual, long memorandum written on the day the White Paper was released, FDR complained that the new policy violated the original 1922 Palestine Mandate, which intended to convert Palestine into a Jewish homeland within a comparatively short time. The British could not legitimately read into the terms of the mandate any policy that would limit Jewish immigration, he noted. As a compromise, he suggested eliminating the ban on Jewish immigration after five years and reconsidering policy at that point. The president wanted to avoid any sign that his government endorsed this new British policy.[8]

When the State Department prepared a release that edged toward acceptance of the White Paper, the president objected. He said that the British would not willingly modify the White Paper, but that British policy could change with shifting circumstances. It was "better to cross the Palestine bridge when we came to it, instead of now," he said. Zionist political pressure he did not think amounted to anything; and "if the pressure group was on Congress, let it stay there." Rising Arab feeling could be met through purchases of more farms for Arabs or drilling wells, "so that any Arab who really felt himself pushed out of the city could go somewhere else." However, as rumors of war grew credible in mid-1939, Roosevelt resigned himself to a fixed British policy, at least for the near future.[9]

When he became prime minister, Winston Churchill quietly favored continued Jewish immigration to Palestine within the framework of the White Paper, but was isolated within the cabinet. He scoffed at the notion that Nazi agents lurked among Jewish refugees, but still hoped to keep calm in Palestine and prevent anything there from interfering with the war effort. British security restrictions and hardships facing Jews trying to reach Palestine legally or illegally kept the White Paper quotas unfilled.[10]

The Jewish Agency for Palestine and the Revisionist Zionists both sponsored illegal immigration to Palestine. British diplomatic and colonial officials viewed this effort as a political maneuver to weaken British control over Palestine, not as a means for resettling Jewish refugees. They also argued, despite the lack of evidence, that the Gestapo had planted spies among Jews arriving in Palestine. One Colonial Office official wrote in April 1941, "The Jews have done nothing but add to our difficulties by propaganda and deeds since the war began. . . . The morally censorious attitude of the United States in general to other people's affairs has long attracted attention, but when it is coupled with unscrupulous Zionist 'sob-stuff' and misrepresentation, it is very hard to bear."[11]

By the late spring of 1941, Germany threatened Palestine on two sides. Pro-Nazi Arab leaders carried out a successful coup in Iraq, and German general Erwin Rommel, after triumphs in the North Africa desert, endangered British control over Egypt. Rabbi Stephen S. Wise wrote to Roosevelt of his fear that British forces alone could not defend the Middle East; they should recruit more Jewish fighters. The hard-pressed British had to enlist both Jewish and Arab supporters, Roosevelt responded. The United States could only offer moral and material support to the British defenders of Palestine.[12]

In December 1941, William Donovan's office, the Coordinator of Information, published a report on Axis propaganda, which targeted Arabs who opposed British rule over their homelands. Meanwhile, Arabs in Syria, Palestine, Egypt, and Iraq ignored Italian imperialism and the German conquests in Europe, the American analysts noted. The Arabs abhorred Britain's alleged support of the Jews in Palestine and its policy of divide and rule in the Middle East. Arabs in Syria and Palestine also believed that the American government stood behind the Zionists and the British. Finally, the report observed that German radio broadcasts to the Middle East had quoted "anti-Jewish passages from the Koran, emphasizing that the Jews are 'enemies of Islam.'" After Pearl Harbor, Radio Berlin also typically accused Roosevelt of acting under Jewish orders to provoke a needless war. FDR's adviser Harry Hopkins received a copy of this report, and the substance probably reached FDR through him or Donovan.[13]

Haj Amin al-Husseini, the grand mufti of Jerusalem, and Rashid Ali al-Gailani of Iraq, the two leaders of the pro-Nazi coup in Iraq in May 1941, had gone to Italy and then to Berlin after British troops ousted their government. From Berlin, they began Arabic shortwave broadcasts to the Middle East. On December 16, 1941, Donovan sent FDR broadcasts from Husseini that asserted that the Arabs and the Axis powers had three great enemies in common—the British empire, Jews, and communism.[14]

In late November 1941, Hitler had told Husseini that a German victory in Europe would liberate the Arab peoples. German troops would surge through the passes in the Caucasus Mountains region and move into the Middle East. Their arrival would free Arab peoples from British and French colonialists. Germany's only objective in the Middle East, Hitler pledged, would be to destroy the Jews.[15]

Although Germany never forced a passage through the Caucasus, in mid-1942 German and Italian forces under Rommel assaulted Egypt from the west, threatening not only the Suez Canal and British shipping lanes, but also the survival of Palestine's Jews. The Libyan city of Tobruk, near the Egyptian border, fell on June 21, and German forces captured 35,000 British troops.

David Ben-Gurion, chairman of the Jewish Agency Executive, then met with key American officials such as William Bullitt, Assistant Secretary of War John J. McCloy, and Undersecretary of War Robert P. Patterson to warn that a Nazi invasion of Palestine could mean "the end of our nation." The Turks had murdered more than a million Armenians during World War I, and German generals would inflict the same grim fate on the Jews, he said. The Jewish Agency chief asked Felix Frankfurter to send Roosevelt his memo advocating a Jewish fighting force.[16]

Declining to meet with Ben-Gurion, Roosevelt conferred instead with Chaim Weizmann, whom he had praised publicly for his scientific and humanitarian achievements. Weizmann wanted the British to transfer Major Orde Wingate from India to Palestine to take command of a Jewish division of 40,000 men. The Scottish Wingate, who had learned Hebrew, was pro-Zionist and had commanded special joint British Jewish units in Palestine during the Arab uprisings of 1936–1939. Roosevelt, however, said he wanted to delay any statement about a Jewish force for ten days, citing British fears that the Egyptian army would turn against them. Weizmann compared this temporizing to appeasing a rattlesnake. FDR told Henry Morgenthau Jr. that the immediate issue was to prevent Cairo and Alexandria from falling to the Germans. Later, if the British could spare enough rifles and machine guns for the Jews, Roosevelt said, Wingate would be a good choice as commander. He was expressing an opinion, not promising any results with Britain.[17]

At an extraordinary conference at the Biltmore Hotel in New York during May 1942, 586 American Zionists and sixty-seven foreign guests reached agreement on supporting the creation of an autonomous Jewish state in Palestine after the war and a Jewish armed force in Palestine during the war. They also called for Jewish Agency control of future immigration to Palestine. Weizmann told the Biltmore group that Nazi brutality and atrocities would wipe out a quarter of Eastern European Jewry. Settlement in Palestine, he said, was the only salvation for millions of other European Jews.[18]

Absent from the Biltmore Conference were the Revisionist Zionists, small in number and led by Peter Bergson, who also favored the formation of a Jewish army. Its prospects were dim. Undersecretary Welles told anti-Zionist Rabbi Morris Lazaron that a Jewish army clashed with the military priority of forestalling Arab unrest and defending North Africa from Nazi invasion. The British and American general staffs, Welles said, insisted that "a Jewish army, per se, would not be helpful nor desirable from the standpoint of increasing the efficiency of the Allied forces in the Middle East." They did not want their decision to become a matter for public debate.[19]

Given their need for support from Jews in Palestine and in the United States, the British created a Jewish and Arab regiment in Palestine from existing companies and some new recruits. When Bergson's group denounced this move as "too little but not yet too late," British representatives in the United States complained that such carping harmed the Allied cause. Assistant Secretary of State Adolf A. Berle said that the "difficulty [for the British] lay with Arab opposition to such a plan [for a Jewish army]." In November 1942, *New York Times* publisher Arthur Sulzberger publicly declared that Zionist efforts and the calls for a Jewish army created enmity among Moslems and added to the difficulties of the Allies: "it serves no useful purpose to continue, at this time, a campaign which not only embarrasses the United Nations, but can be distorted by the Axis in the Arab world."[20]

Unlike mainstream advocates, Bergson fit his call for a Jewish army within the bigger idea that the Jews of Palestine and the "stateless" Jews of Europe constituted a "Hebrew Nation" distinct from Jews who accepted residence in nations of the Diaspora. The "Hebrew Nation," he insisted, should have its own military, whether or not the integration of Palestinian Jews into British forces represented a more efficient use of Jewish manpower than arming, supplying, and training a separate army.[21]

In late May 1942, Senator Robert F. Wagner and Judge Samuel Rosenman drafted a presidential statement on Palestine. With FDR's approval, Wagner read it to the annual meeting of the American Palestine Committee, a bipartisan Christian organization Wagner had founded in 1941 to support implementation of the Balfour Declaration. Among Republicans, prominent Republican Senator Robert A. Taft of Ohio was a co-sponsor of the committee, which eventually won the backing of most members of the U.S. House and Senate.[22]

Noting that he had previously backed the efforts of those trying to establish a Jewish National Home in Palestine, the president praised the development of Palestine over the last two decades. He linked its progress to humanity's march toward the achievement of his Four Freedoms: freedom from fear, freedom from want, freedom of speech, and freedom of worship. If the Allies were fighting to free humanity from tyranny, why should they leave the Jews behind? He avoided specific policy proposals and ringing Rooseveltian phrases that foreign enemies might have seized for propaganda that connected him with Jews. It seemed like a reasonably innocuous document—even though the then anti-Zionist *New York Times* omitted his comment about a Jewish National Home. Weizmann expressed his "profound satisfaction" with FDR's message of "hope and encouragement."[23]

The president had again overridden the preferences of his State Department. The department's Near Eastern Affairs Division had preferred a quite different statement recognizing "the importance to us in the present military effort of the great Moslem bloc which extends from North Africa across the Middle East to Western India." The State Department stressed the numerical superiority of the Arabs so as to "make impossible American support of an all-out Jewish state in Palestine."[24]

Wallace Murray, former head of the Near Eastern Affairs Division and now adviser on political relations, responded positively to an inquiry from a Syrian-Orthodox priest in Georgia about whether Palestine, with its Arab majority, was among the small nations that the Allies would allow to determine its own destiny after the war. The Arabic newspaper *As-Sameer* thereupon published the correspondence under the headline "Glad Tidings for the Arabs."[25]

Circumspection on Palestine extended beyond State Department officials. Roosevelt's speechwriter Robert Sherwood, director of the overseas branch of the Office of War Information, wrote guidelines for its broadcasts known as the Voice of America that called for particular tact and caution with regard to Palestine—no mention of Zionist goals, no mention of a Jewish army. Any "serious outbreak of anti-Jewish feeling which might result among the Arab peoples in this area would jeopardize our strategy in the eastern Mediterranean." Since Jews firmly supported the United Nations and the Arabs did not, "our words must be addressed primarily to Moslem and

Christian Arabs, especially in view of the effectiveness of enemy propaganda." Roosevelt's political enemies at home would exploit any evidence that might show the president mismanaging the war effort, lengthening the fighting, and increasing American casualties.[26]

After British forces ended the immediate German threat to Palestine, American Jewish activists debated its present and future status. Prominent anti-Zionist Jews joined an American Council for Judaism, founded in December 1942, led by Sears magnate Lessing Rosenwald and Reform rabbis Louis Wolsey of Philadelphia and Morris Lazaron of Baltimore. Reform leaders had established the council, Wolsey said, "with the purpose of combating nationalistic and secularistic trends in Jewish life. We are opposed to a Jewish state, a Jewish flag, or a Jewish army." Lazaron questioned whether Jews should even mention Nazi atrocities. Such publicity would not deter the Nazis, he argued, but would boost the Zionists' campaign for unrestricted immigration to Palestine and Jewish statehood there. Although small, this council had access to Undersecretary Welles through his friendship with Lazaron and several influential non-Jewish backers, such as renowned author Dorothy Thompson. It carried out a vigorous campaign against Zionist goals. In turn, Zionist leaders denounced the council for sowing dissension during the greatest crisis in Jewish history.[27]

Even among Reform leaders, the council represented minority opinion. Rabbi James G. Heller of Cincinnati, president of Reform Judaism's Central Conference of American Rabbis, saw Palestine as the natural haven for Jews who could escape Europe. Wise pressed for a wartime refuge in Palestine and for a postwar Jewish state there. Another Reform rabbi, Abba Hillel Silver, leader of the militant wing of American Zionism, had pushed through the pro-statehood declaration at the Biltmore Conference in May of 1942. Still, a small group of well-positioned activists had created the impression of widespread Jewish dissension on Palestine.[28]

In early December 1942, Rosenman suggested that Morgenthau host a meeting for rival Jewish leaders about Palestine. FDR asked Morgenthau to "go easy," because he had made up his mind: 90 percent of Palestine should be Jewish. Arabs should be moved out to land elsewhere in the Middle East and replaced by as many Jewish families as Palestine could absorb. Palestine would then become an independent state. Although he did not say so explicitly, this was a postwar program.[29]

Among non-Jews, the Holocaust advanced the Zionist cause. On December 4, 1942, as reports of the Final Solution circulated in Washington, sixty-three senators and 181 representatives signed a resolution drafted by Senator Wagner. Reports of Nazi efforts to "exterminate a whole people" had moved them to reaffirm their traditional support for a Jewish homeland in Palestine and for moving survivors there at the end of the war.[30]

By late 1942, Allied leaders confronted the "Jewish Question" in Northwest Africa. After landing in Morocco and Algeria as part of Operation Torch, Allied troops faced resistance by French forces loyal to Vichy. The Allies had expected that Free French general Henri Giraud would help them to win over French forces in North Africa, but Vichy's Admiral Jean-François Darlan happened to be in Algiers during the Allied invasion. When Darlan, who had collaborated with the Nazis, tried to deliver control of French forces to the Allies, he became potentially useful. In the short run, the Allied governments dealt with three French rival leaders—Free French leader Charles De Gaulle, Giraud, and Darlan.

The 330,000 Jews in North Africa—110,000 in Algeria, 160,000 in Morocco, and 60,000 in Tunisia—had suffered discrimination and expropriation under Vichy during 1941–1942 and even worse treatment once SS and Italian authorities intervened in Tunisia. American liberals wanted to purge Vichy authorities in North Africa. General George Patton, an admirer of Darlan's subordinate, General Charles-Auguste Noguès, the French resident-general in Morocco, complained to General Dwight D. Eisenhower that the Arabs wanted Noguès retained. His projected removal and the revocation of anti-Jewish decrees in Morocco would provoke so much Arab unrest that he would need 60,000 Allied troops just to maintain order. Eisenhower then told the president he needed French forces to avoid tying down Allied troops for occupation duties and delaying offensive operations elsewhere. In late November 1942, Berle wrote in his diary, "I gather only God could tell whether the Arab tribes would rise."[31]

On November 17, 1942, eight days after the Torch landings, FDR called for the abrogation of all Nazi-inspired laws or decrees and the release of all anti-Nazi political prisoners in French North Africa. He seemed to favor the release of Jewish prisoners and the nullification of a Vichy measure that had stripped Algerian Jews of French citizenship. So too did Eisenhower and Berle. Nevertheless, military considerations intervened.[32]

Patton wrote to Eisenhower that any perception of American favoritism for Jews could provoke Arab violent reprisals.

> Arabs don't mind Christians, but they utterly despise Jews. The French fear that the local Jews[,] knowing how high their side is riding in the U.S.[,] will try to take the lead here. If they do the Arabs will murder them and there will be a local state of disorder. . . . I suggest that you write Gen. Marshall and inform him of the situation so that if some State Department fool tries to foist . . . Jews on Morocco, we will stop it at the source. If we get orders to favor the Jews[,] we will precipitate trouble and possibly civil war.

Patton passed along a report from French officials under Darlan defending Vichy's restrictions on Jews. Special presidential representative Robert Murphy, attached to the Allied High Command and supported by his Jewish adviser Paul Warburg, agreed that any Allied appearance of special privileges for Jews would cause turmoil in North Africa.[33]

After a young French monarchist assassinated Darlan in late December 1942, American officials turned to Giraud for leadership. Although unblemished by service in the Vichy regime, Giraud believed that Moslems despised Jews, who were tradesmen, craftsmen, and usurers by nature. An imperial power had to strike a balance and keep order between the two groups. He tried to uphold the Vichy decree that had stripped Algerian Jews of French citizenship in order not to favor Jews over Moslems, who also lacked citizenship rights. The later architect of European integration, Jean Monnet, told Giraud that his obstinacy was damaging the interests of Free France, but Giraud stood his ground.[34]

Roosevelt and Churchill inspected conditions in the region during a summit conference at Casablanca from January 14–24, 1943. (Stalin declined an invitation to attend.) The Allies agreed to appoint Eisenhower as the Allied Supreme Commander in North Africa and publicly reinforced their opposition to a negotiated settlement with the major Axis countries.[35]

Roosevelt also met with officials opposed to restoring the citizenship of Algerian Jews: Murphy, Patton, and Nogués. After Patton praised Nogués's fine cooperation, Nogués declared that, for the most part, Jews had been released from concentration camps, but Algerian Jews wanted their suffrage restored. Murphy said that Jews were disappointed that Allied liberation had not resulted in their complete freedom. Aware of the views that giving

Jews more rights than Moslems risked civil strife, Roosevelt played to his audience. To provide opportunities for Jews, without unduly antagonizing Moslems, he suggested capping the representation of Jews in the professions at their percentage of the population. This limitation would avoid the kind of "specific and understandable complaints" that the Germans had developed toward the overrepresentation of Jews among lawyers, doctors, and educators. His loose comments only provoked Nogués to further absurdity: it would be "a sad thing for the French[!] to win the war merely to open the way for the Jews to control the professions and the business world of North Africa," he said.[36]

Both French and American officials hesitated to restore Algerian Jewish citizenship when they were not ready to consider reciprocity for Moslems. Even Berle cited concern about Arab reaction as a reason for moving slowly and cautiously. Welles tried to forestall American Jewish pressure for prompt restoration of their rights. In October 1943, Algerian Jews finally regained their citizenship—partly because of expanding Gaullist influence in French North Africa and partly through bureaucratic inertia.[37]

Roosevelt and Churchill took up some regional issues again in May 1943 when Churchill came to Washington for two weeks of meetings known as the Trident Conference. Amid their larger war agenda, they had to decide whether to approve and implement minor agreements reached at the Bermuda Conference on Refugees. The British had agreed to formulate a proposal for moving refugees from Spain or Turkey into temporary havens in North Africa; in return, the Americans had demanded a refugee camp in British-controlled territory in Africa.[38]

In their poorly recorded private talks on Palestine and other Jewish issues, neither man followed the scripts written by his diplomatic officials. According to Vice President Henry Wallace, who participated in one discussion, FDR reiterated his fondness for Isaiah Bowman's strategy of spreading Jews out across the world. Roosevelt, who never lacked a pithy anecdote, said he had added four or five Jewish families in Marietta County, Georgia (the location of FDR's Warm Springs retreat), and at Hyde Park with no adverse local reaction. Roosevelt claimed that Jewish Palestine was not yet economically self-sufficient, but still depended on funds supplied by Jews outside the country. Churchill "cussed out" the various Arab leaders for their pro-German bias. Wallace thought Churchill favored the development of Trans-Jordan for the Jews; it had been part of the original British mandate. Roosevelt would balance concessions to Jews by transforming the Middle East into a bloc of independent Arab states, with Palestine as the exception. This plan left no room for continued British colonialism in the region, which probably dismayed Churchill. The prime minister said non-committedly that Jews had more votes than Arabs in Britain and the United States, and politics could not be ignored. Wallace pointed out that despite some dissenters, most Jews strongly supported Palestine as a homeland.[39]

Churchill proposed to use the former Italian colonies of Eritrea and Tripolitania (part of present-day Libya) as Jewish havens affiliated, if they wished, with a national home in Palestine. Although this notion paralleled Roosevelt's prewar thinking, he could not have seen it as realistic in mid-1943. The American military and the French colonial officials in North Africa had resisted plans generated at the Bermuda Conference for locating a refugee camp in Allied-conquered North Africa, let alone a permanent Jewish colony in the midst of Arab populations. Eventually, Churchill and Roosevelt pushed reluctant subordinates into installing two North African refugee camps, which harbored mostly refugees from Spain. British sources show Churchill taking the initiative, while American sources show him as waiting for approval from London and delaying the process.[40]

During Churchill's visit, Roosevelt conferred with Bowman, who discouraged bringing refugees into both Libya and Palestine. The Johns Hopkins geographer thought that Jewish immigration to Palestine was no guide for Libya because outside aid sustained Palestinian Jewry. Libya might be able to accommodate 20,000 people, but Bowman thought that assistance to (Jewish) refugees must be balanced with aid to the Arabs. He also wanted prior Arab consent for transporting Jews into Libya. Bowman said that any additional settlement of refugees in the Arab world would confirm Nazi propaganda charges that the Allies were using Jews to dominate the Arabs. Incredibly, he charged that creating a Jewish state in Palestine would be the mirror image of Hitler's *Lebensraum* policy.[41]

Bowman was hardly alone: many administration officials favored a pro-Arab course. Former textile manufacturer Colonel Harold Hoskins, born in Syria and attached to Office of Strategic Services (OSS), became a key source of biased information on Palestine. In late 1942, the Arabic-speaking Hoskins had toured the Middle East for the president. Upon his return, Hoskins told Hamilton Fish Armstrong, editor of *Foreign Affairs,* that fighting between Arabs and Jews in Palestine might erupt soon, undermining the

Allies' standing throughout the Arab world, and threatening the war effort. Although Hoskins claimed to support the admission of more Jews to Palestine, up to parity with Arabs, he said he opposed political Zionism. Yet all interested parties knew that the two issues could not be separated; the more Jews who settled in Palestine, the greater the prospects for a Jewish state there.[42]

Two months later, Hoskins delivered a more resolute anti-Zionist report. He predicted that, without remedial measures, Arabs and Jews would begin fighting before the war's end and perhaps during the next few months. One consequence would be the massacre of Jews in Iraq, Syria, and other places in the Middle East. Somehow, despite a pogrom against Jews in Baghdad in June 1941, Hoskins had conjured up an informal wartime truce between Arabs and Jews, which the Jews had violated, through worldwide agitation for a Jewish state. In April 1943, an unnamed OSS analyst agreed that Arab opinion had shifted against the supposedly pro-Zionist United States. In addition, Zionism created tension between the United States and Great Britain, he maintained.[43]

Another anti-Zionist in OSS headquarters was Stephen Penrose, a Middle East expert. One of Penrose's friends, a high administrator of the Meharry Medical College in Nashville wrote to him that talk of two million Jews killed by the Nazis was insignificant next to all the other soldiers and civilians killed during the war "to make the world safe for minorities like the Jews: (Can't you just imagine the three and one-half million Arabs extending a blanket invitation for three million more blonde Aryan Semites or should I say—Termites—out of Europe?)." Driven by intense prejudice, such people rejected the idea of any future Jewish state in Palestine.[44]

On June 11, 1943, Weizmann came to the White House. En route, Welles encouraged him to discuss Palestine with FDR because Allied policy would crystallize soon. Welles warned that King Ibn Saud of Saudi Arabia had recently written "unpleasant" and "childish" letters demanding the end of Jewish immigration to Palestine. That was to put it mildly. Ibn Saud wrote Roosevelt that Palestine was a "sacred Moslem Arab country" that "belonged to the Arabs." Jews, he said, sought to "exterminate peaceful Arabs." He called them vagrants who had nothing but an imaginary claim to Palestine, based on fraud and deceit. The King traced Jewish perfidy to the birth of Islam, when Jews had shown "treacherous behavior" toward Moslems and their prophet. Roosevelt diplomatically responded with his

hope for reconciliation between Arabs and Jews on Palestine and his promise to confer with both before reaching final decisions.[45]

Roosevelt told Weizmann he had persuaded Churchill to attend with
him a postwar conference of Jews and Arabs. Weizmann warned the president against repeating Britain's mistakes of 1939 and failing to control
events. The democracies had to affirm Jewish rights to Palestine before any
meeting of Arabs and Jews. The two world wars had created the prospect of
independent Arab states; the democracies which spent so much "blood and
treasure" on these wars had earned the right to dictate a fair settlement.
Roosevelt responded that the Arabs had behaved badly during the war and
had neglected to develop their own vast territories. He said that Jews and a
postwar United Nations might possibly help them with development: "He
then said that he believes that the Arabs are purchasable, to which I [Weiz-
mann] remarked that I have heard something to that effect." Welles suggested the names of possible envoys to Ibn Saud, but FDR said Churchill
had to agree to any such mission. Roosevelt asked Weizmann whether he
had met with Churchill recently. Weizmann said Churchill had nothing of
substance to tell him. Weizmann concluded that a potential Arab revolt
could be averted "if the Arabs really feel that the democracies mean business" about guaranteeing Jewish settlement. Weizmann found the hour-
long meeting satisfactory, he later told Morgenthau's secretary.[46]

In conjunction with the British Foreign Office, the State Department
plotted a different course. On his route back from the Middle East, Hoskins
had conferred with the highest British officials, who agreed with him that
renewed clashes between Jews and Arabs in Palestine could turn the Arab
world against the Allies. In subsequent meetings with Secretary of State
Hull and officials in the Near Eastern Affairs Division, Hoskins criticized
Zionism as contrary to American interests.[47]

State Department political adviser Wallace Murray prompted Hull to
ask Hoskins to draft a United Nations or a joint American-British statement on Palestine designed to "reduce Arab-Jewish tensions." FDR approved without comment a first draft in May 1943 and a revised version on
June 9. British foreign minister Anthony Eden welcomed this statement
and preferred that it come from both Britain and America. Eventually, the
two sides agreed on a document discouraging "special viewpoints" that might
create "undue anxiety" among friendly governments and peoples during
the war: "[Both governments] consider that it would be helpful to the war

effort if these [public political activities with regard to Palestine] were to cease." Britain also rejected any changes brought about by force in Palestine, and the United States said it agreed with British policy. The statement made Jewish immigration to Palestine and the status of Palestine itself subject to Arab consent and strongly suggested to American citizens that they should not use their constitutional rights to speak out on Palestine during the war.[48]

Murray, whom Morgenthau later called one of the worst anti-Semites in the State Department, was on the verge of getting Washington and London to declare Zionism an impediment to winning the war. Welles would never have let such a politically controversial proposal reach the president without careful discussion. However, Welles was on his way out: his formal resignation came within weeks. Through the joint statement on Palestine, Hull sought to demonstrate his command of foreign policy and his break with Welles. On July 19, Hull forwarded this long draft statement to the president, who simply wrote "OK" on it.[49]

Three days later, Rabbi Wise brought to the president's attention rumors about an Anglo-American statement on Palestine that would restrict public discussion of its future. He warned FDR that American Jewry would rise up with "righteous anger" against any such move. Wise wrote Welles afterwards that the president "did not seem to be familiar with any such proposal and virtually assured me that no such statement would be issued." Roosevelt was dissembling, backtracking, or acknowledging his lack of attention to State Department plans.[50]

The State Department and British Foreign Office had planned to issue their statement on Palestine in late July 1943. The politically sensitive Hull then had second thoughts. The American-British declaration on Palestine was bound to infuriate all Zionists and the sixty-three senators and 182 representatives who had signed the December 1942 statement commemorating the twenty-fifth anniversary of the Balfour Declaration. Did Hull really want to take all the responsibility? Roosevelt had not shown any interest in a presidential statement, and he had a knack for escaping political traps.

Hull again postponed release of the joint statement in order to gain political cover through backing from the all-important War Department. General Strong of Army Intelligence (G-2) firmly supported it, but Assistant Secretary Patterson, acting in Secretary Henry L. Stimson's absence, gave it only qualified approval. Patterson excised the key sentence that irresponsible [Zionist] agitation had dangerous *military* repercussions. Hull then wanted to raise the matter with Stimson. In response to a request from Representative Sol Bloom, FDR's adviser Rosenman reviewed the proposed statement and discussed it with both FDR and Jewish leaders. On August 3, the judge concluded that the State Department was using the War Department for its own ends.[51]

Stimson told Hull he thought the proposed draft was "alarmist" and formally withdrew Patterson's qualified letter of support. Without such blessing, Hull balked at moving ahead with the statement. The State Department sent the bad news to the British, who noted Eden's disappointment. Once again, Roosevelt had declined to follow the State Department's lead on the Middle East. Wise wrote shortly afterwards: "A statement had been threatened which I think has now been averted. Still, I am not sure. We have been dealing with the Chief [Roosevelt] and with the State Department, and all of our best men have been most helpful to us, including Judge S. R. [Rosenman], H. J. Jr. [Morgenthau], and others."[52]

On August 9, columnist Drew Pearson published a partly inaccurate account of this behind-the-scenes controversy, perhaps drawing on information leaked by Welles just before his resignation from government. The main proponent of the joint statement, Pearson claimed, was Major General Patrick Hurley, who had met with Ibn Saud (who had told him, "I hate the Jews more than anyone") and then with FDR. In May 1943, after his visit to the Middle East, Hurley had delivered a generally negative report on American support for Zionist aspirations in Palestine. Wise, however, had dissuaded FDR from issuing this statement, according to the column. That last part might have been correct.[53]

In effect, Murray's declaration on Palestine had inflated Allied military problems in order to justify clamping down on Zionist activity and backing the British White Paper of 1939. Roosevelt's political instincts served him well in avoiding a State Department trap. Nevertheless, the war was far from won, and the president was far from having any clear answers for the future of Palestine.

On the same day that Pearson published his column, Roosevelt asked Bowman, "Isaiah, have you found places enough all over the map for refugees that we will have to look after?" Bowman said he was always ready to give advice, but, in keeping with his earlier memo, FDR should avoid Libya and look to Angola. The president responded that he had received and read

Bowman's earlier report on Libya and given a copy to Churchill. Bowman claimed that settlement at any place in the Arab world would "make terrible trouble" and that Saudi Arabian opposition to Jewish immigration was intensifying. When FDR said that one of Ibn Saud's sons was coming to the United States, Welles, in one of his last official acts, urged postponement of this visit.[54]

Churchill and Roosevelt discussed Palestine again at the Anglo-American conference in Quebec later that month. British officials tried to get the United States to revive the Anglo-American statement on Palestine, but neither leader agreed to do so. Shortly before he died, Roosevelt recounted an exchange with Churchill regarding Palestine that may have taken place during this conference. When Churchill said he was a Zionist, FDR asked him about his plan for Palestine. Churchill said he had no plan. The president commented that "what he really meant was that he could not have a plan for a Jewish state in Palestine that was consistent with the safety of the British empire, and thereupon Mr. Churchill had expressed acquiescence in that view." Whether or not this revealing dialogue happened at this time, the two delegations at Quebec agreed to reassess Palestine as the war situation evolved. The anti-Zionist statement stayed on the shelf.[55]

Roosevelt gained expert advice on Palestine from sources other than Bowman. By 1943, his close adviser John Franklin Carter and anthropologist Henry Field took over the reins of a scholarly investigation of settlement possibilities known as the "M Project." Field drew on the work of Walter Clay Lowdermilk, an Agriculture Department official, whose book *Palestine: Land of Promise* forecast that with sufficient irrigation, Palestine could support many millions of additional settlers. The more conservative M Project report on Palestine, finalized in early 1944, concluded that the territory could receive at least four million Jewish refugees from Europe without displacing the existing 1.8 million Arabs and Jews in Palestine and a western strip of Transjordan. A scornful Bowman opposed passing on such expansive estimates to the president even though it was already too late for four million Jews to emerge from Nazi-dominated territories in Europe.[56]

In late January 1944, Representatives James Wright, Democrat of Pennsylvania, and Ranulf Compton, Republican of Connecticut, introduced a resolution calling for unrestricted Jewish immigration to Palestine and the ultimate—not immediate—establishment of Palestine as a free and democratic Jewish commonwealth. Senators Wagner and Taft sponsored the same measure in the Senate. The possibility that Congress might endorse a Jewish state in Palestine worried Morgenthau, who believed that controversy over this sensitive matter might divert attention from the rescue of Jews facing death in Europe. He told FDR, "I feel the thing is to get out the Jews [of Europe] and get the thirty thousand into Palestine, as permitted under the so-called White Paper, before we raise this whole question of the White Paper." According to Morgenthau, Roosevelt responded, "I am so glad to hear you say that, Henry, because that is the way I feel."[57]

On February 8, Zionist leader Silver and several other Jewish leaders testified in favor of the Palestine resolution before the House Foreign Affairs Committee. The next day, Senator Tom Connally read into the record Secretary of War Stimson's testimony that passage of the resolution would seriously prejudice the war effort by antagonizing the Arabs. Chief of Staff General George C. Marshall and Assistant Secretary of War McCloy both spoke against it as well in closed sessions of the Senate Foreign Relations Committee.[58]

Having spoken earlier with Hull about the resolution, Silver felt betrayed. He had launched a major lobbying effort that enlisted members of temples and synagogues across the country; "telegrams by the tens of thousands and great quantities of letters" had reached both houses of Congress. It was awkward for him to reverse course, he told Breckinridge Long on February 24. He wondered if the State Department had influenced the War Department. Silver noted that American Jews had overwhelmingly backed Roosevelt, and that this resolution's defeat might threaten Jewish loyalty in an election year.[59]

Long claimed that the War Department had acted independently. Stimson, however, told War Refugee Board director John Pehle that the State Department had asked him to oppose the measure, because State would not do so openly. Nonetheless, Stimson sought to avoid any risk of an Arab uprising that would force the army to keep troops in the Middle East that it could better deploy elsewhere. Silver's closest associate, Emanuel Neumann, wrote to the rabbi on February 24, "Even then I am asking myself just what the President will be able to do. He may not be in a position to reverse the action of the War Department."[60]

Although Wallace Murray had failed twice before, he decided to try once again to put the views of the State Department and the Foreign Office into a joint Anglo-American pronouncement on Palestine. Undersecretary of State Edward R. Stettinius Jr. sent Murray's draft letter to FDR under his name. Roosevelt responded just as he had done nine months earlier with Murray's previous draft: "OK, FDR." Stettinius returned the draft to Murray with FDR's handwritten OK, but it was little better than a souvenir.[61]

On March 9, Roosevelt met with Wise and Silver, the cochairs of the American Zionist Emergency Council, a coordinating body of the American Zionist organizations. FDR shared Stimson's worries about Arab unrest and sought a graceful death for the Wright-Compton resolution. The two Zionist leaders needed to show that the efforts of their constituents in support of Wright-Compton had achieved results. At a minimum, they wanted Roosevelt to affirm a future for a larger Jewish population in Palestine.

Roosevelt found Silver, nominally an independent, abrasive and suspected him of Republican loyalties. He had a close relationship with fellow Ohioan, Republican senator Taft. Prior to Pearl Harbor, Taft had been a preeminent leader of the isolationist bloc in the Senate, but he also supported Zionist aspirations in Palestine.[62]

The president asked Silver whether he wanted to take responsibility for the death of 100,000 soldiers. Silver had told people that Roosevelt inspired the War Department's stance against the Palestine resolution: FDR denied this flatly and called Silver's behavior reprehensible. Roosevelt asked Silver how many Jews "could he get out" of Europe if Britain opened the gates of Palestine. Silver optimistically said, "a great many." Roosevelt said he preferred to avoid criticizing the White Paper before immigration had reached its limits. Nearly 30,000 Jews could still immigrate into Palestine under the White Paper once the British agreed to extend the cutoff date. He authorized the two rabbis to state publicly his view that "the American government had never given its approval to the White Paper of 1939." They also quoted him as being "happy that the doors of Palestine are open to Jewish refugees" and promising, in future decisions, full justice to those who seek a Jewish homeland in Palestine. As the American Zionist Emergency Council noted, this was "the first official American statement expressing explicit disapproval of the White Paper." It accurately reflected FDR's views ever since early 1939.[63]

Even the militant Silver hailed this statement by "the great president of the United States" that "is the true heart of America speaking and the conscience of the world." In a memo to supporters, Silver's lieutenant, Harry L. Shapiro, wrote, "The president spoke *after* protests against the pending

Palestine resolution [in Congress] had come in from the officials of seven Arab nations. In a very real sense the President *rebuked* these Arabs." FDR, in effect, had also rebuked high officials in his State Department. A *New York Times* analysis by Arthur Krock noted that Roosevelt's statement was in substance little different from the Wright-Compton resolution that administration spokespersons had opposed.[64]

Still, in response to the War Department's testimony, the Senate Foreign Relations Committee and the House Foreign Affairs Committee tabled the Wright-Compton resolution. Silver tried to use a mass rally in Madison Square Garden and an avalanche of letters and telegrams to revive the measure, but his effort failed. Well-wishers abounded in both houses, but few would take responsibility for what critics might decry as the needless deaths of American troops.[65]

Other matters weighed against the resolution in Congress. Long secretly met with a delegation of senators at the suggestion of Secretary of State Hull. He told them about the vast quantity of oil in Saudi Arabia, and warned them against jeopardizing relations with the Arabs by endorsing a Jewish homeland in Palestine. In Palestine, archaeologist and OSS official Nelson Glueck wrote, "The possibility of Palestine's affording succor to many thousands of desperately homeless Jews has not begun to be realized. . . . The oil game is being played and all those who touch it will have their hands smeared by pitch."[66]

During the 1944 presidential campaign, the Republicans vied with the Democrats to satisfy Jewish concerns about Palestine. Rabbi Silver tired of waiting until the end of the war to achieve his objectives for Palestine. Through an arrangement by Senator Taft, Silver met New York governor Thomas E. Dewey, the front-runner for the Republican nomination. Dewey, like Taft, backed Silver's dual goals of unrestricted Jewish immigration and support for a Jewish commonwealth. Silver got his way at the Republican National Convention in Chicago, with the complication that Dewey's political adviser John Foster Dulles inserted language into the platform condemning Roosevelt for pretending to support the Balfour Declaration, but failing to insist on British fulfillment of it.[67]

It was the first time the Republican Party had supported Zionist goals unconditionally. However, the plank alienated loyal Democrats among Zionists. It also heightened long-standing tensions between Silver and Wise, who turned to his Democratic allies to match or outdo the Republicans.

With the backing of Representatives John McCormack of Massachusetts and Emanuel Celler of New York, at the Democratic National Convention Wise spoke in favor of a pro-Zionist Palestine plank, which Lazaron predictably opposed. Wise announced that he would not support the Democratic campaign if the platform lacked a suitable statement on Palestine. The Democrats ended up adopting a slightly stronger plank than the GOP, pledging support for a free and Democratic Jewish commonwealth and "unrestricted Jewish immigration and colonization."[68]

In September 1944, Senator Taft asked Stimson whether the War Department had relented on congressional resolutions to permit free Jewish immigration to Palestine. After some delay, Stimson conceded that military considerations should no longer constrain the Senate. Meanwhile, Wise pressed hard for FDR to endorse the Democratic plank on Palestine and indicated that, in his next term, he would induce the British to translate it into action.[69]

On October 7, Rosenman told Roosevelt that Wise and Silver wanted a personal meeting with him. Rosenman called Silver "hostile" politically; he was using Dewey to influence presidential policy. FDR could see Wise alone and accomplish just as much, especially if he could now reveal that economic surveys were underway in Palestine to determine its capacity for Jewish immigration.[70]

On October 11, Wise met with FDR in the White House and apparently gave the president a letter drafted by Senator Wagner, designed for Wagner to read at the mid-October annual convention of the Zionist Organization of America. This draft is not in the president's files, but Rosenman commented on it, "It seems to me this takes you out very far in favor of a Jewish Commonwealth—too far."[71]

Roosevelt first suggested an endorsement of the Democratic platform and a tepid corollary: "Efforts will be taken to find appropriate ways and means of effectuating this policy as soon as practical." Wagner rejected this uninspired language and drafted his own statement: "I know how long and ardently the Jewish people have worked and prayed for the establishment of Palestine as a free and Democratic Jewish commonwealth. I am convinced that the American people give their support to this aim, and if reelected, I shall help to bring about its realization." Sitting up in his bedroom the night before the convention opened, Roosevelt told Rosenman that he approved of the new version, and Wagner read it to the convention on October 15.

Delegates responded with a sustained ovation. Even Silver expressed quickly to the president his "profound appreciation and gratitude" for this historic statement.[72]

Over the course of a more than a decade as president, Roosevelt sounded at times like a Zionist, at times like a skeptic about Palestine's capacity to absorb new settlers, and at times, when speaking to anti-Semites, like an anti-Semite himself. Often he would agree with someone only to reverse course weeks or even days later. Beneath such maneuvers and reversals, FDR showed some core beliefs. He approved of the Balfour Declaration, and he disapproved of British retreats from it. He never allowed the State Department to dictate American policy toward Palestine or the region. Not by coincidence, his closest advisers on Jewish issues, Rosenman and Morgenthau, favored continued Jewish immigration to Palestine, but did not pressure the president to endorse to a Jewish state there. For political and military reasons, Roosevelt did not think it wise for him to raise the question of Jewish statehood during the war or to break openly with Britain. He also recognized that many Jewish leaders and their non-Jewish allies (like Senator Wagner) would pursue their own course on Palestine.

FDR's postwar vision of autonomous states in the Middle East meant an independent Palestine. Since he wanted sizable Jewish immigration to continue, he accepted and, at times explicitly endorsed, a future Palestine with a dominant Jewish influence. He leaned toward a personal effort to persuade Ibn Saud of Saudi Arabia that the benefits for the Arab world would outweigh the disadvantages. Circumstances would determine how to proceed if he failed to sway the Saudi ruler.

Churchill, although ostensibly pro-Zionist, was unwilling or unable to get his own government to open Palestine to Jewish immigrants Historian Michael J. Cohen has noted that two weeks after *Kristallnacht* Churchill proposed a ten-year limit on Jewish immigration to Palestine so that it would not alter the balance between Jews and Arabs. Meanwhile, FDR was pressing Chamberlain's government to increase immigration to Palestine.[73]

Through action and not just words, Roosevelt helped stop the Nazis' from extending the Holocaust from Europe to the Middle East and Northwest Africa. Nazi authorities had planned to annihilate the region's Jews. A mobile killing unit called Einsatzkommando Egypt waited in Athens for word that the German armies had conquered Egypt and Palestine, home to roughly half a million Jews. Its commander Walter Rauff flew to Tobruk in

July 1942 after Rommel's pivotal capture of that Libyan port to meet with Rommel and to prepare for the mass slaughter of Jews after the projected German capture of Cairo. German planes dropped propaganda postcards over Egypt with the title "Borders of the New Zionist Kingdom." They showed a disfigured Weizmann standing with Churchill and Roosevelt in front of a map showing Jewish control of Palestine, Trans-Jordan, Syria, and portions of Iraq and Saudi Arabia.[74]

For once, British military priorities synchronized with the protection of Jews. Roosevelt diverted to British forces in Egypt and Libya American A-20 bombers already designated for Russia under Lend-Lease and other bombers promised to China. They helped General Claude Auchinleck and the British Eighth Army hold out against Rommel's forces. At Churchill's request, Roosevelt also sent two shipments (Germans U-boats sank the first one) of 300 Sherman tanks to help stabilize British lines in Egypt. Roosevelt and Chief of Staff Marshall personally cleared away the bureaucratic obstacles that otherwise would have significantly delayed any request for such a massive diversion of American armaments. In November 1942, at the second battle of El Alamein, one of the major turning points of the war, the Sherman tanks, which had greater range and firepower than Rommel's, helped Allied forces end the German threat to Alexandria, Suez, and Palestine.[75]

Roosevelt undoubtedly sent direct military aid to buttress British positions in Egypt and its hold on the Suez Canal—not to aid Palestine's Jews. Still, he was conscious of the Nazi threat to Jews in the region, and his action helped to save them, regardless of his motivation. FDR managed wartime strategy in the region, doing more good for Jews there than his inconsistency and his dissembling did harm. He overrode the preferences of his State Department on Palestine—no easy decision for a president—but he could not just ignore America's military priorities, its relations with Great Britain, and its interests in the oil-rich Arab world. He also legitimately worried about the survival of half a million Jews in a region populated by tens of millions of hostile Arabs. FDR's promise to consult with the Arabs—who had their own grievances about an imperial power dictating the future of a predominantly Arab-settled land—was in his view a minimal but necessary wartime concession. Overall, Roosevelt's course was more consistent than Churchill's, and better for the Jews.

CHAPTER THIRTEEN

The War Refugee Board

IN LATE JUNE 1944, the Nazi newspaper *Völkischer Beobachter* labeled FDR "the twentieth century Moses." The Nazi journalists noted that Roosevelt had just returned from his vacation on the estate of "the Jew Baruch" and that he had surrounded himself with Jews who were plotting to reelect "their president." Nazi propagandists pointed to the new War Refugee Board as the latest evidence of Roosevelt's dependence on Jews and his commitment to a "Jewish war." They hoped that such propaganda would weaken the Allied cause or help defeat FDR in November.[1]

Administration officials had long been sensitive to the charge, however false, of American subservience to Jewish concerns. The Office of War Information's (OWI) psychological warfare experts and its Overseas Planning Board, the State Department, and the Joint Chiefs of Staff had repeatedly rejected proposals for exploiting publicity on Nazi atrocities against Jews. Such propaganda, they feared, would corroborate Nazi claims that international Jewry controlled American leaders. The British had opposed publicizing German crimes against Jews; the Soviets had refrained from it; and the Germans might exploit Allied divisions on the issue. Or so the critics claimed.[2]

Some British officials also thought that in creating the War Refugee Board Roosevelt had responded to Jewish pressures to gain reelection, but they discounted its real significance. British foreign minister Anthony Eden told a cabinet committee on refugees that Roosevelt had created the War Refugee Board as an election year maneuver. Securing British cooperation would remain an ongoing issue for the board.[3]

Roosevelt created the board only at the prompting of Treasury Secretary Henry Morgenthau Jr. and his activist staff, while under pressure from an increasingly assertive Congress. Morgenthau and other outraged Treasury officials wanted to counter forces within the administration still obstructing rescue or relief of Jews and in effect, giving the Nazis more latitude for mass murder.

The other two members of the board—Secretary of War Henry Stimson and Secretary of State Cordell Hull—had no such commitments. With his delicate health and lack of interest in the board's concerns, Hull frequently relied on Undersecretary Edward R. Stettinius Jr., who had a cordial relationship with Morgenthau, but scant experience with refugee issues. Stimson participated reluctantly, but through an adviser, Judge Samuel Rosenman, FDR conveyed to Stimson his personal interest in rescue measures. Stimson responded that he "had a few other things on my hand," but that he would "try to do anything of that kind that the president wanted." Morgenthau was deeply committed to the success of the board and could get the president's attention, but he also sought to avoid the appearance of special pleading on behalf of his fellow Jews.[4]

Roosevelt's standard formula for defusing criticism of his alleged pro-Jewish bias called for an independent and prestigious director, preferably a Republican or a Catholic. With the Nazis killing thousands of Jews each day, however, the board needed someone with the motivation and expertise to start quickly without a steep learning curve. To work successfully within the Roosevelt administration, the new director also needed political skill, tact, and administrative expertise.

Roosevelt suggested Philip Murray, president of the Congress of Industrial Organizations, and Henry Bruère, president of the Bowery Savings Bank, who had organized relief to Britain and France. Morgenthau regarded Murray as uninterested and Bruère as lacking the fortitude for an arduous job. Morgenthau lamented, "when you stop to think of somebody sympathetic, you can't think of anybody." According to Morgenthau, FDR responded, "that is correct." Roosevelt thought of himself as on the righteous side of a politically unpopular and isolated cause.[5]

Morgenthau raised with his Treasury staff the possibility of appointing an independent figure such as Wendell Willkie, Hamilton Fish Armstrong, editor of *Foreign Affairs,* or Frank Graham, president of the University of North Carolina. To FDR, he posed the more practical suggestion that the president appoint his Treasury subordinate John Pehle as director. Roosevelt said he needed a day or two to search for someone of stature. The president approached New York lawyer Morris Ernst, general counsel for the American Civil Liberties Union, who recommended the veteran journalist and high-profile broadcaster Raymond Gram Swing, Supreme Court Justice William O. Douglas, Leon Henderson, former director of the Office of Price Administration, and Harold Stassen, the former Republican governor of Minnesota, who would later become America's best-known perennial candidate for president. None of them had relevant experience, and Henderson had administered unpopular price controls. Stimson alone suggested a Jewish candidate, little known James H. Becker of Chicago, who served on the American Jewish Committee's executive board.[6]

None of the independent candidates made it through the administration's political screening. The White House rejected Willkie, a loose cannon with ambitions to run again as the Republican nominee for president. Willkie had offended Roosevelt and Winston Churchill when he openly criticized the two leaders for meeting at Casablanca in January 1943 without Joseph Stalin.[7]

Stimson learned from Assistant Secretary of War John J. McCloy that administration officials respected Pehle. Without any big-name prospects, War Refugee Board members agreed to recommend Pehle as acting director. A week later, Morgenthau coaxed agreement on Pehle from a reluctant FDR. Still wary of publicity on Jewish issues, Roosevelt recommended trimming the press release that introduced Pehle and the board to the public.[8]

On February 1, Pehle and Morgenthau met privately with Stimson to explain the need for rescue and relief measures to save Jews and to note the availability of private Jewish funds. To his relief Stimson heard nothing that threatened military activities or resources. He even called the meeting interesting and profitable and, in effect, agreed to cooperate.[9]

Although the creation of the War Refugee Board formally committed the administration to rescuing Jews, it confronted the same problems that

Herbert Lehman had found so frustrating when FDR appointed him to direct relief operations in Europe a year earlier. The board operated on a shoestring budget of some $250,000 from FDR's wartime contingency fund. Even the board's proponents agreed on the futility of asking for an appropriation from Congress. It had to depend on private sources of funding, mostly from Jewish organizations, and had a small staff of about twenty-five professionals with no authority to bind administration officials to its policies. Instead, the board had to rely on cooperation from the often resistant diplomatic and military bureaucracies.[10]

High military officials worried that the board's missions would impede their job of fighting the war. In January 1944, the only American troops in Europe were taking heavy casualties as they advanced with their British counterparts up the boot of German-occupied Italy. The Allies also systematically bombed German manufacturing and refining targets at this time to reduce Germany's capacity to wage war and to resist the impending Allied invasion of France. In early 1944, no one in the upper ranks of the Roosevelt administration pressed for military operations to rescue Jews. There were no military means available to stop the Holocaust; until the late spring of 1944 American bombers could not have reached Auschwitz, the only extermination camp still functioning.

In late January, the deputy chief of staff wrote Assistant Secretary of War McCloy that only the speedy defeat of the Axis would save victims of Nazi persecution: "For this reason I share your concern over further involvement of the War Department, while the war is on, in matters such as the one brought up by Secretary Morgenthau." In response to this fear and similar British concerns, Pehle adopted language drafted in the War Department, indicating that the United States would not use combat troops to rescue civilians except as a byproduct of ongoing military operations.[11]

When McCloy's executive assistant Harrison Gerhardt told Colonel Thomas Davis, an official of the War Department's Operations Division, about the War Refugee Board's responsibilities, Davis responded that, "we are over there to win the war and not to take care of refugees." Even after Gerhardt said that Roosevelt had a different view, the Operations Division officer resisted any notion of using military force for humanitarian goals.[12]

Another sign of the military's recalcitrance came when the War Refugee Board sought to persuade Spanish dictator Francisco Franco to shelter some refugees. Ernst of the American Civil Liberties Union suggested Colonel

William O'Dwyer, a Catholic, a New Yorker, and a friend of Francis Cardinal Spellman as an envoy to Spain whom Franco might heed. Pehle agreed, but Undersecretary of War Robert Patterson refused to release O'Dwyer from his job of detecting fraud in the army air force. The president then asked Patterson to "show cause" why he could not temporarily reassign O'Dwyer: "I honestly think that Colonel William O'Dwyer can do relatively a more important job for the War Refugee Board at this time than in any other capacity," FDR said. "I would want him to be under Stettinius and go over to Spain at once. I know no one else who could do as good a job. I do not think this need be called a permanent assignment." Patterson said O'Dwyer had unique skills, and he could not spare him even temporarily. O'Dwyer stayed in the army.[13]

The War Refugee Board could still deploy the power of words. The board staff ventured into the State Department's preserve of foreign relations when it endorsed a new declaration against Nazi atrocities. In the board's view, the Allies could perhaps influence the leaders of Romania, Bulgaria, and Hungary to cease cooperating with Nazi programs of mass murder. Board staff member Josiah DuBois said, "And if this country could really show, as it has never shown, that it really means business when it says it is interested in the Jews . . , it would make an awful lot of difference in the attitude of particularly the subordinates of the Nazi leaders and in the satellite countries. We have in mind the issuance of a strong declaration by the President."[14]

In late January 1944, the World Jewish Congress had requested a new Allied statement that condemned the Nazi killings of Jews. The British Foreign Office believed that the Allies had already covered atrocities against Jews with their declaration of December 17, 1942, with the unfortunate result that "it seemed to indicate to Germans a means whereby they could distress and embarrass Allies." The December 1942 declaration had raised "unrealistic hopes" among Jews, and Britain did not want to repeat this mistake. British officials sought reassurance about American backing if they turned the World Jewish Congress down.[15]

Instead, DuBois and his board colleague Joseph Friedman wrote a powerful draft declaration that denounced the systematic Nazi killings of Jews as one of the blackest crimes of history and urged Germans to repudiate Adolf Hitler's homicidal madness. Their draft committed the United States to help rescue Jews and others threatened by Nazi executioners and called for assistance from the peoples of Europe. DuBois thought that the United

States had to back words with actions and welcome some of the persecuted to its shores. Rather than enter this political thicket, the board staff placed American shelter on a slow track, while it pressed for an immediate presidential declaration.[16]

Morgenthau called the staff's draft, "wonderful, beautiful." Stimson rewrote some provisions, but approved it as well. However, Stettinius warned, "We in the State Department feel that in issuing this statement the President is taking a very important step and we hope he will have an opportunity to study it with great care." On March 8, Stettinius apparently relayed specific State Department objections to the president. State, the OWI, and the Joint Chiefs all preferred to avoid making Jews the headline in any American propaganda. They reacted as if nothing had changed since 1942. Their objections carried some weight with FDR, but not enough to block action from a president accustomed to overriding State Department views.[17]

Roosevelt told Stettinius that he wanted Rosenman and Stephen T. Early to redraft the declaration, making it a statement (not a declaration), and aiming it less directly at the atrocities against the Jews. FDR also wanted clearance from the British. In response to this troubling news, Morgenthau quickly arranged for Pehle to see Rosenman.[18]

Rosenman advised the president not to sign the board's draft. He raised the familiar objection that its "pointed reference to Jews" would likely inflame anti-Semitism in the United States. Rosenman's redrafted "statement" used the standard formula: Nazi and Japanese torture and murder of persons of many nationalities threatened the general goals of the United Nations for a better world. Rosenman, however, retained the board's language that referred specifically to the wholesale systematic murder of the Jews, including the vivid phrase "one of the blackest crimes of all history." Pehle feared that Rosenman had diluted the original too much. The next day, Stimson read over the new version with Pehle and found it improved, which boosted Pehle's spirits.[19]

On March 17, Pehle met with Bernard Baruch, who said that only Roosevelt could push the statement through a resistant bureaucracy. FDR was "right on these things," Baruch said, but something was amiss. Perhaps he meant that State Department officials were giving the president contrary advice. Baruch also thought that a positive response to the perils of European Jewry might help FDR win New York State in the upcoming presidential election. The next day, Morgenthau nudged Roosevelt to issue the statement, but the president said he had to wait for clearance from Britain and consultation with Rosenman before making a final decision.[20]

On March 20, Representative Noah M. Mason of Illinois, the ranking Republican on the House Immigration Committee, charged that the president had circumvented the will of Congress and opened the door to unrestricted immigration through his War Refugee Board. He called the executive order creating the board unconstitutional, and he did Breckenridge Long one better by claiming that 600,000 refugees had already entered the country.[21]

Four days later, Roosevelt read and discussed the revised board statement at his press conference. It would be a great tragedy if Jews who had escaped to Hungary should "perish on the very eve of triumph over the barbarism which their persecution symbolizes," he declared. He announced that Churchill and Stalin had both approved his statement. He called upon German citizens to aid the persecuted escape the Nazi hangman. He urged Germans and Europeans to collect evidence of those who were guilty of carrying out barbaric crimes. He called upon the free peoples of Europe and Asia to open their frontiers temporarily to the victims of oppression. On the same day, the War Refugee Board contacted the Apostolic Delegate in Washington, urging the pope to use his influence to protect Hungary's Jews. The board had succeeded in giving the rescue of Jews new visibility, with Roosevelt's assistance.[22]

At his press conference, Roosevelt also said that American authorities had transferred many refugees from occupied Europe to a camp in North Africa. In response to a direct question, he said that not enough refugees had escaped from Nazi territories to consider admitting them to the United States. He announced that Pehle's appointment as acting director of the board had become permanent. The *New York Times* carried the story on page 1, along with Pehle's picture; it reprinted the presidential statement on page 4, and added an editorial calling for practical plans to save refugees, not just hopeful words.[23]

Stimson and Hull opposed bringing refugees into the United States temporarily without congressional approval. Stimson reiterated old arguments that European Jews did not assimilate well in the United States and should be admitted only in limited numbers after careful scrutiny. Procedurally, he said, the president needed to consult Congress, because opponents viewed temporary havens as a wedge for expanding immigration. The president had already granted many supposedly temporary visitors the right to stay in the United States indefinitely. Politically, the immigration laws reflected the widespread sentiment that any inflow of immigrants should parallel the existing "racial stocks" in the country. After World War I, Congress had curtailed immigration from precisely those countries with throngs of potential refugees now. The war powers of the president did not cover humanitarian initiatives that ran counter to the intent of Congress, Stimson declared. Because of Morgenthau's contrary view, the board did not reject the idea of temporary havens in the United States, but posed it to FDR without an endorsement.[24]

State Department officials remained fixated on the threat of spies and saboteurs supposedly hidden among new arrivals to American shores. In February 1944, Visa Division chief Howard Travers had told two officials of the American Jewish Committee that federal agents had recently captured two Nazi spies posing as Jewish refugees. The Interdepartmental Visa Review Committee properly applied exceedingly strict standards of review, he said, and moved with deliberate caution. If the State Department had admitted more refugees, Travers added, it would have antagonized the large anti-immigration bloc in Congress. Director Pehle complained to his staff in mid-February that "in any refugee-movement people can raise that spy thing if they want to raise it." He added that the State Department tended to defer initiatives for Jews so that "nothing will happen." About a month later Pehle told Undersecretary Stettinius that the board's efforts "are being effectively nullified by the failure of the State Department to act promptly on the Board's programs."[25]

In a memo to the War Refugee Board in early March, DuBois noted that even more than State Department resistance, the most important obstacle to rescuing Jews is "that the United Nations have not been prepared to supply even temporary havens of refuge for substantial numbers of the persecuted peoples of Europe, particularly the Jews." This failure, he said, undermines efforts to persuade satellite leaders to cease cooperating with the Nazis in exterminating Jews. It provides "the pretext of justification that the Allies, while speaking in horrified terms of the Nazi treatment of the Jews, never once offered to receive these people."[26]

About a month later, the *New York Post*'s Samuel Grafton proposed in his popular syndicated column to solve the problem of finding places of refuge by establishing "free ports" for refugees. "A free port," he said, "is a place where you can put things down for a while, without having to make a final decision about them." It was typically used for the temporary storage of foreign goods, but could also become a temporary haven for "refugees fleeing the Hitler terror." He wrote that he was ashamed to pander to antiforeign prejudices and endorse a plan that would give refugees no rights—"store them like corn, and herd them like cattle." Still, time was short, and the United States needed to set a better example for other countries. The Bergson group agreed and launched one of its signature advertising campaigns in support of American havens, as well as other camps for refugees in Palestine, Turkey, and North Africa. Rabbi Wise also pledged that his World Jewish Congress would back the free port initiative.[27]

At the request of White House officials, survey research expert Hadley Cantril conducted a private poll. Some 70 percent of a small national sample approved of temporary havens in the United States; 23 percent disapproved, and only 7 percent said they did not know. Some objected to foreigners entering America, fearing that they would add to the cost of government and endeavor to stay in the United States once the war ended. One respondent said he or she did not want this class of people (Jews). Another suggested that there were enough Jews running things in Washington already. There is no direct evidence that Roosevelt saw the positive results, but it seems likely.[28]

In early May, Pehle and the board staff prepared a detailed report in support of the plan. By admitting refugees, even provisionally, the United States would add moral weight to its denunciation of Nazi atrocities, convince Germans that it meant to punish war criminals, and persuade neutral countries to give shelter themselves. The arrival of refugees on American shores would convey a stronger message to the world abroad than rhetoric alone.[29]

On May 11, Roosevelt told Pehle that he approved his plan for temporary refuge, although he objected to the phrase "free port" because it did not convey the clear message that refugees would leave at the war's end. Pehle pointed to a now vacant camp previously used for Japanese Americans at Jerome, Arkansas, as a way station for refugees, but FDR said he preferred a vacant army camp somewhere on the Atlantic seaboard. Ships transporting American soldiers to Europe could accommodate refugee passengers on their return trip. Pehle showed the president newspaper stories and editorials that backed the plan; he mentioned that the American Federation of Labor, the Congress of Industrial Organizations, the Federal

Council of Churches, the Young Women's Christian Association, and many other organizations had pledged support.[30]

Even so, the fourth Roosevelt remained cautious about harboring refugees within the United States. He said that without congressional approval, he could not announce the admission of large numbers of refugees. Instead, he suggested using some specific situation involving about 1,000 refugees as a test case—eventually the limiting case. FDR would admit them and explain his decision to Congress. He asked Pehle to prepare a justification, and Pehle pointed to an overcrowded camp in Allied territory in Italy a week later.[31]

On May 22, the 1928 Democratic candidate for president, Al Smith, had asked Roosevelt's former law partner Basil O'Connor whether he should endorse a statement by prominent American Christians urging the president to help save a million Jews in Hungary and supporting the establishment of refugee havens in the United States and Allied countries. O'Connor sent the query to the White House. FDR responded that this would be "a fine thing to do," but the statement should insert the word "temporary" in front of refugee havens.[32]

At the cabinet meeting of May 26, FDR stated that roughly 1,500 refugees a week—Jews and non-Jews—were moving from Yugoslavia into Italy; he wondered where they could be housed. Secretary of the Interior Harold Ickes suggested relocating them to the Virgin Islands or Puerto Rico. Morgenthau urged the American military not to discourage the flow of refugees from the Balkans into southern Italy. Hull agreed to send a strong cable to Ambassador Robert Murphy in Algiers to prevent the military from obstructing refugees seeking safety.[33]

Roosevelt at first hoped that those refugees who had reached southern Italy could go to Cyrenaica or Tripolitania (Libya). Pehle again had to convince him of the need for havens in the United States. FDR said he was not averse to the scheme, but he had to convince Congress that larger numbers would go elsewhere. The president personally chose the title "Emergency Refugee Shelter" because it connoted nothing more from the government than temporary shelter. Pehle saw Baruch in the outer office of the White House, and Morgenthau said afterwards that Baruch was very pleased at FDR's approval. Congratulating the War Refugee Board staff, Morgenthau accurately stated, "the best position we can take is that this is a token to the rest of the world."[34]

After Allied forces had landed at Normandy and taken control of Rome on June 6, a relieved Roosevelt was eager to announce that he had set up the new camp for refugees. Once again, military victories gave him the cover needed for humanitarian ventures. The president directed Ambassador Murphy in Algiers to arrange for the transport of approximately 1,000 refugees from southern Italy to the United States. On June 9, he announced at a press conference his plan to establish a temporary home for these refugees at Fort Ontario, a vacant army camp near Oswego, New York, which McCloy had recommended. Then he sent a message to Congress praising the work of the War Refugee Board, explaining arrangements for the camp, and pledging that the refugees, predominantly women and children, would leave at war's end. Roosevelt's announcement elicited little reaction from restrictionists in Congress, who seemed mollified by his reassurances.[35]

The mainstream press mostly lauded the president's initiative, without explicitly mentioning Jews. A *New York Times* editorial praised FDR and called for the United States to shelter temporarily additional victims of Nazi terror, not to promote "unrestricted and uncontrolled immigration," but "to save the lives of innocent people." The *Baltimore Sun* hoped that the plan signified new directions for a government that had been generous with advice to other nations, but "less than generous with practical assistance" to suffering peoples abroad.[36]

Despite its meager resources and authority, the War Refugee Board also influenced American government policy toward Hungary, which held the largest population of Jews remaining in Europe. In late 1943, Hungarian government officials, only nominally loyal to their ally Germany, secretly tried to negotiate peace with the Allies. After intelligence agents informed Hitler of this plot, he ordered the German army to occupy Hungary on March 19, 1944. Adolf Eichmann's team of deportation specialists followed German troops into Hungary, posing a dire threat to roughly 750,000 Hungarian Jews and tens of thousands of Jewish refugees who had reached the country.

The regent of Hungary, Admiral Miklós Horthy, and a new Hungarian cabinet, headed by the pro-German Döme Sztójay, gave cover and legitimacy to Hungarian participation in the Holocaust. Starting in mid-May 1944, the Hungarian police and gendarmerie regularly loaded each day thousands of Jews from newly established ghettos onto freight trains. Unknown to most of the deportees, these trains ran directly to the gas chambers and crematoria of Auschwitz.

On April 7, A. Leon Kubowitzki of the World Jewish Congress wrote the War Refugee Board to recommend broadcasts that warned Hungarian Jews to avoid self-identification through yellow badges and to destroy all registers that might expose Jews in hiding. He also suggested that America should call upon non-Jews to assist Jewish neighbors. By this time, Gerhart M. Riegner, representative of the World Jewish Congress in Switzerland, had already reported that the Germans planned to concentrate, deport, and exterminate 800,000 Jews in Hungary: "suggest Jews [be] advised [to] seek refuge inside and outside Hungary by all conceivable means and warned not make same mistake as Jews in Poland and [the] Netherlands."[37]

On April 22 1944, representatives of the Treasury, State, and War departments met with OWI officials and convinced them to broadcast warnings to Hungary. In mid-May, the War Refugee Board confirmed arrangements with OWI to broadcast warnings to Nazi satellites. The War Refugee Board later reported widespread coverage of Hungary in OWI broadcasts from overseas and from the United States. How much Hungarian Jews were able to hear or learn about such warnings remains unclear.[38]

The United States directed other warnings to the Hungarian government through diplomatic channels. The War Refugee Board asked American missions in neutral countries to express their grave concern to unaligned governments that Nazis and their local collaborators seemed poised to annihilate the Jews of Hungary. It requested these governments and the Vatican to contact their missions in Budapest for information about the fate of Hungarian Jews. The United States also asked neutral governments to expand their missions in Budapest in the hope that additional foreign observers would constrain Hungarian officials. A separate American dispatch called upon the pope to broadcast his concerns about the persecution and impending slaughter of 800,000 Jews to the Hungarian authorities and people, as well as send them through Vatican officials in Budapest.[39]

Roosevelt's June 12 message to Congress also described Nazi intentions as defeat neared, "the fury of their insane desire to wipe out the Jewish race in Europe continues unabated. This is but one example: many Christian groups are also being murdered." FDR's inclusion of Christians broadened the appeal of the message and reduced the risk of adverse political reactions, but he had forthrightly singled out the annihilation of Jews. He said that the War Refugee Board had a solemn duty to translate America's humanitarian principles into action. The *New York Times* published a front-page story on FDR's statement.[40]

On June 21, War Refugee Board director Pehle briefed the House Foreign Affairs Committee on Hungary. Afterwards, Chairman Sol Bloom issued a statement in the name of the committee calling upon Hungary to halt its oppression of Jews, and warning that the Allies would punish the perpetrators of crimes. On June 26, Hull publicly reinforced the House committee's statement. Through the Swiss government, the United States sent a sharp note to the Hungarian leadership calling to their attention Roosevelt's March 24 warning about punishing the guilty. Members of the Senate Foreign Relations Committee participated in a radio program broadcast via shortwave that implored Hungarians to protect the lives of Jews among them through every possible means. In a message transmitted by the OWI, Archbishop Francis J. Spellman of New York warned Hungarians that their nation's anti-Jewish policies contravened the Catholic faith. These warnings and broadcasts not only pressured the Hungarian government, but also broadened the American coalition interested in saving Hungarian Jews. "Hungary has been flooded with broadcasts dealing with the persecution of the Jews," Pehle said. American planes also dropped leaflets with Roosevelt's March 24 statement over Hungary. It was the most concerted effort to date by the American political establishment to aid in the rescue of Jews.[41]

On April 7, 1944, shortly before the Nazis began deporting Hungarian Jews to the extermination camp at Auschwitz, two Jewish prisoners from Slovakia made a daring escape. Rudolf Vrba and Alfred Wetzler, who had survived more than two years at the camp, had studied the facility's vulnerabilities and fashioned a successful plan of escape. Vrba also later claimed he had heard SS guards suggest that Hungarian Jews would begin to arrive soon. They wanted to save themselves and warn the world about the hideous factory-style gas chambers and crematoria at Auschwitz-Birkenau. On April 10, 1944, the escapees emerged from their hiding place and fled south toward their native Slovakia. After they linked up with what remained of the Jewish leadership there, they dictated an amazingly detailed account of facilities at Auschwitz and its methods for the mass slaughter of Jews.[42]

The substance of this Vrba-Wetzler report and corroborating information spread quickly into Switzerland and then to the United States and Britain. Even earlier, on April 10, 1944, American officials had received from sources in the Polish underground a detailed and largely accurate account of the operation of killing factories at Auschwitz, including estimates of the large number of Jews already executed in the gas chambers. Then in May, the press, led by the *New York Times,* began publishing stories about the peril of Hungarian Jews. On May 10, the *Times* reported that Hungary "is now preparing for the annihilation of Hungarian Jews by the most fiendish methods." On May 18, without specifying its sources, the *Times* reported with rough accuracy that more than 80,000 Hungarian Jews already "had been sent to murder camps in Poland," with many more to come. Then, on July 3, the paper published a major story on Auschwitz-Birkenau. Information reaching two private, non-Jewish organizations in Switzerland—likely including the Vrba-Wetzler report—confirmed the existence of death camps at Auschwitz and Birkenau and the murder of more than 1.7 million Jews there through April 15, 1944. Since then, the article claimed with rough accuracy, about 400,000 Hungarian Jews had been deported to Auschwitz. The *Times* also reported that the Nazis were using a poison gas derived from cyanide.[43]

Reports of mass killings of Jews at Auschwitz and Nazi plans to deport perhaps all Hungarian Jews there lent new urgency to ideas for saving Hungarian Jewry. In mid-1944, Hungary represented the only land under Nazi control or influence where a large population of Jews had survived. It remained an open question whether the remaining Jews there could be saved from annihilation. The War Refugee Board had the will, but not necessarily the way. Rescue or relief of Hungarian Jewry involved a process of trial and error in political maneuvers, diplomacy, and feasible military actions.

CHAPTER FOURTEEN

Negotiations and Rescue in Hungary

ON JUNE 6, 1944 (D-Day), Hungarian prime minister Döme Sztójay met with Adolf Hitler to convey a request from Regent Miklós Horthy: now that Hungary had a stable government, Germany should restore full Hungarian sovereignty by withdrawing its troops. Hitler made it plain that German troops would not leave Hungary until the "Jewish Question" there was fully resolved.[1]

The Nazis followed a dual strategy in Hungary. They regularly deported Jews from Hungary, while simultaneously trying to exploit Allied concerns for these victims. Two Hungarians carried to Istanbul an intriguing but suspicious offer to the West on behalf of Nazi officials; it raised several thorny issues for American officials and FDR. Could the Nazis be trusted in any offer they made to the Western Allies? Did the emissaries from Hungary have the authority to broker any deal between Germany and the United Nations? Was it wise to give trucks and other supplies to Nazi forces in return for potentially saving Jews? Although they welcomed serious prospects for rescuing Jews, American officials, including President Roosevelt, who was a target of Nazi maneuvers, eventually answered no to each of these questions.

On May 18, Joel Brand of the Jewish Rescue and Relief Committee of Budapest flew to Istanbul bringing a personal message from Adolf Eichmann: if the Western Allies gave Germany 10,000 trucks and other assorted supplies and food, Germany would use the trucks only on the Eastern front—and it would spare the Jews in Hungary. Brand's colleague Rezsö (Rudolf) Kasztner, head of the Jewish Relief and Rescue Committee of Budapest, advanced another version of Eichmann's offer, which eventually reached Roswell McClelland, who represented the War Refugee Board in Switzerland. The Gestapo declared they would trade 1,000 Jews for every ten tractors. Once delivery of the tractors began, "they would destroy the 'plants' at Auschwitz." McClelland thought the offer reflected a shift in Nazi interest from biological goals to material benefits.[2]

Another Hungarian, Andor Grosz (alias Andreas György), a Jewish convert to Catholicism who was a smuggler and an agent working for several intelligence services, traveled with Brand to Istanbul. Grosz claimed that he had a separate mission authorized by officials of the SS Security Service (SD) based in Hungary. His role was to contact Western Allied authorities and help initiate peace negotiations—a separate peace for Germany with Britain and the United States. Germany then could continue to fight the Soviet Union.[3]

American intelligence officials knew Grosz well as a double agent who funneled information to U.S. representatives in Istanbul while also working for the Gestapo. His presence made them suspicious of the entire mission. After brief discussions in Istanbul with Turkish authorities, representatives of the Jewish Agency for Palestine, and others, Brand and Grosz crossed the border into British-held Syria, trying to reach Palestine. British forces intercepted them in Syria.[4]

On June 12 in Aleppo (Syria), Brand spoke to Moshe Shertok, a high official of the Jewish Agency, while British intelligence officials listened and took notes. Brand said that the Nazis were willing in principle to liberate a large number of Jews, but Eichmann refused to stop deportations while negotiations proceeded. German authorities balked at sending Hungarian Jews to Palestine; they did not want to offend the Arabs or help Jews build a strong state there. Shertok also reported what intelligence officials called "the fantastic theory" that Nazis considered Jews "a disease—a virus which excites, distracts, and upsets society." Purportedly, the Germans wanted Jews distributed widely in the West to spread chaos and weaken resistance to Nazi power. The liberation of numerous Hungarian Jews would also embarrass and divide the Allies, who did not want many Jews resettled within their borders. Perhaps it might even help some SS authorities expiate for the sin of killing millions of Jews.[5]

On May 25, after learning about Brand's mission from Shertok and David Ben-Gurion, British high commissioner for Palestine Sir Harold Mac-Michael dismissed it as a Nazi intrigue with hidden motives. The British War Cabinet rejected the alleged Nazi offer six days later. A. W. G. Randall of the Foreign Office worried that the War Refugee Board and the upcoming presidential election might give the proposal undue consideration in America. The British notified Washington that they opposed any dealings with the Gestapo.[6]

The British Foreign Office urged rejection of the German feeler, saying that Allied responsibility for an additional million persons meant suspending essential military operations, but if Germany released Jews on its own, the Foreign Office said, Britain and the United States would consider prospects for moving them to Spain or Portugal. It was a perfunctory gesture. Calling the Jews-for-trucks deal bizarre, Assistant Secretary of War John J. McCloy agreed with the British.[7]

The War Refugee Board had its own sources of information and analysis. American ambassador to Turkey Laurence Steinhardt had asked Joint Distribution Committee representative Reuben B. Resnik, who also worked with the War Refugee Board, to speak to Brand and others. Resnik summarized Brand's background and movements, reviewed the range of possible Nazi motives for Brand's mission, and concluded that, whether or not the Nazis were laying a trap to split the Allies, Eichmann's conditions were impossible. Nonetheless, he advised keeping negotiations open in the hope of rescuing some Jews.[8]

War Refugee Board director John Pehle thought perhaps the Nazis would release some Jews to Spain or a neutral country for payment in gold, presumably into an account blocked until war's end. On June 8, Pehle and Henry Morgenthau Jr. told Roosevelt about the purported German offer: "We then mentioned to the President the information concerning the alleged German offer received from a Jewish representative from Hungary who came to Ankara [*sic*] with a Gestapo man in a German military plane. The President was very interested in this development and agreed that we should keep the negotiations open."[9]

On June 22, Bloomingdale executive Ira Hirschmann, a special representative of the War Refugee Board, persuaded British authorities in Cairo to let him question Brand, whom authorities had moved to a British prison there. Hirschmann explained that the matter had gained the attention and interest of President Roosevelt and showed them a letter from FDR to Lord Moyne, the British minister of state for the Middle East. Hirschmann concluded, as did officials of the Jewish Agency for Palestine, that Brand was sincere, that Hungarian Jews were in dire peril, and that the British should let Brand return to Budapest with some sign of Allied interest in negotiations. But Office of Strategic Services (OSS) officials in Washington concluded that the Brand mission was an "incredible Nazi black maneuver" designed to embarrass the president: "Roosevelt is the chief target, for the Nazis claim that he is impeding the war effort by his attempts to rescue Jews." In another cable, the officials stated, "the political move motivating this plant [of two German double agents in Istanbul] is the implication that American[s] placed more worth on saving Hungarian Jews than on the war effort."[10]

British officials expressed skepticism about the sincerity of the "offer" to trade Jews for trucks, but also worried that the Nazis might be serious about trying to dump a million Jews on the Allies. In their view, that would cause grave logistical problems and hamper the war effort. As a result, they insisted on notifying the Russians about the offer. On July 19, the British Broadcasting Corporation broadcast a report about the offer, killing off Jewish hopes of confidential negotiations.[11]

The Nazi offer to trade the lives of Hungarian Jews for goods or money was a poisoned chalice, reminiscent of Nazi proposals to ransom Jews after the Évian Conference of 1938, but it still offered some small opportunities. Opposition from the British and the Soviets and the detention of Brand in Cairo limited the chance that Jewish organizations working with or parallel to the War Refugee Board could make something out of Brand's mission. When the Nazis tried to reestablish contact with the Allies through Joseph Schwartz of the Joint Distribution Committee in Lisbon, even Pehle opposed the meeting because it might divide the Allies. He also said, "there is no disposition here or elsewhere in this Government to my knowledge to even negotiate on supplying the German with commodities." Still, by keeping the possibility of negotiations open, the Allies may have saved some Jewish lives. According to the War Refugee Board's McClelland, "the Gestapo in Budapest refrained from sending to Auschwitz during the initial period of deportations . . . groups totaling 17290 souls."[12]

In July, for reasons unrelated to Brand's mission, Hungarian authorities stopped deporting Jews to Auschwitz. In late June, the pope had sent a telegram to Regent Horthy appealing to his noble sentiments to save many unfortunate people from further pain and sorrow. He avoided the word Jews, but his meaning was clear. Only the opening of Vatican archives may reveal whether Pius XII responded to American encouragement or acted independently. Regardless, his intervention and that of the unusually forceful Papal Nuncio Angelo Rotta stung Horthy, who also received a letter from the king of Sweden and continuing warnings from President Roosevelt.[13]

Horthy finally grasped that Germany's deteriorating military situation and its crimes against civilians compromised Hungary's postwar interests. Foreign pressures, a coincidental American bombing of Budapest on July 2, and the threat of an anti-Horthy coup by pro-German elements forced sudden changes in Hungary. On July 7, Horthy suspended deportations of Jews in time to save those left in Budapest. It validated the War Refugee Board's strategy of pressuring Nazi satellites, even if American pressure by itself would not have halted the deportations.[14]

Soon after halting deportations, Horthy's government offered a new plan for saving Jews. The Hungarians proposed to Swiss diplomats in Budapest that they would allow the emigration of Jews under ten years of age ("if possible to Palestine"), and Jews with entry visas for other nations, including Palestine. The Horthy offer would potentially free some 40,000 Hungarian Jews, but it required German approval and authorization for transit through German-occupied territory.[15]

The British government shunned plans that could increase immigration to Palestine or place logistical demands on the military for transporting refugees. To avoid the appearance of openly rejecting an offer to save Jews, the British proposed conditions that would indefinitely delay an authoritative reply. The Roosevelt administration, in contrast, responded quickly and positively to the offer, rejecting British reservations. Pehle said that British "delaying tactics" would "jeopardize lives" and "be interpreted as an admission that the policies of the two governments as proclaimed by their highest authorities are without substance." Washington pressed the British government for a joint declaration agreeing to Horthy's terms, which British equivocation delayed until August 16. In response to British objections, the United States agreed to reword the declaration's commitment to "make arrangements for the care of all Jews," to one limited to "such Jews," that is only the Jews specifically covered by Horthy's offer. The two powers made no mention of Palestine and pledged only to find places of temporary refuge for liberated Jews. Then Germany effectively killed the proposal by refusing to allow Jews to leave Hungary, "except as part of an unacceptable ransom scheme," Hull said on August 28.[16]

If negotiations offered little hope of saving Hungarian Jewry, military actions posed problems as well. Some Jewish advocates urged the Allies first to bomb the rail lines and junctions to Auschwitz and then the killing apparatus there. The operation was conceivable logistically. By early 1944, American bombers based in southern Italy could reach the rail lines in Hungary and the facilities at Auschwitz without refueling. By May, the American Fifteenth Air Force had reached full strength and had begun bombing industrial targets, not far from Auschwitz.[17]

On June 18, 1944, Jacob Rosenheim of Agudath Israel in New York beseeched the War Refugee Board to bomb the railways leading from Hungary to Auschwitz. It was the first of several such requests; Allied censorship of private mail delayed other proposals from abroad. Gerhart M. Riegner, representative of the World Jewish Congress in Switzerland, and representatives of the Czechoslovakian government-in-exile had both suggested bombing the gas chambers and crematoria. Peter Bergson's Emergency Committee to Save the Jewish People of Europe also favored a direct attack on the killing centers. A. Leon Kubowitzki, head of the World Jewish Congress's rescue unit, opposed such an attack because it would kill Jewish prisoners, and the Nazis would use such Allied-induced casualties as propaganda and cover for their own massive killings.

At a June 28 meeting with the War Refugee Board staff, Kubowitzki, a Jewish refugee, urged the Allies to use commandos dropped by parachute to destroy the installations. Pehle thought this proposal unrealistic because it would result in heavy American casualties; he did not refer it to the War Department. Kubowitzki did pass on to American officials requests by other Jewish leaders for the bombing of Auschwitz itself. He also later favored a request to the Polish underground to attack the camp and destroy gas chambers and crematoria. Pehle thought any such request to the Poles pointless, and he did not pass this suggestion on to the military.[18]

The War Department had consistently balked at cooperating with the War Refugee Board. Why would anyone there heed the board's request for a precision bombing raid against a nonmilitary target? Pehle must have pondered this conundrum before he approached Assistant Secretary of War McCloy about bombing the railways that ran from Hungary to Auschwitz.[19]

Still, on June 21 he referred this request to the War Department, and on June 24 he asked McCloy personally to at least explore proposals for bombing the rail lines. In a "memo for the files" written that same day, Pehle said that he told McCloy that he was not "requesting the War Department to take any action on this proposal other than to appropriately explore it." He also said that he expressed to McCloy "several doubts" about the proposal. He reported saying that "it would be difficult to put the railroad line out of commission for a long enough period to do any good" and that even success might not help the Jews of Hungary survive.[20]

All War Refugee Board matters went initially to the War Department's Civil Affairs Division, which fell under McCloy. The Operations Division—on the military side—very quickly decided it wanted no part of a mission to bomb the rail lines, calling it impractical and diversionary. In an internal memorandum on June 26, just two days after Pehle conferred with McCloy, the Operations Division instructed the Civil Affairs Division to prepare a reply "indicating War Department disapproval of proposed operation." The memorandum concluded, "No other action necessary." In support of this position, Major General Thomas T. Handy wrote on behalf of the Operations Division that "The most effective relief to victims of enemy persecution is the early defeat of the Axis, an undertaking to which we must devote every resource at our disposal." This became the War Department's stock formula for responding to all proposals for military missions with humanitarian goals. On July 4, McCloy informed Pehle that the Operations Division had rejected the idea of bombing the rail lines to Auschwitz.[21]

In peremptorily rejecting any air raids to halt or slow down the deportation of Jews to Auschwitz, military officials did not scrutinize the logistics of such a bombing mission, calculate the likelihood of destroying the target, consider the possibilities of collateral damage, or estimate the loss of planes and pilots. Kai Bird, a biographer of McCloy, notes that the office of General Henry H. "Hap" Arnold would have had to determine whether such an operation was viable, but there is no evidence that the matter ever reached him.[22]

Those in charge of military operations simply believed that they had higher priority tasks elsewhere and could not spare resources for a humanitarian mission. The military command devoted its bombers to supporting Allied troops on the ground and striking economic targets, such as German industrial plants and oil refineries. For every target military planners selected, they left other targets untouched. The Operations Division preferred to set priorities in conjunction with theater commanders. Roosevelt did not generally intervene in strategic targeting decisions. McCloy's biographer agrees that there is no evidence the issue ever reached the president, a conclusion that is corroborated by the War Department's nearly immediate rejection of the bombing proposal.[23]

The War Refugee Board also considered proposals to bomb the death camp at Auschwitz itself. On June 29, in response to recommendations from the World Jewish Congress, relayed from McClelland in Geneva, Benjamin Akzin, a Jewish member of the board's staff, wrote up the case for bombing the gas chambers and crematoria. Bombing might kill the prisoners, he said, but they were doomed anyway. By killing perpetrators as well as victims, bombing raids would show that the Allies meant to punish the murderers. More importantly, successful bombing would destroy the machinery of death. These sound arguments had traction, however, only with those convinced that the Nazis in fact operated gas chambers and crematoria at Auschwitz, that they killed thousands of people every day, and that the life-saving potential of a bombing raid outweighed the inevitable losses of planes, the killing of some Jews, and the neglect of other targets.[24]

On July 13, Lawrence Lesser of the War Refugee Board staff drafted a presidential directive that requested that the military investigate missions to rescue civilians. By this time, in a report to the members of the board, Pehle alluded to proposals to bomb concentration and extermination centers "in order that in the resultant confusion some of the unfortunate people might be able to escape and hide." He also mentioned proposals to air-drop weapons to prisoners and to attack the camp with parachute troops. Competent military authorities were examining these proposals, Pehle claimed. He had not given up hope of getting someone in the military or the War Department to reverse McCloy's rejection of humanitarian bombing missions, although he did not officially recommend an attack on the death camp until months later.[25]

On August 2, because of British consideration of similar proposals, General Carl A. Spaatz, commander of the U.S. Strategic Air Forces, expressed sympathy for the idea. Days later, British air marshal Norman Bottomley wrote Spaatz that the Foreign Office advised against the raid; the British would not carry it out and they recommended no further consideration. In mid-August the War Department rejected a request from the World Jewish Congress to bomb Auschwitz and the rail lines from Hungary. McCloy said that the military could not divert military resources for this mission, which was of "doubtful efficacy."[26]

Late in August, for the first time, a request to bomb rail lines to Auschwitz actually reached commanders in the Mediterranean Allied Air Forces in Europe. The intelligence unit of the Mediterranean command rejected this proposal in familiar terms; its analysis concluded that bombing raids might only disable the rail lines for a brief period, given that military priorities of the Fifteenth Air Force precluded the sustained bombing of a nonmilitary target. General Henry M. Wilson, supreme Allied commander in the Mediterranean, accepted this conclusion and on September 6 conveyed it to the War Department in Washington. This rejection likely had no effect on the Holocaust in Hungary since it occurred after Regent Horthy had already ceased deporting Hungarian Jews to Poland. However, the Nazis and their collaborators were still dispatching Jews from other regions to the gas chambers.[27]

In late September, the Orthodox rescue group Vaad ha-Hatzala, with backing from the Polish government-in-exile, urged the Allies to bomb the gas chambers. On October 1, Pehle again approached McCloy. Pehle noted, "I understand that the matter [the possibility of bombing the gas chambers and crematoria] is now in the hands of appropriate theatre commanders." Someone in McCloy's office wrote: "received, no reply necessary." According to McCloy's assistant Harrison Gerhardt, the War Department had previously rejected such requests, and nearby Russian forces should have the responsibility for any missions against Auschwitz.[28]

By the late summer of 1944, the U.S. Fifteenth Air Force, based in Foggia, Italy, was bombing industrial targets in Upper Silesia, including some in the Auschwitz complex of camps. A female employee at the IG Farben synthetic rubber plant at Auschwitz-Monowitz wrote her brother, "On the

20.8.44 we had a heavy attack on Auschwitz; at home they had only an air-raid alarm, but on Auschwitz they threw 1200 bombs. . . . Nothing has changed here in Auschwitz, only we have 3 air-raid alarms a day; even during the night they do not give us peace." She slightly underestimated: on that day 137 Flying Fortresses dropped 1,336 500-pound high explosive bombs on synthetic oil and rubber plants less than five miles from the gas chambers.[29]

The raids on industrial targets in Upper Silesia did not prove that Allied targeting of the gas chambers and crematoria would succeed in hitting such precise targets. They did expose McCloy's justification as hollow, however. In August and September 1944, American planes were available and already bombing targets near the death factories.

The Fifteenth Air Force flew from southern France to Bulgaria. Its priorities were to support the Allied invasion of France, the Allied campaign in Italy, and Soviet forces in the east—all strategic military targets. Unless someone with command authority made the case to add the targeting of gas chambers and crematoria to an existing strategic mission, such as striking the industrial facilities near Auschwitz, the requests had no chance of approval. The War Refugee Board lacked the political clout, military intelligence, and expertise to challenge the War Department.[30]

In November 1944, Pehle sent McCloy a short version of the Vrba-Wetzler report, the reconstruction of the death factories by two Slovak Jews who escaped Auschwitz. He noted that if Allied bombers destroyed these killing installations, the Germans could not quickly rebuild them, given other priorities as its military fortunes declined. McCloy and the Operations Division rejected this proposal with several familiar but specious arguments. Medium bombers and fighter-bombers based in Britain, France, or Italy could not reach the target, and heavy bombers based in Britain would need to fly unescorted for 2,000 miles over enemy territory, they said. Allied losses of planes would be unacceptably high, and the mission would divert resources from military targets.[31]

Remarkably, the full Vrba-Wetzler report did not reach Pehle until late October. He decided to release the report to the press. Elmer Davis, director of the Office of War Information, objected too late that the document lacked credibility. The War Refugee Board had already mailed out press releases. Secretary Stimson objected that Morgenthau and Pehle had authorized release of the report without consulting him. It was another example, he said, of "Morgenthau's further intrusion into matters of policy in respect to the treatment of Germany." He objected to Morgenthau's pushiness on issues involving Jews and said, "He as a Jew is the last man who ought to do it."[32]

Decades after World War II, advocates of humanitarian intervention focused on McCloy's decisive and abrupt rejection of requests to disrupt the executions at Auschwitz through American bombing missions. In response, McCloy in 1983 "remembered" that the War Department general staff had consulted air force operational commanders in Europe and reported their negative conclusions to him. This supposedly happened just when the Allies needed every resource at their command in the struggle to break out from Normandy in late June and July 1944. War Department records lack any trace of McCloy's consulting air force commanders in Europe at this time.[33]

McCloy also recalled that Judge Samuel Rosenman and Harry Hopkins had asked him to investigate the feasibility of bombing the Auschwitz death camp. After he did so and reported his findings to them, they told him that FDR had rejected the idea of a military operation aimed at the gas chambers and crematoria. The papers of Hopkins and Rosenman at the Roosevelt Presidential Library do not document any such discussion. Given contemporary evidence of his nearly immediate pro forma rejection of humanitarian bombing missions, McCloy's recollections seem little more than a self-serving attempt to revise the historical record.[34]

Still, based on the very mixed results of precision bombing missions at the time and even decades later (for example, against Serbia in the late 1990s), destruction of the gas chambers and crematoria would not have been simple or easy. Despite the contrary claims of FDR's critics, the bombing of Auschwitz would not likely have forced the Nazis to cease or reassess the Final Solution. Everything we know about Nazi leaders indicates the contrary: when it came to killing Jews, they were resourceful. Their henchmen could shoot as well as gas Jews.[35]

Fierce debates among scholars and opinion-makers decades after the fact have turned proposals for the bombing of Auschwitz into a cause célèbre. That was not the case at the time in the United States. Even American Jewish leaders knew little about Auschwitz, and most Americans would have agreed that the military's job was to win the war as quickly as possible.

A New York rally of 40,000 persons for saving Jewish lives sponsored by the umbrella American Jewish Conference on July 31 called for the military to work with underground forces to destroy Nazi facilities of mass execution. Speakers at this demonstration and another mass rally held later in Los Angeles, did not mention the bombing of Auschwitz or any other camps. American Jewish leaders did not approach the mainstream press on the bombing issue. Major Jewish groups such as the American Jewish Congress, the American Jewish Committee, and the leading Zionist organizations did not publicly advocate bombing missions. Key Jewish figures such as Rabbi Stephen S. Wise, Joseph Proskauer, and Rabbi Abba Hillel Silver did not lobby the administration to bomb Auschwitz, either publicly or behind the scenes. Proposals to do so reached the War Refugee Board from the Orthodox rescue group, the New York office of the World Jewish Congress, and Bergson, although Bergson focused on his plan to threaten the Germans with retaliatory poison gas strikes.[36]

On August 10, Pehle met with two international Jewish leaders: Nahum Goldmann, head of the Executive Committee of the World Jewish Congress, and Jewish labor leader Israel Mereminski, as well as Kubowitzki. These men proposed that the Polish underground attack the German death camps, but did not raise the question of bombing raids. Six days later, when Pehle met with American Jewish leaders on August 16, he presented his reasons for rejecting the idea of bombing Auschwitz; none present objected.[37]

The destruction of gas chambers and crematoria would have made Nazi killing less efficient and more costly. But later, in October 1944, Hungarians and Germans killed an additional 98,000 Jews in Hungary without any recourse to Auschwitz. American sources in Europe reported the determination of the Germans to kill as many Jews as possible even if faced with imminent defeat. Studies estimate that after the closing of Auschwitz, from January 1945 until the collapse of their regime, the Nazis murdered as many as 250,000 additional Jews. These considerations again illustrate the difficulties of evaluating long after the fact decisions that reflect conflicting priorities and imperfect information.[38]

Decades afterward, the nonbombing of Auschwitz has become a symbol of Roosevelt's alleged failure during the Holocaust. Clearly, the War Department had no interest in devoting resources to a nonmilitary mission for saving Jewish lives. However, there is no evidence beyond an elderly McCloy's highly suspect "recollections" that FDR had any role in this decision-making. The broader record of America's response to the Holocaust in Hungary is mixed. Despite rejecting pleas to bomb rail lines or the death camp itself, American officials pursued other means for aiding the surviving Jews of Hungary.[39]

In mid-September, Assistant Secretary of State Adolf A. Berle noted that the War Refugee Board had sanctioned negotiations to buy time and improve the chances for Jews to escape the Nazis. However, negotiations had reached the point where the Gestapo was threatening hideous reprisals against Jews if the Allies refused to provide them money or war materiel. Berle asked higher authorities for instructions, but they never came—no surprise, given official opposition to any such arrangements. In Switzerland, McClelland worked with Saly Mayer of the Joint Distribution Committee. Mayer had an available credit of $5 million from the War Refugee Board, although U.S. policy against ransom payments prohibited the release of these funds in exchange for Jewish freedom. Still, McClelland and Mayer did what they could to create the impression that the United States was willing to give Nazi officials something in return for the release of some Hungarian Jews, without running afoul of American laws, the suspicions of military authorities, or the doctrine of unconditional surrender, which applied both to Germany and Axis satellite countries.[40]

A more effective pursuit of the War Refugee Board involved a joint effort with the Swedish government and a courageous young Swede sent to Hungary. The Wallenbergs, a family of financiers, industrialists, and diplomats, were among Sweden's first families. Raoul Wallenberg, thirty-one in the spring of 1944, had trained as an architect at the University of Michigan and accumulated business experience in South Africa and Palestine. After he returned to Sweden, he formed a partnership with Koloman Lauer, originally a Hungarian Jew, who still had relatives in Budapest. Wallenberg himself had gone previously to Hungary during the war on business. By the spring of 1944, he had new grounds to return there.[41]

Beginning in mid-May or possibly earlier, representatives of Stockholm's Jewish community, Lauer, and both Swedish and American officials all backed the idea of Wallenberg returning to Budapest. He very much wanted to go, even if he initially thought of it as a short-term mission. In response to American requests that Sweden increase its representation in Budapest, the Swedish Foreign Office appointed Wallenberg as an attaché.[42]

Stockholm wanted Wallenberg simply to report on events in Hungary. Iver Olsen, who represented the War Refugee Board in Stockhom, and Herschel Johnson, the U.S. minister in Sweden, had a different view. Backed by

Lauer, they anticipated that the young Swede would lead a rescue effort that the United States would finance, even if documents about his functions and strategy are sparse. Wallenberg sided with the U.S. view: he would not sit back and write reports, but would attempt to save lives.[43]

Wallenberg's assignment to Budapest posed risks both for the Swede and his American sponsors. His American mission conflicted with his official Swedish role and more conservative Swedish instructions: How would he serve two masters? He would likely have to deal with German officials in Budapest in efforts to rescue Jews, but U.S. representatives had to refrain from any negotiations with the enemy. The War Refugee Board also had to avoid criticism from the State Department and the War Department that it was running its own foreign policy. Wallenberg and board officials kept paper communication to a minimum.

Internally, the War Refugee Board claimed Wallenberg as an ally to demonstrate progress against the Holocaust in Hungary. Morgenthau asked, "and this man, this Wallenberg, is able to get them [Jews] shelter in Hungary?" Pehle responded, "To some extent. Wallenberg is there solely because we put him there. He is really our representative."[44] The board also had plausible deniability in case Wallenberg went too far for American political sensibilities.

Shortly after Wallenberg arrived in Budapest on July 9, Pehle informed the board directors that he had sent a "detailed program to Olsen, suggesting the names of persons in Hungary who might be helpful in arranging rescues and we have indicated various escape routes which might be available from Hungary. We have arranged for private funds to be sent to Olsen to be used expressly for rescue operations from Hungary."[45] Olsen also reported that Wallenberg immediately arranged for an extraterritorial office, which he used to grant refuge to a number of Hungarian rabbis and intellectual leaders.[46]

Pehle told the director of the left-leaning magazine *The Nation* that the German government's attitude—not lack of transportation or of havens for refugees—blocked the emigration of Jews from Hungary. German officials repeatedly suggested that these Jews would end up in Palestine, and Germany could not afford to offend the Arabs. In Switzerland, McClelland strongly recommended continued publicity to pressure the Hungarian government.[47]

Meanwhile, Wallenberg, other Swedish officials in Budapest, and other neutral diplomats there distributed protective papers identifying Jews as citizens of Sweden or other lands, assuming that they remained in dire jeopardy, despite the halt in deportations. In mid-August, the War Refugee Board asked Johnson and Olsen in Stockholm to have Wallenberg answer some critical questions. Had Hungary stopped deportations temporarily or permanently? Did Jews in Hungary have access to food brought in from outside? Was emigration possible? Could the Allies rely on Hungarian promises? In early September, after receiving reports of efforts to save lives by Wallenberg and other Swedish diplomats in Budapest, Johnson told the Swedish government of America's "utmost appreciation" for Sweden's invaluable services in Hungary.[48]

Protective documents for thousands of Jews in Budapest became lifelines in mid-October. When Regent Horthy announced that Hungary had signed an armistice with the Soviet Union, German authorities immediately installed Ferenc Szálazi's extremist Nyilas movement in power, effectively displacing Horthy. Szálasi and Nazi officials then initiated the last phase of the Holocaust in Hungary. Wallenberg sent reports via Stockholm of the deteriorating situation, but also of the German legation's agreement to release Jews with Swedish protective documents from camps. Swedish diplomats also moved Jews into non-Jewish homes and provided them with supplies and medical care.[49]

Besides Wallenberg and his Swedish compatriots, other diplomats issued protective papers or set up safe houses to hide Jews. These figures included Carl Lutz, the Swiss vice-consul in Budapest, and George Mantello, a Jewish diplomat working in the consulate of tiny El Salvador in Switzerland.[50]

From mid-July until mid-October 1944, the Jews of Budapest benefited from the cessation of deportations from Hungary. Once Szálasi's extremists took power, however, the killings resumed, while their government segregated the remaining Jews into ghettos in Budapest. Wallenberg and his compatriots, operating with War Refugee Board backing and Joint Distribution Committee funding, saved many thousands of Jews, but far more perished.[51]

On December 8, Wallenberg reported to the Swedish Foreign Office that about 40,000 Jews had been taken on death marches toward Germany, and at least 69,000—but probably many more—would be housed in the central ghetto in Budapest. By comparison, about 7,000 were placed in houses enjoying Swedish protection, 2,000 in those with Red Cross protection, and 23,000 with Swiss protection. Pehle, who received a summary of this report, sent his own message to Wallenberg via the American legation in Stockholm, the same day:

> My dear Mr. Wallenberg. . . . We have followed with keen interest the reports of the steps you have taken to accomplish your mission and the personal devotion which you have given to saving and protecting the innocent victims of Nazi persecution. . . . I think that no one who has participated in this great task can escape some feeling of frustration [that] our efforts have not met with complete success. . . . [Yet] it is our conviction that you have made a very great personal contribution to the success which has been realized in these endeavors.[52]

Pehle's message never reached Wallenberg. When Soviet troops took Budapest, they arrested Wallenberg for reasons unknown. He died after the war in a Soviet prison. Exactly how, when, and why remains a mystery.

By November 1944, Jewish leaders worried that the Nazis and their collaborators might well unleash their hatred and frustration against defenseless enemies already in their hands. Organizations ranging from the American Jewish Committee to Agudath Israel to Bergson's renamed Hebrew Committee of National Liberation called for sharp Allied warnings against a slaughter of prisoners in the concentration and extermination camps. Proskauer, president of the American Jewish Committee, thought that such a warning would be most telling if it came from General Dwight D. Eisenhower. Pehle agreed, since Eisenhower might be in charge of an American zone of occupied Germany. That meant going through the War Department's maze.[53]

The Adjutant General's Office rejected the idea of a warning, because the German leaders might retaliate against all prisoners, civilian and military. Proskauer, however, had also enlisted the president's assistance through Judge Rosenman. Pehle drafted a memo from FDR to Stimson approving such a warning by Eisenhower. Roosevelt signed it on October 18, adding that Eisenhower "should issue such a statement as promptly as possible." Pehle's draft had warned Germans against harming or persecuting persons in forced-labor battalions or camps "without regard to their nationality and whether they are Jewish or otherwise." The War Department followed the president's expression of approval, but Eisenhower's headquarters changed the language to "without regard to nationality or religious faith." The Allied supreme commander released the warning on November 7, Election Day in the United States, three weeks after FDR's approval.[54]

Earlier Allied warnings against Hungarian cooperation with the Nazis, warnings orchestrated by the War Refugee Board, had helped to convince Regent Horthy to suspend deportations of Jews in July 1944—but only after Eichmann's men had sent more than 400,000 Jews to their deaths in Auschwitz. Considering how late in the war the Nazis brought the Final Solution to Hungary and how much the outside world knew or should have known of Nazi plans, the ultimate deaths of more than 564,000 Hungarian Jews are horrific and infuriating. But it was far easier for the Nazis and their Hungarian counterparts to kill Hungarian Jews than it was for outsiders to save them. The forces of mass murder had the advantage of experience at their task and presence on the scene. Most of the would-be rescuers were far away, and hemmed in by political and military restrictions.[55]

Nonetheless, outside influence mattered. On December 28, 1944, Solomon Adler-Rudel, one of the Jewish officials operating in Stockholm during 1943–1944, wrote, "I have every reason to believe that the constant intervention of the Swedish Legation, the fact that the Hungarian Government was aware of being watched by the Swedish and Swiss Legations considerably hamp[er]ed and delayed the wholesale deportation of Jews from Budapest, even of those who were not protected by Swedish or Swiss documents." Some 115,000 Jews in Budapest survived the Nazi Holocaust in Hungary, at least in part because of efforts by the War Refugee Board and the heroics of Wallenberg and other neutral diplomats.[56]

Holocaust controversies and animosities have endured for generations. Reszö Kasztner, former head of the Rescue and Relief Committee of Budapest, had negotiated with Eichmann and his subordinates for the release of two transports of Jews totaling 1,684 people. However, he had failed to distribute widely the Vrba-Wetzler report about the gas chambers and crematoria at Auschwitz. After the war, many within his adopted country of Israel blamed him for letting hundreds of thousands of Hungarian Jews go to their deaths unknowing, and for including friends and relatives among those he placed on the train to freedom. In 1953, an Israeli writer labeled Kasztner, now an Israeli civil servant and member of the Labor Party, a Nazi collaborator. The Israeli government sued for libel on Kasztner's behalf. Initially, Kasztner lost the case, the verdict in effect incriminating him for selling out Hungarian Jewry in order to save a favored few.[57]

The Kasztner ruling caused a furor in Israel that led to the collapse of the government and to Kasztner's assassination in 1957. A year after his death, the Supreme Court of Israel overturned the adverse verdict. The two Israeli courts reached opposing decisions on whether Jewish leaders during the war were justified in dealing with the Nazis for the salvation of a relatively small number of Jews: Should they have kept to a high moral ground that might have led to the death of all? Leaving aside factual disputes over the number of Jews Kasztner actually saved or whether he warned Jews not to board the trains to Auschwitz, the two rulings presented different models for judging Jewish responses to the Holocaust. Judge Benjamin Halevi of the lower court had accused Kasztner of "selling his soul to the devil," whereas Judge Simon Agranat of the Supreme Court reinterpreted Kasztner's actions as a reasonable response to the stress, uncertainty, and implacable evil of the Nazis' "Final Solution of the Jewish question." The Kasztner controversy has spawned numerous popular and scholarly articles, books, plays, and documentaries, including the recent full-length film *Killing Kasztner: The Jew Who Dealt with Nazis,* directed by Gaylen Ross, which premiered in the United States in late 2009. Many recent interpretations of Kasztner's role in the Holocaust are either exculpatory or laudatory.[58]

As a teenager in 1944, George Klein served as a courier for the Relief and Rescue Committee of Budapest. As he ran his rounds, he used to tell other youths some of what he had learned about Nazi policies and what they meant for the Jews of Budapest. One of the younger boys struck him as particularly sharp and inquisitive.

Like 115,000 other Jews of Budapest, Klein survived the Holocaust. He then emigrated to Sweden, became an accomplished physician, and served on the Nobel Prize Committee. In the mid-1990s, during a visit to New York, Klein received an unexpected and unexplained invitation to come to the office of financier George Soros. When he walked in, Soros greeted him, and he realized that Soros had been the inquisitive younger youth from Budapest in 1944. It was the last time they had seen each other.

As the two men began to reminisce, they found themselves on opposite sides of the still simmering Kasztner controversy: Klein regarded him as a hero, and Soros thought him a villain. Soros abruptly terminated the meeting, and the two Holocaust survivors never talked again. Ironically, more than a decade after his meeting with Klein, Soros found himself accused by right-wing political opponents of collaborating with the Nazis in Hungary, even though he was only thirteen years old when German troops occupied his homeland.[59]

In February 1945, the War Refugee Board staff tried to calculate the number of people in Europe rescued during the board's first year. It reliably confirmed some of its calculations, such as the number who entered Turkey—about 7,000—or those who had received American visas in European countries or temporary shelter at Fort Ontario—a total of about 5,300. However, it also relied on rough estimates and outcomes not directly related to its operations An estimated 45,000 people had reached the Middle East from the Balkans, and 14,000 Hungarian Jews had received protective documents from neutral governments such as Sweden and Switzerland. The overall total rescued, which the board staff estimated at more than 126,000, may have been an exaggeration, but its warnings to Nazi satellites may have saved others not counted. If these estimates are even 50 percent accurate, the scale of rescue compares well with the number who might have been saved through successful bombing raids against gas chambers and crematoria.[60]

The War Refugee Board's count also does not include as many as 75,000 additional Jews who survived the Holocaust in Budapest without special protective papers or other forms of external assistance. These Jews benefited from Horthy's cessation of deportations. Arguably, the board's efforts, combined with other factors, contributed to their survival. Thus, the board may have helped to save approximately 200,000 Jews.

Should twenty-first-century observers blame Roosevelt for his political caution and for the deaths of hundreds of thousands of Hungarian Jews? Under pressure, Roosevelt established the War Refugee Board, which did seek to aid the Jews of Hungary under adverse conditions. Churchill's cabinet in Britain failed to create its own version of the board or to take similar action in Hungary. This comparison must weigh into any retrospective judgment. Roosevelt's decision-making alone was hardly responsible for the tragedy of Hungarian Jewry.

CHAPTER FIFTEEN

Endings

SUFFERING FROM AN enlarged heart and high blood pressure, FDR felt and looked weary in the fall of 1944. Still, he believed it was his duty to remain commander in chief, if the American people willed it, until the war ended. He also apparently harbored the dream of solving the conundrum of Palestine.[1]

Some Republicans saw the 1944 presidential campaign as a crusade against FDR's allegedly dictatorial government and dangerous left-wing policies. "We must beat the 4th Term. It is the 'last round-up' for the American way of life," said the influential senator Arthur Vandenberg of Michigan. The Republicans nominated the safe, sound, and politically moderate Thomas Dewey, the governor of New York, who ran a self-professed campaign of "competence against incompetent bungling." He refused to dredge up what Republican Representative Clare Boothe Luce had identified in 1943 as conservatives' deepest fears: if the liberal Roosevelt government won the war, it would "lose the peace first by destroying the 'free enterprise system' at home, and secondly by an unrealistic attempt abroad to institute

WPA-ism (globaloney)"—a term that Luce had coined to disparage the plans of liberals for a global postwar New Deal.[2]

FDR refrained from raising what Luce called the inner fears of liberals, that conservatives "would lose the peace by returning the government to the Hooverite apostles of Depression, Toryism, etc." and "the economic and military 'isolationism' of the '20s, which would make the next world war inevitable." The nation thus avoided Luce's nightmare scenario of a "political civil war" within the United States "more bitter than the war against the Axis."[3]

If the rescue and relief of Jews in Europe played no significant role in the campaign, Secretary of the Treasury Henry Morgenthau Jr. did. He had criticized State Department and War Department plans for the occupation and reconstruction of Germany as too soft. Roosevelt had come to agree with him that the German people, who had supported the Nazi regime, should not escape the consequences of their actions. The Allies had to resolve a German problem, not merely a Nazi problem. Like many American liberals including FDR, Morgenthau believed that German heavy industry and cartels had contributed to Nazi aggression and that the Allies could not maintain postwar security in Europe without transforming the German economy.

Unfortunately, he formulated a simplified and extreme version of detailed Treasury plans for Roosevelt's review and cabinet discussion. Earlier Treasury plans had targeted Germany's economic potential to wage war; this one would turn Germany into a largely agricultural land. After Roosevelt and Winston Churchill both signed off on this Morgenthau Plan at the Quebec Conference in mid-September, Secretary of War Henry Stimson counterattacked. "It is Semitism gone wild and will lay the seeds for another war in the next generation," he said. Secretary of State Cordell Hull opposed the plan as another misguided intrusion by Morgenthau into foreign policy. When the Republicans began assailing the plan, Roosevelt retreated and laid all responsibility on Morgenthau; the president said he had no idea how he could have initialed the plan. Stimson's comment, along with earlier remarks about Jews not assimilating well into American life, shows the presence of anti-Semitism even in Roosevelt's cabinet.[4]

Neither controversy over the "pastoralization" of Germany nor anything else kept voters from giving FDR a fourth term in office. The war was going well at last, and the economy benefited from war production. Dewey earned no more than Wendell Willkie's 45 percent of the popular vote. Republicans lost eighteen U.S. House seats and picked up one in the Senate, which left the Democrats with better than 55 percent majorities in each chamber. Republican efforts to win the Jewish vote came to naught: Jewish voters again overwhelmingly opted for the president and his party. The war had decisively ended the depression, kept the Democrats in power, and disarmed the opposition. Still, the contretemps over the Morgenthau Plan during the campaign probably reinforced Roosevelt's inclination to tread carefully on controversial proposals involving Jews.

After the election, Roosevelt told advisers that he still wanted to avoid congressional debates on any resolution dealing with the future of Palestine. The loyal Sol Bloom had promised to table the Wright-Compton resolution again in the House Foreign Affairs Committee, but Zionist pressure made him reverse course. The bill reached the House on November 30. FDR told Edward R. Stettinius Jr., whom he had just appointed as secretary of state to replace Hull, "Please tell them on the Hill to please give them [the resolutions?] more time." Roosevelt hoped to use his persuasive diplomacy to settle matters in Palestine and wanted no interference from Congress. "I am going to take a trip [the Yalta Conference] this winter and will see a lot of people," he told Stettinius. "I want to see if I can't unravel this whole situation on the ground." FDR had received word that King Ibn Saud of Saudi Arabia wanted to meet with him after Yalta. In secret testimony Stettinius reminded the House Foreign Affairs Committee that ethnic animosity simmered in Palestine, with the potential for violence coming from both Arabs and Jews. Jewish terrorists, he noted, had assassinated Lord Moyne, the British minister of state in the Middle East. Congress, Stettinius indicated, could gain nothing by passing a resolution that would only create more acrimony in Palestine.[5]

Roosevelt agreed on the dangers of a bloodletting in Palestine. On December 3, 1944, He told Senator Robert F. Wagner,

There are about half a million Jews there [in Palestine]. Perhaps another million want to go. They are of all shades—good, bad, indifferent. On the other side of the picture there are approximately seventy million Mohammadans [*sic*] who want to cut their throats the day they land. The one thing I want to avoid is a massacre. . . . I hope that at this juncture no branch of the Government will act. Everybody knows what American hopes are. If we talk about them too much we will hurt fulfillment.[6]

Five weeks later, the president told Wagner over lunch that he would do everything in his power to help Zionists promptly achieve their objectives. The victorious United Nations would have to impose a fait accompli upon the Arabs, Wagner warned. Otherwise, the Arabs would veto any Zionist program in Palestine. Moreover, those Jews left in Europe could not wait long for a new homeland: the continent had become a charnel house for them. The conferences at Évian and Bermuda had failed to produce other places of refuge; only Palestine was irrevocably tied to the fate of the Jews. Referring to FDR's comment that peacemakers after World War I had failed and "we are now getting a second bite at the cherry," Wagner argued, "That bite must put an end once and for all to the homelessness of the Jewish people. To that end you and I and the great mass of our fellow Americans are pledged."[7]

In an "absolutely confidential" letter to the president, Representative Emanuel Celler praised Roosevelt for his preelection statement read to the Zionist convention, and noted its political benefits: in some precincts in Celler's district, the president had won more than 90 percent of the vote in 1944. Its preponderantly Jewish voters revered FDR as a "modern Moses," ironically echoing a theme of Nazi propaganda. Nevertheless, the scuttling of the Palestine resolutions in both the House and Senate had disappointed and confused them: "It is with sorrow I write. Is there an acceptable explanation for your retreat?" After some delay, Roosevelt answered, "Give me an opportunity to talk with Stalin and Churchill. . . . Naturally I do not want to see a war between a million or two million people in Palestine against the whole Moslem world in that area—seventy million strong."[8]

On December 30, Stettinius reminded the president that he would have to take a position on Palestine by the spring. Agreeing, Roosevelt said he had heard that Rabbis Stephen S. Wise and Abba Hillel Silver had resigned as chairmen of the American Zionist Emergency Council. Stettinius said no, only Silver was out, and Wise was likely in. This news seemed to please the president. Wise had accepted FDR's decision to table the Palestine resolution in Congress; Silver had not. Silver said that Wise had "deliberately wrecked this effort and torpedoed the resolution." He publicly denounced Wise as a "Court Jew" who blindly defended an administration with which he was entangled.[9]

The American Zionist Emergency Council elected Wise as sole chairman in late December. Wise later said that apart from disregarding decisions reached unanimously, Silver had "made the terrible mistake of using the president's pet enemies" among Republicans "to pressure the Boss [FDR] as though the latter could be pressured that way." In actuality, Silver's pressure tactics on the party platforms had worked quite well. Significantly, the two most prominent American Jewish leaders fought hardest over questions of tactics on the future of Palestine—even though both were Zionists—and not over matters of rescue or relief.[10]

By this time, John Pehle's joint responsibilities at the War Refugee Board and the Treasury Department had drained his energies. When Morgenthau offered him a promotion at Treasury, the board staff recommended replacing him with William O'Dwyer. Roosevelt had earlier unsuccessfully sought to release O'Dwyer from the War Department for a War Refugee Board mission to Spain. By late January 1945, the War Department had agreed to reassign him, and the board announced his appointment while FDR journeyed to Yalta. Morgenthau knew that FDR would approve the succession.[11]

In early January, Roosevelt had told Stettinius that when he met with Ibn Saud after Yalta he wanted a map with him showing the small size of Palestine in relation to the region. He intended to say, "he could not see why a portion of Palestine could not be given to the Jews without harming in any way the interests of the Arabs with the understanding, of course, that the Jews would not move into adjacent parts of the Near East from Palestine."[12]

According to Sumner Welles, Roosevelt, like the late Justice Brandeis, thought a Jewish state would become a model of social justice and would raise the standards of living in the region. FDR also knew that Saudi Arabia badly needed outside funds for development. Surely, a farsighted Arab leader would recognize such benefits—along with the advantages of American aid.[13]

Roosevelt had innate confidence that he could personally solve problems that eluded others. After attending a presidential session on the Middle East, State Department economic adviser Herbert Feis said, "I've read of men who thought they might be King of the Jews and other men who thought they might be King of the Arabs, but this is the first time I've listened to a man who dreamt of being King of both the Jews and the Arabs."[14]

FDR miscalculated the depth of prejudice in the region. Before the Yalta conference, Ibn Saud released a statement saying, "As to Palestine, America and Britain have a free choice between an Arab land of peace and quiet or a

Jewish land drenched in blood." The Jews, he said, "are accursed in the Koran and the enemies of Muslims until the end of the world."[15]

Just before Roosevelt left for Yalta, Wise managed to meet with him briefly at the White House. Beforehand, Judge Samuel Rosenman told FDR that Wise wanted to tell his own organization that he had conferred with the president at this historic moment. Roosevelt asked Wise his view of Walter Lowdermilk's conclusion that Palestine could absorb many millions more people. Wise said that although some considered it unrealistic, David Lilienthal, an authority of regional planning who directed the Tennessee Valley Authority, thought it "extremely practical and desirable." An engineer formerly connected with Lilienthal's organization was in Palestine carrying out surveys; he too thought that the land could take in millions. In response to FDR's concern about Arab fears of Jewish domination, Wise said Jews had no desire to infiltrate Arab countries from Palestine. Jews living in Arab countries would undoubtedly move to Palestine instead, he advised. In a follow-up letter, Wise wrote that about a million Jews had an immediate need for a haven, and, given the studies, he thought Palestine could easily accommodate such numbers.[16]

Wise also relayed to FDR that President Edvard Benes of Czechoslovakia had learned from Stalin that if Britain and the United States approved of a Jewish commonwealth in Palestine, the Soviets would go along. In fact, high Soviet authorities had already signaled to Jewish leaders during the previous year that they favored Jewish immigration to Palestine—even from Eastern European countries—and Jewish hopes for statehood. Soviet ambassador to Mexico Konstantin Umanskii, for example, met in Mexico City with World Jewish Congress cofounder Nahum Goldmann to discuss possible Soviet support for a Jewish state. The ambassador even suggested that his government might endorse a joint security guarantee by the Big Three. Umanskii asked Goldmann how many Jews would want to go to Palestine; Goldmann answered as if it were established fact that the Soviets would let perhaps a quarter million Polish and Soviet Jews settle there. A Jewish Palestine would pose challenges for the British empire, and create opportunities for the Soviets.[17]

State Department officials either missed or dismissed the signs of a new Soviet policy on Palestine. In a pre-Yalta memorandum that broadly reflected department views, Secretary Stettinius urged the president not to make any decisions about Palestine without Soviet approval. Otherwise, the Soviets could gain influence in the Middle East by "championing the cause of the Arabs at the expense of United States." He recommended that the president use the Yalta Conference to win agreement from Great Britain and the Soviet Union on a Palestine policy that considered the interests of both Arabs and Jews and avoided uncritical support for the Zionist position. The secretary optimistically hoped that moderate Jews and Arabs would step forward to reach an equitable settlement, although he gave no hint of its terms.[18]

In February 1945, just two months before his death, a seriously ill President Roosevelt made an arduous journey to the Livadia Palace near Yalta on the Ukraine's Crimean Peninsula. There he met with Stalin and Churchill. To reach Yalta, the president had to cruise across the Atlantic and then traverse the Mediterranean Sea to Malta. From there he flew for seven hours to the Crimea and rode to Livadia Palace for eight hours in an automobile over bad roads. Churchill reportedly told FDR's confidant Henry Hopkins, "We could not have found a worse place for this meeting if we had spent ten years looking for it."[19]

After dinner on February 10, Roosevelt informally asked Stalin whether he supported the Zionist program. Stalin was not in Hitler's league as an anti-Semite, but he could not conceal his sentiments. He claimed that he was a Zionist "in principle," but that Jews had not cooperated with Soviet efforts to establish an autonomous Jewish region at Birobidzhan. Roosevelt stated that he would meet with Ibn Saud after Yalta to discuss Palestine. Stalin asked whether the president was going to give the Saudi Arabian something. Roosevelt quipped, "the six million Jews in the United States." Stalin took the comment literally, saying that would be difficult, and calling Jews "middlemen, profiteers and parasites."[20]

Years before, Roosevelt and Hopkins had loosened up Soviet foreign minister Vyacheslav Molotov with liquor and with an exchange of anti-Semitic comments: they claimed that American communists were frustrated, disgruntled, ineffectual, and included a high proportion of distinctly unsympathetic Jews. Molotov responded that not all communists were alike. The three had agreed on a distinction between Jews and "Kikes." Roosevelt resurrected the maneuver of using anti-Semitism as an icebreaker with Stalin at Yalta. Whatever its wisdom or impact, Stalin did not object to Roosevelt's goal of establishing a Jewish homeland in Palestine.[21]

To avoid controversy, Churchill told FDR not to talk about the British White Paper. However, "we will let the Jews come in," he said. Roosevelt came away from his informal soundings at Yalta pleased that he could move forward.[22]

A week before his conversation with Stalin, Roosevelt had asked American officials to set up post-Yalta meetings with the monarchs of Egypt, Ethiopia, and Saudi Arabia somewhere in the Middle East. By this time, administration officials realized that Saudi Arabian oil might be critical to America's future economic growth. Yet the Arabian-American Oil Company (Aramco) seemed fully in charge of discovery and production there, presenting no pressing economic need for a summit.[23]

Roosevelt explained only that he might not "get over here again." Whether or not he recognized that he had little time left, the difficult trip to Yalta and the rigors of the conference left him exhausted. He had every personal reason to want to come home directly from Yalta.

On February 12, FDR had ceremonial meetings in Egypt with King Farouk of Egypt and Emperor Haile Selassie of Ethiopia. On February 14, Ibn Saud arrived aboard the cruiser USS *Quincy* with a party of forty-eight assistants, relatives, and servants. He and FDR were of the same age, and both had a disability, although Ibn Saud only limped. Roosevelt offered the king his spare wheelchair, which he accepted. William Eddy, the pro-Arab American minister to Saudi Arabia, reported that Roosevelt was in top form as a charming host: "However, every now and then I would catch him off guard and see his face in repose. It was ashen in color; the lines were deep; the eyes would fade in helpless fatigue. He was living on nerve."

The State Department and American diplomats in the region had warned the president about Ibn Saud's fixation on Palestine and his hatred of Jews. Roosevelt nonetheless told Ibn Saud that the Jews of Central Europe had suffered "indescribable horrors . . . eviction, destruction of their homes, torture and mass murder." Roosevelt felt responsible for helping them and asked for the king's assistance. Ibn Saud suggested giving them the choicest lands and homes of the Germans. Roosevelt responded that the Jews were afraid to go back to Germany and had a special attachment to Palestine. Ibn Saud pointed out that the Allies would determine policy for Germany, not the Germans. Besides, Jews and Arabs would never cooperate in Palestine or anywhere else. Roosevelt tried again: there were not many Jews, and they would cause no trouble for the Arabs. Ibn Saud, with some impatience, said, "What injury have the Arabs done to the Jews of

Europe? It is the 'Christian' Germans who stole their homes and lives. Let the Germans pay."

Roosevelt persisted. Calling himself a farmer at heart, he suggested that Arabs could profit from irrigation and other methods to improve their lands. Ibn Saud said he could not support an expansion of agriculture if the Jews would inherit the benefits. Stymied, FDR reverted to his traditional formula that the Allies would make no decisions on Palestine without first consulting both Arabs and Jews. He indicated that congressional resolutions were not U.S. policy: he would not help the Jews at the expense of the Arabs. Hopkins, who did not attend the session because he lay ill in his cabin, thought FDR had swayed too far from his pro-Zionist position.[24]

Ibn Saud subsequently referred to the meeting on the *Quincy,* according to Eddy, as the high point of his life. He apparently thought he had triumphed, although he did not recognize FDR's evasions and lack of candor. Days later, Churchill also failed to budge Ibn Saud from his position that compromise with Zionism would be "an act of treachery to the Prophet and all believing Muslims which would wipe out my honor and destroy my soul."[25]

During the final weeks of his life, Roosevelt struggled to get out of a bind on Palestine. Although he had pledged only to consult the Arab leaders, not to give them a veto, he had expressed sympathy for their concerns. However, his belief in a Jewish Palestine—in whole or in part—had not changed. With the end of the war rapidly approaching, it became increasing difficult for him to continue distinguishing between Jewish immigration to Palestine and its formal status after the war. Most American Jewish leaders viewed the two issues as inseparable. Ibn Saud had shown FDR that the Arab states would fight against a Jewish Palestine, and Roosevelt was both unable and unwilling to impose Zionist goals by force of American arms.

On March 1, Roosevelt spoke to Congress about the Yalta Conference. In passing, he commented that Ibn Saud had impressed him and that he had learned much about the Moslem-Jewish problem from their meeting. Many observers seized upon this remark as a sign that Roosevelt had adopted the State Department's line on the Middle East. What he probably meant was that he now understood Ibn Saud's fanaticism. On March 16, FDR met with Wise at the White House to counteract widespread speculation about his March 1 comment. Roosevelt issued no official statement after the meeting, but he allowed Wise to quote him as saying that he had made clear his positive position on Zionism in October 1944 and that his viewpoint had not changed: he would seek ways to bring about its earliest realization. A *New York Times* report that FDR had reaffirmed to Wise his pro-Zionist position generated letters of protest from Arab governments and alarmed State Department officials. In a memo to the acting secretary of state, Political Adviser Wallace Murray warned that FDR's reaffirmation of his October statement would damage America's position among Arabs and create an opening for the Soviets. "The continued endorsement by the President of Zionist objectives," Murray said, "may well result in throwing the entire Arab world into the arms of Soviet Russia."[26]

Wise's private account of the March 16 meeting, which he sent to Chaim Weizmann, shows that Roosevelt virtually apologized to Wise—something he almost never did to anyone. The one failure of his trip, FDR said, was his meeting with Ibn Saud. Roosevelt had arranged this meeting "for the sake of your cause," and he regretted his failure to make any impact upon the Saudi ruler. He now feared that if Ibn Saud united Arab states in a holy war, they could defeat the small contingent of Jews in Palestine. He could only suggest bringing the issue to the new international organization, the United Nations. Wise concluded, "The President remains our friend as much as ever."[27]

Only days afterwards, FDR met with Joseph Proskauer and Jacob Blaustein, key members of the non-Zionist American Jewish Committee. According to Proskauer's reconstruction of the conversation months later, Roosevelt "gravely feared a continuance of the agitation for a Jewish state at this time was provocative of a situation that might cause a third world war and also might cause grave disturbances in Palestine which would be most harmful to the Jewish settlement there." The president also disparaged Churchill's commitment to a Jewish Palestine given his intention to protect the British empire. FDR said that a Jewish state could not be established under current conditions and that Jewish advocates should press for liberal Jewish immigration to Palestine and human rights for Jews across the world. Proskauer added that the president urged him "to moderate the sharpness of the propaganda of the extreme Zionists." The president may have tilted his remarks to fit what Proskauer and Blaustein wanted to hear, and Proskauer may have shaded his reconstruction to fit his own political views. Still, Proskauer's account generally corroborates other sources on Roosevelt's thinking and reasonably reflects conditions at the time, including the numerical superiority of Arabs in Palestine and surrounding states and Ibn Saud's implacable hostility to Zionist goals in Palestine.[28]

Rabbi Silver went astray in thinking that outside pressure alone could move the president on Palestine. Congress could tie a president's hands, as demonstrated by the Neutrality Acts of the 1930s, but could rarely force a president to act against his inclinations in foreign affairs. Jewish advocates, moreover, could hardly rely on Congress, which opposed increased immigration to the United States and had mixed sentiments and a mixed record on rescuing Jews in Europe. Its nonbinding endorsement of Zionist aspirations would not have withstood the combined onslaught of the State Department, the War Department, and the intelligence agencies. Congress could not implement a foreign policy based on ideals; only a responsive president could do so.

FDR continued to placate the Arabs, perhaps to buy time. He could not know that he had almost no time left. He authorized the State Department to convey secretly to Arab leaders that in affirming his earlier pro-Zionist position on Palestine he was referring only "to possible action at some future time." On April 5, FDR wrote directly to Ibn Saud reiterating his promises from their February meeting and assuring the desert leader that he would take no action "which might prove hostile to the Arab people." The State Department's Murray continued to worry that FDR had tilted too far in favor of unrestricted Jewish immigration to Palestine and the establishment of a Jewish state there. If the United States implemented a pro-Zionist policy, Murray wrote on April 6, the results would be disastrous for American interests in the Middle East and its efforts to counter Soviet influence there. Most Americans disagreed. A Gallup Poll from March 1945 found that 59 percent of respondents favored "the idea of establishing a Jewish state in Palestine." Only 19 percent opposed the idea and 22 percent had no opinion.[29]

On April 11, Morgenthau visited Roosevelt at Warm Springs, Georgia— the first time he had seen the president in many weeks. FDR was still planning to attend the opening of the United Nations two weeks later, but Morgenthau noticed immediately that the president was haggard, and his hands shook as he tried to pour cocktails. He managed to transfer himself from his wheelchair to a regular chair only with the greatest difficulty. Simply to watch him was agonizing, but trying to carry on, he asked what the treasury secretary wanted. Morgenthau, among other things, suggested that the president break up the State Department crowd headed by Political Adviser James Dunn. Roosevelt said Morgenthau's ideas about how to accomplish this were wonderful, and he asked Morgenthau to write them down, although he defended Dunn's performance at the Quebec Conference. Morgenthau insisted, "I think Dunn is terrible."[30]

The next morning Roosevelt sat for a portrait by artist Elizabeth Shoumatoff. Shortly before 1:00 p.m. the butler entered to set the table for lunch, but the president asked for fifteen more minutes to work. He suddenly felt a pain in the back of his head, slumped forward, and collapsed. At 3:35 p.m. a doctor pronounced him dead. Shoumatoff's *Unfinished Portrait* still hangs on the wall of FDR's Little White House at Warm Springs, a museum since 1948.[31]

News of Roosevelt's death of a massive cerebral hemorrhage on April 12 reached Adolf A. Berle, now American ambassador to Brazil, in Rio de Janeiro. Berle watched in amazement as a steady stream of Brazilians, some humble laborers without shoes, came to the American embassy to offer their condolences. He wrote in his diary that FDR had been a friend of nations and a friend of peoples. His foreign policy had included friendship with various classes, especially "the large humbler classes who do not usually find expression in their governments." His policies therefore brought into consideration "problems which normally do not find the place to which they are entitled in foreign relations."[32]

For a time, Roosevelt's death unified the usually feuding Jewish community. At a tribute that filled Carnegie Hall and left thousands outside seeking admission, Wise praised FDR as a warrior against Nazi evil and a "warm and genuine supporter of the Zionist cause." FDR, he said, may have "felt a partial sense of failure in respect to his mission to the Near East," but "only because he may have attached too much importance to those counselors in the State Department and the Colonial Office in England who exaggerated the importance and power of the most conspicuous and picturesque of the Near Eastern rulers." Wise assured his listeners that FDR was planning a new and effective means of establishing a Jewish commonwealth in Palestine at the time of his death. Wise's Zionist rival Silver called Roosevelt "a great and good man who served his country and mankind in faithfulness and high devotion in one of the most critical periods in the history of our country and the world. He matched his hour." The non-Zionist American Jewish Joint Distribution Committee recalled "the generous support we have received from Mr. Roosevelt. . . . His unique grasp of world conditions and his unbounded sympathy for the distressed gave him a clear understanding of our efforts to help the persecuted and relieve the needy." The Rabbinical Assembly of America praised him as an "immortal leader of humanity and a peerless servant of God."[33]

About a year and a half after the end of the war in Europe, there emerged the first sign of a reversal in positive contemporary judgments about FDR and the Jews. In a late 1946 address to the World Zionist Congress in Basel, Switzerland, Silver indicted FDR for the death of perhaps millions of Jews, because of his failure to block or change British policy restricting immigration to Palestine. Perhaps Silver was also attempting to send a message about Palestine to President Harry Truman and Prime Minister Clement Attlee. Regardless, his charges remained a discordant note in an otherwise harmonious chorus of Jewish voices. Even after liberators revealed the full horrors of Nazi death camps, most Jewish leaders continued to cherish FDR's memory. In April 1947, upon the two-year anniversary of his death, the *New York Times* noted that FDR was "lauded in Jewish sermons." In a typical tribute, the prominent rabbi Israel Goldstein eulogized Roosevelt "a man of peace," a fighter for "liberty and justice," a "noble architect of democracy," and a "congenial interpreter of man's humanity to man."[34]

Only with the publication in the late 1960s of books critical of FDR did controversy arise in the United States over his response to Jewish concerns. The cover of the paperback edition of the first such work, Arthur D. Morse's *While Six Million Died* (1967), showed a caricature of Franklin D. Roosevelt with "crocodile tears" dripping from his eyes.[35]

Eleanor Roosevelt achieved her greatest prominence during the seventeen years in which she survived her late husband. After the war, she became America's most noted advocate for human rights. In 1945, President Truman appointed her as a delegate to the United Nations General Assembly, making her the only former First Lady to serve in government until Hillary Clinton won election to the U.S. Senate in 2000. At the United Nations she chaired the committee that promulgated the Universal Declaration on Human Rights. Eleanor also emerged in the postwar period as a more forthright and prominent advocate for Jewish concerns than during her years with FDR. Her horrified reaction to the Holocaust and her close friendship with several Jews seemed to have erased any trace of her earlier anti-Semitism. In 1946, she called for increased immigration to the United

States, and in 1947, she pressed the Truman administration to support and enforce the United Nations plan for partitioning Palestine in Jewish and Arab states. She later used her influence in support of the new state of Israel. As her final service to the nation, she chaired the first presidential commission on the status of women, established by President John F. Kennedy in 1961. She died a year later to the accolades of a mourning nation. In his eulogy rabbi and author Arnold M. Goodman said that she will be remembered "thru the many golden deeds she performed and the many vital causes she espoused. White and Negro, Jew and Christian, were alike to Mrs. Roosevelt."[36]

High State Department officials who had dealt with Jewish causes during the Roosevelt years had little to do with such matters afterwards. Hull presided over the San Francisco negotiations about the Charter of the United Nations in 1945. He received the Nobel Peace Prize that year, although he had played a limited role in American foreign policy during the Roosevelt years and poor health had kept him away from performing most of his functions from 1942 on. Hull took no part in debates over the postwar disposition of Palestine. His 1948 memoirs contain many self-serving constructions and are of relatively little use to scholars. He died of a heart attack in 1955.[37]

William Phillips officially retired from government in 1944 after some forty years of service. He briefly returned the following year as a special assistant to Secretary Stettinius. In 1946, he served with James G. McDonald as one of the six Americans on the Anglo-American Committee of Inquiry on Palestine. Phillips fully retired in 1948 and died in 1968. His papers and diaries at Harvard University are an important historical source.

Welles never reentered government after his forced resignation. Mistrustful of Roosevelt's successor, he criticized the Truman administration sharply. In late 1945, he became chairman of the American Christian Palestine Committee of Maryland, and by 1947 he had become a Zionist. The American Jewish Congress gave him a citation in 1948 for his work on Jewish issues. He was the only prominent State Department official to whom Jewish issues mattered significantly after he left office. Welles worked as an author, columnist, and radio broadcaster until his drinking and homosexual escapades brought him down again. He died in 1961 of pancreatic cancer. After his son published Welles's biography in 1997, the family donated his papers to the Roosevelt Library.[38]

Breckinridge Long never recovered politically from his clash with the Treasury Department and his inaccurate testimony in Congress about Jewish immigration. He retired from the State Department late in 1944 and became a director of Laurel Raceway in Maryland, where he oversaw thoroughbreds. Critics of America's response to the Holocaust have targeted Long as the State Department's most notorious anti-Semite who stymied for years any effort on behalf of imperiled Jews. Long contributed to his tarnished legacy with his resentment-filled diaries, available in the Library of Congress. He died in 1958.

Near the end of the war, Roosevelt appointed Berle as ambassador to Brazil, but he served there only for a year. He then returned to Columbia University and headed the Twentieth Century Fund for about two decades. In 1961, he advised President Kennedy on Latin American affairs. Today scholars regard him as a key member of FDR's brain trust, although less important as an influence on policy regarding Nazi persecution of Jews. His published diaries and papers are an important historical source. Berle died in 1971.

Feis resigned from the State Department to pursue a career as an author. He wrote thirteen books, winning the Pulitzer Prize for his work on the Potsdam Conference and the origins of the Cold War. In his book on Churchill, Roosevelt, and Stalin during World War II, he wrote literally nothing about Palestine, Jews, or the Holocaust. Perhaps he feared that an insider's account of the State Department's approach to Jewish issues would have cost him some friends. He died in 1972. Today the American Historical Association honors his memory with a prize for the best work annually by an independent historian.

Isaiah Bowman was a champion and a victim of the Cold War. Before and during World War II he had warned consistently about the Soviet threat to the United States, but he proposed his friend Alger Hiss for membership in the American Geographical Society and gave him an honorary degree at Johns Hopkins in 1947. He also had brought China expert Owen Lattimore into the Geography Department at Hopkins. Representative Richard Nixon of California and Wisconsin senator Joseph McCarthy accused these men of being top Soviet spies in the United States. Bowman defended Hiss, but not Lattimore, making poor choices in both cases. Bowman retired as president of Hopkins in 1948 and died of a heart attack two years later. Today there is little trace of him on the campus, beyond his papers in the Milton S. Eisenhower Library. His reputation as an anti-Semite endures.[39]

McDonald served on the 1946 Anglo-American Committee of Inquiry on Palestine, which recommended increased Jewish immigration to Palestine but, owing to the opposition of the British representatives, declined to endorse partition into Jewish and Arab states. Britain rejected its compromise plan, but bowed to a later, United Nations decision in favor of partition. President Truman appointed McDonald as special representative and then America's first ambassador to the new state of Israel. Thus, fifteen years after he unsuccessfully sought to become America's envoy to Germany, McDonald gained an ambassadorship. He wrote a useful book about his three-year tenure in Israel, but his diaries, now at the United States Holocaust Memorial Museum, are even more important and revealing. McDonald died in 1964.[40]

The birth of Israel in 1948 essentially resolved the battle among American Jews over Zionism. Despite the differences among them, American Zionists leaders such as Wise and Silver had achieved their dream of a Jewish state, likely far sooner than they had expected. Anti-Zionists such as Morris Lazaron lost all credibility within the Jewish community. Six years after Truman recognized Israel, Zionist I. L. Kenen, who had not been prominent during the Nazi era, formed the little noted American Zionist Committee for Public Affairs in support of Israel. In 1959 the leadership changed the group's name to the American Israel Public Affairs Committee, better known as AIPAC. By the 1970s, AIPAC had become one of the most powerful lobby groups in Washington.[41]

Rabbi Wise outlived Roosevelt by four years—long enough to witness Israel's birth and successful military defense. The New York Free Synagogue he had established renamed itself after him, and a temple in Los Angeles also took his name in 1964. The only scholarly biography of Wise is favorable, but in recent decades Wise's reputation in the Jewish community has suffered from his ties with Roosevelt. Some of Roosevelt's critics believe that Wise could have pressed more aggressively for rescue of Jews in Europe. As evidenced by the experience of Silver, however, such an approach may only have antagonized FDR and forfeited the influence that Wise did have.[42]

Silver assiduously mobilized support for a Jewish state during and after the war. His distance from Presidents Roosevelt and Truman and his hard-knuckled lobbying have enhanced his standing in some circles, but probably only antagonized Truman. The president made a lonely decision to recognize the state of Israel. State Department officials had opposed the partition of Palestine and Truman's decision to support the new state of Israel. Many of them thought American opposition to a Jewish state was the only possible decision in the interest of the United States. In a shift of opinion from three years earlier, some 56 percent of Americans, according to a Gallup Poll from March 1948, favored noninterference by the United States in Palestine or had no opinion on American policy there. Only 17 percent backed a Jewish state or the United Nations plan for partitioning Palestine into an Arab and Jewish state; most others favored control by the United Nations or European nations. After the founding of Israel, internal rivalries forced Silver out of his leadership position in the Zionist movement. He died in 1963.[43]

Peter Bergson continued to create controversy in the years after FDR's death, not with American politicians or Jewish advocates, but with fellow Irgun leaders battling the British in Palestine. Bergson clashed with Menachem Begin, the head of the Irgun, and later prime minister of Israel, over whether he should focus on aiding illegal immigrants to reach Palestine or on shipping arms to Irgun fighters there. Begin also objected to Bergson's high public profile, which he believed brought undue attention to Irgun activities. In 1948, Bergson returned home, where he participated briefly in Israeli politics.

Critics of President Roosevelt and America's mainstream Jewish leadership have applauded Bergson for his militant approach to publicizing the Holocaust and demanding the rescue of Jews. In 2012, the Varian Fry Institute, which celebrates those it views as Holocaust heroes, released a highly favorable documentary titled *Not Idly By* on Bergson's effort to rescue Jews. Bergson never met with FDR and created distractions with his quixotic quest for a "Jewish Army" and his claim to represent the "Hebrew nation." Still, by stirring up support for a congressional resolution on rescue and working with Oscar Cox, he likely contributed to the Treasury's effort to establish the War Refugee Board. Bergson died in 2001.[44]

White House insider Benjamin V. Cohen, another Zionist, had concentrated increasingly on foreign affairs during the last years of the war and wanted a high State Department appointment. His fate was tied to James F. Byrnes, whom Roosevelt overlooked when he picked Stettinius as Hull's successor. Harold Ickes picked up rumors that State Department circles objected to Cohen as a Jew and a Zionist. Roosevelt offered him only a subordinate position at State. Cohen sensed that the department did not want him and resigned from government: he suffered from depression throughout much of his life. After Truman named Byrnes secretary of state in July 1945, Cohen regained influence and reentered government service, but had relatively little success in budging State Department officials on Palestine. Cohen became a member of the American delegation to the United Nations General Assembly and he retired at the end of the Truman years. He died in 1983.[45]

Morgenthau resigned as secretary of the treasury early in the Truman administration. His postwar activities mostly revolved around Jewish philanthropy and Israel. Despite his close relationship with Roosevelt, his reputation in the American Jewish community remains stellar, partly because of his effort to establish the War Refugee Board. He died in 1967. His diaries, available at the Roosevelt Library in Hyde Park, and on microfilm, are an essential source for scholars.

Rosenman was perhaps the only member of Roosevelt's inner circle who remained influential in the Truman administration. The new president asked Rosenman to stay on as special counsel, and Rosenman reportedly served Truman as a speechwriter. He continued to publish a series of the papers and addresses of Roosevelt, the last of thirteen volumes coming out in 1950. He served as head of the New York City Bar Association in the mid-1960s, and he died in 1973.

History has been kinder to Louis D. Brandeis than to Felix Frankfurter. When he retired in 1939, Brandeis had already won acclaim as one of the greatest American jurists, and his stature has grown over the decades. He devoted himself to Palestine in his last years. He died in October 1941 after the beginning of the Holocaust. Frankfurter's brilliance had a shorter shelf-life. He moved gradually but steadily toward the right on the Supreme Court and found himself isolated from the liberal majority in the Chief Justice Earl Warren years. Some of his personal characteristics—particularly, his tendency to flatter and ingratiate to get his way—bothered many. He may well have discussed the Holocaust with Roosevelt, but there is little to no trace of it in surviving documents. He had no impact on Truman's policies toward Palestine or other postwar issues of Jewish concern. Frankfurter died in 1965.[46]

FDR had turned to Frankfurter for one key service. Eleanor Roosevelt's younger brother G. Hall Roosevelt died in September 1941. After the funeral Roosevelt summoned Frankfurter to the White House. The next day Frankfurter reconstructed his conversation with FDR while the president was having his hair cut in his office.

> The President seemed under considerable strain and plainly enough he just wanted to talk. After the barber left, talk continued, going hither and yon, and the President told me of a letter to Fred Delano, which the latter had sent to him, from a correspondent who had apparently just discovered that Jackson Park contains the statues of four Revolutionary heroes and that the equestrian statue of Jackson was incongruous in this Revolutionary setting. . . .
>
> When he finished reading the memorandum, this followed:
>
> FDR: "This leads me to say something that I want you to remember because you are much more likely to be here longer than I shall be."
>
> FF (jocosely) "You mean that I shall remain on the Supreme Court longer than you will remain in the White House."
>
> FDR (smilingly but sharply) "No, that isn't what I mean at all. I mean in plain English that I am likely to shuffle off long before you kick the bucket. And if that should happen and if any memorial is to be erected to me, I know exactly what I should like it to be. Now please remember what I am telling you as my wish in case they are to put up any memorial to me. About half way between here and the Capitol is the Archives Building.
>
> Now I have some relation to Archives.

[The construction of the National Archives building on Pennsylvania Avenue had begun under the Hoover administration, but the still unfinished limestone and granite building opened only in 1935, in FDR's first term. Roosevelt continued:]

> And right in front of the Archives Building is a little green triangle [grassy area]. If, as I say, they are to put up any memorial to me, I should like it to be placed in the center of that green plot in front of the Archives Building. I would like it to consist of a block about the size of this (putting his hand on his desk). I don't care what it is made of, whether limestone or granite or whatnot, but I want it to be plain, without any ornamentation, with the simple carving: In Memory of _____. This is all, and please remember that, if the time should come."

FF: "I shall indeed remember and you deeply honor me in putting this wish in the keeping of my memory."[47]

In 1946, Frankfurter told President Truman and others about this conversation. The government built the simple Pennsylvania Avenue block memorial outside the National Archives building soon thereafter. It was the only Washington memorial Roosevelt wanted. Perhaps, anticipating the future challenges of representing his body, he knew he could not control the decisions of later generations. Roosevelt had also established the first presidential library and archive on his beloved Hyde Park estate.

The National Archives and the Franklin D. Roosevelt Presidential Library contain much of the evidence of his achievements, efforts, and failures. His opposition to Nazi Germany comes across very clearly. With his aversion to note-taking and his predilection for oral communication and improvisation, FDR did not make it easy for later generations to sort out his calculation of trade-offs on Jewish issues.

Of the 620 passengers of the *St. Louis* who went back to continental Europe, 365 survived the war, as did virtually all the 288 passengers who landed in Britain. About half of the original 937 passengers eventually immigrated into the United States. One of them later became vice-chair of the United States Holocaust Memorial Council. Others ended up in Argentina, Australia, the Bahamas, Bolivia, Brazil, Canada, Chile, Columbia, Cuba, the Dominican Republic, Israel, South Africa, Mexico, Uruguay, and Venezuela.[48]

CHAPTER SIXTEEN

Perspectives

FDR WAS NEITHER a hero of the Jews nor a bystander to the Nazis' persecution and then annihilation of Jews. No simple or monolithic characterization of this complex president fits the historical record. FDR could not fully meet all competing priorities as he led the nation through its worst economic depression and most challenging foreign war. He had to make difficult and painful trade-offs, and he adapted over time to shifting circumstances. His compromises might seem flawed in the light of what later generations have learned about the depth and significance of the Holocaust, a term that first came into widespread use many years after FDR's death. Still, Roosevelt reacted more decisively to Nazi crimes against Jews than did any other world leader of his time.

The first-term Roosevelt did little to assist Jews in Germany. He failed to speak out against Nazi persecution of Jews, to try to put public pressure on Adolf Hitler, or to rally the world's democracies against Hitler's anti-Semitic policies. During the worst economic crisis in U.S. history, this Roosevelt put recovery, reform, and party-building well ahead of other priorities. He worried about stirring up anti-Semitism in America and believed that the prevention of war required formal relations with the new German government.

FDR could have spoken out against Nazi persecution, especially during the early months of his presidency when a wave of revulsion against Hitler's oppression of Jews swept through the American public and Congress, including the Democratic leadership and some influential Republicans. He also could have followed through on his apparent promise to admit some 10,000 additional Jewish refugees to the United States each year. Organized labor would likely not have broken with the president over admitting so few newcomers into a nation of some fifty million workers. Despite the ubiquity of low-grade anti-Semitism, America's truly virulent anti-Semitic organizations lacked numbers or influence.

A second and more decisive Roosevelt emerged after his landslide reelection in 1936. FDR finally smashed the bureaucratic barriers to the expanded admission of Jewish refugees to the United States. He openly backed Jewish settlement in Palestine and pushed Britain behind the scenes to admit Jews liberally there. In the spring of 1938, FDR personally devised and launched the world's only ambitious international initiative for rescuing Jewish refugees during the Nazi era. "That was *my* proposal," the president proudly told his friend and League of Nations staffer Arthur Sweetser in a private discussion. "I worked that out myself."[1]

Although Roosevelt failed to put his full prestige and influence behind the July 1938 Évian Conference on refugees, even a maximum effort would have foundered against the near-universal resistance of world leaders to admitting significant numbers of Jewish immigrants. Later that year, FDR became the only world leader to call home his ambassador to Germany to protest the violence of *Kristallnacht.* After *Kristallnacht,* the president continued to seek places of refuge for Jews. He also extended visitors' visas for German Jews who could not safely return to their homeland.

From fiscal 1937 to fiscal 1940 the United States admitted some 83,000 mostly Jewish German and Austrian immigrants, compared to about 18,000 for the previous four fiscal years. Some 15,000 German Jews holding visitors' visas gained American residence. FDR also backed negotiations with Germany for the orderly emigration of additional persecuted Jews. In Latin America, administration pressure and incentives led Cuba to take in at least 5,000 Jewish refugees during 1938 and 1939, facilitated the emigration of some 20,000 Jews to Bolivia, and eased immigration restrictions in

Brazil, leading to the entry of about 10,000 Jews there between 1939 and 1942. Although these calculations are approximate, FDR's second-term policies likely helped save the lives of well over 100,000 Jews.[2]

These humanitarian ventures promised no political benefits for a president and party already assured of overwhelming Jewish support. On the contrary, FDR's second-term policies defied public and congressional opinion at a time when he faced a difficult midterm election, internal party strife, and tough battles with Congress over Neutrality Acts and economic policy. His own State Department failed to provide support or political cover for the president. In the blunt words of Secretary of the Treasury Henry Morgenthau Jr., "The point is the President has this. Nobody is helping him." The president also used refugee issues to expose the horrors of a regime determined to punish and persecute Jews, rather than let them emigrate. A solution to Hitler's festering "Jewish Problem," Sumner Welles, FDR's man at State, even speculated, could help defer war.[3]

Preparing for a showdown with Congress on the Neutrality Acts in 1939, FDR did not fight for the Wagner-Rogers bill to admit refugee children outside immigration quotas, which public opinion strongly opposed. He continued to press Britain on keeping Palestine open to Jewish refugees, but threatened no reprisals when the British proposed to slash the admission of Jews. FDR would not go so far as to risk a break in relations with America's most important ally in the event of war.

With encouragement from the American government, Jewish groups found safe havens in democratic nations of Europe for all passengers on the SS *St Louis* denied entry to Cuba. Roosevelt could have admitted the *St. Louis* passengers to the United States only by exceeding the immigration quotas. A quarrel with Congress over the *St. Louis* had the potential to doom his efforts to revise the Neutrality Acts and aid the nations resisting Hitler's aggression. Had such events come to pass, posterity would have judged FDR far more harshly than it has in our time.

The outbreak of World War II led to the emergence of a third Roosevelt, preoccupied with aiding Germany's opponents and protecting the internal security of the United States. FDR believed that Europe's democracies could survive only with an infusion of American aid, which required the dispatch of arms and materiel abroad. With such momentous and difficult battles to fight, the president no longer spent political capital on Jewish refugees or sought to keep admitting streams of Jewish immigrants, who, some feared, might harbor in their midst German spies and saboteurs. FDR salvaged a small number of refugees and planned for a massive postwar resettlement of displaced persons, preferably in sparsely settled places around the world, including Palestine.

After his reelection in 1940, FDR also pushed through a reluctant Congress his Lend-Lease program for aiding the allies resisting Nazi and fascist aggression by all means short of war. Under Lend-Lease, FDR supplied British forces with the Sherman tanks that helped it prevail in the pivotal battle of El Alamein. This victory kept the Nazis from taking Egypt and then overrunning Palestine and killing Jewish settlers there. Without FDR's policies and leadership there may well have been no Jewish communities left in Palestine, no Jewish state, no Israel.

Gerhart M. Riegner, the World Jewish Congress representative who sent so much tragic news about the Holocaust from Switzerland to the West, credits Roosevelt's Lend-Lease program with saving Britain and with it, many Jewish lives and the future of world Judaism. In a 1992 interview, Riegner criticized FDR for not doing enough to help European Jews. But he said world Jewry "owes gratitude to Roosevelt" for preventing the "additional catastrophe" for Jews of Britain's defeat:

> Imagine for a moment what would have happened if Britain would have gone down. It would not be only Britain. It would not only be 400,000 Jews in Britain being under Hitler. It would be the breakdown in Palestine and the Middle East. The 600,000 Jews in Palestine who are today the basis of the Jewish Renaissance and of the Jewish state. Imagine that the British government would have gone down and Alexandria would be open to Rommel, and they would have gone into Israel [sic]. The whole idea of Israel would have disappeared.[4]

After Pearl Harbor, the third Roosevelt and his military and diplomatic advisers sought to unite the nation and blunt Nazi propaganda by avoiding the appearance of fighting a war for the Jews. They tolerated no potentially divisive initiatives or any diversion from their campaign to win the war as quickly and decisively as possible. Britain put a priority on placating Arabs, avoiding unrest among the many Moslems in its colonies and army, and maintaining access to Middle East oil. The British tightly restricted Jewish immigration to Palestine throughout the war.

Roosevelt knew that his domestic political opponents would seize upon any evidence that might show him hindering the war effort, even in small ways. After the midterm elections of 1942, the president faced a Congress largely controlled by a hostile conservative coalition of Republicans and southern Democrats. Success on the battlefield, Roosevelt and his advisers believed, was the only sure way to save the surviving Jews of Europe. It would also determine Democratic prospects in the presidential and congressional elections of 1944.

The president and his administration did not forthrightly inform the American people of Hitler's grisly "Final Solution" or respond decisively to his crimes. The State Department sought to prevent some information about the Nazi extermination of Jews from reaching the American people. In a remarkable turn of history, a private citizen, Rabbi Stephen S. Wise—not the president or high diplomatic officials—presented dramatic evidence that Hitler was systematically murdering millions of innocent civilian Jews. The mainstream press buried this story on the back pages of their newspapers. After meeting with the president in early December 1942, Wise quoted FDR as saying that the United States and its allies were prepared to take every step "which will end these serious crimes against the Jews and against all other civilian populations of the Hitler-ruled countries and to save those who may yet be saved." Then on December 17, the Allies issued a joint statement condemning Germany's "bestial policies of cold-blooded murder" of Jews, but failed to translate words into immediate action.[5]

After the largely cosmetic Bermuda Conference on refugees in April 1943 and later Allied military victories, Roosevelt signaled approval of a World Jewish Congress plan for the deposit of money in blocked accounts to aid in the relief or emigration of Jews in the Balkans and France. State Department obstruction and opposition from the British stalled implementation for many months.

In late November 1943, Secretary Morgenthau and his activist, young, and mostly non-Jewish staff took on the State Department. The Treasury group learned that State had not only checked administration policy on rescue and retribution, but had also sought to cut off sources of information on the Holocaust. A damning report on State by Josiah DuBois of the Treasury, Morgenthau's personal intervention with FDR, a pending resolution on rescue in Congress, and revelation of inaccurate and self-serving testimony by Assistant Secretary of State Breckinridge Long broke the bureaucratic logjam on refugees. Since June, Oscar Cox of the Foreign Economic Administration had circulated a plan for a new American rescue organization with the authority of government behind it. After meeting with Morgenthau and two of his aides in mid-January 1944, FDR quickly approved a version of the Cox plan that became the War Refugee Board, dedicated to saving the lives of Jews and other civilians. The cessation of the Nazis' mass murder of Jews, however, still required the defeat of Germany and her allies.

A fourth Roosevelt, preoccupied with ending the European war and planning postwar arrangements and in failing health, did not match the activism or creativity of the prewar Roosevelt. Still, FDR backed initiatives of the War Refugee Board and a declaration that denounced the Nazi killings of Jews. For the first time he officially dissociated the American government from the British White Paper restricting immigration to Palestine. He also pledged full justice to those who sought a Jewish homeland in Palestine, while continuing to assure Arab leaders that he would make no decision without consulting them. FDR made strenuous efforts, even at the expense of his health, to reconcile King Ibn Saud of Saudi Arabia to a Jewish Palestine. Roosevelt never realized his hope of easing Arab opposition to a Jewish Palestine or finding havens around the world for Jewish refugees.

Roosevelt's policies often defied the preferences of his State Department, which lacked Welles as a balance wheel after July 1943. State opposed most efforts of the War Refugee Board to rescue Jews. It opposed a presidential denunciation of Nazi atrocities against Jews and even opposed open discussion of Zionist aspirations in Palestine.

In the late twentieth century, Auschwitz became the symbol of the Holocaust. Latter-day critics of the Roosevelt administration have seized upon America's failure to bomb Auschwitz's rail lines or death factories in 1944 as a microcosm of government's indifference or worse to the Holocaust. In a 1998 speech at Auschwitz, Israeli prime minister Benjamin Netanyahu claimed that the Allies failed to act on Auschwitz because Jews did not have a state to protect them. Historian Deborah Lipstadt called Netanyahu's comment "using history for political purposes." Fourteen years later in 2012, Netanyahu again cited America's refusal to bomb the death camp, this time as potential justification for a preemptive strike against Iran's nuclear facilities. On a 2008 visit to the Israeli Holocaust memorial Yad Vashem, President George W. Bush, allegedly with tears in his eyes, had told Secretary of State Condoleezza Rice that the United States should have bombed Auschwitz. Bush even alluded to *Franklin Roosevelt's decision* not to bomb the killing sites. As with the case of the SS *St. Louis,* the facts belie the simple lessons politicians draw from them.[6]

Roosevelt played no apparent role in the decision not to bomb Auschwitz. Even if the matter had reached his desk, however, he would not likely have contravened his military. Every major American Jewish leader and organization that he respected remained silent on the matter, as did all influential members of Congress and opinion-makers in the mainstream media.

British rejection of similar requests to bomb Auschwitz has made comparatively little impression upon the American public, possibly because Winston Churchill wrote one memo expressing support for a bombing mission, although neither Churchill nor any official of his government followed up with an operational plan. Nonetheless, American policies during 1944–1945 in response to the Holocaust were clearly more humanitarian than British policies.[7]

Nor were gas chambers and crematoria the only mechanisms of the Holocaust. The SS and German police had shot Jews in large numbers before and after the use of gas chambers. Specialists on Nazi Germany recognize that the Final Solution continued almost to the end of the war, even after the extermination camps ceased operations.[8]

Jewish groups pressured Roosevelt throughout his years in office. Like other religious and ethnic groups, Jews had quarreled among themselves over ideology, political strategy, and tactics. These disputes persisted despite a common enemy in Nazi Germany. Greater cohesion would have strengthened Jewish influence, especially during FDR's critical first year when he used internal dissension among Jews to justify inaction. Still, large ethnic or religious groups are rarely, if ever, fully unified, and even a solid Jewish bloc might not have shifted American policy, given the political pressures and priorities of the times.

The axis of conflict among American Jews also changed over time. Until the outbreak of the war, two old antagonists, the elitist, non-Zionist American Jewish Committee and the more populist and Zionist American Jewish Congress refought familiar battles. After the rise of Hitler in 1933, Rabbi Wise, the most prominent Congress leader, organized mass rallies across America. His organization soon joined the boycott of trade with the Nazis.

American Jewish Committee leaders exerted all their influence and powers of persuasion to stop the rallies, end the boycott, and persuade Jewish leaders to rely on quiet diplomacy with the nation's decision-makers.

During the war, Palestinian Peter Bergson and his small group of followers slammed American Jewish leaders for their deference to the administration, their constricted imagination, their lack of bold initiative, and their only part-time dedication to the rescue of Jews. In turn, most established leaders, including the mainstream Zionists, shunned Bergson as a self-promoter who antagonized important allies and represented no one but a small group of militant, right-wing Palestinian Jews and caring non-Jews. They also believed that Bergson had mistakenly presumed that outside pressure alone could compel a presidential response on Jewish concerns. Bergson helped publicize the need to rescue Jews during the Holocaust and lobbied with some success for a rescue resolution in Congress. Eventually, Bergson alienated both Jews and non-Jews by claiming to be the ambassador of the so-called Hebrew nation.

A rift also opened between America's two leading mainstream Zionists, the veteran Wise, who turned 70 in 1943, and the younger and more militant Rabbi Abba Hillel Silver. Although the two worked together, Silver eventually denounced Wise, the militant of the 1930s, as a "Court Jew" whose deference to the president weakened outside Jewish influence on the administration.

External pressure, especially after the outbreak of war, would not have compelled FDR to elevate his commitment to the rescue of Jews. Beyond moral suasion, Jewish leaders lacked political strength. They did not control the Jewish vote or the political contributions of Jewish donors. They only had a small presence in Washington and lacked political action committees or large numbers of volunteers to sway elections. Jewish leaders also loosely represented only their own community, not a coalition of American minorities groups sympathetic to persecuted Jews abroad. Most of their limited non-Jewish support came from liberal Protestants in the model of FDR or John Haynes Holmes, Wise's ally in New York reform politics, with only weak and sporadic backing from the American Catholic hierarchy or leaders of the African American community.

Wise's unique position as outside advocate and inside presence in the Roosevelt administration yielded some notable benefits for Jews. Wise educated FDR on the importance of Palestine for the Jews and the need to keep the territory open to Jewish immigration. He helped forestall an official government statement aimed at quashing public discussion of Palestine's future. Wise released to America and the world evidence of the Holocaust. He helped launch an initiative for rescuing Jews in the Balkans and France, which the State Department and the British stalled; that controversy contributed to the formation of the War Refugee Board. The advent of the board reflected a combination of Silver's and Bergson's creative, militant advocacy and success with Congress, as well as the inside initiatives of Wise, and, above all, Morgenthau.

Until the Republicans adopted a pro-Palestine plank in their platform for the 1944 elections, they offered American Jews little alternative to FDR and his Democrats. The conservative domestic policies and overt Christian "Americanism" of the Republican Party, with its dominant base of white Protestant voters and financiers, repelled most Jewish leaders and voters. The GOP's restrictive immigration policies would have made the United States far less hospitable to Jewish refugees than under Roosevelt's stewardship. Its isolationist foreign policies would have greatly weakened resistance to German aggression before America entered the war. Even after Pearl Harbor, former president Herbert Hoover and some of FDR's other isolationist opponents hoped that America would fight only Japan and avoid war with Nazi Germany.

Churchill talked responsively about Palestine with Zionist leaders, but did nothing to open its gates to Jewish immigrants or help Jews settle elsewhere in Britain's imperial domains. Preoccupied with access to Arab oil reserves and preserving the heavily Moslem British empire, his government consistently opposed measures to rescue Jews and create a Jewish state in Palestine.

Allied leaders sought an all-out war to complete victory as quickly and efficiently as possible, a decision that seemed reasonable at the time and to many in retrospect. Victory would end the suffering of all peoples subject to Nazi rule, they believed. It thus made military and political sense to focus Allied military resources on that task. Moreover, the Allies had no troops in Western Europe until mid-1944, when most Nazi killings of Jews had already taken place. The Allies also knew that major battles still lay ahead.

Hitler and other Nazi fanatics shrugged off threats of punishment from the West, even after the D-Day invasion in June 1944 and the continued advance of Russian troops toward its western borders. When Hungary indicated its willingness in the summer of 1944 to release Hungarian Jews to go elsewhere and when many Germans recognized that the war was likely lost, German officials still blocked the initiative.

The Nazis sought to eliminate the Jewish people, not as a diversion from their war effort, but as a complementary campaign to annihilate enemies considered racially and politically dangerous. Otto Ohlendorf, the head of a German killing unit that murdered approximately 110,000 Jews, would later say that the Nazis targeted Jewish women and children, as well as men, to insure the total extermination of the Jewish population.[9]

For America and Britain, the rescue of Jews, when considered at all, was far subordinate to the preeminent goal of winning the war and defeating the enemy by unconditional surrender. Some Allied officials even viewed rescue measures as conflicting with those goals. The lack of an Allied military presence in most of Central and Western Europe until late in the war left most Jews in Nazi-controlled and influenced Europe facing near-certain death.

Subordinate Allied officials interpreted the war effort so rigidly that they ruled out all military means—even in conjunction with nearby military operations—to save the lives of Jews and others targeted by the Nazis. Even proposals to mount moderate-scale rescues or provide modest relief despite economic blockades violated their belief that nothing must interfere with winning the war. Some of these rescue or relief proposals were unrealistic, others apparently feasible. It is all but impossible to honestly assess their likely impact, because they remained untried until January 1944. In most cases, Allied officials, with their eyes focused on victory, did not even seriously consider them.

Nazi satellites such as Romania, Bulgaria, Slovakia, and Hungary, which lacked Hitler's all-or-nothing approach, offered the most likely prospects for rescuing Jews. These countries included about 1.4 million Jews, two-thirds of whom perished during the war and the Holocaust. The Allies might have saved some additional Jews beginning in 1943, when the war first turned against Germany, with a combination of direct threats to satellite governments, explicit warnings to Jews, infusion of medical supplies and foodstuffs for suffering Jews, and the issuing of visa documents. The Allies might also have been able with sufficient inducements and guarantees to persuade neutral countries to take in more refugees for the duration of the war.

The fourth Roosevelt came late to the task. His chosen instrument of rescue, the War Refugee Board—the only agency of its kind in the world—lacked the resources and authority for an immensely difficult task. Throughout its tenure, the board remained underfunded, undermanned, and dependent on a military and State Department with decidedly different priorities. Still, the board helped to save as many as 200,000 Jewish lives, in addition to the more than 100,000 saved by FDR's second-term initiatives for refugees. If established earlier, the War Refugee Board would likely have saved some additional Jewish lives, but cessation of the Nazis' mass murder of Jews required the military defeat of Germany and their allies.

Roosevelt's responses to Jewish problems abroad fit into a broader pattern for American presidents. In the first decade of the twentieth century, Theodore Roosevelt had failed to use his big stick to pressure the tsar into containing murderous pogroms against Jews. A decade later the American press had meticulously covered the much greater Turkish slaughter of some one million Armenians during World War I. Henry Morgenthau Sr., America's Jewish ambassador to Turkey, amply documented this "race extermination" for President Woodrow Wilson. Yet a president celebrated for his humanitarian vision did nothing to halt the carnage in Turkey. After World War I, both Wilson and his Republican successor Warren Harding resisted pressure to aid oppressed Jews in Romania and Poland. FDR himself did not respond to atrocities committed by dictators such as Joseph Stalin in Russia and Rafael Trujillo in the Dominican Republic. Ironically, FDR overlooked Trujillo's mass murder of Haitians in part so that the United States could work with him on plans to resettle Jews in the Dominican Republic.

Later presidents, despite American military supremacy and knowledge of Western failures during the Holocaust, typically responded feebly or worse to genocide on their watch. The cries of "never again" that followed the revelation of Nazi horrors became instead the reality of "again and again" in places across much of the world.

President Jimmy Carter, another champion of human rights, sat by while the Cambodian dictator Pol Pot slaughtered more than 20 percent of his country's population. Carter even provided some back-channel support to Pol Pot's regime as a counterweight to Vietnam.[10]

The administration of President Bill Clinton buried information about the genocide in Rwanda that claimed some 800,000 victims. His actions covered the administration's failure to save lives through even a minimal deployment of American troops in Rwanda or American backing for an expanded United Nations force.

Presidents George H. W. Bush and Bill Clinton delayed for several years any strong response to genocidal violence by Serbian armies against Moslem peoples in Bosnia. Clinton had criticized Bush during the presidential campaign of 1992 for lack of response to Serbian atrocities, but failed to change course until late in his second term in office.[11]

The administrations of George W. Bush and Barack Obama failed to act decisively against the genocide by attrition in the Sudanese region of Darfur. An independent estimate based on epidemiological methods indicates that state-sponsored violence had killed some 300,000 persons there by 2008.[12]

Since the 1980s, American presidents have ignored and at times even abetted genocidal violence by the government of Sri Lanka and the Sinhalese majority against the Tamil people that has resulted in several hundred thousand Tamilese deaths and contributed to an ongoing civil war in Sri Lanka. Atrocities against the population of East Timor by Indonesia during its occupation from 1975 to 1999 also failed to generate an American response. Long-delayed intervention by Western powers eventually stopped a quarter century of violence in East Timor.[13]

When President Clinton broke precedent and intervened militarily against alleged Serbian genocide in Kosovo in 1999, he compared events in Kosovo to the Nazi Holocaust against the Jews, and some at the time described this intervention as the world's first humanitarian war. Clinton understood from the caution of past presidents that military intervention abroad for humanitarian reasons brings financial costs, possibly the loss of some American lives, disputes among advisers, and major political controversy, from both the left and the right. He gained North Atlantic Treaty Organization cooperation and opted for the relatively safe technological solution of a bombing campaign that posed minimal risks to Americans. Arguably, the recent focus on drones, unmanned aircraft armed with Hellfire missiles, and secret commando strikes are a direct result of the American public's anathema to foreign intervention.

Still, some conservative Republicans, including Texas governor and presidential aspirant George W. Bush, opposed the intervention in Kosovo, as did left-wing activists such as Ralph Nader, who also had presidential ambitions.

After the war, criticism continued that Clinton had exaggerated the case for genocide in Kosovo and then escalated Serbian violence there with his bombing campaign.[14]

President Obama learned in 2011 that after the protracted wars in Iraq and Afghanistan, Americans have grown skeptical of military operations abroad. In deciding to participate in a joint military effort in Libya, at least partly on humanitarian grounds, he waited for United Nations authorization, participation by European allies, and political cover from the Arab League. This cautious approach still drew mostly skeptical reviews from contemporaries that cut across partisan and ideological lines. Journalist Samantha Power, author of the Pulitzer Prize–winning book *A Problem from Hell: America in the Age of Genocide* (2002), which is critical of American presidents, advocated humanitarian intervention in Libya as a member of President Obama's National Security Staff and head of the Office of Multilateral Affairs and Human Rights. She helped design American policy to take into account the lessons of history. Critics drew upon different interpretations of history to support contrary positions. The intervention in Libya resulted in the overthrow and killing of the dictator Muammar Gaddafi. The passage of time may clarify events in Libya, but hindsight will likely only give rise to fresh controversy.[15]

The appropriate response of an American president to humanitarian crises abroad remains very much in dispute. Abstract principles translate into precise guidelines for action only in untestable, retrospective judgments on past crises. Even the most powerful and persuasive American presidents are hemmed in by public and congressional opinion, bureaucratic pressures, and the views of allied powers. Even well-intentioned decisions may have unintended and perverse results.

During World War II the ferocity, the global reach, and the stakes of the military conflict dwarfed humanitarian concerns. Granted, some American officials recognized even in the midst of a war that took some 60 million lives, the cold horror of what we know today—that the Holocaust was an unprecedented catastrophe. They were exceptions. Humanitarian intervention in the midst of an all-out war for the survival of Western civilization was far more difficult and much riskier than intervention in any late twentieth-century case of genocide or ethnic cleansing. It is regrettable, but not surprising, that the War Refugee Board was established late in the war and failed to secure military resources for its objectives. But critics who have dismissed the significance of the board based on what it failed to try or accomplish are too hasty. It was a new concept in advancing American humanitarian goals—and one that subsequent presidents largely ignored.

Despite these many dispiriting examples of humanitarian tragedies before and since World War II, a special horror still clings to the Nazis' murder of six million Jews. The Holocaust followed centuries of brutal responses in many lands to the world's "Jewish Question." It did not arise from ethnic, religious, economic, or political conflicts within a single nation or region, but represented history's only systematic effort to annihilate an entire people, no matter where they might be found across the globe. The Nazis marshaled all the resources and technical skills of the modern state to achieve this brutal goal. Their contagion spread across much of Europe, infected many non-German collaborators in genocide, and threatened to engulf the entire world. Even some modern-day opponents of humanitarian intervention suggest that the Holocaust stands as a singular exception to their theories.[16]

The Holocaust also profoundly changed postwar life and culture, most obviously in Europe, but in America as well. Hitler's perverse biological theories of race added to increasing scientific and popular skepticism about the once robust disciplines of eugenics and racial science in the United States. The Nazi precedent focused American attention on human rights, which facilitated Eleanor Roosevelt's work in formulating the Universal Declaration on Human Rights that the United Nations General Assembly adopted in 1948. Reactions against the horrors of the death camps and crematoria contributed to a decline of anti-Semitic attitudes and practices in the two decades following the war. Between 1937 and 1965, Gallup Poll respondents who said they would not vote for a qualified Jew for president plunged from 47 percent to 11 percent. Discrimination against Jews in employment, education, and housing eased during this period. These indicators suggest that the Holocaust discredited open anti-Semitism in the United States, and that the significance of the Holocaust expanded over several decades.

Roosevelt lived during the war and the Holocaust, but he inhabited a pre-Holocaust world. Few of his contemporaries recognized the political or moral significance of the events we now scrutinize carefully.

Ironically, our work suggests that American Jews of Roosevelt's own time came close to a balanced and accurate assessment of their president.

Although most American Jews—both leaders and ordinary folk—revered the president, they were not blind to his limitations or the constraints under which he operated. Even Jewish advocates close to FDR recognized that he often failed to turn humanitarian principles into action to benefit Jewish victims of Nazism, especially during his first term and the period from the outbreak of World War II through the formation of the War Refugee Board. They understood, however, that he was the first president to intervene part of the time on behalf of their oppressed brethren abroad—and during world crises of unparalleled scope and gravity. They also knew that without his leadership, the resistance to Nazi aggression would have been much weaker than it was, perhaps even fatally so. For Jews, he posed a far better choice than the political opponents of his era, not just in his response to Jewish peril, but also in his domestic and foreign policies, and his integration of Jews into American government.

In a retrospective on FDR published some two weeks after his death, Felix Frankfurter insightfully wrote that contemporaries no less than later generations have a claim on the legacy of world leaders: "Fluctuations of historic judgment are the lot of great men, and Roosevelt will not escape it. . . . But if history has its claims, so has the present. For it has been wisely said that if the judgment of the time must be corrected by that of posterity, it is no less true that the judgment of posterity must be corrected by that of the time."[17]

Notes

INTRODUCTION

1. The most noted critical work on FDR and the Jews remains David S. Wyman, *The Abandonment of the Jews: America and the Holocaust, 1941–1945* (New York: New Press, 1984). But Wyman dealt selectively with Roosevelt the man. The idea that FDR and his administration were "bystanders" to Nazi persecution of Jews is commonplace even in reasonably balanced scholarship. See, for example, Michael R. Marrus, ed., *Bystanders to the Holocaust* (Westport, CT: Meckler, 1989); David Cesarani and Paul A. Levine, eds., *Bystanders to the Holocaust: A Re-evaluation* (Portland, OR: Frank Cass, 2002). One critic goes so far as to indict both Roosevelt and British prime minister Winston Churchill as "accomplices" in Hitler's crimes against Jews: Alexander J. Groth, *Accomplices: Churchill, Roosevelt, and the Holocaust* (New York: Peter Lang, 2011). For ardent defenses of FDR's policies and decisions see William D. Rubinstein, *The Myth of Rescue: Why the Democracies Could Not Have Save More Jews from the Nazis* (New York: Routledge, 1997), and Robert N. Rosen, *Saving the Jews: Franklin D. Roosevelt and the Holocaust* (New York: Thunder's Mouth, 2006). In *The Holocaust in American Life* (New York: Mariner Books, 2000), Peter Novick calls it an anachronism to judge contemporary responses to the Holocaust, since the concept did not exist at the time of the events.

2. Kenneth S. Davis, *FDR: The War President, 1940–1943: A History* (New York: Random House, 2000), 746–747.

3. Roosevelt to Wise, 9 February 1944, Stephen S. Wise Papers, reel 74-48, American Jewish Historical Society, Center for Jewish History, New York; "Roosevelt Censures Anti-Semitic Groups," *New York Times,* 13 February 1944, p. 36.

4. Carole Fink, *Defending the Rights of Others: The Great Powers, The Jews, and International Minority Protection, 1878–1938* (New York: Cambridge University Press, 2004).

1. THE RISE AND FALL OF FDR

1. Jan Pottker, *Sara and Eleanor: The Story of Sara Delano Roosevelt and Her Daughter-in-Law, Eleanor Roosevelt* (New York: St. Martin's Press, 2004), 288, 309; "Mrs. J. Roosevelt Cited," *New York Times,* 21 March 1938, p. 8; "Misses Guard of Honor," *New York Times,* 13 May 1941, p. 25. We are grateful to Richard Garfunkel for these references.

2. For biographical works devoted to FDR's early life see Geoffrey C. Ward, *Before the Trumpet: Young Franklin Roosevelt, 1882–1905* (New York: Harper & Row, 1985), and Kenneth S. Davis, *FDR: The Beckoning of Destiny, 1882–1928, A History* (New York: G. P. Putnam, 1972).

3. Michael S. Bell, "The Worldview of Franklin Roosevelt: France, Germany, and American Involvement in World War II" (PhD diss., University of Maryland, College Park, 2004), 22–26.

4. Frank Costigliola, *Roosevelt's Lost Alliances: How Personal Politics Helped Start the Cold War* (Princeton, NJ: Princeton University Press, 2012), 36; Geoffrey C. Ward, *A First-Class Temperament: The Emergence of Franklin Roosevelt* (New York: Harper & Row, 1989), 185–186.

5. Stephen Steinberg, *The Academic Melting Pot: Catholics and Jews in American Higher Education* (New York: Transaction Publishers, 1977), 21–23. FDR's extracurricular activities are documented through a search of the *Harvard Crimson* digital archives at www.thecrimson.com/search/newspapers.

6. Thomas H. Greer, *What Roosevelt Thought: The Political and Social Ideas of Franklin D. Roosevelt* (East Lansing: Michigan State University Press, 1958), 4–6.

7. Bell, "Worldview of Franklin Roosevelt," 73–82; FDR quoted in David Cannadine, "Historians as Diplomats? Roger B. Merriman, George F. Trevelyan, and Anglo-American Relations," *New England Quarterly* 72 (June 1999): 219; Davis, *FDR,* 138–139.

8. *Harvard Crimson,* 9 October and 15 December 1903, 2; *Harvard College Class of 1904, Twenty-Fifth Anniversary Report* (Norwood, MA: Plimpton Press, 1929), 642, both in Harvard Archives, Pusey Library, Cambridge, Massachusetts.

9. Diary of Courtney Letts de Espil, 17 January 1938, Library of Congress, Washington, D.C. (henceforth LC).

10. Frank Burt Freidel, *Franklin D. Roosevelt: A Rendezvous with Destiny* (Boston: Little, Brown, 1990), 296.

11. "President Roosevelt Gives the Bride Away," *New York Times,* 18 March 1905, p. 2; "President Attends Wedding of His Niece," *Washington Post,* 18 March 1905, p. 2.

12. Roosevelt Folder, Herbert Hoover Papers, Post-Presidential, box 277, Herbert Hoover Presidential Library, West Branch, Iowa (henceforth Hoover Library).

13. "Charge That Morgan Defeated Sheehan," *New York Times,* 31 May 1911, p. 6.

14. "A Democratic Senator from New York," *Independent,* 6 April 1911, p. 3; "Campaign Brings Young Men to the Front as Leaders," *New York Times,* 14 July 1912, SM13; "Attack on Bosses Stirs Up M'Cabe," *New York Times,* 25 December 1911, p. 8.

15. "Campaign speech Troy, Mar. 3, 1912," Franklin D. Roosevelt, Papers as New York State Senator, box 1, Franklin D. Roosevelt Library, Hyde Park, New York (henceforth Roosevelt Library); Thomas G. Dyer, *Theodore Roosevelt and the Idea of Race* (Baton Rouge: Louisiana State University Press, 1980), 168.

16. See generally Alfred B. Rollins Jr., *Roosevelt and Howe* (New Brunswick, NJ: Transaction, 2002), 3–62.

17. Robert F. Wagner to Franklin D. Roosevelt, 4 April 1913, Papers as New York State Senator, box 16, Roosevelt Library.

18. "Contributors to National Democratic Campaign Fund, 1912," Henry Morgenthau Sr. Papers, reel 30, LC.

19. "Study New Roosevelt," *Washington Post,* 11 March 1913, p. 3.

20. Stephen S. Wise to A. I. Elkus, 22 August 1914, Stephen S. Wise Papers, reel 74-52, American Jewish Historical Society, New York, New York.

21. On Wise see Melvin I. Urofsky, *A Voice That Spoke for Justice: The Life and Times of Stephen S. Wise* (Albany: State University of New York Press, 1982).

22. "The Brandeis Nomination," *New York Times,* 25 May 1916, p. 12.

23. "Jews to Face Famine," *Washington Post,* 18 February 1915, p. 2.

24. Franklin Roosevelt to Eleanor Roosevelt, 9 November 1916, in Franklin Delano Roosevelt, *F.D.R., His Personal Letters,* vol. 1, *The Early Years,* ed. Elliot Roosevelt (New York: Duell, Sloan and Pearce, 1947), 339.

25. On Frankfurter see Liva Baker, *Felix Frankfurter: A Biography* (New York: Coward-McCann, 1969).

26. Pottker, *Sara and Eleanor,* 288, 309; Jean Edward Smith, *FDR* (New York: Random House, 2007), 148.

27. "Wants America to Lead," *New York Times,* 9 March 1919, p. 17.

28. See generally Joseph E. Persico, *Franklin & Lucy: President Roosevelt, Mrs. Rutherfurd and the Other Remarkable Women in His Life* (New York: Random House, 2008), and Pottker, *Sara and Eleanor.*

29. Molly Dewson, "Women and the New Deal," 8 April 1936, in Richard D. Polenberg, *The Era of Franklin D. Roosevelt, 1933–1945: A Brief History with Documents* (New York: Palgrave, 2000), 99–100.

30. Selig Adler, "The Palestine Question in the Wilson Era," *Jewish Social Studies* 10 (October 1948): 307–308.

31. See the treatment in Margaret MacMillan, *Paris 1919: Six Months That Changed the World* (New York: Random House, 2003), 410–418; Hershel Edelheit and Abraham J. Edelheit, *History of Zionism: A Handbook and Dictionary* (Boulder, CO: Westview, 2000), 85–106, quotation at p. 90.

32. "Leaders Believe Cox the Best Nominee," *New York Times,* 7 July 1920, p. 2.

33. Frankfurter to Lewis L. Strauss, 2 February 1920, Lewis L. Strauss Papers, box 25, Hoover Library; "Harding Proposes Immigration Curb," *New York Times,* 15 September 1920, p. 5.

34. Roosevelt to Steve Early, 21 December 1920, in Roosevelt, *F.D.R., His Personal Letters,* 1:514.

35. Allan J. Lichtman, *White Protestant Nation: The Rise of the American Conservative Movement* (New York: Grove/Atlantic, 2008), 44–46.

36. Joseph W. Bendersky, *The Jewish Threat: Anti-Semitic Policies of the U.S. Army* (New York: Basic Books, 2000), xi–226; Adler to Louis Marshall, 19 August 1919, in Ira Robinson, ed., *Cyrus Adler: Selected Letters,* vol. 1 (Philadelphia: Jewish Publication Society of America, 1985), 386.

37. Lichtman, *White Protestant Nation,* 36–42. This view of Jews as a distinctive race was not universally held among social, biological, and psychological authorities of the time. Some divided Jews into two distinct races (e.g., Mediterranean and European). A few denied that Jews were a racial group at all. See also Daniel Kevles, *In the Name of Eugenics: Genetics and the Uses of Human Heredity* (New York: Knopf, 1985); Ann Gibson Winfield, *Eugenics and Education in America: Institutionalized Racism and the Implications of History, Ideology, and Memory* (New York: Lang, 2007); Desmond King, *Making Americans: Immigration, Race, and the Origins of the Diverse Democracy* (Cambridge, MA: Harvard University Press, 2000).

38. U.S. House of Representatives, 66th Congress, 3rd Session, *Committee on Immigration and Naturalization,* "Report: Temporary Suspension of Immigration With Minority Report," 6 December 1920; Max J. Kohler, Memo to American Jewish Committee, undated, 1921, Louis Marshall Papers, box 62, American Jewish Archives, Cincinnati, Ohio.

39. Franklin Roosevelt to Eleanor Roosevelt, 7 July 1916, in Roosevelt, *F.D.R., His Personal Letters,* 1:304.

40. The Todhunter School, *Our Daughters Heritage* (1938), in Dorothy Schiff Papers, box 64, New York Public Library, New York, New York.

41. Hugh Gregory Gallagher, *FDR's Splendid Deception: The Moving Story of Roosevelt's Massive Disability and Efforts to Conceal It from the Public* (New York: Dodd, Mead, 1985), 19–87.

2. FDR RETURNS

1. See Burl Noggle, *Teapot Dome: Oil and Politics in the 1920's* (Baton Rouge: Louisiana State University Press, 1962).

2. U.S. House of Representatives, Committee on Immigration and Naturalization, *Restriction of Immigration,* 68th Congress, 1st Session, 1923–1924, 373–374, 387; *U.S. v. Thind,* 261 U.S. 204 (1923).

3. Desmond King, *Making Americans: Immigration, Race, and the Origins of the Diverse Democracy* (Cambridge, MA: Harvard University Press, 2000), 173; Mae M. Ngai, "The Architecture of Race in American Immigration Law: A Reexamination of the Immigration Act of 1924," *Journal of American History* 86 (June 1999): 67–92; Roger Daniels, *Guarding the Golden Door: American Immigration Policy and Immigrants Since 1882* (New York: Hill and Wang, 2004), 47–58; Allan J. Lichtman, *White Protestant Nation: The Rise of the American Conservative Movement* (New York: Grove/Atlantic, 2008), 37–38; "Alien Law Defended in Biological Study," *Washington Post,* 2 January 1925, p. 3.

4. "Hoover Probes Immigration," *Washington Post,* 25 April 1923, p. 8; "Alien Quota Shift Seen," *Los Angeles Times,* 23 March 1929, p. 1; King, *Making Americans,* 199–228; Marshall to Senator David Reed, 10 April 1926, Jacob Billikopf Papers, box 19, American Jewish Archives, Cincinnati, Ohio (henceforth AJA).

5. "Peru and Paraguay Give Jews Welcome," *Washington Post,* 14 March 1927, p. 2; "Bid European Jews Colonize in Peru," *New York Times,* 8 February 1931, p. 3; Bound reports, No. R-49, *Studies of Migration and Settlement: Report Series Plan for the Cooperative Settlement of Eastern Jews on the Land Grants in Peru,* 11 May 1944, Isaiah Bowman Papers, Milton S. Eisenhower Library, Johns Hopkins University, Baltimore, Maryland.

6. "Roosevelt Offers Name of Governor Smith," *New York Times,* 27 June 1924, p. 4; "Roosevelt Looses Volcano," *Atlanta Constitution,* 27 June 1924, p. 1; Stephen S. Wise to Abram L. Elkus, 16 July 1924, Stephen S. Wise Papers, reel 74-52, American Jewish Historical Society, New York, New York (henceforth AJHS); Frank Freidel, *Franklin D. Roosevelt: The Ordeal* (Boston: Little, Brown, 1954), 180; *Washington Post,* 27 June 1924, p. 6; "Text of Mr. Roosevelt's Speech With Smith's Offer to Quit," *New York Times,* 9 July 1924, p. 1.

7. "Democratic Party's Crushing Defeat Due to the Worship of False Gods, Declares Former Senator Hardwick," *Atlanta Constitution,* 8 November 1924, p. 6.

8. Howe to Roosevelt, undated 1926, Louis McHenry Howe Papers, box 18, Franklin D. Roosevelt Library, Hyde Park, New York (henceforth Roosevelt Library). By the 1920s these terms had come into routine use, with "progressive" largely reserved for Republican followers of the late Theodore Roosevelt.

9. Morgenthau to Roosevelt, 5 July 1928, and Roosevelt to Morgenthau, 7 July 1928, Campaign of 1928 File, box 8, Roosevelt Library.

10. Howe to Roosevelt, 25 September 1928, 29 September 1928, 1 October 1928, Louis McHenry Howe Papers, box 19, Roosevelt Library. For FDR's views on Democratic prospects for 1928, see Roosevelt to Josephus Daniels, 23 June 1927, Josephus Daniels Papers, reel 59, Library of Congress, Washington, D.C. (henceforth LC).

11. Baruch to Churchill, 12 November 1928, Bernard Baruch Papers, unit no. 6, volume 20, Seeley G. Mudd Manuscript Library, Princeton University, Princeton, New Jersey; Billikopf to Julius Rosenwald, 18 June 1928, Jacob Billikopf Papers, box 25, AJA; Adler to Roosevelt, 16 October 1928, in Ira Robinson, ed., *Cyrus Adler: Selected Letters,* vol. 2 (Philadelphia: Jewish Publication Society, 1985), 158; Straus to Hoover, 26 September 1928, Pre-Presidential, General Correspondence, box 23, Herbert Hoover Presidential Library, West Branch, Iowa.

12. Roosevelt to Daniels, 20 July 1928, Daniels Papers, reel 59, LC; Allan J. Lichtman, *Prejudice and the Old Politics: The Presidential Election of 1928* (Lanham, MD: Lexington Books, 2000), 180–183.

13. Roosevelt to Wagner, 8 October 1928, Campaign of 1928 File, box 10, Roosevelt Library.

14. Billikopf to Cardozo, 13 September 1928, and Mack to Billikopf, 29 August 1928, Jacob Billikopf Papers, box 18, AJA; Ochs to Samuel Untermyer, 7 September 1928, Adolph S. Ochs Papers, box 42, New York Public Library, New York, New York.

15. Frankfurter to Billikopf, 4 October 1928, and Billikopf to Cardozo, 8 October 1928, Jacob Billikopf Papers, boxes 4 and 8, AJA.

16. Daru to Roosevelt, 3 October 1928, Campaign of 1928 Papers, box 7, Roosevelt Library.

17. Marshall to Jacob Shulkin, Louis Marshall Papers, box 1600, AJA; Marshall to Billikopf, 2 October 1928, Jacob Billikopf Papers, box 19, AJA.

18. Roosevelt to Daru, 5 October 1928, Campaign of 1928 Papers, box 7, Roosevelt Library; "F. D. Roosevelt Relies on Fairness of Jews," *New York Times,* 19 October 1928, p. 3.

19. "Untermyer Assails Ottinger on Power," *New York Times,* 24 October 1928, p. 18; "Hoover Supporters Urged to Aid Ottinger," *New York Times,* 23 October 1928, p. 6; "Hearst Assails Roosevelt Tactics," *New York Times,* 29 October 1928, p. 12.

20. "F. D. Roosevelt Relies on Fairness of Jews"; Newspaper Interview, 21 October 1928, Franklin Delano Roosevelt: Family, Business and Personal Papers, box 42, Roosevelt Library.

21. Wise to Smith, 11 September 1928; Frankfurter to Julian Mack, 17 October 1928, Stephen S. Wise Papers, reels 74-52 and 74-44, AJHS.

22. Lichtman, *Prejudice and the Old Politics,* 166–198.

23. The statistical methodology used here is described and illustrated in Lichtman, *Prejudice and the Old Politics.* Additional statistical results based on the same methodology are available from the author.

24. Untitled typescript, undated 1928, Franklin Delano Roosevelt: Family, Business, and Personal Papers, box 42, Roosevelt Library.

25. Jean Edward Smith, *FDR* (New York: Random House, 2007), 231.

26. Walter Knabenshue to Secretary of State, 19 September 1929 (received 20 September 1929), in *Foreign Relations of the United States, 1929,* vol. 3 (Washington, DC: U.S. Government Printing Office, 1944), 57; Naomi Wiener Cohen, *The Year after the Riots: American Responses to the Palestinian Crisis of 1929–1930* (Detroit: Wayne State University Press, 1988), 16–49; Sonja P. Schoepf Wentling, "Ambivalence and Ambiguity: The Hoover Administration and American Zionism" (PhD diss., Kent State University, 2002), 217–290.

27. Wilbur J. Carr, Memorandum in regard to the Requests of the Delegation Headed by Judge Lehman, 13 October 1933, RG 59, entry 702, box 148, 150.626J/31 1/2, National Archives and Records Administration, College Park, Maryland.

28. "Immigration Ban to Aid Employment, *Washington Post,* 10 September 1930, p. 2; Louis I. Dublin, "A New Phase Opens Up in America's Evolution," *New York Times,* 17 April 1932, p. XX1.

29. "Roosevelt-for-President Club to Be Formed in Warm Springs," *Atlanta Constitution,* 7 November 1930, p. 1.

30. "Governor Roosevelt Condemns Economic Bias against Jews," Jewish Telegraphic Agency, 25 June 1930, www.archive.jta.org/article/1930/06/25/2785250/governor-roosevelt-condemns-economic-bias-against-jews.

31. Ron Chernow, *The House of Morgan: An American Banking Dynasty and the Rise of Modern Finance* (New York: Grove, 2001), 326–327; Anthony Patrick O'Brien, "The Failure of the Bank of United States: A Defense of Joseph Lucia," *Journal of Money, Credit and Banking* 24 (August 1992): 374–384.

32. Gulie Ne'eman Arad, *America, its Jews, and the Rise of Nazism* (Bloomington: Indiana University Press, 2000), 89; Morris Frommer, "The American Jewish Congress: A History, 1914–1950," vol. 2 (PhD diss., Ohio State University, 1978), 295–296.

33. "40,000 Protest Here on Palestine," *New York Times,* 3 November 1930, p. 1. Ammerman and Stimson quoted in Shlomo Shafir, "The Impact of the Jewish

Crisis on American-German Relations, 1933–1939"(PhD diss., Georgetown University, 1971), 22–23; "Protest Attacks on Jews," *New York Times,* 1 July 1931, p. 52; "Hoover Asked to Help Persecuted Polish Jews," *Washington Post,* 28 November 1931, p. 15; Yehuda Bauer, *My Brother's Keeper: A History of the American Jewish Joint Distribution Committee, 1929–1939* (Philadelphia: Jewish Publication Society, 1974), 305–306.

34. "Cardozo Is Named to Supreme Court," *New York Times,* 16 February 1932, p. 1; Ira H. Carmen, "The President, Politics and the Power of Appointment: Hoover's Nomination of Mr. Justice Cardozo," *Virginia Law Review* 55 (May 1969): 616–659.

35. Herbert Mitgang, *Once upon a Time in New York: Jimmy Walker, Franklin Roosevelt, and the Last Great Battle of the Jazz Age* (New York: Free Press, 2000). On Democratic Party conservatism see Douglas Craig, *After Wilson: The Struggle for the Democratic Party, 1920–1934* (Chapel Hill: University of North Carolina, 1992).

36. Louise Overacker, "Campaign Funds in a Depression Year," *American Political Science Review* 27 (October 1933): 769–783; G. William Domhoff and Michael J. Webber, *Class and Power in the New Deal: Corporate Moderates, Southern Democrats, and the Labor-Liberal Coalition* (Stanford: Stanford University Press, 2011).

37. Wise to Frankfurter, 8 September 1932, Stephen S. Wise Papers, reel 74-69, AJHS; Frankfurter to Wise, 14 September 1932, Felix Frankfurter Papers, reel 105, LC.

38. Franklin Delano Roosevelt, *F.D.R., His Personal Letters,* vol. 2: *1905 to 1928,* ed. Elliot Roosevelt (New York: Duell, Sloan and Pearce, 1950), 244; Klaus P. Fischer, *Hitler and America* (Philadelphia: University of Pennsylvania Press, 2011), 42–45.

3. THE DEMOCRAT AND THE DICTATOR

1. Pittman to James A. Farley, 19 August 1932, Democratic National Committee, Before Election, box 105, Franklin D. Roosevelt Library, Hyde Park, New York (henceforth Roosevelt Library).

2. "Paints Dark Picture of Foreign Affairs," *New York Times,* 20 November 1932, p. F8; James G. McDonald, *Advocate for the Doomed: The Diaries and Papers of James G. McDonald, 1932–1935,* ed. Richard Breitman, Barbara McDonald Stewart, and Severin Hochberg (Bloomington: Indiana University Press, 2007), 20–21.

3. "'Human' Alien Laws Urged by Governor," *New York Times,* 24 October 1932, p. 9.

4. "16 Deeds of Hoover Listed by Warburg," *New York Times,* 1 November 1932, p. 15; "Hoover Cites Twelve Policies," *New York Times,* 16 October 1932, p. 34.

5. Holmes and Wise to Roosevelt, 17 November 1932, Stephen S. Wise Papers, reel 74-42, American Jewish Historical Society, New York, New York (henceforth AJHS).

6. "Rabbis Fear Hitler as Enemy of Jews," *New York Times,* 6 February 1933, p. 13.

7. On the abortive joint protest see Wise to Julian W. Mack, 8 March 1933, Stephen S. Wise Papers, reel 74-74, AJHS.

8. Secretary of State to the Ambassador in Germany, 3 March 1933, in *Foreign Relations of the United States* (henceforth FRUS), *1933,* vol. 2 (Washington, DC: U.S. Government Printing Office, 1949), 320.

9. McDonald, *Advocate for the Doomed,* 48. Copy broadcast speech and interview, August 23, 1933, Hamilton Fish Armstrong Papers, box 99, Seeley G. Mudd Manuscript Library, Princeton University, Princeton, New Jersey; Frederick T. Birchall, "Lengthy Nazi Rule Indicated by Rally," *New York Times,* 6 September 1933, p. 12.

10. Gerhard L. Weinberg, *The Foreign Policy of Hitler's Germany,* vol. 1, *Diplomatic Revolution in Europe, 1933–1936* (Chicago: University of Chicago, 1970); Weinberg, ed., *Hitler's Second Book: The Unpublished Sequel to* Mein Kampf *by Adolf Hitler* (New York: Enigma, 2003).

11. "Atrocious Brutality," *Los Angeles Times,* 16 May 1903, p. 2; "Rivers of Jewish Blood Ran in Kishinev Streets," *Atlanta Constitution,* 14 May 1903, p. 1; Naomi W. Cohen, *The Americanization of Zionism, 1907–1948* (Lebanon, NH: Brandeis University Press, 2003), 29; Alan J. Ward, "Immigrant Minority 'Diplomacy': American Jews and Russia, 1901–1912," *Bulletin. British Association for American Studies,* new series, no. 9 (December 1964): 7–23; "Letter From Roosevelt," 16 November 1905, in *Publications of the American Jewish Historical Society* 14 (1906): 18.

12. "The Jews in Russia," *New York Times,* 10 November 1905, p. 8; "Begs President to Act," *New York Times,* 10 November 1905, p. 2.

13. Cyrus Adler to Oscar S. Straus, 12 November 1905, Cyrus Adler Papers, box 1, AJHS.

14. "Mr. Roosevelt and the Russian Jews," *Washington Post,* November 12, 1905, p. B4; Cyrus Adler to Simon Wolf, 27 December 1905, in Ira Robinson, ed., *Cyrus Adler: Selected Letters,* vol. 1 (Philadelphia: Jewish Publication Society, 1985), 122; "Plan Big Jewish Organ," *Chicago Tribune,* 12 November 1906, p. 4.

15. Adler to Marshall, 1 January 1906, Louis Marshall Papers, box 17, American Jewish Archives, Cincinnati, Ohio (henceforth AJA); Naomi W. Cohen, *Not Free to Desist: The American Jewish Committee, 1906–1966* (Philadelphia: The Jewish Publication Society, 1972), 13; Matthew Silver, "Louis Marshall and the Democratization of Jewish Identity," *American Jewish History* 94 (March–June 2008): 41–70.

16. Eric L. Goldstein, *The Price of Whiteness: Jews, Race, and American Identity* (Princeton, NJ: Princeton University Press, 2006), Marshall quotation at p. 89; Billikopf to Harry Haskell, 13 September 1928, Jacob Billikopf Papers, box 11, AJA.

17. Jerome C. Rosenthal, "The Public Life of Louis Marshall," vol. 1 (PhD diss., University of Cincinnati, 1983), p. 93.

18. Clifford L. Egan, "Pressure Groups, the Department of State, and the Abrogation of the Russian-American Treaty of 1832," *Proceedings of the American Philosophical Society* 115 (August 1971): 328–334; Cohen, *The Americanization of Zionism,* 30; Frank W. Brecher, *Reluctant Ally: United States Foreign Policy toward the Jews from Wilson to Roosevelt* (Westport, CT: Greenwood, 1991), xiv–xv.

19. Carole Fink, *Defending the Rights of Others: The Great Powers, The Jews, and International Minority Protection, 1878–1938* (New York: Cambridge University Press, 2004), 54–64; Sonia P. Wentling, "Prologue to Genocide or Epilogue to War? American Perspectives on the Jewish Question in Poland, 1919–21," paper presented at the Historical Society, Boston University, 5 June 2008, www.bu.edu/historic/conference08/swentling.pdf.

20. Cohen, *Not Free to Desist,* 80.

21. Melvin I. Urofsky, *Louis D. Brandeis: A Life* (New York: Pantheon, 2009), 399–429.

22. Brandeis to Billikopf, 16 June 1916, Billikopf Papers, box 3, AJA; Julian W. Mack, *Americanism and Zionism* (New York: Federation of American Zionists, 1918), 3, 8, in Julian W. Mack Papers, box 2, AJA; Mack to Schiff, 25 November 1917, Jacob H. Schiff Papers, box 460, AJA; Louis Lipsky, "The Festival of Chanukah," Maccabaean, December 1907, 127, in Deborah E. Lipstadt, *The Zionist Career of Louis Lipsky, 1900–1921* (New York: Arno Press, 1982), 63.

23. "Sees Danger in Zionism," *New York Times,* 14 September 1918, p. 7.

24. Louis D. Brandeis, *The Jewish Problem and How to Solve It* (New York: Zionist Publication Committee, 1915), 10; Stephen G. Rich, "The Jews: Race or Conglomerate," *Journal of Educational Sociology,* 8 (April 1929): 472; Goldstein, *The Price of Whiteness,* 86.

25. See Gerald Sorin, *A Time for Building: The Third Migration, 1880–1920,* vol. 3 (Baltimore: Johns Hopkins University Press, 1992), 212–213.

26. Melvin I. Urofsky, *American Zionism from Herzl to the Holocaust* (Garden City, NY: Anchor, 1976), 246–298, Weizmann quotation at p. 296.

27. Lipsky to Mack, 19 April 1921, Louis Lipsky Papers, box 1, AJHS; Urofsky, *American Zionism,* 319–323.

28. "Zionists Here Back New Jewish Agency," *New York Times,* 7 January 1929, p. 20; Minutes of the Emergency Committee for Zionist Affairs, undated 1928, Wise Remarks, Stephen S. Wise Papers, reel 74-63, AJHS; "Hails Harmony on Zionism," *New York Times,* 19 April 1929, p. 18; Herbert Parzen, "The Enlarge-

ment of the Jewish Agency for Palestine," *Jewish Social Studies* 39 (Winter–Spring 1977): 129–158.

29. Adler to Morris S. Lazaron, 13 April 1933, in Ira Robinson, ed., *Cyrus Adler: Selected Letters,* vol. 2 (Philadelphia: Jewish Publication Society, 1985), 262.

30. Stephen S. Wise to Julian W. Mack, April 3, 1933, in Carol Herman Voss, ed., *Stephen S. Wise: Servant of the People, Selected Letters* (Philadelphia: Jewish Publication Society, 1969), 181; Cohen, *Not Free to Desist,* 164.

31. "Other Faiths Join In," *New York Times,* 28 March 1933, p. 1; Cyrus Adler to Affiliated Societies, 22 March 1933, American Jewish Committee Records, RG 347, EXO-29, box 14, YIVO Institute for Jewish Research, New York, New York (henceforth YIVO).

32. "Nazis End Attacks,' *New York Times,* 27 March 1933, p. 1; Diary of Homer S. Cummings, 5 March–1 April 1933, Homer S. Cummings Papers, Small Special Collections Library, University of Virginia, Charlottesville, Virginia.

33. Telephone conversation transcript, Wise and Lehman, 20 March 1933, Stephen S. Wise Papers, reel 74-44, AJHS.

34. "Jews Here Demand Washington Action," *New York Times,* 23 March 1933, p. 1.

35. "Other Faiths Join In," *New York Times,* 28 March 1933, p. 1.

36. Ibid.; "Leaders of Nation Send in Protests," *New York Times,* 28 March 1933, p. 13.

37. Father MacIntyre to Wise, 27 March 1933, Stephen S. Wise Papers, reel 74-61, AJHS.

38. "We'd Like a Break Too, Mr. Alfred E. Smith," *Chicago Defender,* 1 April 1933, p. 11; "Jewish Pogroms in Germany," *Pittsburgh Courier,* 1 April 1933, p. 10.

39. Robert G. Weisbord and Arthur Stein, *Bittersweet Encounter: The Afro-American and the Jew* (Westport, CT: Greenwood, 1970), 40.

40. For the most thorough elaboration of conventional views see Deborah Lipstadt, *Beyond Belief: The American Press & the Coming of the Holocaust, 1933–1945* (New York: Free Press, 1986). The local papers are online in the Newspaper Archives, by subscription at www.newspaperarchive.com.

41. Adler to Laski, 24 April 1933 and 7 June 1933, American Jewish Committee Records, RG 347, EXO-29, box 23, YIVO; Wise to Ochs, 4 April 1933, Adolph S. Ochs Papers, box 84, New York Public Library, New York, New York.

42. Moffat Diary, 29 March 1933, Jay Pierrepont Moffat Papers, Houghton Library, Harvard University, Cambridge, Massachusetts; "Memorandum of Trans-Atlantic Conversation, William E. Phillips to George A. Gordon, Gordon to Phillips," 31 March 1933, in *FRUS, 1933,* vol. 2, 338–344.

43. "Frown on Parades as Hitler Protest," *New York Times,* 28 April 1933, p. 9; Waldman to fellow-members, 1 May 1933, American Jewish Committee Records,

RG 347, EXO-29, box 14, YIVO; Gulie Ne'eman Arad, *America, Its Jews, and the Rise of Nazism* (Bloomington: Indiana University Press, 2000), 168.

44. Moshe Gottlieb, "The Anti-Nazi Boycott Movement in the United States: An Ideological and Sociological Appreciation," *Jewish Social Studies* 35 (July–October 1973): 198; Aaron Berman, *Nazism, the Jews and American Zionism, 1933–1948* (Detroit: Wayne State University Press, 1990), 38.

45. Wise to Felix Frankfurter, 23 May 1933, Stephen S. Wise Papers, reel 74-69, AJHS.

46. "Untermyer Back," *New York Times,* 7 August 1933, p. 4.

47. Wise to Frankfurter, 23 May 1933, Stephen S. Wise Papers, reel 74-69, AJHS; "Jews Here to Push Boycott on Hitler," *New York Times,* 21 August 1933, p. 2; American Jewish Congress, "Resolution on Boycott," 20 August 1933, Louis D. Brandeis Papers, reel 98, Library of Congress, Washington, D.C. (henceforth LC); "Hadassah Pledged to Combat Nazis," *New York Times,* 25 October 1933, p. 4; American Jewish Committee, "The Anti-German Boycott," August 1933, American Jewish Committee Records, RG 347, EXO-29, box 15, YIVO. On the economics of the boycott see Yehuda Bauer, *Jews for Sale? Nazi-Jewish Negotiations, 1933–1945* (New Haven, CT: Yale University Press, 1994), 5–29.

48. Wise to Mack, 30 August 1933, Stephen S. Wise Papers, reel 74-74, AJHS. On the Haavara agreement and the conflicts it sparked among Jewish leaders and on the difficulties of getting good statistics on the Haavara emigrants see Günter Schubert, *Erkaufte Flucht: Der Kampf um den Haavara-Transfer* (Berlin: Metropol, 2009), esp. 173–174.

49. On Hitler's views of America see Klaus P. Fischer, *Hitler and America* (Philadelphia: University of Pennsylvania Press, 2011), and McDonald, *Advocate for the Doomed,* 61–69.

50. Richard Breitman and Alan M. Kraut, *American Refugee Policy and European Jewry, 1933–1945* (Bloomington: Indiana University Press, 1987), 12. Frankfurter's meetings in the White House Usher's Diary, also referred to in Frankfurter to Proskauer, 18 May 1933, Felix Frankfurter Papers, reel 55, LC. Frankfurter's telephone call mentioned in Wise to Frankfurter, 16 April 1933, Stephen S. Wise Papers, reel 74-69, AJHS; Bernard Deutsch, Conversation with James G. McDonald, 4 May 1933, Papers of Julian W. Mack, microfilm, reel 10, Brandeis University Library, Waltham, Massachusetts. Wise's Conversation with Deutsch, 4 May 1933, Stephen S. Wise Papers, reel 74-69, AJHS.

51. FDR quoted in Robert Dallek, *Franklin D. Roosevelt and American Foreign Policy, 1932–1945* (New York: Oxford University Press, 1979), 43; Hull to Davis, 24 April 1933, in *FRUS, 1933,* vol. 1, 102. Hull and Undersecretary of State Phillips met with FDR on April 23, White House appointment diaries, Roosevelt Library.

52. Generally on FDR and Hull see Irwin F. Gellman, *Secret Affairs: Franklin Roosevelt, Cordell Hull, and Sumner Welles* (Baltimore: Johns Hopkins University

Press, 1995), 20–55; Hull to George A. Gordon, 24 March 1933, in *FRUS, 1933*, vol. 2, 330; Roosevelt quoted in Ted Morgan, *FDR: A Biography* (New York: Simon & Schuster, 1985), 371.

53. Maryanne Frances Healey, "'Witness, Participant, and Chronicler': The Role of Herbert Feis as Economic Advisor to the State Department, 1931–1943" (PhD diss., Georgetown University, 1973).

54. Presidential meetings are documented in FDR's appointment diaries, available at the Roosevelt Library.

55. McDonald's inference in Wise conversation with Deutsch, 4 May 1933, reel 74-69, AJHS. FDR's lunch meeting with Schacht, 6 May, and meeting with Schacht and German Ambassador Luther, 8 and 10 May, White House appointment diaries. Manfred Jonas, *The United States and Germany: A Diplomatic History* (Ithaca, NY: Cornell University Press, 1984), 214; Roosevelt to Lehman, 18 May 1933, in Edgar B. Nixon, ed., *Franklin D. Roosevelt and Foreign Affairs,* vol. 1 (Cambridge, MA: Harvard University Press, 1969), 136; McDonald, *Advocate for the Doomed,* 68.

56. Brandeis to Wise, 11 May 1933, Louis D. Brandeis Papers, reel 99, LC; Wise to Julian W. Mack, 7 June 1933, Stephen S. Wise Papers, reel 74-74, AJHS.

57. Lehman to Roosevelt, 24 May 1933, Presidential Personal Files, 446, Irving Lehman, Roosevelt Library.

58. Wise to Julian Mack, 15 April 1933, Stephen S. Wise Papers, reels 74-54 and 74-74, AJHS; Frankfurter to Raymond Moley, 24 April 1933, Felix Frankfurter papers, reel 51, LC; Adler to A. Leo Weil, 3 May 1933, American Jewish Committee Records, RG 347, EXO-29, box 38, folder 6, YIVO; Wise to Mr. and Mrs. Max Lowenthal, 18 April 1933, Stephen S. Wise Papers, reel 74-53, AJHS.

59. "100,000 March Here" and "50,000 Jews Unite in Chicago Protest," *New York Times,* 11 May 1933, pp. 1 and 10; "Anti-Hitler Meeting Held in Cleveland," *New York Times,* 15 May 1933, p. 9.

60. "President Roosevelt to Various Chiefs of State," 16 May 1933, in *FRUS, 1933,* vol. 2, 144; Morgenthau Diaries, 22 May 1933, reel 1, Depression and the New Deal, 1933–1939, LC, Washington, DC; Arad, *America, Its Jews,* 152; Wise to Felix Frankfurter, 17 May 1933, Louis D. Brandeis Papers, reel 99, LC.

61. On FDR and Ellenbogen see Wise to Frankfurter, Mack, and Brandeis, 23 May 1933, Stephen S. Wise Papers, reel 74-69, AJHS.

62. "The Week," *New Republic,* 2 August 1933, p. 300; Frankfurter to Proskauer, 18 May 1933, reel 55, Felix Frankfurter Papers, LC. There is no record in the president's appointment diaries of Felix Warburg having met with FDR in 1933. There is a listing of a "Mr. Warburg" on 2, 4, 18, and 23 April and 9, 15, and 17 May with no first name. Most of these entries, but not necessarily all of them, were likely Felix's nephew and economic adviser James Warburg. Felix Warburg may have passed on his views through James or intermediaries

associated with the American Jewish Committee such as Governor Herbert Lehman.

63. On Rosenman's statement and Wise's response see Wise to Mack, 3 June 1933, Louis D. Brandeis Papers, reel 99, LC.

64. Wise to Frankfurter, 1 June 1933, Stephen S. Wise Papers, reel 74-69, AJHS. Wise to Proskauer, 4 June 1933, Louis D. Brandeis Papers, reel 99, LC; "Senators Decry Persecution of Jews by Hitler," *Chicago Tribune,* 11 June 1933, p. 5. White House appointment diaries, 4 June 1933; Wise, Memorandum of Telephone Conversation with Congressman Sabath, undated, 1933, Louis D. Brandeis Papers, reel 99, LC.

65. Daniel Kadden, "American Jewish Advocacy: The Dynamics of Organizational Structure and Resources" (PhD diss., Brown University, 1996) is an organizational history of the American Jewish Committee and the American Jewish Congress.

66. Jewish Telegraphic Agency, Confidential Report No. 8, July 1933, Louis D. Brandeis Papers, reel 98, LC; McDonald, *Advocate for the Doomed,* 77.

67. On FDR's economic policies and their connection to the improving economy see Gauti B. Eggertsson, "Great Expectations and the End of the Depression," *American Economic Review* 98 (September 2008): 1476–1516.

68. Wise to Julian Mack, 4 May 1933, Stephen S. Wise Papers, reel 74-74, AJHS.

69. "Not Even Roosevelt Can Make Us Change Our Ways, Asserts Nazi Paper in Attack," *Jewish Telegraphic Agency,* 5 July 1933.

4. IMMIGRATION WARS

1. Adler to Louis Ginzberg and to Horace Stern, 7 April 1933, in Ira Robinson, ed., *Cyrus Adler: Selected Letters,* vol. 2 (Philadelphia: Jewish Publication Society, 1985), 260; "Dr. J. B. Wise Sees No Hope in Reich," *New York Times,* 13 May 1933, p. 7.

2. The meeting or conversation is referenced in Lehman to Roosevelt, 21 September 1933, RG 59, entry 702, 150.01/2153, National Archives and Records Administration, College Park, Maryland (henceforth NARA).

3. Wise to Mack, 15 April 1933, Stephen S. Wise Papers, reel 74-74, American Jewish Historical Society, New York, New York (henceforth AJHS); Frankfurter to the President, 16 April 1933, RG 59, 862.4016/586, NARA. Excerpts of the wire included "Time is of the essence," "prayerfully hope for some word by the president," and "progress on plan for admission carefully safeguarded of refugees."

4. Moffat Journal, 20 April 1933, Jay Pierrepont Moffat Papers, MS Am 1407, Houghton Library, Harvard University, Cambridge, Massachusetts (henceforth Houghton Library).

5. Ibid.

6. Ibid.

7. Richard Breitman and Alan M. Kraut, *American Refugee Policy and European Jewry, 1933–1945* (Bloomington: Indiana University Press, 1987), 32–39. On the attitudes of Phillips, Carr, and Moffat see Moffat Journal, 20 April and 23 March 1933, Moffat Papers, MS Am 1407, Houghton Library.

8. On Hull see Irwin F. Gellman, *Secret Affairs: Franklin Roosevelt, Cordell Hull, and Sumner Welles* (Baltimore: Johns Hopkins University Press, 1995), 33–38. Moffat Journal, 9–10 September 1933, Moffat Papers, MS Am 1407, Houghton Library.

9. Perkins to Frankfurter, 25 April 1933, in Raymond Moley Papers, box 67, folder 6, Hoover Institute for War, Revolution, and Peace, Stanford, California; Frankfurter to Perkins, 27 April 1933, Frances Perkins Papers, box 4, Columbia University Rare Book and Manuscript Library, New York, New York (henceforth Columbia Library).

10. Robert Dallek, *Democrat and Diplomat: The Life of William E. Dodd* (New York: Oxford, 1968), 201; Wise to Frankfurter, 5 July 1933, Stephen S. Wise Papers, reel 74-69, AJHS; Max Kohler to Alfred M. Cohen, 5 July 1933, American Jewish Committee Records, RG 347, EXO-29, box 16, YIVO Institute for Jewish Research, New York, New York (henceforth YIVO). On Dodd's claim about the quota see Daniel MacCormack to Isador Lubin, 23 August 1933, Frances Perkins Papers, III B (INS), Connecticut College, New London, Connecticut. According to Dodd's version (recorded in a suspect diary), the president had told him Nazi Germany was treating its Jews shamefully and American Jews were most upset, but this was not a government matter. Instead, he should use his private efforts to ameliorate the situation. On the problems with Dodd's diary see James G. McDonald, *Advocate for the Doomed: The Diaries and Papers of James G. McDonald, 1932–1935,* ed. Richard Breitman, Barbara McDonald Stewart, and Severin Hochberg (Bloomington: Indiana University Press, 2007), 793–795. On the Dodd family in Berlin see Eric Larson, *In the Garden of Beasts: Love, Terror, and an American Family in Hitler's Berlin* (New York: Crown Books, 2011).

11. Breitman and Kraut, *American Refugee Policy,* 17–18; Bat-Ami Zucker, *In Search of Refuge: Jews and US Consuls in Nazi Germany, 1933–1941* (Portland, OR: Valentine Mitchell, 2001), 92, FDR quotation at p. 93.

12. Breitman and Kraut, *American Refugee Policy,* 18–27; Julian W. Mack, Memorandum of Washington Trip, 30 October 1933, American Jewish Committee Records, RG 347, EXO-29, box 16, folder 297, YIVO; William Green to Franklin Delano Roosevelt, 22 September 1933, Frances Perkins, "Memorandum to the President," 5 December 1933, and Roosevelt to Green, 8 December 1933, President's Official File 133, box 1, Immigration, Roosevelt Library. Franklin D. Roosevelt Library, Hyde Park, New York (henceforth Roosevelt Library).

13. Mack to Carr, 1 September 1933, Herbert Lehman Papers, box 2, item 188, Columbia Library; On Mack as a liaison see Mack to Stephen S. Wise, 19 October 1933, Stephen S. Wise Papers, reel 74-74, AJHS; Lehman to President Roosevelt, 21 September 1933, RG 59, entry 702, box 13, 150.01/2153, NARA.

14. There are two summaries of this meeting: the first, undated [September 13] handwritten notes of Judge Mack's telephone call, covering the first part of the meeting; the second a typed summary by Mack or based on information from Mack the next day. Felix Frankfurter Papers, box 137, Library of Congress, Washington, D.C. (henceforth LC). Also, Lehman to FDR, 21 September 1933, RG 59, entry 702, box 13, 150.01/2153, NARA; Jacob Billikopf to Stephen S. Wise, 12 October 1933, Stephen S. Wise Papers, reel 74-66, AJHS; Lowenthal to Billikopf, 20 November 1933, Marvin Lowenthal Papers, box 6, AJHS.

15. Steven Early to Hull, 14 September 1933, OF 133, box 1, Immigration, Roosevelt Library, relates FDR's decision not to attend the meeting, but does not specify his reasons. Memorandum of the Conference . . . , 20 September 1933, and Proskauer to Hull, 22 September 1933, RG 59, entry 702, box 13, 150.01/2145 1/2 and box 148, 150.626J/26, NARA.

16. Diary of William Phillips, 30 October 1933, William Phillips Papers, Houghton Library; Confidential Report by Judge Julian W. Mack of Washington trip, 30 October 1933, American Jewish Committee Records, RG 347, EXO-29, box 16, folder 297, YIVO; Breitman and Kraut, *American Refugee Policy,* 18–22, 33.

17. Breitman and Kraut, *American Refugee Policy,* 21; Bat-Ami Zucker, "Frances Perkins and the German-Jewish Refugees, 1933–1940," *American Jewish History* 89 (May 2001): 43.

18. Wyzanski to Parents, 24 January 1934, private possession of Richard Breitman.

19. McDonald, *Advocate for the Doomed,* 355.

20. Chamberlain to Roosevelt, 10 March 1934, RG 59, entry 702, box 13, 150.01/2193, NARA; "House Committee Kills Sharp Immigration Cuts," *New York Times,* 13 March 1933, p. 2.

21. "Visas Show Reich Jews Pouring In," *Los Angeles Times,* 14 April 1934, p. 3.

22. Breitman and Kraut, *American Refugee Policy,* 13–14. Johnson to Frankfurter, 24 April 1933, Felix Frankfurter Papers, box 137, LC; Stanford M. Lyman, "A Haven for Homeless Intellectuals: The New School and Its Exile Faculty," *International Journal of Politics, Culture, and Society* 7 (Spring 1994): 493–512.

23. Mack to Jewish Leaders, 6 June 1934, Louis D. Brandeis Papers, reel 100, LC.

24. Lehman to Mack, 12 June 1934, Stephen S. Wise Papers, reel 74-44, AJHS; McDonald, *Advocate for the Doomed,* 575–576.

25. "Relaxing Quotas for Exiles Fought," *New York Times,* 4 May 1934, p. 7.

26. "Silver Legion Aims Attacks at Jews," *New York Times,* 6 April 1934, p. 12; "Silver Shirt Head Indicted in South," *New York Times,* 24 May 1934, p. 12; Gerald Winrod, "The Hidden Hand," *Defender,* January 1933, p. 7. See generally Leo P. Ribuffo, *The Old Christian Right: The Protestant Far Right from the Great Depression to the Cold War* (Philadelphia: Temple University Press, 1983); Philip Jenkins, *Hoods and Shirts: The Extreme Right in Pennsylvania, 1925–1940* (Chapel Hill: University of North Carolina Press, 1997).

27. "20,000 Nazi Friends at a Rally Here," *New York Times,* 18 May 1934, p. 1; "McCormack Heads House Nazi Probe," *Washington Post,* 6 April 1934, p. 3; "Secret Hearings on Nazism Begin Here," *New York Times,* 18 May 1934, p. 3; Wilbur J. Carr, Diary, 29 March 1934, LC; Morris Waldman, "Memorandum of an Interview with Solicitor Wyzanski," 15 May 1934, American Jewish Committee Records, RG 347, EXO-29, box 7, folder 144, YIVO.

28. Robert F. Burk, *The Corporate State and the Broker State: The Du Ponts and National Politics, 1925–1940* (Cambridge, MA: Harvard University Press, 1990), 130; Frank Buxton to Bainbridge Colby, 17 June 1934, Papers of Bainbridge Colby, box 30, LC.

29. Meeting of the Republican National Committee, 5 June 1934, *Meetings of the Republican National Committee, 1911–1980,* reel 4, LC; David Sherman Beach to William A. Borah, 4 December 1934, William A. Borah Papers, box 751, LC.

30. "Wirt Probe Agreed by Leaders," *Washington Post,* 28 March 1934, p. 1; "Little Red House Is Said to Rule Us," *New York Times,* 21 April 1934, p. 5.

31. Frankfurter to Corcoran, 7 May 1934, Thomas Corcoran Papers, box 638, LC.

32. "Racial Magazine Denies New Deal 'Jew Hierarchy,' " *Chicago Tribune,* 10 May 1934, p. 12.

33. "Nazis 'Convicted' of World 'Crime' by 20,000 in Rally," *New York Times,* 8 March 1934, p. 1.

34. "Roosevelt Urged to Reprove Reich," *New York Times,* 15 March 1934, p. 18; Phillips, Diary, 16 March 1934; Wise to Billikopf, 17 May 1934, Jacob Billikopf Papers, box 34, American Jewish Archives, Cincinnati, Ohio (henceforth AJA).

35. Catherine Collomp, "The Jewish Labor Committee, American Labor, and the Rescue of European Socialists, 1934–1941," *International Labor and Working-Class History* 68 (October 2005): 115–122.

36. Gail Malmgreen, "Labor and the Holocaust: The Jewish Labor Committee and the Anti-Nazi Struggle," *Labor's Heritage* (October 1991): 20–35, Vladeck quotation at p. 23. The nearly 700 pages of Steven Fraser, *Labor Will Rule: Sidney Hillman and the Rise of American Labor* (Ithaca, NY: Cornell University Press, 1991) include not a single reference to the Jewish Labor Committee or Hitler's persecution of Jews.

37. Vladeck to Deutsch, 12 December 1934, Louis D. Brandeis Papers, reel 102, LC; Moshe Gottlieb, "The Anti-Nazi Boycott Movement in the United States: An Ideological and Sociological Appreciation," *Jewish Social Studies* 35 (July–October 1973): 217.

38. Deutsch to Vladeck, undated December 1934, Louis D. Brandeis Papers, reel 102, LC; Wise, "A Jewish Congress Will Help the Jews of Europe," *Day,* 13 January 1935, translation, American Jewish Committee Records, RG 347, EXO-29, box 48a, folder 10, YIVO.

39. Holmes to Jacob Billikopf, 15 July 1935, Jacob Billikopf Papers, box 12, AJA.

40. White to Wise, 17 May 1934, Louis D. Brandeis Papers, reel 100, LC.

41. McDonald, *Advocate for the Doomed,* 125; Vicki Caron, *Uneasy Asylum: France and the Jewish Refugee Crisis, 1933–1942* (Stanford: Stanford University Press, 1999), 14.

42. Felix M. Warburg, Report for the American Jewish Committee, 1 November 1933, Felix M. Warburg Papers, box 286, folder 6, AJA; McDonald, *Advocate for the Doomed,* 134.

43. Adler to Lewis Strauss, 19 October 1933, Felix M. Warburg Papers, box 286, folder 4, AJA.

44. "America Is Chided on Reich Refugees," *New York Times,* 9 December 1933, p. 7; McDonald, *Advocate for the Doomed,* 134.

45. McDonald, *Advocate for the Doomed,* 233–234.

46. Ibid., 311.

5. TRANSITIONS

1. "40 Parties in City Celebrate the Day," *New York Times,* 31 January 1934, p. 1; "Check Given to Roosevelt for Million," *Washington Post,* 14 May 1934, p. 1.

2. "Complete Tables Showing Results of Election," *New York Times,* 8 November 1934, p. 6; "New Faces in the Senate," *Washington Post,* 12 November 1934, p. 9.

3. Allan J. Lichtman, *White Protestant Nation: The Rise of the American Conservative Movement* (New York: Grove/Atlantic, 2008), 65.

4. Raymond Clapper, "Between You and Me," *Washington Post,* 22 February 1935, p. 2; Charles E. Coughlin, *A Series of Lectures on Social Justice* (Royal Oak, MI: Radio League of the Little Flower, 1936); "National Inquirer Poll," OFC-300, 1936 Campaign, Franklin D. Roosevelt Library, Hyde Park, New York.

5. Arthur Sears Henning, "New Deal's 'Hot Dogs' Fear High Court Rulings," *Atlanta Constitution,* 22 December 1935, p. 4.

6. Cohen, Notes, undated, 1935, Benjamin V. Cohen Papers, box 1, American Jewish Archives, Cincinnati, Ohio (henceforth AJA).

7. William Dudley Pelley, *What Every Congressman Should Know* (Asheville, NC: Pelley Publishers: undated), Herbert Hoover Papers, Post-Presidential, Individual File, box 289; J. Lee Kreader, "Isaac Max Rubinow: Pioneering Specialist in Social Insurance," *Social Service Review* 50 (September 1976): 402–425.

8. Franklin D. Roosevelt, "Our Foreign Policy: A Democratic View," *Foreign Affairs* 6 (July 1928): 385; "League Firmness Surprises Berlin," *New York Times,* 12 October 1935, reference to the *Diplomatische Korrespondenz* on p. 10.

9. James G. McDonald, *Refugees and Rescue: The Diaries and Papers of James G. McDonald, 1935–1945,* ed. Richard Breitman, Barbara McDonald Stewart, and Severin Hochberg (Bloomington: Indiana University Press, 2009), 29; American Jewish Committee, Annual Report, January 1936, in *American Jewish Yearbook, 1935–1936,* 603, American Jewish Committee Archives, www.ajcarchives.org/AJC _DATA/Files/1937_1938_4_YearReview.pdf.

10. McDonald, *Refugees and Rescue,* 71–72; Hull (Simmons) to FDR, 6 December 1935, RG 59, entry 702, box 148, 150.626J/175, National Archives and Records Administration, College Park, Maryland (henceforth NARA).

11. Fields to Wise, 31 October 1935, Stephen S. Wise Papers, reel 74-74, American Jewish Historical Society, New York, New York (henceforth AJHS). Cecilia Razovsky, "Summary of Informal Breakfast Conference with Colonel Daniel W. MacCormack," 6 November 1935, Felix Warburg Papers, box 330, National Coordinating Committee folder, AJA; Adler to Felix Warburg, 22 November 1935, Felix Warburg Papers, box 308, AJA, referring to FDR's letter of 13 November 1935.

12. Statistics on demand for visas in A. M. Warren, Chief, Visa Division, U.S. Department of State to Malcolm Bryan, 23 January 1940, RG 59, entry 702, 811.111 Quota 62/769, NARA.

13. Lichtman, *White Protestant Nation,* 88–90.

14. Alexander Lincoln to Abraham Kraditor, 15 May 1936; Thomas Cadwalader to H. G. Torbert, 22 April 1936; Henry Joy to Joseph Brainin, 6 May 1936, Alexander Lincoln Papers, box 7, Schlesinger Library, Harvard University, Cambridge, Massachusetts. "Lincoln Quits Tax Post," *New York Times,* 24 April 1936, p. 17.

15. Lichtman, *White Protestant Nation,* 71–74.

16. On Howe and Wise see Henry L. Feingold, *The Politics of Rescue: The Roosevelt Administration and the Holocaust, 1938–1945* (New Brunswick, NJ: Rutgers University Press, 1970), 13; Wise to Holmes, 3 February 1936, Stephen S. Wise Papers, reel 86-1, AJHS. Wise to Frankfurter, 2 March and 10 April 1936, Louis D. Brandeis Papers, reel 103, LC and Stephen S. Wise Papers, reel 74-69, AJHS.

17. Stephen S. Wise, Memo, The President Franklin D. Roosevelt at Hyde Park, 5 October 1936, Stephen S. Wise Papers, reel 74-47, AJHS.

18. Secretary of State to the Ambassador in Britain, 27 July 1936, in *Foreign Relations of the United States, 1936,* vol. 3 (Washington, DC: U.S. Government

Printing Office, 1953), 444; "President Endorses Palestine Appeal," *New York Times,* 6 August 1936, p. 6; Stephen S. Wise, Memo, The President Franklin D. Roosevelt at Hyde Park, 5 October 1936, Stephen S. Wise Papers, reel 74-47, AJHS.

19. Michael Patrick Allen, "Capitalist Response to State Intervention: Theories of the State and Political Finance in the New Deal," *American Sociological Review* 56 (October 1991): 679–689; Michael J. Webber, *New Deal Fat Cats: Business, Labor, and Campaign Finance in the 1936 Presidential Election* (New York: Fordham University Press, 2000); Coughlin, *A Series of Lectures;* Francis MacDonnell, *Insidious Foes: The Axis Fifth Column and the American Home Front* (New York: Oxford University Press, 1995), 35–37.

20. "Another Whispering Campaign," *Los Angeles Times,* 1 August 1936, p. 4.

21. On Landon's opposition to anti-Semitism see William Allen White to Jacob Billikopf, 9 July 1936, Marvin Lowenthal Papers, box 5, AJHS; Wise, Memo, The President Franklin D. Roosevelt at Hyde Park, 5 October 1936, Stephen S. Wise Papers, reel 74-47, AJHS. "Pugh" was actually spelled Pew and referred to the ultraconservative brothers who ran Sun Oil and heavily contributed to Republicans and conservative groups; Rosensohn quoted in Frankfurter to Wise, 27 October 1936, Stephen S. Wise Papers, reel 74-69, AJHS; Harry Schneiderman, "Review of the Year 5697," in *American Jewish Yearbook* (Philadelphia: Jewish Publication Society, 1937), 252. Livingston founded the Anti-Defamation League in 1913 to combat domestic anti-Semitism.

22. Stephen S. Wise, Memo, The President Franklin D. Roosevelt at Hyde Park, 5 October 1936, Stephen S. Wise Papers, reel 74-47, AJHS; "Rabbi Stephen S. Wise Sees No Jewish Vote," *New York Times,* 2 November 1936, p. 11.

23. Michael J. Webber and G. William Domhoff, "Myth and Reality in Business Support for Democrats and Republicans in the 1936 Presidential Election," *American Political Science Review* 90 (December 1996): 824–833.

24. Lichtman, *White Protestant Nation,* 92.

25. Richard Breitman and Alan M. Kraut, *American Refugee Policy and European Jewry, 1933–1945* (Bloomington: Indiana University Press, 1987), 48–50.

26. Robert Dallek, *Franklin D. Roosevelt and American Foreign Policy, 1932–1945* (New York: Oxford University Press, 1979), 138–140, Chamberlain quotation at p. 139.

27. Cummings Diary, 8 October, 1937, Notebook 7, Homer S. Cummings Papers, Small Special Collections Library, University of Virginia, Charlottesville, Virginia.

28. "Public Opinion Polls Give Background on World News," *Washington Post,* 2 May 1937, p. B1; "Will America Follow Roosevelt's Lead?" *Washington Post,* 10 October, 1937, p. B1.

29. Wise to Mack, 10 November 1937, Stephen S. Wise Papers, reel 74-74, AJHS.

6. MOVING MILLIONS?

1. Benjamin Welles, *Sumner Welles: FDR's Global Strategist* (New York: St. Martin's Press, 1997), 1. A franker assessment of Welles the man can be found in Irwin F. Gellman, *Secret Affairs: Franklin Roosevelt, Cordell Hull, and Sumner Welles* (Baltimore: Johns Hopkins University Press, 1995).

2. These comments are based on a close reading of the Welles Papers, Franklin D. Roosevelt Library, Hyde Park, New York (henceforth Roosevelt Library).

3. Report of Meeting of S.S.W. with F.D.R., 22 January 1938, copy in Frankfurter Papers, reel 164, Library of Congress, Washington, D.C. (henceforth LC). In July 1937, Will Rosenblatt to Wise, 9 May 1938 (quoting from July 1937 correspondence), and Wise to Rosenblatt, 9 May 1938, Stephen S. Wise Papers, reel 74-46, American Jewish Historical Society, New York, New York (henceforth AJHS).

4. Gerhard L. Weinberg, *Germany, Hitler and World War II: Essays in Modern German and World History* (New York: Cambridge University Press, 1995), 102–105.

5. "Jews Humiliated by Vienna Crowds," *New York Times,* 16 March 1938, p. 6; "3,500 Austrians Seek Visas to U.S. in Day," *Atlanta Constitution,* 28 March 1938, p. 1.

6. On the speech see Edward Moore Bennett, *FDR and the Search for Security* (Wilmington, DE: Scholarly Resources, 1985), 129; Messersmith to John C. Wiley, 16 March 1938, John C. Wiley Papers, box 8, Messersmith folder, Roosevelt Library.

7. Harold L. Ickes, *The Secret Diary of Harold L. Ickes,* vol. 2, *The Inside Struggle, 1936–1939* (New York: Simon and Schuster, 1954), 342–343. The Morgenthau Diaries: Depression and the New Deal, 1933–1939 (henceforth Morgenthau Diaries), 22 March 1938, microfilm, reel 31, LC.

8. Morgenthau, discussing the cabinet meeting of 18 March in his diary, credited FDR with suggesting both combining the German and Austrian quota, and with appealing to other countries to take in 100 to 1,000 families each. "America Offers Haven to Minorities within Our Quota Limits," *Washington Post,* 26 March 1938, p. X1. "Troubleshooter in Berlin," *New York Times,* 23 July 1939, p. SM2. According to figures provided by American Consul General Raymond Geist, between June 30, 1933 and April 30, 1939, more than 286,000 Germans applied for immigration visas to the United States. The waiting-list figure in early 1939 is from Minutes of Refugee Committee, 9 February 1939, American Friends Service Committee, Refugee Service 1939, American Friends Service Committee Archive, Philadelphia.

9. Welles Memo of 22 March 1938, with handwritten comment about FDR's approval, RG 59, 840.48 Refugees 11 1/2, National Archives and Records Administration, College Park, Maryland (henceforth NARA). Morgenthau Diaries, 22

March 1938, on FDR's suggestion of the term political refugees, reel 31, LC. "Hull Plan Upheld" and "Welcome Offered to All," *New York Times,* 26 March 1938, pp. 1, 4.

10. "Aid for Refugees Favored by AFL," *New York Times,* 26 March 1938, p. 4; Wise to Julian W. Mack, 29 March 1938, and to Felix Frankfurter, 30 March 1938, Stephen S. Wise Papers, reels 74-74 and 74-69, AJHS. Welles to Henry Morgenthau Jr., 23 March 1938, Sumner Welles Papers, box 49, folder 10, Roosevelt Library.

11. Feis to Felix Frankfurter, 22 March 1938, Herbert Feis Papers, box 16, and Felix Frankfurter Papers, reel 33, LC.

12. Harold L. Ickes Diaries (unpublished), 30 March and 2 April 1938, reel 2, LC. A slightly varying account is found in Alex Goodall, "Diverging Paths: Nazism, the National Civil Federation, and American Anticommunism 1933–9," *Journal of Contemporary History* 44, no. 1 (January 2009): 49–50.

13. FDR Memorandum for the Secretary of State, 11 February 1937, President's Personal File 506, Arthur Sweetser, Roosevelt Library.

14. All the summary and quotes from Sweetser's detailed reconstruction of this meeting, entitled Interview with President Roosevelt, 4 April 1938, Arthur Sweetser Papers, container 34, Sweetser Memorandum of Interview with President Roosevelt, LC. Obvious typos have been corrected and punctuation standardized. The White House appointment diaries confirm that Sweetser was originally scheduled to meet with FDR at noon and that he actually arrived at 2:45 p.m. That is exactly what Sweetser wrote in his reconstruction.

15. Wise to Frankfurter, 30 March 1938, Stephen S. Wise Papers, 74-69, AJHS; Roosevelt to Lehman, 30 March 1938, OF 3186, box 1, Political Refugees, January–May 1938, Roosevelt Library.

16. "Texan Calls Hull New Refugee Plan Taxpayer Burden," *Chicago Tribune,* 27 March 1938, p. 3. Henry L. Feingold, *The Politics of Rescue* (New York: Holocaust Library, 1970), 34; "Austria Seizure Not US Affair, Borah Asserts," *Washington Post,* 29 March 1938, p. X7.

17. For the most detailed account see Confidential Memorandum on White House Conference on Refugees, 13 April 1938, drafted by Wise, in Stephen S. Wise Papers, reel 74-47, AJHS.

18. Ibid.

19. Transcript of Welles's conference with the American Society of Newspaper Editors, 22 April 1938, Sumner Welles Papers, box 44, folder 12, Roosevelt Library.

20. Stimson to Welles, 25 April 1938, Sumner Welles Papers, box 48, folder 4, Roosevelt Library; unlabeled handwritten notes by Armstrong of conversation with Stimson, 26 April 1938, Hamilton Fish Armstrong Papers, box 77, President's Advisory Committee, Seeley G. Mudd Manuscript Library, Princeton University, Princeton, New Jersey (henceforth Mudd Library); Stimson Diaries, 27 April 1938, reel 5, LC. Feingold, *The Politics of Rescue,* 28. Welles, *Sumner Welles,* 221,

incorrectly states that Welles suggested that he, Hull, and Messersmith represent the United States at the international refugee conference. This claim misinterprets Welles's statement about who ought to be present at the 13 April meeting at the White House.

21. Minutes, 20 May 1938, Copy in RG 59, Lot File 52D408, Alphabetical Subject File, box 9, President's Advisory Committee—Minutes, NARA.

22. Frankfurter stayed over at the White House on 12 and 13 May. Frankfurter to McDonald, 1 July 1938, Felix Frankfurter Papers, reel 49, LC.

23. Memo of 20 May 1938 conversation between Messersmith and Potocki, George Messersmith Papers, item 995, University of Delaware Library, Newark, Delaware (henceforth Delaware Library); Feingold, *The Politics of Rescue,* 28; Memorandum, 4 June 1938, Third Meeting of the President's Advisory Committee on Political Refugees, RG 59, Lot File 52D408, Alphabetical Subject File, box 9, NARA.

24. Feis to Bullitt, 18 May 1938, William C. Bullitt Papers, box 29, Feis folder, Sterling Memorial Library, Yale University, New Haven, Connecticut (henceforth Sterling Library).

25. Welles to NE [possibly Near Eastern Affairs at the State Department or someone's initials] and Mr. Alling, 6 June 1938, Sumner Welles Papers, box 46, folder 2, Roosevelt Library.

26. See Patrick O. Cohrs, *The Unfinished Peace after World War I: America, Britain and the Stabilisation of Europe 1919–1932* (New York: Cambridge University Press, 2008), 90–91. Berle saw Welles and himself interested in a conference that might bring about a European settlement. Adolf A. Berle, *Navigating the Rapids, 1918–1971: From the Papers of Adolf A. Berle,* ed. Beatrice Bishop Berle and Travis Beal Jacobs (New York: Harcourt Brace Jovanovich), 169 (entry of 19 March 1938).

27. "Roosevelt's Popularity Loss," *Washington Post,* 8 June 1938, p. X2. Confidential Report on the Investigation of Anti-Semitism in the United States, American Jewish Committee Archives, Blaustein Center for Jewish Research, New York.

28. Barbara McDonald Stewart, *United States Government Policy on Refugees from Nazism, 1933–1940* (New York: Garland Press, 1982), 298–305; Confidential Memo, Inter-governmental Conference on Refugees Held at Evian, 6 July 1938, American Jewish Committee Records, RG 347, EXO-29, box 19, Immigration-Refugees-Evian, YIVO Institute for Jewish Research, New York, New York (henceforth YIVO).

29. " 'Yes, But—' Attitude Prevails at World Refugee Conference," *Washington Post,* 10 July 1938, p. B7; "Concern for Jews Is Held Insincere," *New York Times,* 22 November 1938, p. 4. See generally Solomon Adler-Rudel, "The Evian Conference," *Leo Baeck Institute Year Book* 13 (1968).

30. Stewart, *United States Government Policy,* 298–315, gives more detailed description and analysis. Hull to Taylor, 17 August 1938, copy in Joseph P. Kennedy

Papers, box 171, John F. Kennedy Presidential Library, Boston, Massachusetts (henceforth Kennedy Library).

31. Memorandum of a conversation between Mr. Rublee and Mr. Max Warburg, 31 August 1938, RG 59, Lot File 52D408, Alphabetical Subject File 1938–1941, box 14, Warren memoranda, NARA. James G. McDonald, *Refugees and Rescue: The Diaries and Papers of James G. McDonald, 1935–1945,* ed. Richard Breitman, Barbara McDonald Stewart, and Severin Hochberg (Bloomington: Indiana University Press, 2009), 106–107, 109 n.10. Wise to Brandeis, 24 or 25 August 1938, Louis D. Brandeis Papers, reel 107, LC.

32. Hull to Myron Taylor and George Rublee, 27 August 1938, in *Foreign Relations of the United States* (henceforth *FRUS*), *1938,* vol. 1 (Washington, DC: U.S. Government Printing Office, 1955), 775; Franklin Mott Gunther to Hull, 23 March 1938, Anthony J. Drexel Biddle, Jr. to Hull, 6 April 1938, in *FRUS, 1938,* vol. 2, 681–683 and 653–654; Hull to Taylor and Rublee, 1 September 1938, in Joseph P. Kennedy Papers, box 171, Kennedy Library; Memorandum of a Conversation Between Rublee and Warburg, 31 August 1938, RG 59, Lot File 52D408, Alphabetical Subject File, box 14, Warren Memoranda, NARA.

33. Cohen's trip and purpose described in Stroock to Adler, 30 August 1938, American Jewish Committee Records, RG 347, EXO-29, box 1, folder 4 (Adler), YIVO; and William Lasser, *Benjamin V. Cohen: Architect of the New Deal* (New Haven: Yale University Press, 2002), 204–207. Pell to Jay Pierrepont Moffat, 10 September 1938, vol. 41, Jay Pierrepont Moffat Papers, Houghton Library, Harvard University, Cambridge, Massachusetts. The charge against Taylor was quite unfair. The claim about fascists in the State Department reflected the anti-Semitic attitudes and pro-appeasement views that were present there.

34. In a "very confidential" letter to Cyrus Adler, Morris D. Waldman, executive director of the American Jewish Committee, said that he had spoken to a distinguished American Jew who had returned from Europe a few days after the Czechoslovakian crisis. The name Benjamin V. Cohen is inserted in hand. Cohen said that British prime minister Neville Chamberlain was perhaps the most sinister man in Europe. Frankfurter quoted R. H. Tawney, in defiance of Chamberlain's "surrender" to Hitler at the Munich Conference: "I'd rather die standing than live on my knees." Waldman to Adler, 6 November 1938, Morris D. Waldman Papers, box 1, Adler Folder, American Jewish Archives, Cincinnati, Ohio; Frankfurter to Jacob Billikopf, 15 November 1938, Felix Frankfurter Papers, box 25, Billikopf folder, LC.

35. Roosevelt expressed disgust with the "Cliveden Set" on 4 April 1938. See McDonald, *Refugees and Rescue,* 127. Michael Beschloss, *Kennedy and Roosevelt: The Uneasy Alliance* (New York: Norton, 1980), 163–180. Edward Renehan, *The Kennedys at War, 1937–1945* (New York: Doubleday, 2002), 29. On Kennedy before and during the Munich crisis, see Barbara Reardon Farnham, *Roosevelt and*

the Munich Crisis: A Study in Political Decision-Making (Princeton: Princeton University Press, 1997), esp. 96–97; Ickes, *Secret Diaries,* 2:406, 415.

36. Cummings Diary, 14–15 October 1938, box 235, notebook 8, Homer S. Cummings Papers, Small Special Collections Library, University of Virginia, Charlottesville, Virginia (henceforth Small Library).

37. Arthur Murray to FDR, 15 December 1938, President's Secretary's File, box 38, Murray 1938, Roosevelt Library; On FDR's views and maneuvers generally see Farnham, *Roosevelt and the Munich Crisis,* 137–162 and 179–180.

38. Rublee's draft enclosed in Pell to Ted [Achilles], 30 September 1938, RG 59, Lot File 52D408, Alphabetical Subject File, box 9, Preparation of Rublee Statement on Settlement, October 7, 1938, NARA; Copy of dispatch in Kennedy Papers, box 163; Undated Kennedy Memorandum, Kennedy Papers, box 152, Kennedy Library. Chamberlain to FDR, 7 October 1938, Official File 3186, box 1, Roosevelt Library; Feingold, *The Politics of Rescue,* 39–40; American Embassy, London [Rublee] to Secretary of State, 12 October 1938, Strictly confidential for the Secretary and Under Secretary, RG 59, Lot File 52D408, Alphabetical Subject File, box 7, 2nd Officer's Meeting, 2 December 1938, NARA. Copy of the message (undated) in Kennedy Papers, box 163, Kennedy Library.

39. Rublee to Acheson, undated, Dean Acheson Papers, box 27, Rublee folder, Sterling Library. We are grateful to Garry Clifford for a copy of this document; FDR's Memorandum for the Secretary and Under Secretary of State, 17 October 1938, Official File 20, box 6, Roosevelt Library.

40. Alan E. Steinweis, *Kristallnacht 1938* (Cambridge, MA: Harvard University Press, 2009).

41. *New York Times,* 10–12 November 1938; *Washington Post,* 12 November 1938, p. X6.

42. Armstrong Memorandum, 13 November 1938, Hamilton Fish Armstrong Papers, box 99, Notebooks and Memoranda, Mudd Library.

43. Messersmith to Secretary of State, 14 November 1938, George Messersmith Papers, item 1075, Delaware Library; Donald B. Schewe, ed., *Franklin D. Roosevelt and Foreign Affairs,* Second Series, *January 1937–August 1939* (New York: Clearwater, 1979), vol. 12, press conference of 15 November 1938, 83–86.

44. On Perkins see George Martin, *Madam Secretary, Frances Perkins: A Biography of America's First Woman Cabinet Member* (Boston: Houghton Mifflin, 1976), 57–62; On Messersmith's opposition, Messersmith to Secretary of State, 17 November 1938, RG 59, Visa Division 1910–1939, 150.01/2607 1/2, NARA. On the press conference, 18 November 1938, see Schewe, *Franklin D. Roosevelt,* vol. 12, 132–134. See also "Roosevelt Finds Quotas Limit Aid," *New York Times,* 18 November 1938, p. 2. Arthur D. Morse, *While Six Million Died: A Chronicle of American Apathy* (New York: Random House, 1967), 246, and Kenneth S. Davis, *FDR: Into the Storm, 1937–1940* (New York: Random House, 1995), 367,

discount Perkins's denial that she and FDR discussed the possibility of mortgaging the quota.

45. The Diaries of William Lyon Mackenzie King, 17 November 1938, pp. 7–9, and 18 November 1938, pp. 1–2. www.canadaonline.about.com/gi/o.htm?zi=1/XJ &zTi=1&sdn=canadaonline&cdn=newsissues&tm=25&f=00&su=p649.3.336.ip _&tt=2&bt=0&bts=0&zu=http%3A//www.collectionscanada.gc.ca/databases/king /index-e.html. After meeting with Perkins on November 17, the president invited Taylor to the White House. An acquaintance of Taylor, Canadian prime minister King, in Washington to sign a Canadian-American trade agreement, was staying at the White House. British ambassador Lindsay joined the group, and Welles and Hull attended the latter part of the gathering before dinner.

46. Ibid.

47. Morgenthau Diaries, 16 November 1938, reel 41, LC.

48. Armstrong to Frederick Keppel, 18 November 1938, Hamilton Fish Armstrong Papers, box 77, President's Advisory Committee, Mudd Library; "Quota Change to Let Jews in Held Unlikely: Borah Hits Refugee Plan," *Washington Post,* 20 November 1938, p. 4. Unless otherwise indicated, our polling data is from Roper Center, Public Opinion Archives, iPoll Databank.

49. See McDonald, *Refugees and Rescue,* 151–152. George Warren, who had also been present, backed up McDonald when McDonald related FDR's November 16 statement on this point to a surprised State Department official seven months later. Morris to Hickerson and Dunn, Governmental Participation, 29 June 1939, RG 59, Lot File 52D408, Alphabetical Subject File, box 3, Coordinating Foundation, NARA.

50. Morse, *While Six Million Died,* 343–344. Davis, *FDR: Into the Storm,* 367.

51. FDR told Brandeis about this conversation with British ambassador Lindsay and from Brandeis Cohen passed the account on to Frankfurter. Lasser, *Benjamin V. Cohen,* 206; Cohen to Frankfurter, 21 November 1938, Felix Frankfurter Papers, box 45, reprinted in McDonald, *Refugees and Rescue,* 153–154.

52. Welles to Moffat, EU, 22 December 1938, Welles Papers, box 48, folder 9, Roosevelt Library. The British embassy memo, dated 20 December, is attached.

53. Schewe, *Franklin D. Roosevelt,* vol. 12, 132–134. Cummings Diary, 18 November 1938, Homer S. Cummings Papers, Notebook 8, Small Library.

54. Cohen to Frankfurter, 21 November 1938, Felix Frankfurter Papers, reel 2, LC.

55. Outline of Plan for Refugee Problem, 23 November 1938, Morgenthau Diaries, reel 42, LC.

56. McDonald, *Refugees and Rescue,* 153–154. FDR to Myron Taylor, 23 November 1938, Myron C. Taylor Papers, box 3, folder 1, Roosevelt Library.

57. Roosevelt to Lehman, 13 October 1938, Herbert Lehman Papers, ldpd _leh_0784_0206, Columbia University Rare Book and Manuscript Library, New

York, New York; "Roosevelt is Gratified by Report Palestine Will Take More Refugees," *New York Times,* 24 November 1938, p. 1; Frankfurter to FDR, 25 November 1938, PSF, Frankfurter, box 135, 1938 folder, Roosevelt Library.

58. Bowman to FDR, 25 November 1938, Morgenthau Diaries, reel 42, LC; Memorandum for the Undersecretary of State, 26 November 1938, box 1, Holocaust/Refugee Collection, Roosevelt Library; Feingold, *Politics of Rescue,* 103–108; Ickes Diary (unpublished), 7 January 1939, Ickes Papers, reel 3, LC. Consistent with FDR's statement as recorded by Ickes, Welles to American Embassy London for Taylor and Rublee, 7 December 1938, strictly confidential, RG 59, 840.48 Refugees/1071B and 1077A, M-1284/reel 23, NARA.

59. "Outline of Plan for Refugee Problem," Morgenthau Diaries, 23 November 1938, reel 42, LC; "Miss Perkins Gets Vast Refugee Plan," *New York Times,* 1 December 1938, p. 12.

60. Morgenthau Diaries, 6 December 1938, reel 43, LC.

61. Geist to Messersmith, personal and confidential, 5 December 1938, George Messersmith Papers, item 1087, Delaware Library; On FDR's similar views at a later date see McDonald, *Refugees and Rescue,* 174.

62. Rublee to Acheson, 8 December 1938, Acheson Papers, box 27, Rublee folder, Sterling Library; Wiley to Messersmith, 8 June 1938, George Messersmith Papers, item 1051, Delaware Library.

63. Feingold, *Politics of Rescue,* 50–53.

64. Messersmith to Geist, 20 December 1938, personal and confidential, George Messersmith Papers, item 1099, Delaware Library. Laski's Note of Interview with the American Ambassador, 7 December 1938, American Jewish Committee Records, RG 347, EXO-29, box 15, folder 186 (Germany-Hitlerism), YIVO.

65. Laski's Note of Interview with the American Ambassador, 7 December 1938, American Jewish Committee Records, RG 347, EXO-29, box 15, folder 186 (Germany-Hitlerism), YIVO.

66. White House appointment diaries, 16 December 1938, Roosevelt Library. Undated Notes, Jewish Problem, 1938–September 1939, Joseph P. Kennedy Papers, box 151, Kennedy Library.

67. Welles to NE and Alling, 6 June 1938, Sumner Welles Papers, box 46, folder 2, Roosevelt Library.

68. Radio Address to the *New York Herald Tribune*'s Eighth Forum on Current Problems, quoted in *American Jewish Yearbook,* vol. 41 (1939–1940): 190.

69. Transcript of conversation among Morgenthau, Grossman, Klapp, Loth, Nevins, Klotz, 25 April 1946: Morgenthau: "Well, it was in '38 that Roosevelt, in his own mind, went from deciding he was not going to run to deciding he was going to be the great war President; he had to lead us out of this thing." Henry Morgenthau Jr. Papers, box 391, Roosevelt Library. We are grateful to Garry Clifford for this document.

70. "Roosevelt Awarded the Hebrew Medal," *New York Times,* 24 December 1938, p. 6.

7. RESETTLEMENT IN LATIN AMERICA?

1. For a brief overview see Judith Laikin Elkins, *Jews of the Latin American Republics* (Chapel Hill: University of North Carolina Press, 1980), 76–99; Herbert A. Strauss, "Jewish Emigration from Germany: Nazi Policies and Jewish Responses II," *Leo Baeck Institute Year Book* 26 (1981): 363–382. James G. McDonald, *Advocate for the Doomed: The Diaries and Papers of James G. McDonald, 1932–1935,* ed. Richard Breitman, Barbara McDonald Stewart, and Severin Hochberg (Bloomington: Indiana University Press, 2007), 632–763, 771.

2. FDR to Bowman, 14 October 1938, and Bowman to FDR, 15 October 1938, President's Personal File 5575, Franklin D. Roosevelt Library, Hyde Park, New York (henceforth Roosevelt Library).

3. Neil Smith, *American Empire: Roosevelt's Geographer and the Prelude to Globalization* (Berkeley: University of California Press, 2003), esp. 87, 180, 295.

4. Ibid., esp. 168, 212.

5. Ibid., 20, 40, 168, 212, 229–234, 239, 244–251, 295, 310–316.

6. Ibid., 246–247.

7. Bowman to FDR, 30 October 1938, and FDR to Bowman, 2 November 1938, PPF 5575, Roosevelt Library. Bowman to FDR, 21 November 1938, PSF, box 177, Refugees, Roosevelt Library. Smith, *American Empire,* 295–296.

8. McDonald to Keppel, 21 November 1938, James G. McDonald Papers, D 357 P8 (President's Advisory Committee), Columbia University Rare Book and Manuscript Library, New York, New York.

9. McBride telegram to Bowman, undated, and Morgenthau to FDR, 21 November 1938, PSF, box 177, Refugees, Roosevelt Library.

10. Smith, *American Empire,* 307–308.

11. Bowman Memo, 16 November 1938, Isaiah Bowman Papers, box 2.32, Morgenthau folder, Milton S. Eisenhower Library, Johns Hopkins University, Baltimore, Maryland (henceforth Eisenhower Library). Smith, *American Empire,* 296–297.

12. McDonald to Liebman, 13 December 1938; Bowman to Achilles, 26 December 1938; and Bowman to Liebman, 27 December 1938, Isaiah Bowman Papers, box 2.27, Liebman folder, Eisenhower Library.

13. Copy of undated study and Bowman to FDR, 10 December 1938, PPF 5575, Roosevelt Library. See also Smith, *American Empire,* 296–297.

14. Undated, unsigned draft, Harry Hopkins Papers, box 118, Refugee Problem, Roosevelt Library. Robert Clark, deputy director of the Roosevelt Library, confirmed that Rosenman wrote this unsigned draft.

15. James G. McDonald, *Refugees and Rescue: The Diaries and Papers of James G. McDonald, 1935–1945,* ed. Richard Breitman, Barbara McDonald Stewart, and Severin Hochberg (Bloomington: Indiana University Press, 2009), 148. Theodore Achilles to Welles, 9 December 1938, and Welles to Achilles, 12 December 1938, RG 59, Lot file 52D408, Country File, box 1, British Guiana, National Archives and Records Administration, College Park, Maryland (henceforth NARA).

16. Henry L. Feingold, *The Politics of Rescue* (New York: Holocaust Library, 1970), 109–111. Bressman to Wallace, 16 June 1939, and Klotz to Wallace, 22 June 1939, Morgenthau Papers, box 106, German-Jewish Refugee Situation, Roosevelt Library.

17. FDR Memorandum for E.R., 4 May 1940; FDR Memorandum for Welles, 4 May 1940; Welles to FDR, 6 May 1940: PSF, box 96, Welles January–June 1940, Roosevelt Library.

18. Bowman to Morgenthau, 28 February 1939, Henry Morgenthau Jr. Papers, box 106, German-Jewish Refugee Problem, Roosevelt Library. Welles to Achilles and Briggs, 1 December 1938, Welles Papers, box 48, folder 9, Roosevelt Library. Allen Wells, *Tropical Zion: General Trujillo, FDR, and the Jews of Sosúa* (Durham, NC: Duke University Press, 2009), 41–42.

19. Wells, *Tropical Zion,* 42, 70–71.

20. Chapin to Hinkle, 7 December 1938, RG 59, Lot File 52D408, Country File, box 3, Dominican Republic, vol. 1, NARA.

21. Wells, *Tropical Zion,* 69–76.

22. Ibid., xix (number of settlers). See generally Marion Kaplan, *Dominican Haven: The Jewish Refugee Settlement in Sosúa, 1940–1945* (New York: Museum of Jewish Heritage, 2008); McDonald, *Refugees and Rescue,* 278–291. Max Paul Friedman, "The U.S. State Department and the Failure to Rescue: New Evidence on the Missed Opportunity at Bergen-Belsen," *Holocaust and Genocide Studies* 19, no. 1 (2005): 26–50.

23. On the younger generation's willingness to adopt new careers and lives see Walter Laqueur, *Generation Exodus: The Fate of Younger Jewish Refugees from Nazi Germany* (Hanover, NH: University Press of New England, 2001), 17–22.

24. McDonald, *Advocate for the Doomed,* 573–574; McDonald, *Refugees and Rescue,* 75.

25. McDonald, *Refugees and Rescue,* 264–267. Caldwell to Secretary of State, 10 December 1938, RG 59, 840.48 Refugees/1082, M-1284, reel 23, NARA.

26. McDonald, *Refugees and Rescue,* 268. Liebman to Bowman, 11 January 1940, and Bowman to Liebman, 18 January 1940: Isaiah Bowman Papers, box 2.27, Liebman 1940, Eisenhower Library.

27. McDonald, *Refugees and Rescue,* 264–276.

28. Hyman to Adolfo Hirsch, 29 November 1938, Record Group AR 33/44, Argentina 1938–1940, folder 1069; Pilpel to Borchardt and Glick, 1 June 1939, and

Conia to Borchardt, 24 June 1939, Record Group AR 33/44, Peru 1939–1940, folder 1128; Pilpel File Memo, 20 December 1939, AR 33/44, Chile, file 1080—all in the Joint Distribution Committee Archives, New York, New York.

29. On the 1929 agreement, see Chapter 2. Steinhardt to Secretary of State, 30 March 1938, RG 59, Lot File 52D408, Country File, box 6, Peru, NARA.

30. Brett to Secretary of State, 17 November 1938, RG 59, Lot File 52D408, Country File, box 6, Peru, NARA.

31. Steinhardt to Secretary of State, 24 November 1938, RG 59, Lot File 52D408, Country File, box 6, Peru, NARA.

32. Armour to Secretary of State, 8 December 1938; Edward A. Dow, Chile Suspends Immigration Applications, 4 March 1939; Trueblood to Secretary of State, 7 July 1939; Flexer, Immigration of Jewish Refugees in Chile, 5 and 11 December 1939: RG 59, Lot File 52D408, country file, box 2, Chile, NARA. Strauss, "Jewish Emigration from Germany," 379.

33. "U.S. to Cut Tariff on Cuban Sugar," *New York Times,* 30 November 1938, p. 1; Robert M. Levine, *Tropical Diaspora: The Jewish Experience in Cuba* (Gainesville: University Press of Florida, 1993), 83. "Haven for Exiles in Cuba Pledged," *New York Times,* 19 November 1938, p. 3; "The New Yorker," by Leonard Lyons, *Washington Post,* 19 November 1938, p. 11.

34. Berenson had ties to both the Joint Distribution Committee and the National Coordinating Committee for Aid to Refugees and Emigrants Coming from Germany. Hull and Welles to American Embassy, Argentina, Urgent, Please Present Personally, 22 November 1938: same to ambassadors to Bolivia, Brazil, Chile, Columbia, Cuba, Dominican Republic, Ecuador, Guatemala, Haiti, Honduras, Mexico, Nicaragua, Panama, Peru, Uruguay, and Venezuela, RG 59, 840.48 Refugees/955A, reel 22, NARA.

35. Welles to J. Butler Wright, American Ambassador to Cuba, undated 1938 and Wright to Welles, 19 December 1938, Sumner Welles Papers, box 50, Roosevelt Library; "Cuba Asks Cut in Sugar Duty," *Washington Post,* 18 November 1938, p. X27.

36. Division of Latin-American Affairs Memorandum, 6 April 1939, RG 59, 837.55J Confidential File, NARA, reprinted in John Mendelsohn, ed., *The Holocaust: Selected Documents in 18 Volumes,* vol. 7 (New York: Garland, 1982), 31. Trager to Waldman, 30 August 1939, American Jewish Committee Records, RG 347, EXO-29, box 9 folder 172, YIVO Institute for Jewish Research, New York, New York (henceforth YIVO). Paul Vincent, "The Voyage of the *St. Louis* Revisited," *Holocaust and Genocide Studies* 25, no. 2 (2011): 256–257.

37. "There is the unanimous opinion that a woman, in the first place, and Miss Razovsky especially, could do no good and probably did some harm." Trager to Waldman, 30 August 1939, American Jewish Committee Records, RG 347, EXO-29, box 9, folder 172, YIVO.

38. Diane Afoumado, *Exil Impossible: L'errance des Juifs du paquebot 'St-Louis'* (Paris: Editions L'Harmattan, 2005), 97–98. Vincent, "The Voyage of the *St. Louis* Revisited," 259–262.

39. Benjamin Welles, *Sumner Welles: FDR's Global Strategist* (New York: St. Martin's Press, 1997), 156–181. Vincent, "The Voyage of the *St. Louis* Revisited," 274–275.

40. Transcripts of Morgenthau's phone conversations with Hull, Welles, and Commander Rose, 5–7 June 1939, Holocaust/Refugee Collection, box 1, Roosevelt Library.

41. The origin of the myth can be found in Arthur D. Morse, *While Six Million Died: A Chronicle of American Apathy* (New York: Random House, 1968), 280; it also appears in Kenneth S. Davis, *FDR: Into the Storm, 1937–1940* (New York: Random House, 1995), 371; Richard Breitman and Alan M. Kraut, *American Refugee Policy and European Jewry, 1933–1945* (Bloomington: Indiana University Press, 1987), 71. Vincent, "The Voyage of the *St. Louis* Revisited," 276, also argues that the admission of the passengers to the United States would have had high political cost.

42. Coert de Bois Memorandum for the Files, 7 June 1939, reprinted in Mendelsohn, *The Holocaust,* vol. 7, doc. no. 3, 85–86. Memorandum of Conversation between Ambassador Wright and Miss Clarkson, 8 June 1939, Holocaust/Refugee Collection, box 1, Roosevelt Library.

43. Vincent, "The Voyage of the *St. Louis* Revisited," 270–273.

44. James N. Rosenberg and Joseph C. Hyman to Morgenthau, 21 June 1939, Holocaust Refugees and the FDR White House, microfilm, reel 7 (Bethesda, MD: University Publications of America, 2006).

45. Berenson to Wise, 14 June 1939, Stephen S. Wise Papers, reel 74-59, American Jewish Historical Society, New York, New York.

46. Sarah A. Ogilvie and Scott Miller, *Refuge Denied: The* St. Louis *Passengers and the Holocaust* (Madison: University of Wisconsin Press, 2006), 174.

47. Levine, *Tropical Diaspora,* 150–165.

48. Harriet Sara Lesser, "A History of the Jewish Community of Mexico City, 1912–1970" (PhD diss., Jewish Theological Seminary and Columbia University, 1972), 18–22.

49. Jeffrey Lesser, *Welcoming the Undesirables: Brazil and the Jewish Question* (Berkeley: University of California Press, 1995), 89–104, 110–116. Scotten to Welles, personal and confidential, 10 March 1939, RG 59, Lot File 52D408, subject file, box 5, immigration statistics, NARA.

50. Lesser, *Welcoming the Undesirables,* 119–122.

51. Haim Avni, *Argentina and the Jews: A History of Jewish Immigration* (Tuscaloosa: University of Alabama Press, 1991), 128–174. Armour to Secretary of State, 22 August 1939, RG 59, Lot File 52D408, country files, box 1, Argentina, NARA.

52. Welles to FDR, 22 May 1939, OF 338, Roosevelt Library. Morgenthau Presidential Diaries, 19 June 1939, microfiche 2, Roosevelt Library. The president held a luncheon for the president-elect of Paraguay on 1 June.

53. Strauss, "Jewish Emigration from Germany," 363, 367, 374–378.

54. Ibid., 363, 367, 374–378, comparison between with Palestine and Latin America at 363.

8. TOWARD WAR

1. Robert Dallek, *Franklin D. Roosevelt and American Foreign Policy, 1932–1945* (New York: Oxford University Press, 1979), 183.

2. *JTA Weekly News Digest*, 11 August 1939, copy in Joseph Chamberlain Papers, RG 278, folder 100, reel 4, YIVO Institute for Jewish Research, New York, New York (henceforth YIVO).

3. Memorandum of meeting with Mussolini, enclosed with Phillips to FDR, 5 January 1939, RG 59, 840.48 Refugees/1306, M-1240, reel 24, National Archives and Records Administration, College Park, Maryland (henceforth NARA).

4. Hitler's Reichstag speech of 30 January 1939, from *The Speeches of Adolf Hitler, April 1922–August 1939*, vol. 1, ed. Norman H. Baynes (New York: Howard Fertig, 1969), 736–741. Many observers so desperately hoped to avoid war that they accepted at face value Hitler's declarations that he sought peace and mutually beneficial trade. Wesley K. Wark, *The Ultimate Enemy: British Intelligence and Nazi Germany, 1933–1939* (Ithaca, NY: Cornell University Press, 1985), 218.

5. Castle Diary, 25 August 1939, MS Am 2012, Houghton Library, Harvard University, Cambridge, Massachusetts (henceforth Houghton Library).

6. Gaffney to Tully, 16 January 1939, and FDR to Gaffney, 20 January 1939, Holocaust and Refugee Collection, box 1, Franklin D. Roosevelt Library, Hyde Park, New York (henceforth Roosevelt Library).

7. Letts de Espil Diary, 27 January 1939, Library of Congress, Washington, D.C. (henceforth LC).

8. On Ickes see Ickes Diary, 12 February 1939, reel 3: Propaganda, attached to Ickes to Spiro, 14 March 1939, Harold Ickes Papers, box 205, LC.

9. Kenneth S. Davis, *FDR: Into the Storm, 1937–1940* (New York: Random House, 1995), 390–391. Joseph Lash's biographical introduction to Lash, ed., *From the Diaries of Felix Frankfurter: With a Biographical Essay and Notes* (New York: W. W. Norton, 1975), 64. Welles to Roosevelt, 17 October 1938, Sumner Welles Papers, box 150, folder 3, Roosevelt Library; Cohen to Jacob Billikopf, 25 January 1939, Jacob Billikopf Papers, box 4, American Jewish Archives, Cincinnati, Ohio (henceforth AJA); Frankfurter to Billikopf, Felix Frankfurter Papers, reel 14, LC.

10. Note by Samuel Rosenman, Samuel Rosenman Papers, box 1, Frankfurter folder, Roosevelt Library; Lash, *From the Diaries of Felix Frankfurter,* 65–66. If Frankfurter had been thirteen at time of entry, as McCarran claimed, then the naturalization of his parents five years later would not have covered him too.

11. The 8 percent is derived from 10 percent of the 79 percent who opposed but felt sympathetic toward a widespread campaign against the Jews.

12. "Warns on Measures to Admit Refugees; Celler Says Opposition in South and West Is Too Strong," *New York Times,* 27 February 1939, p. 4.

13. Judith Tydor Baumel, *Unfulfilled Promise: Rescue and Resettlement of Jewish Refugee Children in the United States, 1934–1945* (Juneau, AK: Denali Press, 1990).

14. Louise London, *Whitehall and the Jews 1933–1948* (Cambridge: Cambridge University Press, 2000), 98–109. Unpublished ms. by Paul Vincent, Keene State University, to whom we are grateful. James G. McDonald, *Refugees and Rescue: The Diaries and Papers of James G. McDonald, 1935–1945,* ed. Richard Breitman, Barbara McDonald Stewart, and Severin Hochberg (Bloomington: Indiana University Press, 2009), 157–158.

15. On Lubin and Rosenwald, we drew from unpublished ms. by Paul Vincent. On Perkins and Alaska, Perkins to Messersmith, 3 December 1938, RG 174, Frances Perkins, entry 20, box 97, folder State Department 1938, NARA. Welles quote in Welles memorandum, 10 December 1938 attached to Messersmith to Welles, 15 December 1938, RG 59, entry 702, 150.01/2617 1/2, NARA.

16. Excerpt of letter from Eleanor Roosevelt to Justine Wise Polier, 4 January 1939, Polier Oral History, Holocaust/Refugee Collection, box 11, Roosevelt Library. Polier was the daughter of Rabbi Stephen S. Wise.

17. Kenworthy's narrative summary, 15 January 1939, cited and discussed by Paul Vincent in unpublished ms. See also David S. Wyman, *Paper Walls: America and the Refugee Crisis, 1938–1941* (Amherst: University of Massachusetts Press, 1968), 76.

18. Messersmith to Secretary and Undersecretary, Moffat, and Achilles, 23 January 1939, RG 59, entry 702, 150.01 Bills/99, NARA.

19. Ibid.; Messersmith to Welles, 25 January 1939, Sumner Welles Papers, box 54, folder 08 (Marvin McIntyre 1939), Roosevelt Library; Wyman, *Paper Walls,* 76.

20. Telegrams of 22 February 1939, OF 200, Roosevelt Library, cited by Wyman, *Paper Walls,* 97. "First Lady Backs Move to Open U.S. to 20,000 Exiles," *Washington Post,* 14 February 1939, p. 1. On FDR and the heritage of the Old Testament see www.presidency.ucsb.edu/ws/index.php?pid=15721.

21. Among other Protestant luminaries, Samuel McCrea Cavert, executive secretary of the Federal Council of Churches; Canon Anson Phelps Stokes of the Washington Episcopal Cathedral; and Albert Wentworth, president of the Chicago Theological Seminary, endorsed the bill. Wyman, *Paper Walls,* 78–79. "Aid to

Child Exiles in U.S. Is Mapped," *New York Times,* 31 March 1939, p. 4; Barbara McDonald Stewart, *United States Government Policy toward Refugees from Nazism, 1933–1940* (New York: Garland Press, 1982), 533–536. "Hoover Backs Bill to Waive Quota Act for Reich Children," *New York Times,* 23 April 1939, p. 1; "Landon Backs Bill to Admit Child Exiles," *Washington Post,* 25 April 1939, p. 1.

22. Billikopf to Ben M. Seligman, 18 March 1939, Jacob Billikopf Papers, box 8, AJA. Castle Diary, 26 May 1939, MS Am 2012, Houghton Library; Stewart, *United States Government Policy,* 506–514.

23. Richard Gutstadt to Lessing Rosenwald, 1 May 1939; General Robert E. Wood to Moseley, 11 May 1939; Wood to Rosenwald, 11 May 1939; Gutstadt to Wellens, 29 May 1939—all in Lessing Rosenwald Papers, box 2, LC. On Moseley's anti-Semitism see Joseph W. Bendersky, *The Jewish Threat: Anti-Semitic Policies of the U.S. Army* (New York: Basic Books, 2000), 249–258. On the other department stores see Theodore S. Hamerow, *Why We Watched: Europe, America, and the Holocaust* (New York: Norton, 2008), 214.

24. Memorandum of Conversation, April 13, 1939, and Messersmith to Moffat, 14 April 1939, RG 59, entry 702, 150.01 Bills/102 and 103, NARA. On Ready see Wyman, *Paper Walls,* 80–81.

25. On private polls see Wyman, *Paper Walls,* 82–84. Taft to Carl E. Pritz, 10 May 1939, copy in Jacob Billikopf Papers, box 3, folder 3, AJA; On the House see Stewart, *United States Government Policy,* 537–539, and Wyman, *Paper Walls,* 90–91.

26. Wyman, *Paper Walls,* 97. Stewart, *United States Government Policy,* 536–542. Warren to Messersmith, 10 August 1939, RG 59, entry 702, 150.01 Bills/151, NARA.

27. The most detailed and personal account is in Geist to Messersmith, 22 January 1939, personal and confidential, George Messersmith Papers, item 1136, University of Delaware Library, Newark, Delaware (henceforth Delaware Library).

28. Ibid. Rublee to Acheson, 24 January 1939, Dean Acheson Papers, box 27, Rublee folder, Sterling Memorial Library, Yale University, New Haven, Connecticut. On Nazi rigidity, see Martin Dean, *Robbing the Jews: The Confiscation of Jewish Property in the Holocaust, 1933–1945* (New York: Cambridge University Press. 2008), 128–129.

29. Robert Pell's analysis of the agreement, undated memo entitled Intergovernmental Committee, RG 59, 840.48 Refugees/2122, NARA.

30. Minutes of the Twentieth Meeting of the President's Advisory Committee on Political Refugees, 24 February 1939, Hamilton Fish Armstrong Papers, box 27, PACPR January–March 1939, Seeley G. Mudd Manuscript Library, Princeton University, Princeton, New Jersey. Wise to Harold Fields, 16 March 1939, Stephen S. Wise Papers, reel 74-44, American Jewish Historical Society, New York, New York (henceforth AJHS). Messersmith to Geist, 16 February 1939, George Messer-

smith Papers, item 1158, Delaware Library. Emerson was a poor choice. See London, *Whitehall,* 152–160.

31. Pell to Moffat, 8 March 1939, and Moffat to Pell, 30 March 1939, RG 59, Lot File 52D408, Alphabetical Subject File, box 7, Wohlthat-Berlin, NARA. Pell's long letter went to Welles, who sent a copy to FDR. Geist to Messersmith, confidential, 4 April 1939, George Messersmith Papers, item 1139, Delaware Library. Geist stated all this to a correspondent for the Jewish Telegraphic Agency, who published it in garbled form. Geist privately gave Messersmith the correct version. See also the knowledgeable account in S. Adler-Rudel to Borchardt, 21 February 1939, Joseph Chamberlain Papers, RG 278, folder 98, reel 4, YIVO.

32. "Rublee Is Hopeful," *New York Times,* 10 March 1939, p. 5; "President Gets Rublee Report on Refugees," *Washington Post,* 10 March 1939, p. 4.

33. Geist to Messersmith, confidential, 4 April 1939, George Messersmith Papers, item 1139, Delaware Library.

34. Pell to Messersmith and Welles, 23 February 1939, RG 59, Lot File 52D408, Alphabetical Subject File, box 9, President's Advisory Committee—Minutes, NARA. Adler-Rudel to Borchardt, 21 February 1939, Joseph Chamberlain Papers, RG 278, folder 98, reel 4, YIVO.

35. McDonald, *Refugees and Rescue,* 169–170. Robert Szold to Brandeis, 19 April 1939, Robert Szold Papers, PEF IX/14, Central Zionist Archive, Jerusalem. Wise's undated handwritten notes of this meeting in Stephen S. Wise Papers, reel 74-46, AJHS.

36. Welles to FDR, 29 April 1939, Official File 3186, Political Refugees, January–June 1939, Roosevelt Library.

37. Judge Samuel Rosenman, Judge Joseph Proskauer, Lewis Straus, Henry Ittleson, Sol Stroock, Paul Baerwald, Nathan Straus Jr., and Rabbi Stephen Wise were the Jewish representatives at the White House. Welles to LeHand, 29 April 1939; press release of 4 May 1939; both in Official File 3186, box 2, Political Refugees January–June 1939, Roosevelt Library; Moffat Journal, 4 May 1939, MS Am 1407, Houghton Library.

38. Quote from Moffat Journal, 4 May 1939, MS Am 1407, Houghton Library. On the warnings from the embassy, see Geist to Messersmith, confidential, 4 April 1939, George Messersmith Papers, item 1139, Delaware Library. Luncheon Meeting at the Office of Myron C. Taylor, 18 May 1939, AR/33/44, #255, Joint Distribution Committee Archives, New York, New York.

39. McDonald, *Refugees and Rescue,* 178. Quote from Moffat Journal, 4 May 1939, Call number MS Am 1407, Houghton Library. Welles to FDR, 20 May 1939, OF 3186, box 2, Political Refugees, January–June 1939, Roosevelt Library. Welles to Taylor, 22 June 1939, Sumner Welles Papers, box 56, folder 07 (Taylor), Roosevelt Library.

40. List of directors in Morris to Berle, 22 August 1939, RG 59, Lot File 52D408, Alphabetical Subject File, box 3, Coordinating Foundation, NARA.

41. McDonald, *Refugees and Rescue,* 179–180.

42. Waldman to Stroock, 18 March 1940, American Jewish Committee Records, RG 347, EXO-29, box 49, folder World Jewish Congress 4, YIVO.

43. McDonald, *Refugees and Rescue,* 185.

44. Ibid.

45. Strauss to Hoover, 22 August 1939, Strauss folder, Herbert Hoover Papers, Post-Presidential, Herbert Hoover Presidential Library, West Branch, Iowa; Pell to Welles, 5 September 1939, and Welles and Hull to American Embassy London, 6 September 1939, RG 59, 840.48 Refugees/1843 and 1832 respectively, M-1284, reel 26, NARA; Kennedy to Secretary of State, 25 and 29 September 1939, RG 59, 840.48 Refugees/1865 and 1874 respectively, M-1284, reel 26, NARA.

46. FDR to Undersecretary of State, 4 December 1939, RG 59, Lot File 52D408, Alphabetical Subject File, box 6, Jewish Refugees, NARA. FDR to Welles, 17 October 1939, copy Harry Hopkins Papers, box 118, Refugee Problems folder, Roosevelt Library.

47. On Perkins and Alaska see Perkins to Messersmith, 3 December 1938, RG 174, Frances Perkins, entry 20, box 98, State Department 1938, NARA. Confidential Memorandum of Meeting in the Office of Dr. Isador Lubin, 14 January 1939, Joseph Chamberlain Papers, RG 278, folder 80, reel 4, YIVO.

48. Flournoy to Secretary of State, Hackworth, and Warren, 7 February 1941, RG 59, entry 702, 150.01/Bills 287, NARA.

49. Henry L. Feingold, *The Politics of Rescue* (New York: Holocaust Library, 1970), 94–97. Harold L. Ickes, *The Secret Diary of Harold L. Ickes,* vol. 3, *The Lowering Clouds, 1939–1941* (New York: Simon and Schuster, 1954), 56–57.

50. Billikopf to Hexter, 18 September 1939, Jacob Billikopf Papers, box 11, AJA; Emergency Committee for Zionist Affairs, undated memo, October 1939, Louis Lipsky Papers, box 6, AJHS.

51. Wyman, *Paper Walls,* 99–112. Tom Kizzia, "Sanctuary Alaska, the Nazis, and the Jews: The Forgotten Story of Alaska's Own Confrontation with the Holocaust," *Anchorage Daily News,* four-part series, 16–19 May 1999.

9. TIGHTENED SECURITY

1. Francis MacDonnell, *Insidious Foes: The Axis Fifth Column & the American Home Front* (New York: Oxford, 1995), 23–28, quotation at p. 23.

2. Ibid., 49–65.

3. "International Spy Systems Increase," *Washington Post,* 26 June 1938, p. B2, and "German Spy Film Brings Nazi Threat," *Washington Post,* 19 December 1938, p. X4.

4. MacDonnell, *Insidious Foes,* 137, 167; "Roosevelt Bolsters U.S. Defense," *Washington Post,* 9 September 1939, p. 1; "Spies and Spy Mania," *New York Times,* 24 September 1939, p. 76.

5. Houghteling Memorandum for the President, 5 January 1940, Official File 133; FDR's Memorandum for the Secretary of Labor, 27 January 1940, Official File 2030, Franklin D. Roosevelt Library, Hyde Park, New York (henceforth Roosevelt Library). In July, Congress passed and the President signed the Smith Act, requiring the registration and fingerprinting of all aliens. It also imposed fines or prison sentences for speech or writing that could subvert the armed forces.

6. Congressman Albert Gore to FDR, 6 February 1940, and FDR to Watson, 9 February 1940, President's Personal File 15-D, Roosevelt Library.

7. War Refugees and the U.S. Immigration Law," *Baltimore Sun,* 15 June 1940, p. 12; "Sharp Limit Is Set on Entry of Aliens," *New York Times,* 15 June 1940, p. 9; Stephen R. Alton, "Loyal Lieutenant, Able Advocate: The Role of Robert H. Jackson in Franklin D. Roosevelt's Battle With the Supreme Court," *William & Mary Bill of Rights Journal* 5 (1997): 527–618.

8. FDR to Murray, 4 March 1940, PSF Diplomatic, box 38, Arthur Murray, Roosevelt Library. Gerhard L. Weinberg, *A World at Arms: A Global History of World War II* (New York: Cambridge University Press, 2005), 121.

9. MacDonnell, *Insidious Foes,* 113–121. On Bullitt's charges of Jewish agents for the Nazis see Ted Morgan, *FDR: A Biography* (New York: Simon and Schuster, 1986), 498–499. Despite views tinged with anti-Semitism, Bullitt was among the targets of American anti-Semites who listed him among FDR's Jewish advisers. His mother's maiden name was Horwitz, and her family was once Jewish.

10. MacDonnell, *Insidious Foes,* 100, 167–168. On British internment of refugees see Louise London, *Whitehall and the Jews, 1933–1948* (Cambridge: Cambridge University Press, 2000), 169–171. On the relationship between British Security Coordination and the FBI see H. Montgomery Hyde, *Room 3603: The Story of the British Intelligence Center in New York during World War II* (New York: Farrar Straus and Giroux, 1963), 52.

11. Breckinridge Long Diary, 8 May 1940, Breckinridge Long Papers, box 5, Library of Congress, Washington, D.C. (henceforth LC). There is a similar, follow-up entry on 10 May that again praises Warren as efficient and competent and raised the prospect of new legislation to stem the influx of "undesirable persons whose purpose is contrary to the best interests of the United States."

12. Confidential, 29 November 1938, accompanied by a note from FDR to Welles, 13 December 1938: "to read and return. This is only for your eyes. FDR." Cohen's name does not appear on this memo, but no one else could have written it. Sumner Welles Papers, box 150, folder 05 (FDR: December 1938), Roosevelt Library.

13. Berle to Hull and Welles, 5 July 1940, copy in Adolf A. Berle Papers, box 57, State Department Correspondence, Hull, Roosevelt Library. Kirk to Secretary of State, 16 February 1940; Berle memorandum to EU, 17 February 1940; Berle to Secretary of State, 23 February 1940: RG 59, 862.4016/2172 and 2162 1/2,

National Archives and Records Administration, College Park, Maryland (henceforth NARA). Long to EU, 23 February 1940, Breckinridge Long Papers, box 195, LC. Berle to Biddle, 6 June 1940, Adolf A. Berle Papers, box 29, Biddle folder, Roosevelt Library.

14. MacDonnell, *Insidious Foes,* 121.

15. Berle Diary, 23 April and 8 May 1940, Adolf A. Berle Papers, box 211, Roosevelt Library. The cases he cited involved leftists: Bertolt Brecht and Spanish refugees who allegedly supported the Soviet invasion of Finland had nothing to do with Nazi Germany or Jews under Nazi control. But Berle started worrying about refugees in general, and eventually he got around to Jewish refugees. MacDonnell, *Insidious Foes,* 169. Joseph W. Bendersky, *The Jewish Threat: Anti-Semitic Policies of the U.S. Army* (New York: Basic Books, 2000), 281–282.

16. Long Diary, 10 May 1940, Breckinridge Long Papers, box 5, LC. Strictly Confidential Memo attached to Messersmith to Welles, May 22, 1940, George Messersmith Papers, items 1360 and 1361, University of Delaware Library, Newark, Delaware. See also Messersmith to Long, 31 May 1940, Breckinridge Long Papers, Correspondence: State Department 1917–1944, box 199, Messersmith 1940 folder, LC. Messersmith to Secretary of State, 21 June 1940, "Confidential" Letter, Subject: "With reference to the alleged pro-German attitude on the part of Jewish refugees in Habana awaiting an opportunity to proceed to the United States on immigration visas." RG 59, entry 702, 150.626 J/798, NARA. Harold L. Ickes, *The Secret Diary of Harold L. Ickes,* vol. 3, *The Lowering Clouds, 1939–1941* (New York: Simon and Schuster, 1954), 197.

17. Morgan, *FDR,* 524. One biographer of J. Edgar Hoover called this intelligence a triumph of quantity over quality. Richard Gid Powers, *Secrecy and Power: The Life of J. Edgar Hoover* (New York; Free Press, 1987), 238. FDR's memo reprinted in Francis Biddle, *In Brief Authority: From the Years with Roosevelt to the Nürnberg Trial* (New York: Doubleday, 1962), 167.

18. *Complete Presidential Press Conferences of Franklin D. Roosevelt,* vols. 13–14 (New York: Da Capo Press, 1972), 495–496, June 5, 1940.

19. Castle Diary, 29 August 1940, MS Am 2012, Houghton Library, Harvard University, Cambridge, Massachusetts (henceforth Houghton Library).

20. State Department Circular Telegram to Consuls, 5 June 1940, Quoted by Pell to Secretary of State, 6 September 1940, RG 59, 840.48 Refugees/2599; State Department Circulars to Consuls, 5 and 29 June 1940, described in Steinhardt to Secretary of State, 2 October 1940, RG 59, 811.111 Refugees/397, NARA.

21. Long to Berle and Dunn (then political adviser), 26 June 1940, Breckinridge Long Papers, box 211, Visa Division file, LC. Long Diary, 29 June 1940, box 5, LC, quoted by Wyman, *Paper Walls,* 174.

22. Wyman, *Paper Walls,* 117–120. Judith Tydor Baumel, *Unfulfilled Promise: Rescue and Resettlement of Jewish Refugee Children in the United States 1934–1945*

(Juneau, AK: Denali Press, 1990), 31–33. Coulter to George Nickel, 20 September 1940; Coulter Memo for the Files, 10 October 1940: RG 59, Visa Correspondence, 1940–1945, 811.111 Refugee Children/1 and 8, NARA; Dorsz, Consulate Stuttgart to Secretary of State, 16 April 1941, RG 59, Visa Correspondence 1940–1945, 811.111 Refugee Children/40, NARA.

23. Executive order 8430 issued on 5 June allowed the Secretary of State to waive passport and visa requirements for nonimmigrants in emergencies. On the mid-1940 efforts of the Presidential Advisory Committee on Political Refugees see James G. McDonald, *Refugees and Rescue: The Diaries and Papers of James G. McDonald, 1935–1945,* ed. Richard Breitman, Barbara McDonald Stewart, and Severin Hochberg (Bloomington: Indiana University Press, 2009), 200–216; 38th Meeting of the President's Advisory Committee, 18 July 1940; Armstrong to Watson, 3 July 1940, both in Hamilton Fish Armstrong Papers, box 78, PACPR July–December 1940 folder, Seeley G. Mudd Manuscript Library, Princeton University, Princeton, New Jersey.

24. Laurel Leff, *Buried by the Times: The Holocaust and America's Most Important Newspaper* (New York: Cambridge University Press, 2006), 49, had access to the memo Nussbaum wrote in September 1940, which is in private hands. On the luncheon see Nussbaum oral history, 30 July 1958, 01/222 (Collection Ball-Kaduri), Yad Vashem, Jerusalem. We are grateful to the late David Bankier for a copy of this document.

25. See *Refugees and Rescue,* 208–210.

26. Pell to Secretary of State, 6 September 1940, RG 59, 840.48 Refugees/2599, NARA.

27. Neumayer to Rogers, 26 September 1940, Refugee Service 1940, Letters from Austria, American Friends Service Committee Archive, Philadelphia, Pennsylvania. Librarian of Congress Archibald MacLeish asked Frankfurter whether someone should ask Warren to confirm or deny he made such statements. MacLeish to Frankfurter, 12 November 1940, Archibald MacLeish Papers, box 8, LC.

28. Allan J. Lichtman, *White Protestant Nation: The Rise of the American Conservative Movement* (New York: Grove/Atlantic, 2008), 97–98.

29. Roosevelt to Taylor, 13 February 1940, Holocaust/Refugee Papers, box 1, Roosevelt Library. "Kennedy Backs FDR: Denies Any War Promises," *Chicago Tribune,* 30 October 1940, p. 4.

30. Hilles to Henry W. Marsh, 22 October 1940, Charles Hilles Papers, box 130, Sterling Memorial Library, Yale University, New Haven, Connecticut (henceforth Sterling Library).

31. George Ellis to Nicholas Butler, 17 October 1940, Charles Hilles Papers, box 129, Sterling Library; Charles Peters, *Five Days in Philadelphia: The Amazing "We Want Willkie" Convention and How It Freed FDR to Save the Western World* (Washington, DC: Public Affairs, 2005).

32. Elizabeth Dilling, "Round Table Letter," 22 October 1940, *National Republic* Collection, reel 144, Hoover Institution for War, Revolution, and Peace, Palo Alto, California; "Clerics Charge Dictator Plot," *Chicago Tribune,* 28 May 1940, p. 12.

33. Roosevelt to Stimson, 21 May 1940, PSF, War Department, box 106, Stimson 1940, Roosevelt Library; 20 May 1940, Morgenthau Presidential Diaries, reel 1, frame 0562, both quoted by MacDonnell, *Insidious Foes,* 139. Castle Diary, 3 January 1940, MS Am 2012, Houghton Library.

34. Long's Memorandum of Conversation, 24 September RG 59, 811.111 W.R./349, NARA. McDonald, *Refugees and Rescue,* 215–217. Also, Steinhardt to Loy Henderson, 5 October 1940, Loy Henderson Papers, box 1, LC.

35. Wise to Otto Nathan, 17 September 1940, and Wise to Cohen, 15 June 1939, Stephen S. Wise Papers, reels 74-52 and 74-47, American Jewish Historical Society, New York, New York (henceforth AJHS).

36. Long to FDR, 3 October 1940, RG 59, 811.111 Refugees/397, NARA. 30 October 1940, Minutes of the 41st meeting of the President's Advisory Committee, James G. McDonald Papers, D367 (PACPR), P64, Columbia University Rare Book and Manuscript Library, New York, New York.

37. See various documents excerpted in McDonald, *Refugees and Rescue,* 217–225.

38. FDR to the Secretary of the Interior, 18 December 1940, Official File 3186, Roosevelt Library. See the general treatment in Wyman, *Paper Walls,* 112–115.

39. Berle to FDR, 13 November 1940, Adolf A. Berle Papers, box 67, FDR, July–December 1940, Roosevelt Library. Although this written message was not sent, Welles transmitted Berle's view to FDR. Journalist Pat Frank wrote that army and navy intelligence had placed a bee in FDR's ear regarding Nazi placement of spies among Jewish refugees. Pat Frank confidential memo, 5 December 1940, American Jewish Committee Records, RG 347, EXO-29, box 41, State Department 1937–40 folder, YIVO Institute for Jewish Research, New York, New York (henceforth YIVO). Ickes, *Secret Diary of Harold L. Ickes,* 3:21, December 1940, 398–399. State Department regulations prohibited giving a visitor's visa to anyone who had on file an application for an immigration visa. The State Department view, which had held up action, was that this required new legislation. President Roosevelt did consult the attorney general—see Margold to Ickes, 26 December 1940, and FDR Memorandum, 27 December 1940, FDRL, Official File 3186, Roosevelt Library. Nonetheless, the plan remained blocked.

40. Blake to Secretary of State, 27 February 1941, RG 59, 811.111 Refugees/1048, NARA; Berle to Hull, Welles, and Long, 28 February 1941, RG 59, 811.111 Refugees/1883, NARA. Berle Diary, 5 March 1941, Adolf A. Berle Papers, box 211, Roosevelt Library. "U.S. Sifting Immigrants for Nazi Spies," *Washington Post,* 20 July 1941, p. 9.

41. Pell to Taylor, 7 March 1941, Myron C. Taylor Papers, box 5, folder Intergovernmental Committee on Political Refugees, Correspondence, October 1939–1941, Roosevelt Library.

42. Visas issued at German issuing offices by months from 1 July 1940 to 31 March 1941, United States Holocaust Memorial Museum, Washington, DC, 1994.A.0342, reel 48.

43. Long to Welles, 17 March 1941, and Welles to Long, 20 March 1941, RG 59, 811.111 W.R./356, NARA. Roosevelt to Hull, 21 April 1941, Official File 20, Holocaust/Refugee Collection, box 1, Roosevelt Library.

44. Eleanor Roosevelt to McDonald, 2 March 1941, Eleanor Roosevelt Papers, box 1612, Roosevelt Library.

45. Leahy to Welles, 24 May 1941 and Welles to Eleanor Roosevelt, 26 May 1941, personal, Sumner Welles Papers, box 72, folder 11 (ER), Roosevelt Library.

46. Copy in Biddle to Secretary of State, 21 June 1941, RG 59, 811.111 W.R./391, NARA. "Congress Sets Up Checks on Aliens," *New York Times,* 21 June 1941, p. 1.

47. Flournoy Memorandum, 2 May 1941, RG 59, 811.111 Refugees/1507, NARA; Circular Telegram, 5 June 1941; Circular Telegram, 17 June 1941, RG 59, 811.111 W.R./359 1/2 and 408, NARA.

48. "U.S. Bars Refugees with Kin in Reich," *New York Times,* 18 June 1941," p. 1. "U.S. Bars Refugees Nazis Can Coerce," *Washington Post,* 19 June 1941, p. 1. "Refugee Visas," *Washington Post,* 25 June 1941, p. 6. "U.S. Sifting Immigrants for Nazi Spies," *Washington Post,* 20 July 1941, p. 9.

49. Biddle to Welles, 20 June 1941, RG 59, 811.111 W.R./359 1 /2, NARA.

50. Long to Welles, 25 June 1941, Breckinridge Long Papers, box 211, Visa Division folder, LC. Biddle to Welles, 18 July 1941, 811.111 W.R./364 1/2; handwritten note on draft letter from Hull to FDR, RG 59, 811.111. W.R./366A, NARA.

51. See McDonald, *Refugees and Rescue,* 254–258, for more details.

52. See ibid., 260–263, for more details.

53. American Jewish Committee Archives, Blaustein Center for Jewish Research.

54. Biddle, *In Brief Authority,* 165–169. The Justice Department paid for its stance. Months later, FDR's administrative assistant and political adviser James H. Rowe Jr. wrote confidentially to his friend Biddle that for months the public unfortunately had regarded Biddle and the Justice Department as "civil liberties boys" and "softies." Rowe thought that the verdict of history would ultimately sustain Justice's positions. In the meantime, however, other agencies critical of Justice were undermining it with the president. Justice got its reputation, Rowe noted, by insisting that that most aliens were loyal. Instead, it needed to emphasize how tough it was on those few who were disloyal. Rowe to Biddle, 23 March 1942, Francis Biddle Papers, box 2, propaganda domestic folder, Roosevelt Library.

55. Transcript of Goldmann's speech in Sao Paolo, 5 August 1941, RG 347, EXO-29, box 49, World Jewish Congress 4 folder, YIVO.

56. Robert Dallek, *Franklin D. Roosevelt and American Foreign Policy, 1932–1945* (New York: Oxford University Press, 1979), 246–250. "President Moves," *New York Times,* 31 October 1940, p. 1.

57. Roosevelt to Rosenman, 13 November 1940, Samuel Rosenman Papers, box 3, FDR folder, Roosevelt Library. Ickes to Wise, 6 November 1940, Stephen S. Wise Papers, reel 74-52, AJHS. "De Gaulle Assails Anti-Jewish Laws," *New York Times,* 14 November 1940, p. 10.

58. Alfred L. Castle, *Diplomatic Realism: William R. Castle, Jr. and American Foreign Policy, 1919–1953* (Honolulu: Samuel and Mary Castle Foundation, 1998), 106–118. "Leaders Warn of Dangers in Roosevelt Talk," *Chicago Tribune,* 7 January 1941, p. 2. James T. Patterson, *Mr. Republican: A Biography of Robert A. Taft* (Boston: Houghton Mifflin, 1972), 288. See generally Warren F. Kimball, *The Most Unsordid Act: Lend-Lease, 1939–1941* (Baltimore, MD: Johns Hopkins University Press, 1969).

59. F. H. Hinsley, C. F. G. Ransom, R. C. Knight, and E. E. Thomas, *British Intelligence in the Second World War,* vol. 2 (Cambridge: Cambridge University Press, 1981), 67. David E. Murphy, *What Stalin Knew: The Enigma of Barbarossa* (New Haven: Yale University Press, 2005), esp. 185–189.

60. Weinberg, *A World at Arms,* 243–244. Detailed account in Kenneth S. Davis, *FDR: The War President, 1940–1943: A History* (New York: Random House, 2000), 219–247.

61. Jon Meacham, *Franklin and Winston: An Intimate Portrait of an Epic Friendship* (New York: Random House, 2003), 104–105.

10. WARTIME AMERICA

1. Saul Friedländer, *Nazi Germany and the Jews: The Years of Extermination* (New York: HarperCollins, 2007), 205; Jeffrey Herf, "Narratives of Totalitarianism: Nazism's Anti-Semitic Propaganda during World War II and the Holocaust," *Telos* 135 (Summer 2006): 43–47. Klaus P. Fischer, *Hitler and America* (Philadelphia: University of Pennsylvania Press, 2011), 159–160.

2. Jeffrey Herf, *The Jewish Enemy: Nazi Propaganda during World War II and the Holocaust* (Cambridge, MA: Harvard University Press, 2006), 105–110, 117–120. Morris to Secretary of State, 18 October 1941, RG 59, 862.4016/2206, National Archives and Records Administration, College Park, Maryland (henceforth NARA).

3. Gerhard L. Weinberg, *A World at Arms: A Global History of World War II* (New York: Cambridge Universisty Press, 2005), 250. Ian Kershaw, *Hitler, 1936–1945: Nemesis* (New York: Norton, 2000), 443. Also, Special State Depart-

ment Interrogation of Erich Kordt, 7 January 1946, copy in RG 226, entry 19, XL 34409, NARA.

4. On the campaign generally see Christopher R. Browning with Jürgen Matthäus, *The Origins of the Final Solution: The Evolution of Nazi Jewish Policy, September 1939–March 1942* (Lincoln: University of Nebraska Press, 2004); on the significance of the conference of 16 July and general killings of Jews by early August see Friedländer, *Nazi Germany and the Jews,* 206.

5. Brief description in Richard Breitman, *The Architect of Genocide: Himmler and the Final Solution* (New York: Alfred A. Knopf, 1991), 212.

6. Goebbels's speech quoted by Herf, *Jewish Enemy,* 122; on Germany's efforts at secrecy see Richard Breitman, *Official Secrets: What the Nazis Planned, What the British and Americans Knew* (New York: Hill and Wang, 1998), 64–67, 74–78, 84–87.

7. In early June Roosevelt had written that he was bringing the country along slowly but surely with his view. FDR to the Murrays, 2 June 1941, PSF, Diplomatic, box 38, Arthur Murray, Franklin D. Roosevelt Library, Hyde Park, New York (henceforth Roosevelt Library). Japan did not join Germany and Italy in the war against the Soviet Union.

8. David Reynolds, *From Munich to Pearl Harbor: Roosevelt's America and the Origins of the Second World War* (Chicago: Ivan R. Dee, 2001), 116–119, 129–132.

9. Robert Dallek, *Franklin D. Roosevelt and American Foreign Policy, 1932–1945* (New York: Oxford University Press, 1979), 291. "Willkie Calls Idea of Peace 'Delusion'," *New York Times,* 19 October 1941, p. 3.

10. Quoted by Kenneth S. Davis, *FDR: The War President, 1940–1943* (New York: Random House, 2000), 324. On Nazi objectives in the Western Hemisphere see Norman J. W. Goda, *Tomorrow the World: Hitler, Northwest Africa, and the Path Toward America* (College Station: Texas A&M University Press, 1998).

11. Report on Axis Broadcasts during the week ending 31 October 1941, PSF, box 128, Coordinator of Information 1941, Roosevelt Library.

12. "Flyer Names 'War Groups'," *Los Angeles Times,* 12 September 1941, p. 3; Justus D. Doenecke, *In Danger Undaunted: The Anti-Interventionist Movement of 1940–1941 as Revealed in the Papers of the America First Committee* (Stanford: Hoover Institution, 1990), 400.

13. Hufty to Ethyle Stevenson, 19 September 1941, America First Committee Records, box 1, Hoover Institution for War, Revolution, and Peace, Palo Alto, California; America First Committee, press release, 25 September 1941, Philip C. Jessup Papers, box A 207, Library of Congress, Washington, D.C. (henceforth LC); Hoover to Mr. and Mrs. Jeremiah Milbank, 14 September 1941, Post-Presidential, Individual Files, box 124, Herbert Hoover Presidential Library, West Branch, Iowa (henceforth Hoover Library).

14. Philip Roth, *The Plot Against America* (New York: Vintage, 2004), 8; Doenecke, *In Danger Undaunted,* 30.

15. "President Denies Movies Pressure," *New York Times,* 17 September 1941, p. 12.

16. "President Hits Film Inquiry," *Los Angeles Times,* 17 September 1941, p. 1.

17. "Jews Listed Fifth in Pro-War Groups," *New York Times,* 24 October 1941, p. 7.

18. Davis, *FDR: The War President,* 329. Morris to Secretary of State, 18 October 1941, RG 59, 862.4016/2206, NARA.

19. Davis, *FDR: The War President,* 335–338; "FDR's War Plans!" *Chicago Tribune,* 4 December 1941, p. 1. According to Garry Clifford, to whom we are grateful, the *Washington Times-Herald* published this account at the same time.

20. Davis, *FDR: The War President,* 340, 347–352.

21. Kershaw, *Hitler: Nemesis,* 446. Davis, *FDR: The War President,* 352.

22. Doenecke, *In Danger Undaunted,* 469; Lindbergh to "Members of the America First Committee," 14 December 1941, Robert E. Wood Papers, box 9, Hoover Library. Hoover to Robert Taft, 8 December 1941, Taft Papers, box 286, LC.

23. Arnold Krammer, *Undue Process: The Untold Story of America's Alien German Internees* (Lanham, MD: Rowman & Littlefield, 1977), 31–34. Francis MacDonnell, *Insidious Foes: The Axis Fifth Column & the American Home Front* (New York: Oxford, 1995), 141–142. Rowe to Biddle, 23 March 1942, Francis Biddle Papers, box 2, propaganda—domestic, Roosevelt Library.

24. Krammer, *Undue Process,* 45–52. See also James G. McDonald, *Refugees and Rescue: The Diaries and Papers of James G. McDonald, 1935–1945,* ed. Richard Breitman, Barbara McDonald Stewart, and Severin Hochberg (Bloomington: Indiana University Press, 2009), 293. Brian Masaru Hayashi, *Democratizing the Enemy: The Japanese American Internment* (Princeton, NJ: Princeton University Press, 2004).

25. FDR to J. Edgar Hoover, 21 January 1942, PSF, box 57, Justice: Hoover 1941–1944; Biddle notes of conference with FDR, 22 April 1942, Francis Biddle Papers, box 2, FDR folder; Rowe to Biddle, personal and confidential, 23 March 1942, Francis Biddle Papers, box 2, propaganda—domestic; Biddle notes of cabinet, 7 May 1942, Biddle Papers, box 1, cabinet meetings—all in Roosevelt Library.

26. Allan J. Lichtman, *White Protestant Nation: The Rise of the American Conservative Movement* (New York: Grove/Atlantic, 2008), 119–120.

27. Joseph W. Bendersky, *The Jewish Threat: Anti-Semitic Policies of the U.S. Army* (New York: Basic Books, 2000), 291–292.

28. Memorandum on the Reputed Danger to National Safety in the Admission of Refugees Based on the Experience of Private Agencies, 1942, Hamilton Fish Armstrong Papers, box 78, President's Advisory Committee 1942, Seeley G. Mudd Manuscript Library, Princeton University, Princeton, New Jersey.

29. MI5 files on Borchardt, KV 2/2429–2430, National Archives (United Kingdom). We are grateful to Stephen Tyas for this document. "Three Spy Ringleaders Get Twenty-Year Terms," *New York Times,* 14 March 1942, p. 1.

30. For a good British account of this relationship between Stephenson and Donovan see H. Montgomery Hyde, *Room 3603: The Story of the British Intelligence Center in New York during World War II* (New York: Farrar Straus and Giroux, 1963). For debriefings of German-Jewish refugees see RG 226, entry 210, boxes 241–242, 244–245, 248, NARA.

31. On Donovan's trips to Britain, the Balkans, and the Middle East see Anthony Cave Brown, *The Last Hero: Wild Bill Donovan* (New York: Times Books, 1982), 149–158; Hyde, *Room 3603,* 43–47. On Donovan generally see Douglas Waller, *Wild Bill Donovan: The Spymaster Who Created the OSS and Modern American Espionage* (New York: Free Press, 2011).

32. Donovan to FDR, 25 April 1942, COI White House Books, RG 226, entry 180, M-1642, reel 23/f 154, NARA.

33. Richard Breitman, *Official Secrets,* 91–100.

34. Military Attaché Report, 10 November 1941, Harry Hopkins Papers, box 188, Central European Documents, vol. 12, Roosevelt Library.

35. "President Flays Hostage Killings," *New York Times,* 26 October 1941, p. 1. Arieh Kochavi, *Prelude to Nuremberg: Allied War Crimes Policy and the Question of Punishment* (Chapel Hill: University of North Carolina Press, 1998), 15. Laurel Leff, *Buried by the Times: The Holocaust and America's Most Important Newspaper* (New York: Cambridge University Press, 2006), 105, 123–131.

36. "Timely Topics: Tragic Silence," *Congress Weekly,* 31 October 1941; Louis Segal to Early, 3 November 1941—both in Holocaust/Refugee Collection, box 1, Roosevelt Library.

37. Rothschild to Louis Wirth, 29 September 1941, American Jewish Committee Records, RG 347, EXO-29, Waldman Files, box 30, Nazism, YIVO Institute for Jewish Research, New York, New York (henceforth YIVO).

38. See Breitman, *Official Secrets,* 128–129. Leff, *Buried by the Times,* 139–142. "Vilna Massacre of Jews Reported," *New York Times,* 16 June 1942, p. 6; "Allies Are Urged to Execute Nazis," *New York Times,* 2 July 1942, p. 6; "Estimate 1,000,000 Jews Died Victims of Nazis," *Chicago Tribune,* 30 June 1942, p. 7.

39. See Richard Breitman, Norman J. W. Goda, Timothy Naftali, and Robert Wolfe, *U.S. Intelligence and the Nazis* (New York: Cambridge University Press, 2005), 11–25.

40. Donovan to FDR, 12 February 1942, RG 226, COI White House Books, entry 180, M-1642, reel 22/f 1029, NARA. For a discussion of the collection see Breitman et al., *U.S. Intelligence,* 22. Because of the way the Central Intelligence Agency later handled these documents, it is extremely difficult today to determine who wrote which stories and who received copies of them. Redacted copies of these

semi-news documents were declassified in 2000; the originals no longer exist. Dulles's role is visible only through the fact that some journalists wrote their stories as letters to "Dear Allen." Later, the new Office of War Information, which took over propaganda and information programs from the Coordinator of Information, probably controlled the operation.

41. Confidential, 28 June 1942, RG 226, entry 16, 26896, reel 170, NARA. For more discussion see also Breitman, *Official Secrets,* 129–130; Breitman et al., *U.S. Intelligence,* 22–24.

42. Berle Diary, 30 April 1942, in Adolf A. Berle, *Navigating the Rapids, 1918–1971: From the Papers of Adolf A. Berle,* ed. Beatrice Bishop Berle and Travis Beal Jacobs (New York: Harcourt Brace Jovanovich, 1973), 411. Berle to FDR, 9 May 1942, Adolf A. Berle Papers, box 67, folder FDR 1942, Roosevelt Library. Clayton Laurie, *The Propaganda Warriors: America's Crusade against Nazi Germany* (Lawrence: University of Kansas Press, 1996), 89–91.

43. Laurie, *The Propaganda Warriors,* 95. Committee on War Information Policy, meeting of 2 September 1942, RG 208, entry E-1, box 3, meetings-4, NARA. On the general subject of information about the Holocaust and the difficulties of comprehending it see Walter Laqueur, *The Terrible Secret: Suppression of the Truth about Hitler's "Final Solution"* (New York: Holt, 1998). On official British skepticism in the fall of 1941 and December 1942 see Kochavi, *Prelude to Nuremberg,* 15–16, 141.

44. Roosevelt to Wise, 17 July 1942, copy in Stephen S. Wise Papers, reel 86-1, American Jewish Historical Society, New York, New York (henceforth AJHS). Wise used FDR's words at the rally of July 21.

45. Text of both statements in "Nazi Punishment Seen by Roosevelt," *New York Times,* 22 July 1942, p. 1.

46. Wise to Mack, 19 July 1942, Stephen S. Wise Papers, reel 74-74, AJHS; and Wise draft, undated, in Stephen S. Wise Papers, reel 74-47, AJHS.

47. Kubowitzki to Wise et al., 21 August 1942, World Jewish Congress Records, box A78, folder 14 Executive Committee, American Jewish Archives, Cincinnati, Ohio (henceforth AJA).

48. Ibid.

49. For the most detailed account see Walter Laqueur and Richard Breitman, *Breaking the Silence: The German Who Exposed the Final Solution* (Hanover, NH: University Press of New England, 1994).

50. Ibid., 145–152.

51. Wise to Welles, 2 September 1942, and Atherton to Welles, 3 September 1942, RG 59 840.48 Refugees/3080, NARA. Wise to Frankfurter, 4 September 1942, reprinted in Stephen S. Wise, *Stephen S. Wise: Servant of the People: Selected Letters,* ed. Carl Hermann Voss (Philadelphia: Jewish Publication Society, 1969), 248–249; and Wise to Goldmann, 4 September 1942, Stephen S. Wise Papers, reel 74-70, AJHS.

52. Cablegram to Dr. Jacob Rosenheim, 4 September 1942, Stephen S. Wise Papers, reel 74-74, AJHS. On the Agudath Israel sources and background see Joseph Friedenson and David Kranzler, *Heroine of Rescue: The Incredible Story of Recha Sternbuch* (New York: Mesorah Publications, 1984). Wise to Frankfurter, 4 September 1942, reprinted in Wise, *Stephen S. Wise,* 249–250; and Wise to Goldmann, 4 September 1942, Stephen S. Wise Papers, reel 74-70, AJHS.

53. Schuster to Waldman, 8 September 1942, and Rosenblum to Wertheim, 9 September 1942, RG 347, EXO-29, box 34, folder 9 (Poland 1942), YIVO.

54. Wise to Holmes, 9 September 1942, Stephen S. Wise Papers, reel 74-40, AJHS. Wise, Goldmann, Perlzweig to Easterman, 17 September 1942, World Jewish Congress Records, box A24, folder 2 (reports, reactions to extermination), AJA. McDonald and Warren to Welles, 30 September 1942, Sumner Welles Papers, box 80, folder 14 (McDonald 1942), Roosevelt Library.

55. Memorandum of Conversation, 25 September, PSF, box 71, Vatican: Myron C. Taylor, Roosevelt Library. See also Laqueur and Breitman, *Breaking the Silence,* 155.

56. "Roosevelt Says U.S. Will Join in Investigation of Atrocities," *New York Times,* 8 October 1942, p. 1; Kochavi, *Prelude to Nuremberg,* 32–36. Welles to Winant, 5 October 1942, PSF Diplomatic, box 38, Roosevelt Library.

57. Richard Breitman and Alan M. Kraut, *American Refugee Policy and European Jewry, 1933–1945* (Bloomington: Indiana University Press, 1987), 152. "U.S. Rebukes Vichy on Deporting Jews," *New York Times,* 5 September 1942, p. 3.

58. Breitman and Kraut, *American Refugee Policy,* 161–162. "U.S. Rebukes Vichy on Deporting Jews," *New York Times,* 5 September 1942, p. 3.

59. See McDonald, *Refugees and Rescue,* 298–300.

60. Breitman and Kraut, *American Refugee Policy,* 163–164.

61. "Laval Indicts U.S. on Africa, Pins Hope on Nazi Entente," *New York Times,* 21 November 1942, p. 1.

62. Laqueur and Breitman, *Breaking the Silence,* 156. Easterman to Taylor, 7 October 1942, copy in RG 59, 740.00116 European War 1939/634; Tittmann to Welles, 16 October 1942, RG 59, 740.00116 European War 1939/605 CF—both in NARA.

63. Taylor Memorandum for the President and Secretary of State, 20 October 1942, Sumner Welles Papers, box 84, folder 1 (Taylor September–October 1942), Roosevelt Library.

64. "President Asks Trade Barrier End," *New York Times,* 3 November 1942, p. 1; Cabinet notes, 20 November 1942, Francis Biddle Papers, box 1, cabinet meetings, July–December 1942, Roosevelt Library. Dallek, *Franklin D. Roosevelt and American Foreign Policy,* 446.

65. Laqueur and Breitman, *Breaking the Silence,* 158–160. Welles to Wise, 13 November 1942, and Wise to Welles, 17 November 1942, Sumner Welles Papers, box 86, Wise 1942 folder, Roosevelt Library.

66. Breitman, *Official Secrets,* 145–146. "Himmler Program Kills Polish Jews," *New York Times,* 25 November 1942, p. 10.

67. Laqueur and Breitman, *Breaking the Silence,* 160. Irwin F. Gellman, *Secret Affairs: Franklin Roosevelt, Cordell Hull, and Sumner Welles* (Baltimore: Johns Hopkins University Press, 1995), 287, 308–309. Leff, *Buried by the Times,* 155, 255–257.

68. See Leff, *Buried by the Times,* 154.

69. On the relationship between Welles and Hull see Gellmann, *Secret Affairs,* 308–309.

70. Leff, *Buried by the Times,* 155–156. "Wise Gets Confirmation," *New York Times,* 25 November 1942, p. 10.

71. Watson Memo, 30 November 1942, and Memo of 1 December 1942, OF 76-c, box 8 (September–December 1942), Roosevelt Library.

72. Michaela Hoenicke Moore, *Know Your Enemy: The American Debate on Nazism, 1933–1945* (New York: Cambridge University Press, 2010), 105–130. Morgenthau Presidential Diary, 3 December 1942, microfilm, reel 2, Georgetown University Library, Washington, DC.

73. Donovan Memo, For Meeting with the President, 21 October 1941, attached to Morris to Secretary of State, 17 October 1941, copy in PSF, box 128, Coordinator of Information, Roosevelt Library; Michael P. Rogin and Kathleen Moran, "Mr. Capra Goes to Washington," *Representations* (Autumn 2003): 241.

74. Diary of Mackenzie King, 5 December 1942, www.canadaonline.about.com /gi/o.htm?zi=1/XJ&zTi=1&sdn=canadaonline&cdn=newsissues&tm=14&f=10& su=p649.3.336.ip_&tt=2&bt=1&bts=1&zu=http%3A//www.collectionscanada.gc .ca/databases/king/index-e.html.

75. Wise to FDR, 2 December 1942, and Wise to Niles, 2 December 1942, Stephen S. Wise Papers, reels 74-47 and 83-9, AJHS. Also, FDR to General Watson, 4 December 1942, Official File 76-c, box 8 (September–December 1942), Roosevelt Library.

76. Held's account of the meeting, part 3, section 1, no. 15, Jewish Labor Committee Archives, today available at www.jewishvirtuallibrary.org/jsource /Holocaust/fdrmeet.html.

77. Wise to Niles, 9 December 1941, Stephen S. Wise Papers, reel 83-9, AJHS.

11. DEBATING REMEDIES

1. "President Renews Pledges to Jews," *New York Times,* 9 December 1942, p. 20.

2. See treatments in Richard Breitman, *Official Secrets: What the Nazis Planned, What the British and Americans Knew* (New York: Hill and Wang, 1998), 150–153; Bernard Wasserstein, *Britain and the Jews of Europe, 1939–1945* (Oxford:

Clarendon Press, 1979), 170–174; Arieh Kochavi, *Prelude to Nuremberg: Allied War Crimes Policy and the Question of Punishment* (Chapel Hill: University of North Carolina Press, 1998), 141–142. Copy of Eden's statement in RG 59, 740.00116 E.W. 1939/749, National Archives and Records Administration, College Park, Maryland (henceforth NARA).

3. "11 Allies Condemn Nazi War on Jews," *New York Times,* 18 December 1942, p. 1.

4. On events in Turkey see, for example, Simon Payaslian, *United States Policy Toward the Armenian Question and the Armenian Genocide* (New York: Palgrave, 2005); Peter Balakian, *The Burning Tigris: The Armenian Genocide and America's Response* (New York: HarperCollins, 2003); Jay Winter, ed., *America and the Armenian Genocide of 1915* (New York: Cambridge University Press, 2003); Vahakn N. Dadrian, *The History of the Armenian Genocide* (Providence, RI: Berghahn, 1995); Robert Melson, *Revolution and Genocide: On the Origins of the Armenian Genocide and the Holocaust* (Chicago: University of Chicago Press, 1992); and Donald Bloxham, *The Great Game of Genocide: Imperialism, Nationalism, and the Destruction of the Ottoman Armenians* (New York: Oxford University Press, 2005).

5. Morgenthau to Bryan, 27 April 1915; Bryan to Morgenthau, 29 April 1915; Morgenthau to Lansing 18 June 1915; and Morgenthau to Lansing, 16 July 1915—in RG 59, 867.4016/58, 70, 76, NARA.

6. "Chamber of Horrors," *Los Angeles Times,* 22 October 1915, p. 11; "Only 200,000 Armenians Now Left in Turkey," *New York Times,* 22 October 1915, p. 3; "Thousands Protest Armenian Murders," *New York Times,* 18 October 1915, p. 3.

7. "Roosevelt Heaps Blame on America," *New York Times,* 1 December 1915, p. 4; Keith Pomakoy, *Helping Humanity: American Policy and Genocide Rescue* (Lanham, MD: Lexington Books, 2011), 74–75. Payaslian, *United States Policy,* 58–122.

8. Henning, "Wilson Warns Turkey to Stop Massacres," *Los Angeles Times,* 19 February 1916, p. 11; "Armenians Get Relief," *New York Times,* 8 March 1916, p. 22; Lansing to Morgenthau, 12 February 1916, RG 59, 867.4016/258a, NARA.

9. Balakian, *The Burning Tigris,* 195–196; 123–160; Payaslian, *United States Policy,* 123–188. Hitler's statement comes from the unofficial "Lochner" version of his 22 August 1939 speech at Berchtesgaden to the commanders in chief of the armed forces. See Winfried Baumgart, "Zur Ansprache Hitlers vor den Führern der Wehrmacht am 22. August 1939: eine quellenkritische Untersuchung," *Vierteljahrshefte für Zeitgeschichte* 16 (1968): 120–129.

10. Charles R. Vickrey to FDR, 28 August 1921, Family, Business, Personal Papers, box 33, Near East Relief, Franklin D. Roosevelt Library, Hyde Park, New York (henceforth Roosevelt Library). Pomakoy, *Helping Humanity,* 101, initially called our attention to Henry Morgenthau Jr. and Roosevelt's Armenian connection.

11. Henry Morgenthau Sr. to my dear children, 13, 23, and 28 February 1915, Henry Morgenthau Jr. Papers, box 474, letters to family 1915; Phillips to Morgenthau Sr., 1 November 1915; Henry Morgenthau Jr. Papers, box 474, letters to nonfamily 1915: Roosevelt Library.

12. "Uncle Henry," in Governorship Papers, box 56, Henry Morgenthau Sr., Roosevelt Library; "Zionism a Fallacy Says Morgenthau," *New York Times,* 27 June 1921, p. 4.

13. Durbrow Memo of 9 February 1943, RG 59, 860C.4016/644 1/2 and 862.4016/2256a, NARA.

14. Richard Breitman and Alan M. Kraut, *American Refugee Policy and European Jewry, 1933–1945* (Bloomington: Indiana University Press, 1987), 183–184. This episode played a significant role in the late 1943 battle between State Department and Treasury Department officials.

15. Matthews to Secretary of State, 20 February 1943, paraphrase in RG 59, Lot File 52D408, box 3, Bermuda Conference background, NARA.

16. Ibid., 179–181.

17. Wise to Rabbi Morton Berman, 15 February 1943, Stephen S. Wise Papers, reel 74-66, American Jewish Historical Society, New York, New York (henceforth AJHS).

18. "Saved Doomed Jews, Huge Rally Pleads" and "Proposals for Aiding Jews," *New York Times,* 2 March 1943, pp. 1, 4; David S. Wyman, *The Abandonment of the Jews: America and the Holocaust, 1941–1945* (New York: New Press, 1984), 87–89, treats this mass meeting at some length, but casts it partly as an effort to undercut the Bergson group's scheduled rally for March 9 entitled "We Shall Never Die."

19. The Joint Emergency Committee included the American Jewish Committee, the American Jewish Congress, B'nai B'rith, the Jewish Labor Committee, the Synagogue Council of America, Agudath Israel, the Union of Orthodox Rabbis of the United States and Canada, and the American Emergency Committee for Zionist Affairs. The Joint Distribution Committee and United Palestine Appeal sent representatives as observers, but wanted to avoid participating in political goals. David Rosenblum to Trager and Rothschild, 17 March 1943, American Jewish Committee Records, RG 347, EXO-29, box 23, Joint Emergency Committee for European Jewish Affairs, YIVO Institute for Jewish Research, New York, New York (henceforth YIVO).

20. "Jews' Fate Pondered: Conference Proposed," *Washington Post,* 4 March 1943, p. 9.

21. David S. Wyman and Rafael Medoff, *A Race against Death: Peter Bergson, America, and the Holocaust* (New York: New Press, 2002), 22–27. Monty Noam Penkower, *The Jews Were Expendable: Free World Diplomacy and the Holocaust* (Detroit: Wayne State University Press, 1988), 12–13; Judith Tydor Baumel, *The "Bergson Boys" and the Origins of Contemporary Zionist Militancy* (Syracuse, NY:

Syracuse University Press, 2005), 37–81. Examples of ads in *New York Times,* 3 January 1942, p. 11; 5 January 1942, p. 13.

22. Interviews with Bergson in *Not Idly By: Peter Bergson, America and the Holocaust,* 2012 film directed by Pierre Sauvage. Rose to David Niles, 23 February 1943; Pringle to Hassett, 3 March 1943; Early to Rose, 4 March 1943, Official File 76-C, box 8, January–July 1943, Roosevelt Library. Wyman, *Abandonment of the Jews,* 90–91. Breitman and Kraut, *American Refugee Policy,* 175.

23. "20,000 Plead: 'Act Now to Rescue Jews,'" *Chicago Tribune,* 15 April 1943, p. 1. Interviews with Bergson in *Not Idly By*; Baumel, *The "Bergson Boys,"* 116–119.

24. Interviews with Bergson in *Not Idly By.*

25. Monty Penkower, "Eleanor Roosevelt and the Plight of World Jewry," *Jewish Social Studies* 49 (Spring 1987): 125–136.

26. Ibid. Eleanor Roosevelt, "My Day: Mass Memorial for Jewish Dead," *Atlanta Constitution,* 15 April 1943, p. 18, and "My Day: Race Issues," *Atlanta Constitution,* 14 August 1943, p. 18. For example, Doris Kearns Goodwin, *No Ordinary Time: Franklin and Eleanor Roosevelt: The Home Front in World War II* (New York: Simon & Schuster, 1995), 174–176, relies on the 1982 oral history of Eleanor's friend Justine Polier (also the daughter of Rabbi Stephen S. Wise) for claims that Eleanor pressured Franklin privately on Jewish concerns.

27. Warren to McDonald, Armstrong, Baerwald, Cavert, and Chamberlain, 11 March 1943, and McDonald and Warren to Welles, RG 278, Joseph C. Chamberlain Papers, folder 72, reel 3, YIVO. James G. McDonald, *Refugees and Rescue: The Diaries and Papers of James G. McDonald, 1935–1945,* ed. Richard Breitman, Barbara McDonald Stewart, and Severin Hochberg (Bloomington: Indiana University Press, 2009), 309.

28. Memorandum, 10 April 1943, Berle Diary, microfilm reel 4, Adolf A. Berle Papers, Roosevelt Library; Breitman, *Official Secrets,* 182.

29. Penkower, *The Jews Were Expendable,* 107. The list of participants at the meeting comes from FDR's appointment books. Proskauer to Wise, 29 March 1943, American Jewish Committee Records, RG 347, EXO-29, box 23, Joint Emergency Committee, YIVO.

30. Minutes of the Joint Emergency Committee on European Jewish Affairs, 10 April 1943, American Jewish Committee Records, RG 347, EXO-29, box 23, Joint Emergency Committee, YIVO. Long Diary, 20 April 1943, Library of Congress, Washington, D.C. (henceforth LC).

31. "Senate Condemns Nazis," *New York Times,* 10 March 1943, p. 12; "Congress Sets Nazi Guilt," *New York Times,* 19 March 1943, p. 11. Abram S. Magida to Herman Shulman, 3 May 1943, Robert F. Wagner Papers, PA-2, F-24, Georgetown University Library, Washington, D.C.

32. Press Release, 31 March 1943, Jewish Labor Committee Records, reel 15, New York University Library, New York, NY. "Rally at Capital Asks Aid for Jews,"

New York Times, 31 March 1943, p. 12. "U.S. Lead in Rescuing Jews Urged," *Washington Post,* 31 March 1943, p. B1.

33. FDR's appointments for 31 March 1943. Wyman, *Abandonment of the Jews,* 108–109.

34. On Lucas's career see Brian S. Deason, *Eye of the Storm: A Political Biography of U.S. Senator Scott W. Lucas of Illinois* (Carbondale: University of Southern Illinois Press, 2000); Richard P. Stevens, *American Zionism U.S. Foreign Policy, 1942–1945* (New York: Pageant Press, 1962) contains information on Bloom's leadership during this period, esp. 44–53. Henry L. Feingold, *The Politics of Rescue* (New York: Holocaust Library, 1970), 192–197.

35. Watson to Long, 1 April 1943, Official File 3186, box 3, 1943 folder, Roosevelt Library. Watson wrote diplomatically, "They were a little critical of the Army, Navy, etc." Celler's views and statements recounted in Minutes of the Joint Emergency Committee on European Jewish Affairs, 10 April 1943, American Jewish Committee Records, RG 347, EXO-29, box 23, Joint Emergency Committee, YIVO. Tuvia Friling, *Arrows in the Dark: David Ben-Gurion, the Yishuv Leadership and Rescue Attempts during the Holocaust,* vol. 1, trans. Ora Cummings (Madison: University of Wisconsin Press, 2005), 167. There is no meeting with a Jewish delegation after April 1 listed in FDR's appointment books.

36. Minutes of the Joint Emergency Committee on European Jewish Affairs, 10 April 1943, and Joint Emergency Committee to Welles, 14 April 1943, American Jewish Committee Records, RG 347, EXO-29, box 23, Joint Emergency Committee, YIVO. Wyman, *Abandonment of the Jews,* 112–113. Memorandum for Mr. Ladd, 13 April 1943, file 64-23000 Bermuda Conference, RG 65, NARA.

37. "20,000 Plead: 'Act Now to Rescue Jews'," and "12 Point program Adopted for Direct Action to Aid Jews," *Chicago Tribune,* 15 April 1943, pp. 1, 15. Allis Radosh and Ronald Radosh, *A Safe Haven: Harry S. Truman and the Founding of Israel* (New York: HarperCollins, 2010), 50–51.

38. Breitman, *Official Secrets,* 183. Friling, *Arrows in the Dark,* 1:185–188.

39. For details see Radu Ioanid, *The Holocaust in Romania: The Destruction of Jews and Gypsies under the Antonescu Regime, 1940–1944* (Chicago: Ivan R. Dee, 2000), 245–250; Dennis Deletant, *Hitler's Forgotten Ally: Ion Antonescu and His Regime, Romania, 1940–1944* (London: Palgrave Macmillan, 2006), 207–214. Both sources mention an alleged warning from Secretary Hull to the Romanians in September 1942; State Department records contain no such initiative. Deletant specifies also the effect of Roosevelt and Churchill's July 1942 message to the American Jewish Congress meeting, as well as threats against the Romanians by Soviet foreign minister Molotov (p. 208). On Roosevelt's and Churchill's warnings, see Chapter 10 in this volume.

40. Wyman, *Abandonment of the Jews,* 82–87. Wise to John Hayes Holmes, 22 March 1943, Stephen S. Wise Papers, reel 74-40, AJHS. In this document Wise

called it the Ben Hecht group—Hecht had signed this ad. Friling, *Arrow in the Dark,* 1:206–208.

41. Michael J. Cohen, "Churchill and the Jews: The Holocaust," *Modern Judaism* 6 (February 1986): 31.

42. Morning Conference, 20 April 1943, Confidential Memorandum for the Chairman, RG 59, Lot File 52D408, Subject File, box 3, Bermuda Conference Minutes, NARA. "Permanent Board on Refugees Posed," *New York Times,* 24 April 1943, p. 2. Deletant, *Hitler's Forgotten Ally,* 217. Breitman and Kraut, *American Refugee Policy,* 179. Friling, *Arrow in the Dark,* 205–211.

43. Morning Conference, 20 April 1943, Confidential Memorandum for the Chairman, RG 59, Lot File 52D408, Subject File, box 3, Bermuda Conference Minutes, NARA. Penkower, *The Jews Were Expendable,* 110. Louise London, *Whitehall and the Jews, 1933–1948* (Cambridge: Cambridge University Press, 2000), 216. Breitman and Kraut, *American Refugee Policy,* 178–180.

44. Foreign Office 371/36661 (W 7186/49/48), National Archives (United Kingdom).

45. William D. Hassett, *Off the Record with F.D.R.: 1942–1945* (New Brunswick, NJ: Rutgers University Press, 1958), 151–152.

46. Perlzweig to Alex Easterman, 12 January 1943, World Jewish Congress Records, box A10, folder F8, American Jewish Archives, Cincinnati, Ohio; Lehman to Roosevelt, 30 August 1943, Herbert Lehman Papers, ldpd_leh_0784_0359, Columbia University Rare Book and Manuscript Library, New York, New York.

47. Meredith Hindley, "Blockade before Bread: Allied Relief for Nazi Europe, 1939–1945" (PhD diss., American University, 2007), 414–422.

48. Churchill to Eden, 21 May 1943, FO 115/3953, National Archives (United Kingdom), cited by Hindley, "Blockade before Bread," 423. Francis Pickett Journal, 15 June 1943, American Friends Service Committee Archive, Philadelphia, Pennsylvania.

49. "6 Weeks' Mourning Begins for Jews," *New York Times,* 27 April 1943, p. 15. Captain Kades to Morgenthau, 11 August 1943, The Morgenthau Diaries: World War II and Postwar Planning, 1943–1945 (henceforth Morgenthau Diaries), microfilm, reel 23, LC; Cox to Morgenthau, 16 June 1943, Morgenthau Diaries, reel 11, LC. Milton Handler to Cox, 18 June 1942, Oscar Cox Papers, box 101, Refugees folder, Roosevelt Library.

50. Penkower, *The Jews Were Expendable,* 110. Wise to FDR, 28 April 1943, Stephen S. Wise Papers, reel 85-6, AJHS. Celler to Wise, 14 May 1943, American Jewish Committee Records, RG 347, EXO-29, box 23, Emergency Committee, YIVO.

51. Wise to FDR, 23 July 1943, PPF 3292, Roosevelt Library. Paul to Morgenthau, 12 August 1943, Morgenthau Diaries, reel 23, LC. Roosevelt to Wise, 30 August 1943, Stephen S. Wise Papers, reel 74-48, AJHS.

52. Cox to Hopkins, 6 July 1943, Hopkins Papers, box 137, Cox folder, Roosevelt Library. E. Thomas Wood and Stanislaw M. Jankowski, *Karski: How One Man Tried to Stop the Holocaust* (New York: John Wiley & Sons, 1994), 197–201.

53. Jan Ciechanowski, *Defeat in Victory* (Garden City: Doubleday, 1947), 182. Walter Laqueur, *The Terrible Secret: Suppression of the Truth about Hitler's "Final Solution"* (New York: Holt Paperbacks, 1998), 232. Wood and Jankowski, *Karski,* 201.

54. O'Connell and Pehle to Morgenthau, 1 July 1943, Morgenthau Diaries, reel 12, LC. Stephen Wise, *Challenging Years: The Autobiography of Stephen Wise* (New York: 1949), 193–194, which is inaccurate on some details; Wise to FDR, 23 July 1943, RG 59, 840.48 Refugees/4212, NARA; FDR to Morgenthau, 30 July 1943, and Morgenthau to Wise, 11 August 1943, PPF 3292, Roosevelt Library; Morgenthau to Hull, 5 August 1943, and Paul to Morgenthau, 12 August 1943, Morgenthau Diaries, reel 23, LC.

55. Irwin F. Gellman, *Secret Affairs: Franklin Roosevelt, Cordell Hull, and Sumner Welles* (Baltimore: Johns Hopkins University Press, 1995), 312–317. Frank Costigliola, *Roosevelt's Lost Alliances: How Personal Politics Helped Start the Cold War* (Princeton: Princeton University Press, 2012), 188–190. Adolf A. Berle, *Navigating the Rapids, 1918–1971: From the Papers of Adolf A. Berle,* ed. Beatrice Bishop Berle and Travis Beal Jacobs (New York: Harcourt Brace Jovanovich, 1973), 449 (entry of 6 January 1944).

56. Paul to Morgenthau, 12 August 1943, Morgenthau Diaries, reel 23, LC. Gellman, *Secret Affairs,* 312–317. Berle, *Navigating the Rapids,* 449 (6 January 1944). Costigliola, *Roosevelt's Lost Alliances,* 188–190.

57. Transcript of Morgenthau-Lehman Conversations, 15 and 20 September 1943; Paul to Morgenthau, 2 November 1943; British Embassy, Washington to Pehle, 13 November 1943; Harrison to Secretary of State, 20 November 1943—all in Morgenthau Diaries, reel 23, LC.

58. Berle to Hull, 16 September 1943, Adolf A. Berle Papers, box 58, Hull August–December 1943, Roosevelt Library.

59. Van Paassen to FDR, 4 September 1943, RG 59, 840.48 Refugees/4679, NARA; Wyman, *Abandonment of the Jews,* 193–194. Bergson to Cox, 15 September 1943, Oscar Cox Papers, box 2, Bergson folder, Roosevelt Library.

60. Testimony of Stephen S. Wise, Executive Session, U.S. House of Representatives, Committee on Foreign Relations, 78th Congress, "Establishment of a Commission to Effectuate the Rescue of the Jewish People of Europe," 2 December 1943, 217–221. For examples of works criticizing mainstream Zionist for advocating on Palestine at the expense of rescue measures see Louis Rapoport, *Shake Heaven and Earth: Peter Bergson and the Struggle to Rescue the Jews of Europe* (Jerusalem: Geffen, 1999); Rafael Medoff, *The Deafening Silence: American Jewish Leaders and the Holocaust, 1933–1945* (New York: Shapolsky, 1987); and Sarah

E. Peck, "The Campaign for an American Response to the Nazi Holocaust, 1943–1945," *Journal of Contemporary History* 15 (April 1980): 367–400.

61. Transcripts of Morgenthau's phone conversations with Lehman, 15 and 20 September 1943, Morgenthau Diaries, reel 23, LC. Cox to Stettinius, 20 November 1943, Edward R. Stettinius Jr. Papers, box 727, Refugees; Reams to Stettinius, 8 October 1943, RG 59, 840.48/Refugees/4683 1/5, NARA.

62. Efraim Zuroff, *The Response of Orthodox Jewry in the United States to the Holocaust: The Activities of the Vaad Ha-Hatzala Rescue Committee, 1939–1945* (Jersey City, NJ: KTAV Publishing, 2000), 257.

63. Hassett, *Off the Record with F.D.R.,* 209.

64. Zuroff, *The Response of Orthodox Jewry,* 258–259. "Rabbis Present Plea to Wallace," *New York Times,* 7 October 1943, p. 14. Hassett, *Off the Record with F.D.R.,* 209–210.

65. Zuroff, *The Response of Orthodox Jewry,* 259.

66. Samuel Grafton, "I'd Rather Be Right," 22 July 1943, *Baltimore News-Post.*

67. FDR to Stimson, 10 November 1943, PSF, box 84, Stimson 1943–45, Roosevelt Library.

68. Meeting of the Under Secretary with the Assistant Secretaries, the Political Advisers, and the Geographic Division Heads, 11 November 1943; Cox to Stettinius, 20 November 1943, Edward R. Stettinius Jr. Papers, boxes 732 and 727 respectively, refugees, Small Special Collections Library, University of Virginia, Charlottesville, Virginia. On FDR's views of Germany see Steven Casey, *Cautious Crusade: Franklin D. Roosevelt, Public Opinion, and the War Against Germany* (New York: Oxford University Press, 2001), esp. 130–161.

69. Wyman, *Abandonment of the Jews,* 195–197.

70. Ibid., 197–198.

71. Jewish Evacuation, 23 November 1943, Morgenthau Diaries, reel 23, LC.

72. Transcripts of Jewish Evacuation, 6 and 17 December 1943, Morgenthau Diaries, reel 23, LC.

73. DuBois Memorandum for the Files, 9 December 1943, Morgenthau Diaries, reel 23, LC.

74. Quote from Winant to Secretary of State, 15 December 1943; Morgenthau Diaries, reel 24, LC; also in Wasserstein, *Britain and the Jews of Europe,* 247. Hull to American Embassy, London, 18 December 1943; 19 December 1943, Memorandum for Secretary Hull, Morgenthau Diaries, reel 24, LC.

75. Morgenthau to Hull, 18 December 1943, Cox's statement, transcript of Jewish Evacuation meeting, 20 December 1943, Morgenthau Diaries, reel 24, LC.

76. Hull to American Embassy, London, 18 December 1943; transcript of Jewish Evacuation, 20 December 1943, Morgenthau Diaries, reel 24, LC.

77. Transcript of Jewish Evacuation, 19 December 1943, Morgenthau Diaries, reel 24, LC.

78. "The decks are clear" was Morgenthau's description of Hull and Long's attitude. Transcript of Jewish Evacuation, 20 December 1943, Morgenthau Diaries, reel 24, LC.

79. Breitman and Kraut, *American Refugee Policy,* 189.

80. Personal Report to the President, Morgenthau Diaries, 1943–45, reel 25, LC. Cox to Rosenman, 1 January 1943 [should be 1944], Samuel Rosenman Papers, box 1, Oscar Cox folder; Cox to Morgenthau, 20 December 1943, Oscar Cox Papers, box 24, Morgenthau folder—all in Roosevelt Library.

81. Transcripts of Jewish Evacuation, 10 and 15 January 1944, Morgenthau Diaries, reel 25, LC.

82. Pehle Memorandum for the Secretary's Files, 16 January 1944, Morgenthau Diaries, reel 25, LC.

83. On the collapse of the White House team see Costigliola, *Roosevelt's Lost Alliances,* 59–85.

84. The Treasury group recognized Bergson's contribution. See Meeting Transcript, 24 May 1944, Morgenthau Diaries, reel 35, LC.

85. Berle to Stettinius, 20 January 1944, Adolf A. Berle Papers, box 70, Stettinius folder, Roosevelt Library.

12. ZIONISM AND THE ARAB WORLD

1. FDR Diary, 11 November–17 December 1943, OF 200, box 64, Franklin D. Roosevelt Library, Hyde Park, New York (henceforth Roosevelt Library). For details of the president's flight see Log of the President's trips, Africa and the Middle East, Cairo and Teheran Conference, November–December 1943, Grace Tully Papers, box 7, Roosevelt Library.

2. Arthur Murray to FDR, 15 December 1938 and 20 December 1938; FDR to Faith and Arthur Murray, 19 January 1939, President's Secretary's File, box 38, Arthur Murray folder, Roosevelt Library. On FDR's attempt to pressure Chamberlain see also Chapter 6.

3. Cohen to Missy LeHand, 24 January 1939, OF 700, Roosevelt Library.

4. Brandeis to FDR, 16 March 1939; FDR to Brandeis, 23 March 1939, PSF, Diplomatic Correspondence, Palestine, box 46, Roosevelt Library. On four times see Melvin I. Urofsky, *Louis D. Brandeis: A Life* (New York: Alfred A. Knopf, 2009), 740.

5. Intelligence report entitled *Haj Amin el Husseini: Grand Mufti of Jerusalem: Seen against the Background of Recent Palestine History,* 28, RG 263, Haj Amin al-Husseini Name File, National Archives and Records Administration, College Park, Maryland (henceforth NARA). It is likely that Ragheb Nashashibi, a member of the Arab delegation in London, supplied this report. The unnamed author is described as a native Arab Moslem of Jerusalem, one of the best-educated and smartest Palestinians.

6. FDR to Hull and Welles, 10 May 1939, Official File 700 (Palestine), 1939–1943; FDR to Brandeis, 12 May 1939, PSF, Diplomatic, box 46, Palestine; Transcript of Telephone Conversation, 12 May 1939, 9:50 a.m., Sumner Welles Papers, box 53, folder 11 (Kennedy)—all in Roosevelt Library.

7. Bernard Wasserstein, *Britain and the Jews of Europe 1939–1945* (Oxford: Clarendon Press, 1979), 20.

8. FDR's Memorandum for the Secretary of State, 17 May 1939, PSF, box 46, Palestine folder, Roosevelt Library.

9. Adolf A. Berle, *Navigating the Rapids, 1918–1971: From the Papers of Adolf A. Berle,* ed. Beatrice Bishop Berle and Travis Beal Jacobs (New York: Harcourt Brace Jovanovich, 1973), 223 (entry of 26 May 1939).

10. Michael Makovsky, *Churchill's Promised Land: Zionism and Statecraft* (New Haven: Yale University Press, 2007), 172–174, 183–186. Michael J. Cohen, *Churchill and the Jews* (London: F. Cass, 1985), 185–305.

11. Wasserstein, *Britain and the Jews of Europe,* 49–50.

12. Roosevelt to Wise, 9 June 1941, Stephen S. Wise Papers, reel 74-47, American Jewish Historical Society, New York, New York (henceforth AJHS).

13. Bulletin no. 2, Coordinator of Information, Axis Propaganda for the Moslem World, 23 December 1941, cited by Jeffrey Herf, *Nazi Propaganda for the Arab World* (New Haven: Yale University Press, 2009), 84–86. Harry Hopkins Papers, box 139, Enemy Propaganda folder, Roosevelt Library.

14. Donovan to FDR, 16 December 1941, Coordinator of Information, White House Books, RG 226, M-1642, reel 22/f 725, NARA. See discussion in Herf, *Nazi Propaganda for the Arab World.* Richard Breitman and Norman J. W. Goda, *Hitler's Shadow: Nazi War Criminals, U.S. Intelligence, and the Cold War* (Washington, D.C.: National Archives and Records Administration, 2011), 19.

15. Herf, *Nazi Propaganda for the Arab World,* 76–78; and Klaus-Michael Mallmann and Martin Cüppers, *Nazi Palestine: The Nazi Plan for the Extermination of the Jews in Palestine* (New York: Enigma Books, 2010), 89–91.

16. Tuvia Friling, *Arrows in the Dark: David Ben-Gurion, the Yishuv Leadership, and Rescue Attempts during the Holocaust,* vol. 1, trans. Ora Cummings (Madison: University of Wisconsin Press, 2005), 58. "World's Leaders Honor Weizmann," *New York Times,* 11 June 1942, p. 21. Noam Monty Penkower, *The Jews Were Expendable: Free World Diplomacy and the Holocaust* (Detroit: Wayne State University Press, 1988), 14–15.

17. Penkower, *The Jews Were Expendable,* 14–15.

18. Aaron Berman, *Nazism, the Jews, and American Zionism, 1933–1948* (Detroit: Wayne State University Press, 1990), 85–95.

19. Welles to Lazaron, 31 March 1942, Sumner Welles Papers, box 80, folder 8 (Lazaron January–May 1942), Roosevelt Library.

20. Wasserstein, *Britain and the Jews of Europe,* 275–285. "British Will Form Palestine Force," *New York Times,* 7 August 1942, p. 8. "Too Little But Not Yet Too Late" [advertisement], *New York Times,* 18 August 1942, p. 18. Minutes of the Joint Committee on Information Policy, 26 August 1942, RG 208, entry 1, box 5, policies and procedures-3, NARA; Berle's statement in Minutes of the 16th Meeting of the Interdepartmental Committee for Foreign Nationality Problems, RG 226, entry 86, box 1, NARA. Sulzberger's statement in "Sulzberger Bids Jews Drop Plan for Own Army," *New York Herald Tribune,* 6 November 1942.

21. U.S. State Department, Division of European Affairs, Memorandum: Committee for a Jewish Army, 23 September 1943; U.S. Department of Justice, Memorandum: Conference with Free Palestine Committee, 1 March 1944; Bergson to Cordell Hull, 19 June 1944, Papers of the Palestine Statehood Committee, microfilm, reels 3 and 5, Sterling Memorial Library, Yale University, New Haven, Connecticut (henceforth Sterling Library).

22. Rosenman Memorandum for the President, 23 May 1942, PPF 601, Zionist Organization of America, Roosevelt Library. On the American Palestine Committee see Caitlin Carenen, "The American Christian Palestine Committee, the Holocaust, and Mainstream Protestant Zionism, 1938–1948," *Holocaust and Genocide Studies* 24 (Fall 2010): 273–296.

23. "President Offers Hope for Palestine," *New York Times,* 26 May 1942, p. 13. For the full statement see "Developments in Palestine Are Praised by Roosevelt," *Baltimore Sun,* 26 March 1942, p. 3.

24. Wiley to Donovan, 27 May 1942, RG 226, entry 180G, Microfilm A-3556, reel 49, NARA.

25. "Welles Predicts Postwar World Policed by Allies," *New York Times,* 31 May 1942, p. 6. OSS Foreign Nationalities Branch, Foreign Politics in the United States, no. 54, 17 July 1942, "Arabic and Zionist Activities in the United States," RG 226, entry 368, box 350, Foreign Politics in the U.S., NARA.

26. Office of War Information Directive re Palestine, 15 November 1942, copy in Archibald MacLeish Papers, box 52, Library of Congress, Washington, D.C. (henceforth LC).

27. "New Jewish Group Being Formed Here," *New York Times,* 12 December 1942, p. 20; Lazaron to Welles, 30 November 1942, Sumner Welles Papers, box 80, folder 9 (June–December 1942), Roosevelt Library. On the council's campaign see Louis Newman to Rabbi William F. Rosenblum, 11 February 1943, Stephen S. Wise Papers, reel 74-63, AJHS. On Lazaron's reactions to mass meetings see Lazaron telephone message for Welles, 30 March 1943, Sumner Welles Papers, box 89, folder 7 (Lazaron 1943), Roosevelt Library.

28. See the hostile summary of and commentary on Heller's 1 February 1943 speech in Nashville by M. Don Clawson, dean of the school of dentistry at Meharry Medical School. Clawson to Penrose, 1 February 1943, RG 226, entry

210, box 377, WN 14476, NARA. On Silver and the Biltmore Conference see Marc Lee Raphael, *Abba Hillel Silver: A Profile in American Judaism* (New York: Holmes and Meier, 1989), 85–86.

29. 3 December 1942, The Morgenthau Diaries: Prelude to War and War, 1940–1942, microfilm, reel 112, LC.

30. Ibid. "Senate, House Join in Palestine Plea," *New York Times,* 5 December 1942, p. 9.

31. Kenneth S. Davis, *FDR: The War President, 1940–1943* (New York: Random House, 2000), 703. Berle, *Navigating the Rapids,* 428 (entry of 28 November 1942).

32. "President's Statement on Darlan" and "President Eases Fears of French," *New York Times,* 18 November 1942, p. 4. Landau to Berle, 27 January 1943 (referring back to their conversation of November), American Jewish Committee Records, RG 347, EXO-29, box 8, folder 169a, Crémieux Decree, YIVO Institute for Jewish Research, New York, New York (henceforth YIVO).

33. Patton to Eisenhower, 22 November 1942, RG 331, Film 71D, File 091, NARA. Michel Abitbol, *The Jews of North Africa during the Second World War,* trans. Catherine Tihanyi Zentelis (Detroit: Wayne State University Press, 1989), 114, 152–153.

34. Abitbol, *The Jews of North Africa,* 112–113, 153–157.

35. Gerhard L. Weinberg, *A World at Arms: A Global History of World War II* (New York: Cambridge University Press, 2005), 436–438.

36. *Foreign Relations of the United States* (henceforth *FRUS*), *The Conferences at Washington, 1941–42 and Casablanca 1943* (Washington, DC: U.S. Government Printing Office, 1968), 608. Some have suggested that FDR's remarks indicated that he favored quotas for Jews, which is contradicted by his appointment of Jews to professional positions in the federal government far beyond Jewish representation in the population. He had also withstood considerable opposition to appoint a Jew to the Supreme Court.

37. Berle to Landau, 9 March 1943; Proskauer to Welles, 17 March 1943; Welles to Backer, 24 March 1943; Gottschalk to Rosenblum, 16 April 1943; Proskauer to Welles, 17 May 1943; Welles to Proskauer, 20 May 1943—all in American Jewish Committee Records, RG 347, EXO-29, box 8, folder 169a, YIVO. Abitbol, *The Jews of North Africa,* 155–165. Officials failed to maintain the abrogation of Vichy's Crémieux Decree.

38. William D. Hassett, *Off the Record with F.D.R.: 1942–1945* (New Brunswick, NJ: Rutgers University Press, 1958), 169. Weinberg, *A World at Arms,* 439–442. Warren F. Kimball, ed., *Churchill and Roosevelt: The Complete Correspondence* (Princeton: Princeton University Press, 1984), 212–227. Richard Breitman and Alan M. Kraut, *American Refugee Policy and European Jewry, 1933–1945* (Bloomington: Indiana University Press, 1987), 178–179.

39. Henry A. Wallace Diary, 23 May 1943, University of Iowa Libraries, Special Collections, Iowa City, Iowa.

40. Makovsky, *Churchill's Promised Land,* 189. On the American military and Jews in North Africa see Joint Chiefs of Staff to Secretary of State, 26 April and 7 May 1943, in *FRUS,* 1943, vol. 1 (Washington, DC: U.S. Government Printing Office, 1943), 296–299. On the North African camps see Breitman and Kraut, *American Refugee Policy,* 178. Long Memorandum of Conversation with Campbell re Refugees to North Africa, 4 June 1943, RG 59 840.48 Refugees/3880, NARA.

41. Bowman's notes after meeting with FDR, 18 May 1943, and Bowman to FDR, 22 May 1943; also Bowman Memo of Conversation with Sumner Welles, 10 December 1942, Isaiah Bowman Papers, Section XIV.6, Franklin Rooosevelt 1943, and XIV.7, Welles, Milton S. Eisenhower Library, Johns Hopkins University, Baltimore, Maryland (henceforth Eisenhower Library).

42. Memorandum of H.F.A's Talk with Lieutenant Colonel Harold Hoskins, 16 March 1943, Hamilton Fish Armstrong Papers, box 100, Notebooks and Memoranda 1943, Seeley G. Mudd Manuscript Library, Princeton University, Princeton, New Jersey. It is possible that Hoskins tempered his views for Armstrong, who served as a member of the President's Advisory Committee on Political Refugees.

43. Hull to FDR, 7 May 1943; Undated Summary of Colonel Hoskins's Report on the Near East OSS Trend Memorandum, 16 April 1943, Holocaust/Refugee Collection, boxes 11, 9, Roosevelt Library.

44. M. Don Clawson, dean of the school of dentistry at Meharry Medical School. Clawson to Penrose, 1 February 1943, RG 226, entry 210, box 377, WN 14476, NARA.

45. Weizmann's summary attached to Weizmann to Klotz, 15 June 1943, The Morgenthau Diaries: World War II and Postwar Planning, 1943–1945 (henceforth Morgenthau Diaries), microfilm, reel 11, LC. Makovsky, *Churchill's Promised Land,* 204–205.

46. Weizmann to Klotz, 15 June 1943, Morgenthau Diaries, reel 11, LC. But Weizmann had justified fears about the United States sending Harold Hoskins to see Ibn Saud. Weizmann to Welles, 25 June 1943, Sumner Welles Papers, box 93, folder 9, Roosevelt Library.

47. Murray to Hull, 17 August 1943, and Murray's Chronology, 12 August 1943, RG 59, 867.01/1908 1/2, NARA; Chronology of Extracts from Documents on the Arab-Jewish Controversy attached to Memorandum for the President, 30 July 1943, RG 59, 867N.01/1890 1/2, NARA. Although signed by Hull, the second document was also prepared by Murray. They also drew support from diplomatic, OSS, and military intelligence reports from June 1941 complaining about the damaging effects in the Middle East of Zionist activities and pro-Zionist statements by politicians in the United States, including Wendell Willkie. The Office of War

Information's representative in Beirut, for example, complained about the widespread Moslem belief that a circle of Jewish advisers in the White House determined American policy.

48. Hull to FDR, 19 July 1943, and Statement for Issuance by the Governments of the United States and the United Kingdom regarding Palestine, RG 59, 867N.01/1882 1/2, NARA. On Weizmann's views in writing see Weizmann to Welles, 1 February 1943, RG 59, 867N.01/1834, NARA.

49. Morgenthau's statement on Murray in Morgenthau's comment in transcript of Jewish Evacuation Meeting, 8 March 1944, Morgenthau Diaries, reel 28, LC. Welles to FDR, 19 May 1943, Welles Papers, box 93, folder 9, Roosevelt Library. Hull to FDR, 19 July 1943, and Statement for Issuance by the Governments of the United States and the United Kingdom regarding Palestine, RG 59, 867N.01/1882 1/2, NARA. At the top: CH, OK, FDR.

50. Wise to Welles, 23 July 1943, Sumner Welles Papers, box 93, folder 12, Roosevelt Library.

51. "Wise Asks Roosevelt Aid," *New York Times,* 23 July 1943, p. 11. This account is largely based on the chronology prepared by Murray, attached to Murray to Hull, 17 August 1943, RG 59, 867N.01/1908 1/2, NARA.

See also Morgenthau Memo regarding conversation with Rosenman, 3 August 1943, Morgenthau Diaries, reel 14, LC. Drew Pearson's column of 9 August follows the main thrust of Murray's version, adding Major General Pat Hurley and Berle to those responsible for the State Department's venture. "Merry-Go-Round," *Washington Post,* 9 August 1943, p. 4.

52. Chronology prepared by Murray, attached to Murray to Hull, 17 August 1943, RG 59, 867N.01/1908 1/2, NARA. Wise to Billikopf, 19 August 1943, Stephen S. Wise Papers, reel 74-66, AJHS.

53. "Merry-Go-Round," *Washington Post,* 9 August 1943, 4. On Hurley and Ibn Saud see Makovsky, *Churchill's Promised Land,* 205. Hurley to FDR, 5 May 1943, in *FRUS,* 1943, vol. 4 (Washington, DC: U.S. Government Printing Office, 1943), 776–780. Hurley, however, had little influence at State. Roosevelt accepted Welles's resignation on 11 August.

54. For Bowman's 10 August 1943 memo recounting the previous day's events see Isaiah Bowman Papers, Section XIV.6, FDR 1943, Eisenhower Library.

55. *FRUS, The Conferences at Washington and Quebec, 1943* (Washington, DC: U.S. Government Printing Office, 1943), 930–932. Roosevelt recounted his conversation with Churchill to Joseph Proskauer in April 1945. See Draft Confidential Memorandum for the President [Truman] Submitted by the President of the American Jewish Committee [Proskauer], undated [June 1945], American Jewish Committee Records, RG 347, EXO-29, box 31, folder 11, YIVO, and Proskauer to Truman, 6 July 1945, cited by Zvi Ganin, *Truman, American Jewry, and Israel* (New York: Holmes and Meier, 1979), 31.

56. On Bowman's detachment from the M Project see Neil Smith, *American Empire: Roosevelt's Geographer and the Prelude to Globalization* (Berkeley: University of California Press, 2003), 302–305. On Field's enthusiasm for the absorptive capacity of Palestine augmented by a strip of Transjordan, and Bowman's severe criticism, see Bowman Memo of Meeting with Henry Field, John Carter, Strauss-Hupé, and Jacobsen, 28 October 1943, Isaiah Bowman Papers, Section XIV.6 FDR 1943; The Absorptive Capacity of Palestine, 27 March 1944, Section IX.21—both in Eisenhower Library.

57. Transcript of Treasury group meeting, 4 and 13 February 1944, Morgenthau Diaries, reel 27, LC. For the text of the Wright-Compton resolution see Cyrus Adler and Aaron Morris Margaith, *With Firmness in the Right: American Diplomatic Action Affecting Jews, 1840–1945* (Philadelphia: Jewish Publication Society, 1946), 399.

58. Raphael, *Abba Hillel Silver,* 99–100.

59. Long's Memorandum of Conversation with Silver, 24 February 1944, RG 59, 867N.01/2248, NARA. Interview with David Niles, 23 February 1944, Abba Hillel Silver Papers, Microfilm, reel 103, Eisenhower Library.

60. Neumann to Silver, 24 February 1944, Abba Hillel Silver Papers, reel 103, Eisenhower Library. Long's Memorandum of Conversation with Silver, 24 February 1944, RG 59, 867N.01/2248, NARA. Transcript of Jewish Evacuation Meeting, 9 March 1944, Morgenthau Diaries, reel 29, LC.

61. Murray to Stettinius, 4 March 1944 and Stettinius to Murray, 8 March 1944, RG 59, 867N.01/2275A, NARA.

62. The next day, Roosevelt related parts of their conversation to the cabinet, and Morgenthau repeated his summary to Treasury officials. Transcript of Jewish Evacuation Meeting, 11 March 1944, Morgenthau Diaries, reel 29, LC. Clarence E. Wunderlin, *Robert A. Taft: Ideas, Tradition, and Party in U.S. Foreign Policy* (Lanham, MD: Rowman and Littlefield, 2005), 133.

63. Transcript of Jewish Evacuation Meeting, 11 March 1944, Morgenthau Diaries, reel 29, LC. "Roosevelt Backs Palestine Plan as Homeland for Refugee Jews," *New York Times,* 10 March 1944, p. 1.

64. American Zionist Emergency Council, Confidential Bulletin, 29 March 1944; Silver, Address, 9 March 1944; Shapiro, Memorandum, 24 March 1944—all in Abba Hillel Silver Papers, reel 102, Eisenhower Library; "President on Palestine," New York Times, 29 March 1944, p. 3.

65. Raphael, *Abba Hillel Silver,* 100–102.

66. Long's Memorandum of Conversation with Senators Connolly, Barkley, George, Vandenberg, and LaFollette, 5 February 1944, copy in Palestine Statehood Committee Papers, reel 3, Sterling Library. William Hicks [codename of Nelson Glueck] to Jacob Marcus, 1 May 1944, censorship intercept, RG 226, entry 210, box 369, folder 17, NARA.

67. Raphael, *Abba Hillel Silver,* 110–112.

68. Ibid. 110–115.

69. Taft to Stimson, 12 September 1944, Robert A. Taft Papers, box 734, Palestine and the Jews 1944, LC. Raphael, *Abba Hillel Silver,* 119. Wise to Rosenman, 26 September 1944; Rosenman to Wise, 27 September 1944, Samuel Rosenman Papers, box 4, Wise folder, Roosevelt Library.

70. Rosenman Memorandum for the President, 7 October 1944. Samuel Rosenman Papers, box 4, Wise folder, Roosevelt Library.

71. Rosenman to FDR, 12 October 1944, Samuel Rosenman Papers, box 4, Wise folder, Roosevelt Library.

72. FDR to Wagner, 13 October 1944, PPF 601, Zionist Organization of America, Roosevelt Library. Silver telegram to FDR, 15 October 1944; Leo Sack telegram to FDR, 15 October 1944; Israel Goldstein telegram to FDR, 15 October 1944; Sack to General Watson, 20 October 1944—all PPF 601, Roosevelt Library.

73. Michael J. Cohen, "The Churchill-Gilbert Symbiosis: Myth and Reality, Martin Gilbert, *Churchill and the Jews," Modern Judaism* 28, no. 2 (2008): 204–228, esp. 218.

74. Interrogation of Hoth, March 15, 1946/PWIS (Norway)/83, RG 319, Hoth IRR D 33387, NARA; RG 226, entry 119a, box 25, folder 639, NARA. Mallmann and Cüppers, *Nazi Palestine,* 110.

75. Davis, *FDR: The War President,* 534–536. Weinberg, *A World at Arms,* 350–351. Mallmann and Cüppers, *Nazi Palestine,* 106. Andrew Roberts, *Masters and Commanders: How Four Titans Won the War in the West, 1941–1945* (New York: HarperCollins, 2009), 206–207.

13. THE WAR REFUGEE BOARD

1. Randolph L. Braham, The *Politics of Genocide: The Holocaust in Hungary,* vol. 2 (New York: Columbia University Press, 1981), 1110. Translated copy of newspaper article in War Refugee Board records, box 33, vol. 1, Franklin D. Roosevelt Library, Hyde Park, New York (henceforth Roosevelt Library).

2. Memorandum for the Policy Committee, 6 March 1944, RG 59, Lot File 53D289, box 1, War Refugee Board—Miscellaneous January–March 1944, National Archives and Records Administration, College Park, Maryland (henceforth NARA). See also Michaela Hoenicke Moore, *Know Your Enemy: The American Debate on Nazism, 1933–1945* (New York: Cambridge University Press, 2010), 152–153, 194–195. The operations of the Jewish Anti-Fascist Committee were an exception to general Soviet policy. The Soviets hoped to generate some Jewish support abroad with their efforts.

3. Bernard Wasserstein, *Britain and the Jews of Europe, 1939–1945* (Oxford: Clarendon Press, 1979), 233.

4. Stimson diary entry, 18 January 1944; see also 1 February 1944—both reel 8, Library of Congress, Washington, D.C. (henceforth LC).

5. Transcript of Treasury group meeting of 26 January 1944 and transcript of Morgenthau's phone call with Stettinius, 26 January 1944, The Morgenthau Diaries: World War II and Postwar Planning, 1943–1945 (henceforth Morgenthau Diaries), microfilm, reel 26, LC.

6. Transcript of Treasury group meeting of 26 January 1944 and transcript of Morgenthau's phone call with Stettinius, 26 January 1944, Morgenthau Diaries, reel 26, LC. Ernst to FDR, 27 January 1944, PSF, box 173, War Refugee Board, Roosevelt Library. Stimson also recommended State Department official Thomas Finletter, Office of Strategic Services official Allen Dulles (who was in Switzerland), and Allen Wardwell, president of the New York City Bar Association. Stimson Diary, 26 January 1944, reel 8, LC.

7. "Willkie Critical on Roosevelt Trip," New York Times, 27 January 1943, p. 5. On the rejection of Willkie, David S. Wyman, The Abandonment of the Jews: America and the Holocaust, 1941–1945 (New York: New Press, 1984), 210–211, calls Willkie an ideal candidate. On Willkie's problems see Kenneth S. Davis, FDR: The War President, 1940–1943 (New York: Random House, 2000), 632–641, 701.

8. Stimson Diary, 26 January 1944, reel 8, LC. Stimson to Morgenthau, 26 January 1944, Morgenthau Diaries, reel 26, LC. On FDR's approval of Pehle see transcript of Treasury group meeting, 4 February 1944, Morgenthau Diaries, reel 27, LC.

9. Stimson Diary, 1 February 1944, reel 8, LC.

10. Richard Breitman and Alan M. Kraut, American Refugee Policy and European Jewry, 1933–1945 (Bloomington: Indiana University Press, 1987), 191–194. Wyman, Abandonment of the Jews, 210–211. The most detailed record of War Refugee Board operations is an institutional history, which is in the War Refugee Board records at the Roosevelt Library.

11. Jewish Evacuation Meeting, 10:30 a.m., 13 February 1944, Morgenthau Diaries, reel 27, LC. Memo for Record, 23 June 1944, Proposed Air Action to Impede Deportation of Hungarian and Slovak Jews, tracing the history of War Department statements, RG 165, entry 418, box 1304, OPD 383.7, NARA. War Refugee Board to American Embassy, London, 9 February 1944, copy in Edward R. Stettinius Jr. Papers, box 745, War Refugee Board folder, Small Special Collections Library, University of Virginia, Charlottesville, Virginia (henceforth Small Library).

12. Wyman, Abandonment of the Jews, 292–293.

13. Ernst to FDR, 21 February 1944; FDR Memo for the Under Secretary of War, 24 February 1944; Patterson Memorandum for the President, 26 February 1944—all PSF, box 173, War Refugee Board, Roosevelt Library. An alternative mission eventually led Franco, in late 1944, to issue up to 2,000 passports and

letters of patronage to Hungarian Jews who claimed Spanish descent. On Spanish protection in the fall see Breitman and Kraut, *American Refugee Policy,* 208–210.

14. Pehle to Stettinius, 11 February 1944, RG 59, 840.48 Refugees/5278, NARA. Transcript of Jewish Evacuation Meeting, 13 February 1944, Morgenthau Diaries, reel 27, LC.

15. Foreign Office Memorandum, 25 January 1944, attached to Raynor to Pehle, 5 January 1944, War Refugee Board Records, box 30, Roosevelt Library. Copy in Morgenthau Diaries, reel 27, LC.

16. Transcript of Jewish Evacuation Meeting, 13 February and 8 March 1944 and draft undated Report to the War Refugee Board, Morgenthau Diaries, reels 27 and 28, LC.

17. Stettinius to Early, 6 March 1944, Holocaust/Refugee Collection, box 7, Roosevelt Library. Transcript of Jewish Evacuation Meeting, 8 March 1944, Morgenthau Diaries, reel 28, LC; Stettinius to Long, Dunn, Berle, and Hackworth, 25 February 1944, Edward R. Stettinius Jr. Papers, box 215, Long, October 1943, Small Library; Memorandum for the Policy Committee, 6 March 1944, RG 59, Lot File 53D289, box 1, War Refugee Board—Miscellaneous January–March 1944, NARA.

18. Stettinius to Long, Shaw, Murray, McDermott, Achilles, 8 March 1944, Edward R. Stettinius Jr. Papers, box 215, Long folder October 1943, Small Library. Stettinius to Early, 8 March 1944, Holocaust/Refugee Collection, box 7, Roosevelt Library. Transcript of Jewish Evacuation Meeting, 11 March 1944, Morgenthau Diaries, reel 29, LC.

19. Pehle Memorandum for the Files, 8 March 1944, Morgenthau Diaries, reel 28, LC. Stimson Diary, 9 March, 1944, reel 8, LC. Transcript of Jewish Evacuation Meeting, 9 March 1944, Morgenthau Diaries, reel 29, LC.

20. Transcript of Jewish Evacuation Meeting, 17 March 1944, and [Morgenthau's] Conversation with the President, 18 March 1944, Morgenthau Diaries, reel 30, LC. Minutes of the Third Meeting of the War Refugee Board, 21 March 1944, RG 59, Lot File 53D289, box 1, War Refugee Board—Miscellaneous January–March 1944, NARA.

21. "FDR Assailed in Creating of Refugee Board," *Democrat and Chronicle,* 21 March 1944, copy in Morgenthau Diaries, reel 30, LC.

22. "Roosevelt Warns Germans on Jews," *New York Times,* 25 March 1944, p. 1. On March 24, Soviet ambassador Andrei Gromyko said he had already seen the president's statement. Landau strictly confidential memo, 27 March 1944, American Jewish Committee Records, RG 347, EXO-29, box 17, Hungary 1944, YIVO Institute for Jewish Research, New York, New York (henceforth YIVO). Braham, *The Politics of Genocide,* 1070.

23. "Roosevelt Warns Germans on Jews" and "Aid for Axis Victims," *New York Times,* 25 March 1944, pp. 1, 4.

24. Minutes of the Third Meeting of the War Refugee Board, 21 March 1944, RG 59, Lot File 53D289, box 1, War Refugee Board—Miscellaneous Jan.–March 1944, NARA. Ruth Gruber, *Haven: The Unknown Story of 1000 World War II Refugees* (New York: New American Library, 1984), 32. Stimson diary, 9 and 21 March 1944, reel 8, and 8 May 1944, reel 9, LC. Stimson to Pehle, 31 March 1944, Morgenthau Diaries, reel 31, LC.

25. Confidential Memorandum [Morris D. Waldman], February 1944, American Jewish Committee Records, RG 347, EXO-29, box 41, folder 3 U.S. Government—Waldman, YIVO; Transcript of War Refugee Meeting, 13 February 1944, Morgenthau Diaries, reel 27, LC; Pehle, Memorandum for Mr. Stettinius, 10 March 1944, RG 59, Lot File 52D 408, box 2, folder IGC-WRB, NARA.

26. DuBois, Report to the War Refugee Board, 6 March 1944, Morgenthau Diaries, reel 28, LC.

27. Gruber, *Haven,* 32. Samuel Grafton, "I'd Rather Be Right," *Zanesville Signal,* 6 April 1944, p. 4. Wise to Pehle, 3 April 1944, copy in Morgenthau Diaries, reel 31, LC.

28. Cantril to Niles, 14 April 1944, Samuel Rosenman Papers, box 14, Princeton Public Opinion Poll, Roosevelt Library. William D. Hassett, *Off the Record with F.D.R.: 1942–1945* (New Brunswick, NJ: Rutgers University Press, 1958), 241.

29. Undated Memorandum re Establishment of Temporary Havens of Refugee in the United States, and Memorandum for the President, 8 May 1944, RG 59, Lot File 53D289, box 1, War Refugee Board, Emergency Shelter, NARA.

30. Ibid.; Pehle to Hull, Morgenthau, and Stimson, confidential, 20 May 1944, RG 59, Lot File 53D289, box 1, War Refugee Board, Emergency Shelter, NARA.

31. Pehle to Hull, Morgenthau, and Stimson, confidential, 20 May 1944, RG 59, Lot File 53D289, box 1, War Refugee Board, Emergency Shelter, NARA.

32. Tully Memorandum for the President, 22 May 1944, PSF, box 158, Refugees, Roosevelt Library.

33. Biddle's cabinet notes, 26 May 1944, Francis Biddle Papers, box 1, Cabinet Meetings, January 1944–May 1945, Roosevelt Library. Stimson Diary, 26 May 1944, reel 9, LC. Pehle Memorandum for the Files, 1 June 1944, Morgenthau Diaries, reel 37, LC. See also Gruber, *Haven,* 13 and 33, which is inaccurate on some details.

34. Pehle Memorandum for the Files, 1 June 1944, and transcript of Jewish Evacuation Meeting, 2 June 1944, Morgenthau Diaries, reel 37, LC.

35. Transcript of Telephone Conversation between Morgenthau and McCloy, 2 June 1944; Pehle Memorandum for the Files, 8 June 1944; FDR to Murphy, 8 June 1944—all in Morgenthau Diaries, reel 37, LC.

36. "Port of Refuge," *New York Times,* 10 June 1944, p. 14; "Asylum for Some of the Refugees," *Baltimore Sun,* 10 June 1944, p. 6.

37. Kubowitzki to Lesser, 21 April 1944, War Refugee Board Records, box 35, World Jewish Congress, vol. 1, Roosevelt Library.

38. Minutes of the Executive Committee, World Jewish Congress, 25 April 1944, World Jewish Congress Records, box A 78, folder 15, American Jewish Archives, Cincinnati, Ohio. OWI to Control Desk, New York, and Sherwood and Backer, London, 25 April 1945, RG 208, entry 359, box 116, folder refugee policy, NARA. War Refugee Board developments during the week of 8–13 May 1944, copy in Morgenthau Diaries, reel 35, LC. Summary of steps taken by War Refugee Board with respect to the Jews of Hungary, copy in RG 107, entry 180, box 644, ASW 400.38 Jews, NARA.

39. Report of War Refugee Board for Week of 15–20 May 1944, copy in Morgenthau Diaries, reel 35, LC. Secretary of State to Tittmann via American Legation, Bern, 26 May 1944, copy in Morgenthau Diaries, reel 36, LC.

40. "President Predicts Murder Orgy by Nazis to Wipe Out Minorities," *New York Times,* 13 June 1944, p. 1.

41. "Hungary Warned by Congressmen," *New York Times,* 22 June 1944, p. 12. "Hull Backs Move to Warn Hungary," *New York Times,* 27 June 1944, p. 6. Report of the War Refugee Board for Week of 29 May–3 June 1944, and the Week 19–24 June 1944, Morgenthau Diaries, reels 37 and 38, LC. Braham, *Politics of Genocide,* 1110–11. Pehle to Morgenthau, 6 September 1944, War Refugee Board Records, box 34, Hungary, vol. 1, Roosevelt Library.

42. Rudolf Vrba, *I Escaped from Auschwitz* (New York: Barricade Books, 2002). Copy of the report, appendix 3, 327–363. Randolph L. Braham, "Hungary: The Controversial Chapter of the Holocaust," in *The Auschwitz Reports and the Holocaust in Hungary,* ed. Randolph L. Braham and William J. vanden Heuvel (Boulder, CO: East European Monographs, 2012), 45–46, expresses skepticism that Vrba heard in 1944 that Hungarian Jews would soon begin to arrive.

43. Description of the Concentration Camp at Oswiecim [Auschwitz], from F. L. Belin to William L. Langer, 10 April 1944, RG 226, entry 16, #66059, NARA;"Jews in Hungary Fear," *New York Times,* 10 May 1944, p. 5; "Savage Blows Hit Jews in Hungary," *New York Times,* 18 May 1944, p. 5; "Inquiry Confirms Nazi Death Camps," *New York Times,* 3 July 1944, p. 3.

14. NEGOTIATIONS AND RESCUE IN HUNGARY

1. Randolph L. Braham, *The Politics of Genocide: The Holocaust in Hungary,* vol. 2 (New York: Columbia University Press, 1981), 744–745.

2. Leland Harrison to Secretary of State, 11 August 1944, from McClelland to War Refugee Board, War Refugee Board Records, box 118, WRB History— Documents, Franklin D. Roosevelt Library, Hyde Park, New York (henceforth Roosevelt Library).

3. Richard Breitman and Shlomo Aronson, "The End of the Final Solution: Nazi Attempts to Ransom Jews in 1944," *Central European History* 25, no. 2 (1992): 177–203; Shlomo Aronson, *Hitler, the Allies and the Jews* (New York: Cambridge University Press, 2006), 227–231, 237–247.

4. Aronson, *Hitler, the Allies, and the Jews,* 254–256.

5. Assistant Defense Security Office, Northern Syria, 12 June 1944, copy in RG 226, entry 196, box 76, folder 196, National Archives and Records Administration, College Park, Maryland (henceforth NARA); OSS, Hungary, Political: Exchange of Refugees, 17 July 1944, RG 226, entry 16, no. 85291, NARA. On the views of the Jewish Agency see Tuvia Friling, "Nazi-Jewish Negotiations in Istanbul in mid-1944," *Holocaust and Genocide Studies* 13, no. 3 (1999): 405–436.

6. Braham, *The Politics of Genocide,* 1104.

7. Transcript of Stettinius-Morgenthau Conversation, 5 June 1944, and Aide Mémoire, 5 June 1944; The Morgenthau Diaries: World War II and Postwar Planning, 1943–1945 (henceforth Morgenthau Diaries), microfilm, reel 37, Library of Congress, Washington, D.C. (henceforth LC). McCloy to Stettinius, 10 June 1944, and Stettinius to McCloy, 14 June 1944, Edward R. Stettinius Jr. Papers, box 742, War Department, Small Special Collections Library, University of Virginia, Charlottesville, Virginia (henceforth Small Library).

8. Resnik's strictly confidential memorandum for the American Ambassador [Steinhardt], 4 June 1944, copy in RG 226, entry 168A, box 1, folder 12, NARA. See also Aronson, *Hitler, the Allies, and the Jews,* 248–249.

9. Stettinius Memorandum of Conversation, 7 June 1944, Edward R. Stettinius Jr. Papers, box 274, Memorandum of Conversation L-2, Small Library; Pehle's Memorandum for the Files, 8 June 1944, Morgenthau Diaries, reel 37, LC.

10. Braham, *Politics of Genocide,* 2:1077–1089. Hirschmann, Memorandum to Ambassador Steinhardt, 22 June 1944 and Hirschmann Interrogation of Mr. Joel Brandt, 22 June 1944, RG 226, entry 196, box 76, folder 196, NARA; OSS to Ustravic London, 4 and 7 July 1944, RG 226, entry 134, box 245, folder 1499, NARA.

11. Braham, *The Politics of Genocide,* 1105, 1109. Aronson, *Hitler, the Allies, and the Jews,* 252–253.

12. Pehle to Stettinius, 27 July 1944 and Harrison to Hull, 11 August 1944 (containing McClelland communiqué) War Refugee Board Records, box 70, Joel Brand Proposal, and box 113, WRB History, respectively, Roosevelt Library.

13. Report of the War Refugee Board for Week of 29 May–3 June 1944, Morgenthau Diaries, reel 37, LC; Braham, *Politics of Genocide,* 2:752–763, 1070–1073.

14. Braham, *Politics of Genocide,* 2:743–62.

15. For statistics see Bela Vago, "The Horthy Offer: A Missed Opportunity for Rescuing Jews in 1944," in Randolph L. Braham, ed., *Contemporary Views on the Holocaust* (Boston: Kluwer-Nijhoff, 1983), 38.

16. Pehle to Stettinius, 29 July 1944, RG 59, Lot File 53D, 289, box 2, WRB June–July 1944, NARA; John G. Winant [American Ambassador to Great Britain] to Hull, 16 August 1944, and Hull to Winant, 28 August, in *Foreign Relations of the United States* (henceforth *FRUS*), *1944, vol. 1* (Washington, DC: U.S. Government Printing Office, 1966), 1125–1127, 1138–1139.

17. David S. Wyman, *The Abandonment of the Jews: America and the Holocaust, 1941–1945* (New York: New Press, 1984), 15.

18. Martin Gilbert, "The Contemporary Case for the Feasibility of Bombing Auschwitz," in *The Bombing of Auschwitz: Should the Allies Have Attempted It?*, ed. Michael J. Neufeld and Michael Berenbaum (New York: St. Martin's Press, 2003), 65–67. Wyman, *The Abandonment of the Jews*, 289–291. Martin Gilbert, *Auschwitz and the Allies* (New York: Holt, Rinehart and Winston, 1981), 256. Kubowitzki to Frischer, 2 August 1944, War Refugee Board Records, box 4, Censorship Intercepts, Roosevelt Library. Pehle Memorandum for the Files, 11 August 1944, and Pehle to Morgenthau, 6 September 1944, What we have done with respect to Hungary, War Refugee Board Records, box 34, Hungary, I, Roosevelt Library.

19. Wyman, *Abandonment of the Jews*, 292–293. Tami Davis Biddle, "Allied Air Power: Objectives and Capabilities," in Neufeld and Berenbaum. *The Bombing of Auschwitz,* 43.

20. Pehle Memorandum for the Files, 24 June 1944, War Refugee Board Records, box 35, Hungary, Roosevelt Library. See also Gilbert, "The Contemporary Case," 66. Pehle to Morgenthau, 6 September 1944, What we have done with respect to Hungary, War Refugee Board Records, box 34, Hungary I, Roosevelt Library.

21. Proposed Air Action to Impede Deportation of Hungarian and Slovak Jews, 26 June 1944, and McCloy to Pehle, 4 July 1944, RG 107, entry 180, box 44, ASW 400.38 Jews, NARA.

22. Kai Bird, *The Chairman: John J. McCloy and the Making of the American Establishment* (New York: Simon & Schuster, 1992), 217.

23. Biddle, "Allied Air Power," 35–48. Bird, *The Chairman,* 218.

24. Gilbert, "The Contemporary Case," 68.

25. Lesser Draft Memorandum for the President, 13 July 1944, War Refugee Board Records, box 34, Hungary folder I, Roosevelt Library. Memorandum for the Members of the War Refugee Board, 15 July 1944, RG 107, entry 180, box 44, ASW 400.38 Jews, NARA.

26. Gilbert, *Auschwitz and the Allies,* 301, 319.

27. This paragraph is drawn from Kevin A. Mahoney, "An American Operational Response to a Request to Bomb Rail Lines to Auschwitz," *Holocaust and Genocide Studies* 25 (Winter 2011): 438–446.

28. Gilbert, *Auschwitz and the Allies,* 306. Michael Makovsky, *Churchill's Promised Land: Zionism and Statecraft* (New Haven: Yale University Press, 2007),

182. Mann to War Refugee Board, 29 September 1944, Morgenthau Diaries, reel 49, LC. Pehle to McCloy, undated, received 1 October 1944, and Gerhardt Memorandum for McCloy, 5 October 1944, RG 107, entry 180, box 44, ASW 400.38 Jews, NARA.

29. Private letter from Luzie Klaja to Erich Klaja, 23 August 1944, captured on the Isle of Rhodes, distributed by Anglo-Egyptian censorship, 23 October 1944, RG 226, entry 136, box 509, folder 14, NARA. Wyman, *Abandonment of the Jews,* 299.

30. Mahoney, "An American Operational Response."

31. Virginia M. Mannon Memorandum to Files, 22 November 1944, War Refugee Board Records, box 6, German Extermination Camps, Roosevelt Library; Pehle to McCloy, 8 November 1944; Hull Memorandum for the Assistant Secretary of War, 14 November 1944; and McCloy to Pehle, 18 November 1944, RG 107, entry 180, box 44, ASW 400.38 Germany, and RG 165, box 390, ABC-383.6 (8 November 1943)—all in NARA. Wyman, *Abandonment of the Jews,* 297–298. Bird, *The Chairman,* 221.

32. Stimson diary entry, 27 November 1944, reel 9, LC.

33. McCloy presented his version through a writer with whom he worked on a book and in the form of a long letter to the editor. Edward T. Chase, "Why We Didn't Bomb Auschwitz," *Washington Post,* 21 May 1983, p. 13.

34. Ibid. Mortin Mintz, "Why We Didn't Bomb Auschwitz: Can John McCloy's Memories Be Correct?," *Washington Post,* 17 April 1983, p. D1.

35. See, for example, Wyman, *Abandonment of the Jews,* 304. For debates on the feasibility of a successful air raid see the articles in Neufeld and Berenbaum, *The Bombing of Auschwitz,* 59–179. See also J. R. White, "Target Auschwitz: Historical and Hypothetical German Responses to Attack," *Holocaust and Genocide Studies* 16 (2002): 54–76.

36. "40,000 Here Seek Way to Save Jews," *New York Times,* 1 August 1944, p. 17; "Jewish Relief Discussed at Mass Meeting," *Los Angeles Times,* 29 August 1944, p. 1. Interview of Bergson in *Not Idly By: Peter Bergson, America and the Holocaust,* 2012 film directed by Pierre Sauvage.

37. Pehle, Memorandum for the Files, 10 August 1944, War Refugee Board Records, file Hungary No. 1, Roosevelt Library. I. L. Kenen, American Jewish Conference, Report of Meeting with John W. Pehle," 16 August 1944, in Neufeld and Berenbaum, *The Bombing of Auschwitz,* 274–275.

38. On intelligence warnings see, Herschel Johnson, American Minister to Sweden to Hull, 26 June 1944, Morgenthau Diaries, reel 38, LC. For statistics on Hungary see Leni Yahil, Ina Friedman, and Haya Galai, *The Holocaust: The Fate of European Jewry, 1932–1945* (New York: Oxford University Press, 1990), 646, and overall see Daniel Blatman, *The Death Marches: The Final Phase of Nazi Genocide,* trans, Chaya Galai (Cambridge, MA: Harvard University Press, 2011).

39. For an example of this critique of FDR and U.S. policy see Wyman, *The Abandonment of the Jews,* xv, 288–307.

40. Berle to Stettinius, 16 September 1944, Adolf A. Berle Papers, box 70, Stettinius Report, Roosevelt Library.

41. The latest of many biographies is Paul Levine, *Raoul Wallenberg in Budapest: Myth, History, and Holocaust* (London: Valentine Mitchell, 2010).

42. Levine, *Raoul Wallenberg in Budapest,* 137–138.

43. Ibid., 139–149.

44. Ibid., 150–151. Transcript of Jewish Evacuation Meeting, 17 August 1944, Morgenthau Diaries, reel 45, LC.

45. Memorandum for the Members of the War Refugee Board, 15 July 1944, RG 107, entry 180, box 44, ASW 400.38 Jews, NARA.

46. Summary of Steps Taken by War Refugee Board with Respect to Jews of Hungary [August 1944], War Refugee Board Records, box 118, Raoul Wallenberg Materials, Roosevelt Library.

47. War Refugee Board to Ambassador Winant, 25 August 1944, copy in Morgenthau Diaries, reel 46, LC. Pehle to Shultz, 31 August 1944; American Legation Bern to Secretary of State, from McClelland to Board, 26 August 1944, War Refugee Board Records, boxes 34 and 35, Hungary, vols. 1 and 3, Roosevelt Library; Report of the War Refugee Board, 25–30 September 1944, Morgenthau Diaries, reel 50, LC.

48. War Refugee Board cable to Johnson and Olsen, 11 August 1944, copy in Morgenthau Diaries, reel 45, LC. Johnson to Secretary of State for War Refugee Board, 30 October 1944, copy in Morgenthau Diaries, reel 51, LC.

49. Braham, *The Politics of Genocide,* 820–919. Levine, *Raoul Wallenberg in Budapest,* 238–239, 256–62.

50. Theo Tschuy, *Dangerous Diplomacy: The Story of Carl Lutz, Rescuer of 62,000 Jews* (Grand Rapids, MI: William B. Erdmans, 2000); David Kranzler, *The Man Who Stopped the Trains to Auschwitz: George Mantello, El Salvador, and Switzerland's Finest Hour* (Syracuse, NY: Syracuse University Press, 2000).

51. Braham, *The Politics of Genocide,* 834–844, 1143.

52. Johnson to Secretary of State, for War Refugee Board, 22 December 1944, War Refugee Board Records, box 118, History—Documents, Roosevelt Library. Pehle to Wallenberg, 8 December 1944, quoted by Levine, *Raoul Wallenberg in Budapest,* 318.

53. Rosenheim to McCloy, RG 107, entry 180, box 43, Countries A–Z, X-Jacob Rosenheim, NARA. Proskauer telegram to Pehle, 26 September 1944, War Refugee Board Records, box 18, Poland, Roosevelt Library. Pehle to Morgenthau, 3 November 1944, Morgenthau Diaries, reel 53, LC.

54. Proskauer to Rosenman, undated, American Jewish Committee Records, RG 347, EXO-29, box 10, Emergency Committee 1944, YIVO Institute for Jewish

Research, New York, New York. Pehle to Morgenthau, 3 November 1944, Morgenthau Diaries, reel 53, LC. "Eisenhower Warns Reich on Prisoners," *New York Times,* 8 November 1944, p. 21.

55. Braham, *The Politics of Genocide,* 1143.

56. S. Adler-Rudel, Intervention of the Swedish Government on behalf of the Jews of Hungary, 28 December 1944, document given us by Shlomo Aronson, to whom we are grateful.

57. For a short account of Kasztner in Israel see Yechiam Weitz, "Rudolf Kasztner," in *The Holocaust Encyclopedia,* ed. Walter Laquer and Judith Tydor Baumel (New Haven: Yale University Press, 2001), 379–382.

58. Leora Bilsky, "Judging Evil in the Trial of Kastner," *Law and History Review* 19 (Fall 2001), with comments and responses at 117–188; "Kasztner: Hero or Devil?," *Forward,* 23 October 2009, p. 11. See also Anna Porter, *Kasztner's Train: The True Story of an Unknown Hero of the Holocaust* (New York: Walker & Co., 2008), and Laura Bilsky, *Transformative Justice: Israeli Identity on Trial* (Ann Arbor: University of Michigan Press, 2004). Yehuda Bauer, *Jews for Sale? Nazi-Jewish Negotiations, 1933–1945* (New Haven, CT: Yale University Press, 1994), 199–201, rejects charges against Kasztner as farfetched and credits him with saving as many as 20,000. But see the very recent rejoinder by Eliahu Reichental, "The Kasztner Affair: A Reappraisal," in *The Auschwitz Reports and the Holocaust in Hungary,* ed. Randolph L. Braham and William J. vanden Heuvel (Boulder, CO: Rosenthal Institute for Holocaust Studies and Social Science Monographs, 2012), 211–253.

59. Information from Dr. George Klein to Richard Breitman. Klein also related this story in his oral presentation at International Conference on the Auschwitz Reports and the Holocaust in Hungary, City University of New York Graduate Center, 7 April 2011. On Klein's experiences generally, see his "Confronting the Holocaust: An Eyewitness Account," in *The Auschwitz Reports,* 255–283.

60. McCormack to Executive Director, 19 February 1945, War Refugee Board Records, box 33, War Refugee Board, vol. 3, Roosevelt Library. There is still a need for a thorough study of the War Refugee Board.

15. ENDINGS

1. Jean Edward Smith, *FDR* (New York: Random House, 2008), 602–606, 617–618. On Palestine, see pp. 297–298.

2. Vandenberg to Samuel Pettengill, 24 August 1943, Samuel Pettengill Papers, box 2, University of Oregon Library, Eugene, Oregon. Luce to MacArthur, 3 May 1943, Clare Boothe Luce Papers, box 380, Library of Congress, Washington, D.C. (henceforth LC).

3. Luce to MacArthur, 3 May 1943, Clare Boothe Luce Papers, box 380, LC.

4. Michaela Hoenicke Moore, *Know Your Enemy: The American Debate on Nazism, 1933–1945* (New York: Cambridge University Press, 2010), 295–303. Smith, *FDR,* 624.

5. Stettinius to Long and Murray, 15 November 1944, and Stettinius to Long, 27 November 1944, Edward R. Stettinius Jr. Papers, box 215, Long October 1943 folder, Small Special Collections Library, University of Virginia, Charlottesville, Virginia. Edward R. Stettinius Jr., *The Diaries of Edward R. Stettinius, Jr., 1943–1946,* ed. Thomas M. Campbell and George C. Herring (New York: New Viewpoints, 1975), 187–190.

6. FDR Memorandum for Senator Wagner, 3 December 1944, in Franklin Delano Roosevelt, *F.D.R., His Personal Letters,* vol. 2, *1928–1945,* ed. Elliot Roosevelt (New York: Duell, Sloan and Pearce, 1950), 1559–1560, cited by Allis Radosh and Ronald Radosh, *A Safe Haven: Harry S. Truman and the Founding of Israel* (New York: Harper Perennial, 2009), 18.

7. According to Wagner's description of their conversation in a follow-up letter, Wagner to FDR, 15 January 1945, PSF, box 46, Palestine, Franklin D. Roosevelt Library, Hyde Park, New York (henceforth Roosevelt Library).

8. Celler to FDR, 15 December 1944, absolutely personal and confidential; FDR to Dear Manny, 16 January 1945, PSF, box 46, Palestine, Roosevelt Library.

9. Stettinius, *The Diaries of Edward R. Stettinius,* 208. Statement by Dr. Abba Hillel Silver, undated December 1944, Abba Hillel Silver Papers, reel 102, Milton S. Eisenhower Library, Johns Hopkins University, Baltimore, Maryland.

10. Marc Lee Raphael, *Abba Hillel Silver: A Profile in American Judaism* (New York: Holmes and Meier, 1989), 128.

11. Transcript of Treasury group meeting, 12 January 1945, The Morgenthau Diaries: World War II and Postwar Planning, 1943–1945 (henceforth Morgenthau Diaries), microfilm, reel 58, LC. Morgenthau to FDR, 27 January 1945, PSF, box 173, War Refugee Board, Roosevelt Library. On the smooth transition from Pehle to O'Dwyer see "Washington Memo," *New York Post,* 29 January 1945, p. 7.

12. Stettinius, *The Diaries of Edward R. Stettinius,* 211.

13. Radosh and Radosh, *A Safe Haven,* 19–20.

14. Ibid., 21. Herbert Feis, *The Birth of Israel: The Tousled Diplomatic Bed* (New York: Norton, 1969), 17.

15. Ibn Saud's statement in The Minister in Saudi Arabia to the Secretary of State, 1 February 1945, in *Foreign Relations of the United States* (henceforth *FRUS*), *1945,* vol. 8 (Washington, DC: U.S. Government Printing Office, 1969), 687.

16. Wise's appointment with FDR, 22 January 1945. The conversation summarized in Wise to FDR, 24 January 1945, OF 700, Palestine 1944–1945, Roosevelt Library. See also Radosh and Radosh, *A Safe Haven,* 23.

17. Albert Kaganovitch, "Stalin's Great Power Politics, the Return of Jewish Refugees to Poland, and Continued Migration to Palestine, 1944–1946," *Holocaust and Genocide Studies* 26, no. 1 (2012): 59–94.

18. Memorandum from Stettinius to Roosevelt, undated [probably December 1944], in *FRUS, 1944,* vol. 5 (Washington, DC: U.S. Government Printing Office, 1944), 655–657.

19. Fraser J. Harbutt, *Yalta 1945: Europe and America at the Crossroads* (New York: Oxford University Press, 2010), 280–282.

20. Radosh and Radosh, *A Safe Haven,* 24–25.

21. Frank Costigliola, *Roosevelt's Lost Alliances: How Personal Politics Helped Start the Cold War* (Princeton: Princeton University Press, 2012), 168–169. Radosh and Radosh, *A Safe Haven,* 25.

22. Michael Makovsky, *Churchill's Promised Land: Zionism and Statecraft* (New Haven: Yale University Press, 2007), 219; S. M. Plokhy, *Yalta: The Price of Peace* (New York: Penguin Books, 2011), 245–247.

23. Ross Gregory, "The Conference of Franklin D. Roosevelt and King Ibn Saud in February 1945," in *Presidents, Diplomats, and Other Mortals: Essays Honoring Robert H. Ferrell,* ed. J. Garry Clifford and Theodore A. Wilson (Columbia: University of Missouri Press, 2007), 116–119. Unless otherwise noted, all subsequent information about this meeting comes from this brilliant article by Gregory (pp. 116–133). We are grateful to Garry Clifford for calling it to our attention.

24. In addition to Gregory, "The Conference," see Radosh and Radosh, *A Safe Haven,* 28.

25. Gregory, "The Conference," 131. Radosh and Radosh, *A Safe Haven,* 29.

26. Radosh and Radosh, *A Safe Haven,* 30–31. "President again Asks Palestine's Freedom," *New York Times,* 17 March 1945, p. 13; Murray to Acting Secretary of State, 20 March 1945, in *FRUS, 1945,* vol. 8, 694–695.

27. Radosh and Radosh, *A Safe Haven,* 31–323.

28. Proskauer, Conference with the President [Roosevelt], Memo to President Truman, undated June 1945, RG 347, EXO-29, box 31, folder 11, YIVO Institute for Jewish Research, New York, New York. The earliest evidence of what transpired at this meeting, and the date of it, are in Blaustein to FDR, 24 March 1945, OF-76-C, box 9, folder 1, Roosevelt Library.

29. Acting Secretary of State Joseph Grew to the Charge in Iraq, 24 March 1945, Roosevelt to Ibn Saud, 5 April 1945; Murray to Assistant Secretary of State James Dunn, 6 April 1945, in *FRUS, 1945,* vol. 8, 696–702.

30. William D. Hassett, *Off the Record with F.D.R.: 1942–1945* (New Brunswick, NJ: Rutgers University Press, 1958), 332. Morgenthau Diaries, 11 April 1945, reel 66, LC. See also Smith, *FDR,* 635–636.

31. Smith, *FDR,* 635–636.

32. Adolf A. Berle, *Navigating the Rapids, 1918–1971: From the Papers of Adolf A. Berle,* ed. Beatrice Bishop Berle and Travis Beal Jacobs (New York: Harcourt Brace Jovanovich, 1973), 527. On the global impact of FDR's speeches and principles generally see Elizabeth Borgwardt, *A New Deal for the World: America's Vision for Human Rights* (Cambridge, MA: Harvard University Press, 2007).

33. "Roosevelt Tribute by Free Synagogue," *New York Times,* 16 April 1945, p. 8; "Tributes Paid to Franklin D. Roosevelt," *New York Times,* 15 April 1945, p. 4.

34. "Deaths of Many Jews Charged to FDR Policy," *Chicago Tribune,* 11 December 1946, p. 20; "Roosevelt Lauded in Jewish Sermons," *New York Times,* 13 April 1947, p. 49.

35. See also David S. Wyman, *Paper Walls: America and the Refugee Crisis* (Amherst: University of Massachusetts Press, 1968).

36. Goodman, "Letter to the Editor," *Chicago Tribune,* 14 November 1962, p. 20. Mary Ann Glendon, *A World Made New: Eleanor Roosevelt and the Universal Declaration of Human Rights* (New York: Random, 2001); Michelle Mart, "Eleanor Roosevelt, Liberalism, and Israel," *Shofar* 24 (Spring 2006): 58–89; Allida M. Black, *Casting Her Own Shadow: Eleanor Roosevelt and the Shaping of Postwar Liberalism* (New York: Columbia University Press, 1996).

37. On Hull's health see Irwin F. Gellman, *Secret Affairs: Franklin Roosevelt, Cordell Hull, and Sumner Welles* (Baltimore: Johns Hopkins University Press, 1995), 290–291, 310–311, 336, 359. Cordell Hull, *The Memoirs of Cordell Hull* (New York: Macmillan, 1948).

38. Gellman, *Secret Affairs,* 390–391. Benjamin Welles, *Sumner Welles: FDR's Global Strategist* (New York: St. Martin's Press, 1997).

39. Neil Smith, *American Empire: Roosevelt's Geographer and the Prelude to Globalization* (Berkeley: University of California Press, 2003), 374–462.

40. See James G. McDonald, *Advocate for the Doomed: The Diaries and Papers of James G. McDonald, 1932–1935,* ed. Richard Breitman, Barbara McDonald Stewart, and Severin Hochberg (Bloomington: Indiana University Press, 2007), and McDonald, *Refugees and Rescue: The Diaries and Papers of James G. McDonald, 1935–1945,* ed. Richard Breitman, Barbara McDonald Stewart, and Severin Hochberg (Bloomington: Indiana University Press, 2009).

41. David Howard Goldberg, *Foreign Policy and Ethnic Interest Groups: American and Canadian Jews Lobby for Israel* (Westport, CT: Greenwood, 1990), 16–28.

42. Melvin I. Urofsky, *A Voice that Spoke for Justice: The Life and Times of Stephen S. Wise* (Albany: State University of New York Press, 1982).

43. Marc Lee Raphael, *Abba Hillel Silver: A Profile in American Judaism* (New York: Holmes & Meier, 1989), 85–222. On Truman's decision to recognize the state of Israel see Radosh and Radosh, *A Safe Haven,* 36–354.

44. For an example of celebratory work on Bergson, see David S. Wyman and Rafael Medoff, *A Race against Death: Peter Bergson, America, and the Holocaust* (New York: New Press, 2002). See also Judith Tydor Baumel, *The "Bergson Boys" and the Origins of Contemporary Zionist Militancy* (Syracuse, NY: Syracuse University Press, 2005).

45. Cohen wrote FDR, "It is now abundantly clear to me that I am not really wanted in the State Department unless I wish to accept some undefined, subordinate position and unless I understand that my services do not rank with those holding Presidential appointment." Cohen to FDR, 16 January 1945, PSF, box 127, Cohen, Roosevelt Library. William Lasser, *Benjamin V. Cohen: Architect of the New Deal* (New Haven: Yale University Press, 2002), esp. 277.

46. Melvin I. Urofsky, *Louis D. Brandeis: A Life* (New York: Alfred A. Knopf, 2009).

47. Frankfurter Memorandum for the Files, 27 September 1941, President's Secretary's Files, box 135, Felix Frankfurter 1937–1941, Roosevelt Library.

48. Sarah A. Ogilvie and Scott Miller, *Refuge Denied: The* St. Louis *Passengers and the Holocaust* (Madison: University of Wisconsin Press, 2006), 174–175.

16. PERSPECTIVES

1. See p. 104.

2. See Chapters 5–7 in this volume.

3. See p. 108.

4. Richard Breitman, video interview of Gerhart M. Riegner, 28 April 1992, Records Group 50.030*0189, United States Holocaust Memorial Museum.

5. See Chapters 10–11 in this volume.

6. On Netanyahu's speech at Auschwitz in 1998 see Richard G. Davis, "The Bombing of Auschwitz: Comments on a Historical Speculation," in *The Bombing of Auschwitz: Should the Allies Have Attempted It?*, ed. Michael J. Neufeld and Michael Berenbaum (New York: St. Martin's Press, 2003), 214, 226; Deborah Lipstadt, "The Failure to Rescue and Contemporary American Jewish Historiography of the Holocaust: Judging from a Distance," in Neufeld and Berenbaum, *The Bombing of Auschwitz*, 236. On Bush's statements see "Bush Leaving Israel," *New York Times*, 12 January 2008, p. 3; "Playing the Holocaust Card," *Jerusalem Post*, 5 April 2012, p. 5.

7. Richard Breitman, *Official Secrets: What the Nazis Planned, What the British and Americans Knew* (New York: Hill and Wang, 1998), 209–210, 229.

8. David S. Wyman, *The Abandonment of the Jews: America and the Holocaust, 1941–1945* (New York: New Press, 1984), 304–305. Gerhard L. Weinberg, "The Allies and the Holocaust," in *The Bombing of Auschwitz*, 24–26. Shlomo Aronson, *Hitler, the Allies, and the Jews* (New York: Cambridge University Press, 2006),

290–297. Daniel Blatman, *The Death Marches: The Final Phase of Nazi Genocide,* trans, Chaya Galai (Cambridge, MA: Harvard University Press, 2011).

9. Ohlendorf testimony at http://law2.umkc.edu/faculty/projects/ftrials /nuremberg/Ohlentestimony.html.

10. Kenton Clymer, "Jimmy Carter, Human Rights, and Cambodia," *Diplomatic History* 2 (April 2003): 245–278.

11. For American responses to the atrocities in Cambodia, Rwanda, and the former Yugoslavia see Samantha Power, *A Problem from Hell: America in the Age of Genocide* (New York: Basic Books, 2002), 247–474.

12. Olivier Degomme and Deborati Guha-Sapir, "Patterns of Mortality Rate in Darfur Conflict," *The Lancet* 375 (January 2010): 294–300.

13. Geoffrey Robinson, *"If You Leave Us Here, We Will Die": How Genocide Was Stopped in East Timor* (Princeton, NJ: Princeton University Press, 2011). The civil war in Sri Lanka, with abuses on both sides, creates difficulties in analysis as illustrated by Asoka Bandarage, *The Separatist Conflict in Sri Lanka: Terrorism, Ethnicity, Political Economy* (London: Routledge, 2009).

14. Robert A. Rankin, "GOP is Quick to Criticize Clinton," *Philadelphia Inquirer,* 28 March 1999, p. 26. For critical views of American and NATO involvement in the Kosovo War see Tariq Ali, ed., *Masters of the Universe: NATO's Balkan Crusade* (New York: Verso, 2000). For a critique of moral intervention see Alan J. Kuperman, "The Moral Hazard of Humanitarian Intervention: Lessons from the Balkans," *International Studies Quarterly* 52 (March 2008): 49–80. For a still critical, but more nuanced, view of moral intervention see Arman Grigoryan, "Third Party Intervention and the Escalation of State-Minority Conflicts," *International Studies Quarterly* 54 (December 2010): 1143–1174.

15. "While Avoiding Limelight, Obama Aide Backs Action," *International Herald Tribune,* 31 March 2011, p. 5.

16. Kuperman, "The Moral Hazard," 50.

17. Grace Tully Collection, Tully, box 1, folder Felix Frankfurter, 1939–1946, Frankfurter, Franklin Delano Roosevelt, reprinted from *Harvard Alumni Bulletin,* 28 April 1945, Franklin D. Roosevelt Library, Hyde Park, New York.

Acknowledgments

Helpful and knowledgeable archivists contribute heavily to successful research. At the Franklin D. Roosevelt Presidential Library and Museum, we benefited greatly from our conversations with Deputy Director Robert Clark and the assistance of Mark Renovitch, Virginia Lewick, Matthew Hanson, and in earlier years, Robert Parks. They helped us find what an enigmatic man often preferred to hide. They were wonderful custodians of the raw materials of history and biography.

At the National Archives, William Cunliffe, Greg Bradsher, and David Langbart all aided us in our search for relevant materials in a vast archive. We would also like to thank now-retired Assistant Archivist Michael Kurtz for his general helpfulness. At the Library of Congress, we are grateful for the assistance of the competent and efficient staff in the manuscript reading room. At the Center for Jewish History in New York, Gunnar Berg and Jesse Cohen offered insight into YIVO collections and helped us find specific documents. Director Gary Zola and Archivists Kevin Proffitt and Elisa Ho guided us to many relevant collections at the American Jewish Archives in Cincinnati. Kelly Spring at the Eisenhower Library at Johns Hopkins University assisted us with the Bowman Collection, and Rebecca Johnson Melvin and Timothy Murray at the Rare Book and Manuscript Collections at the University of Delaware helped us with the Messersmith Papers there. At the United States Holocaust Memorial Museum, Benton Arnovitz, Michlean Amir, and Vincent Slatt were all helpful in a variety of ways, as was Judy Cohen in the photo archive. Archivists were also helpful at many other institutions, among them Columbia University, Georgetown University, Harvard University, New York University, Yale University, the New York Public Library, and the Herbert Hoover and John F. Kennedy presidential libraries.

Joyce Seltzer, our editor at Harvard University Press, helped to polish our interpretation and style, insisting on improvements in earlier drafts. We thank her for taking so much time and care with this book. We are responsible for any defects that remain. Joe Spieler, our agent, called for a book that dealt with FDR's entire life and kept us focused at early stages of the project.

Erwin Gellman and John (Garry) Clifford could not have been more generous and helpful in reading multiple drafts and in offering detailed critiques. We appreciate greatly all the time they put in—far beyond the call of duty. Their insights have enriched our work tremendously. Norm Goda and our American University History Department chair, Pamela Nadell, both offered a wealth of suggestions for the penultimate draft. We only hope we have taken sufficient account of all their guidance.

Max Friedman, our American University colleague, offered time and substantive expertise in diplomatic history. He helped us avoid a number of errors and gave us greater confidence in our argument. We consulted our colleague Laura Beers on some points of British history and historiography. Johanna Neuman read the entire manuscript and suggested ways to make it more readable. Peter Starr, dean of the College of Arts and Sciences at American University, offered practical support for this project and for our work generally. Daniel Ballentyne and Jason Weixelbaum helped with proofreading. We are grateful to the whole American University crew.

Stephen Tyas and the late David Bankier consulted distant archives for us and filled in a few gaps in our documentation. David Engel was kind enough to advise us on some conceptual problems and on Palestine material.

Carol Breitman and Karyn Strickler helped us surmount the stresses of any long and large collective enterprise. We dedicate this book to them and to the memory of Gerhart M. Riegner, who sent news of Hitler's Final Solution to the West.

Index